Managing Project Risk and Uncertainty

A Constructively Simple Approach to Decision Making

**Chris Chapman and
Stephen Ward**

School of Management
University of Southampton

JOHN WILEY & SONS, LTD

Other Wiley Editorial Offices

John Wiley & Sons, Inc., 605 Third Avenue,
New York, NY 10158-0012, USA

WILEY-VCH Verlag GmbH, Pappelallee 3,
D-69469 Weinheim, Germany

John Wiley & Sons Australia, Ltd., 33 Park Road, Milton,
Queensland 4064, Australia

John Wiley & Sons (Asia) Pte, Ltd., 2 Clementi Loop #02-01,
Jin Xing Distripark, Singapore 129809

John Wiley & Sons (Canada), Ltd., 22 Worcester Road,
Rexdale, Ontario M9W 1L1, Canada

British Library Cataloguing in Publication Data

A catalogue record for this book is available from the British Library

ISBN 0-470-84790-5

Typeset in 10/12pt Times Ten by Footnote Graphics, Warminster, Wiltshire.
Printed and bound in Great Britain by Antony Rowe Ltd, Chippenham, Wiltshire.

This book is printed on acid-free paper responsibly manufactured from sustainable forestry,
in which at least two trees are planted for each one used for paper production.

To optimists

Contents

Contents

Preface

This book is about managing uncertainty in managerial decision processes from a project management perspective. One way to decompose the whole of managerial decision processes involves three areas: project management (the management of change), operations management (the management of ongoing operations) and strategic management (deciding what to change). But marketing, contracting, safety, and financial management are four examples of aspects of management which cut across all three areas, and the boundaries of what some see as 'functional silos' defined by both areas and aspects are ambiguous. This book takes a holistic view of these areas and aspects. The focus is project management oriented, but the aim is to help managers deal with uncertainty more effectively and more efficiently, whatever the area and aspect of primary concern.

This book includes 'project' in the title because its primary market is those with a project orientation, and its focus is projects and programmes, but we hope it will prove of interest to others, because of its holistic view of management decision processes and the generality of the constructive simplicity concept. It includes 'risk' in the title because its primary market is those who are interested in risk management, but we hope it will stimulate wider use of uncertainty management to reflect a holistic view of what is needed. With these qualifications this book is about managing uncertainty in organizations in holistic terms.

Effective uncertainty management requires effective understanding of uncertainty. Efficient uncertainty management requires an effective process for sorting out which aspects of uncertainty need to be understood at a deeper level than that currently available, and which aspects are not worth the bother. Making this process efficient is also a direct concern. Organizations should use managers' time wisely, and managers have to choose how much time to spend on each issue wisely.

To achieve effective and efficient uncertainty management, this book recommends 'constructive simplicity' in terminology, analysis and associated decision support processes. What this term means is outlined in Chapter 1, illustrated by ten tales (short stories based on case studies) in Chapters 2 to 11, and summarized in Chapter 12.

Each tale is based on one or more cases the authors were involved in, and all tales endeavour to tell it like it is. However, some contexts are deliberately transformed, and all the organizations, people and stories are composites, to integrate issues and simplify discussion. We are direct in our criticism of some commonly used approaches, but no direct or implied criticism of particular organizations or people is intended. None of the tales should be taken literally in relation to particular organizations or people. Others authors have used stories to develop management concepts. The 'novels' of Eliyahu Goldratt (e.g. 1997) were most in mind when shaping this book, but there are many others (e.g. Ackoff, 1986; Rivett, 1994).

The specific processes employed in the individual tales are used to illuminate the general concepts. In this way the book attempts to build a systematic set of process rules of thumb, by synthesizing lessons from the tales, and integrating them in the overall perspective developed chapter by chapter. The reader will find it helpful to read the tales in sequence, although each tale is complete in itself, and there is no simple progression of issues and concepts between the tales. Most management decision contexts involve multiple interrelated issues, and all the tales reflect this. The primary role of the tales is to illustrate the insights a constructively simple approach can provide when used in any uncertainty management context. However, each tale may be of direct interest in its own right, in the sense that each tale also provides guidance about the nature of effective and efficient uncertainty management in the context it involves, and guidance about the models and decision support processes which might be used directly.

Most of the tales involve the use of simple models and decision support processes in an operational form. However, this book is not about particular operational techniques or tools per se. It is primarily about how to conceptualize the analysis of uncertainty, in the sense of breaking it down, then synthesizing it, putting it back together along with relevant issues not analysed, in order to understand it better. Synthesis based directly on any given piece of analysis is clearly essential, but synthesis also has to draw on what the organization has learned earlier, in terms of knowledge about models, processes, hard facts about the context, and soft information about the context. Synthesis also needs to encourage creative leaps, possibly triggered by analysis, but driven by intuition, emotion and creative will. The role of analysis using formal models is important, but it is subordinate to holistic synthesis.

The book assumes an understanding of basic probability and statistics at the level of a first-year university course in quantitative methods plus a willingness to work with numerical examples. Abstract mathematics is avoided, but sophisticated concepts (like separability) are addressed in simple terms when they are useful. The aim is to make most of the ideas accessible to anyone who may be interested, without being simplistic.

Employing a series of tales facilitates understanding of unfamiliar and sometimes complex ideas. Generic discussions abstracted from any illustrative context can be very difficult to follow, and often give rise to scepticism about their application in practice. The use of tales allows complex ideas to emerge a bit at a time through material which is engaging because it is immediate and concrete. The basic idea is to convey key ideas as simply and clearly as possible in a sequence designed to aid understanding, with supporting discussion which explains how the key ideas develop and can be exploited in practice.

The rationale for the use of tales also flows from the needs of readers which this book attempts to meet. Some readers may be interested in the insights these tales provide with a view to influencing the way their organizations think about managing uncertainty. They may not wish to undertake any analysis themselves, but they may want to know what can be done to set agendas and pose questions. These readers might be characterized as shapers. We hope shapers will find this book directly focused on their needs.

Some readers may be interested in using the insights these tales provide to deliver new organizational processes. They may have less direct control over deciding what needs to be done in the organization in question, but more direct responsibility for doing it. They might be characterized as doers. We hope doers will also find this book focused on their needs in terms of the first step in instigating developments that will have to go beyond the issues discussed here. We are very concerned with the operational needs of doers, but we could not meet them fully in this book without detracting from the primary aim of providing a basis for an enhanced understanding of uncertainty management at a conceptual level. In our view this enhanced understanding is an essential first step for doers, before they attempt to make operational use of that understanding. Some doers will want to explore supporting literature and ideas and the operational details of approaches outlined in this book alongside alternative operational and conceptual frameworks. We hope sufficient references are provided to help start this process.

Some readers, aspirants in the sense of students who are aspiring doers or shapers, should have an interest in supporting literature and ideas and critical analysis of alternative frameworks which goes beyond that provided here. However, we hope this book will help to inform and stimulate the wider study these readers need to undertake. This book has not been written as a course text, with exercises. However, it raises lots of questions to explore, and we believe it should be suitable for a range of courses.

This book is not addressed to academics or consultants who might wish to defend specific approaches we have criticized or ignored, in the sense that we have not attempted to provide a comprehensive academic argument to support our suggested approaches. The standard of proof we have applied is obvious relevance to shapers and doers. However, the authors hope fellow travellers will find the book of interest, and a basis for ongoing dialogue.

For all readers this book can be viewed as an exploration of emerging themes in the management of uncertainty which the reader is invited to share. This book is about trying to understand the nature of key issues, as well as providing an overview of some effective answers. Some new answers are offered, which we hope readers will find relevant and immediately useful. Some new questions emerge as well, which we hope readers will find thought-provoking and useful in improving future practice.

Acknowledgements

The ten tales of Chapters 2 to 11 are based on cases taken from our employment, consulting and related research contract experience. In chronological order in terms of initial contact, the organizations involved are IBM Canada, Ferranti (London), Singer UK, Economic Models Limited, Buckinghamshire County Council (Third London Airport Enquiry), Spillers Foods Limited, Acres Consulting Services Limited (Canada and US), Ministry of State for Urban Affairs (Canada), Canadian Arctic Gas Study Group, Canadian International Project Managers Limited, The Boots Company plc, Newfoundland and Labrador Hydro, National Westminster Bank Operational Research Group, BP International (London), Potomac Electric Power Company, US Department of Energy, Petro Canada, Northwest Alaska Pipeline Company, Fluor Engineers and Contractors Inc., Alaska Power Authority, UK Ministry of Defence, Gulf Canada Resources Inc. (Calgary), Gulf Research and Development Company (Houston), British Gas Southern, Alberta Utilities Consortium, Petroleum Directorate of the Government of Newfoundland and Labrador, The Channel Tunnel Group, Gresham CAP, Sir William Halcrow and Partners, Spicers Consulting Group, British Aerospace, National Power, IBM UK, ESCW/ Bombardier, British Marine Technology (BMT), BMT Reliability Consultants Ltd, UK Nirex Limited, Independent Power Producers Society of Ontario (IPPSO), National Westminster Bank, Ricardo Hitech Ltd, Defence Research Establishment (DRA), Statoil (Norway), Southern Water, John Mowlem and Company, Railtrack, BNFL Engineering Ltd (BEL), and Project Management Professionals Learning Ltd. We are very grateful to these organizations and all the people involved for the opportunities and insights provided.

It is not possible to single out all the individuals in these organizations who had a significant impact, but special mentions are due to Oscar Sigvaldison, Robin Charlwood, Gavin Warnock, Chuck Debelius, Peter von Lany, Mike Howden, Jeff Thomson, Jim Lambert, Peter Wakeling, Ian Barrett and David Hillson. We would particularly like to thank Per Willy Hetland, who triggered this book, via discussions about Statoil's use of uncertainty management rather than risk management and the importance of complexity and ambiguity. We would also like to particularly thank Brenda Trickey and Julie Cardy, who gave up weekends to finish word processing this book by the publisher's deadline. Others who deserve a special mention include Ian Harwood (who prepared the figures), other members of secretarial staff of the School of Management of the University of Southampton who contributed to its production, Diane Taylor and other Wiley staff, who contributed to its shape as well as its production, and four very helpful referees. All of them are optimists in the sense implied by this book's dedication, defined by the quote for Chapter 1. So are our wives, Jean Chapman and Mary Ward, who warrant a special kind of thanks for the power and durability of their optimism.

1 Introduction

*A pessimist sees the difficulty in every opportunity,
an optimist sees the opportunity in every difficulty.*
Sir Winston Churchill

Managing Uncertainty, Risk, Threat And Opportunity

'Uncertainty' in the plain English sense of 'lack of certainty' has important implications for what can be achieved by organizations. All management decisions should take uncertainty into account. Sometimes the implications of uncertainty are 'risk' in the sense of 'significant potential unwelcome effects on organizational performance'. Then management needs to understand the nature of the underlying threats in order to identify, assess and manage the attendant risk. Failure to do so is likely to result in adverse impacts on performance, and in extreme cases, major performance failures. Sometimes the implications of uncertainty are an upside form of risk, significant potential welcome effects. Then management needs to understand the nature of the underlying opportunities in order to identify and manage the associated upside risk. Failure to do so can result in a failure to capture good luck, which can give rise to downside risk. For example, a sales campaign which generates unexpectedly high demand for a new product may prove a disaster if that demand cannot be met and this stimulates a competitor to enter the market; a project activity which finishes early may not result in a following activity starting early, and later delays will not be neutralized by this good luck if it is wasted; a contractor may have more resources available than anticipated, but may not be motivated to use them to a client's benefit, ultimately leading to problems for both parties.

In any given decision situation both threats and opportunities are usually involved, and both should be managed. A focus on one should never be allowed to eliminate concern for the other. Opportunities and threats can sometimes be treated separately, but they are seldom independent, just as two sides of the same coin can be examined at one time, but they are not independent when it comes to tossing the coin. Courses of action are often available which reduce or neutralize potential threats and simultaneously offer opportunities for positive improvements in performance. It is rarely advisable to concentrate on reducing risk without considering associated opportunities, just as it is inadvisable to pursue opportunities without regard for the associated risk. Because resources expended on risk management may mean reduced effort on the pursuit of opportunities, and vice versa, effort on each needs to be balanced, in addition to balancing the total effort expended in relation to the benefits.

To emphasize the desirability of a balanced approach to opportunity and threat management, the term 'uncertainty management' is increasingly used in preference to the more established terms 'risk management' and 'opportunity management'. However, uncertainty management is not just about managing perceived threats and opportunities and their risk implications. It is also about managing the various sources of uncertainty which give rise to and shape risk, threat and opportunity. Understanding the nature and significance of this uncertainty is an essential prerequisite for its efficient and effective management.

Uncertainty is in part about variability in relation to performance measures like cost or duration or quality. But uncertainty is also about ambiguity. Both variability and ambiguity are associated with lack of clarity because of the behaviour of all relevant players, lack of data, lack of detail, lack of structure to consider the issues, working and framing assumptions being used to consider the issues, known and unknown sources of bias, and ignorance about how much effort it is worth expending to clarify the situation. Clarification is primarily about improving effectiveness and efficiency. Improved predictability is sometimes a useful by-product. Uncertainty management as addressed in this book is about effective and efficient decision making given this comprehensive and holistic view of uncertainty.

The Scope For Uncertainty In Managerial Decision Processes

The scope for uncertainty in any managerial decision situation is considerable. A useful way to see part of this scope is by considering a generic managerial decision process defined as a sequence of stages, each of which involves associated sources of uncertainty, as shown in Table 1.1. The decision stages in Table 1.1 are similar to those used to describe a generic decision process in many textbooks on managerial decision making.

The first stage in the decision process involves continuous monitoring of the environment and current operations in the organization. At some point issue recognition occurs, when those with sufficient influence realize there is a need to make one or more decisions to address an emergent issue. However, uncertainty

Table 1.1—Sources of uncertainty in a managerial decision process structure

Stage in the decision process	Uncertainty about
Monitor the environment and current operations within the organization	Completeness, veracity and accuracy of information received, meaning of information, interpretation of implications
Recognize an issue	Significance of issue, urgency, need for action
Scope the decision	Appropriate frame of reference, scope of relevant organization activities, who is involved, who should be involved, extent of separation from other decision issues
Determine the performance criteria	Relevant performance criteria, whose criteria, appropriate metrics, appropriate priorities and trade-offs between different criteria
Identify alternative courses of action	Nature of alternatives available (scope, timing and logistics involved), what is possible, level of detail required, time available to identify alternatives
Predict the outcomes of courses of action	Consequences, nature of influencing factors, size of influencing factors, effects and interactions between influencing factors (variability and timing), nature and significance of assumptions made
Choose a course of action	How to weigh and compare predicted outcomes
Implement the chosen alternative	How alternatives will work in practice
Monitor and review performance	What to monitor, how often to monitor, when to take further action

associated with ambiguity about the completeness, veracity and accuracy of the information received, the meaning of the information, and its implications, may make ambiguity associated with the emergence of issues important. Further, defining issues may not be straightforward. Different parties in an organization may have different views about the significance or implications of an existing situation, and differing views about the need for action. Issues may be recognized as threats or opportunities which need to be addressed either reactively or pro-actively. Alternatively, issues may be expressed in terms of weaknesses in organizational capability which need to be remedied, or particular strengths which could be more extensively exploited. Issues may involve relatively simple concerns within a given ongoing operation or project, but they may involve the possible emergence of a major organizational change programme or a revision to a key aspect of strategy. The decisions involved may be first-order decisions, or they may be higher-order decisions, as in process design choices, deciding how to decide. Ambiguity about the way issues are identified and defined implies massive scope for uncertainty.

'Scope the decision' will depend on how an issue is defined. It involves determining which organizational activities are relevant to addressing the issue, who is already involved with the issue, who should be involved, and importantly, the extent to which other areas of decision making need to be linked with this decision process. 'Determine the performance criteria' involves identifying the performance criteria of concern, deciding how these will be measured, and determining appropriate priorities and trade-offs between the criteria. As with issue recognition, the tasks comprising these two stages can present significant difficulties, particularly if multiple parties with differing performance criteria or priorities are involved. The 'identify alternative courses of action' stage may involve considerable effort to search for or design feasible alternatives. The 'predict outcomes of courses of action' stage builds on this to identify the factors that are likely to influence the performance of each identified course of action, estimating their size and estimating their combined effect. The 'choose a course of action' stage then involves comparing the evaluations obtained in the previous stage, often by comparing relative performance on more than one performance criterion. Ambiguity about how best to manage all these stages and the quality of their output is a further massive source of uncertainty.

The final two stages, 'implement the chosen alternative' and 'monitor and review performance', might be regarded as outside the decision process. However, if the concern is issue resolution then it is important to recognize these two steps and consider them in earlier stages of the decision process.

Most decision processes are not adequately described in terms of this simple sequence of separate stages. It has an operations management flavour, project or strategic management contexts warranting a modified shape to reflect context differences. In any context, the distinction between separate stages becomes blurred by simultaneously working on more than one stage at a time, and by iterative loops between various stages to incorporate revised perceptions and additional information. For example, the determination of performance criteria may be merged with the identification of alternative courses of action, or their evaluation, because views about what performance criteria are relevant are initially ill-defined, and need to be developed in the light of what alternatives are identified. Identification of alternatives and their evaluation is an iterative process involving search and screening processes to produce a shortlist of alternatives which are developed and evaluated in more detail. In the case of major investment decisions, often only one alternative is fully developed and evaluated because alternative courses of action and alternative design choices have been dismissed in earlier iterations through the 'choose a course of action' stage. However, Table 1.1 is a useful portrayal of what is involved in outline.

Experience, as well as this brief overview of sources of uncertainty in a generic decision process structure, tells us that the scope for making poor quality decisions is considerable. Difficulties arise in every stage. The uncertainties listed in Table 1.1 indicate the nature of what is involved. Have we correctly interpreted information about the environment? Have we correctly identified issues in a timely manner? Have we adopted the most appropriate scope for our decision? Are we clear about the performance criteria and their relative importance to us? Have we undertaken a sufficiently thorough search for alternatives? Have we evaluated alternatives adequately in a way that recognizes all relevant sources of uncertainty? And so on.

In order to manage all this uncertainty, decision makers seek to simplify the decision process by making assumptions about the level of uncertainty that exists, and by considering a simplified version or model of the decision components. Often this is done intuitively or informally using judgement and experience. For decisions that are important, where time and other resources permit, decision makers may use formal decision support processes incorporating explicit, documented models to assist with various stages in the decision process. Decision support need not imply formal computer-based information system support, though it often does. The key is formal models and associated analysis and synthesis to help make decisions, without attempting to exclude any relevant decision-maker input. The value of this approach is a starting position for this book. A key aim is to demonstrate that the quality of decision making can be greatly improved by the use of formal decision support processes to manage associated uncertainty.

Ten Tales About Uncertainty Management

The ten tales in Chapters 2 to 11 of this book focus on different stages of the decision process in a number of important contexts. They illustrate how uncertainties associated with particular stages of the decision process can be explored in order to improve the quality of the decision process. Each tale involves the use of formal analysis, and holistic synthesis, to help the protagonists understand the decision context and the implications of associated uncertainty more clearly. Several tales focus on understanding and evaluating the implications of uncertainty in the 'predict outcomes' stage of the decision process. Others range more widely, implicitly addressing each decision stage in a sequence which involves iterative loops. For example, some tales begin with issue recognition, then move to prediction of outcomes for certain alterative courses of action, but as insights from the analysis emerge, the narrative describes a return to earlier stages in the decision process to reconsider issues, decision scope, performance criteria, possible additional courses of action, or re-evaluation of alternatives. All the tales involve situations where uncertainty has significant consequences for the decision owners. The need to understand the extent of threats to organizational performance is a common theme, but the tales also illustrate the linkage between threats and opportunities. In most tales the emphasis is on identifying and creating opportunities, rather than on merely neutralizing perceived threats. And in most tales the need to manage both variability and ambiguity, including deciding whether or not to seek more clarity, is a central issue.

For easy reference each tale is designated by the main protagonist, who typically manages the decision support process at the centre of the tale. However, other parties are involved, and their perceptions and motives are invariably important. This reflects the fact that a key source of uncertainty in most decision contexts relates to the identification of performance criteria together with the relative priorities and trade-offs that decision makers and other influential parties place on these criteria. Taken together the tales range over most of the stages in the generic decision process, and consequently address many of the uncertainties associated with each stage. They also cover the project management, operations management and strategic management areas, and aspects which include marketing, contracting, safety and financial management. The scope of each tale is summarized briefly below.

Nicola's tale

Nicola's tale involves an example of buffer management in a supply chain. The tale begins with a proposal to change the size of replenishment orders for a particular component used by a family business which manufactures lawnmowers. Nicola starts by using a basic inventory control model to explore the effects of different reorder levels. However, the main body of the tale concerns the identification of assumptions made in the initial analysis and how this suggests a much wider-ranging review of supply chain strategy, including revised arrangements with other suppliers and all major customers. The tale demonstrates the relative importance of variability and ambiguity, and the way analysis can trigger creativity – very general issues which set the scene for other tales. The tale also suggests an approach to managing other forms of resource buffer. Time between activities and budget contingencies are project-oriented examples, but it is useful to see buffers in general terms and to start with a comparatively simple context.

Martha's tale

Martha's tale deals with the common problem of determining an appropriate bid in a competitive tendering context. Concerned with her company's recent lack of success in competitive tenders, the regional marketing manager of an international computer systems supplier institutes the design of a new process for bid development. This incorporates cost estimation and consideration of the probability of winning with different levels of bid. Using an iterative process to discriminate between uncertainty which matters and uncertainty which doesn't matter, in order to spend more time on what matters, is a general issue at the centre of this tale. Decomposing the uncertainty which matters most (pricing issues associated with competitor and buyer behaviour), not the uncertainty best understood (cost), is facilitated by the process described.

Eddy's tale

Eddy's tale describes an approach to preliminary cost estimation of a possible offshore North Sea pipe-laying contract. It provides further consideration of cost estimation issues arising in the previous tale. Eddy's approach demonstrates how a minimalist first-pass approach can be used to focus subsequent analysis on important sources of uncertainty. The ideas presented here can be applied in any performance measurement uncertainty estimation context. The focus is understanding what variability measures mean, separating out ambiguity issues associated with 'conditions' in so far as this is possible, and thinking ahead in an iterative process, all very general issues.

Ian's tale

Ian is an independent consultant called in to comment on the risks associated with a property development project which his client wishes to undertake. Central to the project is a contract Ian's client has been offered by a property developer. Using a formal project risk analysis and management process, Ian demonstrates the significant moral hazard risk associated with the contract. He then outlines the structure of an incentive contract which would address the moral hazard problems and make the deal acceptable to all parties. A general issue of importance in this tale is the relationship between estimates which are conditional on assumptions and actual outcomes, whatever the ambiguities which separate the two, including the extent to which contracts motivate parties (or not) in an aligned manner.

Roger's tale

Roger's tale continues with the moral hazard theme, but shifts the initial emphasis to internal relationships between departments in a project-based organization. The central issue is the need for the project manager to meet performance targets in terms of cost, time and quality, while relying on the performance of the various contributing departments. Part of the tale focuses on the development of internal incentive arrangements for the design department to ensure that the benefits of better than expected performance in the design department are extended to the project as a whole. This approach to formally capturing good luck is then extended to a linked set of contractors. Aligning the motivation of parties with or without formal contractual boundaries to manage good or bad luck is the general issue addressed.

Sarah's tale

Unlike all the other tales, Sarah's tale concerns events which have only adverse consequences such as accidents or acts of God, events which the insurance industry often refers to as pure risks. This tale focuses on assessing uncertainty about the likelihood and possible consequences of a particular risk event. Subsequent analysis considers the need for trade-offs between costs and benefits, the problem of unambiguously identifying the benefits of reducing levels of risk, and the politics of basic framing assumptions in the context of a mandatory insurance approach. The tale addresses the management of safety in a railway system, but the form of analysis and synthesis presented is applicable to a wide range of related risk management problems. It can be very important to link issues like safety to other aspects of project conception, development and selection, breaking down functional silo boundaries.

Norman's tale

Norman's tale addresses the problem of evaluating uncertain costs and benefits over time. Starting with a basic net present value (NPV) discounting framework, it explores the usefulness of a parametric approach employing sensitivity analysis of the key parameters to arrive at evaluations which reflect underlying uncertainties. It then goes on to explore related probabilistic and 'real options' approaches to evaluating possible future courses of action. Norman's analysis is concerned with the problem of nuclear waste disposal and appropriate costing of a deep mine repository project. However, the concepts and issues discussed apply to most capital investment appraisal problems.

Tess's tale

Tess's tale concerns an investment decision problem for a small manufacturer. To begin with, the decision problem is formulated by Tess as a simple choice between a small number of alternative options, amenable to analysis via a decision matrix and then a decision tree model. However, this formulation is shown to be inadequate. Tess's journey towards a broader perception of the issues, and a wider range of strategic options, involves general issues of relevance in many contexts and most stages of Table 1.1 as well as all areas and all aspects of management. A portfolio of projects requiring multiple-attribute evaluation is the conceptual framework which emerges, with specific process recommendations.

Sam's tale

Sam's tale is about portfolio analysis in its most general sense: analysing the collective uncertainty associated with a set of component assets. The analysis starts with a basic Markowitz mean–variance model of a portfolio of financial securities and the formalization of the important concept of risk efficiency. It then extends the analysis to exploit the concept of separability. The modelling framework provided then facilitates further extension of the analysis to address issues associated with corporate structure, staff motivation, staff training, staff selection and retention. This tale underpins many of the constructive simplicity notions used in most of the other tales.

Conrad's tale

Conrad is a consultant contracted to advise a Canadian electric utility on how best to embed uncertainty management into their corporate strategy formulation process. Conrad's analysis distinguishes three levels of planning: short-, medium- and long-term. It considers separability and dependence of the uncertainties associated with each of these horizons. For example, long-term uncertainties involve political and economic issues which drive the mix of hydro, nuclear, thermal and 'conservation' approaches to the energy portfolio of the utility. Given uncertainties about the growth in demand for electricity, medium-term planning for new power stations presents considerable difficulty because of the long lead times associated with the construction of new generating capacity. Conrad's analysis demonstrates that provision and operation of new capacity should lag behind expected growth in demand for electricity because the costs associated with providing capacity excess to requirements are significantly higher than the costs associated with a shortfall in capacity, a profoundly counter-intuitive result for the utility. However, the focus of the tale is the way the framework developed by Conrad facilitates reflection about alternative short-, medium-, and long-term strategies, the linkages between them, and the way synthesis can incorporate bottom-up emergent strategy development as well as top-down analysis. These are all issues of general interest.

Tales in context

The nature of the tale format employed means that each tale addresses a particular context, but the approaches used in each tale are directly transferable to most other similar contexts, and many other contexts which may seem very different. Managers who deal with contexts like the ones described should find the concepts and approaches discussed directly relevant to their own organizations. However, the ideas presented are relevant to a much wider set of contexts, and collectively the ten tales provide a comprehensive sample of the implications of the constructively simple approach adopted throughout. All the tales are based on cases, but all the organizations, people and stories are composites, to integrate issues and simplify discussion. None of the tales should be taken literally in relation to specific organizations or individuals.

A General Process For Supporting Managerial Decision Making

Each tale can be viewed from two perspectives: first, as an approach to addressing uncertainty in particular contexts and related situations; and second, as an illustration of key principles in devising analytical approaches that are both efficient and effective. This second perspective is the primary concern of this book. The ten tales illustrate a number of general methodological issues concerning the use of analysis and synthesis to understand and manage uncertainty which are not specific to particular areas of application.

In identifying principles involved in the design of effective and efficient processes for supporting managerial decision making, we do not need to start from scratch. In management science, broadly defined to include operational research (OR) – some prefer operations research, what some may see as separate perspectives provided by soft systems and soft OR, and cognate aspects of what some may see as the separate disciplines of economics, finance, and so on, there is a long tradition of employing models of real management decision situations to understand the key features of a decision and guide subsequent decision making. The tales draw on this experience. In particular, the process adopted in each tale is based on a typical general process followed in OR interventions as depicted in Figure 1.1. This process

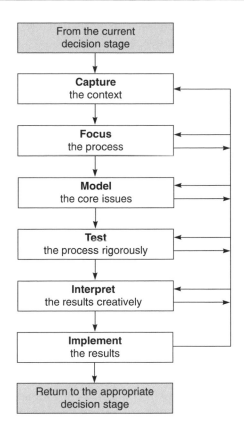

Figure 1.1—The general decision support process.

may be applied to support one or more stages of the decision process in Table 1.1. As with most decision support processes, this process is not a simple linear process. The need for an iterative approach arises because of the presence of uncertainty and learning that takes place as the process progresses. Efficient and effective processes to support decision making usually warrant an iterative approach involving multiple passes through one or more phases in the process.

The six-phase structure of Figure 1.1 captures the spirit of modern OR-based management science approaches to decision support processes in a manner shaped to reflect the constructive simplicity notion this book develops. The term 'decision support' itself reflects the spirit of constructive simplicity as explored by this book, briefly described later in this chapter. In particular, it is worth emphasizing that the process of Figure 1.1:

- Supports decision making, it does not make decisions
- Enhances the skills of decision makers, it does not downgrade the role of decision makers

- Involves synthesis which attempts a holistic perspective
- Requires thoughtful interpretation, and is concerned with stimulating creativity
- Involves facilitation and guidance, and embraces corporate learning processes
- Can accommodate the idea of specific and general processes (see page 25).

Nicola's tale in Chapter 2 is concerned with clarifying this process in basic terms, and later chapters explore its enhancement in various ways, but the following outline may help to explain it.

Capture the context

The process of Figure 1.1 begins with 'capture the context', the capture phase. This involves developing a description of the prevailing state of the decision process in terms of the stage reached, the information and understanding obtained, and the uncertainties present.

Focus the process

The next phase is 'focus the process', the focus phase. This involves identifying the purpose of the support to be provided and selecting an approach which is fit for purpose. The purpose of the process will reflect the stage the supported decision process has reached. For example, if the decision process has only reached the stage of determining performance criteria in a first pass, then the purpose of the analysis may be to help those involved in the decision process to consider appropriate measures for possible performance criteria and identify their preferences in terms of plausible trade-offs. If the decision process has progressed to 'predicting the outcomes of course of action' then the purpose of analysis may be to estimate the outcomes of the alternative courses of action using the previously determined measures of performance.

In a basic context as illustrated in Nicola's tale, choices about the approach have to start with two basic options. First, we can choose a soft systems (Checkland and Scholes, 1990) or a more broadly cast soft OR (Rosenhead, 1989) initial position, perhaps embedding a more traditional OR approach (Ackoff and Sasieni, 1968) at a later stage if appropriate. Second, we can start with a traditional OR perspective, embedding soft OR approaches as appropriate. This book presumes the latter, because this is the authors' preference in the contexts considered, for reasons illustrated in the tales.

Given this choice, another choice has to be made, about the degree of focus on qualitative models or quantitative models. If quantitative models are the focus, a choice has to be made between a modelling approach which is descriptive or prescriptive. A prescriptive model may involve optimizing techniques designed to identify the best course of action given that the decision maker has adopted particular performance criteria and trade-offs. A descriptive model may simply describe the likely consequences of particular decisions. Decision makers or analysts can then vary model parameters to see the effect of different assumptions or choices. Simulation is commonly employed as a descriptive modelling technique. Both prescriptive and descriptive modelling approaches can help decision makers understand more about the associated decision context and guide future choices.

For some purposes a qualitative modelling approach is appropriate and quantification is unnecessary. For example, qualitative modelling techniques can be very helpful in clarifying and addressing uncertainties present in the decision stages of 'issue recognition', 'scoping the decision', 'determining performance criteria', and 'identifying alternative courses of action'. Soft OR approaches like the use of influence diagrams and cognitive mapping (Eden, 1988) can be very useful here. However, quantitative models are often desirable because:

- Numbers form a common language for more effective communication of some issues
- Some decision situations can be more precisely defined and ambiguity minimized
- The logic of the decision process becomes more explicit
- Decisions, and subsequent changes in decisions, can be defended in a rational and consistent manner

In practice, qualitative and quantitative modelling approaches are best used together in a complementary manner. The use of qualitative models can often induce use of a quantitative model, and vice versa. Each of the tales describes a process which focuses on the relationship between quantitative modelling of some issues and qualitative modelling or informal consideration of other issues. As the analysis and synthesis process in each tale progresses, a recurring issue is whether or not it is worth modelling relevant factors in quantitative terms, and the level of precision and detail worthwhile where quantitative modelling is used.

Model the core issues

A first step in a basic version of the 'model' phase in the process of Figure 1.1 involves the design of an appropriate conceptual model which incorporates structure and detail to reflect the focus and purpose of the process. A second step is to obtain data in an appropriate form which provides relevant values for all model parameters. Such data may not be readily available, and may require estimating. A third step is to solve the model, to determine results using input data.

Test the process rigorously

The test phase explores important sources of uncertainty introduced by the process which in a basic context include:

- Uncertainty about the accuracy of calculations
- Uncertainty about the pedigree of parameter estimates incorporated
- Uncertainty about the importance of individual model parameters
- Uncertainty about the validity of explicit assumptions which structure the analysis
- Uncertainty about implicit assumptions

This involves scrutinizing the model solution, form and assumptions for accuracy, sensitivity and robustness. It also involves scrutinizing the process used to obtain the model for robustness, implicit assumptions posing particular difficulties. This scrutiny may suggest a need to loop back to earlier phases in the process, typically to revise the model construction, but potentially to consider a different modelling approach, or even to re-examine the decision context. Framing assumptions can be particularly important. All the feedback loops in Figure 1.1 are important, but the loops in the test phase are particularly important.

A useful first step is a reality check, to see if the results are consistent with common sense expectations. If not, then check the model construction, check the quality and pedigree of the data, and check the calculations for errors. Counter-intuitive results which can be explained and defended are the pearls of wisdom being sought, but counter-intuitive results which cannot be explained are a serious risk to the process.

Sensitivity analysis is important because it indicates the extent to which changes in the value of a parameter can affect the model results. If model results are extremely sensitive to small changes in the value of a parameter, then uncertainty about the value of this parameter is important; it needs to be investigated and managed. If model results are relatively insensitive to changes in the value of a parameter, this is useful information about the level of variability or uncertainty associated with the parameter that can be tolerated without significantly affecting the situation being modelled.

A management science approach to model-based analysis following a process like that of Figure 1.1 emphasizes the importance of explicitly analysing the robustness of the assumptions embedded in models. This goes much wider and deeper than sensitivity analysis of model parameters. For example, if someone with statistical training uses a statistical test based on a model which assumes a Normal (Gaussian) distribution for data, he or she should have confidence that the extent to which the data is not Normally distributed is not a critical issue. This is robustness as understood by statisticians. The concern for robustness addressed in the test phase is similar but much more fundamental. The essence of the robustness issue is that we need to pay very careful attention to assumptions, ensuring that no assumptions are made which clearly depart from reality without testing their effect. If we fail to do this, then our models will generate new uncertainty, rather than reduce existing uncertainty. If the theory our models incorporate is a distortion of reality, this can distort associated perceptions and decisions in unpredictable ways. Such theory is not useful. Indeed, it is positively harmful and counterproductive.

Looking for insight from all earlier aspects of this phase and the process more generally is the crucial final step in this phase, and the rationale for the formal modelling aspects of the process.

Interpret the results creatively

The interpret phase in the process of Figure 1.1 continues the synthesis begun in the previous phase. It involves critical reflection on the results of the previous phases and drawing conclusions which can be used to enhance decision makers' understanding about the decision context and to guide their future actions. It needs to address the implications of all aspects of the previous phase, especially assumptions which are not robust and issues not captured by the formal analysis and the synthesis thus far. It should also involve standing back from the modelling effort to consider the big picture. These deliberations may well suggest that it is desirable to revisit earlier phases of the process or earlier stages of the decision process, in order to pursue more refined analysis, develop alternative modelling approaches, or reframe the decision context altogether, for example.

An important part of reflections in the interpret phase should be to address the implications of:

- Uncertainty about the nature of implicit assumptions
- Uncertainty about the appropriateness of the modelling approach
- Uncertainty about the depth to which the analysis should be conducted
- Uncertainty about aspects of the decision context which have been overlooked

These uncertainties may be addressed to some extent in earlier phases of the process, but a more informed assessment and consideration of the implications of these uncertainties is possible after completing at least one pass through the preceding phases. Reflections about the above uncertainties usually warrant revisiting early phases of the process, and sometimes result in significant shifts in the focus of analysis and changes in the form of model employed.

It is particularly important that reflection here should include consideration of uncertainties associated with the decision context that have not been adequately captured by the preceding analysis and synthesis. For example, the analysis may prompt questions about who should be involved in the decision process, or what other related decision processes should be taken into account. Further consideration of such questions might warrant major changes in approach. It also might shift attention away from the current decision support process back to the underlying decision process stage, and the desirability of revisiting earlier stages of this decision process, to redefine the decision issue, rescope the decision, or revise the relevant performance criteria, for example.

Implement the results

The implement phase is included because experience suggests that the need to implement results must be designed into the whole process from the outset. It is also included because it is important to emphasize that this process is about results which can be implemented. A process of this kind can have embedded scientific methods, but it is not about doing science (adding to knowledge without any particular decision in mind) unless it is embedded in a scientific process, an issue not addressed in this book.

Nicola's tale in Chapter 2 provides a direct illustration of the use of a basic version of the process of Figure 1.1, illustrating and developing the discussion of this section, as indicated earlier. The concept of constructive simplicity also builds on this basic version of the process of Figure 1.1, and it requires some exploration at a conceptual level in this chapter.

Constructively Simple Models

A key concern in the process of Figure 1.1 is deciding how much detail to incorporate in a model of the decision situation, and in what manner to introduce it. Models which attempt to mirror reality in every detail are not usually appropriate or feasible, but at the same time, excessive reduction in complexity must be avoided if the model is not to obscure issues or produce misleading inferences. What is needed is a model that captures all the key features of the decision context which matter a lot, but ignores all the detail which matters relatively little. What matters depends critically on the immediate purpose of the model. For example, detailed 2 cm to 1 km scale maps produced by the Ordnance Survey are useful for planning a walk, but a one-page map of the whole country is more useful for planning a 500 km car trip. Both are graphical models of geographic features, but each is designed for and best suited to particular uses.

In terms of model construction there are good reasons to start with a model which is simple in terms of construction detail, whatever the purpose of the model or the decision context (Ward, 1989). This simplicity can be incorporated into a model by:

- Restricting the number of variables in the model, e.g. by definition of a boundary to the problem
- Quantifying simple relationships between variables, e.g. hypothesizing linear relationships
- Limiting the amount of uncertainty incorporated, or perhaps even ignoring uncertainty altogether
- Assuming a well-defined objective function or set of decision criteria
- Aggregating variables with certain shared characteristics; for example, rather than considering all customers individually, they are grouped for modelling purposes according to size, products purchased, industry or location

Constructively simple models generally have a number of advantages over their counterparts, along the following lines:

- **Transparent assumptions** Assumptions are more apparent and more accessible (transparent) in a constructively simple model. In a complex model it can be difficult and time-consuming to keep track of every assumption incorporated in the model. Even with detailed documentation, some assumptions may be overlooked when model outputs and their implications are being discussed. In particular, the arbitrary or inappropriate nature of some assumptions may go unnoticed.
- **Simple data requirements** Constructively simple models require less data, and where data is limited, a simple model may be the only practicable approach (Cohen and Durnford, 1986). Even when data is available, the larger amounts of data required for a complex model may be difficult or onerous to obtain, prepare, and check. Where the quality of data is low, constructively simple models are more appropriate than complex ones. In this respect, a disadvantage of complex models is that output from such models can imply a degree of precision which is not justified by the quality of the input data. There is always a need to maintain a healthy suspicion of the data used and the processed results.
- **Simple sensitivity analysis** Sensitivity analysis is more practical with a constructively simple model. Unless the number of variables is small, the effect of individual assumptions on model output can be very difficult or impractical to determine (Eilon, 1979). In particular, it can be difficult to carry out detailed sensitivity or robustness analysis by varying combinations of model variables. Even complete sensitivity analysis of each variable individually may be onerous in a model with many variables. A notable exception is a linear programming (LP) model formulation. Sensitivity analysis on individual model variables and constraints is readily available on most LP software; the weakness is that simultaneous sensitivity analysis of two or more variables is not conveniently performed. Unless sensitivity analysis can be carried out conveniently, there will be a tendency to rely on 'best estimate' values for model data, with consequent model unreliability in the face of uncertainty.

- **Simple development and maintenance** Constructively simple models can be less time-consuming and costly to develop and maintain. Complex models take a long time to construct and test, often much longer than intended. Delays in producing them do not inspire confidence. Complex models require more extensive documentation.
- **Flexibility** Constructively simple models are easier to alter. Complex models can be very difficult to alter quickly and correctly when new features are required, or assumptions built into the logic need updating.

These advantages of constructively simple models are particularly relevant in decision contexts involving high levels of uncertainty. In the presence of high uncertainty, beginning with a constructively simple model in a first pass through the decision support process, followed by subsequent iterations, is usually preferable to attempting a single pass with a model that may be overly complex. For example, if decision criteria and their relative importance are ill-defined, or the relationships between decision variables are not fully understood, some relevant features may not be identified until later in the process. In these circumstances an initial model may be more useful in terms of refocusing the analysis in a second pass through the phases of the decision support process than in terms of producing immediate guidance for the decision maker. First and subsequent passes through the test and interpret phases lead to correction of errors, changes in model formulation, or the decision maker learning something new about the problem and 'updating intuition' (Roberts, 1977; Little, 1970). To facilitate this, flexible, easily amended models are needed, rather than models of great technical accuracy and complexity (Fripp, 1985).

Other Aspects Of Constructive Simplicity

Constructively simple models provide the foundation for what we shall term 'constructive simplicity' in a decision support process like that of Figure 1.1. The term 'constructive simplicity' captures the idea of simplicity in model or process detail, and the idea of simplicity which is helpful or constructive. Complementary to constructive simplicity is the notion of constructive complexity, incremental complexity which adds value efficiently at a level appropriate to the context. Two obvious opposite concepts are destructive simplicity and destructive complexity. Destructive simplicity is simplistic, it oversimplifies and obscures, and obstructs the ability to develop understanding. Destructive complexity is overelaborate, adding details or complexities which are not cost-effective in contributing to understanding, and which may even be counterproductive. For example, some forms of model are mathematically attractive but counterproductive for practical decision-making insight purposes, because they obscure more than they reveal.

Simplicity efficiency in modelling

The tales in this book are concerned with approaches which are as simple as possible, or no more complex than necessary to achieve an appropriate level of understanding of uncertainty in the context considered. We believe that the best way to achieve this balance is to begin with constructive simplicity, only adding complexity when it is constructive to do so. This involves adding the minimum amount of complexity necessary to provide needed insight, or maximizing the amount of additional insight provided by an additional level of complexity. Simplicity efficiency implies seeking efficient trade-offs between insight and complexity. Destructive simplicity or destructive complexity is implied by a serious failure to achieve simplicity efficiency, involving simplification of a starting position or added complexity which is counterproductive. What these terms mean and how we can achieve simplicity efficiency is a central theme in the ten tales of this book.

One immediate implication of a seeking simplicity efficiency is that model development should involve a number of iterations or passes. To begin with we need a first pass model deliberately designed in a minimalist style (introduced in Eddy's tale of Chapter 4). Constructive complexity is then added in the most efficient way possible as it becomes clear what is needed (also illustrated in Chapter 4). To achieve this kind of simplicity efficiency more generally we need to design a very flexible model set for variability issues, which can be used on their own or linked in a nested fashion to all other relevant models. Collectively the models used in the ten tales illustrate what this model set ought to look like, without any attempt to be definitive.

Risk efficiency

In this book, risk efficiency is central to a constructively simple approach to uncertainty. It has three aspects. Static risk efficiency is risk efficiency in relation to decisions at a point in time, as developed by Markowitz (1959) in relation to a 'variance efficiency' version of risk efficiency. This involves ensuring that decisions at a point in time involve the minimum level of risk (potential variability on the downside) for any given expected level of performance. An inefficient choice in these circumstances involves more risk than necessary for a given expected outcome. Chapter 10 addresses this aspect in the portfolio analysis context which is its birthplace, but all other chapters make use of it.

The second aspect of risk efficiency involves identifying an appropriate risk/expected value trade-off from risk-efficient alternatives. Risk efficiency leads to an efficient set of choices which involve less and less risk as expected performance is adjusted to a less favourable level, and in the limit to a choice which minimizes risk. How much expected performance it is worth giving up to reduce risk (if any), or vice versa, can be seen as a simple matter of preference or taste, a behavioural issue. This book suggests a minimal backing away from risk as a matter of policy, driven by the third aspect of risk efficiency, dynamic risk efficiency.

Dynamic risk efficiency is risk efficiency in relation to all the decisions over time which are relevant. Over the long haul it is important to optimize expected values unless this involves a chance of catastrophic outcomes which are more of a problem than a more risk-averse stance with respect to each decision. For example, a contractor who never takes a chance that a particular contract will lead to bankruptcy may be certain of bankruptcy through lack of business: the issue may be balancing the risk of bankruptcy on each contract against the risk of going bankrupt through lack of business. Dynamic risk efficiency does not eliminate the preference aspects of balancing risk and expected value, but it couples opportunity management and threat management at a basic conceptual level. It does not in general lend itself to direct mathematical optimization, but it provides a direct rationale for favouring a bold approach to risk taking which is central to this book.

Simplicity efficiency in basic concepts and terminology

Risk management, opportunity management and other aspects of uncertainty management have become increasingly fashionable over the past decade. However, these terms mean different things to different people. Current applications are building on many decades of pioneering work by many different groups of people with different perspectives and different concerns. Constructive simplicity requires a simple set of basic uncertainty concepts and associated terms which are common across these groups. In particular, we need to avoid terms and concepts which are restrictive and which inhibit our approach because of framing assumptions. For example, many people working in the area of safety analysis (and some others) define 'risk' as 'probability times impact', assuming the use of objectively determined probabilities that hazards (threats) will occur, and objectively assessed impacts if they occur. In our terms, 'probability times impact' is an expected value measure, 'risk' is the implications of significant departures from expectations, and any available objective assessments must be embedded in subjective judgements. The implications of this broader perspective in terms of safety are explored in Sarah's tale (chapter 7). The point here is that anyone who insists on defining risk in probability times impact terms cannot make use of 'risk efficiency', a core issue in risk and opportunity management in terms of the perspective of this book. They gain simplicity but lose generality. This is simplistic, and it implies destructive simplicity. Destructive complexity might be associated with attempting to use this narrow definition of risk and a more general inconsistent or contradictory definition.

Constructive complexity may involve additional meanings for basic terms, providing the context makes the meaning clear and more than one meaning is useful. For example, the term 'risk' is often used by many people to mean 'threat' in the sense of a source of uncertainty with downside risk implications. This is a useful and acceptable second meaning for the term 'risk', but in this book the term 'risk' is used in a wider sense to mean the implications of significant uncertainty. Constructive complexity may also involve additional terms for the same basic concepts in a different context when this is useful. For example, 'threat' in a project risk management context usually becomes 'hazard' in a safety context, in terms of the common language of the context. It would not be constructive to attempt to avoid additional terms for the same basic concept in such circumstances in general, although this book avoids doing so. It is very important to eliminate the use of restrictive meanings for basic terms and concepts, but it is also important to avoid terminology imperialism. This book is about setting people free to take a wider view of their concerns, not limiting them to particular terms when other terms are more familiar and equally effective.

All ten tales preserve the same common basic uncertainty concepts and terminology, in an attempt to achieve simplicity efficiency. Some readers may not welcome unfamiliar terminology and associated concepts. However, this book uses a common basic uncertainty concept and terminology set to attempt to explain how to manage uncertainty in any context, using ten fairly different example contexts, and those who wish to develop a similarly broad perspective will need similar common terminology and concepts. This principle of constructively simple basic concepts and associated terminology has been extended beyond 'uncertainty' issues in a limited number of related cases. The use of 'decision support' to describe the nature of the process of Figure 1.1 is one example. The general use of plain English wherever possible is another. Our view is that the simplest concepts and terminology in terms of constructive simplicity are the most robust to changes in context or approach or form of model. They are portable and flexible and unrestrictive. They are also plain English, which helps to avoid or minimize the need for jargon and to simplify communication.

Simplicity efficiency in processes

In this book we are not just concerned with simplicity efficiency for models, concepts and terminology. We are also concerned that the process of organizing and carrying out analysis and synthesis is efficient and effective in terms of desirable numbers of iterations, the resources the process requires in terms of cost and time, and the extent to which spending more (or less) time on the planning process, or doing it differently, might better meet the expectations of those responsible for the associated decisions. This is a higher-order concern, in the sense that it is a higher level of decision making which should be addressed before the nature of the concepts and models employed is considered. In practice this management of the decision support process is extremely important. We do not have infinite time, information and other resources to perform analysis and make decisions. The way we undertake analysis and synthesis has to reflect the practical difficulties decision processes must contend with.

The previous section identified several reasons for preferring constructively simple forms of model. A further important reason for preferring constructively simple models is that they facilitate an efficient and effective decision support process. Typically, at the beginning of the process, understanding of the relative importance of features of the decision context is limited. Setting out to formulate a model incorporating all identifiable situation variables may be unnecessarily complicated – many variables may subsequently prove to be relatively unimportant. For example, in evaluating a number of decision alternatives against multiple criteria, an initial constructively simple analysis may be sufficient to show that one option is always preferred for a wide range of possible futures, rendering further more detailed analysis unnecessary (Belton, 1985). A more efficient approach would involve starting with a constructively simple model and incorporating additional detail only as necessary and as understanding of the decision context develops. In any decision support process, if we know we are going to use an iterative, multiple-pass approach, it makes sense to simplify early passes to focus on what we hope to achieve in early passes, adding complexity constructively in subsequent passes. This idea is developed in Martha's tale (Chapter 3) and Eddy's tale (Chapter 4), and used in the rest of this book. It is an important aspect of simplicity efficiency, with implications for models as well as processes.

Effective processes also need to facilitate and encourage the involvement of the decision owner and their subsequent commitment to making use of the findings from the analysis. Most of the tales in this book involve scenarios where these requirements are a consideration for the analyst in adopting an approach to the decision support process. An in-depth study requiring much time and resources before any answers or help to the decision owner are forthcoming may not be the best way to proceed. Most OR practitioners in this situation recognize the need for early results, something that will help their client *and* help the client appreciate the practitioner. The real trick is for the analyst to identify an immediately helpful perspective on the issues, and useful objectives for the analysis which can be delivered with a high degree of certainty in an acceptable timescale. Such considerations play an important part in determining the nature of analysis that is carried out. More sophisticated models and solutions may need to wait.

Frequently decision owners will express considerable scepticism over an analyst's claim to be able to help with what the decision owner regards as a difficult or complex situation. Any analysis is seen as likely to be too simplistic. A common example arises in corporate studies of branch or area networks. Each branch or area manager claims that his branch or area has special problems which cannot be adequately considered in a model which uses a similar approach to model all branches or areas. Nevertheless, once persuaded that analysis might be useful, decision owners often express a preference, other things being equal, for a constructively simple form of analysis, particularly in the early stages of the work. Why?

Partly decision owners may see constructive simplicity as a way of ensuring model transparency in the face of untried and perhaps overenthusiastic analysts. Once a degree of understanding develops between decision owner and analyst, the decision owner is usually much more willing for complexity to increase. However, decision owners may also prefer constructively simple models for reasons not connected with making models more transparent to them. These reasons relate to the time available to consider a problem, implementing recommendations, and involvement of third parties (Ward, 1989).

In many cases decision owners see lack of time as an effective constraint on the complexity of analysis that is feasible. Indeed, lack of time due to pressure of other work is often a reason for seeking assistance with a decision problem. In this situation analysts must temper the complexity of analysis undertaken by the need to explain progress and results adequately to a decision owner with limited time available to study and contribute to the analysis. Also significant are situations where there are specific deadlines for making decisions. Then decision makers are often prepared to make decisions with less information than they would require if they had more time. The costs of delay imposed by attempting a detailed analysis may be regarded as prohibitive when compared with the likely additional benefits. Even when a detailed analysis *is* feasible within the time constraint, a relatively simple level of analysis may be preferred by a decision owner because:

- It is more rapidly understood
- It reduces the likelihood of unexpected delays due to technical difficulties with the models or data acquisition
- It reduces pressure on analysts and therefore reduces the chance of mistakes
- It allows more time for sensitivity analysis
- It allows more time to reflect on model results

This reasoning is consistent with earlier comments characterizing decision support processes as learning processes, although it reflects the decision owner's typically more pragmatic attitude to problem solving.

The level of detail worth including in a model will also depend to a certain extent on the precision with which decision options can be implemented, and the associated processes. Complex models which specify desirable courses of action in fine detail will be of limited value if such courses of action cannot be precisely implemented and controlled. Furthermore, decision owners are only too aware that no model can take *all* factors into account. It may be necessary to respond to events and effects which were not considered in the model. Models which produce detailed, precise recommendations will not be welcome if they remove or reduce the decision owner's ability to control events directly. Where uncertainty about future developments is high, the overriding need may be to devise courses of action which preserve flexibility for future actions. Existence of a changing situation and a limited amount of relevant data suggests an emphasis on rough appraisals sufficient to evaluate courses of action in broad terms, and facilitate the consideration of qualitative factors.

For themselves, decision owners may be happy with a relatively complex analysis, but may prefer a simpler form of analysis if third parties need to be persuaded by the results. Where implications of a model need to be understood and appreciated more widely, it is useful to have a form of analysis that can be easily understood by managers other than the decision owner, who may not have the inclination or the need to understand a more complex analysis. Insights that are the product of a constructively simple and transparent model may be easier to sell than recommendations derived from a complex and opaque black-box model.

The foregoing observations illustrate the particular importance of the relationship between the models, the decision support process, the decision context, and the parties involved as decision owners or analysts. The decision support process is the overall vehicle. The model is the engine which powers it. The two have to be designed or selected to complement each other, with due attention to the purpose of the vehicle, the (decision) terrain it has to operate in, and how it is to be driven. Most of the tales in this book discuss models and their relationship with the process and the parties involved, with joint consideration driven by a concern for the relative return for effort expended.

The aspects of simplicity efficiency discussed here are implicitly part of Ward's original (1989) 'constructive simplicity' concept, and to some extent they are implicit in any effective decision process, but it is worth making them explicit. Several other aspects receive explicit attention in this book.

Constructively simple models of variability

According to the adage, if the only tool in your box is a hammer, every problem looks like a nail. Management scientists operating as consultants usually pride themselves on having a large toolbox and a wide range of tools, borrowed from all feasible sources. They also pride themselves on knowing when to use them. However, modelling uncertainty issues using the full range of tools developed by OR, economics, finance, safety engineers, technology forecasters and others, raises a number of difficulties. For example, traditional decision analysis models are focused on discrete events and discrete choices, whereas traditional portfolio analysis models are focused on continuous variable allocations and continuous variable outcomes, and the utility theory behind decision analysis is not really compatible with the mean–variance basis of portfolio analysis. The models explored in this book attempt to break down these barriers. The end goal is a compatible family of models of the variability aspects of uncertainty that allow us to start with a very simple model appropriate to any context and add complexity in a constructive way whenever necessary without the need to set aside an approach because it cannot deal with required new features another model could provide. Tess's tale (Chapter 9) and Sam's tale (Chapter 10) explore the intersection between decision analysis and portfolio analysis. These tales and the others illustrate the portable, flexible and unrestrictive nature of the approach to modelling variability which this book suggests. This builds on a synthesis of the risk engineering approach to model building developed by Chapman and Cooper (Chapman and Cooper, 1983a; Cooper and Chapman, 1987) and Ward's (1989) original constructive simplicity ideas. For expository purposes this book makes extensive use of simple analytical procedures to combine measures of variability, but in practice Monte Carlo simulation methods or other algorithms could be used, employing generic software like @Risk (e.g. Grey, 1995).

Constructive complexity via separability

Separability and associated modularity can add complexity to models and processes, but used effectively, very powerful constructive complexity can be achieved. This notion is largely implicit in early chapters, but explicitly touched on in Chapter 3 and developed in Chapters 9 to 12. The use of separability in mathematical programming and utility theory are classic examples, with implications of relevance in these later chapters. The role of statistical independence as an extreme (and often unrealistic) form of separability is directly relevant throughout this book. At a conceptual level, a core notion for this book is refusing to see either opportunities and threats or variability and ambiguity as independent concepts. We can treat them as separable for some purposes, but they are not independent. The distinction is constructive simplicity at its most fundamental level.

Constructively simple processes which are specific or generic, with portable components

The decision support process of Figure 1.1 is generic, in the sense that it is suitable for any context or decision stage, as illustrated by Nicola's tale in Chapter 2. In Martha's tale (Chapter 3) this process underlies the analysis, but the target deliverable is a specific version of the process of Figure 1.1 to be used every time Martha's organization makes a bid. That is, because the same sort of analysis is required time after time, it is worth designing and refining a bidding analysis process specific to the problem context to make bidding more efficient and effective. Constructive simplicity in this book includes this idea of designed processes for repetitive use in very specific circumstances. Chapman and Cooper's 'risk engineering' design concept is the basis of this notion, as discussed in Chapman (1992) and illustrated extensively in Cooper and Chapman (1987), which draws on a series of earlier papers.

A key notion here is the extent to which process ideas are portable; portability makes it simpler to design new processes. For example, the foundation of the risk engineering approach was Chapman's development of project risk management processes and models for BP International's offshore North Sea projects (Chapman, 1979). The next step was a very similar reliability analysis process for Petro Canada (Chapman, Cooper and Cammaert, 1984), followed by a related but quite different engineering design strategy analysis for Fluor Engineers and Contractors Inc. (Chapman *et al.*, 1985), followed by an entirely different economic desirability assessment methodology for the Alaska Power Authority (Chapman and Cooper, 1983b). Constructively simple synthesis needs to draw on all relevant similar processes as appropriate, to simplify the design of suitable processes and avoid reinventing similar wheels.

In Ian's tale (Chapter 5) a central role is played by PRAM (project risk analysis and management), a generic project risk management process developed by the Association for Project Management (Simon, Hillson and Newland, 1997), as elaborated by Chapman and Ward (1997) and subsequent papers. For some purposes it can be seen as a halfway position between a general process like Figure 1.1 and a specific process like the one in Martha's tale. It is specific to project risk management but generic to all projects and organizations.

Chapman and Ward (1997) can be used as a practical basis for understanding, enhancing and implementing any of the generic guidelines for project risk management. This book can be used as a practical basis for further understanding, enhancing, expanding the scope, and implementing any of the generic guidelines for project risk management. This book and Chapman and Ward (1997) can be read in any order or used independently. They intersect in Chapter 5 of this book. This book can also be used in a much broader context, with a focus shifted to bidding, safety, security portfolio management, or strategic management, for example, building on an intersection with these aspects of management in Chapters 3, 7, 10 and 11.

Keep It Simple Systematically

Keep it simple stupid (KISS) is an old adage some people have taken to heart. One way to portray constructive simplicity is as a modified version of KISS: keep it simple *systematically*. What we mean by 'systematically' is characterized by the process notions developed through this book. 'Stupid' is no longer appropriate, because keeping it simple is one objective, but avoiding simplistic approaches which are inappropriate for a range of reasons is another objective. Everyone understands the desirability of 'keeping it simple'. The trick is doing so without being simplistic.

William of Occam (circa 1285–1349) is widely credited with Occam's Razor, an ancient philosophical principle some believe has much earlier origins. Here is how the Oxford Concise Dictionary of Quotations puts it: no more things should be presumed to exist than are necessary. Ward's (1989) original 'constructive simplicity' concept in terms of models has been equated to Occam's razor by several participants in our seminars, and this is quite a useful analogy for some people. Some readers may find it useful to see the generalized version of 'constructive simplicity' used in this book as a refinement of Occam's razor, with what is 'necessary' varying according to circumstances.

Practical OR studies are often described as 'quick and dirty'. Constructive simplicity can be linked to a competent 'quick and dirty' first-pass analysis, followed by thoughtful and effective subsequent passes if time permits and the circumstances warrant it. However, the adjective 'dirty' is not one we favour; 'quick and constructively simple' suits us rather better. More generally, what the reader calls 'constructive simplicity' does not much matter. What matters are the concepts it embodies, which the authors hope the ten tales will clarify.

This book attempts to build a systematic set of rules for producing efficient and effective decision support processes, by building on the foregoing considerations and synthesizing lessons from the tales. However, the overall paradigm is still emerging, and these are working conclusions not definitive guidelines. The opening quote for this chapter is clearly relevant to those who wish to manage uncertainty. It is also apt for those who wish to further develop constructive simplicity. It sets the tone for the whole book, and it is reflected in the dedication.

2 Nicola's tale: Sizing inventories and other buffers

*Predictable variability is often the most certain
and least important aspect of uncertainty.*

Nicola

Introduction

Our first tale concerns decisions about the level of inventory to hold in a small manufacturing company. This is a useful context to begin with for three reasons. First, it is a convenient context to illustrate key features of the general process introduced in Figure 1.1 and employed in all subsequent chapters. Second, it is important to clarify the opening quote for this chapter at the outset. Third, the tale of this chapter illustrates a useful basic uncertainty management strategy for dealing with buffers, a feature of several later tales.

Buffers are a basic component of many systems of interest, operating at the interface between other system components. It is difficult to address the other system components, never mind complete systems, without reference to associated buffers. Inventories are a prime example of the use of buffers. Holding inventories of raw materials, components, work in progress, and finished goods is an obvious way of maintaining continuity of operations in the face of variability in supply and demand. However, organizations who wish to operate efficiently and effectively need to carefully control inventory levels. Holding high levels of inventory incurs costs in a variety of ways, while holding too little inventory runs the risk of interrupted operations and related costs. Determining appropriate levels of inventory means considering replenishment policy, understanding the nature of associated costs, and the trade-offs involved between holding and procurement costs. It can also involve more fundamental and wide-ranging consideration of the way operations are configured. For example, the well-known just-in-time (JIT) approach to supply chain management seeks to manage uncertainty about supply and demand directly without the need for inventory buffers. Such systems can be effective in certain contexts, but they may be inefficient in some parts of the supply chain, and they are vulnerable if unexpected variability in supply or demand occurs. Using a relatively simple context, the tale in this chapter illustrates how decisions about inventory buffers can be addressed. And towards the end, we briefly consider other types of buffer.

The relatively simple inventory sizing issue addressed in the tale of this chapter also provides a convenient context to illustrate the role of models in helping to understand and manage uncertainty. Such models need not address uncertainty directly. Their basic role is to lend structure to issues, to reduce ambiguity. The tale demonstrates the useful role of simple deterministic (non-probabilistic) models in capturing the basic features of a decision problem and guiding further analysis. The tale also demonstrates the useful role of simple stochastic (probabilistic) models which capture some uncertainty explicitly. Of particular importance, for all relevant models, the tale explores the importance of understanding associated assumptions, ranging from simple explicit 'working' assumptions to 'framing' assumptions which may be implicit and difficult to identify. A particular concern is the relationship between assumptions made to construct an appropriate model and the reality being modelled, uncertainty in terms of ambiguity if the implications of these assumptions are not understood, and how this ambiguity aspect of uncertainty is related to uncertainty modelled as variability. The tale also highlights the usefulness of creative leaps which may go beyond formal models, although formal modelling processes can directly facilitate such creative leaps.

The central character in this first tale is Nicola. In 1989 Nicola completed a degree in mechanical engineering. She then took a year out to see the world. On her return, Nicola took her mother's advice and asked her Uncle George for a job. Uncle George was the general manager of a traditional family business of modest size which manufactured a limited range of lawnmowers in the UK's industrial Midlands, near Birmingham. George hired Nicola because she was his sister's daughter, and his sister was a silent partner in the business. During the first few days Nicola worked for George without a clearly defined role, learning the ropes and doing odd jobs.

A Stockholding Issue

On the Monday of her second week in her new job, Nicola was accompanying her uncle round the premises when George was approached by the firm's driver, Dave, who appeared somewhat agitated. Dave used a large van to pick up components from local suppliers. Finished lawn mowers were usually shipped to customers via a range of delivery services, according to order size and destination location, but Dave made some local deliveries. Dave was not very socially adept.

About a month before Nicola's arrival, he offended the dispatch staff of a supplier of engine speed controls used for all the firm's mowers by complaining about the quality of the tea and biscuits they offered him. Their response when Dave returned for another order about the time of Nicola's arrival was to stop giving him any refreshment. After brooding about this, Dave had resolved to try and persuade George that less frequent trips to the speed control supplier would be in order.

With Nicola listening in, Dave suggested to George it was silly for him to pick up the standard order of 2000 speed controls about once a month when his van was big enough to cope with about 12 000 every six months. He pointed out the costs involved in each trip in terms of his time and wear and tear on the van. He also suggested some of the time saved might be used to deliver more of the finished goods, saving external delivery service charges, which were expensive compared to the cost of sending him.

George was aware that Pete, his production manager, would not mind larger orders of components, and could find space for them. However, he was also aware that Arvind, his accountant, would object to the extra funds tied up in larger inventories unless it could be demonstrated that overall costs would be reduced. George explained both these concerns to Dave and Nicola, and suggested it might be useful if Nicola undertook some analysis to test Dave's suggestion. Dave had made an issue of the order size which needed resolution, although George's intuition suggested 2000 actually was about right.

Focusing The Process

As part of her degree studies, Nicola had taken a management course which provided an introduction to uncertainty management using basic inventory models in a similar context to the present situation (Chapman, Cooper and Page, 1987, Chs 12 and 13). Consequently, Nicola was aware of a range of models that could be used to represent inventory decisions, in the sense of being deliberate abstractions of reality which could be used to capture the key features of the current context in a useful manner. Nicola spent several days talking to people, observing what went on, and developing her ideas about modelling the issue context. This confirmed the desirability of an analysis that would focus on the costs associated with reordering and holding inventory given different order levels.

Nicola then prepared for George a presentation which reflected the iterative nature of her deliberations. It was as if she were going through the process with George, eliminating the blind alleys she had explored along the way, glossing over the incidentals, and making appropriate simplifications. She acknowledged her sources, in a carefully timed manner, but she presented the analysis as 'her creation shared with George'.

Constructing A Model

Nicola's chosen modelling approach involved starting with an economic order quantity (EOQ) basic inventory control model described in most management science textbooks. Nicola began constructing her model by identifying what had to be decided; this is the primary decision variable, the order quantity Q_o.

Nicola next identified key parameters that would influence the order quantity. An obvious key parameter was the demand rate for speed controllers, R_d. As a simplifying working assumption, R_d was assumed to be constant, corresponding to a constant monthly total output of mowers of all types. Nicola set R_d at about 2000 controls per month, as indicated by Dave and confirmed by Pete, the production manager.

Nicola then identified the order cost C_o, all costs which vary with the number of orders. C_o posed problems in terms of measurement precision. Arvind had pointed out that C_o could be as low as £10: about £5 for vehicle wear and tear plus fuel, and a further £5 to cover the cost of processing the associated invoice. This would be an appropriate assessment for midwinter. During midwinter Dave and his van had periods of idle time, and the staff who processed the associated invoices also had spare time. Arvind had also pointed out that C_o could be as much as £50 if serious opportunity costs or overtime/extra staff were involved, say an extra £35 opportunity cost for Dave and his van plus an extra £5 to cover the cost of processing the associated invoice using agency staff. This would be an appropriate assessment for the spring. In the spring the upturn in demand for gardening equipment meant Dave working overtime and the firm still had to use expensive external delivery services for low-volume local deliveries which Dave could deal with given more hours in the day. In the spring, inexperienced agency accounting staff had to be taken on and managed carefully by permanent staff to avoid mistakes.

To begin with, Nicola suggested using a midpoint estimate of £30 per order – the average $(10 + 50)/2$ – noting she would return to the associated extremes later. A key issue was the seasonal variation in this parameter, a form of variability which was partially predictable but not captured by the model.

Nicola next identified the holding cost C_h, all costs which vary with the number of speed controls in stock per unit time (months for present purposes). Arvind had suggested C_h was about £0.06 per control per month, involving two components. Assuming an average cost of capital of about 20% per annum and a value per control of £3, about £0.05 per control per month was the cost of capital component. He assumed other holding costs of the order of £0.01 per control per month (an allowance for pilfering, security, insurance, etc). Pete had confirmed that space was not a problem, and he could think of no other holding costs.

Nicola indicated that C_h was subject to cost of capital variations noted by Arvind, but they were not as important as the variations associated with C_o, because they were smaller and less systematic.

Continuing her presentation to George, Nicola then showed him Figure 2.1. She explained that it was a simple representative picture of a typical order cycle which indicated working assumptions like a constant demand rate R_d and no planned shortages. This representation led to the definition of T_0, the order interval, a secondary decision variable defined by Q_0 and R_d.

Nicola then defined C_c as the cost per order cycle, where

$$C_c = C_o + C_h T_o Q_o / 2$$

using Figure 2.1 to explain the obvious C_o term and the less obvious C_h term: the area of the triangle (half the base times the height) defines the number of speed control months (one speed control held in stock for one month = one speed control month) which has to be multiplied by C_h, the cost per speed control per month. Nicola explained that C_c was a convenient place to start looking at joint holding and order cost because it relates clearly to Figure 2.1. However, of more interest is C_t, the average joint cost per month, where

$$C_t = C_o / T_o + C_h Q_o / 2$$

Next Nicola used the identity $Q_o = T_o R_d$ (the order quantity must be equal to the order interval times the demand rate) in the form

$$T_o = Q_o / R_d$$

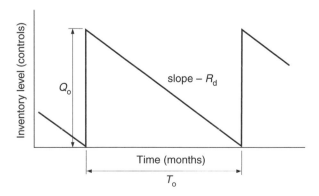

Figure 2.1—Order cycle relationships.

substituting it into the C_t expression to obtain

$$C_t = C_o R_d/Q_o + C_h Q_o/2$$

Nicola explained that the model was concerned with minimizing C_t, to minimize the average joint cost of orders and holding per month. Nicola explained that the structure of this model could be understood via Table 2.1 and Figure 2.2.

Table 2.1 and Figure 2.2 show how the holding cost component of C_t is a simple linear function of Q_o, defined by $C_h Q_o/2$ (with $C_h = 0.06$). If Q_o approaches zero, $C_h Q_o/2$ approaches zero. As Q_o increases by 500 controls, $C_h Q_o/2$ increases by £0.06 × 500/2 = £15 for each successive 500 controls. Table 2.1 and Figure 2.2 also show how the order cost component of C_c is a non-linear function of Q_o, defined by $C_o R_d/Q_o$ (with $C_o = 30$ and $R_d = 2000$). Each time Q_o is doubled, the order cost component is halved; each time Q_o is halved, the order cost component is doubled. In addition, Table 2.1 and Figure 2.2 show how C_t has an optimal value, C_t^*, in the region of £85 per month, associated with an optimal order quantity, Q_o^*, in the region of 1500 controls. They also show that C_t^* is not very sensitive to rounding Q_o^*. For example, rounding Q_o^* from 1500 to 1000 or 2000 (plus or minus 500) increases C_t by only 90 − 85 = £5 per month. However, they show that sensitivity associated with rounding errors is not symmetric: increasing Q_o from 1500 to 2500 (plus 1000) increases C_t by 99 − 85 = £14, while decreasing Q_o from 1500 to 500 (minus 1000) increases C_t by 135 − 85 = £50. This asymmetry suggests 'round up when in doubt'. More importantly, it suggests any errors in analysis which are biased towards larger Q_o^* than an underlying true Q_o^* are less serious than errors which are biased towards smaller Q_o^*. This is one of the more important insights in the analysis to this stage, and Nicola made sure George understood it.

Nicola then explained that the optimal values C_t^* and Q_o^* were defined by the point of zero slope of the C_t curve in Figure 2.2, in turn defined by the point where the negative slope of the order cost component curve became equal in absolute terms to the positive slope of the holding cost component curve, and calculus could be used to determine Q_o^*, which is given by

$$Q_o^* = (2R_d C_o/C_h)^{1/2}$$

the classic EOQ formula, also known as the economic lot size or Wilson formula, after one of its earliest proponents.

Table 2.1—Joint cost and its components as Q_o changes

Order quantity Q_o	500	1000	1500	2000	2500	3000
Order cost component	120	60	40	30	24	20
Holding cost component	15	30	45	60	75	90
Joint cost C_t	135	90	85	90	99	110

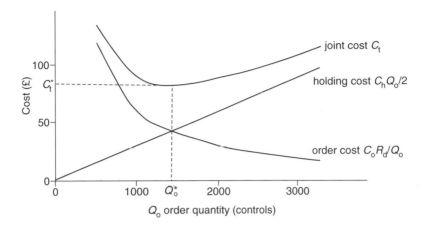

Figure 2.2—Joint cost relationships.

In this case, setting $R_d = 2000$, $C_o = £30$ and $C_h = £0.06$ implies $Q_o^* = 1414$, but it is convenient and sensible to round this to 1500, to avoid implying spurious precision (the sensitivity in C_t^* terms is low, involving an increase of £1.56 per month).

Nicola developed this spurious precision issue further. She explained that this simple model would provide limited accuracy in its assessments because both the model and the parameters involved uncertainty. She suggested rounding the answer to 2000 might (or might not) be appropriate. One merit of 2000 is that it confirms the status quo. This confirms Pete's judgement in choosing 2000 some time ago, and it avoids making matters worse for Dave. The way Table 2.1 shows how C_t changes from $Q_o^* = 1500$ to $Q_o = 2000$, illustrating the lack of sensitivity to this kind of adjustment, is a very useful feature of the model and of the joint tabular/graphical presentation of Table 2.1 and Figure 2.2.

Nicola explained that further strengths of this model were its lack of sensitivity in terms of C_t^* to variations in the parameters R_d, C_o and C_h. For example, if the assumed value of C_o involves an error relative to a true value, a tabular presentation of the lack of sensitivity of C_t to such errors is provided by Table 2.2.

Table 2.2 shows that overestimating the true C_o value by £15 involves only a 6% increase in C_t relative to the true optimum, highlighting these values for easy identification, but showing all the detail so the construction of the table is clear. Nicola pointed out the asymmetry here as in Table 2.1. Underestimating the true C_o value by £15 involves only a 2% increase in C_t relative to the true optimum, and a 6% increase in C_t relative to the true optimum corresponds to underestimating the true C_o value by £30. These values are also highlighted for easy interpretation of the key messages provided by Table 2.2.

Nicola also explained that further strengths of this model were its robustness in terms of C_t^* sensitivity to relaxing both explicit and implicit assumptions used

Table 2.2—C_o sensitivity analysis, assuming $C_o = 30$

True C_o	15	30	45	60
C_o error	**+15**	0	**−15**	**−30**
Calculated Q_o^* using assumed C_o	1414	1414	1414	1414
True Q_o^*	1000	1414	1732	2000
Q_o^* error	414	0	−318	−586
Realized C_t	64	85	106	127
True C_t^*	60	85	104	120
Extra cost (£)	4	0	2	7
Extra cost (%)	**6**	**0**	**2**	**6**

to construct the model. For example, she explained that the model assumes no planned shortages. Planned shortages in this context are equivalent to deliberately producing a lawnmower for finished goods inventory without a speed control. Nicola suggested that the cost of a stockout per unit of inventory per unit time would be about 100 times the cost of holding inventory per unit of inventory per unit time, because a mower without a speed controller ties up about 100 times as much capital. Extending the model to allow this possibility, the new optimal order quantity is 1428 (compared with 1414), with a planned shortage of 28 (Chapman, Cooper and Page, 1987, p. 182). Taking the model literally, it is worth being out of speed controls for about (28/1428) × 100 = 2% of the time production takes place, about 2 hours each month, to avoid carrying the extra 28 controls for the rest of the cycle. Nicola indicated it would be silly to take this extended model too literally, and both versions provide an answer which rounds to $Q_o^* = 1500$, but the idea that limited planned stock outage is not a disaster is a useful insight.

Refining The Analysis: Considering Safety Stock Policy

George was very impressed by Nicola's presentation to this point and he was now following her arguments carefully. She then built on his attention to develop the model in a way good practice required, suggesting that they needed to refine the model to incorporate additional aspects of the decision context.

During her investigations Nicola observed that Pete keeps a safety stock of 300 controls, in the sense that he places an order for another 2000 when there are still about 300 left. This is because most times Dave delivers an order almost immediately (the same day), but sometimes other jobs take priority and it takes a day, very occasionally it takes 2 days, and Pete is concerned that it might take 3 days. The firm produces for about 20 days a month, about 100 mowers per production day, so Pete's safety stock equates to about 3 days of production. Nicola suggested that the chances associated with Dave taking 0 to 3 days to replace the stock might be defined as in Table 2.3. She indicated that she had not yet confirmed these figures with Pete, but they were the orders of magnitude suggested by their conversation on the issue. She indicated that this analysis treats 'days' as a discrete variable, which is a simplifying working assumption.

Nicola illustrated the implications of such numbers in a stochastic (probabilistic) safety stock model using the previous assumption that a mower without a speed controller held in inventory costs about 100 times as much as a speed controller held in inventory. Nicola prepared the following analysis of discrete alternatives:

- **Policy 1**: Pete's current policy (base case)
  - Safety stock of 300, 3 days of production
  - No chance of a stockout, no stockout costs
  - Total cost per month = holding cost per month = $300C_h = £18$

- **Policy 2**: Modest reduction in safety stock
  - Safety stock of 200, 2 days of production
  - Probability of a stockout of 100 for 1 day = 0.01
  - Expected cost of stockouts per month = $0.01 \times 100C_h \times 100/30 = £0.20$; this is the probability $P(n)$ times $100C_h$ times the 100 controls times 1/30 of a month
  - Holding costs per month = $200C_h = £12$
  - Total expected cost per month = 0.20 + 12 = £12.20

- **Policy 3**: Aggressive reduction in safety stock
  - Safety stock of 100, 1 day of production
  - Probability of a stockout of 100 for 1 day = 0.05, 200 for 1 day = 0.01
  - Expected cost of stockouts per month is
    $(0.05 \times 100C_h \times 100/30) + (0.01 \times 100C_h \times 100/30) = 1 + 0.40 = £1.40$
  - Holding cost per month = $100C_h = £6$
  - Total expected cost per month = £1.40 + 6 = £7.40

- **Policy 4**: Elimination of safety stock
  - Zero safety stock; reorder when stockout occurs
  - Probability of a stockout of 100 for 1 day = 0.20, 200 for 1 day = 0.05, and 300 for 1 day = 0.01
  - Expected cost of stockouts per month is
    $(0.20 \times 100C_h \times 100/30) + (0.05 \times 100C_h \times 100/30) + (0.01 \times 100C_h \times 100/30)$
    $= 4 + 2 + 0.6 = £6.60$
  - Holding cost per month = 0
  - Total expected cost per month = £6.60

Table 2.3—Days to replace stock probability distribution

Number of days n	3	2	1	0
Probability $P(n)$	0.01	0.04	0.15	0.80
Cumulative probability $CP(n)$	0.01	0.05	0.20	1.00

George was taken through this analysis of the four policies fairly quickly; he wanted to understand how it was done but not the calculation details. A summary table prepared for George was the focus of most discussion, provided here as Table 2.4. The final line of Table 2.4 was rounded to the nearest pound as a reminder to avoid attributing spurious accuracy to the results.

Nicola acknowledged that stockouts have an important nuisance value for Pete and his staff, with possible extra fitting costs, which this model does not capture. She suggested that a zero safety stock would probably not be a good idea, despite its apparent slight advantage prior to rounding, and the case for planned stockouts made earlier. She recommended a safety stock of 100, policy 3, highlighted in Table 2.4. She suggested that Pete was adopting a cautious 'zero risk of stockouts' policy that was not a good idea. Policy 3 involves 0.01 probability of a 2 day stockout and 0.04 probability of a 1 day stockout. This sounds (and feels) significant to Pete in the context of a cost 100 times C_h. But in the context of a monthly order of 2000, a safety stock of 300 involves 100 controls which are only needed for 1 day every $1/0.01 = 100$ months, and another 100 which are only needed for 1 day every $1/0.05 = 20$ months, on average. The consequences of a stockout are irritating for Pete and serious for the firm, but not catastrophic for either. And communication between Pete and Dave about priorities could make the recommended safety stock of 100 fairly free of hassle as well as cost-effective.

Pete's current policy was probably costing the firm about £10 per month more than a safety stock of 100, which she characterized as 'an aggressive reduction in safety stock' policy. Adjusting Q_0 from 1500 to 2000 might increase C_t by about £5 per month, which might (or might not) be overlooked because of other considerations. However, regardless of whether the order quantity is 1500 or 2000, adjusting the safety stock reorder rule from 3 days of production to 1 day of production would save about £10 per month ($18 - 7.40 = 10.60$ rounded).

Nicola finished this part of her presentation by indicating that if both changes suggested by her analysis were implemented, a Q_0 of 1500 and a 1 day reorder rule, about £15 per month could be saved. This would involve an EOQ-based monthly order and holding cost of about £85, plus a safety stock holding and storage cost component of about £10, a total cost of about £95 per month. The major saving would be associated with a more aggressive approach to shortages which would involve a culture shift, and it would greatly benefit in operational terms from more

Table 2.4—Summary of safety stock issues

Policy number	1	2	**3**	4
Safety stock, days production	3	2	1	0
Safety stock, number of controls	300	200	100	0
Expected holding cost per month (£)	18	12	6	0
Probability of stockout	0	0.01	0.05	0.20
Expected stockout cost per month (£)	0	0.20	1.40	6.60
Expected total cost per month (£, rounded)	18	12	7	7

communication between Pete and Dave about priorities. Simply letting Dave know that Pete needed replacement stock within a day to avoid a stockout would be a useful step in the right direction.

Further Refinements: Influences On Holding Costs

By now George was seriously impressed. He could see clearly that the issues raised went beyond speed controls and savings of £15 per month. Nicola then explained to George that she needed the first two passes at modelling the decision context to win George's confidence, but more importantly, she needed to take George on the same learning curve she had travelled because they both needed a shared basis for understanding what was to follow. Building on George's growing confidence and respect, Nicola suggested they needed to further refine the model to incorporate additional aspects of the decision context.

During her investigations Nicola had observed that invoices for speed control orders take about 15 days to arrive, payment falls due in 30 days, and there are usually payment transfer delays of another 15 days, leading to a free credit period T_c of about 2 months. She pointed out that during this period C_h is only £0.01, because the £0.05 cost of capital component does not apply. Further, Nicola observed that inflation on components like speed controls was currently running at about 16% per annum, implying a capital appreciation C_a of about £0.04 per control per month.

Nicola explained that the EOQ model used in the first pass could be extended to consider the impact of both the capital appreciation and the free credit period. She explained that the mathematics of this model was considerably more complex but the basic approach was the same. She indicated that the details were developed in her course materials (Chapman, Cooper and Page, 1987, Ch. 12), but all George needed to understand was that Figure 2.3 was the equivalent of Figure 2.1, where T_c is the credit period, Table 2.5 was the equivalent of Table 2.1, Figure 2.4 was the equivalent of Figure 2.2, and Tables 2.6 and 2.7 were useful additional tables.

Helping George to interpret Figure 2.3, Nicola indicated that the area of the shape *abcd* could be associated with the £0.01 holding cost component less appreciation of £0.04, but no cost of capital. This involved a negative cost (positive appreciation net of holding cost) of £0.01 − £0.04 = −£0.03. She indicated that the rest of the usual holding cost triangle could be associated with £0.06 holding cost component less appreciation of £0.04. This involved a positive cost of £0.06 − £0.04 = £0.02.

Helping George to interpret Table 2.5 (and the associated Figure 2.4), Nicola

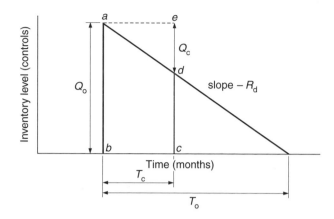

Figure 2.3—Order cycle relationships: credit period allowed.

explained that the order cost component was the same as in Table 2.1. She explained that a more complex expression was used to derive the holding cost component, with negative costs (net appreciation savings) which reached a minimum between $Q_o =$ 6000 and 7000, when the rate of growth of further appreciation costs was overtaken by the rate of growth of further holding costs. Nicola explained that this effect, together with the continually declining order cost component as Q_o increased, meant that average joint cost per unit time, C_t, reached a minimum of about −£64 per month at a Q_0 of about 7000, highlighted for easy identification.

Helping George to understand Table 2.6, Nicola explained this was a summary portrayal of parameter sensitivity, comparable to Table 2.2, but simplified to focus on how Q_o^* changes as the true C_a changes (to demonstrate a reasonably insensitive impact on Q_o^* unless C_a approaches $C_h = 0.06$) and associated C_t^* error (to demonstrate the cost implications). She drew attention to the highlighted values. If the true C_a is 0.02 instead of the assumed 0.04, the Q_o^* error is negligible and the C_t error is only £3 per month. But if the true C_a is 0.06, the Q_o^* becomes infinite and the C_t error is £24 per month, eight times bigger. Nicola pointed out that appreciation had to be predicted with respect to the future; recent (and more distant) past appreciation is no more than a guide. Indeed, a large recent price increase for controls might suggest no further price increases for some time. One

Table 2.5—Joint cost and its components as Q_o changes

Order Quantity Q_o	1000	2000	3000	4000	5000	6000	**7000**	8000
Order cost component	60	30	20	15	12	10	9	8
Holding cost component	−15	−30	−45	−60	−70	−73	−73	−70
Joint cost C_t	45	0	−25	−45	−58	−63	**−64**	−63

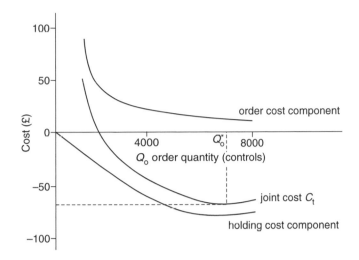

Figure 2.4—Joint cost relationship: graph for $T_c = 2$ months.

important risk (or mistake) was a relatively large order based on assumed appreciation when none took place or a slump led to price decreases. But a much more important risk (or mistake) was a relatively small order based on assumed stable prices when large price increases took place. The relationship between the relative sizes of the holding cost (including the cost of capital) and the rate of appreciation was a key issue here. Infinite order quantities were clearly a nonsense, but they indicated a transition from inventories as costs (a bad thing) to inventories as appreciating assets (a good thing), and associated asymmetry.

Helping George to understand Table 2.7, Nicola explained that the free credit

Table 2.6—C_a sensitivity analysis assuming $C_a = 0.4$, $T_c = 0$

True C_a	−0.02	0	**0.02**	0.04	0.05	**0.06**
Q_o^*	1225	1414	2000	2449	3464	**infinite**
C_t^*	98	85	70	49	35	0
Realized C_t	122	98	73	49	37	24
C_t^* error	24	13	3	0	2	**24**

Table 2.7—T_c sensitivity analysis

T_c	0	1	2	3	4	5	6	12
Q_o^*	2449	4000	6782	9798	**12 884**	16 000	19 131	38 026
C_t^*	49	−20	−64	−104	**−142**	−180	−217	−439

period was not uncertain in the sense that appreciation was, but the credit period was a directly or indirectly negotiable parameter which the value of C_t was clearly very sensitive to.

Nicola finished this part of her presentation by indicating that these results might be implemented directly with a rule: safety stock = 1 day of production. Relative to the current standard order quantity of 2000, in terms of order, holding and appreciation costs as captured by the revised EOQ model, Table 2.5 indicates savings of about £64 per month should be feasible with an increased order quantity of 7000. The safety stock implications (risk of stockout every 3–4 months instead of every month) should save a further £16 per month relative to the 3 day rule with $Q_o = 2000$, say £80 a month in total, £65 a month more than her initial refinement.

Interpreting The Results Of Analysis Creatively

By this stage George was congratulating himself on his great wisdom when hiring Nicola, and glowing with family pride for his niece. Nicola, who fancied an early promotion to the board, now moved in for the kill.

Nicola observed that an important assumption underlying Table 2.5 and Figure 2.4 was that inventory was paid for when used during the free credit period. If this assumption was not made, C_t was affected by the free credit period, but not Q_0^*.

Nicola then observed there would be no point in offering to pay for inventory when it was used (not the case now) unless this could be used to argue for a longer free credit period. For example, the highlighted numbers in Table 2.7 indicated that controls paid for when used with the balance of unused stock paid for after 4 months justified an order of about 12 000 (12 884), 6 months' supply. If an order of 12 000 was on offer, the control supplier might be persuaded to offer an inducement comparable to 4 months of free credit on unused stock. This would generate a further cost saving of about £80 per month ($142 - 64 = 78$).

Nicola then indicated that she had approached the managing director of the control supplier, and indicated that Bob, George's buyer, might be interested in placing a six-monthly order of about 12 000, provided they could be paid for at a uniform rate over the 6 month period at the end of each month, roughly equivalent to paying for them as used, providing a further saving for the mower firm she had not costed directly.

Nicola next indicated she had let the managing director of the controls firm negotiate her to a situation where the 12 000 would not have to be made available for collection by Dave every 6 months. They could be delivered to the mower firm by the controls firm as and when the controls firm wished and in whatever delivery size they wanted, with the guarantee that the mower firm would not have a stockout, in return for a discount on the agreed price. Bob would have to negotiate what the discount would be. This was all further gravy, because the mower firm did not want the order costs or the physical inventory with its holding costs, especially the cost of capital components. All it wanted was a reliable supply at a low price which offered protection from rising prices. Indeed, having a large physical inventory at the start of each cycle would be distinctly unhelpful.

Nicola observed she knew the managing director of the controls firm would wish to push her in the direction agreed because it was clearly in his interests to do so. The flexible approach to production of speed controls, the stable revenue and pre-agreed prices should be worth a significant discount from the speed control firm, sharing that benefit with the mower firm. Nicola also observed that the exact size of the discount was clearly Bob's province, but she could do some further work on what such a deal would be worth to both firms if Bob or George wished. What was involved was supply chain management, taking a partnership view of linkages to share the benefits of integrated practices.

Starting to elaborate on the implications of this approach for the mower firm, Nicola made a number of observations:

- Pete would have to keep an eye on stocks in a control sense, but life should be easier for him
- Arvind and the accounting staff who paid the bills should be pleased with the outcome, because the workload would be smoother
- Dave would never have to visit the controls firm again, and he would have more time for delivering finished goods inventory or other tasks throughout the year
- Bob would no longer have to be a price taker with respect to speed control price; instead he could establish a new negotiating position which should please him and strengthen his hand

Nicola indicated there was clearly scope for extending this analysis to other components for the firm's mowers, further reducing raw material and components inventory holding costs, routine input invoice payment costs, Dave's routine input delivery efforts, and increasing Bob's buying power.

She then indicated that the real opportunity probably lay in applying this thinking to finished goods inventory, working with Sita, George's sales manager. That is, to maintain reasonable production costs and quality control, the mower firm used a fairly steady production rate with large mower stock build-ups over the winter to meet the peak spring demand. Overtime was used to cope with unexpected upturns, but was not usually planned. It would make sense to hold these stocks on the premises of the firms selling them to the public (or their warehouses), persuading vendors to allow this using a combination of pegged prices and discounts and payment only when mowers are sold (it would be important to retain ownership of mowers until they are sold, and manage the risk of related bankruptcies and fraud). If Sita used this approach effectively, she would no longer be a price setter who took orders. She would be in a position to influence or even orchestrate special sales campaigns by the vendors of the firm's mowers in an effective manner.

The speed controller firm would be sharing the benefits of this approach with the mower firm, the key idea flowing from the earlier analysis. Even bigger benefits could be shared between the mower firm and the vendors of its mowers, the key area of application of this idea. Knock-on effects would include a smoother work profile for Dave and the accounting staff. Much more important would be the knock-on effect for Bob and Sita.

Nicola knew that a snappy label for her consignment inventory management approach would help to sell it to George and the others involved, in the tradition of leading management consulting firms. Following the just-in-time label, she called her approach 'my place your timing' for upstream management of controls and other inputs, 'your place my timing' for downstream management of lawnmower and other outputs. George was impressed by this worldly professionalism in his young niece, despite his natural cynism about stylistic issues of this kind.

Nicola finished her presentation without making any promises about the impact of knock-on effects. They would be highly dependent on a range of factors that were beyond her control. However, she indicated that if George approved of her work so far, perhaps she should start talking to Bob and Sita. George readily agreed, and Nicola was on her way to achieving her ambitions.

Nicola worked quite hard to show a saving of £5 per month in her first-pass analysis, using the EOQ model. She managed to save another £10 per month with a comparatively simple stochastic safety stock model in the second-pass analysis, increasing the improvement by a factor of 3. By tackling ambiguities in the form of key assumptions in a third pass, she had suggested a further £65 saving, increasing the improvement by a further factor of 5. However, by interpreting the results of this analysis creatively in a much broader redefinition of the context, the improvements increased by a further very large factor, perhaps 10 or even 100. The hard work of the early analysis was very focused. Its real rewards lay in the creative leaps illustrated in this section. The early analysis was in part an investment in insight and understanding, a learning process. To fail to look for and make associated creative leaps was to waste this investment.

Alternative Creative Interpretations

A seasoned cynic might ask, What if capital appreciation were not an issue because the context was ten years later, or what if Nicola had missed the idea of a free credit period? In this event the results of the second pass would still warrant creative use, and for our purposes it is useful to explore briefly an alternative ending to Nicola's tale. Pretend for the moment that the third pass did not happen, and consider an 'interpret the results creatively' phase which builds directly on the second pass.

Nicola might have started by indicating that speed controls should not be considered in isolation. Dave's comment about spare space in his van is even more important with a reduced order quantity. Next she might have indicated that the economic lot size model form of analysis can be used to size T_o^*, the optimal order interval, rather than Q_o^*, using the identity $T_o = Q_o R_d$. This leads to a periodic review approach to inventory management, conceptually linked to the EOQ approach but operationally quite different. The difference is important if it is convenient, perhaps because of shared transport, to collectively restock items on common cycle patterns. The stochastic safety stock model of the second pass can be used with either. Nicola might then have suggested that it would be useful to perform a crude T_o^* analysis on all production inputs, not just speed controls, and see how the results cluster when plotted on a timescale graph with stock item names listed vertically and a horizontal time plot for T_o^* values. For speed controls, an order quantity of $Q_o = 1500$ units with a monthly demand for 2000 units implies restocking every 3 weeks. If the restocking intervals for all components cluster around 3 weeks like speed controls, a 3 week reorder cycle for all items could be used to set up collection routes for Dave which would minimize mileage to a number of adjacent suppliers and result in a nearly full van each trip.

If restocking intervals were clustered around 1, 4 and 26 weeks, for example, separate weekly, monthly and six-monthly cycles might be developed. Similar ends could be achieved, albeit with more complexity. However, this approach in itself starts to generate some further sources of uncertainty and risk which would have to be managed. For example, if the overall system does not resolve the swings in reorder costs between $C_o = 10$ and $C_o = 50$ between winter and spring associated with speed controls, and similar swings for other items, Table 2.2 suggests somewhat bigger orders in the busy spring time, say 2000 speed controls, and somewhat smaller orders in the slack winter time, say 500 speed controls. This complicates the whole idea of standard collection routes.

A key attraction of the supply chain strategies identified after the third pass is the simplicity on the supply side coupled to the greater flexibility on the output side, and we will not find this in the alternative ending explored here. It is arguable that these strategies are critical even if appreciation and free credit periods are not relevant issues. What matters is a trigger during the analysis and synthesis process which sets the thinking going in the directions that will yield the biggest improvements when the results are finally used in practice. The process of analysis has to be used with this in mind if serendipity (happy unplanned outcomes) is an intended feature of the process, what some people might call making your own luck.

A key insight which underlies sharing benefits via a supply chain partnership is the idea that the ownership and management of both systematic and random variability of inventories is an issue which has to be addressed in terms of both providers and users of those inventories if the cake they are going to divide is to be as large as possible, and it is in both parties' interests to make the cake as big as possible. Put another way, it was the implicit assumption that individual party interests could be addressed independently that was tested and rejected after the third pass. We did not need a formal model to see the benefit of relaxing this assumption given the earlier analysis, although formal analysis could be applied to develop these ideas further.

One of the biggest sources of uncertainty in terms of both risk and opportunity is implicit assumptions. It is important to understand clearly that it is the searching for and testing of assumptions which drives the looping back for successive passes in the decision support process illustrated in this chapter. Looking for fresh insight is made operational in terms of looking for explicit and implicit working assumptions and framing assumptions which matter, in the sense that they constrain our effectiveness.

Other Stock Control Contexts

It would be unwise to suppose that all inventory management contexts could or should be approached via the use of EOQ models plus stochastic safety stock inventory modelling or linked periodic review approaches in the manner employed here.

One implicit assumption in all the previous discussions is that we are dealing with a small number of input items and a small number of output items. If the firm produced 1000 products using 10 000 components, a quite different approach is needed, even if the same models are still viable. For example, Nicola might have started by grouping the speed controls and all other inputs into 10 to 100 categories defined by value, rate of demand, and potential for treatment via the supply chain strategies identified after the third pass. She might then have developed two portfolios or sets of input inventories, one associated with a post third pass treatment, one associated with a post second pass treatment. That is, in terms of horses for courses, we may have to deal with more than one horse for more than one course.

Another implicit assumption in all the previous discussion is that we are dealing with low value items. High-value items like spare engines for commercial airliners require more sophisticated procurement rules, analogous to Pete placing a standard order for more controls with Dave if the stock drops to 100, telephoning him on his mobile at 80, looking for someone else to send at 60, and so on, varying the rules to achieve effectiveness and efficiency. If Nicola's uncle George was in the airline business, her tale might look quite different.

Other Buffer Contexts

Inventories are just one common example of uncertainty management involving the use of a buffer reserve of resources, or slack, in a system. Other forms of buffer raise additional issues about understanding and managing uncertainty. To broaden the discussion, consider the management of time as a buffer.

Suppose that as part of his frequent business trips, George has to drive to London's Heathrow airport, fly to Frankfurt for a meeting expected to last 2–4 hours, and then return. Suppose that he asked Nicola to arrange his tickets and schedule soon after her arrival, prior to her presentation on inventory management. Focusing her analysis, Nicola might suppose that ideally George would like to reach the airport with just an assumed minimum boarding time to spare before take-off. However, uncertainty about the duration of the journey to the airport needs to be factored into the schedule to be reasonably sure that George makes his flight. Arriving too late might be costly for George (and Nicola). Arriving early would also involve costs in terms of inefficient use of George's time. Therefore an appropriate buffer or level of slack needs to be introduced into George's schedule. For example, George's existing practice might involve a 60 minute buffer, implying that if the minimum boarding time is 15 minutes he plans to arrive $15 + 60 = 75$ minutes before take-off.

To address this problem Nicola could have used the stochastic inventory model for the lawnmowers to optimize the buffer time between arriving at Heathrow and Frankfurt airports and the last chance to board, being explicit about the sort of trade-offs George would make intuitively if he made the arrangements himself. Nicola might have started by estimating the $P(d)$ probabilities associated with various lengths of delay over and above the minimum feasible time required to reach the airport check-in desk. Based on her own experience of driving to Heathrow, Nicola might set out estimates in the format of Table 2.8, assuming George would confirm or adjust these figures if the results of her analysis interested him. An initial working assumption is that delays within a given range are all equally likely. The assumed ranges might exclude major delays caused by motorway pile-ups and any other reasons for extending the actual journey by more than 120 minutes over the minimum, on the grounds that a buffer would not be appropriate in such cases.

Nicola might then have developed the following analysis, summarized in Table 2.9, assuming she knows her uncle well enough to characterize the base case as his current practice, and it would be diplomatic to choose parameter values which show his current practice as an optimal solution, although a different solution was the recommended outcome. The initial analysis might assume that the value of time spent at Heathrow waiting for the flight booked is costed at £1 per minute, and that missing a flight is costed at £100. The £100 would have to include a valuation of the time spent waiting for a subsequent flight, the opportunity cost associated with delaying (or missing) the appointment, and any costs associated

Table 2.8—Probability of relevant delay driving to Heathrow

Relevant delay range (minutes)	0–30	30–60	60–90	90–120
Probability $P(d)$	0.4	0.3	0.2	0.1
Cumulative probability $CP(d)$	0.4	0.7	0.9	1.0
Associated buffer choices	30	60	90	120

with rebooking. In terms of appropriate decisions, it is the relative costs that matter.

Nicola might have evaluated three possible policies as follows:

- **Policy 1**: George's current practice (base case)
  - Buffer of 60 minutes
  - Probability of missing plane = 0.3
  - Expected cost of missing plane = $0.3 \times 100 = £30$
  - Expected cost of waiting for booked flight is
    $(0.3 \times (60 - 45) \times 1) + (0.4 \times (60 - 15) \times 1) = 4.5 + 18 = £23$
  - Total expected cost = $30 + 23 = £53$

- **Policy 2**: 50% increase in buffer time
  - Buffer of 90 minutes
  - Probability of missing plane = 0.1
  - Expected cost of missing plane = $0.1 \times 100 = £10$
  - Expected cost of waiting for booked flight is
    $(0.2 \times (90 - 75) \times 1) + (0.3 \times (90 - 45) \times 1) + (0.4 \times (90 - 15) \times 1)$
    $= 3 + 13.5 + 30 = £47$
  - Total expected cost = $10 + 47 = £57$

- **Policy 3**: doubling the buffer
  - Buffer of 120 minutes
  - Probability of missing plane = 0
  - Expected cost of missing plane = 0
  - Expected cost of waiting for booked flight is
    $(0.1 \times (120 - 105) \times 1) + (0.2 \times (120 - 75) \times 1)$
    $+ (0.3 \times (120 - 45) \times 1) + (0.4 \times (120 - 15) \times 1)$
    $= 1.5 + 9 + 22.5 + 42 = £75$
  - Total expected cost = £75

Table 2.9 shows the effect of changing the cost of a missed flight from £100 to £200 and £300. Nicola might have thought £300 was appropriate, using the £100 to explain the base case. Nicola might have started to help George interpret Table 2.9 by suggesting that £100 per missed flight is probably too low, but if £100 is appropriate, and the $P(d)$ values are appropriate, then George's current policy has the lowest expected cost and is appropriate. She might have pointed out that

Table 2.9—Summary of the buffer time issues

Policy number	1	2	3
Buffer time allowed	60	90	120
Probability of missing flight	0.3	0.1	0
Expected cost of waiting for booked flight	23	47	75
Expected cost of missed flight using £100 per flight	30	10	0
Expected total cost using £100 per missed flight	53	57	75
Expected cost of missed flight using £200 per flight	60	20	0
Expected total cost using £200 per missed flight	83	67	75
Expected cost of missed flight using £300 per flight	90	30	0
Expected total cost using £300 per missed flight	103	77	75

even in this case, moving to policy 2 only increases the expected total cost by £4, and it drops the probability of missing the plane from 0.3 to 0.1.

She might then have pointed out that £200 per missed flight clearly switches the lowest expected total cost choice to policy 2. If George was happy with the probabilities, Nicola could have determined the decision flip-point in terms of the cost per missed flight; it is around £140. She might then have pointed out that £300 per missed flight clearly switches the lowest expected total cost policy to policy 3. At this point she might have revealed her view that £300 might be a more appropriate value than £100.

George might well have wanted to change the $P(d)$ values, and the relative costs, but it is likely such an analysis would suggest he generally cuts it too fine, and that a significant increase in the planned buffer would be appropriate. In support of this change of policy, Nicola could have interpreted the results creatively by suggesting a change in attitude on George's part. She could have encouraged George to stop thinking about the time waiting for the booked flight as wasted, and start thinking about it as an opportunity to spend an hour or so away from interruptions to think about strategic issues, read material he needs to catch up on, and so on. She could have suggested he arranges access to an executive lounge to make this more pleasant and effective. This is analogous to Sita explaining to the sellers of the firm's mowers that for them to hold large stocks of mowers in the winter is not a bad thing, because they don't have to pay for them, they will be given discounts which pay for the physical storage costs, and they will be helped via national advertising campaigns to hold special sales periodically to shift large numbers of mowers at bargain prices. The trick is turning a problem into an opportunity.

If Nicola wanted to build further on her reputation for comprehensive understanding of uncertainty, she might have explained this link between inventories, George's time in airports, and the way George runs the firm's projects. In the general context of project planning, all slack time between the finish of some activities and the start of others is a buffer. Some people treat all such buffers as a bad thing, to be eliminated by starting all activities as late as possible. As Goldratt

(1997) argues, this is a wasted opportunity to understand and manage the uncertainty in projects. This issue is explored further in Chapter 6.

Other buffers George's firm might consider include spare resource provision, factors of safety in designs in the overengineering sense, margins of reliability in components, factors of safety in terms of the way systems concerned with health and safety are operated, contingencies in budget estimates, and many more.

If Nicola really wanted to impress upon George the ubiquitous nature of buffers, she might use some examples from his favourite hobby or recreational activity. For example, if he is a sailor, carrying a bit less sail than the present wind allows is a buffer in relation to unexpected increases in wind strength, and the same models can be used to analyse different policies for racing or casual cruising.

Conclusions

Constructive simplicity

Simple, explicit, deterministic models are very valuable, as illustrated by the basic EOQ model used in Nicola's first-pass analysis. The basic structure such simple models provide is a useful starting point for examining and understanding key features of a decision situation and guiding further analysis. The deterministic nature is an asset, not a liability, because it clarifies ambiguity without the complexity of associated variability. Simple, explicit, probabilistic models are also very useful, as illustrated by the basic safety stock model used in Nicola's second-pass analysis. Complexity is added, but in the spirit of constructive simplicity.

All passes through the general decision support process of Figure 1.1 involve keeping the models as simple as possible, but facilitating the introduction of useful constructive complexity, as and when appropriate, is important. This is illustrated by Nicola's second-pass analysis, further illustrated by the consideration of inflation and free credit in Nicola's third-pass analysis. Central to this incremental addition of constructive complexity is the transparency of assumptions, the rigorous testing of assumptions, the highly iterative nature of the process, and the concern for holistic synthesis which extends to 'interpret the results creatively'. Constructive simplicity as a whole involves features not yet touched on but which subsequent chapters will illustrate. However, Nicola's tale provides a useful starting point.

Appreciating trade-offs

An important aspect of any decision is the role of trade-offs between basic performance measures. In Nicola's tale the trade-off between order costs and holding costs was a central issue. Simple, explicit deterministic models can be very useful in clarifying the nature of the trade-offs involved for different parties in the decision context.

Informal, intuitive approaches are usually biased by the provider of the intuition to a greater extent than related formal processes. For example, Pete's intuitive approach led to a slightly larger order quantity than the first-pass analysis. This is marginally more expensive for the firm, and marginally more convenient for Pete. This result should not come as a surprise. Pete might not be familiar with EOQ models, but he will have an intuitive grasp of the trade-offs involved, for himself and for his firm. On a learning by doing basis, Pete will tend to settle on a reasonably appropriate solution in these terms. However, even a very simple formal model may provide the insight for a modest improvement, in terms of separating out what is in the best interests of the individuals and the organization, as well as in terms of classifying what key trade-offs need attention. Managing the motivation aspects of the stockholding issue was important with respect to Pete and other parties.

Explicit treatment of uncertainty associated with Pete's safety stock was useful to capture further trade-offs, in this case between holding costs and stockout costs. This provided much more fertile grounds for improvements in cost, despite the very low level of uncertainty involved, in terms of 0, 1 or 2 day replenishment of stock and the corresponding small size of the safety stock relative to the order quantity.

The importance of questioning assumptions

A key turning point in Nicola's analysis as presented to George was the recognition that an assumption of zero appreciation (inflation) and immediate payment for goods delivered (cash on delivery), implicit in the basic EOQ model, was not true and that using more realistic assumptions matters. The authors, along with most others familiar with the use of EOQ models, did not realize the import-ance of these hidden assumptions until the late 1970s, fifty years after these models were first used. The resulting paper (Chapman et al., 1984) flushed out some earlier papers and generated considerable discussion; a stream of subse-quent papers addresses the impact of both inflation and free credit periods. However, for half a century most people who wrote about or used a very popular basic inventory model were not aware of key implicit assumptions. Yet the consequences in Nicola's tale are orders of magnitude more important than the stochastic model.

In terms of Nicola's tale, most of the variability aspect of uncertainty was simply and effectively addressed via a safety stock. This aspect of uncertainty was of trivial importance and difficulty relative to the ambiguity aspects of uncertainty in the sense of assumptions made without realizing them. The assumptions which surrounded the models used were the key source of uncertainty. Later chapters will pay much less attention to framing assumptions, but their importance in all contexts should not be underestimated, although it is very easy to do so.

Nicola's tale also illustrates different levels of ambiguity associated with assumptions. For example, the successively more general models introduced in the first, second and third passes involve successively more complex sources of ambiguity associated with working assumptions which can be modelled directly. Whether or not Nicola reached the best possible strategy development direction, discussed briefly after the third pass, is clearly not amenable to modelling. In between these levels of ambiguity is the implicit assumption that stocking policy can be optimized independently with respect to the organizations whose supply chain links are upstream and downstream. In principle this issue of dependence might be modelled, but it may not be appropriate to do so. What matters is the need to understand the full range of ambiguity, and to use a process of analysis and synthesis which addresses the whole range.

A failure to understand the scope for ambiguity is sometimes closely linked to confusion between models and theory. Ward, Chapman and Klein (1991) explore this issue in the context of the newsboy safety stock model used in the second pass from a constructively simple perspective.

The importance of creative interpretation

Another key turning point in Nicola's analysis was her use of creative flair when recognizing the opportunities unleashed by the insights generated by the third-pass analysis. The final approach to the procurement of speed controls suggested by Nicola, her 'my place your timing' approach, was orders of magnitude more effective than the third-pass analysis results, and generalizing it to all buying and selling has a clear potential to deliver even more benefits. What is at issue here is the recognition of all levels of ambiguity in respect of framing assumptions. Nicola looked at all inputs and all outputs for the mower firm, and other firms linked in the supply chain. She relaxed assumptions concerning the scope of her brief, and identified interdependencies beyond her brief.

Significantly, Nicola went well beyond her brief in terms of her synthesis. She was guilty of constructive insubordination. And constructive insubordination is an important aspect of creative interpretation of results. Making sure that the dialogue which can be triggered by constructive insubordination is rewarded, not punished, was for George an important part of the process of understanding uncertainty. It was even more important than removing the ambiguity illustrated by the hidden assumptions about appreciation and free credit periods. Ironically perhaps, explicitly encouraging constructive insubordination can help with the more subtle hidden assumption issues. It is also part of the business of managing motivation.

The models employed in analysis and synthesis are a map that we use to guide us in this search for any hidden assumptions or inappropriate constraints on scope. The modelling process is the way we use the map to get to our goals. The quality of the map matters, but the way we use it is even more important. The bottom line is achieving our goals in the broadest sense.

Downside variability and other aspects of risk

Minimizing expected cost has been the focus throughout this chapter. Risk, in the usual sense of potential downside variability relative to expected outcomes, has not been addressed. In particular, there are some serious supply chain risks associated with Nicola's analysis which might be addressed somewhat separately by other analytical processes. For example, if the firm producing speed controls had gone into liquidation or had suffered a major industrial dispute and there were no alternative suppliers, George would have been in serious difficulties. Other buffers associated with other risks might also be addressed somewhat separately. The buffer for planning driving to Heathrow flagged this by its focus on relevant delays. A 50-car pile-up on the motorway which involves George is a risk for George in more ways than one, but considering this risk is not relevant to the size of the buffer, because buffers cannot deal with this kind of risk. Subsequent chapters will develop this issue at some length.

Alternative approaches

There are of course quite different approaches which could be taken to this kind of situation. Christopher (1998) and Ballow (1999) are examples of general references on logistics and supply chain management which cover a range of alternative approaches. The spirit of alternative approaches might be captured in modified versions of Nicola's approach, or aspects of Nicola's approach might be embedded in these alternative approaches. Our concern here is not to recommend a unique way to approach supply chain management, but to illustrate the nature of associated uncertainty and the insights provided by a constructively simple approach.

3 Martha's tale: Setting bids and other pricing decisions

If you can keep your head when all about you, others are losing theirs and blaming it on you, perhaps you don't understand the situation.
Adapted from 'If' by Rudyard Kipling

Introduction

Bidding to obtain work from other organizations or from other parts of the same organization is found in one form or another in many organizations. It is a process which involves addressing two basic sources of uncertainty. One is uncertainty about the cost of carrying out work. The other is uncertainty about what price to offer the customer. A high bid price increases the chance of making a profit if the bid is accepted, but reduces the chance of the bid being accepted. A low bid price increases the chance of winning work, but decreases the chance of the work being profitable.

The tale of this chapter is about the development of an efficient and effective formal process for formulating competitive bids by a major player in the computing and information systems field. The tale focuses on the initial development of a formal process using a particular contract as a vehicle to illustrate both the nature of the analysis required and the nature of the uncertainty management issues that ought to be addressed. Although the tale is set in a specific context, using a particular example contract with associated data, the ideas and experience described here are readily transferable to a wide range of other situations. Many organizations would benefit substantially from adopting a process directly comparable to the bid preparation process described here.

If the reader is not directly interested in bidding, the principles discussed in this chapter are still worth understanding at a reasonably detailed level, as part of the overview provided by the book as a whole, and as a basis for the development of linked ideas in later chapters. The details shape and clarify the principles, in addition to the obvious converse dependence. For example, a context discussed briefly on page 112, to illustrate the generality of bidding processes, is the disposal of UK intermediate-level nuclear waste by UK Nirex. The process described in the main body of this chapter would require significant transformations to accommodate this alternative context. However, the reader will have a much clearer view of what is required to deal with the nuclear waste context if the details of the computing and information systems example used in this chapter are understood at a general level.

This tale includes detailed discussion of several aspects, including analysis of cost uncertainty (pages 73–88), and assessment of the probability of winning (pages 88–96). The reader might like to skim over these sections on a first reading, and focus on the overall form of the bid preparation process. As the section headings indicate, the process involves multiple passes with each pass addressing different kinds and levels of uncertainty using successively more detailed analysis. In terms of the general problem-solving process of Figure 1.1, the bid preparation process described here emphasizes the iterative nature of a constructively simple approach, with different forms of modelling and analysis in successive passes. In the present tale, the scope of first, second, third and subsequent passes is an important illustration of the need to scope and plan the analytical effort to ensure efficient as well as effective uncertainty management.

A Bidding Opportunity for Astro

Martha and Barney were a perfect pair, a 'study of syncopated synergy in management teamwork', as their colleague Trevor liked to put it after the way they worked together became legend. Trevor invariably generated audible groans from his colleagues when he indulged in this kind of music hall language, but everyone agreed with his judgement.

Barney attracted the nickname 'Barney the Beaver' from his friends at school. He ascribed this to his hardworking approach to sport and chasing girls as well as his studies. Barney's detractors at school called him 'Boring Barney'. He was very pleased to become just plain Barney at university, although this did not reflect any change in his approach to life. He graduated with a degree in accounting and economics in 1985. He was 'saved from a lifetime as an accountant', as he liked to put it, by Astro Computer Systems. He was recruited by Astro's London office, but based in Cardiff, in Astro's head office for Wales. There he soon became known as 'Barney the Bid'. Welsh humour of this kind did not greatly amuse Barney, but he found this nickname quite useful in the establishment of his initial role within Astro Wales. Barney reported to Martha, marketing director for Astro Wales.

The morning Barney started working for Astro Wales, Martha was very upset. Astro Wales had just lost the third of three unsuccessful bids that month for major 'systems integration' projects. 'Systems integration' was Astro jargon for a complete system, including hardware, software, physical facilities and training, normally incorporating the functionality of heritage systems, existing hardware and software, in addition to providing new functionality, usually tendered for on a fixed price basis with performance penalties. Martha knew that the loss of three major systems integration bids in a row was not just bad luck. There were clear symptoms of serious problems in Astro Wales. Sales representatives were complaining to Martha that Systems people were taking far too long to cost things, they were taking far too long to get approval for their costs from their managers, and their solutions to problems were often far too conservative (safe and expensive). Systems people were complaining to Martha that Sales people were putting unreasonable pressure on them to provide quick responses to difficult questions and to cut corners, that most of their efforts were wasted because of lost bids, and that the bids that were won were the wrong ones. Both groups were implying the problem was serious and that it was up to Martha to resolve it. Neither group seemed to understand why they were so unsuccessful, and it was clearly up to Martha to clarify the situation. The panic level was rising.

Astro Wales was a division of Astro UK, which was part of Astro Inc., a US-based worldwide major player, with a premium end of the market image. Astro worldwide was experiencing difficulties similar to Martha's. The word on the street was that Astro Inc. had lost its way and was in danger of losing the plot altogether. Martha's view was that the competition had simply become much tougher, and Astro Inc. had not yet adjusted in terms of organizational structure, process or culture. Martha had been promoted to her current post six months earlier. She had spent this time largely focused on the strategic or macro-management aspects of her new job, which were unfamiliar. She had deliberately avoided getting involved in the details of individual bids or the bid process. However, Martha was aware of the opening quote for this chapter, and knew she did not understand what Astro's problems were. More specifically, she needed to get to grips with the details of Astro Wales' difficulties with systems integration projects. Martha saw the present systems integration sales crisis as a spur to sort out bidding processes more generally in Astro Wales, and to start to address the much more difficult associated culture issues. For Martha there was no such thing as a problem, only opportunities. If she could sort out Astro Wales, she might get the opportunity to sort out Astro UK on the way to Astro worldwide.

Martha knew that Barney had studied operational research (OR) as part of his economics and accounting degree, and assumed he should know something about bidding models and associated processes. Martha's academic training was philosophy. This gave her a very structured approach to business issues, with a strong concern for the internal consistency of sets of assumptions, and clear logic. Martha asked Barney to act as coordinator and facilitator for a new bidding process. Martha and Barney would design this process as they went, using as a test case a systems integration bid for Transcon. Transcon was a containerized freight road transport company recently formed from the merger of two successful firms, one based in Wales, one based in Hampshire, with a view to attracting the growing container freight market in Europe.

Astro had a tradition of throwing new staff in at the deep end, and rewarding them if they learned to swim the requisite strokes quickly. Martha made this clear to Barney, and she made it clear that she expected him to take the lead in the bidding model and process design. However, she reassured him that all his ideas could be tried out on her first, she would contribute as required to their development, and her authority would be behind him when they had an agreed approach. Martha let it be known that she was marketing director for Wales by her late twenties because she had been given similar tests in Astro Scotland, and she was now on a fast track. If Barney succeeded, he could expect similar rapid promotion.

The Transcon invitation to tender had just arrived on Martha's desk that morning, out of the blue. Trevor was the obvious Astro sales representative for Martha to make responsible for the Transcon bid, because of his transport sector experience. Martha introduced Barney to Trevor. Martha indicated that she wanted Trevor to use Barney as a bid coordinator and facilitator for the Transcon bid, so that she and Barney could design a new systems integration bidding process for Astro Wales. Martha made it clear to Trevor that his input would help to shape the process as a whole. Trevor knew Martha well enough to know what that meant, in terms of both carrots and sticks. Martha also introduced Barney to Sian. Sian was responsible for the Systems people who would cost the Transcon systems integration project, and those Systems people who would implement some of it if the bid was won. Martha made Barney's role clear to Sian, and also emphasized the importance of Sian's input to shaping the process as a whole. Sian knew Martha even better than Trevor. Sian and Martha were technically on the same management level, both reporting to Rhys, manager for Astro Wales, but Martha had an edge because Astro was a market-driven organization.

Martha indicated that she wanted Barney to prepare a document for her which summarized what this bid was about, in the sense that everyone involved could agree that this document was the starting point for formal analysis of the Transcon bid. Martha provided Barney with a desk and left him to it. It wasn't even time for lunch on his first day with Astro Wales.

A Preliminary Proposal Document

During their initial discussion, Trevor suggested that Barney should start by visiting Transcon with him. Trevor would naturally do most of the talking, but Barney could take notes which, subject to Trevor's approval, would form the basis of the documentation Sales passed to Systems to facilitate a technical specification and costing. Trevor was very happy to start this way. Barney would be making himself useful as Trevor's gopher, and Trevor could control the shape of the document Martha wanted. Barney was also very pleased to start this way. He needed guidance from someone, and Trevor was the obvious choice. By lunchtime Trevor had arranged an appointment that afternoon with key Transcon staff.

Following the afternoon's meeting, Barney proceeded to write up his notes on the meeting to provide an initial working document for Astro Wales. Trevor loved acronyms and similar abbreviations, usually with three letters. Although most Astro staff winced each time a new one was invented, they usually adopted it, for convenience as well as to humour Trevor, who everybody liked. Trevor referred to Barney's document based on his initial enquiries as the draft PPD (preliminary proposal document). The draft PPD began with some general background information. For example, Transcon had been formed eight months earlier by the merger of Eurofleet Containers and Continental Haulage. The new company would be operating from 15 depots, all in the UK. The head office was in Cardiff. The managing director of Transcon had commissioned an assessment of Transcon's future information system needs by a leading firm of consultants. The consultants had reported that about half the systems being used in the former companies would remain useful, but they should be converted for a single new-generation mainframe. The rest of the systems should be scrapped and replaced with proprietary software packages, and a major new scheduling system would be required, with capability distributed to the 15 depots. The consultants went on to recommend that Transcon should go out to tender for a new computer system capable of taking over the existing work and providing additional capacity to cope with the new scheduling system. Their offer to develop the invitation to tender was duly accepted, executed, and sent to Martha at Astro Wales among others.

The draft PPD provided a brief summary of the technical details in terms of Trevor's views on what should be provided. This involved a simple five-item breakdown of the work to be included in the bid. The draft PPD also provided a brief summary of the marketing issues in terms of information gleaned by Trevor, shaped to some extent by Barney's questions.

Following their meeting with Transcon, Barney pushed Trevor to give him an estimate of what he referred to as the preliminary maximum bid, and Astro's chance of winning at this level, to size the upper end. Trevor put the preliminary maximum bid at about £20 million, with a 10% chance of winning. Barney also pushed Trevor to give him an estimate of what he called the preliminary minimum bid, and Astro's chance of winning at this level, to size the lower end. Trevor put the preliminary minimum bid at about £15 million, with an 80% chance of winning. Barney incorporated this in the draft PPD, noting that a senior manager of Transcon had let slip (probably deliberately) that Transcon's budget for this contact was a maximum of £20 million, but that no information on competitive bids was available as yet. Barney finished the draft PPD that evening. Trevor agreed with it next morning, apart from editing with a bold red pen, never allowing three words if two would do. Barney then approached Sian. Barney indicated that the draft PPD was a very preliminary document, designed to consider the bid in a preliminary way. It did not require any commitments on Sian's part. It needed completing by Sian at the simple level set out in the draft. Sian agreed that her staff would flesh out the PPD in terms of Trevor's simple five-item breakdown of the work required. Here is a summary of Trevor's five-item breakdown and the elaborations of Sian's staff, provided later that week, which were incorporated in the revised PPD.

Preliminary Proposal Document

Item 1: Central Site Equipment

One new mainframe computer was required to replace both existing machines. It would be located in Transcon's Cardiff head office. It must run the converted subset of existing application software plus the new scheduling system. The proposed equipment should have a spare capacity of at least 50% in terms of the converted and new software as installed, to allow for proprietary packages and other post-installation growth. Contractual guarantees on capacity were required. An Astro mainframe computer and peripherals were specified and the direct cost to Astro Wales for this equipment (from Astro Inc.) was £3.6 million. This compared with a usual selling price for this equipment of £5.0 million. Sian's estimator noted a high degree of confidence in the utilization estimates for the proposed new equipment, based on extensive experience of similar bids, but a source of risk for this component (implying a possible need for additional memory) linked to item 4.

Item 2: Computer Suite Modifications

The new mainframe computer would be installed in a room adjacent to the existing mainframe machine room at Transcon's head office, to avoid disturbing existing operations. The two existing mainframe machine rooms would be emptied and released for alternative use as soon as parallel operation was no longer required. Astro would design the new facility and provide a project manager to supervise the work. A subcontractor, Zenith Controls, would undertake the installation work for a fixed price. The Astro direct cost estimate was £0.30 million. The Zenith preliminary quote was £1.00 million. Sian's estimator noted a high degree of confidence in the Astro component estimate but indicated that actual prices contracted with Zenith were usually between 10% and 30% higher than preliminary quotations.

Item 3: Initial Operation and Training

Operators would be provided to run the new systems in parallel with the old systems initially. Transcon's staff would then be trained to take over, and supported during the takeover process. The transition should be complete within 6 months from the installation of the new system. Sian's estimator noted that two options were available.

(a) Zoro Computing would undertake this task on the Transcon site for a fixed fee. Zoro's preliminary quote was £1.00 million.

(b) An existing Astro computer site, an Astro service bureau close to Transcon's head office, could be used for initial operation, with a service contract for training the customer's operators on Astro premises. An estimate of the direct cost was £0.8 million.

Sian's estimator indicated that experience with Zoro on previous contracts suggested that fixed prices actually contracted were between 20% and 40% higher than preliminary quotations. Zoro had a very good track record of success on Astro and other contracts. However, they were currently the subject of a hostile takeover bid. Astro had two contracts in progress similar to option (b), both going reasonably to plan, but no other similar contract experience. The Astro estimate was based on estimated hours effort by Astro service bureau staff with back-up from Astro's training staff (not local). Both existing contracts were close to completion. One was currently 10% below budget, the other 40% over budget. The estimator recommended option (b).

Item 4: Convert Existing Programmes

A subset of Transcon's existing financial programmes would be converted and associated documentation would be updated. Runtime savings of 25% would be required. Current documentation was 'believed to be reasonable – 95% accurate', according to the invitation to tender. Sian's estimator indicated two options here:

(a) Datapol systems would undertake this task, using new-generation languages to rewrite the software. Datapol was willing to commit now to the required runtime savings and a firm fixed price of £1.20 million.

(b) Sysdoc Autocode would undertake this task, using an automatic converter to translate about 90% of the code, manual patching to deal with the balance of about 10% which proved non-viable for automatic translation. Sysdoc had provided an initial estimate of £0.50 million based on a fixed fee rate per man day.

Sian's estimator indicated that Datapol was a large well established company. Sysdoc was a relatively new company, with only 100 employees, but it had a good record of success on smaller projects. Sysdoc would not commit to a fixed price, but would commit to a measured day rate contract. Cost variability was associated with the proportion of the translation achieved automatically, programme documentation, house standards, and so on.

Sian's estimator indicated that either approach could give rise to a requirement for more memory than that assumed in relation to the central site equipment (item 1). The estimator believed there was a 50% chance that additional memory would be needed to meet the capacity and performance guarantees. He estimated that if sufficient additional memory to meet this contingency was specified and installed at the outset, the additional cost would be £0.50 million. If installed subsequently, he estimated the additional cost would be £1.0 million. The estimator recommended option (a) and pre-installing the additional memory.

Item 5: Distributed Scheduling System

A distributed scheduling system would have to be developed, to operate in each of the 15 depots, linked to the mainframe. Subsecond response time was required. Sian's estimator indicated two options in this case as well. Both involved 15 Astro workstations with a direct cost of £3.00 million (usual selling price £4.20 million) However, the development and installation of the system involved a choice between:

    (a) Astro (Sian's) staff, man years direct cost £1.10 million, plus a 20% contingency, for an estimated total of £1.32 million

    (b) Zoro subcontract, preliminary estimate £1.00 million

Sian's estimator noted that Astro had completed three successful projects very similar to option (a), and drew attention to the comments on Zoro associated with initial operation and training (item 3), in terms of high-quality deliverables but a potential hostile takeover, and 20–40% uplifts from preliminary quotes to fixed prices.

Sian's estimator also noted that either approach might give rise to a need for more powerful distributed computing equipment. The estimator believed there was a 50% chance that additional performance would be required to meet response time performance guarantees. She estimated that if higher-performance equipment to meet this contingency was specified and installed at the outset, the additional cost would be £1.00 million. If installed subsequently, she estimated that the additional cost would be between £1.5 million and £2.5 million.

Sian's estimator recommended option (a) and pre-installing the additional performance.

Sian was pleased with the form and content of the PPD, although she was as handy with a red pen as Trevor. Sian ensured that the quality of the drafting matched Trevor's, and she was confident that the level of the detail provided would be seen as useful. When Barney received the PPD with the Systems contribution incorporated and edited, he was very impressed. He showed it to Martha, and Martha reviewed the PPD quickly while Barney waited. They then discussed what to do next.

Martha indicated that current Astro UK policy was a normal overhead recovery rate of 30% on all Astro direct costs and subcontract costs, and a normal further 10% profit margin on total (direct and indirect) cost for all contracts. Martha and Barney agreed that this information should be part of the PPD, even though this policy was generally known. Martha and Barney also agreed that the PPD as completed to date should now be copied to Trevor and Sian, with a copy of the invitation to tender attached as an annex.

Martha and Barney then spent some time working through what they anticipated would be the formal analysis built on the PPD. On the basis of this, Martha arranged a meeting with Trevor and Sian to review the PPD, and to outline the associated bidding process.

A Proposed Multiple-Pass Process

Martha opened the review meeting by suggesting that bid preparation ought to involve a multiple-pass process. The first pass should be concerned with identifying and eliminating from further consideration contracts which were non-starters in feasibility or risk terms. The second pass should be concerned with identifying and eliminating from further consideration no-hopers, contracts which were feasible but which did not look promising enough in terms of potential profit to analyse any further. The third pass should be concerned with deciding an approximate bid price and bidding strategy for remaining candidates. Each of these three passes involved managing different kinds and levels of uncertainty best addressed by different styles of successively more detailed analysis. Further passes would also be involved, but they would not be discussed directly at this meeting.

Martha indicated that she thought the outline information provided by Trevor in the PPD was perfect for a second-pass uncertainty management process, aimed at identifying no-hopers. Martha indicated that she thought that the more detailed information provided by Sian in the PPD was perfect for a third-pass uncertainty management process, aimed at deciding an approximate bid price and bidding strategy, given a potential contract had passed the second stage. However, she thought Sian's input was too good for analysing a second pass. In Martha's view, there was a serious mismatch between the level of effort provided by Trevor and Sian. Martha said she appreciated that Trevor may have expected this level of detail from Sian in the past, and Sian may have felt a professional approach required it, but Astro could not afford to invest this much effort in a bid proposal which might be revealed as a no-hoper with relatively simple input from Sian's staff. Martha further elaborated by saying that the PPD was completely missing a suitable basis for a first-pass uncertainty management process, concerned with identifying non-starters as distinct from no-hopers.

Martha indicated that the exercise to produce the PPD was not a waste of time – it was a crucial first step. What Trevor and Sian had produced was of good quality, perfect in the right context. Also, it was important to begin with a clarification of the best of current practice before considering change, and Martha would regard the PPD as an approximation to the best of current practice. However, they now had to address change, starting with the development of a suitable first-pass uncertainty management process and an associated basis for that process.

First-Pass Uncertainty Management: Identifying Non-starters

In general, by non-starters Martha meant contracts Astro did not want to get involved with for reasons which were not necessarily profit-related in a simple or direct sense. Martha began by suggesting there were a number of quite different kinds of uncertainty associated with non-starters. The first kind of uncertainty which needed to be addressed, as a separate first-pass process, involved a series of questions for identifying a non-starter. These could be addressed in qualitative form, largely with a qualified yes or no answer. For example, early in the list of first-pass uncertainty management process questions there should be a series of questions designed to identify a potential client who was a poor credit risk. Simple tests of creditworthiness should be tried first. If they proved inconclusive, more onerous tests should be used next. Expensive checks might be left until a decision to proceed to a bid had been made. However, if simple tests revealed doubtful creditworthiness, the proposal should be dropped at the outset of the first pass, before any serious analysis effort was wasted. Later in the first-pass uncertainty management process there should be a series of questions designed to identify a serious lack of synergy, or very strong synergy, between what the client needs and Astro objectives. Here are some examples:

- Would the contract require the use of Astro resources which are currently overstretched (or very underutilized)? If so, which resources?
- Is the contract in an area Astro are withdrawing from (trying to get into)? If so, indicate the area.
- Is the contract with an undesirable client (e.g. a major source of pollution receiving a lot of press)? If so, explain the potential fallout for Astro's reputation.

One question revealing a lack of synergy might not define a non-starter, but two or more might make such a definition likely. Questions which reveal very strong synergy would be useful for later bid development, for opportunity management in the third and later passes of the uncertainty management process. Their immediate purpose would be counterbalancing negative answers, and it would be important to identify them as part of the first pass for this reason.

Martha indicated that she was opposed to the use of any simple scoring scheme, adding up pluses and minuses, because this would involve adding apples and oranges. She wanted a no more than a one-page executive summary which argued a view for or against a bid on balance, with the detailed questions and answers available as back-up. Martha would expect Sales to operate this first-pass bidding process, with support from Systems, Accounts (e.g. on credit checks), and other departments as appropriate. She would expect this process to be formal, focused, carefully designed, updated in the light of experience, and documented on each application. She would expect it to be both efficient and effective.

As a target to be used to develop early versions of the first-pass analysis, Martha suggested that Sales and those supporting them should apply about 1% of the effort required for a complete bid, and that about 60% of the potential contracts should be rejected at this stage. If significantly more or less than 60% of the potential contracts survived this first-pass analysis, its balance in relation to later passes should be reconsidered early in careful formal terms. In any event, both the 60% and the 1% targets should be subjected to careful review over time, to see if adjusting these targets would improve the efficiency and effectiveness of the bidding process as a whole. The 60% target was Martha's best educated guess of what to expect, which she would associate with a confidence band of about ±20%, given her uncertainty about how many potential contracts ought to fall into such a category. She wanted the use of separate first-pass uncertainty analysis in relation to the subsequent passes to refine the 60% target. The 1% effort target should also be interpreted as a target to be revised with experience. She would expect a rationale for proposed changes as experience was gained.

Martha indicated that Barney would coordinate the development of this first-pass process, initially working with Trevor, then with other Sales staff, and later with other Astro staff as appropriate. Martha indicated that the deliverable documentation for the first pass should be electronically based throughout its development, and Barney would coordinate this aspect. That is, the questions would be presented to the sales staff responsible for each bid electronically, and their responses would trigger the follow-on question.

Martha finished outlining the first-pass uncertainty management process by emphasizing the separability (not independence) she wanted to see between the different passes, in terms of their objectives and the resulting processes and outputs. In particular, the first pass was a test for non-starters, which would be qualitative in nature, and quite different in character from subsequent passes. To drive home this separability notion, Martha suggested they adapt Trevor's terminology for the preliminary proposal document (PPD) to call the deliverable from the first pass proposal document 1 (PD1). The invitation to tender would be a formal annex to the PD1. Martha would not expect to see or approve PD1s, and Sales personnel would move directly to a second-pass process if a potential contract survived the first pass. However, subsequent contract audits would include non-starters as well as those potential contracts which progressed, to monitor the system and the players in the system rather than individual decisions.

That concludes this chapter's treatment of the first-pass uncertainty management process. It is a simple concept and there is no need to say any more. Simplicity does not imply lack of importance.

Second-Pass Uncertainty Management: Identifying No-hopers

Martha began considering the second-pass uncertainty management process by suggesting that its focus was a preliminary view of profitability. She suggested that its nature was quite different from the first pass. It would be based on a simple quantitative analysis addressing a different kind of uncertainty. It might be usefully characterized as a preliminary quantitative analysis to identify a no-hoper. By no-hoper she meant a potential contract with too little potential profit to make it worth anything beyond rejection after the effort of a second-pass process. She was looking to reject about 40% of those potential bids which survived the non-starter tests, with about 1% of the effort required for a complete bid evaluation process. The second-pass uncertainty management process was similar to the first pass in terms of the level of effort required, but it was expected to reject a significantly lower proportion of potential projects (40% rather than 60%), and in all other key respects it could be very different. As with the first pass, Martha wanted the 40% and 1% figures to be interpreted as initial targets to be refined over time as experience was gained. Martha indicated that she had in mind five separate sequential components for the second-pass uncertainty management process. She would consider them in turn, as steps 1 to 5, producing PD2.1 to PD2.5.

Second-pass initiation to produce PD2.1

Martha indicated that the information provided by Trevor in the PPD was a good basis for the first step of producing a PD2. If a member of the Sales staff progressed a bid beyond a PD1, they should note why, then proceed as Trevor had, visit the client, and make summary notes. The resulting document, a PD2.1, could then be sent by Sales to Systems, for cost input. It should have the completed PD1 as an annex. Martha might have added that preparation of the PD1 prior to visiting the client might focus the discussion in a useful manner in areas of uncertainty flagged by the first-pass uncertainty management process. However, she knew Trevor and other Sales staff would make good use of the PD1 in this way, and did not wish to threaten Trevor's pride any more than necessary.

Second-pass cost uncertainty analysis to produce PD2.2

Martha then indicated that if the PD2.1 as just described had been sent to Sian in Systems, in Martha's view Sian ought to be able to suggest an expected direct cost estimate of £12 million plus or minus about £1 million associated with a preliminary range of actual outcomes of £10–£20 million, on the basis of an hour's consideration, without referring it to other staff. If Sian preferred, she could ask someone else to do the whole hour, but it would have to be someone with an overview based on experience, like Sian. This is the level of input from Systems which Martha wanted for the second pass. Could Sian provide this sort of precision with that level of effort?

Sian had not actually read the PPD or the invitation to tender before passing it on to her staff, but her subsequent close reading of their detailed estimates suggested an expected cost of about £13 million. She was happy to agree that an estimate of expected direct cost of £12 million plus or minus about £1 million associated with a £10–£20 million anticipated outcome range was a preliminary estimate that she or one of her staff with wide experience could produce in an hour or so. Sian liked the way the discussion was going.

Martha then indicated that adding this preliminary cost estimate to the PD2.1 would make it a PD2.2, which could be sent to Barney. Martha then asked Barney to take the floor and explain how he would create a PD2.3.

Second-pass probability of winning analysis to produce PD2.3

Barney started his presentation by reminding everyone that Trevor had provided a preliminary maximum bid and a preliminary minimum bid and associated estimates of the chance of winning in the PPD, now assumed to be incorporated in the PD2.1. He indicated that these estimates could be used to produce a corresponding preliminary estimate of the probability of winning curve. He suggested that the solid straight line between a and b in Figure 3.1 was an appropriate preliminary estimate. Figure 3.1 added to the PD2.2 would define the PD2.3.

Barney indicated that it was important to spend some time discussing what the curve between a and b implied and what underlay it. To begin with, Trevor had indicated a preliminary maximum bid of £20 million, with a chance of winning at this level of about 10%. This information had been used to plot point a on Figure 3.1. Point a was linked to the information slipped, deliberately or otherwise, by a Transcon senior manager, that £20 million was their budget figure. The £20

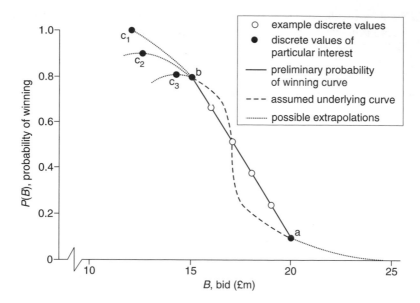

Figure 3.1—Preliminary probability of winning curve.

million figure was presumably based on a recommendation from the consultants who prepared the invitation to tender. It was sensible to use such a figure as a preliminary maximum bid. It was also sensible to then estimate the associated probability of winning to the nearest 10%, as Trevor had done.

Trevor had also identified a preliminary minimum bid of £15 million, with a chance of winning at this level of about 80%. This information had been used to plot point b. The basis of point b was not clear, and this uncertainty might be important. In Barney's view, point b was not necessarily an appropriate preliminary minimum bid. However, for the moment this concern would be ignored. It would be assumed that Trevor had chosen £15 million because he was unsure about the shape of the probability of winning curve below this value, and he did not think it was worth worrying about it. By implication he was reasonably confident about the shape of the curve for bids above £15 million. Trevor looked uncomfortable when Barney suggested that point b might not be an appropriate preliminary minimum bid. Trevor had good reason to be, in the sense that he was not clear why he had selected this value. However, he readily grasped the lifeline Barney had thrown. He indicated that Barney was quite right in assuming he was reasonably confident over the range £15–£20 million, but not below £15 million, and he doubted that below £15 million would be of interest, given the level of information available. Barney thanked Trevor for confirming his interpretation of point b. He then indicated that he had joined points a and b with a solid straight line to define a preliminary probability of winning curve over the preliminary bid range £15–£20 million.

Barney had added the dashed curve between a and b to indicate the nature of the underlying curve. He had also added the dotted curve beyond the preliminary bid range at the top end, and he had added three dotted curves at the bottom end, for bid values below £15 million, to indicate the range of possibilities which might be involved. For example, the curve through c_1 implied a bid of about £12 million would win for sure: Transcon could be convinced that such a bid was a question of buying the work to keep Astro staff busy, and it represented value no competitor could touch. At the other extreme, the curve through c_3 implied a bid below about £14 million would lead to a decrease in the probability of winning because it would suggest to Transcon that Astro lacked credibility: Astro were desperate for work because they were inferior to others in the marketplace, and/or they did not understand what the job was about. The curve through c_2 was an intermediate case, with a peak probability of winning of about 0.9 at a bid of about £13 million. Barncy encouraged a discussion about these dashed and dotted curves, to gain understanding of (and approval for) his simple linear probability of winning curve by exploring the nature of the underlying true curve it approximated. When Barney was pushed about the obvious lack of data associated with this preliminary curve, Martha interjected that it would become clear shortly that such a curve is used implicitly if not explicitly, and explicit use was better than implicit use for a number of reasons, one being the basis it provided for gathering appropriate data.

Barney suggested they leave the question of which of the c_1, c_2 or c_3 curves was most appropriate for the moment, and assume that the preliminary linear curve between a and b provides sufficient precision over a suitable range for a preliminary quantitative (second-pass) analysis. Trevor indicated he was happy with this, although he was not too sure where it was leading. Sian looked puzzled but intrigued. There were no more questions, so Barney pressed on with his presentation, moving to step 4.

Second-pass uncertainty synthesis to produce PD2.4

Barney indicated that the PD2.3 deliverable illustrated by Figure 3.1 and the preliminary cost estimate provided by the PD2.2 now needed to be brought together to produce a preliminary bid setting summary table, as illustrated by Table 3.1. Added to the PD2.3, it would define the PD2.4.

The top line of Table 3.1 indicates the PD2.2 expected direct cost estimate of £12 million plus or minus about £1 million and the associated range of actual outcomes of £10–20 million. The E notation for expected direct cost, $E(C)$, is partially to clarify the computations in the columns which follow. However, the $\pm£1$ million is a measure of potential error in the expected value cstimate, not a measure of spread associated with anticipated actual outcomes. That is why the standard deviation notation was introduced. That is, $V(E(C)) = £0.5$ million

Table 3.1—Summary table (second pass) for preliminary bid setting

Expected direct cost $E(C)$ = £12m ± £1m with an outcome in the range £10–20m anticipated, $V(E(C))$ = £0.5m and $V(C)$ = £2.5m
Probability of winning for a bid of £15m = 0.1, for a bid of £20m = 0.8, linear interpolation, $V(P(B))$ unknown

Bid values B (£m)	Corresponding probabilities $P(B)$	Corresponding margins (conditional) $M = B - E(C)$			Corresponding expected margins $E(M) = P(B)M$		
		$E(C) =$ 11	$E(C) =$ 12	$E(C) =$ 13	$E(C) =$ 11	$E(C) =$ 12	$E(C) =$ 13
15	0.8	4	3	2	3.20	2.40	1.60
16	0.66	5	4	3	3.30	2.64	1.98
17	0.52	6	5	4	3.12	2.60	2.08*
18	0.38	7	6	5	2.66	2.28	1.90
19	0.24	8	7	6	1.92	1.68	1.44
20	0.1	9	8	7	0.90	0.80	0.70

*Maximum $E(M)$ if $E(C)$ is about £13m.

suggests a standard deviation or standard error associated with $E(C)$ of the order of £0.5 million, which implies a 95% confidence interval for $E(C)$ of the order of ±£1.0 million (two standard deviations); the interpretation of $E(C)$ = £12 million ± £1 million is that Sian is about 95% confident the expected value of the direct cost lies in the range £11–13 million. A $V(C)$ value of £2.5 million would imply a 95% confidence interval for the direct cost C in the range £10–20 million, plus or minus two standard deviations, if C had a symmetric approximately Normal (Gaussian) probability distribution. It does not, but citing $V(C)$ helps to clarify the difference between $V(C)$ and $V(E(C))$.

Martha anticipated the slightly glazed looks on Trevor and Sian's faces, and stepped in before Barney got too carried away with this discussion. She indicated that as a philosopher by training, the $V(E(C))$ and $V(C)$ notation left her cold. But all that she, Sian and Trevor needed to understand was that what really mattered was an unbiased estimate of $E(C)$ for the second pass, a tolerable level of error in this estimate, as approximated by $V(E(C))$ and measured roughly during a third pass if they got there, and a range of outcomes approximated by $V(C)$ which Astro could live with on a swings and roundabouts basis over successive contracts. The $E(C)$ = £12 million value was fit for purpose for the second pass in her view, as was the £10–20 million range for outcomes. However the ±£1 million associated with the $E(C)$ = £12 million suggested more precision might be needed if they decided to make a serious bid. Martha, Sian and Trevor agreed they would drop the $V(E(C))$ and $V(C)$ notation in future, to Barney's not very well concealed disgust. But he had made the difference between the £11–13 million range (in $(E(C))$ and the £10–20 million range (in C) reasonably clear, which was what really mattered.

The second line of Table 3.1 indicates the preliminary minimum and maximum bid provided by Trevor in the PD2.2 and the use of the PD2.3. The notation '$V(P(B))$ unknown' indicates that they have no information about the error which might be associated with the $P(B)$ values, the probability of winning with a bid of B. Barney recovered his charm and suggested that this note and notation should be dropped as well, but it was important to be clear that uncertainty associated with $P(B)$ might be much more important than uncertainty associated with $E(C)$. Barney explained that the notation for the table columns was just to clarify the calculations. The concepts here were all straightforward. Six integer values of B define the six-row body of the table. The first column indicates the potential bid values to be considered, working to the nearest £1 million over the preliminary bid range. About half a dozen alternative bid scenarios is a suitable level of detail for preliminary analysis, but more detail could be provided if deemed useful. The second column indicates the probabilities of winning taken from the preliminary linear curve of Figure 3.1, the PD2.3. A second decimal place has been used to aid interpretation. The third column indicates the margin, Astro-speak for contribution to overhead and profit, equal to the amount bid less direct cost (conditional upon winning the bid). The fourth column indicates the expected margin, the expected contribution to overhead and profit. The final column provides a note indicative of the discussion which needs to take place as a basis for selecting a preliminary bid and using it to assess whether or not Transcon was a no-hoper.

Second-pass bid setting to produce PD2.5

Barney indicated that the fifth and final step of the second-pass process was the use of the PD2.4 to discuss bid setting given the information available to date, and in particular the potential profitability of this contract suggested by such bids. A summary of this discussion added to the PD2.4 would define the PD2.5. He suggested they have such a discussion to illustrate what was involved. For example, if the preliminary estimate of the expected direct cost is £13 million, expected margin is maximized at a value of 2.08 (bold in Table 3.1) with a bid of about £17 million and a chance of winning of about 0.52. If the preliminary estimate of the expected direct cost is taken as £11 million, expected margin is maximized with a bid of about £15.5 (interpolating midway), a chance of winning of about 0.73 (also interpolating midway). A bid of £17 million assuming a direct cost of £13 million involves a margin of £4 million ($17 - 13$), about 31% ($4 \times 100/13$). A bid of £15.5 million assuming a direct cost of £11 million involves a margin of £4.5 million ($15.5 - 11$), about 41% ($4.5 \times 100/11$). Even the £17 million bid scenario looks reasonable and the £15.5 million bid scenario looks extremely attractive. Barney suggested that Table 3.1 clearly indicated to him that the Transcon bid is *not* a no-hoper. Transcon is a preliminary goer, requiring a more detailed third pass.

At this point Sian suggested that the Transcon contract would be a useful one to win. However, she suggested it was 'nice to have' rather than critical. She suggested that a bid of £18 million with an assumed margin of £5 million on a £13 million expected cost looked about right to her (she would be happy to get the work, but with a high expected cost, playing by the rules on margin). Trevor rejoined that he thought a bid of £15 million with an assumed mark-up of £4 million on an £11 million expected cost looked about right to him. There was no point, in his view, in risking the loss of this important contract (and his commission) in what was clearly a tough market. He was not keen to chance four lost Astro Wales Systems integration contracts in a row, which would seriously damage his credibility, and playing by the rules on margin was not a big concern for Trevor. Martha then suggested that Sian and Trevor had both raised important issues that should be noted. However, before they were addressed, along with a number of other issues, it would be worth undertaking a third-pass analysis. It would be helpful to clarify the expected direct cost, and the shape of the probability of winning curve. Sian had already done what was needed to clarify the expected direct cost, but much more needed to be done on the shape of the probability of winning curve.

Third-Pass Initiation

To maintain useful consistency between the five-step structure of the second pass and all subsequent passes, and to acknowledge the importance of formally agreeing to start a further pass and planning its execution, Martha indicated that the first step of the third pass would be a formal initiation step, to produce a PD3.1. The PD3.1 would be comparable to a PD2.1 in that it was kicked off by a formal decision to proceed to another pass, taken directly by the person responsible, with subsequent audit. However, it would not involve the equivalent of Trevor's visit to Transcon, or the notes he prepared for the PD2.1, and it would build on the PD2.5. Martha suggested that they started the PD3.1 by agreeing that Transcon was a preliminary goer, a third pass was appropriate, and it would be reasonable for Sales staff to make such judgement. They readily complied. Martha then indicated that this decision noted on the PD2.5 should be taken to define the start of the PD3.1, the deliverable of the first step of the third-pass analysis process. Plans indicating how and when the other four steps would be executed would complete the PD3.1. In effect, executing the third pass was a project. The planning (and perhaps control) of this project was part of producing the PD3.1. Martha suggested that as part of these plans, Sian and Barney should be asked to produce an enhanced cost estimate to form the PD3.2, the deliverable of the second step of the third pass. This would be an enhanced version of the preliminary cost estimate of PD2.2. Martha also suggested that Trevor and Barney should produce what Martha would call the PD3.3, the deliverable of the third step of the third pass, an enhanced probability of winning curve, an enhanced version of PD2.3. These would then be combined by Barney to produce an enhanced bid setting summary table, defining the PD3.4, the enhanced version of Table 3.1. The PD3.5 would follow, analogous to the PD2.5. Sian and Trevor both agreed that this made sense.

Martha now indicated that Sian had already provided a basis for the third pass cost estimate, in terms of the details in the current PPD, which Martha had excluded from the PD1 and PD2 documents. Martha revealed that Barney had already used this input of Sian's, to completed a draft of the PD3.2 deliverable. Barney would present this draft now. Martha suggested that in practice Sian and Barney should discuss Barney's contribution to this document before it was released to Trevor and herself; Sian and Barney did not need to agree on all issues, and would be important to highlight any differences in view.

Third-Pass Cost Uncertainty Analysis

Barney began his presentation by reiterating that the basis of the PD3.2 enhanced estimate was the detail provided by Sian's staff in the PPD. He provided copies of this material, and indicated that he had drafted an analysis based on this information. He revealed that Martha had very carefully reviewed his draft analysis. She had clarified its structure greatly, elaborating on his draft in some areas, simplifying it in others. Sian could of course change her initial views of the Transcon information provided. But what mattered most at this point were views from Sian and Trevor on process, the way Barney, with significant help from Martha, had analysed the information from Sian's staff.

Barney then revealed the first part of Table 3.2, to the end of item 1. He indicated that the whole of Table 3.2 would be revealed, item by item, as he explained each item, using associated figures in some cases. Table 3.2 as a whole would be his part of the PD3.2.

Starting with item 1, the central site equipment, Barney indicated that the base cost was the direct cost to Astro Wales of £3.6 million. He indicated that this could be taken as the minimum, maximum and expected cost. There was no uncertainty of interest here (Astro Inc. to Astro Wales transfer costs were beyond the current remit). Barney noted that, for present purposes, direct cost was the issue, not selling price, and it was important to maintain this focus. An overall overhead cost recovery and profit (margin) would be determined later, in terms of standard list prices and suitable discounts as part of drafting the presentation package for the client. Barney also indicated there was no choice to be made here. This item

Table 3.2—Summary table (third pass) for enhanced bid

Items	Item components and options	Direct costs (£m)				Choices and assumptions
		Base	Minimum	Maximum	Expected	
1 Central site equipment	Astro main frame plus peripherals	3.6	**3.6**	**3.6**	**3.6**	No choice
2 Computer suite modifications	Astro	0.30	0.3	0.3	0.3	
	Zenith	1.00	1.1	1.3	1.2	
	Total	1.30	**1.4**	**1.6**	**1.5**	No choice
3 Initial operation and training	(a) Zoro	1.00	1.2	1.4	1.3	No hostile takeover effect
	(b) Astro	0.8	**0.7**	**1.1**	**0.9**	Preferred option
	Adjustment to (b)	−0.5	**−0.5**	**−0.5**	**−0.5**	Direct cost overstated, nominal discount
4 Convert existing programmes	(a) Datapol	1.2	1.2	1.2	1.2	No non-compliance effects or additional costs
	(b) Sysdoc	0.5	**0.5**	**2.0**	**1.0**	Preferred option, Sysdoc 2 best estimate, Sysdoc 3 maximum
Additional memory	(a) Pre-install	0.5	0.5	0.5	0.5	
	(b) Post-install if necessary	1.0	**0**	**1.0**	**0.1**	Preferred option
5 Distributed scheduling system	Astro equipment	3.0	3.0	3.0	3.0	
	(a) Astro software	1.1	1.2	1.4	1.3	Preferred option?
	(b) Zoro software	1.0	1.2	1.4	1.3	No hostile takeover effect
	Total (a) or (b)		**4.2**	**4.4**	**4.3**	
	Adjustment to (a)	+5				Switch preference to (b), no other impact
Additional performance	(a) Pre-install	1.0	1.0	1.0	1.0	
	(b) Post-install if necessary	1.5–2.5	**0**	**2.5**	**0.4**	Preferred option
Contract nominal direct cost			9.9	15.7	11.3	**Say £11m in range £10–16m**
Overhead at 30%					3.4	
Nominal total cost					14.7	
Profit at 10%					1.5	
Nominal price					16.2	**Say £16m**
Nominal margin					4.9	**Say £5m**

provided the simplest possible example of the cost analysis required in the third-pass cost estimate format of Table 3.2. Barney indicated that the issue of possible additional memory could be addressed as part of item 1, but he would deal with it as part of item 4, following Sian's estimator's approach to the descriptive material. Everyone nodded approval with the analysis to this stage, so Barney moved swiftly on to item 2 (computer suite modifications).

Barney indicated that the item 2 base cost estimate of £0.30 million for Astro's direct costs was the £0.30 million provided by Sian's estimator, as was the £0.3 million maximum, minimum and expected value, apart from rounding to the nearest tenth of a million. He indicated that spurious precision wastes time and, more importantly, is misleading. He suggested that working to the nearest £0.1 million (about 0.5% of total expected cost) would be useful for most purposes in this case, to remind everyone of the precision needed and provided by a third-pass cost estimate. Barney indicated that the £1.00 million base cost for Zenith was as provided by Sian's estimator. In this case the minimum, maximum and expected values were different. The range of 10% to 30% uplift from preliminary quotes to actual prices for Zenith as reported by Sian's estimator had been used to determine what Barney called nominal minimum and maximum values (£1m × (10 + 100)/100 and £1m × (30 + 100)/100). He suggested values outside this range were clearly possible, but in the present context it was not worth being too concerned about the chances of this so long as they were reasonably consistent across the analysis as a whole. A nominal 5% or 10% chance of being outside the bounds at either end would be the usual assumptions (5–95 or 10–90 percentile values). He indicated that the midpoint expected value of £1.2 million ((1.1 + 1.3)/2) could be associated with a uniform probability distribution density function between the nominal minimum and maximum values, or between more extreme minimum and maximum values, provided the tails defining the extremes were similar. Table 3.2 showed a single total for the two components of item 2. The label 'no choice' applied to the total, and by implication both components. The highlighting (in bold) makes later interpretation of totals easier. Barney's presentation on item 2 finished with a request for questions or comments, but none were forthcoming, so he moved on to item 3 (initial operation and training).

Barney began his discussion of item 3 by indicating that when two choices involve continuous probability distributions, a useful conceptual and operational framework which is widely employed is provided by plotting cumulative probability distributions for both choices on the same graph (Figure 3.2) using simple linear cumulative curves (not so widely employed). Both curves in Figure 3.2 are plotted using the associated maximum and minimum value from Table 3.2. The Astro curve uses the item 3 Astro choice (b) base value provided by Sian's estimator (£0.8 million) less 10% to provide a nominal minimum of £0.7 million (0.8 × (100 − 10)/100), plus 40% to provide a nominal maximum of £1.1 million. The −10% and +40% figures were provided by Sian's estimator. The straight line between these values implies a uniform probability distribution density function, with whatever tails extend beyond the nominal minimum and maximum cut-off.

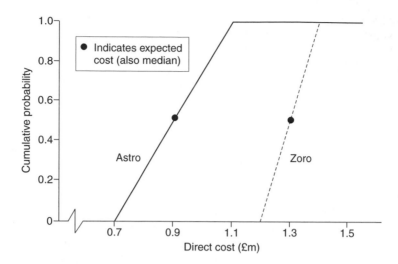

Figure 3.2—Uniform distribution comparison: item 3 (initial operations and training) example.

The expected value of £0.9 million follows whatever the tails, provided they are similar in shape, because it is a simple midpoint ((0.7 + 1.1)/2). These three plotted values (0.7, 1.1 and 0.9) are highlighted in Table 3.2. The Zoro curve uses the item 3 Zoro choice (a) base value provided by Sian's estimator (£1.0 million) plus 20% to provide a nominal minimum of £1.2 million (1.0 × (20 + 100)/100), plus 40% to provide a nominal maximum of £1.4 million. Again the adjustments are as provided by Sian's estimator, and the expected value is the midpoint £1.3 million. This curve ignores the possible implications of the hostile takeover bid.

Barney indicated that because the expected cost of the Astro option was lower (£0.9 million compared to £1.3 million, a difference of £0.4 million), and the Figure 3.2 curves did not cross, the Astro choice was risk efficient – Astro had a lower expected cost, and the probability of exceeding any given cost was less. The Astro choice involved more variability but it was less risky. Unless qualitative benefits (non-quantified benefits) worth £0.4 million could be associated with the Zoro choice, Astro was the preferred choice, as indicated in this section of Table 3.2, which Barney displayed at this point. The highlighting of Astro minimum, maximum and expected values in Table 3.2 corresponds with the highlighting of the Astro curve in Figure 3.2. Trevor and Sian were both comfortable with the implications of this part of the presentation. Neither had come across the concept of risk efficiency but it seemed clear enough in this context. No questions or comments were forthcoming.

Martha then indicated that non-quantified benefits associated with the Astro choice could be given a negative spin by the client and their competitors. A competitor who could not provide the equivalent of option (b) might argue that it was better for Transcon to have their staff trained on their own site on their own new equipment. They could argue that their proposal, which did this, offered a non-price advantage of importance. Astro should propose that Transcon could have the Zoro option (a) for an additional £0.4 million, but recommend option (b). Option (b) would allow the training to start well in advance of the Transcon facility being ready, spreading it out for the convenience of Transcon staff (and Astro staff), and it would decouple training from the risk of any delays with the new computer suite in addition to saving £0.4 million. These features for option (b) should be described as non-price advantages for Astro. The Zoro hostile takeover risk was a serious threat if the Zoro option (a) appealed to Transcon, but not if Transcon favoured the Astro option (b) because of the lower cost.

Barney then indicated that the Figure 3.2 format was a basic tool for considering choices, but once Astro staff were comfortable with its operational use and its implications, Table 3.2 could be used on its own. That is, the risk efficiency of the Astro option (b) for this item was indicated by a lower expected value and a lower nominal maximum value in Table 3.1. There was no need to draw Figure 3.2. Figure 3.2 could become a background conceptual device which only required operational use when someone did not understand direct use of Table 3.2 to make risk-efficient choices. Trevor and Sian both nodded again, and Sian smiled, indicating she appreciated the efficiency of the simple procedure which was emerging to justify clear-cut decisions.

Martha now interjected as agreed with Barney in advance. She indicated that Sian's staff had used standard costing procedures to estimate the Astro option (b) base cost of £0.8 million. This was an appropriate starting point. It might be the basis which should be used to present the analysis to Transcon, although it might not be. Presentation was an issue to be discussed later for list prices and discounts. However, Martha, Sian and Trevor were aware that the Astro service bureau site in question had idle capacity. Indeed, it was in danger of being shut down because of its underutilization. The marginal cost to Astro Wales was about £0.5 million less than Sian's £0.8 million if the Astro site were used. Martha indicated that it was the marginal cost which would affect the bottom line of Astro Wales at year end, in terms of the bottom line for the manager of this site, and Martha's bottom line. She had spoken to the manager concerned, and he confirmed the £0.5 million figure. She had agreed with him a nominal discount of £0.5 million, recognizing that he was in effect bidding to Martha to be included in this proposal, and it was in his interests that Astro get the contract in order to make use of his idle capacity. In this case the £0.5 million reduction would not affect the option (a) or (b) choice, but it would affect the bid and the chances of winning. At this point, Barney revealed the adjustment entries for item 3. Martha indicated that the Astro internal accounting did not, at present, allow this kind of discounting. However, she liked to ensure that as many people as possible owed her a favour. The service bureau site manager had agreed he would owe her one if she made this adjustment. Martha went on to explain that Astro Inc.'s normal 30% and 10% mark-ups for overhead and profit were what she would call nominal, for use as a guideline, to indicate what was needed as a minimum on average. In very tough market conditions, they would have to accept less or go out of business. Conversely, in very good market conditions, they would have to take much more, in order to achieve at least the company norms on average. Trevor was well aware of this when considering a bid like Astro's bid to Transcon, and it made sense to Sian too.

What was less obvious to both of them, so Martha pointed it out, was the process of choosing between options (a) and (b) for this item involved a lower-level bidding process with one part of Astro in competition with Zoro. The same principles applied to this lower-level bidding process. And the Astro site associated with option (b) was truly desperate for the work, in a very tough market for them. The fact that the Astro option (b) was already cheaper than the Zoro option (a) should not be allowed to obscure the low marginal cost for the Astro option. Overall optimization of the Astro Wales position required the use of adjusted costs whenever this kind of consideration was relevant. In effect, it was part of Martha's brief to ensure that underused capacity in the Astro Wales service bureau was pushed, with the support of Sales and Systems. This kind of adjustment was the instrument they all needed to use to help push the marketing of underused capacity. Of course Astro could not sustain consistent negative adjustments of this kind in any area, and would look to the elimination of such areas in the medium term. However, in the short term it was important to make explicit negative adjustments which made direct cost as computed using internal accounting conventions, more accurately reflect actual marginal cost. The flip side of this, protecting high demand capacity from overuse via positive adjustments to reflect opportunity costs, would arise in item 5. Trevor and Sian were a bit stunned by this revelation, but they were both smiling, and Sian could already see part of what was coming in item 5.

Barney then moved on to item 4 (convert existing programmes), beginning with Figure 3.3. Barney indicated that Datapol's firm fixed price of £1.2 million implies a vertical cumulative probability curve in Figure 3.3, provided compliance is assumed. If a failure to comply or successful additional cost claims against Astro which could not be passed on to Transcon were a significant risk, the Datapol curve should have a tail moving to the right at the top. The possibility of Datapol going broke would imply a long tail to the right at the top, perhaps going off the page. Figure 3.3 assumes a nominal maximum for Datapol of £1.2 million in the same spirit of ignored tails as earlier nominal values. The Datapol curve of Figure 3.3 corresponds to line 1 of item 4 in Table 3.2.

Barney indicated that Sysdoc's nominal minimum of £0.5 million was derived from the base value and Sian's estimator's discussion in a straightforward way. There might be a chance of a lower cost, but too little chance to be of practical interest. The obvious difficulty with Sysdoc was a basis for defining a complementary nominal maximum. The unknown nature of this nominal maximum cost was an understandable basis for Sian's estimator's suggested choice of Datapol. However, the unknown nature of such a maximum cost should not induce an automatic preference for a known cost alternative, such as Datapol. When there is

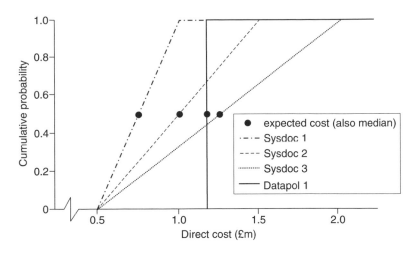

Figure 3.3—Uniform distribution comparison: item 4 (convert existing programmes) example.

uncertainty about a nominal maximum cost, different scenarios are worth considering. For example, to choose between Datapol and Sysdoc, Figure 3.3 portrays three illustrative maximum values which provide a useful basis for discussion:

- Sysdoc 1: maximum £1.0 million, 100% more (minimum × 2)
- Sysdoc 2: maximum £1.5 million, 200% more (minimum × 3)
- Sysdoc 3: maximum £2.0 million, 300% more (minimum × 4)

Putting aside non-quantified benefits (including non-price advantages) for the moment, assuming that both Astro and the client perceive no difference in the two approaches, a Sysdoc choice in terms of each of these three scenarios can be compared with the Datapol choice. If the Sysdoc 1 curve applies, then Sysdoc is a clearly preferred choice in terms of risk efficiency. It may be more variable, but it is always cheaper, and the expected cost saving is £0.45 million (1.2 − (0.5 + 1.0)/2), using a second decimal place at this stage to clarify comparisons. If the Sysdoc 2 curve applies, there is still an expected cost saving of £0.20 million (1.2 − (0.5 + 1.5)/2), but a Sysdoc choice is not risk efficient on its own, because it involves a risk of costs in the range £1.2 million to £1.5 million not associated with Datapol. A trade-off is involved in terms of this particular decision. However, taken in the context of all decisions being made on the basis of minimizing expected cost unless unacceptable risks are involved, in order to aggressively minimize costs and maximize profits over time on average, achieving risk efficiency over time, there is a clear case for Sysdoc. Put another way, the possibility of an additional cost up to £0.3 million (1.5 − 1.2) with a fairly small probability is an acceptable risk in the context of an expected saving of £0.20 million on this particular decision. In the context of a £15–20 million contract, this is not really risk at all, it is just variability or noise. Hence Astro should choose Sysdoc if the Sysdoc 2 curve applies. If the Sysdoc 3 curve applies, then Datapol becomes the risk-efficient choice, with an expected cost advantage of £0.05 million ((0.5 + 2.0)/2 − 1.2).

Barney suggested that it would be important to verify that the Sysdoc 3 curve or a curve even further to the right was a best estimate of the reality if Datapol were to be selected without reference to qualitative benefits. If Sysdoc 2 was a best estimate, Sysdoc should be the initial choice prior to considering qualitative benefits. He and Martha suggested using the Sysdoc 2 curve as a best estimate in the expected value sense, with the Sysdoc 1 and 3 curves as nominal bounds in the nominal maximum and minimum sense, a second-order probability model which explicitly treats the nominal maximum as uncertain. This approach had some of the characteristics of a parametric analysis, finding the value of an unknown parameter which flips the decision, in this case a nominal maximum of £1.9 million or more. However, it places this flip value in the context of a best estimate and bounds (an approach to be explored further in Chapter 8). Barney also pointed out that more sophisticated curves for Sysdoc (tilted S shapes) and a tail for the Datapol distribution would enhance the case for Sysdoc. The simple modelling used was robust, supporting the choice of Sysdoc.

Barney then indicated that with respect to items 1 to 3, based on the information from Sian's staff, the third-pass cost estimation approach was very efficient and easy to use. The features illustrated by the Sysdoc versus Datapol choice and the cost adjustment for item 3 showed that the third-pass approach was effective as well. It provided a clear and cost-effective way of making the more difficult decisions that were easy to get wrong. Barney revealed the item 4 part of Table 3.2 at this point. He indicated that Sysdoc 2 had been assumed as the basis of the expected cost of £1.0 million, but the nominal maximum reflected the Sysdoc 3 maximum of £2.0 million. Barney indicated that as with respect to Figure 3.2, Figure 3.3 was not necessary if the rationale was clear just using Table 3.2. However, the more complex the issues, the more useful it was to employ back-up diagrams like Figures 3.2 and 3.3.

Trevor and Sian were impressed by this part of the presentation, and they were both comfortable with the Sysdoc choice given the analysis. Sian did not feel threatened by the modification to her estimator's recommendation in terms of expected cost. However, both Trevor and Sian wanted to talk about qualitative benefits to the client (non-price advantages) of the Datapol approach, and Barney let them have the floor to do so. In brief, a new-generation language rewrite would be a much better basis for future changes, and as such it would provide value-added relative to a Sysdoc approach for Transcon. Martha then made the point that all these arguments were sound, and they should be documented as part of the PD3.2 in order to make them clear to the client, but it would be a serious mistake to add cost to the bid by making this kind of choice for the client, behaving like a nanny contractor. It was important to bid on the basis of the lowest expected cost choices which are compliant, and offer options at extra cost in cases like this.

That is, if Sysdoc 2 is the accepted basis in terms of minimum expected cost, Transcon should be told the bid minimized the cost to Transcon by using Sysdoc, but for the difference in expected costs, currently estimated at £0.2 million, Transcon could have Datapol as a costed option. Trevor indicated that he would normally expect to do this, but Sian's uncomfortable look suggested he was not always given the choice.

Barney then suggested they move on to the linked issue of possible additional memory, a source of uncertainty requiring a decision. Figure 3.4 portrayed the uncertainties associated with the two choices available in terms of a simple decision tree.

If additional memory was required, Martha's reading of Sian's estimator's documentation in the PD3.2 suggested a probability of 0.2 that Astro would have to pay for it. This probability was clearly linked to the choice for item 4 (convert existing programmes) and less strongly linked to the choice for item 5 (distributed scheduling system). It should be seen as conditional on the choice associated with these items, yet to be confirmed. Assuming for the time being that the probabilities 0.5 and 0.2 were correct, there was a 0.1 probability (0.5 × 0.2) that 'post-install if necessary' would cost Astro £1 million, but a 0.9 probability (1 − 0.1) of no additional memory cost. The expected cost (a best estimate of what it should cost on average) was £0.1 million. This was £0.4 million less than the 'pre-install' expected cost (in this case a certain cost) of £0.5 million. Barney recommended 'post-install if necessary' on the grounds that the expected cost difference between the options was likely to favour this choice, and currently the best estimate of their

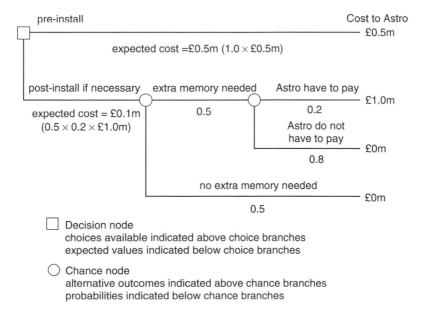

Figure 3.4—Additional memory decision tree.

cost difference was £0.4 million. He indicated that there were some clear qualitative benefits to Astro associated with pre-installation which should not be overlooked, like making it easier for those developing the new systems associated with items 4 and 5, but at present he and Martha took the view that the sum of all such benefits could not be assessed in terms of a value exceeding the £0.4 million difference in expected costs. Trevor was very comfortable with this. Sian was not. Sian felt wrong-footed by the implicit oversight by her estimator of the scenario involving extra memory not paid for by Astro. Sian's challenge was that Martha's approach put only £0.1 million into the budget as a provision for an event which might cost zero but might cost £1 million, and would never cost £0.1 million. Surely, she argued, the long-term average cost might be £0.1 million if this was done time after time, but this was a one-shot project. Putting £0.5 million in the budget for the pre-install option was a prudent safe policy, while a provision of only £0.1 million with a 1 in 10 chance of a £1 million hit was a high-risk gamble. Martha responded by saying that if extra memory was needed which Astro had to pay for, the Transcon project would have to take a £1 million hit. But this should average out with other reasons for cost variations on this and other projects. Her policy was always to minimize expected costs and maximize expected profits unless this posed a threat which was more serious than not doing so. This combined risk efficiency for individual choices with risk efficiency over time. Risk efficiency involved a minimum level of risk for a given level of expected cost or profit. Astro should be doing this consistently for all decisions. At present this was not the case. For cultural reasons with which she sympathized, Astro staff took low-risk decisions, like adding the extra memory in this case, which increased expected costs. This lowered the chances of winning bids. In the context of winning bids it was a high-risk choice, not a low-risk choice, in the sense that it led to a high risk of losing bids. Across all bids it increased the chances of Astro going broke (being broken up in practice), because Astro did not have enough business, now a very serious threat. There was no such thing as a no-risk business, just as there was no such thing as a free lunch. Astro could balance the risk of losing money on some contracts and the risk of going out of business (as currently structured) because it did not get enough contracts. But Astro was no longer in a position to avoid addressing this issue.

Sian was still not happy, but she realized Martha had anticipated this challenge. She didn't really understand the risk efficiency argument, and she felt it was not sensible to prolong the discussion at this stage. Barney then eased Sian's discomfort by indicating that the decision tree format of Figure 3.4 did make discrete events (like a need to post-install additional memory at Astro's expense) seem risky, but the cumulative distribution format of Figures 3.2 and 3.3 could be used for discrete as well as continuous variable outcomes as indicated in Figure 3.5. He suggested that in this format the choice was clearly one analogous to the Sysdoc 2 versus Datapol choice in Figure 3.3, and it might seem less threatening in this format. Indeed, if the risk of Datapol going broke at a critical point was properly reflected in Figure 3.3 with a curve going right off the page to the right at

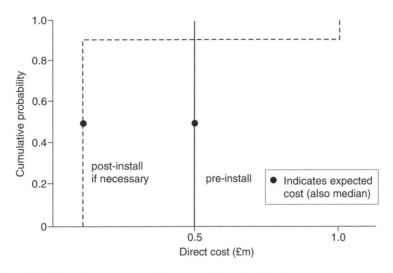

Figure 3.5—Additional memory decision cumulative distributions.

a very low probability, post-installing additional memory if needed might look much less risky than using Datapol. Barney also offered to spend time with Sian later exploring the risk efficiency concept in more detail, in the context of its origins in portfolio theory (Chapter 10).

Barney then moved on to item 5 (distributed scheduling system). He began this time with the appropriate part of Table 3.2, excluding the adjustment line. Barney indicated that the 20% to 40% uplift from preliminary quotes to agreed prices for Zoro noted under item 3 implied the £1.2–1.4 million range associated with the base as in earlier examples. He indicated the Astro potential variability was unclear, but a base cost of £1.10 million and a 20% contingency for a total of £1.32 million suggested a directly comparable range and expected value to the nearest £0.1 million. Diagrams like Figures 3.2 and 3.3 could be used, but they would probably not suggest a significant difference in terms of the quantified costs. He suggested that Sian's estimator's preference for the all-Astro option seemed reasonable given the Zoro hostile takeover risk, and the presumed desirability of keeping the work in house given the recent spate of lost contracts. He put a question mark beside the preferred choice in Table 3.2 because the expected costs for the two options were identical and it was qualitative issues that would drive the choice between options (a) and (b) as things stood. Trevor and Sian both seemed comfortable with this. Martha then indicated that she had three serious problems with the all-Astro approach, option (a). First, the hostile takeover bid for Zoro emanated from one of Astro's key competitors. If it went ahead, Zoro would probably become an effective instrument of the competition, no longer available to Astro. Astro's position would become seriously restricted in relation to work like that on item 5, competition on cost would become very difficult for this kind of work, and work like that associated with item 2 could become a further problem. This implied an opportunity cost associated with the all-Astro approach which should cause them to switch to option (b).

Second, in this case they had another opportunity cost issue which was the flip side of the item 2 adjustment. Sian's staff who would execute the all-Astro option were very busy, with major contracts from Astro Inc. to develop software for worldwide markets. Delay on this work would be serious. This implied a further opportunity cost associated with the all-Astro approach which should cause them to switch to option (b). No doubt Sian's preference for an £18 million bid and £13 million cost estimate in the context of PD2.5 reflected this concern.

Third, the application of a 30% overhead cost uplift on an efficient, well-managed subcontractor like Zoro and the same 30% overhead charge on all in-house development like this was biased against the use of efficient subcontractors. Astro overheads on their own staff time were higher than 30%, perhaps closer to 50%. Astro overheads on a contractor like Zoro were lower than 30%, perhaps only 10%. If this kind of bias forced ineffective choices then it was a major problem. Even if it didn't force ineffective choices, it would adversely affect the level of bid chosen. This implied they should use another opportunity cost associated with the all-Astro approach.

Martha indicated that she did not know what these three effects together amounted to in terms of a total opportunity cost adjustment to option (a), but £5 million seemed a modest (conservative) assessment, with a focus on the first of her three concerns. At this point, Barney revealed the adjustment line in Table 3.2. Martha then revealed that as soon as this had become clear to her, she had started moves for Astro UK to make a friendly takeover offer to Zoro. She was pleased to say that the outcome was still confidential, but it would be favourable. This meant that the £5 million adjustment could be associated with a switch to option (b) but no actual change to the item cost for bid purposes.

From Martha's perspective, the need for a friendly takeover of Zoro was a key strategic insight which came from her involvement in the details of the Transcon bid. She made this clear to Trevor and Sian as part of a general effort to ensure they were comfortable with her ongoing involvement in the PD3.5 and would not see it as just looking over their shoulder all the time. At this point, Martha made it clear that the PD3s would be assessed by her on a case-by-case basis initially, perhaps by sample audit later on. The reason was the learning processes involved. Even the PD1 and PD2 involved learning processes, like identifying strong synergies between a contract and Astro's objectives in the PD1. However, the insights provided by the PD3 process were much deeper and more general, and there was a much stronger and wider need to share the learning involved.

Barney noted that it was now very clear that the Zoro choice was preferred, because of the opportunity cost adjustment and the Zoro friendly takeover success. However, as a process issue, it was very important to understand that Astro did not usually need to commit to decisions where there was no direct cost benefit either way at the bid stage. All that mattered for bidding purposes in such cases was an unbiased estimate of the expected cost. That is, had the takeover and appropriate average overhead and other opportunity cost issues not been present, it might have been useful to assume an expected direct cost of £4.3 million for this item without making a commitment to option (a) or (b), to keep Astro's options open.

Barney then suggested they move on to the issue of additional performance, in terms of Figure 3.6, indicating that the format was much like Figure 3.4, used to consider additional memory. However, in this case Martha had suggested a 0.4 probability Astro would have to pay for it if additional performance was needed. And in this case Sian's estimator had suggested a spread of costs, from £1.5 million to £2.5 million, which he had treated as a nominal range between nominal minimum and nominal maximum values as earlier, with a midpoint of £2.0 million ((1.5 + 2.5)/2). The latter would slightly complicate the additional performance equivalent of Figure 3.5, but the only complication for Figure 3.6 was reducing the nominal range of £1.5 million to £2.5 million with its £2.0 million expected value prior to computing the expected value of the option 'post-install if necessary'. Barney then showed the corresponding part of Table 3.2, and noted that he recommended 'post-install if necessary' because of the £0.6 million (1−0.4) advantage relative to 'pre-install' given the assumed probabilities.

Martha considered the probability Astro would have to pay given that extra performance was needed; she pointed out it was higher (0.4) than in the additional memory case (0.2). This was primarily because, in the additional memory case, the invitation to tender statement about current documentation 'believed to be

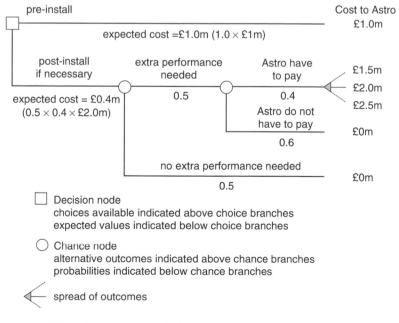

Figure 3.6—Additional performance decision tree.

reasonable – 95% accurate' was an 'invitation to make claims', which could be linked to insisting that the client pay for the additional memory in full or share the cost. However, she suggested that the 0.4 probability that Astro had to pay if additional performance was required would be higher still if Astro took on the whole of item 5, because Astro Wales could not pass the cost of extra performance on to its own staff, but Astro Wales could probably pass at least some of it on to Zoro. Even if Astro UK owned Zoro, this structural difference mattered.

This comment, coupled to Martha's third reason for the £5 million adjustment just discussed, caused Sian to twitch noticeably. However, she did not fully understand the oblique hint. Martha could probably pass some of the 'additional performance' risk on to Zoro, and Zoro's staff had incomes geared to Zoro's profits, which would help Zoro to manage it. Zoro staff were motivated to perform in a way Astro had never contemplated for Systems staff. Although Astro Sales staff used to have incomes highly geared to sales commissions, the trend had been to reduce the gearing for many years. The Astro reward structures for performance were very clear in terms of promotions for fast-track staff like Martha, but comparatively woolly and ineffective for most other staff. An inability to deal with this was in part what was driving the 'redefining core business' approach to outsourcing currently sweeping through Astro Inc. This insight was part of the key strategic spin-offs of Martha's involvement in the details of the Transcon bid, and a key motivation for the friendly takeover of Zoro which Martha proposed. Had Sian's staff not been very productively occupied with other kinds of work, they might have found their transfer to Zoro part of the takeover deal. However, given the positive opportunity cost, it would have been inappropriate to raise this possibility here. Sian was aware Martha was sending an oblique message, despite her inability to decipher this message. This took away her appetite for discussing the particular probabilities associated with Figure 3.6 or Figure 3.4. She would revisit them later.

Barney then drew attention to the highlighted total direct cost of £11.3 million in the final portion of Table 3.2, rounded to £11 millon to reflect the nominal precision of this estimate as a whole. Barney indicated that it was important to use a nominal precision level like £0.1 million earlier for individual items to clarify choices, and some of these choices might benefit from slightly more precision, like the Sysdoc 1 to 3 choices. When adding up item cost estimates to obtain a total cost estimate, we can expect independent errors (not systematic bias) to cancel out on a swings and roundabouts basis. This means the total cost estimate should be more precise than the individual items. However, Astro staff would be misleading themselves if they believed the Transcon PD3.2 of Table 3.2 provided an accuracy level greater than the nearest £1 million for expected total cost, and it was useful to acknowledge this now to simplify the analysis to follow. It was clearly very important that the implied accuracy in percentage terms, an expected value accurate to within 10%, was sufficient. In Barney's view this was the case, in addition to it being plausible and a credit to Sian's staff. That is, Barney was suggesting $V(E(C))$ was about £0.25 million or less, a very credible level of accuracy. Barney also noted the associated nominal range of £9.9–15.7 million for the actual outcome anticipated, rounded to £10–16 million to reflect the same common level of nominal precision for all the 'whole project' estimates. Barney indicated that it was important to associate the £10–16 million range with a 5–95 or 10–90 percentile range consistent with the use of other nominal ranges throughout the analysis. The interpretation chosen did not matter but consistency did matter. This internal consistency implied perfect positive correlation when defining the nominal range for total cost in terms of the nominal ranges for each of the five items, a coefficient of correlation of 1.0.

Barney indicated that this assumption of perfect positive correlation was slightly conservative (pessimistic). A coefficient of correlation of order 0.8 might be a more accurate assumption. However, assuming independence (a coefficient of correlation of 0) was the only other simple assumption, this was much further from the truth, and wildly optimistic, and it was important to use a conservative (pessimistic) assumption for this simple analysis. Despite the conservative nature of this correlation assumption, the nominal range of £10–16 million revealed no significant threat to Astro Wales from cost variations as estimated, although a £16 million outcome which could not be explained might be a threat to the careers of those involved in the Transcon bid and the execution of the project. Barney indicated that the official reason for assuming perfect positive correlation was that Astro should not decide to ignore uncertainty unless it can be confident that it was estimated with a bias which was conservative, if bias existed. Other useful reasons from Sian's perspective included the simplicity of this assumption and the fact that it provided a wider range which made it easier to explain departures from expectations. The last comment was to some extent designed to cheer up Sian, although Barney was making what he knew to be very important practical points. Sian managed a smile, although her unease remained. She resolved to see Martha afterwards, which Martha anticipated.

Barney then drew attention to the 30% overhead and 10% profit margin calculations which finished off Table 3.2, indicating a highlighted nominal price of £16 million with a nominal margin of £5 million. He made the point that this nominal price was a cost-based price as a guide to what Astro Inc. normally expected. It was not a market-based price.

Martha thanked Barney for his presentation to this point, and indicated she hoped it was clear to Sian how her input to the PD3.2 was transformed in an efficient and effective way. She emphasized the need for Sian and herself to pursue further some important issues which the process highlighted, part of the purpose of the process. But she suggested they all had a good basis to proceed with a third pass at the Transcon bid. Martha indicated that five things should come out of the PD3.2 process, and their pursuit should be the clear and conscious goals:

1. An unbiased estimate of the expected direct cost, without being concerned about choices associated with project execution at this stage, except in so far as they affected expected cost; that is, the expected cost of £11 million.

2. Insights about negative and positive adjustments to direct costs as normally assessed were critical to reflect lower marginal costs or opportunity costs associated with other uses.
3. Insights about qualitative benefits of the options chosen which could be played up as non-price advantages in the bid, like those associated with starting to train Transcon staff earlier on a nearby Astro site, were also critical.
4. Insights about more general issues which go beyond the case in question, like the need to mount a friendly takeover for Zoro, and the need to consider differential overhead rates, were of strategic importance.
5. Comfort with the upper end of the nominal range for anticipated outcomes was important, in this case £10–16 million, recognizing that some contracts are going to lose money, and this should not be a problem provided it is not an unexplainable surprise.

In summary, third-pass cost uncertainty analysis was not just a matter of refining estimates of the expected cost and anticipated range of actual outcomes. It was about an enhanced understanding of all the issues which drive such cost estimates, including associated non-price advantage and other qualitative benefit issues.

Third-Pass Probability of Winning Analysis

While Sian was still trying to take in the full implications of the PD3.2 process, Martha turned her fire on Trevor, moving on to what she earlier designated the PD3.3, obtaining an enhanced probability of winning curve. Martha indicated that Barney and Trevor had not yet addressed this issue, but she had worked with Barney to develop and then illustrate what she wanted. She began by explaining that even Figure 3.1 was new to Astro as an explicit tool, although Trevor and other sales staff had obviously used such a curve intuitively. This was not unusual. Very few organizations made use of an explicit Figure 3.1 equivalent. Astro was going to obtain significant competitive advantage by using a refined version of Figure 3.1. She then explained that the key advantage of Figure 3.1 was that it enabled the use of Table 3.1, explicitly bringing together costing and pricing issues in a manner which indicated the price that maximized expected margin (for various cost assumptions if appropriate) and the trade-offs, as the bid was changed, between the expected margin, the actual (conditional) margin, and the probability of winning. The more refined version of Table 3.1 which the third pass would enable was going to be a major competitive weapon for Astro.

Among the other advantages of Figure 3.1 was the ability to record the estimated $P(B)$ for whatever bids are chosen over time, to record how many bids are won over time, and to compare predictions and outcomes in these terms to provide feedback on the accuracy of the $P(B)$. That is, only if $P(B)$ values associated with bids are explicitly recorded can data be collected which will help to improve the estimation of $P(B)$. The third pass would refine this capability as well. Useful as Figure 3.1 was, it was very crude relative to Sian's initial expected direct cost estimate, $E(C)$, £12 million plus or minus about £1 million, never mind the refined estimate provided by Table 3.2. It should be clear that significant benefit was attached to using the PD3.2 process just discussed, relative to Sian's direct cost estimate in the PD2.2. Martha was looking for even more benefit from the PD3.3 process. Martha suggested that one of the keys to the benefits provided by the PD3.2 was the decomposition of the contract into five items. This decomposition allowed a clearer view of what was involved, the use of different people with different expertise to work on different items, and the use of past experience with similar items to facilitate more effective use of past experience data than was possible for Sian working directly at the 'whole contract' level. A comparable decomposition was required for the third-pass enhanced probability of winning curve, for similar reasons.

Martha then asked Barney to illustrate how they might approach the Transcon case if they decomposed all the anticipated competitors into just two nominal competitors, i and j, where competitor i was the strongest and most important competitor, competitor j was a composite of all the rest, and competitor k was a composite of all competitors. She explained this approach could be generalized to deal with any decomposition structure Trevor wanted. Barney indicated they might start by grounding the analysis on the best available estimate of the Astro nominal price, £16 million. Next they might ask all those who had insight into competitor i's past and present bidding situation to estimate i's nominal minimum bid on this occasion (given the £16 million nominal Astro price), at some approximate level of confidence to the nearest £1 million. For example, the 'nominal minimum' might be defined in terms of a 10% chance of lower values, and i's nominal minimum bid might be assessed as £14 million, £2 million below the Astro nominal price. Then this group and other Astro staff with knowledge of the non-price advantages and disadvantages of i's bid relative to Astro's might be asked to adjust the £14 million to an adjusted bid value, defined as the value of Astro's bid which would make Transcon indifferent between competitor i bidding at the £14 million value and Astro bidding at the associated adjusted bid. For example, the adjusted bid might be £15 million. This implies that, in the bidding region being considered, competitor i must bid £1 million lower than Astro to win because of relative non-price advantages which favour Astro – an actual winning bid of £14 million by competitor i is equivalent to an adjusted bid of £15 million in terms of a 'lowest bid wins' assumption. That is, if competitor i bids at £14 million, then competitor i will win if Astro bids at £15.1 million, lose if Astro bids at £14.9 million. Next this expanded group of Astro staff might be asked to use the nominal minimum bid and its adjusted bid equivalent to define a discrete adjusted bid value scale and estimate associated probabilities that competitor i will bid these values. To provide a simple example, assume the competitor i estimates of Table 3.3.

A bid by competitor i of £14 million is associated with an adjusted bid of £15 million (an adjusted bid in the range £14.5–15.5 million) and a probability of 0.2, consistent with the percentile interpretation of the nominal minimum. A bid by competitor i of £15 million (given a consistent midpoint of a range and adjusted bid interpretation) is held to be the most likely and expected value, with an adjusted value of 16 and a probability of 0.6. A bid of £16 million by competitor i is held to be as likely as a bid of £14 million, with an adjusted value of 17 and a probability of 0.2. Any distribution could be used. This example was chosen for simplicity. If Astro is assumed to be the price-setting market leader, the example might be taken to imply that competitor i has an unbiased estimate of Astro's nominal price, give or take £1 million, and is attempting to bid £1 million less, or competitor i overestimates Astro's nominal price by £1 million and is attempting to bid £2 million less, or similar interpretations which could be explored and modelled explicitly in a more detailed structure if appropriate.

The same group or a different group of Astro staff might then be consulted, individually by Barney or collectively, to develop a similar estimate for nominal competitor j. To provide a simple example, assume the competitor j estimates of Table 3.3, repeated for each i value. This example has a slightly wider range, with lower probability value tails than the example competitor i estimates, to illustrate the fact that combinations of several competitors will result in a wider range with

Table 3.3—Calculating the probability of different bids from a composite competitor k defined by competitors i and j

Competitor i		Competitor j		Adjusted bid probability contribution for a bid of			
Adjusted bid	Probability	Adjusted bid	Probability	14	15	16	17
15	0.2	14	0.1	0.02			
		15	0.2		0.04		
		16	0.4		0.08		
		17	0.2		0.04		
		18	0.1		0.02		
16	0.6	14	0.1	0.06			
		15	0.2		0.12		
		16	0.4			0.24	
		17	0.2			0.12	
		18	0.1			0.06	
17	0.2	14	0.1	0.02			
		15	0.2		0.04		
		16	0.4			0.08	
		17	0.2				0.04
		18	0.1				0.02
Column sums				0.10	0.34	0.50	**0.06**
Cumulative probabilities			1.0	0.90	0.56	0.06	0.00
for plotting at bids of			13.5	14.5	15.5	16.5	17.5

lower probability value tails. It might be taken to imply a £2 million non-price advantage for Astro, price-setting market leadership by Astro and competitor *i*, and the same sort of attempts to bid below Astro by all competitors embodied in the composite nominal competitor *j*.

Barney would then combine these two distributions, using a computation scheme of the kind illustrated by Table 3.3, to produce Figure 3.7. The body of Table 3.3 is a tabular form of probability tree, with probability contributions to common result values collected on the right-hand side. For example, line 1 involves an adjusted bid of 15 by *i*, an adjusted bid of 14 by *j*, with a joint probability of 0.02 (0.2×0.1), associated with a winning adjusted bid of 14, the lower of 15 and 14, and puts the probability in the column which is appropriate for the result. All the other lines do the same, for each of the possible combinations of *i* and *j* bids, giving 15 (3×5) lines in all. The column sums collect these probability calculations together, to define a probability distribution for the adjusted bid with respect to competitors *i* and *j*, associated with the composite competitor *k*. These figures are then used to produce a probability of winning curve for Astro, interpreting discrete bids as £1 million ranges. For example, the probability of 0.06 of a bid of 17 (bold entry in the 'column sums' row) is associated with a 0 probability of Astro winning with a bid of 17.5, rising to 0.06 by 16.5. This, in conjunction with a probability of 0.50 of a competitor adjusted bid of 16 (next to the bold entry), implies a chance of Astro winning with a bid of 15.5 rising to 0.56. Similarly, Astro's chance of winning with a bid of 14.5 is 0.9, and Astro is certain to win with a bid of 13.5. Figure 3.7 (now shown by Barney) simply plots the final row values of Table 3.3, a rectangular probability histogram assumption being used in its

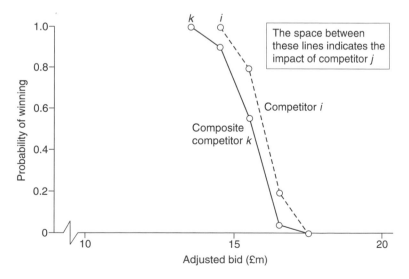

Figure 3.7—Probability of winning curves from Table 3.3 for competitors *i* and *k*.

equivalent piecewise linear cumulative probability distribution form, as the probability of winning curve for composite competitor k, defined by i and j.

Figure 3.7 also displays the comparable distribution for competitor i on its own. The gap between the i and k curves indicates the impact of competitor j. This provides a useful basis for building up an understanding of the impact of successive competitors. Barney indicated that understanding the way this build-up occurred in terms of i plus j yielding k was important. The curve for k would always be to the left of the curve for i. If i dominated j, they might coincide. If i and j were a fairly even match, a shift like that in Figure 3.7 would be observed. If i was dominated by j, a significant shift to the left would be observed. Barney made the point that Table 3.3 might look a bit complicated, but he could write simple computer software to produce Figure 3.7 from the basic inputs. Sales staff, and Martha, needed to be confident they understood what was going on, but they did not have to crunch the numbers. Table 3.3 or a computer software equivalent would allow the definition of Figure 3.7 with an explicit underlying grouping of competitors related to as many or as few individual competitors as Trevor wished, combining probability curves in any structure desired. For example, Figure 3.8 (now shown by Barney) portrayed the likely Transcon competition structure as Barney understood it.

Barney indicated that bid probabilities might be estimated separately for competitors 1 and 2, their two closest and most obvious competitors, both international organizations with bases in Wales. Barney's version had named companies beside all the numbers. This would define probability of winning curves $i = 1, j = 2$ and allow a composite probability of winning curve associated with both competitors to be calculated and associated with $k = 7$, the composite of i and j. 'Composition' in this context implies combination without a loss of information.

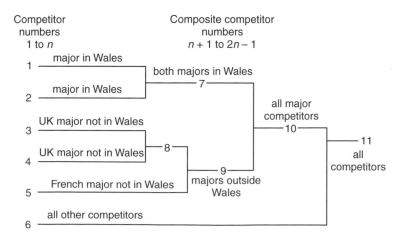

Figure 3.8—Competitor grouping structure.

Similarly, bid probability distributions and probability of winning curves could be estimated for other groups of competitors. The pair designated $i = 3$ and $j = 4$ to define $k = 8$ could address two UK-only majors with no base in Wales, and $j = 5$ could be a French major with no base in Wales, all three being known competitors. Then a probability of winning curve for $k = 9$ could compose known major competitors with no base in Wales, and a probability of winning curves for $k = 10$ would compose all known major competitors. He indicated that $i = 6$ could be all other competitors, and $k = 11$ would then define the probability of winning curves for all competitors, the third-pass equivalent to Figure 3.1. Barney indicated that Martha wanted Trevor and other sales staff, with help from Barney as needed, to provide adjusted bid distributions 1 to 6. Barney would then provide Figure 3.7 format probability of winning curves for composite competitors $k = 7$ to 11.

Barney indicated that this approach assumes the probability distributions for adjusted bid values for competitors i and j are independently distributed in terms of probability distribution shapes which can be estimated approximately by a rectangular histogram probability density function and combined using a discrete probability tree approximation. Rectangular histogram forms can approximate any distribution to whatever level of precision required, so that is not a restrictive assumption, simply a useful working assumption. Discrete probability arithmetic is approximate when continuous variables are involved, but error is modest and it can be controlled or eliminated (Chapman and Cooper, 1983a), or standard Monte Carlo simulation software (Grey, 1995) can be used to achieve the same ends. Statistical independence in this case is a reasonable assumption if collusion between competitors is not involved, and dependence could be modelled, if appropriate, to reflect possible collusion. The key framing assumption is the ability of Astro staff to estimate the input distributions for the Table 3.3 equivalents for Figure 3.8 i and j corresponding to competitors 1 to 6. Martha interjected here on cue. She suggested that Figure 3.7 had to be estimated for $k = 7$ to 11 because she had to have a refined version of Table 3.1 in order to refine the bid price. If Astro sales staff were uncomfortable estimating the competitor bid distributions like Table 3.3, they were just going to have to get over it. In her view, an inability to estimate the equivalent of Figure 3.7 for all competitors ($k = 11$) and appropriate subsets of competitors was tantamount to not understanding the marketplace in a way which was directly useful to her and Astro more generally. However, she could assure them that it was not as difficult as it might seem, and successive use of figures of the form of Figure 3.7 would help them to understand the implications of their base-level assumptions. Further, the kind of decomposition provided by Figure 3.8 would yield benefits analogous to those observed from the five-item breakdown of costs. For example, Astro could start to acquire data on winning bids by individual major competitors relative to Astro's nominal price, to develop a database relevant to their probability distribution estimates. As this data grew, Astro could start to look for formal analysis explanations for changes in these distributions over time, systematic variations due to the state of the market, the state of the competitors' order books, and so on. The models would also provide a framework to test hypotheses about the implications of strategy changes by competitors.

The curve for the final composite, all competitors ($k = 11$), would be the bottom line, what sales staff had to provide to Martha before any bid was considered. No curve meant no bids, and no sales, no commissions, and no jobs for sales staff. How they produced it would be up to Sales with Barney's support. But it would be audited initially by Martha on a case by case basis, to see if it made sense at all levels. Obviously there was no guarantee any Figure 3.7 k-curve would be correct. However, Martha could apply two tests. First, did all the underlying assumptions seem to make sense? Second, as data accumulated, did it confirm the order of magnitude of the estimates used at the final 'all competitors' level and at the level of individual known competitors? Martha stressed that it would be some time before significant data was available, but the first of these tests would be used with immediate effect, with some intensity, until she was convinced that everyone understood what they were doing. The technical details of this approach could clearly take a while to get used to, but Martha did not want to spend more time on them now. Barney would arrange for special seminars to take everyone through the basics, and workshops to develop the details. She wanted to finish off the meeting with a formal presentation by Barney on the enhanced bid setting summary table and discussion based on that table.

Third-Pass Uncertainty Synthesis

Barney started his final presentation of the meeting with Table 3.4, indicating it had the same basic structure as Table 3.1, with three changes of note. First, he had removed the offending $V(E(C))$, $V(C)$ and $V(P(B))$ notation. Second, the table no longer showed different results for alternative $E(C)$ values, because it was assumed that Sian now had $E(C)$ estimated to the nearest £1 million. There was no further need for sensitivity analysis in relation to $E(C)$. Although the range of potential outcomes was still large, this was not an issue. Third, the table now showed different results for the alternative probability of winning curves of Figure 3.7 and 3.1 (assuming the curve through point c_1). He would focus on this difference.

Barney began by emphasizing that the Figure 3.1 curve through c_1 was not necessarily what Trevor had in mind. Its choice here was purely illustrative. Indeed, the Figure 3.7 estimate was certainly not intended as a revision to Trevor's Figure 3.1 estimate. Its role in Table 3.4 was to show the extent to which differences of the scale illustrated by these two curves matter. By way of comparison, at a bid B of £15 million, the second (Figure 3.1) column of Table 3.4 indicates

Table 3.4—Summary table (third pass) for enhanced bid setting

Expected direct cost $E(C) = £11m$ with an outcome in the range £10–16m anticipated

Bid values B (£m)	Corresponding probabilities $P(B)$		Corresponding margins (conditional) $M = B - E(C)$	Corresponding expected margins $E(M) = P(B)M$		Comments
	Figure 3.1*	Figure 3.7		Figure 3.1	Figure 3.7	
13	0.97	1.00	2	1.94	2.00	Suggested bid range if Figure 3.7 used
14	0.94	0.95	3	2.82	2.85	
15	0.80	0.72	4	3.20	2.88	Maximum $E(M)$ range if Figure 3.7 used
16	0.66	0.30	5	3.30	1.50	
17	0.52	0.03	6	3.12	0.18	Maximum $E(M)$ range if Figure 3.1 used
18	0.38	0	7	2.66	0	
19	0.24	0	8	1.92	0	
20	0.10	0	9	0.90	0	

*Using the dotted line through point c_1 on Figure 3.1 for illustrative purposes.

$P(B) = 0.8$, while the third (Figure 3.7) column indicates $P(B) = 0.72$, which is within the sort of noise or acceptable variations they should expect between second- and third-pass estimates. As B is reduced to £14 million and then £13 million, the probability of winning rises more steeply using the Figure 3.7 column than even the dotted line through point c_1 in Figure 3.1, but the two curves cross and then remain close. Over the B range £13–15 million, the two curves roughly coincide if the extension through point c_1 of Figure 3.1 is assumed. The difference starts to show with B values above £15 million. As B rises to £16 million and £17 million, the probability of winning drops much more steeply when using the Figure 3.7 curve than when using the Figure 3.1 curve. It is in this range that the curves differ to a significant extent.

The $E(M)$ column of Table 3.4 associated with the Figure 3.1 curve suggests a maximum expected margin of 3.30, with a bid of £16 million, the nominal price, and a 0.66 probability of winning. This looks quite attractive. However, if the Figure 3.7 column of Table 3.4 is the reality, the chance of winning with this bid of £16 million is only 0.30, and the expected margin is only 1.50, less than half that assumed. Further, if Figure 3.7 is the reality, a maximum margin is achieved with a bid between £14 million and £15 million, and a bid between £13 million and £14 million is suggested because a probability of winning approaching 1.0 can be obtained with very little loss of expected margin. It clearly matters that we know which curve we are dealing with. Figures 3.1 and 3.7 may be roughly the same in the range $B = £13$–15 million, but the differences outside this region are of crucial importance. Astro need to confirm (or revise) and refine Trevor's probability of winning estimates. To get started, Barney recommended working with best estimates associated with close competitors in the structure of Figure 3.8 to define a Figure 3.7 equivalent, then associated nominal optimistic and pessimistic bounds, showing the best estimate and its bounds on the equivalent of Table 3.4. But he suggested this would not be so necessary once they got used to the approach, and Trevor became more confident of his Figure 3.7 equivalents.

Third-Pass Bid Setting Discussion

Barney finished his final presentation of the meeting by indicating that the sort of discussion that Sian and Trevor started in the context of Table 3.1 and the PD2.5 would clearly be much better informed by Table 3.4 and the PD3.5. The discussion would not just be working with more precise numerical estimates; it would be working with a quite different level of understanding of all the uncertainties involved.

Martha reminded Sian and Trevor that the first and second passes should target the use of about 2% (1% + 1%) of all the effort required for the full bid pre-paration process for a bid of the size and importance involved. They should target the elimination of about 80% of the potential bids on the first two passes (60% followed by 40% of the remaining 40%, rounded to the nearest 10%), leaving a residual of about 20% of the bids as hopeful starters or potential goers. She indicated that the third pass should target the use of about 20% of the effort required for the full bid preparation process. The remaining effort should be devoted to building on the insights provided by the third pass, in subsequent passes and parallel bid management processes, to make bids that Astro wanted to win more attractive to the potential clients. It is not just a matter of refining earlier estimates; it is a matter of addressing different kinds of uncertainty in different ways as appropriate. PD3.5 should address these kinds of issues as a basis for possible further passes and other forms of analysis.

Martha then reminded Trevor and Sian that Barney would support the PD3 processes, and make the provision of necessary information as easy as possible for them, Sian's Systems staff, other Sales staff, and any other Astro staff involved. They did not have to understand the technical issues in detail, just the basic principles. She knew Trevor and the Sales staff would find the new approach particularly new and challenging to get to grips with, but they would find it very rewarding as well. She was determined to make Astro Wales a success story that would attract widespread attention. She would now leave them to recover from the information overload of this meeting, and let Barney help them get on with it, starting the next day.

Managing Requisite Change

Martha had synthesized six key steps from her analysis of the change management literature and the project risk management literature:

- Make sure everyone involved understands that no change is not an option.
- Make sure that the strategic direction of the change and the key deliverables from the change are clear.
- If you cannot change the people, then change the people. Redeploy (transfer, retire or fire) anyone who, given reasonable support, is not willing or able to make the change as soon as feasible, to minimize the negative effects of unconstructive dissent on morale, as well as the operational burden of people who are not pulling their weight.
- Manage the whole change process as a very high risk programme (portfolio of high-risk projects), with a focus on flexibility and effectiveness rather than efficiency (doing things right is less important than doing the right things).
- Facilitate joint development of the new models and processes that the change requires by everyone involved so that they have ownership.
- Facilitate learning processes as everyone involved develops the skills necessary to implement the new models and processes.

Martha had done what she could for the moment to minimize uncertainty with respect to the first four steps. It was time to address the remaining two, starting with facilitating joint development of the mechanisms and processes with Trevor and other Sales staff.

Managing the change in Sales

To initiate change, towards the end of her focus on the enhanced probability of winning curve with Trevor, Martha had deliberately played what Trevor would characterize as a tough cop role. The complementary kind cop role was Barney's, although Trevor would not see it as such. Martha now coached Barney carefully, so he could be an effective kind cop while seeming to be just a facilitator. Barney was a natural in this role. Indeed, much of the effectiveness of Barney and Martha as a team was driven by the complementary nature of their roles, skills, personalities and goals. In particular, Barney was able to move the model and process development forward with a steady hand which was largely invisible from Trevor's perspective (the best way to sell people an idea is to let them think they thought of it first). Trevor saw himself as in charge again, with Barney serving as his gopher.

Barney's first step was to arrange a meeting with Trevor. He began the meeting by seeking Trevor's advice on what sort of approach to Figure 3.8 the Sales people might find useful, and what would be a good way to deal with the obvious uncertainty associated with the bid adjustment process. Trevor quickly responded to this opportunity, with a view to making his mark on the new bidding models and processes. He thought out loud with a whiteboard and marker pen for the whole of a morning, while Barney made notes and prompted him. Trevor then put together a presentation for other sales staff, with Barney's help. This was used to trigger further ideas. Trevor then made a presentation to Martha of the initial Sales view of how to approach these issues as perceived by Trevor, with Barney's support and guidance.

One of Trevor's key ideas was to start the focus on competitor 1, defined as the key competitor, with the question, Is competitor 1 the market leader? If the answer was no then Astro was the market leader by definition. Another of Trevor's key ideas was adapting the structure of Table 3.3 to what Trevor called the key competitor equivalent bid table. Table 3.5 illustrates the idea for Taurus, a key competitor who was assumed to be the market leader on the Transcon bid, as formulated by Trevor and Barney at an early stage in the development of this concept.

The rationale behind Table 3.5 was the focus of a very productive meeting of all Astro Wales Sales staff. Trevor introduced Table 3.5 at this meeting by explaining his thinking as follows. Instead of estimating as in Table 3.3 the competitor i input assuming a known and common £1 million adjustment between all actual and adjusted bids and then doing the same for competitor j, each competitor could be associated with a formal modelling of the uncertainty associated with the adjustment process. They would concentrate on $i = 1$, Taurus, but all other competitors could be assessed initially via Table 3.5 formats, then combined via derived Table 3.3 formats, using computer software to keep the input requirements minimal. Formally modelling of the uncertainty associated with the adjustment process would help to give them confidence that the expected outcomes were unbiased, because they could express their lack of certainty visibly and explicitly.

Taurus are expected to be a very aggressive market leader in the context of the Transcon bid, and they have very low costs relative to Astro's. Astro's £16 million nominal price will be high relative to a comparable nominal price for Taurus. Taurus would only bid as high as £16 million if they were very busy and did not particularly want the job. If Taurus wanted the job very badly, they might put in a bid as low as £14 million. A bid of £15 million is most likely, given their cost base and no obvious reasons for high or low bids. The Taurus bid probability distribution in the first two columns of Table 3.5 defines three Taurus bid scenarios which reflect the range of actual bids anticipated, with initial probabilities estimated by Trevor. The high to low ordering of Table 3.5 simplifies considering the associated entries in columns 3 and 4, with initial probabilities estimated by Trevor. If Taurus bid at £16 million, Transcon will recognize that Taurus are not particularly keen to get the job, and Astro might be able to bid as high as £17

Table 3.5—Key competitor equivalent bid table: Taurus

Probability tree estimates				Adjusted bid probability contributions for a bid of						
Bid (actual)	Probability	Adjusted bid	Probability	0	12	13	14	15	16	17
16	0.2	17	0.1							0.02
		16	0.2						0.04	
		15	0.5					0.10		
		14	0.2				0.04			
15	0.6	15	0.1					0.06		
		14	0.2				0.12			
		13	0.4			0.24				
		12	0.3		0.18					
14	0.2	13	0.1			0.02				
		12	0.3		0.06					
		11	(0.6)	(0.12)						
Column sums			(1.0)	(0.12)	0.24	0.26	0.16	0.16	0.04	0.02
Cumulative probabilities for plotting at bids of			(0)	0.88 / 11.5	0.64 / 12.5	0.38 / 13.5	0.22 / 14.5	0.06 / 15.5	0.02 / 16.5	0 / 17.5

million and still win, ascribed a 0.1 conditional probability. This scenario, Taurus bidding £16 million and Astro bidding £17 million, assumes a £1 million non-price advantage for Astro relative to Taurus as perceived by Transcon. Astro is bidding in its 'premium end of the market' manner, and Transcon are presumed to be prepared to pay for the quality given a perceived lack of enthusiasm on the part of Taurus. This defines line 1 of the body of Table 3.5, and we can now work down, line by line. Line 1 is a convenient starting point, combining the highest plausible Taurus bid and the highest plausible Astro bid, the most optimistic plausible scenario.

Lines 2 to 4 of Table 3.5 consider successively lower adjusted bid values and associated probabilities until the probabilities sum to 1. This defines a probability distribution of adjusted bids (and associated non-price advantages) conditioned on Taurus bidding £16 million. With Taurus bidding at £16 million, Trevor is confident that Astro could win for sure with a bid of £14 million, assuming a non-price advantage of no more than £2 million being ascribed to Taurus as perceived by Transcon. Put another way, given a Taurus bid of £16 million, the most likely equivalent bid as perceived by Transcon and estimated by Trevor is £15 million, a non-price advantage to Taurus of £1 million (16−15), with a probability of 0.5.

Line 5 of Table 3.5 associates a maximum adjusted bid value of £15 million with a Taurus bid value of £15 million, because it is assumed that Transcon will see a £15 million bid from Taurus as a reasonably competitive bid, with no chance of Astro doing any better than parity in non-price advantage terms. Lines 5 to 8 consider decreasing adjusted bid values (increasing non-price advantages to Taurus) until the probabilities sum to 1. This defines a probability distribution of adjusted bids (and associated non-price advantages) on Taurus bidding £15 million. With Taurus bidding at £15 million, Trevor is confident that Astro could win for sure with a bid of £12 million, a non-price advantage of up to £3 million being ascribed to Taurus as perceived by Transcon and estimated by Trevor, but no more. Put another way, with Taurus bidding at £15 million, the most likely equivalent Astro bid as perceived by Transcon is £13 million, implying a non-price advantage to Taurus of £2 million (15−13), with a probability of 0.4.

Line 9 is associated with a maximum adjusted bid of £13 million, because it is assumed that Transcon will see a £14 million bid from Taurus as very competitive, with no chance of Astro doing any better than a £1 million deficit in non-price advantage terms. Line 10 starts the definition of a probability distribution as above, but in line 11 a bid of £11 million is associated with a zero probability of winning, a discontinuity, because a non-price advantage of £3 million or more when Taurus are bidding in a highly competitive manner at £14 million would be seen as non-credible by Transcon. Trevor suggested that this scenario should be called a zero bid equivalent to signify that Astro couldn't give it away below £12 million in the face of a £14 million Taurus bid. Instead of putting a zero beside the adjusted bid entry of £11 million in column 4, a 0.6 entry in brackets was used, defined by (1 − 0.1 − 0.3), so the adjusted bid probabilities associated with a Taurus bid of £14 million sum to 1. The brackets signify this is the probability of a zero bid equivalent for Astro bids in the range 0 to 11, a simple way of dealing with the discontinuity. The columns collecting together the adjusted bid probability contributions incorporate the zero bid equivalent with a 0.12 entry (0.2×0.6) in brackets. As soon as Trevor thought the Sales staff understood roughly how Table 3.5 worked, he showed them Figure 3.9, and watched them squirm as he had done when Barney had developed Table 3.5 and Figure 3.9 from Trevor's thinking out loud on the whiteboard.

Trevor explained that, as illustrated by Figure 3.7, any competitor i curve plus competitor j curve yields a composite competitor k curve result which is to the left of i or j. If i dominates j, the shift to the left will be negligible. If j dominates i, the shift to the left will be substantial. The curve for k will never shift to the right. This means the curve of Figure 3.9, if correct, is the best they can do, ignoring all other competitors. As they consider other competitors, things can only get worse. Figure 3.9 shows only a 0.04 probability of winning with a bid of £16 million, only a 0.14 probability of winning with a bid of £15 million, rising to 0.30 for £14 million, 0.51 for £13 million. Trevor suggested that if this assessment were remotely correct, they would need to work out how to attack the massive non-price and cost advantages Taurus have before worrying about other competitors. Trevor indicated this result had surprised him greatly – relative to his preliminary assessment, it was very pessimistic. But he believed addressing the specifics of their key competitor relationship provided a much more realistic view of the competition as a whole.

Trevor then used the framework provided by Barney to stimulate what he called a search for value-added. Using the Astro site for training illustrated what

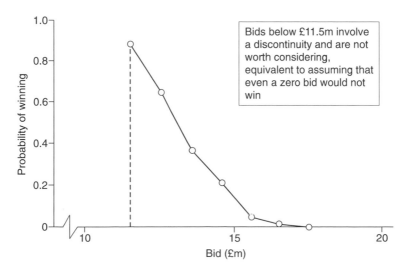

Figure 3.9—Probability of winning graph from Table 3.5, considering only the key competitor.

he was after. More value-added was needed to be competitive with the market leader, Taurus, and other strong competitors. With Barney's support, increasingly recognized and acknowledged as invaluable, Trevor and the other Sales staff worked with Sian's staff to find more value-added. This was an important part of the start of the turnaround in the fortunes of Astro Wales. Only about 20% of the effort put into a full bid was associated with the three-pass bidding process per se. The other 80% was in part associated with later-pass refinements, but was largely associated with parallel value-added searches. What emerged from this exercise as a general consensus was summarized as follows:

- Starting with Astro's key competitor was crucial. A quick stab at a key competitor curve was probably the best basis for the preliminary probability of winning curve of PD2.3 as well.
- Table 3.5 provided a simple framework for capturing the key issues which needed to be quantified, in particular the range and relative likelihood of actual bids by the key competitor, and the associated possible non-price advantage scenarios which defined adjusted bids.
- It was important to explicitly consider uncertainty associated with non-price advantages and to make this uncertainty dependent on the assumed key competitor bid, because this dependence and uncertainty are very important, and require open, explicit, focused discussion by those with relevant knowledge.
- Figure 3.9 provided a useful framework for interpreting Table 3.5, and having a single key competitor underlie Table 3.5 and Figure 3.9 made the graph very credible. Everyone could accept that it approximated reality, the story it told was clear, and messages it sent were clear. Its basis was subjective but sound.
- Once a way of improving the picture portrayed by Figure 3.9 had been managed, it was relatively straightforward to consider an equivalent of Table 3.5 and Figure 3.9 for the next most important competitor. The approach used in Table 3.3 and Figure 3.7 could then be applied to combine these two competitors. Again, the results were accepted as subjective but sound. A second wave of value-added searches, perhaps in slightly different directions, could follow if needed. This process could continue as necessary, as the basis of PD3.3. However, the dominance of the first few competitors, because of the ordering approach, made everyone reasonably confident of a final 'all other competitors' component estimated directly from the results of the first few individual competitors, once the process and the model results became reasonably familiar.
- There was a need to use this basic approach to PD3.3 when no data was available to confirm or deny the validity of subjective estimates agreed by relevant staff, but there was also a need to start thinking about data acquisition from the outset.

As soon as the Sales staff were comfortable with the basic approach, Barney persuaded Trevor to initiate discussion and thinking about the relationship between the purely subjective basis of Table 3.5 and Figure 3.9 and related data which could be acquired over time. Trevor started by suggesting that Table 3.5 could be used to define Figures 3.10 and 3.11. Trevor indicated that Figure 3.10 portrayed the non-price advantage transformations of Table 3.5. For example, if Taurus bid £15 million, the most likely non-price advantage for Taurus as perceived by Transcon is £2 million, and the expected non-price advantage is £1.9 million, with a probability distribution involving a 0.3 probability over the range 3.5–2.5, a 0.4 probability over the range 2.5–1.5, a 0.2 probability over the range 1.5–0.5, and a 0.1 probability over the range 0.5 to −0.5.

Figure 3.11 portrayed the Taurus bid probability distribution in a more conventional format. Data points might be marked directly onto such graphs as observations occurred. For example, if Astro won the Transcon project with a bid of £16.3 million, in the face of a bid of £15.3 million by Taurus, point *a* in Figure 3.10 and point *c* in Figure 3.11 might be marked as indicated. Point *c* in Figure 3.11 uses a small square to indicate an observation (of £15.3 million) which does not conflict with the assumed subjective probability distribution. A lot of points like *c* would be required to start to confirm or slightly shift the distribution. However, point *a* in Figure 3.10 uses a small triangle pointing downwards to indicate the observation of a data point which does conflict with the assumed subjective probability distributions. It points downwards to indicate that interpolating between the assumed Taurus non-price advantage distributions for Taurus bids of

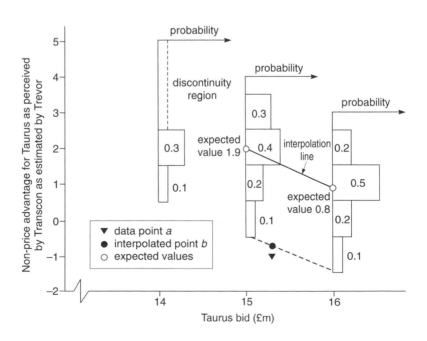

Figure 3.10—Non-price advantage probability distributions from Table 3.5.

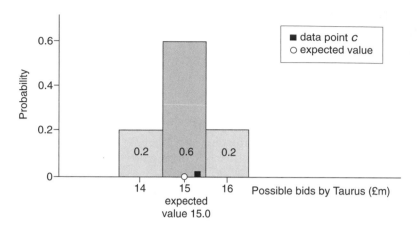

Figure 3.11—Taurus bid probability distributions from Table 3.5.

£15–16 million (to define point *b*) suggests both distributions should accommodate the possibility of more negative non-price advantage for Taurus. There is a discrepancy between the assumed distributions and the data of at least £0.25 million. Trevor pointed out that even one observation like point *a*, if not explainable as a genuine outlier, could force revision outwards of the spread of the subjective probability distributions. However, it would take a lot of observations like point *c* to justify a narrowing of the spread. He suggested that the additional detail provided by Figure 3.10 relative to Figure 3.11 made the use of data more effective.

Trevor suggested that, given a number of data points like this, Sales staff might prefer to start with graphs like Figures 3.10 and 3.11, with Table 3.5 defined subsequently. He labelled this approach to data collection and interpretation 'getting to know the enemy'. He suggested this should be the starting point for their data-based analysis of all key competitors for all relevant market sectors. He suggested different market sectors would lead to different relationships for each of their key competitors. Taurus was not as strong in the retail area for example, where Gemini became the key competitor and market leader. They could start this kind of analysis for Taurus on the Transcon contract. They could undertake similar analysis for Gemini on the Transcon contract, competitor 2 in Figure 3.8. They could accumulate data over time to provide a basis for future Table 3.4 equivalents. Data need not be limited to winning bid observations, and useful data was often much more widely available than commonly assumed. For example, if they lost, some potential clients might indicate why with a range of information which would be useful even if it did not readily lend itself to standardized analysis.

In summary, Martha initiated and provided direction for the change, and Barney facilitated and provided the basis for appropriate models and processes for the change, but Trevor was the visible leader for Sales staff. The models chosen and the processes evolved were simple but effective. The new ideas were an unqualified success. Trevor and Barney established reputations which soon went beyond Astro Wales. Martha shared the glory, and Rhys, the manager in charge of Astro Wales, felt the benefits too. All their careers took a strong turn for the better because of these bidding process developments.

Managing the change in Systems

To initiate change in Systems, towards the end of her focus on the enhanced cost estimate process with Sian, Martha had deliberately made it clear that not all Sian's staff would attract favourable cost adjustments, and all Astro Wales Systems groups had to be competitive to survive beyond the very short run. Martha would try to ensure that underutilized groups had work generated for them in the short run if they could compete on price and quality in the medium term. But nobody could be carried for long if Astro Wales was going to succeed as she intended.

The degree of difficulty inherent in adopting the new models Sian and her staff had tried to make use of in Table 3.2 was trivial in comparison to those Trevor had to develop. Nevertheless, the new internal bidding process which Table 3.2 cost adjustments made explicit involved a major culture change, what Trevor would call a 'character-forming experience'. Sian did not need Barney's support to a significant extent with the costing of bids. Table 3.2 and the supporting figures could be facilitated with software tools, and Barney helped with the specification and testing of these tools. However, Barney's support for Sian was negligible compared to his support for Trevor and other Sales staff, in terms of developing formal models and processes to implement these models. Sian did need Martha's support to a significant extent, and she got it. She also needed and got support from Rhys. Further, in this context Sian, Martha and Rhys all received useful support from Barney as a more general process facilitator, helping to guide their thinking.

Sian's Astro career had always been in Systems, and she had always seen the role of a head of systems like herself in terms of a conventional matrix-based 'service' organization: Sales people were responsible for getting the work and making a profit on the sales, Systems people were responsible for doing the work and ensuring that the quality generated a good reputation and future work. This built in a quality/profit tension management process with clear champions for each. Sian had recognized the growing use of subcontractors like Zoro as a complication of the simple historical situation, but she had never seen marketing her Systems people in competition with external suppliers of the same or similar skills as a key part of her job. Nor had she fully appreciated the conflict of interests inherent in her current role as judge in a process which entailed her Systems staff bidding against external subcontractors. She now recognized these complications were critical. Her job, as she currently saw it, involved serious conflicts of interest, and it was not clear to her what ought to be done. Massive uncertainties she had not seen previously suddenly revealed themselves, in a 'career-threatening manner' as Trevor would put it.

Rhys, the manager in charge of Astro Wales, had a Systems background like Sian. He was a native of Wales, but most of his modestly successful career had been spent in various locations in the UK and the US. Martha and Sian were both keen to involve him in Sian's difficulties from the outset, and he was very keen to be involved. He had held his post longer than Martha or Sian, but he had never been very comfortable telling either of them or their predecessors what to do. He felt 'put out to grass' to some extent, and kept himself busy acting as a front man for Astro Wales in ways which did not seem all that useful. He was as uncertain about his proper role as Sian had suddenly become. Five significant changes emerged from their four-way discussions:

- Sian should ensure that each of her Systems groups had a strong group head who would take full responsibility for the quality and cost of work by that group, with requisite authority to hire, promote, and recommend redeployment in order to maintain a group size agreed with Sian. Sian would be responsible for the performance of her group heads, but not the groups, so long as a group head was not in obvious trouble as a manager. In effect, important roles Sian currently played would be devolved to group heads, drawing lines around what was devolved and what Sian kept with a view to effective management of uncertainty without direct conflicts of interest for any of the players. Sian was subcontracting part of her job in order to enhance her performance with the residual responsibilities, analogous to Astro Wales subcontracting parts of systems integration projects in order to enhance overall performance. Barney was the one who guided their thinking in this direction, and who suggested the subcontracting analogy, but the solution was obvious to all of them as soon as they saw it.
- Each Systems group would be regarded as a profit centre, not just a cost centre, with a focus on profit in both the short term and the longer term. Each group head was responsible for cost and quality, but Sian would accept responsibility for the profit aspect, in conjunction with group-sizing decisions. The size of each group would be a focus of discussions between Sian and her group managers. Groups which made a profit would grow; groups which did not would shrink or relocate.
- Sian would see the main focus of her job as an internal marketing manager for her Systems groups, to Martha's Astro Wales projects, to Astro UK, and to Astro Inc. more generally. She would take a reasonably reactive role to the first, but a highly proactive role to the second and third. That is, she would trust and rely on Martha to take a proactive interest in generating local (Welsh) work for

her people, given support and guidance, but she would proactively seek Systems contracts with Astro UK and Astro Inc., because Martha was not really geared to this kind of sales, and in the past such contracts did not really have a champion.

- Rhys would serve as Sian's front man and chief salesman for internal sales to Astro UK and Astro Inc., making effective use of his extensive network of connections and his wide experience. Martha would also support Sian's internal sales in the Astro UK and Astro Inc. areas in terms of the marketing experience which Sian and Rhys lacked. Barney would provide back-up analytical support as well. Sian would be in charge of marketing in this internal markets sense, but she would be fully supported by all Astro Wales staff whenever they could contribute, whether they were technically a level above (Rhys), on the same level (Martha), or somewhere below in someone else's reporting structure (Barney). Martha's responsibility for Sales would have a local (Welsh) focus, explicitly restricted to non-Astro markets in terms of proactive leadership.

- Rhys would take personal responsibility for developing and maintaining a suitable list of partnership external subcontractors, and for looking after their interests in any competition with Astro Wales Systems groups on Martha's contracts unless and until this task warranted a separate manager. Rhys, Martha, Sian and Barney all agreed that an internal bidding process involving sealed bids, replicating what Martha faced with customers like Transcon, would not be helpful. However, an open process with a level playing field was necessary. A partnership relationship with subcontractors was a productive way of levelling the playing field, putting them on a par with internal Systems groups, rather than the other way around. It also had direct benefits, which business fashion was beginning to recognize. The concept of non-price advantage was central to these considerations; one key non-price advantage was trust that subcontractors or groups could deliver what they promised, when they promised, without arguments and without close management. Another was confidence that partners would be open and honest about uncertainties which could become sources of risk.

Sian, Martha, Barney and Rhys did not attract the immediate attention with these developments that Trevor, Barney and Martha generated with their bidding models and processes. To some extent they were competing with other Astro UK and Astro Inc. groups, so they did not want to shout about these changes too loudly too soon. However, within a few years Astro Wales became prominent for attracting many large systems development contracts from other parts of Astro, as well as for working effectively with a wide range of partner subcontractors in a growing volume of local business, and it was clear where the credit was due. Zoro was one of their partners, as were several Astro groups which were floated off as separate businesses, usually to everyone's benefit, although sometimes these float-offs failed and sometimes very few people were surprised by such failures.

The uncertainties to be faced, the uncertainties associated with the best way to handle them, and the uncertainties generated by associated changes which Sian had to address, were all quite different to those Trevor and the other Sales staff had to address. The support Sian needed was very different as a consequence. The 'softer', less clear-cut nature of the issues made formal models less useful, but the need for formal processes and attention to organizational structure correspondingly more important. There was no need to redefine Sian's job and the organizational structure around her in formal terms for all to see, but there was a very important need to redefine Sian's roles in agreement with those she worked with. Equally important was the flexibility implied in both Martha and Rhys 'working for Sian' in some contexts when this was useful. The senior staff of Astro Wales worked as a close team, with role changes according to context, to effectively manage the opportunities inherent in the complex uncertainty associated with redefining Sian's role in relation to their own roles. The experience was 'character forming' in a very positive sense for Martha and Rhys as well as Sian, and enlightening for everyone else involved. Barney regarded it as a 'defining moment' in his understanding of what management was all about.

The impact of the changes more generally

The example set by Rhys, Sian and Martha in terms of their approach to teamwork was infectious. It was supported by Trevor and other Sales staff turning to Systems staff to help in the search for value-added in order to develop winning bids. It was reinforced by heads of Systems groups seeking a degree of marketing expertise from Trevor and other Sales staff as well as Martha. There was a visible flow of ideas and help from Sales to Systems and from Systems to Sales, which expanded to include the service bureau operation, accounting and other support groups. To a lesser but significant extent it also embraced the partner external subcontractors. Apart from the direct benefits of the ideas and help, as barriers went down, trust grew and new synergy was identified and exploited. 'Managing upwards' and 'managing across' became operational aspects of the office jargon, and natural complements to 'managing downwards', which glues together closely bonded teams. Because managing the uncertainties facing Astro Wales as a whole was very much a team sport, teamwork became the key. Uncertainty management models and processes helped to shape the key and lubricate the lock. Astro Wales as a whole prospered. Astro Wales was seen to be in the vanguard of the turnaround in Astro UK, and a very useful contributor to the turnaround in Astro Inc. Effective and efficient external bidding processes were often held up as illustrative of their contribution. Those directly involved knew these bidding processes were a catalyst or a driver, depending on the perspective, quite certainly only a small part of the whole Astro Inc. recovery story, but arguably a critical part.

Some General Implications

Managing expectations is often the bottom line when managing uncertainty. In the case of Astro, the iterative bidding process Martha and Barney initiated required significant adjustment of the expectations Astro staff had for bidding.

First, Astro staff should not expect to bid in response to every invitation to tender. Some potential bids should be identifiable as unsuitable (non-starters) with a very simple qualitative process, the first-pass PD1 process of page 64. About 1% of the effort required for a full bid evaluation expected in these cases was a reasonable target, to adjust with experience. Some potential bids should be identifiable as unprofitable no-hopers with a very simple quantitative approach, the second-pass PD2 approach of page 66. About 1% of the effort required for a full bid evaluation was also a reasonable target in these cases, to be adjusted with experience. About 80% of the potential bids rejected by these two passes, leaving 20% for third and subsequent passes, seemed a reasonable starting target for Astro, to be adjusted with experience. Jointly, these targets imply a significant variant of the classic 80:20 rule – use 2% of effort to reject 80% of the potential bids, and allow 98% of effort to be focused on the remaining 20% of the bids. Other organizations might require different starting points, and endpoints might be quite different, but the orders of magnitude should be comparable.

A second adjustment of expectations was that Astro staff should not expect to finish the third pass ready to bid. A target of 20% of the effort available expended on this pass is an appropriate starting position, with 80% left to enhance the bid further using further passes or parallel processes like Trevor's 'search for value-added'. This is another simple variant of the 80:20 rule: 20% of the effort allocated to identify where the remaining 80% should be spent. This simple rule is much less specific to the nature of the organization and its market than the first- and second-pass rules. Although it too may need adjustment, the orders of magnitude are much more universal.

Most people involved in bidding processes have rather different expectations to those noted above. Their expectations need to be changed, with support in terms of making them comfortable with highly iterative processes rather than the 'one-shot' processes most organizations use. 'Right first time' may be a very effective and efficient way to manufacture, but it is inexcusably inefficient and ineffective as an approach to decision processes involving significant uncertainty. If appropriate versions or variants of the 80:20 rules are not built into the process for any organization, with models and processes reflecting the changing objectives and the changing nature of the uncertainties addressed by each pass, the process as a whole will be hopelessly inefficient, and ineffective. Putting this another way, Astro staff should not expect to spend 80% of the effort available to prepare a bid developing a specification and costing it, 20% considering the competition and pricing the bid. These ratios should be reversed. Bidding is about persuading a potential client to buy in the face of competitive offers, if it is worth doing so. The expectations of the potential client need to be carefully managed. The details of the specification actually delivered and the costs at a detailed level, which are normally the focus of 80% of the effort in a bid, are generally of limited relevance. Most organizations reflect Sian's overly detailed approach to cost estimating relative to Trevor's approach to bidding strategy when developing the starting point for the formal analysis of a bid. This reflects the common preference for spending a lot of time discussing what is understood and rather less time on what is unfamiliar or not well understood. Most people involved in the details of bid preparation know a lot about specifying and costing, but not much about assessing competitive pricing and non-price advantages. Their expectations need to be changed, with appropriate learning support. As part of this, the mix of people involved also need to be changed; in Astro's case this implied more Sales and less Systems.

A clear and explicit modelling framework for competitive bidding has been available for some time (e.g. Friedman, 1956), and many authors have built on this (e.g. Ruthkopf, 1983; King and Mercer, 1985 and 1991; Tweedley, 1995). A clear and explicit process framework for competitive bidding has also been available for some time (e.g. Ward and Chapman, 1988). However, very few organizations even approach the effective implementation of these ideas in the way achieved by Astro. The authors' use of a related case study (developed for Astro) on professional short courses for more than a decade provides considerable evidence of this (Chapman, Ward and Bennell, 2000). The perception of organizations which avoid such formalizations must be that such formalizations will not be helpful, or that they do not want to change their ways, and the competition will not force them to do so. These perceptions need to be changed. The power of formalizations which can effectively separate the quantitative and the qualitative is increasingly recognized, as such formalizations become better developed. If one significant player in any given marketplace adopts the effective use of such approaches, their competitors will have to follow suit or pay a heavy price. There is no longer room for complacency.

The third-pass approach to enhanced cost estimation of page 73 has been tested and validated as appropriate for more than a decade in the context of bids like Astro's Transcon bid, and published (Chapman, Ward and Bennell, 2000). The formalizations concerning bid levels developed by Trevor and Barney of pages 88 and 97 are key new material on model and process details provided by this chapter. The authors believe that one of the reasons most organizations have not successfully used formal bidding processes in the past is the lack of simple explicit ways of considering important individual competitors, and then relating this to other competitors in a way which balances the value of detailed attention to individuals and simple aggregation of the rest. We hope this new material will help to break the logjam.

To close this section on what might initially seem a very specific point, a £20 million maximum budget for Transcon's contract as indicated by a senior Transcon manager might seem out of line with the figures which Trevor's later analysis suggested. To some extent it might just reflect the consultant's uncertainty about the market. However, it is very important to understand the difference between a fixed contract price and final cost to the client. This issue will be further explored in later chapters. They will suggest a maximum budget of £20 million might be entirely consistent with an anticipated contract price of £15 million or less.

Other Bidding Contexts

Bidding on the basis of a fixed price, sealed bid, one-stage process as discussed for Astro's bid to Transcon is clearly a strictly defined specialized form of bidding. One common variant involves further stages with clarifications or adjustments to winning bids. For example, Transcon might inform Astro that Transcon would accept Astro's bid provided Datapol was used and the price based on Sysdoc applied, in effect asking for the costed option without the extra cost, equivalent to a discount. To some extent such requests had to be anticipated, with appropriate hints in some cases. Astro sometimes became involved in formal multi-stage bidding processes. A field of 10 or 12 competitors for a £200 million project might be reduced to 3 or 4 on the basis of a formal preliminary tender, followed by a formal second-stage bidding process, and then perhaps an informal third stage of negotiation. Both informal and formal multi-stage bidding processes can be modelled using decision trees, building on the ideas developed in this chapter. Astro did this very successfully. This kind of analysis helps to develop a sound feel for how much needs to be held back in the earlier stages, in order to have something to give away later. The models can be controlled and focused on the issues that matter. The perspectives that the models encourage matter more than the precision of the associated arithmetic.

Much of the business Astro Wales undertook did not involve bidding in the usual sense. It involved selling based on standard prices with a range of standard discounts and discretionary discounts in some cases. If discounts are discretionary then each sale can be viewed as a multi-stage bidding process, and this can be a useful perspective for a salesperson. However, for some purposes it can prove useful to see bidding as simply one special case of selling, with a wide range of market mechanisms for the selling process. For example, Trevor and the rest of Sales, working with Martha on all Astro Wales local sales, need to set nominal prices for particular bids and actual prices for direct sales in a coordinated manner, reflecting both direct cost and what prices the market will bear. Furthermore, selling is just one aspect of marketing, which includes a wide range of related decisions that need to be addressed in a coordinated manner. This broader view of bidding as part of selling, which is in turn part of marketing, in a global marketplace, is beyond the scope of this chapter, but it is important, and will be touched on again later, particularly in Chapter 11. At a conceptual level, it is also important to link bidding as discussed here to marketing as discussed by authors like Kotler (1984).

Sian's use of the same basic pricing principles in a very different internal bidding and management context illustrates the very wide range of bidding contexts that can be identified in practice. Markets, where buyers and sellers interact and do a deal (or not) are not restricted to the interface between conventional customers and vendors. Consider two examples to illustrate this ubiquitous nature at the extremes of what we normally perceive as a market, although pricing is clearly the central issue. The first example relates to the disposal of nuclear waste, the second to criminal prosecution policy.

In the early 1990s UK Nirex, set up by the UK government to dispose of UK intermediate-level nuclear waste, asked all the generators of such waste how much of this kind of waste they would have to dispose of over an extended time horizon. Nirex designed a disposal concept based on the reported volumes, and indicated the cost per cubic metre. The reported volumes then began to shrink to a marked extent, the rate of shrinkage becoming a major source of uncertainty for Nirex. Although Nirex was owned by the waste producers (except the UK MoD), in effect, Nirex had bid for disposal contracts at a price per cubic metre which led waste producers to find alternative routes to disposal. For example, planning to entomb waste from decommissioned nuclear power stations on site for extended periods became a favoured option because this was a cheaper disposal route given the high immediate disposal costs and high discount rates imposed by the Treasury. This example will be considered further in Chapter 8, but the point here is that we do not normally think about nuclear waste as a commodity with associated demand and supply curves. However, we overlook at our peril price responses by producers of it (buyers of safe storage). Extensions of the bidding framework outlined in this chapter could be usefully applied to pricing analysis for this sort of situation. This would provide insights that a basic marketplace economic analysis could not, because the key uncertainties as viewed by all the parties can be addressed, including potential changes in environmental and safety legislation.

To further illustrate the potential range of relevance for bidding processes and the underlying pricing issues, consider the formulation of policing policy. In the mid 1990s, the New York police and the associated criminal prosecution system introduced a 'zero tolerance' policy for offenders, coupled to a national 'three strikes and you're out' (of circulation) policy. This resulted in a sharp increase in arrest rates and the severity of prison sentences. The 'price' of crime to the criminal as bid by the policing system suddenly became much higher. The number of 'buyers' declined sharply. The idea of studying the economics of crime in terms of supply and demand using conventional economic and econometric models is not a new idea. However, it would be feasible to experiment with the kind of models and processes discussed in this chapter to assess alternative perspectives on the uncertainties involved in a new and informative manner. The non-price advantage to the prospective criminal of life on the outside (of prison) will clearly be as important as the economic trade-offs in terms of income. Assessing what drives this in terms of all the relevant certain and uncertain factors should be important when assessing the demand for crime. The non-price advantage of citizens feeling safer will be equally important when assessing the supply of prison places in terms of arrest, prosecution, sentencing policy and political pressures for change. The fact that ethical issues and a range of social policy issues are involved does not mean that pricing and market forces are not relevant. It means that we have to be very, very careful to disentangle the issues involving certainties and uncertainties, some of them ethical and social issues, in a way which provides insight. The key is avoiding arguments which are founded on the consequences of particular lines of thinking, rather than on the framing assumptions which led to these lines of thinking. We do not have to be rational in the rather narrow sense of the economists' 'economic man'. But it is generally useful to conduct discussions or debates on the basis of a clear understanding of what does and does not matter, and what the ethical and social choices actually mean.

Conclusion

In the general process of Figure 1.1 the core issues are often perceived as particular decisions like determining the appropriate size for the inventory of speed controllers in Chapter 2. However, the core issues can involve the choice or the design of appropriate models and processes for addressing a common set of problems. In this chapter the issue receiving the bulk of the attention was 'designing an appropriate systems integration bidding process'. A related issue was 'redesigning Sian's roles and those of her fellow senior managers'. The steps embedded in the iterative general process for modelling uncertainty of Figure 1.1 underlie the approach Martha and Barney adopted in Astro Wales. It is important to understand this background role for Figure 1.1, as a rationale for why Barney and Martha proceeded as they did.

This chapter presumes the use of this general process in the background and illustrates a specific process designed to make systems integration bidding decisions for Astro. Figure 3.12 illustrates this specific process in a manner linked to Figure 1.1. In practice, selling this specific bidding process to all involved would be facilitated by portraying the details of the whole integrated process directly.

The specific nature of the process means that its loss of generality carries a price. What the price buys is an increase in efficiency and effectiveness in the

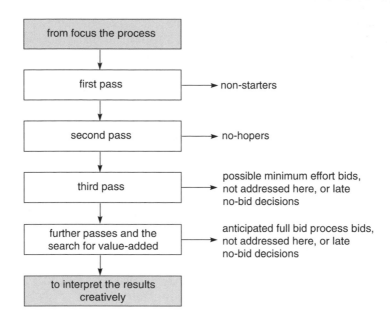

Figure 3.12—The embedded Astro systems integration bidding process: this embedded process serves as the focused process in the 'apply the process' phase of Figure 1.1.

context the process was designed for. There is no such thing as a best process for all situations. Each time the bid process is used in the Figure 3.12 context it needs some further focusing, to reflect the characteristics of that bid, like its comparative importance. But prefocus activity in terms of the design of a specific bidding process provides high efficiency and effectiveness gains. It is like the difference between an all-purpose monkey wrench and a wrench designed by a car manufacturer for a particular difficult and awkward job on a particular model of vehicle.

The highly iterative nature of effective and efficient processes is a theme of importance throughout this book. In the case of a highly specific process, like the one illustrated in this chapter, it is worth being specific about what issues are addressed using what models and what processes in a separate and distinct way for each of the early passes. That is, the first, second and third passes addressed in the body of this chapter are quite different. They address different kinds of uncertainty in different ways with different objectives. Later chapters will develop this idea in somewhat different ways.

Risk efficiency is a central concept in uncertainty management, and the whole of this book. In relation to any particular single decision it involves a minimum level of risk for a given level of expected outcome. In a context like Astro's bidding situation, risk efficiency over time and associated trade-offs can be shown to reduce to always maximizing expected profit provided the risk associated with any given decision is not potentially catastrophic, and if a catastrophic outcome is involved which is not worth the gamble, backing off until the gamble is acceptable. This is an important notion with far-reaching consequences, returned to often in various chapters. In Astro's case the concept of risk efficiency was certainly an important element of this general approach to uncertainty and related trade-offs.

Martha's notion 'there is no such thing as a problem, only opportunities', was a standing joke in Astro, because the culture explicitly encouraged this perspective. A popular rejoinder was 'but there are insurmountable opportunities'. However, to their very great credit, the organization which served as a model for Astro UK was the first organization the authors worked with who instigated a major risk management awareness and education programme aimed at taking more risk, not less, opportunity management as distinct from threat management. They understood and embraced the concept of risk efficiency because they realized that if they did not they faced bankruptcy (break-up). It is arguable whether this realization was the real driver for their turnaround. The bidding process was simply one particular manifestation of this change in attitude, used in fact to illustrate the need for change and the implications of this change.

4 Eddy's tale: Estimating measures of uncertain performance

Chance only favours the prepared mind.
Louis Pasteur

Introduction

Chapters 2 and 3 employed estimating procedures to assess expected values and associated variability, but the focus of the discussion was elsewhere. The focus of this chapter is estimating expected values and associated variability in terms of measures of uncertain performance. It can be viewed as taking the enhanced cost estimation aspects of Martha's tale further, providing more attention to cost estimation for those who are interested in bidding, especially those who are interested in bidding for high-risk projects. However, the models and processes of this chapter are basic to understanding and managing uncertainty in general, as will become clear in subsequent chapters.

This chapter considers cost estimation for a project defined by a single activity. This ignores some key complexities associated with projects defined as sets of activities, and programmes defined as portfolios of projects, which are addressed later. However, the activity in question, laying an offshore oil pipeline, is fairly complex as activities go. Its treatment here is simple enough to convey the intended messages to those who know nothing about offshore projects and have no wish to do so. But it is rich enough to illustrate a wide range of relevant issues, drawing on more detailed treatments which those who want to explore the details can use (e.g. Cooper and Chapman, 1987).

Estimating expected values and associated variability as measures of uncertain performance cannot be decoupled from evaluating this uncertainty. Estimation and evaluation of uncertainty are separable tasks for some purposes, but they are not independent unless a very simple one-pass approach is used, and one-pass approaches are hopelessly ineffective and inefficient. This chapter treats estimation and evaluation as closely coupled tasks in an iterative process, with a focus on estimation in the first pass.

Some Basic Concepts

Eddy felt quite relaxed as he settled in a quiet alcove at his favourite pub. Christmas 2000 was a week away, and Eddy was looking forward to a new job as a cost estimator for a contracting firm based in Aberdeen starting in January. It would be rather different from his current London-based estimator's job with a large civil engineering company, and it offered new challenges. The new job involved more responsibility and a clear requirement to address uncertainty in developing cost estimates. It was because of this latter requirement that Eddy had asked to meet Thomas in the pub that evening for some friendly advice. Thomas was a recently retired friend of Eddy's father. Eddy knew Thomas quite well but had never discussed work-related issues with him. The offer of advice had followed a brief conversation at a family party the week before. Eddy wasn't sure how useful Thomas's advice would be, but it seemed sensible to take up the offer.

If asked what he did before he retired, Thomas usually replied, 'I worked for the government.' If pressed, he might say, 'I was a spy, and cannot talk about it,' with a mischievous grin. Thomas cherished numerous eccentricities, and cultivated a subversive manner, but he had spent his career trying to understand very difficult practical problems and then explain his understanding in very simple terms to senior civil servants, military officers and politicians.

Thomas arrived right on time, carrying a large notepad. They spent twenty minutes in general conversation, and during this time Eddy outlined his new job and his feeling that he could benefit from some pointers on treating cost uncertainty from someone with Thomas's experience. Eddy could see from Thomas's grin and the appearance of the notepad and a pen on to the table in front of them that Thomas was ready to oblige.

Expected values and best estimates

Thomas began by explaining that he was very much in favour of keeping estimates transparent and simple, but not simplistic. In his view, single-figure estimates of any kind were undesirable in any context where uncertainty was important. It was particularly unfortunate that single-figure estimates like the most likely value or the most probable value were used when the expected value was a more appropriate single figure to use, but even expected values had their limitations.

Estimates of expected value (mean or average) should be a key output of any estimation process, as a best estimate of what should happen on average. It is the key decision parameter when comparing alternatives, provided we can afford to live with associated risk (implications of variability). If probability distributions are symmetric, the expected value is the same as the most likely value (most probable value) and the median (50 percentile value). If distributions are not symmetric, these three parameters are different. Most construction cost and time probability distributions are heavily skewed – there is much more scope for things to go badly, relative to the most likely outcome, than there is for things to go well. In such cases the expected value (mean) is generally greater than the median, which in turn is generally greater than the most likely value. The gap between the most likely value and the expected value is usually in the range 5–25%, depending on the level of uncertainty in the project and the level of dependence between components. It is generally important for risk analysts and users of risk analysis to understand the difference.

A convenient way of setting out estimates incorporating uncertainty is a table of discrete possible values and associated probability estimates. As he spoke, Thomas quickly set out Table 4.1 on his notepad. He then illustrated with Figures 4.1 and 4.2 how the discrete estimates in Table 4.1 could be transformed

Table 4.1—Example discrete value specification of a probability distribution

Value	Probability	Product
5	0.15	0.75
6	0.35	2.10
7	0.25	1.75
8	0.15	1.20
9	0.10	0.90
Mean		6.70

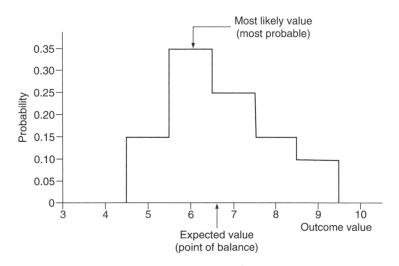

Figure 4.1—Density format diagram (rectangular histogram) for the Table 4.1 probability distribution.

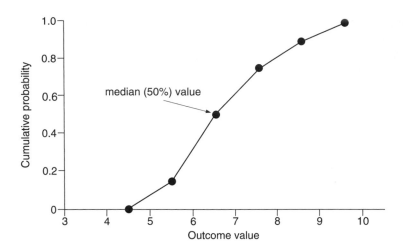

Figure 4.2—Cumulative format diagram (piecewise linear) for the Table 4.1 probability distribution.

into a more useful continuous variable interpretation and cumulative probability form.

Figures 4.1 and 4.2 are derived from Table 4.1 by interpreting the discrete values as class marks for a rectangular histogram: a value of 5 is interpreted as a value between 4.5 and 5.5 with the 0.15 probability uniformly distributed over this range. From Figure 4.2 one can read off the probability of a given outcome being exceeded or not being exceeded. For example, the probability of an outcome of 8.5 or less is 0.9, and the probability of exceeding an outcome of 8.5 is 0.1 (given by $1 - 0.9$). For a distribution skewed this way it is easy to see that the probability of exceeding the expected value of the outcome is always less than 0.5.

The most likely value is 6.0, defined using Table 4.1. The median value is 6.5, defined using Figure 4.2. The expected value (mean) is 6.7, defined by the sum in Table 4.1. The median is 8% bigger than the most likely value. The expected value is 12% bigger than the most likely value. For a smooth curve approximated by this simple example, the most probable nature of the value 6 would be clearer on Figure 4.1, and these differences would be larger.

An important property of expected values is that they are sometimes additive: the expected value of a sequence of activities (not a network with parallel paths) or a set of cost items is the sum of the expected values provided complex dependence is not involved. Most likely or median values are not additive unless perfect positive correlation is assumed, or all probability distributions are symmetric.

Thomas correctly anticipated that Eddy was familiar with these basic concepts, but reviewing them in this way provided a useful starting point. The next idea Thomas wanted Eddy to consider was the inherently subjective nature of estimates, particularly estimates of probabilities.

Rational subjectivity and irrational objectivity

An obvious general concern in estimating is the basis of estimates. In principle we would like all estimates to be entirely objective, based on an unambiguous interpretation of underlying data. However, in attempting to estimate variability in project parameters, or any other decision parameters, this is virtually impossible. For all practical purposes there is no such thing as a completely appropriate objective estimate of any probability distribution model which is suitable for rational decision making. Assumptions are almost always involved in the estimating process, even when lots of relevant data is available, and any assumptions which are not *strictly* true make associated estimates subjective. Given that objectivity is not feasible, it should not be an issue. What is always an issue is the rationality of the numbers used. Irrational objective probabilities have to be avoided.

If we wish to make decisions which are consistent with our beliefs, we must use subjective probabilities. This means our decisions will be non-optimal to the extent that our beliefs are misguided. However, if we make decisions which are inconsistent with our beliefs, the chances of non-optimality will be much higher if our beliefs are rational. This is rational subjectivity in its simplest form, now widely understood and subscribed to, and the basis of most modern decision analysis textbooks, like Thomas's favourite by Raiffa (1968).

To illustrate the nature of rational subjectivity, and the dangers of irrational objectivity, Thomas explained that he would use a slightly disguised estimating example taken from a report he had written before he retired. The organization in question, like many others, had a significant case of irrational objectivity. Thomas explained that his example was developed from an example provided by a senior programme manager to illustrate another linked common corporate culture condition, a conspiracy of optimism – significant corporate pressure to avoid revealing bad news. Thomas then launched into this part of his tutorial as follows.

Suppose that a project manager wants to estimate for planning purposes how long it will take to obtain head office (corporate centre) approval for a particular potential design change with expenditure approval implications. Assume there is a standard time of 3 weeks for approval of design changes. It is clearly important to know what this standard is, and to bear in mind the assumptions which underlie it, including a proposal which is free from potential defects. Assume the project manager recorded how long similar approvals had taken on earlier projects he was involved with, as shown in Table 4.2. These outcomes suggest that the standard time of 3 weeks ought to be interpreted as a target, something sensible to aim for given no problems. But 3 weeks is not a sensible estimate of what is likely to happen on average. If data was not available, the project manager might just use a 3 week estimate. However, this would not be rational if such data was available to the organization as a whole. It is never rational to use objective numbers which are known to be inconsistent with reasonable expectations.

A basic objective probability textbook approach to probability would assume 7 weeks is our best estimate of the expected duration, the simple mean or average

Table 4.2—Example data for design change approval

Project	Duration of approval (weeks)
1	3
2	7
3	6
4	4
5	15

Mean = (3 + 7 + 6 + 4 + 15)/5 = 7 weeks

duration, using all relevant available data, as indicated in Table 4.2. This is a frequentist view of objective probability, the basis of most classical probability theory.

Some people with a classical statistical training might wish to invoke a Bayesian approach, arguing that the standard 3 weeks is a form of prior probability distribution, the data provides 'posterior' information, and the two need to be combined. The key effect is a mean closer to 3 weeks than the 7 weeks defined by the simple mean, because the standard 3 weeks is considered as well as the 3 week observation. Assuming that 3 weeks with a probability of one (no variability) is a suitable prior is a highly questionable approach, but this is a way of using an objective axiomatic probability in a classical objective probability framework which Thomas had encountered in other studies.

Some seasoned users of PERT (Moder and Philips, 1970) might prefer assuming a standard Beta distribution approximation. This raises the obvious problem, What is the most likely value? If 6 is assumed, the mean estimate is (3 + (4 × 6) + 15)/6 = 7, an optimistic estimate (3) plus 4 times the most likely value plus a pessimistic estimate (15) all divided by 6, assuming 3 is a plausible optimistic estimate and 15 is a plausible pessimistic estimate. This is clearly highly subjective with respect to all three parameters used, and rather rough and ready. It is reasonably robust, but it does not lend itself to either simplification or generalization via additional complexity. Generalization may be important if the 15 week observation has implications which need *managing* as well as *measuring*.

Some people with a classical statistical training might wish to reject the 15 week observation as an outlier, because it is not typical of the variability of interest. Presuming this is legitimate is a questionable assumption, but this is a way of subjectively altering the data set employed within an objective paradigm which Thomas had frequently encountered, and it can be given a more objective presentation. For example, the other four observations can be assumed to be Normally distributed, and the 15 weeks can be shown to have a low probability of coming from the same population. However, an objective estimate of 5 based on the mean of the four 'normal' observations, excluding the 15 weeks, is clearly highly irrational. It assumes only normal circumstances matter, which is inconsistent with the very point of the exercise. More appropriately, the 15 week observation might be assumed to have come from a different population representing 'abnormal situations' which need to be taken into account.

The problem this immediately raises is as follows. It is plausible to assume we have four observations to define a Normal distribution for the 'normal situation'. However, we have only one observation of 'abnormal situations'. Abnormal situations clearly matter a lot. They matter much more than normal situations. However, to model them in a meaningful manner requires subjective probabilities. More generally, the past may be of interest when considering the future, but it is irrational to assume the future will replicate the past. Rationality requires conscious consideration of how the future may differ from the past. Put succinctly, the only rational approach in this situation involves the use of rational subjective probabilities. Any attempt to cling to objective probabilities will lead to estimates which are inconsistent with the judgement of the project manager and his team. The purpose of the estimation exercise at this stage is not objectivity. It is rational judgement, within a process framework which recognizes the costs as well as the benefits of more or less structure, detail, and data for the models used.

A multiple-pass approach

If the costs of the estimation effort and the costs of erroneous decisions are considered, a multiple-pass process which begins by filtering out what does not matter is an essential feature of any rational subjective probability approach. Subjective judgements are involved in this process, but this subjectivity is rational, what Simon (1979) has called procedural rationality.

A rational subjective approach warrants consideration of a first-pass estimate based on Table 4.3. The key working assumption is a uniform distribution, which is deliberately conservative (biased on the pessimistic side) with respect to the expected value estimate, and deliberately conservative and crude with respect to variability.

This is a rational approach to take because we know people are usually too optimistic (e.g. Kahneman, Slovic and Tversky, 1982), and we wish to use a simple process to identify what clearly does not matter so it can be dismissed. The residual sources of variability which are not dismissed on a first pass may or may not matter, and more effort may be needed to clarify what is involved in a second-

Table 4.3—Estimating the duration of design change approval: first pass

Optimistic estimate	3 weeks (lowest observed value, a plausible minimum)
Pessimistic estimate	15 weeks (highest observed value, a plausible maximum)
Expected value	9 weeks (central value, (3 + 15)/2)

Working assumptions: the data comes from a uniform probability distribution, 3 and 15 corresponding very approximately to 10 and 90 percentile values.

pass analysis. If both the 9 weeks expected value and the ±6 weeks plausible variation are not a problem, no further estimating effort is necessary. If either is a potential problem, further analysis to refine the estimates is required.

A second pass at estimating the time taken to obtain approval of a design change might start by questioning a possible trend associated with the 15 weeks. In broad terms this might involve looking at the reasons for possible outliers from what normally happens, developing an understanding of reasons for variability within what normally happens, and developing an understanding of what defines abnormal events. It might be observed that the reason for the 15 weeks outcome was a critical review of the project as a whole at the time approval was sought for the design change. However, similar lengthy delays might be associated with a number of other identified reasons for abnormal variation such as bad timing in relation to extended leave taken by key approvals staff, perhaps due to illness; serious defects in the project's management or approval request; and general funding reviews. It might be observed that the 7, 6 and 4 week observations are all normal variations, associated with, for example, pressure on staff from other projects, or routine shortcomings in the approval requests involving a need for further information. The 3 weeks standard, achieved once, might have involved no problems of any kind, a situation which occurred once in five observations.

These second-pass deliberations might lead to a probability model of the form outlined in Table 4.4. This particular model involves subjective estimates related

Table 4.4—Estimating the duration of design change approval: second pass

Normal situation		
Optimistic estimate	3 weeks	Objective estimate?
Pessimistic estimate	7 weeks	Objective estimate?
Expected value	5 weeks	(3 + 7)/2
Abnormal situation		
Optimistic estimate	10 weeks	Subjective estimate
Pessimistic estimate	20 weeks	Subjective estimate
Expected value	15 weeks	(10 + 20)/2
Probability that an abnormal situation is involved		
Optimistic estimate	0.1	Subjective estimate
Pessimistic estimate	0.5	Subjective estimate
Expected value	0.3	(0.1 + 0.5)/2
Combined view		
Optimistic estimate	3 weeks	Normal minimum
Pessimistic estimate	20 weeks	Abnormal maximum
Expected value	8 weeks	(5 × (1 − 0.3) + 15 × 0.3)

Working assumptions: the 'normal' data comes from a uniform probability distribution, 3 and 7 corresponding very approximately to 10 and 90 percentile values. The 'abnormal' data comes from uniform probability distributions. Probabilities of 0.1 and 0.5, and durations of 10 and 20 weeks, both correspond very approximately to 10 and 90 percentile values, defined subjectively (based on unquantified experience), in this case in relation to an observed 1 in 5 chance (probability 0.2) of an observed 15 week outcome, a sample of one.

to both the duration of an abnormal situation and the probability that an abnormal situation is involved, in the latter case using the range 0.1–0.5 with an expected value of 0.3. The one observation of an abnormal situation suggests a probability of 0.2 (a 1 in 5 chance), but a rational response to only one observation requires a degree of conservatism if the outcome may be a decision to accept this potential variability and take the analysis no further. Given the limited data about normal situations, which may not be representative, even the normal situation estimates of 3–7 weeks are best viewed as subjective.

If no data were available, the Table 4.4 approach would still be a sound rational subjective approach if the numbers seemed sensible in the context of a project team brainstorm of relevant experience and changes in circumstances. However, *project managers* may tend to focus on reasons for delay attributable to *approvals staff*, while *approvals staff* will understandably take a different view. Everyone is naturally inclined to look for reasons for variability which do not reflect badly on themselves. Assumptions about how well (or badly) this particular project will manage its approvals request is an issue which should significantly affect the estimates, whether or not data is available. And who is preparing the estimates will inevitably colour their nature.

The second-pass model produces an 8 week expected value which is less than the 9 week first-pass value. The ±6 weeks crude 10–90 percentile value associated with the first pass remains plausible, but the distribution shape is considerably refined by the second-pass estimate. If the 9 week expected value was the source of concern about the first-pass estimate, a third pass might now be required, to explore the 'abnormal' 10–20 week possibility, or its 0.1–0.5 probability range, and to refine understanding of abnormal events.

Thomas sums up

At this point Thomas put down his pen. He felt he had given Eddy some useful pointers in preparation for his new job. Eddy thought so too. Even though Thomas had related an example based on estimating durations for a project activity, Eddy could see that the core ideas could be applied to cost estimation, the focus of Eddy's new job.

Thomas reminded Eddy that his approach to estimating rational subjective probabilities was based on a first-pass approach which was deliberately very simple and plausibly conservative, with a view to subsequent more refined analysis wherever uncertainty seems important. Probabilities needed to be explicitly recognized as subjective models, within a constructively simple structure, allowing more complexity whenever this is useful. The goal is rational decisions. When rationality and objectivity are in conflict, in general it is objectivity which needs to be sacrificed, not rationality. Any relaxation of this priority involves irrational objectivity. Irrational objectivity is a concern which needs direct attack. So is the conspiracy of optimism, which can be attacked at the same time within the same approach.

As they said goodbye, Thomas suggested Eddy should make use of a paper by Chapman and Ward (2000) which developed some of these ideas in a cost estimation context, and Eddy suggested they continue their discussion when he had some experience of his new job to report on.

Eddy Starts Work

Two weeks after his meeting with Thomas, Eddy started his new job in Aberdeen. Eddy's new employers specialized in laying and servicing offshore oil and gas pipelines for operators in the North Sea. Eddy reported to Charlie, the chief estimator (the only estimator until Eddy arrived). Charlie was an estimator of the old school. He knew all there was to know about offshore pipelines, as he saw it. He had worked for oil companies as well as for contractors on North Sea projects since the initial boom of the early 1970s. His experience and wisdom were respected by his colleagues.

The contracting firm had no direct experience of formal risk management. Charlie had been aware of some of the risk management processes used by other companies on North Sea projects since the 1970s. However, he interpreted these processes as formalizations of the common sense which he could apply intuitively. One of the reasons Charlie liked working for a small contracting organization (relative to oil and gas companies) was the freedom from imposed bureaucratic processes. He was well aware that nine times out of ten the actual cost of projects was very different from his estimates. However, he was able to persuade himself, and his managing director Dougal, that this was because of the uncertainties inherent in the business. There were always good reasons why the estimate and the reality were different. He saw no reason to suppose that a formal risk management process would change this fact of life, or improve the contracting firm's performance.

Charlie was due to retire in six months. The risks this posed to the organization had finally risen to the top of Dougal's agenda, and Dougal had arranged for Eddy to be hired. He had instructed Charlie to ensure that Eddy was in a position to cope without Charlie in six months' time. Charlie and Eddy agreed that, for starters, Eddy would take the lead on all future first-pass estimate preparation for bidding purposes, using his knowledge of the latest project risk management processes. Eddy would use Charlie as a consultant, mentor, source of guidance on data, source of judgement on technical choices, and source of judgement on estimates of time and cost. Eddy would move on to taking charge of later passes and later processes at a later stage in his takeover of Charlie's role. A special concern was using the six months to transfer structured knowledge from Charlie to Eddy. Both wanted to be confident that Eddy could operate effectively on his own after six months. Charlie was more concerned about this than Eddy, because he thought he had a clearer idea of what was involved, and in many respects he was right.

Within hours of this agreement, before Eddy had finished his first week's familiarization programme, an invitation to tender arrived on Charlie's desk. It involved a 200 km pipeline, to be constructed on a fixed price basis. Charlie passed it to Eddy, and asked him to report back with a preliminary view of the cost in a few days time. Charlie suggested that Eddy should use this task as a learning process, to structure his thoughts. He suggested that Eddy should consult him as much as necessary, but try to interrupt his work on other jobs as infrequently as possible. That is, Eddy should manage Charlie as a resource and use him efficiently as well as effectively. Modifications to Eddy's views would be discussed with Charlie before Dougal saw Eddy's work, and further refinements would be feasible prior to bidding.

Eddy was particularly concerned to establish a framework to identify where he needed judgements from Charlie, and where refinement prior to bidding might be useful, to explicitly manage the short-term learning process. He was also concerned about the longer-term corporate learning process which he would become responsible for when Charlie retired.

Eddy decided to follow Thomas's advice and use a version of the minimalist first-pass estimation process (Chapman and Ward, 2000). 'Minimalist' meant that the process was as simple as possible by design, in terms of use and interpretation, without sacrificing any of the functionality of what Eddy called 'an optimal p-pass approach to estimation and evaluation, where $p = 1, \ldots, p^*$ and the total number of passes required, p^*, was usually unknown at the outset. Determining p^* was part of the optimization process. The optimality of this first pass had to reflect all the passes to come, despite their unknown number and nature. It also had to reflect the context, including Charlie's dislike of bureaucracy and Dougal's expectations, as well as the technical features of offshore oil and gas pipelines, and the form of bidding and contracting involved.

The minimalist first pass which Eddy designed could be interpreted as a further enhancement and basis for generalizing the third-pass enhanced cost estimation process of Chapter 3. However, Eddy did not see it in these terms. He saw it as a suitable first pass for the 200 km offshore pipeline example he currently faced, and similar projects. Eddy was not concerned with the equivalent of Martha's first and second passes, and in his view the first pass had to lay the foundations for much more sophisticated analysis as and when required, because of the nature of the uncertainties involved. This should not be taken to imply that Eddy could not learn something from Martha and her Astro colleagues about prior passes and about pricing as distinct from costing.

Having designed the minimalist first-pass approach in outline, Eddy obtained the inputs he needed for the example from Charlie. He used these inputs to refine and polish his design. He then prepared a presentation for Charlie, to try it out.

Like any 'minimalist' design, it has to be interpreted in holistic terms. Eddy knew that he and Charlie would get bogged down in the detail before the whole picture was clear unless he managed Charlie's reactions to his presentation very carefully. He decided the best way to do this was to start the presentation with what he called the bare bones of the minimalist approach – a basic description of the minimalist approach – to outline the whole before discussing the details of the parts under a number of headings, in an order which allowed the discussion to build on itself. The next section outlines the initial bare bones portion of Eddy's presentation to Charlie.

Eddy's First-Pass Minimalist Approach

Eddy started his presentation with background we have already covered, and then introduced the six-step minimalist process of Figure 4.3, the road map he referred to as he outlined what each step involves.

Step 1: Identify and structure the parameters and other preliminaries

The first step involves preliminaries, which include setting out the basic parameters of the situation, the composite parameter structure, and associated uncertainty factors. Table 4.5 illustrates the format used by Eddy, which he explained section by section in the following manner.

The first section of Table 4.5 identifies the proposed parameter structure of the cost estimate using a top-down sequence. 'Cost' might be estimated directly as a basic parameter, as might associated uncertainty. However, if cost uncertainty is primarily driven by other factors, it is worth separating out these factors. Time is a key driver in this case, so a 'duration × cost rate' composite parameter structure is appropriate. Further, it is often useful to break 'duration' down into 'length/ progress rate', to address more basic parameters and uncertainties within specific time frames. In this case it is also useful to break 'progress rate' down into 'lay rate × productive days per month'. 'Lay rate' reflects uncertainty about the number of kilometres of pipe that can be laid per day, given that pipe laying is feasible. 'Productive days per month', the number of days in a month when pipe laying is feasible, reflects a different set of uncertainties. Finally, it is convenient in this case to express 'productive days per month' in terms of a days lost rate.

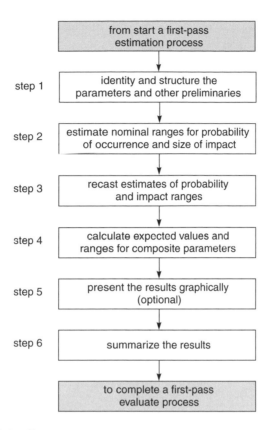

Figure 4.3—The minimalist process.

The second section of Table 4.5 provides base values for all the basic parameters. The 2 km per productive day lay rate and the £2.5 million per month cost rate assume a particular choice of lay barge which Charlie identified as a conservative first choice. Eddy anticipated later consideration of less capable barges with lower nominal lay and cost rates.

The third section of Table 4.5 identifies sources of uncertainty associated with each of the basic parameters, and asks in relation to each whether or not probabilistic treatment would be useful. 'Length' has 'client route change' identified as a key source of uncertainty, defined in terms of client-induced route changes associated with potential collector systems. 'Other (length)' refers to any other reasons for pipeline length change; for example, unsuitable seabed conditions might force route changes. These are examples of risks which it is not sensible to quantify in probability terms because they are more usefully treated as basic assumptions or conditions which need to be addressed contractually. That is, the contract should ensure that responsibility for such changes is not borne by the contractor, so they are not relevant to assessment of the contractor's cost.

Table 4.5—Relationships, base values, uncertainty factors and assessment modes

Composite parameter relationships		Units
Cost = duration × cost rate		£m
Duration = length/progress rate		months
Progress rate = lay rate × productive days per month		km/month
Productive days per month = 30 − days lost rate		days/month

Basic parameters	Base values	
Length	200 km	
Lay rate	2 km per productive day	
Days lost rate	0 productive days/month	
Cost rate	£2.5m month	

Basic parameters	Uncertainty factors	Probabilistic treatment?
Length	Client route change	no
	Other (length)	no
Lay rate	Barge choice	no
	Personnel	yes
	Other (lay rate)	yes
Days lost rate	Weather	yes
	Supplies	yes
	Equipment	yes
	Buckles	yes
	Lay barge sinks	no
	Other (days lost rate)	no
Cost rate	Market	yes
	Other (cost rate)	no

Ensuring that this happens makes listing such risks essential, even if in its simplest terms a standardized list of generic exclusions is used.

'Lay rate' identifies 'barge choice' as a factor not suitable for quantification. This is an example of a variable not suitable for probabilistic treatment because it is a decision parameter usefully associated with assumed values. The implications of changes are best determined in a separate analysis. 'Lay rate' is also influenced by two uncertainty factors deemed appropriate for probabilistic treatment because the contractor must manage them and bear financial responsibility within the contract price. 'Personnel' reflects the impact on the 'lay rate' of the experience, skill and motivation of the barge crew, with potential to either increase or decrease 'lay rate' with respect to the base value. 'Other (lay rate)' reflects minor equipment, supply and other operating problems which are part of the pipe-laying daily routine.

'Days lost rate' identifies four uncertainty factors usefully treated probabilistically because the operator must own and deal with them within the contract price. 'Weather' might result in days when attempting pipe laying is not feasible because the waves are too high. 'Supplies' and 'equipment' involve further days which might be lost because of serious supply failures or equipment failures which are the contractor's responsibility. 'Buckles' is associated with 'wet buckles', when the pipe kinks and fractures, allowing water to fill it, necessitating dropping it, with very serious repair implications. 'Dry buckles', a comparatively minor problem, was part of 'other (lay rate)'. In all four cases, the financial ownership of these effects is limited to direct cost implications for the contractor, with an assumption that any of the client's knock-on costs are not covered by financial penalties in the contract at this stage. 'Days lost rate' also identifies two uncertainty factors best treated as conditions or assumptions. 'Lay barge sinks' is deemed not suitable for probabilistic treatment because it is a *force majeure* event, responsibility for which the contractor would pass on to the lay barge supplier in the assumed subcontract for bid purposes at this stage, avoiding responsibility for its effects on the client in the main contract. 'Other (days lost rate)' is associated with catastrophic equipment failures (passed on to the subcontractor), catastrophic supply failures (passed back to the client), or any other sources of days lost which the contractor could reasonably avoid responsibility for.

'Cost rate' involves a market uncertainty factor associated with normal market force variations which must be borne by the contractor, usefully quantified. 'Cost rate' also involves the uncertainty factor 'other (cost rate)', placing abnormal market conditions with the client, and therefore not quantified.

In this example most of the uncertainty factors treated as assumptions or conditions are associated with financial ownership of the consequences for contractual purposes. The exception is the decision variable 'barge choice'. In general, there may be a number of 'barge choice' decisions to be made in a project. Where and why we draw the lines between probabilistic treatment or not is a key uncertainty management process issue, developed with further examples elsewhere (e.g. Chapman and Ward, 1997). Eddy pointed out this distinction, but did not labour it.

Step 1 as a whole held no surprises for Charlie. The probabilistic treatment decisions reflected cost uncertainties which could not be passed on to subcontractors or passed back to the client as he had explained to Eddy. The associated uncertainty factor structure reflected the way he intuitively thought about sources of uncertainty, although his informal thinking was not as 'neat and tidy' as Eddy's, as Charlie would put it. The parameter structure was the one he used to compute estimates, as he had told Eddy, and Charlie had provided Eddy with all the basic parameter base values. Charlie thoroughly approved of the simple summary structure provided by Table 4.5, and the back-up notes Eddy provided, explaining what labels like 'client route change' meant in terms of how and why this source of uncertainty might arise and associated assumptions about its contractual implications. Charlie declared step 1 'shipshape and Bristol fashion' and waved Eddy on to step 2.

Step 2: Estimate nominal ranges for probability of occurrence and size of impact

The next step involved estimating crude but credible ranges, in terms of nominal optimistic and pessimistic values, for the probability of occurrence and the size of impact of the uncertainty factors which indicated yes to probabilistic treatment in Table 4.5. Table 4.6 illustrates the format used by Eddy. Table 4.6 is in three parts, each part corresponding to a basic parameter. All estimates are to a minimal number of significant figures, to maintain the simplicity which is important in practice as well as for example purposes.

Eddy addressed the two 'impact' columns first. They show estimated pessimistic and optimistic scenario values, assumed to approximate to 90 and 10 percentile values, rather than absolute maximum and minimum values. Eddy explained that extensive analysis (e.g. Moder and Philips, 1970) suggests that the general lack of

Table 4.6—Nominal estimates of probabilities and impacts

Lay rate					Impact scenarios: percentage decrease		
	Event probability		Impact		Probability times impact		
Uncertainty factors	pessimistic p_p	optimistic p_o	pessimistic i_p	optimistic i_o	pessimistic $p_p \times i_p$	optimistic $p_o \times i_p$	midpoint
Personnel	1	1	10	-20	10	-20	-5
Other	1	1	20	0	20	0	10
Combined			30	-20			5

Days lost rate					Impact scenarios: days lost per month		
	Event probability		Impact		Probability times impact		
Uncertainty factors	pessimistic p_p	optimistic p_o	pessimistic i_p	optimistic i_o	pessimistic $p_p \times i_p$	optimistic $p_o \times i_o$	midpoint
Weather	1	1	10	2	10	2	6
Supplies	0.3	0.1	3	1	0.9	0.1	0.5
Equipment	0.1	0.01	6	2	0.6	0.02	0.31
Buckles	0.01	0.001	60	20	0.6	0.02	0.31
Combined			79	2			7.12

Cost rate					Impact scenarios: percentage increase		
	Event probability		Impact		Probability times impact		
Uncertainty factors	pessimistic p_p	optimistic p_o	pessimistic i_p	optimistic i_o	pessimistic $p_p \times i_p$	optimistic $p_o \times i_o$	midpoint
Market	1	1	30	-20	30	-20	5
Combined			30	-20			5

an absolute maximum, and confusion about what might or might not be considered in relation to an absolute minimum, makes 95–5 or 90–10 confidence band estimates much easier to obtain and more robust to use. A 90–10 confidence band approach was chosen rather than 95–5 because it better reflects the minimalist style, and it lends itself to simple refinement in subsequent iterations. This is why Eddy had obtained the 'lay rate' 'personnel' i_p value by asking Charlie, nine times out of ten what is the maximum percentage decrease in 'lay rate' you would attribute to 'personnel'? He adopted a similar approach to all the other i_p and i_o values.

Eddy then indicated that the two 'event probability' columns show the estimated range, also assumed to be a 90–10 percentile range, for the probability of some level of impact occurring. A probability of one indicates an ever-present impact, as in the case of 'personnel', 'weather' or 'market conditions'. A probability of less than one indicates uncertainty about a factor's occurrence, associated with a different 'nominal' pessimistic and optimistic value. Eddy acknowledged that a standard approach assumes probabilities are known, but pointed out that, as Charlie had observed, probabilities were often more uncertain than impacts, and authorities like Raiffa (1968) indicated that second-order uncertainty modelling was possible.

Eddy explained that the 'probability times impact' columns indicated the implied product ranges and provided midpoints (interpreted as expected values) for the individual uncertainty factors. Eddy then explained what was involved for each basic parameter.

For the 'lay rate' section of Table 4.6, impacts are defined in terms of percentage decrease (for estimating convenience) to the nearest 10%. The 'combined' uncertainty factor estimate involves an expected decrease of 5% in the nominal lay rate, defined by the 'midpoint' column, and plus or minus 25% bounds (a range of +30% to −20%), defined by the i_p and i_o values. These 'combined' values are all simple sums of the individual uncertainty factor values.

The 'days lost rate' section treats 'weather' as ever present in the context of an average month, but other factors have associated probabilities over the range 0 to 1, estimated to one significant figure. Impact estimates are also to one significant figure, in terms of days lost per month. The 'combined' uncertainty factor estimate provided in the final row shows an expected impact 'midpoint' of 7.12 days lost per month. It shows a corresponding optimistic estimate of 2 days lost per month, reflecting the possible non-occurrence of 'supplies', 'equipment' and 'buckles'. However, 79 days might be lost if a buckle occurs together with 'pessimistic' values for 'equipment', 'supplies' and 'weather'. The pipe laying process could finish the month behind where it started in progress terms. The bounds here are clearly not obtainable by adding $p_p \times i_p$ and $p_o \times i_o$ values, the reason i_p and i_o values are used to define bounds for the 'combined' row in general. The 'cost rate' section is a simplified version of the 'lay rate' section.

Step 2 as a whole also held no surprises for Charlie. Eddy had explained the nature of the notional values he wanted, and why, when seeking all the parameter values of Table 4.6. Charlie could not resist suggesting that Eddy would make 'a good management consultant because he knew how to borrow someone's watch in order to tell them the time' but he waved Eddy on. Eddy took this joke as an indication of success so far, as intended.

Step 3: Recast the estimates of probability and impact ranges

Eddy indicated that the next step was to recast the estimates in Table 4.6 to reflect more extreme probability and impact ranges, and associated distribution assumptions. This step can also convert units from those convenient for estimation to those needed for combinations, if necessary. Further, it can simplify the uncertainty factor structure, if appropriate. Table 4.7 illustrates what is involved, building on Table 4.6. Apart from changes in units, 10% has been added to each

Table 4.7—Recast estimates

Lay rate					Impact scenarios: km/day		
	Event probability		Impact		Probability times impact		
Uncertainty factors	very pessimistic p_{vp}	very optimistic p_{vo}	very pessimistic i_{vp}	very optimistic i_{vo}	very pessimistic $p_{vp} \times i_{vo}$	very optimistic $p_{vo} \times i_{vo}$	midpoint
Combined	1	1	1.3	2.5			1.9

Days lost rate					Impact scenarios: days lost per month		
	Event probability		Impact		Probability times impact		
Uncertainty factors	very pessimistic p_{vp}	very optimistic p_{vo}	very pessimistic i_{vp}	very optimistic i_{vo}	very pessimistic $p_{vp} \times i_{vo}$	very optimistic $p_{vo} \times i_{vo}$	midpoint
Weather	1	1	11	1	11.00	1	6
Supplies	0.32	0.08	3.2	0.8	1.02	0.06	0.54
Equipment	0.11	0	6.4	1.6	0.70	0	0.35
Buckles	0.011	0	64	16.0	0.70	0	0.35
Combined			84.6	1			7.25

Cost rate					Impact scenarios: £m/month		
	Event probability		Impact		Probability times impact		
Uncertainty factors	very pessimistic p_{vp}	very optimistic p_{vo}	very pessimistic i_{vp}	very optimistic i_{vo}	very pessimistic $p_{vp} \times i_{vo}$	very optimistic $p_{vo} \times i_{vo}$	midpoint
Combined	1	1	3.38	1.87			2.63

$(p_p - p_o)$ and $(i_p - i_o)$ range at either end. This approximates to assuming a uniform probability distribution for both the Table 4.6 probability and impact ranges and the extended Table 4.7 ranges. Strictly, given 10 and 90 percentile figures in Table 4.6, ranges ought to be extended by 12.5% at each end so the extensions are 10% of the extended range. However, using 10% extensions is computationally more convenient and it emphasizes the approximate nature of the whole approach. It also helps to avoid any illusion of spurious accuracy, and it offers one simple concession to optimism, whose effect is both limited and clear. Eddy explained what was involved in Table 4.7 section by section.

The 'lay rate' section combines the 'personnel' and 'other' entries of Table 4.6 directly, using the combined entries from Table 4.6 as its basis, on the grounds that Table 4.6 revealed no serious concerns. It first converts the 30% 'pessimistic' impact estimate of Table 4.6 to a 'very pessimistic' estimate of 35% $(30 + 0.1 (30 - (-20)))$ adding 10% of the $(i_p - i_o)$ range. It then applies this percentage decrease to the base lay rate to obtain a 'very pessimistic' lay rate of 1.3 km per day $(2 \times (100 - 35)/100)$, to move from units convenient for estimation purposes to units required for analysis. Table 4.7 converts the i_o estimate of a 20% increase in a similar way. Converting from percentage change figures to kilometres per day figures is convenient here for computational reasons (it must be done somewhere).

The 'days lost rate' section retains a breakdown of individual uncertainty factors, on the grounds that Table 4.6 reveals some concerns, and it would not be useful to combine them directly. Event probability values less than one are converted to 'very pessimistic – very optimistic' $(p_{vp} - p_{vo})$ ranges in the same way as impact ranges. In this case the 'combined' entries mirror the 'combined' entries of Table 4.6 on a 'very pessimistic' and 'very optimistic' basis.

The 'cost rate' section is obtained in a similar way to the 'lay rate' section. The impact range in Table 4.6 is extended by 10% at either end and these extreme values for percentage increase are applied to the base cost rate of £2.5 million per month.

Eddy briefly addressed the obvious question, Why do we need 'very pessimistic' and 'very optimistic' values as well as the 'pessimistic' and 'optimistic' values of Table 4.6? The answer is to make graphical presentation feasible in step 5. If graphical presentation is not required, and a simple automated spreadsheet model conversion from Table 4.6 to Table 4.7 is not available, we could skip the 'very pessimistic' and 'very optimistic' conversions, reducing the process to one more directly akin to Barney's approach to the cost estimation tables of Chapter 3, but in practice the time saved will be negligible. Eddy wanted to show Charlie and Dougal the graphical possibilities. The term 'minimalist' was chosen to imply minimal effort appropriate to context, ensuring that sophistication and generality to deal effectively with all contexts is preserved. Graphs are often useful, if not essential.

Charlie thought step 3 was looking dangerously academic, in a pejorative sense, but he liked graphs and he bit his tongue while nodding for Eddy to proceed.

Step 4: Calculate expected values and ranges for composite parameters

Eddy explained that the next step was to calculate expected values and ranges for the composite parameters of Table 4.5 using the range and midpoint values in Table 4.7. The calculations are shown in Table 4.8. They work through the composite parameter relationships in the first section of Table 4.5 in reverse (bottom-up) order. The 'midpoint' columns use midpoint values from Table 4.7. The 'very optimistic' columns use i_{vo} values from Table 4.7. Because a 'very pessimistic' or even a 'pessimistic' calculation on the same basis would involve never finishing the pipeline, a 'plausibly pessimistic' column uses $i_{pp} = i_{vp}$ values except in the case of 'days lost rate', when 20 days replaces the i_{vp} value of 84.6 days. The source of this $i_{pp} = 20$ days figure might be a simple rule of thumb like 'the downside range is twice the upside range' ($i_{pp} = 2(\text{midpoint} - i_{vo}) + \text{midpoint}$, rounded to one significant figure). Later estimation and evaluation passes might call for more effective but more time-consuming approaches to estimating a 'plausibly pessimistic' value, should such a value prove important. Eddy indicated that this particular rule of thumb had been suggested by Charlie, but others were possible.

The title of Table 4.8 summarizes the results, rounding the bottom line midpoint to the nearest £1 million, its 'very optimistic' based lower limit to the nearest £1 million, and its 'plausibly pessimistic' based upper limit to reflect an order of magnitude relationship with the lower limit.

Charlie liked the look of the bottom line of Table 4.8 in one respect. It accorded with his view of the actual uncertainty involved. However, it portrayed this uncertainty in a very naked way, which he thought might rattle Dougal. Charlie always provided an estimate which had a much greater air of precision, because it was a relatively precise estimate given the framing assumptions which he did not clarify for himself, never mind spelling them out for Dougal. That is, both Charlie and Dougal were used to greater precision with an ambiguous basis. Charlie could

Table 4.8—Results: current estimate of expected cost is £12 million in the range £5–50 million

Composite parameters	Computation			Results		
	plausibly pessimistic	very optimistic	midpoint	plausibly pessimistic	very optimistic	midpoint
Productive days per month (30-days lost rate)	30 − 20	30 − 1	30 − 7.25	10	29	22.75
Progress rate (productive days × lay rate)	10 × 1.3	29 × 2.5	22.75 × 1.9	13	72.5	43.23
Duration (months) (length × progress rate)	200/13	200/72.5	200/43.23	15.38	2.76	4.63
Cost (£m) (duration × cost rate)	15.38 × 3.38	2.76 × 1.87	4.63 × 2.63	52.0	5.2	12.18

see the sense in less precision with a less ambiguous basis, but he was not clear how Dougal would react.

Notice how there is a clear link to the bottom line of the cost estimation tables of Chapter 3.

Step 5: Present results graphically (optional)

For key areas of concern, additional graphical representation of assessments may be worthwhile, using formats like Figures 4.4 and 4.5. Eddy was very keen to use both of these graphs, so he explained them to Charlie with care.

Figure 4.4 illustrates a probability impact picture (PIP), which can be produced directly from Table 4.7. Eddy explained that he had produced Figure 4.4 because 'days lost rate' is a key area of concern, and he anticipated discussion of assumptions in this area with Dougal. Charlie had indicated that Dougal likes a probability impact matrix (PIM) format, a widely used approach which can be interpreted in a PIP format.

Figure 4.4 can be a useful portrayal of Table 4.7 information in terms of confirming estimation assumptions. It captures the key probability density function information for all the uncertainty factors in both event probability and impact dimensions. Each L_f line plotted corresponds to an uncertainty factor, $f = 1, \ldots, f^*$, for $f^* = 4$ factors which contribute to the 'days lost rate'. If the L_f lines are interpreted as diagonals of associated boxes defining the set of possible combinations of probability and impact, the absence of these boxes can be interpreted as a perfect correlation assumption between event probability and impact for each

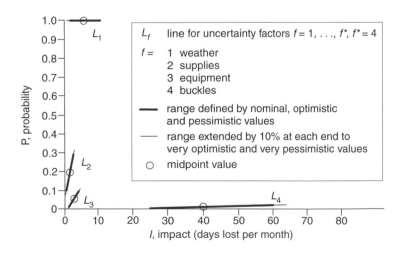

Figure 4.4—Probability impact picture (PIP): example for days lost rate.

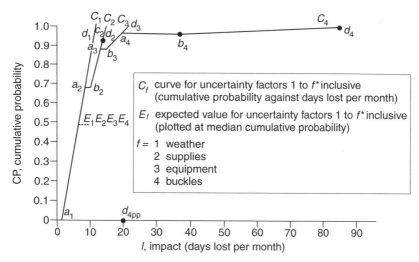

Figure 4.5—Cumulative impact picture (CIP): example for days lost rate.

uncertainty factor f, but nothing can be inferred about correlation between the different factors. A horizontal L_f, like L_1, implies some impact uncertainty but no event probability uncertainty. A vertical L_f would imply the converse. A steep slope, like L_2, implies more uncertainty about the event probability than impact uncertainty. Slope measures necessarily reflect the choice of units for impact, so they are relative and must be interpreted with care. For example, L_3 and L_4 involve the same expected impact 'mid-point' (0.35, as indicated in Table 4.7), but order of magnitude differences with respect to event probability and impact, a relationship which is not captured by Figure 4.4 (although non-linear, isoproduct midpoint values could be plotted).

Figure 4.4 is a very useful way to picture the implications of the 'days lost rate' part of Table 4.7 for those who are used to using the PIM approach. However, in the context of the minimalist approach it is redundant as an operational tool unless the use of computer graphics input makes it an alternative way to specify the data in Tables 4.2 and 4.3. Eddy wanted to explore Dougal's possible interest in software which might do this, not as an immediate concern, but as a low-priority project to be pursued during lulls in other tasks. He also wanted to kill Dougal's interest in a conventional PIM approach. He indicated to Charlie that he would initiate discussion with him of both these issues once their 'bare bones' discussion was complete.

For evaluation purposes, the information in Table 4.7 is more usefully viewed as a cumulative impact picture (CIP) like Figure 4.5 than as a probability impact picture like Figure 4.4. In the longer term, Eddy anticipated going straight to Figure 4.5 unless software to use Figure 4.4 as an input format was developed. Figure 4.5 shows the potential cumulative effect of each of the uncertainty factors contributing to days lost. It uses layered cumulative probability distributions to do this, the gaps between successive curves indicating the contribution of each factor. For convenience the uncertainty factors are considered in order of decreasing event probability values. In Figure 4.5 the curve C_1 depicts the potential impact of weather on days lost. It is plotted linearly between point a_1 ($i_{vo} = 1$, CP = 0) and point d_1, ($i_{vp} = 11$, CP = 1), as for any transformation of an unconditional uniform probability density function into a cumulative distribution form.

The curve C_2 depicts the potential additional impact on days lost of supply failures in a manner which assumes a degree of positive correlation with impacts from the weather. The idea is to incorporate a degree of plausible pessimism reflecting Son of Sod's law. Sod's law is well known: if anything can go wrong it will. Son of Sod's law is a simple extension: if things can go wrong at the same time they will. C_2 is plotted in three linear segments via four points, generalizing the C_1 curve procedure to accommodate a conditional uniform probability density function with a minimalist Son of Sod (MSS) form of correlation:

- $p_{vp} = 0.32$ is used in the transformation $1 - 0.32 = 0.68$ to plot point a_2 on C_1.
- $i_{vo} = 0.8$ is used to move from point a_2 horizontally to the right 0.8 days to plot point b_2.
- $p_{vo} = 0.08$ is used in the transformation $1 - 0.08 = 0.92$, along with $i_{vp} = 3.2$, to move from a point on C_1 at CP = 0.92 horizontally to the right 3.2 days to plot point c_2.
- $i_{vp} = 3.2$ is used to move from point d_1 to the right 3.2 days to plot point d_2.
- a_2, b_2, c_2 and d_2 are joined by linear segments.

This implies the following correlation between 'weather' and 'supplies':

- If 'weather' impact is in the 0–68 percentile value range (0.68 defined by $1 - p_{vp}$ for the 'supplies' event), the 'supplies' event does not occur.
- If 'weather' impact is in the 92–100 percentile value range (0.92 defined by $1 - p_{vo}$ for the 'supplies' event), the 'supplies' event occurs with impact i_{vp}.
- If weather impact is in the 68–92 percentile value range, the 'supplies event' occurs with a magnitude rising from i_{vo} to i_{vp} in a linear manner.

A similar procedure is used for curves C_3 and C_4 associated with equipment failures and 'buckles', but with $c_3 d_3$ and $c_4 d_4$ coinciding since $p_{vo} = 0$ in each case.

Figure 4.5 plots expected values (E_f) defined by midpoint values along the median (CP = 0.5) line. Given the uniform probability density distribution assumption for the unconditional 'weather' distribution, E_1 lies on C_1 and no new assumptions are involved. Given the conditional nature (event probability less than one) of the other three uncertainty factors, interpreting Table 4.7 midpoint values as E_f is an additional assumption, and plotting them off the C_f curves resists employing the optimistic nature of these curves in the 0–68 percentile range.

The 'combined very optimistic' value (1 day lost per month) is plotted as point a_1, the 'combined very pessimistic' value (84.6 lost days per month) is plotted as point d_4. Figure 4.5 also shows the 'plausibly pessimistic' impact value (20 days lost per month) plotted on the impact axis (CP = 0) as point d_{4pp}, to avoid a prescriptive probabilistic interpretation in CP terms. The 'plausibly pessimistic' value should not be associated with a CP = 0.99 or 99% confidence level in general because it is conditional upon the MSS correlation assumption, although that interpretation is invited by Figure 4.5.

Eddy was very keen to use graphs of the form of Figure 4.5, in the short run and in the long run. He regarded software to make this easy to do as a high priority. Charlie had never liked the idea of probability impact diagrams, and he had resisted frequent urging by Dougal to use them, so he was very interested in Figure 4.4, and looked forward to Dougal's reaction, as well as prior discussion with Eddy.

Charlie could see immediately the useful story which Figure 4.5 told. He had not followed the details of the points used to plot the curves, but he understood Sod's law and its offspring. He took Eddy's word for the validity of the plotting algorithm and the value of computer software which could produce Figure 4.5 directly from any section of Table 4.7 on a simple command instruction.

Step 6: Summarize results

Eddy now indicated that whether or not he had produced Figures 4.4 and 4.5, a summary of his analysis results would have the following thrust:

- A £12 million expected cost should be used as the basis for bidding purposes at present.
- This £12 million expected value should be interpreted as a conservative estimate because it assumes a more capable barge than may be necessary. Given weather data and time to test alternative barges, it may be possible to justify a lower expected cost based on a less capable barge. If this contract were obtained, it would certainly be worth doing this kind of analysis. If a bid is submitted without doing it, committing to a particular barge should be avoided, if possible, to preserve flexibility.
- A cost outcome of the order of £50 million is as plausible as £5 million. This range of uncertainty is inherent in the fixed price contract offshore pipe laying business: *no abnormal risks are involved*. The organization should be able to live with this risk, or it should get out of the fixed price offshore pipe laying business. On this particular contract, a £50 million outcome could be associated with no buckles but most other things going very badly, or a moderately serious buckle and a very modest number of other problems, for example. Further analysis will clarify these scenarios, but it is not going to make this possibility go away. Further analysis of uncertainty should be primarily directed at refining expected value estimates for bidding purposes or for making choices (which

barge to use, when to start, and so on) if the contract is obtained. Further analysis may reduce the plausible cost range as a spin-off, but this should not be its primary aim.

This concluded the bare bones summary presentation which Eddy provided for Charlie. Eddy had questioned Charlie for views to put together the whole of his analysis at numerous points in its construction. But Charlie had not been exposed to the implications of his advice in this integrated framework until Eddy's presentation. Charlie was impressed. He and Eddy spent some time discussing its implications, as summarized in the following sections.

First-Pass Interpretation and Anticipation Of Further Passes

A key driver behind the shape of the minimalist approach of the last section is the need for a simple first-pass sizing of uncertainties which are usefully quantified. What matters most can then receive further attention if appropriate.

Table 4.6 (or Table 4.7) makes it very clear that 'days lost rate' is the major source of uncertainty. The 5% expected decrease from the base rate value implied by the midpoint value of the 'lay rate' is important, as is the 5% expected increase from the base rate value implied by the midpoint value of the 'cost rate' distribution. However, refining the basis of these adjustments is a low priority relative to refining the basis of the 7.12 (7.25) days lost per month adjustment, because of the size of that adjustment, and because of its associated variability. In any refinement of the first pass of the last section, 'days lost rate' is the place to start.

Within 'days lost rate' uncertainty, Table 4.6 (or Table 4.7 or Figure 4.5) should make it clear that 'weather' is the dominant source of uncertainty in terms of the 6 day increase in the midpoint value relative to the base value (E_f contribution). In E_f terms, 'weather' is an order of magnitude more important than 'supplies', the next most important uncertainty factor.

To refine the $E_1 = 6$ days lost per month estimate there is no point in simply refining the shape of the assumed distribution (with or without attempting to obtain more detailed data). Implicit in the Table 4.6 estimate is pipe laying taking place in an 'average month', associated with the summer season plus a modest proportion in shoulder seasons. This average month should be roughly consistent with the Table 4.8 duration midpoint of just 4.63 months. However, the range of 2.76 months to 15.38 months makes the average month concept inherently unreliable because this range must involve 'non-average' winter months. To refine the $E_1 = 6$ days lost per month estimate it is sensible to refine the average month concept.

The first step is to estimate an empirical 'days lost' distribution for each month of the year, using readily available wave height exceedance data for the relevant sea area, and the assumed barge's nominal wave height capability. The second step is to transform these distributions into corresponding 'productive days' distributions. A Markov process model can then be used to derive a completion date distribution given any assumed start date, with or without the other 'days lost rate' uncertainty factors and the 'lay rate' uncertainty of Table 4.6 (Table 4.7). Standard Monte Carlo simulation methods (Grey, 1995), discrete probability or controlled interval and memory (CIM) arithmetic (Cooper and Chapman, 1987) can be used.

Markov process models involve a state probability distribution which defines where the system is (in this case, how many kilometres of pipe have been laid), and a transition distribution which defines what happens each subsequent time period (how many kilometres of pipe are laid). These distributions are combined to step the process through time one period at a time, starting with suitable initial conditions, in a recursive manner. An understanding of Markov processes would make it clear that over the number of months necessary to lay the pipeline, 'weather', 'supplies' and 'equipment' uncertainty will cancel out on a swings and roundabouts basis to a significant extent, despite significant dependence. This will reduce the residual variability associated with these factors to the same order of magnitude as 'lay rate' and 'cost rate' uncertainty. However, 'buckles' involves an extreme event that has to be averaged out over contracts, not months on a given contract. A provision must be made for 'buckles' in each contract, but when a buckle happens its cost is not likely to be recovered on that contract, and it would endanger winning appropriate bids if attempts were made to avoid making a loss if a buckle occurs.

It is important to ensure that high-impact and low-probability risks like 'buckles' are identified and expected value provisions are made at an appropriate organizational level. It is also important to ensure that the risk they pose is an acceptable one. However, one buckle could happen, two or more are possible, and whether the appropriate provision is 0.35 days lost per month, twice or half that figure, is a relatively minor issue. In the present context, the first pass would not suggest second-pass attention should be given to buckles as a priority relative to other 'days lost rate' sources of uncertainty or their dependence.

If the 'weather' uncertainty factor equivalent of C_1 on Figure 4.5 is available for each relevant month, it makes sense to model the C_1 to C_4 relationships illustrated by Figure 4.5 plus the 'lay rate' uncertainty via a standard Monte Carlo simulation sampling process for each month, prior to running the Markov process. Further, it makes sense to then model, via a sampling process, the 'cost = duration × cost rate' relationship. This means layered cumulative probability distribution representations of the CIP form of Figure 4.5 can be used to show a top-level cumulative probability distribution for cost, including confidence bands, and this can be decomposed to provide built-in sensitivity analysis for all components of the overall uncertainty. A second-pass approach might seek to do this as simply as possible. A tempting assumption to achieve this is assuming all the Table 4.6 distributions other than 'weather' still apply, and independence is appropriate. However, independence on its own is not a reasonable default option. For example, if the 'lay rate' distribution has a low value in the first month (because the barge is not working properly), it is very likely to be low for the next month, and so on. The simplest acceptable default option short of perfect positive correlation is to assume independence for one run, a form of perfect positive correlation comparable to MSS for a second run, and interpolate between the two for expected values at an overall level of dependence which seems conservative but appropriate. This will size the effect of dependence at an overall level as well as the component uncertainty factors. The next simplest default option, which the authors strongly recommend, involves some level of decomposition of this approach (Chapman and Ward, 1997; Cooper and Chapman, 1987). For example, the four uncertainty factors associated with 'days lost rate' might be associated with one pair of bounds and interpolation, but the 'lay rate' distribution might be associated with another level of dependence between periods in the Markov process analysis, and the 'duration' and 'cost rate' dependence interpolation assumption might be different again.

In general, a second pass might refine the estimation of a small set of key uncertainty factors (just 'weather' in our example), using a sampling process (Monte Carlo simulation) and some degree of decomposition of factors. This second pass might involve consideration of all the first-pass uncertainty factors in terms of both independence and strong or perfect positive correlation bounds with an interpolated intermediate level of dependence defining expected values, some level of decomposition generally being advisable for this approach to dependence. Default correlation assumptions of the kind used in Figure 4.5 should suffice as plausible correlation bounds in this context.

A third pass is likely to address and refine dependence assumptions and associated variability assumptions in the context of particularly important uncertainty factors. Further passes could refine the analysis as and where issues are identified as important, relative to the attention paid them to date.

The number of passes required to reach any given level of understanding of uncertainty will be a function of a number of issues, including the level of computer software support. The Table 4.8 summary might be appropriate to formulate a bid, the second and third passes described above being reserved for successful bids.

When Charlie and Eddy finished discussing these issues, Charlie could see that the multiple-pass formalization of analysis which Eddy was pursuing would allow even someone comparatively inexperienced like Eddy to sort out what mattered and what didn't matter on the first pass, given access to suitable basic parameter information. Charlie could also see that later passes might be very useful if the contract were obtained and the objectives of the exercise had moved on to questions like choice of barge and choice of start date for the subcontract. Charlie could see that Eddy's minimalist first-pass approach was a valuable starting point, with a great future for each and every bid, and all subsequent uncertainty analysis for that project. Charlie was an old dog who could learn new tricks, and he was beginning to regret his forthcoming retirement.

Anticipation Of Corporate Learning

The minimalist approach can play a central role in a corporate learning process which embraces all projects. The idea of learning in an iterative process needs to address subsequent project learning. For example, the uncertainty factor breakdown used in this case could be used again in subsequent projects. Data on 'days lost rate' events caused by supplier or equipment could be distinguished to test and adjust as necessary the parameter estimates used as more experience is gained. Even uncertainty factors like 'lay rate', 'personnel' and 'other', combined directly when moving from Table 4.6 to Table 4.7, could be calibrated separately by experience across projects, provided the structuring of parameters and uncertainty factors is stable, and data is acquired in a way which reflects this structuring. Unfortunately it is often the case that data is not collected in a way which is useful because of the lack of such a structure.

Charlie was quick to see that the formalizations which he had spurned while working largely on his own were a very important part of the learning process for Eddy. Further, they would allow Eddy to involve Dougal in the process as appropriate, and they allowed all of them to understand how different sources of data, judgement and experience could be put together to address a single decision in an integrated manner. The process did not have to be bureaucratic. Indeed, it should not be bureaucratic in the prescriptive, rigid and boring sense; it should be a guide for flexible and interesting integration of insight and the creation of new ideas. Charlie and Eddy rightly concluded that capturing corporate knowledge in this way was a key benefit of the approach, and Dougal could be persuaded that this was the case.

Chapman and Ward (1997) develops this kind of corporate learning approach in this context in more detail, but this aspect of managing uncertainty needs much more attention. For examples of more general discussions which are relevant see, Cook and Brown (1999), Roberts (2000) or Cross and Baird (2000).

Scope For Automation

The minimalist approach was deliberately designed for simple manual processing and no supporting software requirements in the first instance. However, it was also designed to benefit from appropriate computer support. The Table 4.5 specification, input to a suitable package, could be used to present the user with Table 4.6 formats, and a request for the necessary information in Table 4.6 format. The analysis could then proceed automatically to Table 4.7 outputs and Figure 4.5

formats with or without Figure 4.4 portrayals (as pure outputs) in the same manner. The Figure 4.5 format diagrams might be provided assuming independence as well as a variant of MSS, with a request to use these results to select an appropriate intermediate dependence level. As discussed in the context of a second-pass approach, this 'sizes' dependence as well as associated parameter variability, and it could (and should) be decomposed. Relatively simple hardware and inexpensive commercially available software with a generic spreadsheet basis (like @Risk and the wide variety of more recently developed products) could be used to make the input demands of such analysis minimal, the outputs easy to interpret and rich, and the movement on to second and further passes relatively straightforward. In general, specific software should be developed once it is clear what analysis is required, after significant experience of the most appropriate forms of analysis for first and subsequent passes has been acquired. If such software and associated development experience is available, a key benefit is analysis on the first pass at the level described here as second or third pass, with no more effort or time required.

A firm operating lay barges on a regular basis would be well advised to develop a computer software package, or a set of macros within a standard package, to automate the aspects of uncertainty evaluation which are common to all offshore pipe laying operations, including drawing on the relevant background data as needed. Following the example of BP (Clark and Chapman, 1987), software could allow the selection of a sea area and a wave height capability, and automatically produce the equivalent of all relevant Figure 4.5 C_1 diagrams for all relevant months using appropriate weather data. Given a start date and the Table 4.5 base parameters, it could then run the Markov process calculations, with or without other 'days lost' uncertainty factors, to derive completion date (duration) probability distributions. Similar comments would apply in other contexts.

The use of a Figure 4.4 format as an input in place of Table 4.6 is an interesting application for those interested in advanced computer software and hardware possibilities. It could follow in the tradition of light-pen screen input for critical path analysis (CPA) diagrams, which is very popular with some users. Eddy was interested in it as a technical challenge he would enjoy if more pressing matters did not need attention, a view endorsed by Charlie. Neither saw it as a key issue.

Charlie was very pleased that Eddy had designed his minimalist approach so that it was simple enough to apply manually, with no black-box simulations he could not understand. He knew Dougal would warm to this too. However, Charlie was also very pleased that modern widely available software packages could be used to save effort as appropriate. He knew Dougal would be greatly impressed by the more sophisticated possibilities, although unlikely to fund them himself.

Eliminating The Use of Probability Impact Matrices

Readers who have never heard of probability impact matrices (PIMs) might be tempted to skip to the next section, but they should know what PIMs are in case they meet one, either in the present context or in other contexts (e.g. Chapter 7).

In brief, PIMs use the same probability and impact dimensions as Figure 4.4. However, each dimension is divided into high, medium and low ranges (sometimes using more than three categories), prior to assessing sources of uncertainty. Sometimes these labels are totally ambiguous, but usually they are given a semi-numeric interpretation. For example, high probability might be 0.8–1.0, high cost might be £5 million or more (sometimes defined as a percentage of overall project cost). Each source of uncertainty is assessed by a tick in a box, rating it high-high or high-medium or medium-high, for example. For comparisons between sources and sets of sources, an index may be used which will equate high-medium and medium-high, for example, in order to aggregate. Those who favour this approach 'sell' it as a qualitative approach which avoids the need to use numbers in a direct way, making it easier to deal with ambiguity.

The key reason Eddy included the Figure 4.4 probability impact picture (PIP) in the bare bones part of his presentation was because Charlie had warned him that Dougal liked a PIM approach. Like the majority of users of current project risk management processes, Dougal had been sold the PIM approach as a simple first-pass qualitative approach to estimating uncertainty. Charlie was not sold on this, but could not clearly articulate why. Charlie and Dougal had an uncomfortable stand-off on this issue. Eddy was determined to tactfully but firmly eliminate the use of PIMs in any organization employing him. He would use PIPs as a weapon, and as a partial replacement if withdrawal symptoms were evident. The real replacement would be CIPs.

The authors hope that Figure 4.4 in the context of the minimalist approach will help to end the use of conventional PIM approaches, illustrating the inherent and fatal flaws in these approaches from a somewhat different angle than used elsewhere (Ward, 1999; Chapman and Ward, 1997). The essence of the case can be summarized as follows:

- Those who use PIM approaches typically take (or should take) longer to assess uncertainty in this framework than it would take in a Figure 4.4 format for those used to this PIP format, and the minimalist approach can put the information content of Figure 4.4 specifications to simple and much more effective use than a conventional PIM approach.
- The PIP format of Figure 4.4 accommodates the estimator's uncertainty about the probability of occurrence and the size of the impact in terms of crude but credible nominal ranges and simple associated distribution tails.

- Because uncertainty about uncertainty is accommodated, it should be easier to estimate first-order uncertainty. It is easier to confront ambiguity than it is to bury it if you actually want to understand what is going on.
- There is no need for prior definition of high, medium and low probability of occurrence and impact size ranges appropriate to the project or part of the project or risks being considered. Nor is there any need to fit each tick in a box into preset categories. Comparable appropriate ranges are selected directly for each source of risk. Put another way, those who are adamant about sticking to a PIM approach could be constrained to replacing their tick in a box with a tick-equivalent point plotted on a PIP diagram like Figure 4.4. High, medium and low ranges could then be defined later in relation to clustering of the tick-equivalent points.
- Uncertainty about uncertainty is not accommodated just to make first-order uncertainty easier to estimate. It is captured by PIPs. It may be relevant in terms of decisions about the project in question. It is even more likely to be relevant in terms of decisions about the need for further data or analysis. This makes it a valuable part of the iterative process which underlies the minimalist approach.
- Uncertainty about uncertainty defined in terms of parameter ranges is of direct and immediate importance in terms of the assumed expected values for probability of occurrence and size of impact. A PIM approach implicitly puts all the ticks in the centres of all the boxes; it does not allow the expected values to be anywhere other than the centre of the preselected boxes. This loses information about the expected values as well as losing information about the associated uncertainty. It also makes the process difficult and ambiguous when a tick representing an expected value is not clearly in one box, but could be in several. Further, as there is no mid-point to a 'high' impact box like '£5 million or more', this box is a particular source of ambiguity for PIMs.
- Any attempt to convert the ticks in boxes into a numeric risk index further distorts and loses information. For example, a high-low combination and a low-high combination may involve comparable expected values but very different risks in terms of variability relative to expected outcome. Such 'risk indices' are more accurately interpreted as 'expected value indices' which are biased and crude to the extent that they do not accurately reflect expected value. They make no attempt to measure risk in the sense of a potential for departures from expected values. An ambiguous measure of expected value is not a proper measure of risk in any meaningful sense (although many users of PIMs have an ambiguous notion of risk that is based on probability times impact). Any attempt to combine such 'risk indices' further compounds the confusion they are based on.

To the authors it is easy to see why a PIM approach is attractive, but difficult to understand why repeatedly spelling out their obvious defects continues to be necessary. We sympathize with Charlie rather than Dougal on this issue. By contrast, an explicit or implicit PIP approach lends itself to all the advantages of a quantification approach, none of the defects of a PIM approach, with less effort, and a much richer capture of information.

Another way to look at this draws on the distinction between composition and aggregation used by economists (e.g. Green, 1964) and employed in other contexts in this book. Aggregation involves a loss of information, composition does not. Bottom-up analysis can preserve information via composition. Top-down analysis, which is not based on prior bottom-up composition, involves implicit aggregation. The minimalist approach, and associated PIPs and CIPs, involves a bottom-up composition process for top-down interpretation. The PIM approach involves aggregation and associated ambiguity as to what 'risk indices' means. The PIP and CIP approaches are designed to capture and clarify uncertainty, including uncertainty about uncertainty. The PIM approach makes all forms of uncertainty ambiguous and uncertain, and those who use PIM-based 'risk indices' to make decisions do not understand the risks such decisions involve as a consequence of the PIM analysis.

PIM approaches hide more than they reveal. They are a dangerous waste of time. Eddy had no intention of putting it so bluntly to Dougal, but he was prepared to argue the case against PIMs for as long as it took, using PIPs as an acceptable but non-essential alternative, CIPs as a replacement. Charlie was delighted by Eddy's put-down of the PIM approach, and quite taken by the PIP approach. He could see that they addressed explicitly, via the composition process idea, the ambiguities associated with aggregation which he had intuitively understood but had never felt able to articulate.

Managing And Shaping Expectations

The minimalist approach uses ranges primarily to obtain an estimate of expected impact in terms of cost or time which is simple, plausible, and free of bias on the low side. Any estimator should be confident that more work on refining any cost or time analysis is at least as likely to decrease the expected value estimate as to increase it. A tendency for cost or time estimates to drift upwards as more analysis is undertaken indicates a failure of earlier analysis. The minimalist approach has been designed to help manage the expectations of those the estimator reports to in terms of expected values. Preserving credibility should be an important concern. Charlie had no difficulties with this, although he had never thought about it in this way.

The minimalist approach provides a lower bound on impacts which is plausible and free of bias. However, in the current tale, the approach does not provide a directly comparable upper bound (in simpler contexts it will, as illustrated in Chapter 3). In the current context it resorts to a very simple rule of thumb in a first pass to define a plausible upper bound. The resulting ranges are wide. This should reflect the estimator's secondary interest in variability and associated downside risk at this stage, unless major unbearable risks are involved. It should also reflect a wish to manage the expectations of those reported to in terms of variability. Those reported to should expect variability to decline as more analysis is undertaken. Charlie could see the validity of this too, but the naked nature of the £50 million 'plausibly pessimistic' estimate worried him, in terms of Dougal's reaction.

The extent to which Dougal accepts Eddy's view that no abnormal risks are involved would be tested by the plausible upper bound of £50 million in Table 4.8. Charlie could see the point of this. As noted in step 6 (page 140), one implication of this plausible upper bound is that a pipe laying company in the business of bidding for fixed price contracts with a base cost estimate of the order of £12 million must be prepared for a very low probability extreme project to cost four times this amount. A 4.63 month expected duration and Figure 4.5 should suggest a one-season project is the most likely outcome (say probability = 0.90–0.99), but being unable to complete before winter weather forces a second season is an outcome with a significant probability (say 0.01–0.10), and a third season is unlikely but possible. The £50 million upper bound could be viewed as a scenario associated with three moderately expensive seasons or two very expensive seasons, without taking the time to clarify the complex paths that might lead to such outcomes at this stage.

Regarding this risk as bearable does not mean that realizing it cannot be disastrous. But it does mean adopting the preferred basis or the default basis:

- Accepting this level of risk involves acceptable swings and roundabouts – the preferred basis
- Not accepting this risk would involve an even higher risk of going out of business, because competitors will bid on the basis of accepting such risks – the default basis

Firms working on the default basis can balance the risk of going out of business in terms of one project or a series of projects, but they cannot eliminate the risk of going out of business. Being sure you will never make a loss on any project is a sure way to go out of business. A firm operating on the default basis should have some idea what both probabilities are if a balance is to be achieved consistently. The pipe laying contractor may approach this issue operationally by preparing each bid using the barge that is believed to be the highest capability/cost rate option likely to win the bid (a conservative, lowest possible risk approach), and then testing the attractiveness of successive lower capability/cost rate options. Consideration of such options will focus attention on the question of what level of risk defines the limit of bearability for the contractor. This limit can then be assessed in relation to the need to take risk to stay in business, which may have merger implications. In this sense the estimator can help the organization to shape expectations in a very general sense.

As it turned out, Charlie need not have worried about Dougal's reaction. Although Charlie's estimates always had the air of greater precision, Dougal was too canny not to see the inherent risk. Dougal found the idea of explicitly trading off the risk of going out of business because of a loss on any one project with the risk of going out of business because of a lack of work most intriguing. He regarded the issue as one to be further explored as he and Eddy gained the requisite experience of working together.

Robustness Of The Minimalist Approach

How might Eddy defend and explain the minimalist first-pass approach from all the substantive criticisms others might put? This is the rhetorical question Eddy used to start this discussion with Charlie. The issue of interest is not robustness in terms of the sensitivity of specific parameter assumptions, but robustness in a more fundamental process sense. This section addresses the robustness of the approach in a sequence chosen by Eddy to facilitate further clarification of the rationale for the approach. The concern is more with clarifying the rationale for the general form of the approach rather than with defending the details of each step. The authors have no wish to defend example parameter values or associated rules of thumb.

The parameter structure

The example used to illustrate the minimalist approach employed four basic parameters and four composite parameters. This may seem excessively complex, and in many contexts it would be. For example, Chapter 3 adopts a comparatively simple structure. However, in the present example this detail offers a decomposition structure for the estimation process which is extremely useful. The combinations which it makes formal and explicit in Table 4.8 would have to be dealt with intuitively and implicitly in Tables 4.5 to 4.7 if they were not broken out in the first section of Table 4.5. Saving time by using a simpler structure is possible, but it would not be a cost-effective short cut in the authors' view.

If eight parameters are better than six or seven, what about nine or ten? The answer here is less clear-cut. For example, 'cost rate' might be decomposed into a 'lay day cost rate' (associated with days when the weather is good and pipe laying takes place) and an 'idle day cost rate' (associated with bad weather), the £2.5 million being an average linked to about 7 idle days and 23 lay days per month, consistent with Table 4.6. Uncertainty as to which rate applies might be explicitly negatively correlated with weather uncertainty, reducing variability considerably. This might be useful. Certainly it would be useful to decompose in this way if a subcontract defined the cost this way.

However, the spirit of the minimalist approach is not to introduce complications which don't have a clear benefit provided the simple assumptions are conservative (biased on the pessimistic side). Deliberate bias on the conservative side is justified on the grounds that, by and large, people underestimate variability, so a failure to build in appropriate conservative bias will lead to inevitable optimistic bias. How far this conservatism needs to be taken can only be determined empirically. When more projects come in under cost and ahead of time than the original estimates suggest is statistically valid, a less conservative approach is warranted. BP achieved this using the SCERT approach (Chapman, 1979), but they are unique in the authors' experience. Few organizations have this 'problem', and it is relatively easy to deal with if they do.

The uncertainty factor structure

It might be tempting to use a single uncertainty factor for some or even all basic parameters which are given a quantitative treatment. However, in the present example, wide-ranging experience suggests that this would produce a much lower estimate of potential variations, since estimators tend to underestimate variability consistently. Identified contributing factors should yield wider ranges which are closer to reality. Further, different contributing uncertainty factors lend themselves to different sources of expertise and data, different responses including different ownership, and a better understanding of the whole via clear definition of the parts. It is difficult to see what would be gained by recombining any of the uncertainty factors associated with the probabilistic treatment in Table 4.5. The most attractive possible simplification would seem to be combining 'supplies' and 'equipment', but apart from different sources of data and expertise, it might be possible to transfer the 'supplies' risk to the client if pipe supplies is the key component. Combining uncertainty factors which are not treated probabilistically saves minimal analysis effort, but it is worth considering in terms of interpretation effort. A collection of non-quantified 'other' categories is the risk analyst's last refuge when risks occur which have not been explicitly identified. However, this should not make it a last refuge for scoundrels, and examples not worth separate identification should be provided.

Pushing the argument the other way, there is a declining benefit as more sources of uncertainty are individually identified. There is no suggestion that the set of 13 uncertainty factors in Table 4.5 is optimal, but 10 is the order of magnitude (in a range 5–50) that might be expected to capture the optimum benefit most of the time for a case involving the level of uncertainty illustrated by the example.

Treatment of low-probability high-impact events

In our example context, suppose 'catastrophic equipment failure' has a probability of occurring of about 0.001 per month, with consequences comparable to a buckle. It might be tempting to identify and quantify this uncertainty factor, but doing so would lead to a variant of Figure 4.5 where the additional curve cannot be distinguished from the CP = 1.0 bound and an expected value impact observable on Table 4.7 of the order of 0.035 days lost per month. The minimalist approach will communicate the spurious nature of such sophistication very clearly, to support the learning process for inexperienced estimators. This is extremely important, because making mistakes is inevitable, but making the same mistakes over and over is not. Nevertheless, it may be very useful to identify 'catastrophic equipment failure' as an uncertainty factor not to be quantified, or to be combined with other low-probability high-impact factors like 'buckles'.

Now suppose some other uncertainty factor has a probability of occurring of about 0.01 per month, directly comparable to a buckle, with consequences comparable to a buckle. The expected value impact is small (0.35 days per month, about a day and a half over the project), but the additional downside risk is significant, and clearly visible on the equivalent of Figure 4.5. It is important not to overlook any genuine 'buckle' equivalents, while studiously avoiding spurious sophistication.

There is no suggestion that one uncertainty factor equivalent to 'buckles' of Table 4.5 is an optimal number of such factors to consider, but one factor of this kind is the order of magnitude in a range 0–5 that we might expect to capture the optimum most of the time for cases involving the level of uncertainty illustrated by the example.

In our example context, the event 'lay barge sinks' might have a probability of order 0.1 that of a buckle, and implications a factor of 10 worse, giving an expected value of the same order as a buckle, but with much more catastrophic implications when it happens. In expected value terms, quantification is of very modest importance, but recognizing the risk exposure when bidding is of great importance if insurance or contractual measures are not in place. The minimalist approach recognizes the need to list such risks, but it clarifies the limited advantages of attempting quantification.

The assumption of perfect positive correlation

Assuming less than perfect positive correlation would affect the expected value interpretation of midpoint values of Tables 4.6 to 4.8 and Figure 4.5, and the Figure 4.5 curves C_2 to C_4 would develop S shapes. For example, in Table 4.6 the 'supplies' event probability midpoint is $(0.3 + 0.1)/2 = 0.2$ and the impact midpoint is $(3 - 1)/2 = 2$. If these two distributions are combined assuming independence, the expected impact of 'supplies' should be $0.2 \times 2 = 0.4$ and the product distribution will not be symmetric. However, the 'supplies' midpoint expected impact is 0.5, rising to 0.54 in Table 4.7.

There are several reasons for avoiding the sophistication of less than perfect positive correlation for a first-pass approach, although more refined assessments later may focus on statistical dependence structures:

- Some form of perfect positive correlation should be the default option rather than independence, because perfect positive correlation is usually closer to the truth, and any first-order approximation should be inherently conservative.
- Successive attempts to estimate uncertainty tend to uncover more and more uncertainty. This is part of the general tendency for people to underestimate uncertainty. It makes sense to counterbalance this with assumptions which err on the side of building in additional uncertainty. If this is done to a sufficient level, successive attempts to estimate uncertainty ought to be able to reduce the perceived uncertainty. Failure to achieve this clearly signals failure of earlier analysis, throwing obvious shadows over current efforts. An assumption of perfect positive correlation is a key element in the overall strategy to control bias and manage expectations in the minimalist approach.
- It is particularly important to have a first-pass approach which is biased on the pessimistic side if one possible outcome of the first pass is subsequently ignoring areas of uncertainty or variability.
- Perfect positive correlation is the simplest assumption to implement and to interpret, and a minimalist approach should keep processes and interpretations as simple as possible.
- Perfect positive correlation clearly proclaims itself as an approximation which can be refined, avoiding any illusions of truth or unwarranted precision, and inviting refinement where it matters.

The assumption of uniform probability density functions

An assumption of uniform probability density functions involves a relatively crude specification of uncertainty. Other forms of distribution would assign lower probabilities to extreme values and higher probabilities to central values, and allow a degree of asymmetry to be incorporated. Dropping the uniform probability distribution assumption is likely to affect expected value estimates of both cost and duration because such distributions are usually considered asymmetric. Typically cost and duration distributions are perceived to be left skewed, implying a reduction in expected values compared with an assumption of a uniform distribution over the same range of values. However, employing uniform distributions in a first pass is useful for a number of reasons which are similar to the reasons for assuming perfect positive correlation:

- The first pass is a first-order approximation which should be inherently conservative.
- It is useful to build in enough conservative bias in expected values and variability assessments to overcome inherent tendencies to underestimate risk and make successive measurement of uncertainty diminish the perceived uncertainty.
- Linearity in density and cumulative probability functions has the elegance of simplicity that works. It clarifies issues which smooth curves can hide.
- A uniform distribution clearly proclaims itself as an approximation which can be readily modified if later analysis warrants more sophisticated distribution shapes.

Eddy had all the ideas of this section clear and well rehearsed. He thought they were very important, as do the authors. Charlie was very pleased that Eddy had thought things through so carefully, and knew Dougal would be pleased too. But he advised Eddy as gently as possible that he did not wish to discuss the details, and he thought Dougal would feel the same.

The User Perspective: Conditional Estimates And Cube Factors

Three months after Eddy started work in Aberdeen, he met Thomas again. Eddy recounted the progress he had made with the minimalist approach and Thomas was suitably impressed. Thomas then asked how Eddy would regard estimates prepared by other parties, such as subcontractors to Eddy's firm. The problem, Thomas pointed out, was that one party might submit an estimate based on certain assumptions which might not be true, might not be acceptable, or might not be apparent to other users of the estimate. This commonly occurred with the use of what Thomas called the conditional estimate cop-out, an extreme form of irrational objectivity.

To illustrate this, Thomas asked Eddy to recall their previous discussion about a project manager attempting to estimate how long it would take to get head office approval for a particular potential design change. The standard time of 3 weeks for approval of design changes did not appear to be a sensible estimate of what was likely to happen on average, and therefore it was better regarded as a target to aim for given no problems. A multiple-pass process, involving analyses like Tables 4.2 to 4.4, might produce a rather higher expected value for the time required, together with a range of possible durations. However, rather than undertake this analysis and risk appearing unduly pessimistic (or incompetent), the project manager might report an estimate of 3 weeks duration with an attached condition that approval is assumed to be provided in the standard time of 3 weeks. This would amount to a conditional estimate cop-out, which implicitly acknowledges that 3 weeks is a very suspect expected value, but that the risk of exceeding it is no longer the responsibility of the project manager. Clearly it would be important in project performance terms to ensure that other users of the project manager's 3 week estimate understood this and agreed with it.

Despite its lack of rationality, in a 'conspiracy of optimism' environment the conditional estimate cop-out can appear very attractive. If data is not available, which is often the case, and everyone is concerned about being objective, it can be very difficult to avoid a conditional estimate cop-out, even if the project manager thinks the Table 4.4 estimate is about what should be expected.

If any estimate involves assumptions which may not be true, the conditional nature of the estimate, in terms of its dependence on those assumptions being true, may be very important. Treating such an estimate as if it were unconditional – i.e. not dependent on any assumptions being true – may involve a serious misrepresentation of reality. Unfortunately, there is a common tendency for estimate-related assumptions to be subsequently overlooked or not made explicit in the first place, often condoned and reinforced by bias driven by a conspiracy of optimism. Such treatment of assumptions is especially likely where people do not like uncertainty and they prefer not to see it. A conspiracy of optimism is more than enough to make this issue crucial. If messengers get shot for telling the truth, people will be motivated to be economical with the truth. In Thomas's view, this was a serious root cause of cost and time overruns and other failures to live up to performance expectations.

Understanding the conditional nature of estimates is particularly important when estimates prepared by one party are to be used by another party. As a simple example, assume the project manager concerned with estimating the approval duration used a second-pass estimate of 8 weeks, and similar kinds of estimates for all activity durations in the project as a whole. How should the customer, the head office, or any other party who is a user of the project manager's estimates, interpret the project manager's estimate of project duration?

Maintaining simplicity, suppose the user of the project manager's estimate takes a sample of one activity to test the validity of the project duration estimate as a whole, and selects the approval duration for this purpose. Thomas suggested that three adjustment factors ought to be applied to the project manager's estimate, F_k, F_u, and F_b, related to three basic sources of uncertainty: known unknowns, unknown unknowns, and bias. Each adjustment factor is 1 ± 0 if a negligible adjustment effect is involved, but expected values greater than one for each factor and an associated rational subjective probability distribution with a non-zero spread will usually be involved.

F_k is an adjustment factor for known unknowns. These are any *explicit* assumptions which matter. If the project manager has identified a list of sources of uncertainty embodied in the 'normal situation', and another list of sources of uncertainty embodied in the 'abnormal situation', these lists look appropriate, and the quantification of associated uncertainty looks appropriate, a negligible adjustment for known unknowns is involved, and $F_k = 1 \pm 0$ is reasonable. However, if the estimator does not use rational subjective probabilities, the user of those estimates ought to use rational subjective probabilities to make a suitable adjustment. For example, if the project manager has recorded a conditional estimate cop-out for approval duration of 3 weeks, this should suggest an expected F_k greater than 2 with an anticipated outcome range of 1–10 if the user is familiar with data like that of Table 4.2 and analysis like that of Table 4.4. It would not be rational for the user to fail to make such an adjustment.

F_u is an adjustment factor for unknown unknowns. These are any *implicit* assumptions which matter. If the project manager made a provision for unknown unknowns when quantifying approval duration estimates in a Table 4.4 format, which the user deems suitably conservative in the light of the quality of the identification of explicit assumptions, an $F_u = 1 \pm 0$ may be reasonable. In contrast, an expected F_k greater than 2 with an anticipated outcome range 1 – 10 may suggest comparable values for F_u, depending on the user's confidence about F_k estimation and the quality of the project manager's estimates more generally.

F_b is an adjustment factor for bias. This is derived from any *systematic* estimation errors which matter. If $F_k = 1 \pm 0$ and $F_u = 1 \pm 0$ seem sensible conservative estimates, and the organization involved has a history of no bias, $F_b = 1 \pm 0$ may be reasonable. However, if F_k or F_u are thought to be understated relative to recent organizational history, a suitably large F_b expected value and associated spread are warranted.

Combining these three scaling factors provides a single 'cube' factor, short for known unknowns, unknown unknowns, and bias (KUUUB), designated F^3 and equated (for simplicity) to $F_k \times F_u \times F_b$, although this is not strictly equivalent to the useful geometric interpretation provided by Figure 4.6. This F^3 factor is applied as a scaling factor to conditional expected value estimates. This factor can be estimated in probability terms directly, or via these three components, to clarify the conditional nature of the output of any quantitative risk analysis. This avoids the very difficult mental gymnastics associated with trying to interpret a

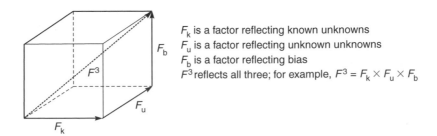

Figure 4.6—A visual representation of the cube factor F^3.

quantitative risk analysis result which is conditional on exclusions and scope assumptions (which may be explicit or implicit) and no bias without underestimating the importance of the conditions.

The key value of explicit quantification of F^3 is forcing those involved to think about the implications of the factors which drive the expected size and variability of F^3. Such factors may be far more important than the factors captured in the prior conventional estimation process where there is a natural tendency to forget about conditions and assumptions and focus on the numbers. Not considering an F^3 factor explicitly can be seen as overlooking Heisenberg's principle: we have to remember that what we observe is not nature itself, but nature exposed to our method of questioning. Attempting to explicitly size F^3 makes it possible to try to avoid this omission. Different parties may emerge with different views about an appropriate F^3, but the process of discussion should be beneficial. If an organization refuses to estimate F^3 explicitly, the issues involved do not go away, they simply become unmanaged risks, and many of them will be betting certainties.

In practice a sample of one activity (such as duration of design change approval) yielding an F_k significantly greater than 1 ought to lead to much larger samples of other activity estimates. Conversely, if no sample activity estimates are examined, this ought to lead to a large F^3 value for a whole-project estimate, given the track record of most organizations. Project teams *and all users of their estimates* need to negotiate a jointly optimal approach to producing original estimates and associated F^3 factors. Any aspect of uncertainty which is left out by an estimate producer which is of interest to an estimate user should be addressed in the user's F^3.

Thomas acknowledged that large F^3 values will seem worryingly subjective to those who cling to an irrational objectivity perspective, but explicit attention to F^3 factors is an essential part of a rational subjectivity approach. It is seriously irrational to assume $F^3 = 1 \pm 0$ without sound grounds for doing so. At present most organizations fail this rationality test.

Thomas pointed out that Eddy would increasingly be dealing with other project parties, including subcontractors, and he would need the F^3 factor concept to interpret their views on the likelihood of events in order to make rational decisions from Dougal's perspective. Perspective was an important driver of what was rational. For example, in one organization Thomas had worked with, estimates prepared by project planners of what something would cost were almost invariably about half what cost estimators thought the same thing would cost. Project planners seemed to be born optimists, while project cost estimators were born pessimists. Moreover, they self-selected themselves into suitable jobs. Both thought they were rational. Yet if the conditions or assumptions used in estimates were known to be debatable, a rational third-party view might be outside the range defined by the most pessimistic cost estimator or the most optimistic planner.

Interpreting another party's subjective or objective probabilities requires explicit consideration of an F^3 factor, and component F_k, F_u and F_b factors. The quality of the modelling and the quality of the associated parameter estimates need to be assessed to estimate F^3. This includes issues like dependence. Estimators and users of estimates who do not have an agreed approach to F^3 factors are communicating in an ambiguous fashion that is bound to generate mistrust. Trust is an important driver of F^3.

Thomas admitted that his F^3 factor concept was not well developed, and it clearly involved a high level of subjectivity. Nevertheless, on the basis of what gets measured gets managed, it looked like a useful way to highlight important sources of uncertainty and prompt consideration of underlying management implications. For the most part, high levels of precision in F^3 factors and component factors were not practical or needed. The reason for sizing F^3 factors was 'insight not numbers'.

Eddy could see that Thomas had hit on an important issue in estimating. He thought that Thomas's F^3 concept was fairly rudimentary, but it did offer a way of raising awareness of key sources of uncertainty which needed to be addressed. Encouraged by success with his minimalist approach to estimating, Eddy resolved to apply Thomas's F^3 concept at the earliest opportunity.

Conclusion

'Chance only favours the prepared mind' is a remark Louis Pasteur is said to have made more than a century ago in the context of understanding the implications when his vaccination for anthrax only worked successfully for the first time after it had been left exposed to the air for two weeks by a lazy laboratory worker who was keen to go on holiday. It is an appropriate quote for the beginning of this chapter in the sense that Eddy's concern was to be the Louis Pasteur of estimators, with a mind prepared to learn by experience and from the experience of others, as well as a mind prepared to see opportunities when they arose. Like Louis Pasteur, Eddy was prepared to be a lateral thinker and a maverick, challenging the established wisdom by following Thomas's example.

This chapter describes a minimalist first-pass approach to estimation and evaluation of uncertainty which is aimed at achieving a cost-effective approach to uncertainty assessment. The minimalist approach defines uncertainty ranges for probability of occurrence and size of impact for each source of uncertainty that is usefully quantified. Subsequent calculations preserve expected value and measures of variability, while explicitly managing associated optimistic bias.

The minimalist approach departs from the first-pass use of rectangular probability density histograms or other convenient probability assumptions which the authors and many others have used for years in similar contexts. Readers used to first-pass approaches which attempt considerable precision may feel uncomfortable with the deliberate lack of precision incorporated in the minimalist approach. However, more precise modelling is frequently accompanied by questionable underlying assumptions, like independence, and lack of attention to uncertainty in original estimates. The minimalist approach forces explicit consideration of these issues. It may be a step back in terms of taking a simple view of the big picture, but it should facilitate more precise modelling of uncertainty where it matters, and confidence that precision is not spurious.

The minimalist approach also departs from the qualitative probability impact matrix (PIM) approach, which is widely used in project management and safety analysis. It was in fact developed to stamp out such approaches, when an earlier attempt using a simple scenario approach failed to achieve this end (Chapman and Ward, 1997).

The way rational subjectivity and irrational objectivity were introduced to Eddy by Thomas on page 121 provides a useful starting point for the interpretation of Eddy's minimalist approach. Rational subjectivity is a form of Simon's (1979) notion of 'procedural rationality' coupled to conventional subjective probability ideas as outlined by authors like Raiffa (1968) that underpins the validity of the minimalist approach. Thomas's project duration example is simple enough and extreme enough to make obvious what is usually obscured by irrational objectivity, often in conjunction with a conspiracy of optimism.

The F^3 (cube factor) concept Thomas introduced on page 154 is a useful endpoint for the interpretation of Eddy's minimalist approach because it completes the synthesis of the whole of the estimation process, including the framing assumptions which underlie any estimates. Not only are all estimates based on subjective probabilities, they all embody an F^3 factor, unless we remember and separately consider the implications of their conditional nature, unknown conditions, and bias. The more estimators identify sources of uncertainty, choosing to quantify some but not others, the more obvious it becomes that F_k aspects are involved. The more obvious the role of F_k greater than 1 with significant variability, the more obvious the role of F_u. F_b closes the loop, reflecting perspective and trust as well as technical estimation issues. The distinction between what is F_b and what is F_u or F_k can remain ambiguous, but acknowledging their separate existence is useful in practical terms.

Estimation and evaluation of uncertainty are core tasks in any process involving the management of uncertainty. The constructively simple probability approach to these core tasks demonstrated by Eddy's tale involves a number of important objectives which contribute to cost-effective uncertainty assessment:

- **Understanding uncertainty in general terms** Understanding uncertainty needs to go beyond variability and available data. It needs to address ambiguity and incorporate structure and knowledge, with a focus on making the best decisions possible given available data, information, knowledge, and understanding of structure.

- **Understanding sources of uncertainty** One important aspect of structure is the need to understand uncertainty in terms of sources of uncertainty, because some (not all) appropriate ways of managing uncertainty are specific to its source.
- **Determining what to quantify** In terms of decision-making effectiveness, distinguishing between what is usefully quantified and what is best treated as a condition or assumption is very important. Knight's (1921) classical distinction between risk and uncertainty based on the availability of objective probabilities is not appropriate. Subjective probabilities are the starting point for all quantification in terms of probabilities, in the decision analysis tradition (Raiffa, 1968). At best, objective probabilities based on data will address only part of the uncertainty of interest with a less than perfect fit between source and application, and a subjective view of the quality of coverage and fit is required. Knowledge gaps and the role of organizational learning need direct explicit treatment.
- **Using iterative processes effectively and efficiently** To facilitate insight and learning, uncertainty has to be addressed in terms of an iterative process, with process objectives which change on successive passes. An iterative approach is essential to optimize the use of time and other resources during the uncertainty management process, because initially where uncertainty lies, whether or not it matters, and how best to respond to it, are unknown. At the outset, the process is concerned with sizing uncertainty about both risk and opportunity to discover what matters. Subsequent passes are concerned with refining assessments in order to effectively manage what matters. Final passes may be concerned with convincing others that what matters is being properly managed. The way successive iterations are used needs to be addressed in a systematic manner. A simple one-shot, linear approach is hopelessly ineffective and inefficient.
- **Starting with a constructively simple first pass at estimation and evaluation** A constructively simple approach to the first pass at estimation and evaluation in order to optimize the overall process is critical. A constructively simple first-pass approach to estimation should be so easy to use that the usual resistance to appropriate quantification due to lack of data and lack of comfort with subjective probabilities is overcome. It may be desirable in some circumstances to make a constructively simple approach more complex than the 'minimalist' approach of this chapter, but the minimalist approach should serve as a default option, to be replaced only if additional complexity is constructive.
- **Avoiding optimistic bias** The optimistic bias of most approaches to estimation and evaluation, which leads to systematic underestimation of uncertainty, needs direct and explicit attention to manage expectations. If successive estimates associated with managing risk do not narrow the perceived variability and improve the perceived expected cost or profit on average, then the earlier analysis process is flawed. Very few organizations have processes which meet this test. They are failing to manage expectations. The more sophisticated the process, the more optimistic bias damages the credibility of estimation and evaluation processes in general.

- **Avoiding irrational objectivity** Corporate culture can drive people to displaying irrational objectivity. An important objective is neutralizing this pressure, via rational subjectivity.
- **Integrating the implications of the F^3 factor** It is very easy to make assumptions, then lose sight of them, between the basic analysis and the ultimate use of that analysis. The F_k factor forces integration of the implications of such explicit assumptions. The F_u factor picks up the implicit assumptions. And the F_b factor integrates any residual bias. Ensuring this is done is an important objective.
- **Avoiding probability impact matrices (PIMs)** Any approach which introduces uncertainty in the form of ambiguity is inherently counterproductive. Eliminating the use of PIMs is an important objective.
- **Constructive simplicity** Simplicity is an important virtue in its own right, not just with respect to the efficiency of a minimalist first-pass approach, but because it can amplify clarity and deepen insight. However, appropriate constructive simplicity must accommodate added complexity as and when appropriate. Getting the best balance between simplicity and complexity is partly a question of structure and process, partly a question of skills which can be learned via a process that is engineered to enhance learning.

No alternative approaches to estimating and evaluating the authors are aware of explicitly address this set of ten objectives or anything like them in a holistic manner. In our view they are all important, as is holistic treatment.

This chapter makes use of a particular example context to illustrate the constructively simple probability approach, but the focus is important generic assessment issues. Nevertheless, context-specific issues cannot be avoided, and there is considerable scope for addressing the relevance of the specific techniques and the philosophy behind the constructively simple probability approach in other contexts. For example, a modification of the process outlined in this chapter is used as the basis for safety management purposes in Chapter 7. Implicitly, if not explicitly, constructively simple probabilities are used throughout this book.

The core of the minimalist approach has been published earlier (Chapman and Ward, 2000), as has the F^3 factor concept (Chapman, 2000b), but Eddy's tale integrates them with rational subjectivity into a constructively simple probability approach.

One way to characterize constructively simple probabilities is an informal subjectively based Bayesian approach within the $p = 1, \ldots, p^*$ (p^* unknown) framework suggested by Eddy, with F^3 squaring the circle (F_b in particular) for *any* assumptions. More formal Bayesian approaches may be more elegant mathematically, but they involve residual assumptions which are overlooked. The issue is, Do you want to be approximately right or precisely wrong?

5 Ian's tale: Aligning buyer and supplier motivation

What doesn't get measured doesn't get managed.

Introduction

The perspective in Chapters 3 and 4 was an organization operating as a contractor or supplier, although aspects of subcontracting were involved. The tale of this chapter concerns a client organization or buyer, Medical Essentials Delivery and Sourcing (MEDS) Ltd. This chapter uses a different focus and a broader perspective to consider the implications of different perceptions of uncertainty by different parties to a project and the need to more formally address alignment of motivation.

In autumn 2001 MEDS was contemplating a new headquarters building. MEDS had been presented with an opportunity to acquire an office development project which included a proposed construction contract with a design and build contractor. Its bankers agreed to finance the deal, but only subject to a due diligence assessment of the proposal and an accompanying risk analysis which had been previously undertaken by the contractor.

The central character in this tale is Ian, the consultant hired by MEDS to carry out the due diligence assessment. Much of this chapter is based on key sections of Ian's report to MEDS. This may be of interest in itself, as an example of a helpful form of consultancy. However, the direct purpose of the tale is twofold: first, to introduce a generic framework for project risk management, aspects of which can be adapted to cope with uncertainty management in general; and second, to discuss the concept of a balanced incentive and risk sharing (BIARS) contract, aspects of which also generalize on a broad basis.

A Development Project

In autumn 2001 MEDS was a rapidly growing business based on contracting to operate hospital medical equipment and supplies information systems, and/or manage associated purchases, and/or deliver the goods. Some clients wanted to outsource their information systems, some wanted to enjoy the leverage MEDS could exert on suppliers, and all valued an efficient inventory and associated logistics management service that meant 'no stockouts, no large inventory requirements, low costs, and no fuss', as the sales manager of MEDS liked to put it. MEDS had a nationwide distributed operation for most customer-facing functions. MEDS also had a growing head office operation based in a small town in North Wiltshire. The head office operation included sales, systems, and the usual corporate support functions, currently housed in a collection of rented premises, some of which were not very suitable. Mai, the managing director of MEDS, wanted to rehouse the headquarters operation on a single site which would facilitate growth without the need to move in the near future. She wanted a prestige building on a prestige site in or near the same town as the current headquarters. She had in mind raising the funding to buy a suitable building, and leasing out space that was not currently needed.

Through the commercial property brokers MEDS used nationwide, MEDS was put in contact with Property Reconstructions of Particular Style (PROPS) Limited. Several years earlier PROPS had acquired a prestige site near the town in question comprising a run-down 1860s hotel building (once a private house) and extensive grounds with a river frontage. PROPS had immediately contracted Design and Build Solutions (DABS) Limited to prepare preliminary designs, and associated plans and cost estimates, for the first phase of an office park on the site, incorporating a stylish restoration of the old hotel and the adjacent river frontage. DABS' ownership was dominated by the same directors as PROPS. These links were not hidden, but they were played down by PROPS and DABS. The proposals prepared by DABS received outline planning approval, and PROPS had subsequently contracted DABS to prepared detailed designs, associated plans and cost estimates. These were near completion, and ongoing liaison with planning authorities had revealed no serious difficulties.

Given this progress, PROPS had negotiated a design and build management contract with DABS to construct the first phase of the development. This contract involved DABS acting as the designer and project manager, subcontracting the construction to other firms. DABS would be reimbursed for the cost of staff time plus overheads, currently estimated at £1.6 million. DABS would receive a fee which represented an 'appropriate minimum profit' of £0.1 million. DABS would also receive a bonus equal to 100% of the fee if the project was completed by the agreed target date (36 months after starting) for the agreed target capital cost of £11 million. A 5% reduction in the capital cost would double the bonus, with a pro rata linear relationship over the range ±5%. Completion 6 months early would also double the bonus, with a pro rata linear relationship over the range ±6 months. The bonus was capped on the high side by 300% of the fee and on the low side by zero. Thus the bonus for a simultaneous 5% reduction in capital cost and completion 6 months early would be 300% of the fee; a 5% increase in capital cost accompanied by completion 6 months early would attract a bonus of 100% of fee; and so on. Neither the DABS fee nor the DABS costs were at risk.

PROPS' original intention had been to finance the development itself, then sell the completed office park to a property company which specialized in leasing, or a mixture of leasing and unit sales. Unfortunately, PROPS' ability to finance such a venture on its own was killed by the recent financial failure of a similar project, set up as a separate company with overlapping directors, which was currently in receivership. The enquiry from MEDS was interpreted by PROPS as a welcome opportunity to sell off its interest in the development.

Following MEDS' initial contact, PROPS offered to sell its interest in the office park development for £4 million. This would include the contract for the first-phase redevelopment which PROPS had negotiated with DABS. That is, if everything went according to plan, the total capital cost for MEDS would be as follows:

	£m
Payment to PROPS	4.0
Target capital cost	11.0
DABS cost	1.6
DABS fee	0.1
DABS bonus	0.1
	16.8

As PROPS pointed out, if DABS were 6 months early and 5% under cost, the DABS bonus would increase to £0.3 million, but the 5% reduction in capital cost alone would be worth £0.55 million. PROPS also pointed out that increases beyond the target capital cost of £11 million were possible, and delays were possible. However, PROPS stressed that the potential for a 300% increase in the £0.1 million fee would provide a strong incentive to DABS to deliver under budget and ahead of schedule. Further, DABS had undertaken a risk analysis of the preliminary plans and associated costs used to obtain outline planning permission. As a result, DABS had suggested an 80% confidence level could be associated with both the £11 million capital cost estimate and the 36 month construction period estimate used as the basis for DABS' current target contract with PROPS.

MEDS' staff viewed the PROPS/DABS deal as 'the only game in town', and they were very keen to proceed. Mai immediately contacted MEDS' bankers, who were prepared to fund the PROPS deal for MEDS subject to a satisfactory due diligence review of PROPS' proposal.

A Consultant Is Hired

Following a friend's suggestion, endorsed by her bank, Mai approached a small but successful international management consultancy practice specializing in project risk management, for assistance. Shortly after this Ian, the consultancy's senior partner, was commissioned by MEDS to undertake a due diligence review of the DABS risk analysis on behalf of MEDS. Ian's contract anticipated about 5 days of his time, and capped it at 10 days.

Ian was an experienced management consultant in his late thirties. He had served his time as a gopher and as a senior consultant in a large international consultancy. He was a proficient spreadsheet jockey, and an effective team leader and marketeer. He had progressed to, and particularly enjoyed, difficult assignments with important 'soft' issues requiring novel perspectives. Ian saw himself as an integrator – someone who could put together different ideas, different perspectives, different agendas, and so on, to form a coordinated whole. Ian was the partner who had triggered the formation of his practice, and his integrator skills were an important part of the glue which held the practice together. Ian had many other strengths, but his integration skills are a defining characteristic for this tale.

Right from the beginning, Mai made it very clear to Ian that approval of the DABS risk analysis was expected. It was obvious to Ian that quite apart from commercial motives, Mai rather fancied the prospect of a large office in the restored hotel, with a view of the river. On his first morning everyone else Ian met on the MEDS staff seemed to have less overt but equally strong personal motives to favour accepting the PROPS/DABS proposal. They all emphasized how important the move would be for MEDS as a whole, in terms of corporate image, team spirit, and so on.

Ian's view of the DABS contract

This enthusiasm rather concerned Ian, not least because his initial impression of the DABS contract was that it was likely to involve substantial risks for MEDS. In Ian's experience a key fundamental risk in most projects is a failure to be clear about the motives of all key players, and a failure to align these motives via suitable contractual arrangements which embrace design (deliverable characteristics) as well as time, cost and resource usage. Therefore, a vital due diligence test for any project is ensuring that motivation is aligned for the key parties. The current offer by PROPS to MEDS seemed to fail this fundamental test in a way which was blindingly obvious to Ian.

PROPS was the supplier until a deal was done, then DABS became the supplier. The key motive from a PROPS/DABS viewpoint was maximizing income.

PROPS' income would be fixed if a deal were done. DABS income would not be fixed. What would matter most to DABS would be its costs (with overheads). DABS' fee would be icing on the cake. The bonus payments offered very limited incentives, in Ian's view. If the current proposition were accepted, DABS would in effect have a cost-plus contract with MEDS, and DABS would be motivated to maximize cost by stealth.

Key commercial motives from a MEDS viewpoint were high revenues from rented space and high-value accommodation for their own use, low operating costs, low capital costs, and short project duration, broadly in that order, but these should be balanced in a weighted manner which reflected MEDS' priorities in actual and opportunity cost terms.

What was required was an effective partnering agreement between MEDS and PROPS/DABS in which all parties perceived themselves as winners. If any party perceived themselves as a loser, all would become losers. This agreement must involve significant pain for DABS if they did not pursue *all* MEDS' objectives, and significant gain if they did. The drivers of these pain and gain incentives must be weighted to reflect the relative priorities of MEDS as defined by actual and opportunity costs for MEDS. Such a contract would need to be a better proposition for PROPS and DABS than their next best alternative. It should be in their interests to accept such a contract and pursue its execution in a way which would serve their interests as well as MEDS'. In short it was clear to Ian that MEDS needed to renegotiate a win-win contract with PROPS/DABS.

Ian's preliminary assessment of the DABS risk analysis

After this preliminary assessment of the DABS contract, Ian skimmed through a copy of the risk analysis for the preliminary plans undertaken by DABS which had been used to support the key figures in the contract. At first glance this was an impressive document, but to Ian's practised eye a number of basic shortcomings were readily apparent. The kind of analysis produced by DABS was rather similar to what he routinely found in working for other clients who were developing a risk management capability. It was *common* practice but it was not *best* practice.

For planning purposes and risk analysis purposes, the project had been broken down into several hundred component activities, and a large number of risks had been identified within this activity structure, with the top 50 risks separately highlighted. The risks considered were somewhat technical and tactical in nature. The softer or strategic risks were not addressed, nor were they clearly cited as scope assumptions. Potential variability in parameters was expressed exclusively in terms of triangular probability distributions. This suggested a rather mechanical process which might not have paid much attention to possible extreme values. Also, while the analysis referred to sets of risk sources that could give rise to variability in relation to each probability distribution, the basis for the various estimates of variability was not explained. For due diligence purposes, this lack of an audit trail was a clear problem.

Overall it was clear to Ian that the DABS risk analysis was focused on the evaluation of the net impact of all risks which the analysts were comfortable dealing with, rather than understanding which risks of a much broader set were most important and how these should be managed. The DABS report acknowledged there was scope for opportunity management which could reduce expected cost and risk via response generation and testing. However, this had not been addressed. The intent (hope) that it would happen seemed to be an underpinning assumption for the validity of the variability ranges in the DABS evaluation. Ian's misgivings about the basic form of the DABS contract merely reinforced the view that capturing any scope for opportunity management was critical to MEDS. DABS must be motivated to ensure this happened, it needed to have enough time, and it needed expert facilitation assistance. The risk of this not happening in the context of the current proposal was a key concern.

Ian's approach

By the end of his first day, Ian had a reasonable outline view of the key problem. He did not know how he was going to recommend resolving it, or how he was going to sell his recommendation. He did know he was going to have to start by selling MEDS and its bank a particular perspective for project risk management – his perspective. This was because what people mean by 'project risk management' is very ambiguous, and Ian was concerned that his client should have an appropriately sophisticated understanding of what was involved. Ian decided that he would need to include a general description of the project risk management process in his report. He would then structure his discussion and critique of the DABS risk analysis to reflect the phases of this process, before developing proposals to address the key issues. Ian's description of the project risk management process would need to be concise, and make clear reference to the origins and status of the process to promote this as an appropriate approach to take. The following section is based on material Ian prepared for his report.

A Framework For Project Risk Management

MEDS needed to understand the risks associated with the PROPS/DABS proposal, but its also needed to consider how these risks should be managed. This was best carried out by following a structured process which incorporated both evaluation and management of uncertainty using current best practice. Current common practice was not good enough.

In the UK, at an institution or association level, a directly relevant process was described by the *Project Risk Analysis and Management Guide* (*PRAM*), produced by the Association for Project Management (APM), developed by twenty members of an APM Project Risk Management Specific Interest Group working party (Simon, Hillson and Newland, 1997). The subsequent guide *Risk Analysis and Management of Projects* (RAMP) (Simon, 1998), produced by the Institution of Civil Engineering and the Faculty and Institute of Actuaries, describes a process that is similar to the PRAM process, broader in scope in some respects, less detailed in others. The US equivalent was Chapter 11 of *A Guide to the Project Management Body of Knowledge* (Project Management Institute, 2000), which reflected PRAM to a significant extent. In a construction context in the UK another relevant guide (Godfrey, 1996) had been published by the Construction Industry Research and Information Association (CIRIA). Whichever guide was adopted, the leading edge at a more detailed level as Ian saw it, was defined in the book *Project Risk Management: Process, Techniques and Insights* (Chapman and Ward, 1997) updated by Chapman and Ward (2000) and Chapman (2000b). (Chapters 4 and 6 of this book update these papers.) The book *Project Risk Management* elaborates the process described in Chapter 3 of the PRAM guide, and provides an operational framework for RAMP concerns. It had been reprinted six times, sales were worldwide, and a second edition was planned. Observations to follow would use this book as a conceptual basis and reference. The other publications mentioned above take a similar line, but with different emphasis, terminology and structures. Ian was very concerned about the emphasis his report adopted, although he did not say so in his report explicitly. Most people prefer a familiar terminology and structure, and Ian was no exception.

The guides indicated above, and Chapman and Ward (1997), reflect the shift from concern about the models and mathematics to concern for process and insight in the developments at the leading edge over the decade 1987 to 1997. The PRAM process has nine phases, outlined in Table 5.1. Each phase is usefully viewed as a project, the nine projects forming a programme for process management purposes. They must be implemented with some concurrence and overlap in an iterative (multiple pass) process, as illustrated by Figures 5.1 and 5.2.

Applied at any stage of a project's life cycle, effective and efficient use of risk management resources demands an iterative (multiple-pass) approach because we do not know when we start what will turn out to be important. A single-pass process invariably spends too much time on things that do not matter, and not enough time on things that matter a great deal. The objective of the first pass is to size and shape the problems to be addressed further in subsequent passes. To illustrate a typical risk management process, Figure 5.2 shows three complete iterations for illustrative purposes, and one sub-iteration between the estimation and evaluation phases. However, the process is unlikely to follow a set pattern because the most effective process depends on what earlier analysis uncovers.

Table 5.1—The nine phases of the PRAM risk management process (RMP)

Phases	Purposes
Define the project	Consolidate relevant existing information about the project. Fill in any gaps uncovered in the consolidation process
Focus the process	Scope and provide a strategic plan for the RMP. Plan the RMP at an operational level
Identify the issues	Identify where risk might arise. Identify what we might do about this risk, in proactive and reactive responses terms. Identify what might go wrong with our responses
Structure the issues	Test simplifying assumptions. Provide more complex structure when appropriate
Clarify **ownership**	Client/contractor allocation of ownership and management of risks and responses. Allocations of client risks to named individuals. Approval of contractor allocations
Estimate sources of variability	Identify areas of clear significant uncertainty. Identify areas of possible significant uncertainty
Evaluate overall implications	Synthesis and evaluation of the results of the estimation phase
Plan for implementation	Preparing base plans ready for implementation and associated risk management contingency plans
Manage implementation	Monitoring. Control. Responding to crises. Ongoing development of action plans for immediate implementation

Phases in the project risk management process

The first phase of the process is the 'define the project' phase: defining the project in a form suitable for risk management purposes. A decade ago most project management professionals would have seen this in terms of a suitable high-level activity structure summary and a related cost item structure. It is now clear that an activity structure is only one of six aspects which need consideration, the 'six Ws' (Chapman and Ward, 1997):

- Who – parties or players involved
- Why – motives of the parties
- What – design or deliverable
- Which way – activities
- Wherewithal – resources
- When – project schedules

All six aspects are interconnected as indicated in Figure 5.3, and all six aspects need joint consideration in the pursuit of project performance. This includes con-

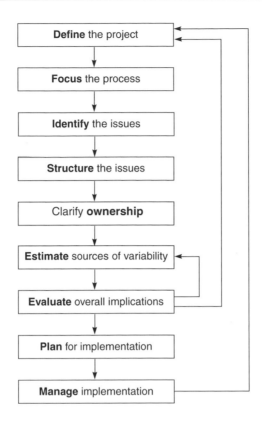

Figure 5.1—Project risk management process (PRAM).

sideration of appropriate and effective trade-offs between cost, time and quality. Quality involves performance measures other than capital cost and time, like operating cost (including maintenance and periodic refurbishment) over the life cycle of the delivered product. Simultaneous improvement in all three areas of cost, time and quality should be achievable in early risk management exercises concerned with improving risk efficiency (a form of value management), but will not usually be achievable later when managing realized project risk, and it is important to be clear what appropriate degrees of freedom are available at any stage in the risk management process and project life cycle. Any attempt to pre-serve performance in all three areas in the face of a realized problem usually results in uncontrolled degradation of all three. In a deterministic context (no uncertainty), we can focus on what is most important. For risk management purposes, when anticipating or reacting to realized problems it is also vital to be clear about what is least important – what can be sacrificed.

Concurrent with the 'define the project' phase is a second phase, 'focus the process'. This is a separate phase in the PRAM phase structure because it is so important, although it is not even mentioned in some risk management

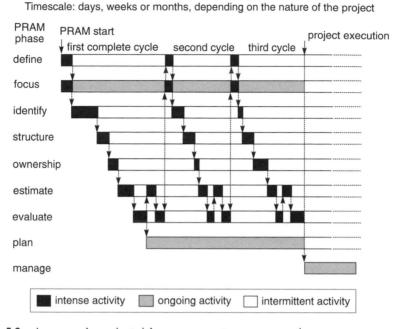

Figure 5.2—An example project risk management process over time.

frameworks. This phase involves focusing the generic risk management process to the particular application in hand for a particular project, what might be thought of as 'planning the planning'. A decade ago many people involved in project risk management were seeking the best way to do all project risk management. It is now clear that developing the best risk management process for a particular project is a mini project in its own right, requiring attention to the six Ws of the *process* (distinct from the six Ws of the project) and everything else we know about good project management. The particular project risk management process applied to a particular analysis of a particular project should be shaped by key drivers, like who wants it done (buyer or supplier), why (e.g. for internal initial planning or for due diligence), where the project is in its life cycle, how experienced the people doing it are, and so on. Key fundamental risks to achieving effective risk management can arise from a failure to be clear about the motives of the players. For example, a threat perceived by a buyer (owner, client, employer) may constitute an opportunity for a supplier (contractor, project manager) if the motivations of different project parties are not compatible, and risk management is not a joint effort. If project-related motivations are not compatible between parties like a buyer and a supplier, then separate attention to risk management by each party is essential. As another example, risk management processes to support a project and risk management processes to audit a project may be quite different.

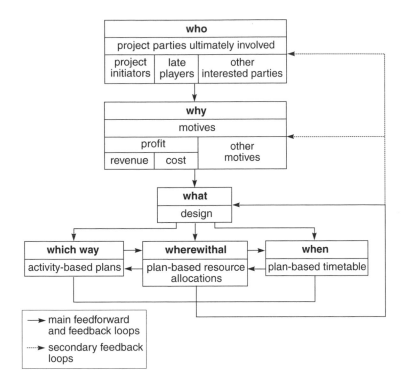

Figure 5.3—The project definition process.

The third phase of the process is 'identify the issues', the sources of uncertainty (risks) and responses, within an appropriate basic structure. For example, major risks which change the name of the game and need to be managed separately need to be identified separately, but minor risks which can be managed collectively need to be grouped (not ignored).

The fourth phase is 'structure the issues'. It involves testing the robustness of the structuring assumptions which are part of the earlier phases, and some additional assessments. For example, are there important causal or statistical dependencies? Are there possible general responses which can deal with sets of risks, perhaps including unidentified risks, as distinct from responses which are specific to particular problems? It is important to develop general responses to build flexibility into the overall strategy, in the sense of the ability to deal with any combination of known or unknown risk.

The fifth phase is concerned with 'clarification of ownership'. It involves developing and testing the robustness of risk ownership in financial terms and in management terms (which may be different). It involves testing contract strategy initially (on a first pass), and subsequently ensuring that all risks have named managers. This is a separate phase in the PRAM process because it is so important. It is an explicit part of other phases in most other risk management process descriptions.

The sixth phase is 'estimate sources of variability', in terms of base or starting point values, and potential variability. Usually variability is addressed in terms of quantitative risk analysis with a limited focus, given a set of conditions or scope assumptions. Initial passes are concerned with sizing variability and finding out what matters. Later passes are about testing alternative responses to important potential problems. Final passes may be about justifying key sensitive decisions. Data is inevitably scarce or non-existent. Estimates of variability are a way of systematically integrating the best judgements of available people in order to make decisions consistent with the best judgements available in a cost-effective manner. There are no right or wrong answers. But quality can be judged in terms of internal consistency, process, use of what data there is, and so on.

The seventh phase is 'evaluate overall implications'. This involves putting together individual sources of uncertainty, including those not quantified, to understand the overall impact. This is closely coupled to 'estimate', especially in early exploratory passes. It is important to express results in a way which shows clearly what matters and what does not matter. Analysis that has been built bottom-up needs to be interpreted top-down in a selective manner. For example, the way sources of uncertainty add to form a whole is usefully portrayed using a nested structure of cumulative probability curves which shows half a dozen sources at each stage like the example in Figure 5.4. This provides a built-in sensitivity analysis. It allows the analyst to understand what is driving results, and to manage the risks in terms of responses, while building the analysis bottom-up. It then allows the analyst to explain the final proposed approach top-down. For example, risk 5 in Figure 5.4 is the most significant, risk 2 relatively minor, so attention needs to focus on risk 5 first.

The purpose of the 'evaluate' phase is ultimately to verify a view of the project which allows progress to the next phase. However, until the final pass of the 'evaluate' phase passes this test, the purpose of evaluation includes:

- Guiding iterations back through earlier phases
- Reviewing base plans and contingency plans to achieve the least expected cost or most expected profit for a given level of risk (risk efficiency)
- Reviewing base plans and contingency plans to achieve the least expected cost or most expected profit the organization can afford to go for, at a suitable level of risk (risk balance)

Effective project risk management is about achieving risk efficiency and risk balance. Comfort is a by-product, not a primary purpose for the process. The 'plan for implementation' phase is about using the risk analysis to develop detailed base plans and contingency plans for project implementation. The 'manage implementation' phase is concerned with ongoing monitoring, controlling, reacting to crises

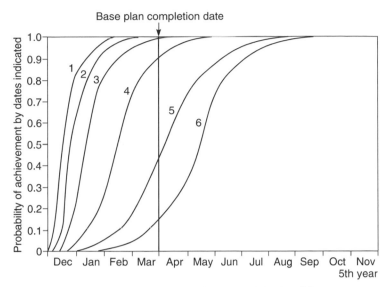

Probability curves show the cumulative effect on the following risks:

1. Yard not available or mobilization delays   4. Material delivery delays
2. Construction problems/adverse weather   5. Industrial disputes
3. Subcontracted nodes delivery delays   6. Delayed award of fabrication contract

Notes
• The curves assume a minimum fabrication period of 20 months
• No work is transferred off site to improve progress
• No major fire, explosion or other damage

Figure 5.4—Initial level output for an offshore project.

(significant unanticipated problems), and rolling forward detailed action plans as the project proceeds.

In his report Ian concluded this outline of the project risk management process with a brief note about expected values, probability distributions, and the F^3 factor. This was similar to the material presented in Eddy's tale (Chapter 4), so it is not repeated here.

A Critical Assessment Of Current Common Practice

In the days following his appointment to the MEDS brief, Ian worked with MEDS' staff to introduce them to the key ideas involved in the risk management process framework outlined in his report. He also spent time with DABS' staff discussing their risk analysis, improving his understanding of their approach, and developing the next section of his report, which would present a critical assessment of the DABS analysis. It was clear to Ian that DABS' staff had put a lot of effort into their risk analysis, that they probably believed they knew what they were doing, and that they would not take kindly to having their analysis criticized. He was also mindful that if the deal went ahead, MEDS would have to work as a partner with DABS, so he did not want to sour relationships. However, MEDS had to understand the shortcomings of the DABS analysis, and the implications for MEDS. He also knew that DABS would need to come to terms with these implications and shortcomings if a deal was done. Ian proposed to square the circle in his report by portraying the DABS risk analysis as favourably as possible in relation to common current practice, but clearly portraying the defects common in current practice which MEDS needed to understand in order to draw conclusions. He wanted to avoid detailed arguments with DABS, but provide MEDS with clear grounds to agree to differ.

To begin as gently as possible, Ian indicated in his report that DABS staff he had talked to about their risk analysis seemed to understand most of the key issues. He made it clear they had the necessary practical understanding of what the project entailed. Ian then indicated that he found the DABS approach 'understandable given DABS' commercial position'. He elaborated by pointing out that DABS has an agreement in place with PROPS which is very favourable to DABS. It is a cost-plus-plus contract, with incentive payments tied to the second plus, and no risk on the costs (including overheads) or fee (the first plus). DABS would want to protect that position. Ian characterized the DABS risk analysis approach overall as understandable in the context of what most organizations tend to do in a similar situation if they have avoided an ambiguous qualitative approach (based on PIMs as discussed in Chapter 4), but they do not have reasonably sophisticated up-to-date risk management expertise. Most of the failings relative to up-to-date best practice were consistent with the motives of DABS. He did not wish to infer deliberate bias, but he needed to point out that unconscious bias is inevitable and should be expected. In discussions about this issue with MEDS staff, Ian carefully and explicitly avoided the word 'reasonable', and the word 'misleading', although he might have used them liberally. Ian indicated that in his view, the DABS estimate of project duration would probably be of the right order of magnitude, *provided* DABS was properly motivated to reflect MEDS' interests and more up-to-date risk management processes were put in place. A duration of 36 months was feasible, but optimistic given the current proposition. The DABS target cost estimate in the context of the current proposition was not a credible estimate for MEDS to use to make decisions without a major adjustment.

Following these preliminary comments, Ian then continued his report with a detailed critique of the DABS risk analysis. He explicitly compared the DABS approach with the nine-phase risk management process he had set out in the previous section of his report. This critique compared the DABS analysis with each phase of the PRAM process in turn, elaborating on key concepts where he felt this was important. The following sections closely follow what Ian drafted for his report.

The focus phase

The 'focus the process' phase of the PRAM project risk management process is about aligning the methodology used to the purpose of the analysis. The DABS risk analysis told a story which is consistent with its position. DABS wanted to convince other parties that its target cost and duration estimates were appropriate as a basis to proceed. These estimates were appropriate as a basis to proceed from a DABS perspective, but not from a MEDS perspective. In short, they would say that, wouldn't they, as the saying goes. Anyone with enough cynicism to survive in the real world ought to expect this.

The define phase

The DABS analysis focused on the project activities and linked cost items. It ignored other aspects of the six Ws structure (and the associated project life cycle structure). Ten years ago this would have been leading-edge practice, but it was seriously defective in terms of current best practice, particularly from a buyer's perspective. It was vital to consider the impact of design (quality) issues. And DABS failure to do so was a show-stopper.

The level of activity decomposition chosen by DABS, with several hundred activities identified, was much too detailed to see the wood for the trees. A target of 5–10 activities, and an upper limit of 50 activities, would be more appropriate for a project of this size.

The identify phase

DABS identified a large number of risks using a top 50 approach. This provided useful focus, but it was not clear that the residual was accounted for adequately. Risks were assumed to be managed by those responsible for the associated work at a detailed level with no justification for these assumptions. Risks should be explicitly structured into composite or aggregate sets, given feasible responses, and their collective impacts assessed. The failure to do this implied optimistic bias.

The risks considered were somewhat technical and tactical in nature. Softer or strategic risks were not addressed, nor were they cited as conditions or scope assumptions. This was a very serious source of optimistic bias. Only one risk-response structure was used for identification purposes, a simple branching model for poor ground conditions. Project-wide risks were considered separately from risks specific to particular project components. The way this was done was appropriate for fairly straightforward risks. However, it was not used very much.

The structure phase

A 'structure' phase equivalent was not really visible in the material available, with the exception of specifying a very small amount of statistical dependence in a way which was not clearly defined and not easy to interpret in causal terms. This was another source of serious optimistic bias. There might be scope for substantial development of effective general responses, building in flexibility. However, there was no evidence of this having been done to date, or of it being likely to happen as things currently stood. This was a wasted opportunity of considerable magnitude and a big risk. It needed to be sized.

The ownership phase

The 'ownership' phase needed attention at the MEDS–DABS/PROPS interface. DABS had addressed particular partnership contracts for its prime contractors and subcontractors, but what was proposed did not look very effective. For a partnering approach to work properly, at any level, the partners need a significant post-contract working partnership period to bring each other on board before work begins. There was no reason at present to believe this would happen. This was an important risk. Fair weather partnerships, which only work when every-thing is going well, are inefficient in general, and they are ineffective as well when storm conditions arise. Partnering is just an added cost if it is not done properly. This risk needed to be managed at a high level. There might be scope to improve the target contract approach adopted by DABS with respect to its prime contrac-tors and subcontractors along the lines of page 191).

The estimate phase

DABS' estimating involved clear evidence of lack of statistical sophistication and leading-edge risk management expertise. Variability was addressed in terms of quantitative risk analysis with a limited focus, given a set of conditions or scope assumptions. To assess the plausibility of estimates of expected values and ranges, we need to consider the effect of known unknowns, unknown unknowns, bias, and the size of the corresponding F^3 factors, F_k, F_u and F_b.

Sources of bias

The DABS analysis made exclusive use of triangular distributions for input. This did not much matter in terms of the direct mathematical implications, but it did matter in terms of suggesting a fairly mechanical approach which could produce significant bias when estimating parameters. For example, consider a triangular distribution with an optimistic (10 percentile) value of 90, a most likely (most probable) value of 100, and a pessimistic (90 percentile) value of 140. What we are attempting to approximate in such a case is a long, low right-hand probability tail, probably asymptotic. It is not clear that a statistically unsophisticated facilitator and data provider will capture such a tail effectively if this approach is always used. DABS always used this approach. Optimistic bias with respect to the assessed high-side variability of significant order can be anticipated in such a case. Additionally, optimistic bias on the range estimate also generates linked optimistic bias on the expected value estimate. Some of this lack of statistical sophistication matters in terms of the direct mathematical implications as well. For example, the term 'most likely estimate' was sometimes used to mean the median, and the median was used as if it was an expected value. This matters at a direct mathematical level as well as suggesting related estimation bias if a realistic view of the uncertainty ranges involved is addressed.

Like many practising risk analysts who lack statistical sophistication, DABS analysts interpreted results in a way which clearly confused these three parameters (expected value or mean, median, and most likely value). Given the very limited variability associated with the target cost and completion dates by DABS, the difference was not very great in mathematical terms. But this variability was seriously understated, and the difference was very important in general. This was one indication of a lack of statistical sophistication in the DABS risk analysis. The overall resulting probability distribution for cost looked very tight, with a 5–95 percentile range that was very narrow and probably very optimistic, and a significantly wider 0–100 percentile range that was certainly even more optimistic. Possible reasons and adjustments had been discussed with MEDS staff, but they amounted to a need to refine DABS' models to overcome a combination of:

- Limited causal modelling of knock-on effects
- Limited modelling of complex relationships of any kind
- Limited attention to extreme events
- Limited statistical dependence modelling in a form linked to causal explanations
- Limited modelling of key specific sources of risk

With the exception of the tactical nature of the risks considered and the lack of statistical dependence, the net effect of these shortcomings was a pessimistic bias on project duration which probably cancels out much of the optimistic bias associated with assumed lack of dependence and forms of optimistic bias noted earlier, apart from *force majeure* extreme circumstances. This was in part why the 36 ± 6 months remained a plausible estimate given appropriate attention. However, the net effect of all these shortcomings was massive optimistic bias on the cost side. In effect, the DABS models ignored the fact that in practice when things go wrong we respond to the delay implications by revising our plans, selecting more expensive options to get back on track. As users of simple PERT models (Moder and Philips, 1970) since the late 1950s should have realized by now, such models automatically encourage optimistic bias with respect to activity duration variability estimates to avoid what would otherwise look like a highly risky timetable (because the model ignores responses). This automatically induces massive optimistic bias into associated cost estimates by ignoring the cost of responses, and transferring common optimistic independence variability bias. DABS was by no means alone in experiencing this problem. It was a problem for many organizations who do not have the sound commercial motivation for such bias which DABS enjoys. However, MEDS could not afford to believe such models, no matter who used them in the belief they produce unbiased results. Such models are no better as approximations to reality than Lewis Carroll's *Alice in Wonderland*, and it was vital that MEDS recognized their fairy-tale nature.

An effective counter to optimistic bias in a first-pass quantitative analysis is to adopt a very simple minimalist approach (Chapman and Ward, 2000) as discussed in Chapter 4. This simple minimalist approach is sophisticated in the sense that it builds in pessimistic bias to minimize the risk of dismissing as unimportant risks which more information might reveal as important, and it is set in the context of an iterative approach which leads to more refined estimates wherever potentially important risks are revealed. Sophistication does not require complexity. It requires constructive simplicity, increasing complexity only when it is useful to do so.

So far, this section of Ian's report had primarily addressed sources of bias associated with the form of the DABS models and the way associated probability distributions were assessed. The aggregate effect of all these sources of bias might be captured in an approximate way by applying an F_b factor to results. In the absence of time to redo the DABS capital cost risk analysis, Ian indicated that it was not appropriate to estimate an F_b value, but a plausible range might be 1.2 to 2 or 3, given the current proposition. This plausible range should be held confidential to MEDS, although the reasons given above could be revealed to PROPS/DABS.

The impact of exclusions

Even more important than the impact of bias is the impact of known unknowns, or exclusions, which are captured in an F_k factor. DABS' estimates involve a number of exclusions. A complete analysis was not attempted, but some examples illustrated what is involved. One exclusion was unusual market conditions. Abnormal market 'boom effects' on labour, materials and other components are an obvious source of extra cost. Discussions with DABS staff suggested that price increases 2% or 3% above inflation would be viewed as a boom. This exclusion was worded by DABS to potentially exclude downside variations. It was therefore asymmetric. Abnormal variations upwards would count, but not abnormal variations downwards. As departures more than 2% or 3% either way are almost inevitable, this builds in a biased upward adjustment. For example, suppose the cost distribution faced were as indicated in Table 5.2. The expected upward adjustment for an exclusion operating for +5% (interpreted as +2.5% to +7.5%) and above would be 7.5% (values below +5% are all zero impact). This is clearly significant. An asymmetric probability distribution could make a much larger expected percentage and expected F_k plausible. And even if the expected F_k is small, the range is clearly an important source of risk when considering joint downside scenarios.

Another exclusion was any client-induced design changes. This risk was a certainty, the question being one of degree. It was ignored by the DABS estimates. MEDS staff had confirmed that the DABS approach to design was explicitly driven by minimizing capital costs, without visible regard for operating costs, based on a vision of quality which reflected initial rental income and a market price for the property based on initial rental income. Any changes imposed by MEDS now would significantly impact the capital cost. Some major changes would be essential, and further major changes desirable. This would be an ongoing source of tension between MEDS and DABS as the proposed contract currently stood, in terms of quality control as well as change management. In effect, 'changes in client brief' and 'quality control' would be the visible points of realization of the show-stopper risk 'lack of alignment of motivation'. If this issue

Table 5.2—Upward cost 'ratchet' model

Variation (%)	Probability	Product for time variation
−20	0.1	
−15	0.1	
−10	0.1	
−5	0.1	
0	0.1	
5	0.1	0.5
10	0.1	1.0
15	0.1	1.5
20	0.1	2.0
25	0.1	2.5
Expected outcome (% increase in cost)		7.5

were not addressed, the appropriate F_k factor was very difficult to assess, but an expected value of 1.5 to 3 or even 4 might be a plausible guestimate. Its exact size did not matter. It simply would not be sensible to proceed with PROPS' current proposal. It was important to keep any view of F_k confidential to MEDS, but equally important to explain to PROPS/DABS that MEDS has to address F_k to assess the expected cost to MEDS, and what MEDS concerns are. It might be useful to focus on these concerns rather than F_b, to avoid challenging DABS' credibility in a direct way.

Further adjustments for unknown unknowns via an F_u factor are particularly difficult in general, and not possible here given limited exposure to the project and the players.

A combined adjustment – the F^3 factor

Each of the factors F_b, F_k and F_u are important, and it could be useful to address them separately, but their combined effect, F^3, is the bottom line. F^3 cannot be ignored if effective understanding of uncertainty is required, whether or not specific distributions are used for each component factor. It was difficult to identify a specific value or distribution for F^3, but putting earlier F_b and F_k estimates together with an allowance for F_u then a plausible range was 1.5 to 10, and a plausible most likely F^3 value was 2 or 3 (to the nearest integer). Every project which has doubled in cost had an implicit F^3 of 2. Lots of projects have experienced an F^3 of 2 or more. Some have experienced an F^3 of 10 or more. Very few projects have had an implicit F^3 less than 1. MEDS needed to overcome the obvious problems associated with lack of congruent motivation, and then give very careful thought to the F^3 factor. The question was not, Do you believe DABS or not? The question was, If you fix the unacceptable lack of congruent motivation, how much is the project going to cost MEDS, and will the expenditure provide good value in terms of MEDS' use of the property, rental income and operating costs?

An effective MEDS–DABS partnership should be able to drive down and control F^3. This would probably still lead to a larger expected cost than the current target suggested. This would not indicate a more expensive project, it would imply that project risk was better understood. Often projects whose cost has doubled or trebled, or worse, have large implicit F^3 factors because those involved refuse to face or reveal the reality. And the reality is often that motives for different parties were not clear, not reconciled, or not compatible. PROPS/DABS had very clear motives which were not congruent with MEDS' motives in terms of the current proposition. Proceeding with this lack of congruence of motives would inevitably lead to a major capital cost overrun coupled to quality control problems and on-going operating cost problems, a disaster which MEDS should not contemplate.

However, MEDS had no need to contemplate such a disaster because MEDS' motives and PROPS/DABS' motivation could be made congruent in a redefinition of the agreement in a win-win manner.

The evaluate phase

Apart from shortcomings in the identification of risks and estimation of variability in cost estimates, the evaluation of this data provided further evidence of a lack of sophistication in the DABS approach to quantitative risk analysis. Only the final combined effect of all sources of uncertainty was shown. There were no figures showing how the various sources of uncertainty contributed to the overall picture. Consequently, it was difficult to learn much from the results of the analysis. Perhaps more importantly, it suggested that the DABS analysts had not addressed understanding the results as they built them up, or managing the risks and responses in the process. Rather than an iterative learning process, the DABS risk analysis was a fairly linear process designed to confirm an established position, as suggested on page 177 under the focus phase.

Formulating An Incentive Contract

Ian was well aware of the need to ensure, if at all possible, that a solution is available before convincing a client they have a show-stopping problem. He explained his solution along the following lines in the third section of his report.

The target cost concept used to define the MEDS–PROPS/DABS contract involves limited incentives, which are unbalanced, with negligible risk sharing. It provides a financial incentive for DABS with respect to cost and time defined in terms of a bonus. However, both the cost and time incentives are too small to motivate DABS, and even these limited incentives are likely to be lost due to upward cost drift and delays. If DABS were to hit a major problem, the likely increase in overheads associated with DABS' cost would provide significant compensation for any decrease in bonus. For all practical purposes, this is a cost-plus contract. Overhead on DABS' cost is what really matters for DABS. The bonus payments are just noise.

The DABS contract is a conventional target contract designed to provide incentive without reference to balancing the incentives in terms of all the drivers of interest to the buyer (client, owner or employer). In this case these drivers include performance criteria reflecting capital cost, operating costs, revenue and delivery date. They also include risk, the relative abilities of the buyer and the supplier (seller or project manager) to manage and take the risk (threats and opportunities) and the degree of motivation to work as a collaborative partner.

Principles guiding risk sharing

In terms of the available range of incentive contracts, it may be useful to see this conventional target contract as level 1 in terms of sophistication. A second level of sophistication of incentive contracts, addressing effective risk sharing, has been explored at length. For example, more than a decade ago, Ward and Chapman had UK government research council funding to explore this issue for three years (1987–89). This resulted in a CIRIA book (Curtis, Ward and Chapman, 1991) and several papers (Ward, Chapman and Curtis, 1991; Ward and Chapman, 1994a, 1995). The thrust of a risk-sharing approach to target contracts a decade ago was developing an understanding of the relative ability to manage risk and the relative ability to take risk. Basic conclusions of this work can be summarized in terms of three points:

- Fixed price contracts are best if the supplier is best able to manage the risk, the supplier can afford to take the risk, and the buyer can prespecify what they want.
- Cost-plus contracts are best if the buyer is best able to manage the risk, the buyer can afford to take the risk, and the buyer cannot prespecify what they want.
- Any intermediate situation requires appropriate risk sharing with appropriate incentives.

This implies breaking a contract into three parts, one corresponding to each of the three circumstances described above, or breaking a project into phases to achieve similar ends. These principles clearly need to be applied here, suggesting significant risk sharing with balanced incentives ought to be a feature of a revised proposal. However, this is not the limit of what can be done.

Another basic conclusion of the risk-sharing research cited was that 'as soon as a contract comes out of the drawer, all the parties are in trouble'. Current research in progress (Chapman, 2000b, as developed in Chapter 6) suggests that this involves several important sets of issues not addressed earlier, which apply to internal contracts (e.g. between a project manager and the project manager's own organization) as well as external contracts. One is the need to ensure that good luck and opportunity are managed proactively and effectively. A second is the need to expose any ambiguity about the motives of all relevant parties in relation to all available performance measures that matter, and ensure that explicit contracts align all the relevant motives for all the key parties in a balanced manner.

Incorporating trade-offs

Operationally it may be convenient for a buyer to freeze the performance specification in terms of one or more measures. For example, if MEDS knew exactly what was best in terms of quality for the delivered office park in terms of revenue, operating costs and the physical characteristics of the property required to deliver this quality, and delivery of a specification involved no uncertainty, MEDS could prespecify what it wants, removing the associated degrees of freedom. All risks would then have to be managed in terms of trade-offs between capital cost and duration. If MEDS also knew what was 'best' in terms of duration, risk could be reduced to a capital cost dimension. However MEDS was clearly not in a position to do this.

If two or more degrees of freedom are involved, the contract has to ensure that pain and gain are experienced by the supplier in a manner which reflects both the implications for the buyer and the buyer's desired trade-offs between the degrees of freedom in project performance. This provides congruence of motives so that a supplier acting in its best interests will also act in the best interests of the buyer. The basic principle is very old basic management theory. But it does not seem to have received attention in this particular way in a contracting context when two or more degrees of freedom need to be used, because all performance criteria involve important interrelated uncertainty.

In the present context, MEDS might start by taking the quality level as given, excluding operating costs, and asking what level of quality MEDS wants in terms of expected operating costs. The balance between operating cost components may also need analysis together with income and other considerations. These complications are ignored at present. Expected operating cost then needs to be related to expected capital cost and expected project duration to identify feasible trade-offs as best as MEDS can estimate these relationships in order to identify an optimum level for all three and related trade-off rates. These relationships would be uncertain for obvious reasons, but they still need to be explicitly addressed. It would not be cost-effective to hold DABS to a specific minimum quality. Problems realized late in the day may make it cost-effective in terms of MEDS' interests to decrease quality, rather than increasing capital cost or delay, and it was important to motivate DABS to aim above absolute minimums. What is more effective than minimum quality limits is to develop an incentive payment scheme with quality as a driver which motivates DABS to manage trade-offs between capital cost, time, and quality in a way which reflects MEDS' interests.

Risk sharing and triggers

The simplest scheme incorporating risk sharing involves a 50:50 sharing of variation in a performance measure relative to a trigger value based on MEDS' best estimate of the actual cost implications for MEDS of any changes. For example, under a 50:50 risk-sharing arrangement in respect of capital cost, MEDS would pay DABS only half of any increase in cost above the capital cost trigger value, and MEDS would pay DABS half of any decrease in cost below the trigger value. The trigger value in this case should be the estimated expected value of the relevant performance criterion. It is important to use the term 'trigger' as a parameter defining the payment scheme which is not a target in the aspirational sense. The word 'target' should be reserved for an aspirational target with a fairly low probability of achievement. The distinction becomes very important in terms of the way the duration of a sequence of contracts is handled (as addressed in Chapter 6) and it is very important in terms of balancing different incentive measures.

Once a trigger value and a scale of incentive payments for quality are defined, a similar approach can be taken to time (delay) and capital cost, using 50:50 sharing in both cases for the financial consequences of deviation from the trigger (expected) values. The partners (MEDS and PROPS/DABS) would need to work together on this and agree the results. If the agreed approach involved trigger (expected) values for time, cost and quality which reflect an optimal balance for MEDS, and if DABS had an incentive payment scheme in terms of each performance criterion which reflected exactly the cost to MEDS of deviations from trigger values scaled down by 50%, then DABS should act as if it were MEDS when managing the uncertainty. And DABS will be taking 50% of the risk.

However, this basic approach would feed 50% of the variation in DABS' own costs (plus overheads) back to DABS as part of the capital cost risk sharing if DABS had a cost-plus contract for its costs, as at present. This introduces a potential flaw in the approach. If DABS is supposed to be acting in MEDS' interests, this feedback unbalances the scheme, in the sense that DABS would still be motivated to spend more on its own staff cost and overheads than serves the best interests of MEDS. The simplest solution is to insist that the MEDS–DABS contract for DABS' costs (plus overheads) is fixed price, based on the expected level of DABS effort given the trigger values for capital cost, operating cost and duration. This would maintain the strict alignment of relative importance for capital cost, operating cost, and duration.

Balanced risk sharing

However, if the negotiated risk-sharing ratio were moved from 50:50 to say 40:60, with 60% of the variations in MEDS' overall cost from expected value taken by MEDS and 40% taken by DABS, it might be argued that a 60:40 share of DABS' own cost variations would be a reasonable second-order adjustment. That is, if DABS picks up 40% of the overall project risk faced by MEDS, a tit-for-tat suggests that MEDS should pick up 40% of the risk faced by DABS in terms of DABS' own costs. One implication of this second-order adjustment is the way it balances risk sharing and motivation with different risk-sharing ratios for different costs. The more of MEDS' risk PROPS/DABS are prepared to take, the more of PROPS/DABS' risk MEDS is prepared to take. In the limit, if PROPS/DABS take 100% of MEDS' risk, MEDS would grant a cost-plus contract to DABS for its effort under this regime. Under no other conditions would MEDS grant a cost-plus contract to DABS. The current proposal involves a cost-plus contract for DABS' effort (MEDS takes all DABS' risk), but PROPS/DABS take virtually none of MEDS' risk.

A 10:90 ratio is the minimum level of risk sharing which makes sense from a MEDS perspective. That is, PROPS/DABS should take at least 10% of MEDS' risk. This minimum level is essential to ensure PROPS/DABS are motivated to some extent towards MEDS' objectives. It could be argued that a 100:0 ratio is the sensible place to start for a contract like this. That is, MEDS should have a fixed price contract in relation to all relevant costs, with PROPS/DABS taking 100% of the risk on MEDS' cost. This is a plausible scenario, consistent with the thrust of the UK government's private finance initiative (PFI) and many related developments. However, the key issue was not risk-sharing to reduce variability of costs, it was the alignment of motives in a balanced way which the balanced risk-sharing ratios provide. Table 5.3 shows an illustrative incentive contract based on a 40:60 risk sharing ratio (as a plausible middle-ground position and starting point for negotiation) as used in Ian's report. PROPS/DABS' numbers cited on page 165 were used to define B, C and D trigger values. The trigger value for A is defined by an associated £0.5 million operating cost estimate. D and E involve suggested increased payments by MEDS to initiate negotiations with concessions: a fee increase for DABS from £0.1 million to £0.5 million, and a £5 million price for PROPS instead of £4 million.

In Table 5.3 the risk-sharing ratios are assumed to be negotiable, but not separately. The incentives are balanced. The 40% figure might be revised to any value in the range 100% to 10%. So might the revised fee to DABS and the revised purchase price to PROPS. The £1 million increase in purchase price for PROPS and the £0.4 million increase in fee to DABS would have to be linked to the risk sharing accepted by PROPS/DABS. However, an increase in these terms for PROPS/DABS of the order of £1.4 million should be a very attractive approach if their initial figures were even remotely viable. And if it bought the alignment of motivation implied, it would be a bargain for MEDS. The key was to give PROPS/DABS a significant portion of the risk in a way which reflects MEDS' actual and opportunity costs for delay, in relation to similarly defined risk sharing for capital costs, and operating costs. This would ensure that DABS was motivated to act as if they were MEDS when assessing trade-offs. The current proposal involved negligible risk sharing and perverse incentives. The lack of risk sharing was important, but the perverse incentives guaranteed perverse outcomes. Perverse outcomes were not a risk in the sense that they were uncertain. They were a

Table 5.3—An example of a balanced incentive contract

Trigger	Possible trigger value	Risk-sharing ratio DABS:MEDS (%)	Payment arrangement	Commentary
A. Operating costs Expected operating cost associated with current design specification	£0.5m	40:60	PROPS/DABS pay MEDS 40% of the operating cost above the trigger value. MEDS pays PROPS/DABS 40% of any cost reduction below the trigger value	MEDS provides PROPS/DABS with a very strong operating cost incentive. This incentive would be balanced in relation to the capital cost and completion date incentives. A withholding scheme would be used until performance was established. There would be no capping. At present PROPS/DABS have no financial incentive of this kind
B Completion date Expected completion date associated with current plans	36 months	40:60	PROPS/DABS pay MEDS 40% of the MEDS opportunity cost of any delay above the trigger value. MEDS pays PROPS/DABS 40% of any cost saving due to early completion	MEDS provides PROPS/DABS with a delivery date incentive which is balanced in relation to the capital cost and the operating cost incentives. At present PROPS/DABS have no financial incentive of this kind
C. Capital cost Expected capital cost associated with the target cost	£11m	40:60	MEDS pays PROPS/DABS 60% of the cost above the trigger value. MEDS is the beneficiary of 60% of any cost reduction below the trigger value	MEDS provides PROPS/DABS with a very strong incentive to manage opportunities and reduce risks associated with capital cost to MEDS, which is balanced with completion dates and operating cost incentives. There is no capping. At present PROPS/DABS have no effective incentives of this kind
D. DABS costs Expected cost billed to MEDS (best estimate of actual outcome)	£1.6m	60:40	MEDS pays DABS a fee of £0.5m. MEDS pays PROPS/DABS 40% of DABS' costs above the trigger value. MEDS has its DABS bill reduced by 40% of any cost saving below the trigger value	MEDS makes the expected cost-plus fee outcome for DABS more attractive, to directly reflect the risk DABS will be taking. The fee is increased from £0.1m to £0.5m. DABS takes 60% of the cost risk associated with variations in DABS' effort from the agreed expected level. At present DABS has no financial incentives to control its own costs as paid for by MEDS
E. Payment to PROPS	N/A	N/A	MEDS pays PROPS £5m	The purchase price paid by MEDS to PROPS is increased from the proposed £4m to £5m, to reflect the risk sharing PROPS is now involved in via DABS

sure thing. Ambiguity was hiding them. But they were rocks hidden by a fog from
the view of an approaching ship, not just possible rocks.

Under the illustrative scheme in Table 5.3, PROPS/DABS would be significantly better off unless they did not believe they could deliver what was acceptable to MEDS within agreed estimates. If PROPS/DABS refuse to negotiate such
a contract, this would provide convincing proof of the need for it. If PROPS/
DABS were to accept such a contract, PROPS/DABS and MEDS should all be
better off. This was the purpose of a partnering approach. If an acceptable deal
with PROPS/DABS could be reached, the balanced incentive and risk sharing
(BIARS) approach outlined above could be applied by DABS to its contractors,
to further improve the position for DABS and MEDS, and to protect the viability
of the scheme as a whole. Where a series of activities is involved, the new features
of the approach at this level include ensuring good luck does not get lost at activity
interfaces. Normal practice means delays are passed on, but potential early com-
pletions are not exploited. Instead of swings and roundabouts it is all roundabouts, driving time and cost upwards. The mechanics are similar to the ratchet
effect associated with market price variations (page 180). They are discussed
directly in Chapter 6. This is a form of bias in the sense that it is a reason why cost
and time overrun. It is also a lost opportunity which needs to be managed.

The Way Forward

Ian was well aware of the risks attached to a breakdown in negotiations between
MEDS and PROPS/DABS. If MEDS staff were correct in their assessment that
'this was the only game in town', it was important to stay in it. Ian was also well
aware of the fourth law of consulting, which is to make sure your recommendations include more work for your firm which your client cannot afford to do
without. With these concerns in mind, Ian drafted a final section in his report
which first summarized five key points about how MEDS should proceed:

- It would be extremely unwise to trust PROPS/DABS to deliver what they are
  currently proposing to deliver with the current contract proposal. It would
  almost certainly lead to a cost-plus contract out of control with respect to the
  quality of the delivered development, the delivery date, and the capital cost.
  This would be a disaster scenario for MEDS. There is no need for MEDS to
  take this risk.
- At this stage it would be reasonable to assume that PROPS/DABS are reasonable and ethical people. They are simply doing what commercially minded
  people in their position do. If you put the bears in charge of the honey, you
  should know what to expect.

- If PROPS/DABS are reasonable people, and they need MEDS, and MEDS offers the kind of contract proposed, PROPS/DABS should be willing to negotiate a reasonable contract which MEDS can proceed with.
- If PROPS/DABS are not reasonable people, during negotiations it should be remembered that they need funding from an organization like MEDS to proceed. Prior to contracting, MEDS should be assertive and tough, and indicate it will be assertive and tough. After contracting, MEDS should make sure it owes PROPS/DABS money, not the other way round. In the limit, if MEDS judges PROPS/DABS untrustworthy, then MEDS might find it expedient to ensure that PROPS goes bankrupt. More generally, going for a win-win solution does not mean MEDS can afford to forget about win-lose, lose-win and lose-lose possibilities.
- MEDS needs a relationship which involves trust. MEDS should be prepared to let PROPS/DABS expect to make a good profit if PROPS/DABS can be trusted to deliver what MEDS wants. PROPS/DABS should be prepared to deliver what MEDS wants if a good profit can be expected. Sharing risk and aligning motivation is aimed at building trust. Partnership contracts are about trust. Trust has value in the sense that it reduces policing costs and claims costs, as well as ensuring that both parties get what they want and expect. Trust has a price in the sense that both parties need to build it, and look after it by paying attention to the interests of their partners. The guiding principle of the incentive contract proposed is 'good fences make good neighbours', and good neighbours trust each other and look after each other without having to be friends. It is a form of enlightened, mutual self-interest that does not require emotional commitments and unfounded expectations which may be counterproductive.

Ian then indicated that if MEDS decided to proceed along these lines, a plan should be developed to manage the changes that would follow. This was a high-risk change management project in its own right. It would be useful to apply a reasonably sophisticated project risk management process to this project. This risk management process would start by being clear what MEDS wishes to achieve. It would then attempt to define what PROPS/DABS want to achieve. It would also attempt to define the motives of any other key players, like the planning authorities and the banks. That is, it would define the parties (the who), and their motives (the why) in the Figure 5.3 context. The design (the what) is the form of partnership agreement with PROPS/DABS which MEDS wants the change process to deliver. Identification of risks and responses can start with design-based risks: what if MEDS attempts to transfer too much risk to PROPS/DABS, or too little, for example? Once the design starts to take shape, some attention can shift to defining the negotiating activities (the which way), resources (the wherewithal) and time (the when). When these are defined, identification of associated risks and responses can be addressed. All risks and responses can be managed collectively once they are identified. Ian's firm would be very pleased to assist with this, and the development project itself when a deal was done.

BIARS Contracts

Ian's proposed MEDS–PROPS/DABS contract is an example of a balanced incentive and risk sharing (BIARS) contract. Given the adoption of buyer and supplier as a useful general characterization of the parties to a contract, use of the term BIARS (pronounced 'buyers') seems apt. A number of principles in designing effective BIARS contracts are clear from Ian's report to MEDS.

- **Congruence of motivation** The best way to obtain congruence between the motivation of a supplier and the motivation of a buyer is to ensure that the actions of the supplier result in pain and gain balanced in the same proportions as the buyer will experience for all criteria of significant interest to the buyer which are not predetermined in a precise deterministic way, free of uncertainty and ambiguity. This will ensure that the best interests of the buyer will be served by the supplier acting in the supplier's best interests. Trust can thrive between the parties precisely because there is no moral hazard (potential advantage to be gained by improper behaviour). The supplier has to trust the buyer will pay the bill, but regular instalments paid on an agreed basis can minimize the strain on trust this involves. The buyer has to trust the supplier will act in the supplier's best interests, but this should involve no strain on trust whatsoever.
- **Triggers based on expected values** Trigger values which are unbiased expected values of performance measures are an appropriate basis for all incentive payments in a case like this. Most likely values or median values or some other common percentile values might seem attractive, but expected values are the simplest basis for incentive contracts with respect to the control of bias. Also, expected values are the most appropriate single values for decision making, and there are no compelling arguments for alternatives in this case. Chapter 6 uses 80 percentile values, a useful alternative in some contexts.
- **Consistent risk sharing ratios** Pain and gain adjustments to the expected cost or price should be driven by sharing a consistent proportion of the risk associated with ambiguity and uncertainty for each of the measured performance criteria of direct interest to the buyer, to preserve balance in the dimensions of performance. The proportion of risk taken by the supplier might vary over a range like 10% to 100%. If the supplier takes none of the risk then there is no incentive, the contract is cost-plus, and the basic principles of the BIARS contract are forfeit. In a MEDS–PROPS/DABS context, if the supplier takes 100% of the risk, we have a fixed price rental agreement, with the rent pre-fixed in terms of the expected capital and operating costs. This is a common special case, but one that is frequently fraught with a lack of trust and moral hazard problems. For incentive purposes we might expect risk-sharing agreements in the range 10% to 50%, with 40% serving as a useful starting point for negotiations. Second-order adjustments to risk-sharing ratios may prove useful for negotiation purposes. For example, Ian suggested that MEDS might take

40% of the PROPS/DABS risk on DABS staff and associated overhead costs if PROPS/ DABS take 40% of the MEDS risk on capital cost, operating cost, and delay.

These principles provide initial guidance, but there are a number of issues involved in formulating BIARS contracts more generally that were not discussed in Ian's report to MEDS. These issues are related to developing an optimum balance between performance criteria, and deciding on an appropriate level of risk sharing.

Developing an optimum balance between performance criteria

An obvious question is, Can you measure all the relevant criteria for the buyer on a common scale in order to ensure they are all balanced? The short answer is yes, in principle, although comparisons may be crude. It may be difficult, but buyers must try their best, because what doesn't get measured won't get managed *in your favour* (it probably will get managed in the supplier's favour). This is a slight but important clarification of an ambiguity in the quote at the beginning of the chapter. A corollary is that what doesn't get measured is out of control if you only manage what gets measured. This is important to remember when designing trigger contracts, or any other kind of contract which might be interpreted as a trigger contract. The MEDS contract example involved three such performance measures which could and probably should be considered for all construction procurement contracts: capital cost, duration, and operating costs.

Those who argue for expressing risk in terms of PIMs using qualitative impact labels such as low, medium and high sometimes argue that these labels can be usefully applied to time and cost separately, and then jointly and simultaneously to evaluate time and capital cost risk to trade off time against capital cost by adjusting the scales, equating cost impacts to time impacts. For example, if a medium time impact is 1–2 weeks and a medium cost impact is £0.1–0.2 million, a 1 week delay is equated with £0.1 million, and a 2 week delay is equated with £0.2 million. A linear relationship over this range might be assumed, implying (misleadingly) more precision. Unfortunately such simple comparisons bear no relationship to appropriate trade-offs. The problem is that such comparisons do not address the question, What is the value of delay (or early completion)? Unless this basic question is answered, there is no basis for evaluating trade-offs.

Answering this question can be pursued through an appropriate iterative process, with or without uncertainty. That is, having developed in outline a plan with what seems a suitable expected cost and duration, replan it to answer the following questions: How much would it cost to take a week (or month) off the schedule, and would it be worth it? If a week (month) is worth it, what about two? If a shorter duration isn't worth it, what about a longer duration? If these questions have not been addressed then an appropriate trade-off between duration and capital cost has not been addressed, and there is no reason to assume that what is proposed is appropriate. This indicates a very basic project planning failure, whether or not uncertainty is an issue.

Balancing capital cost and duration against operating cost seems a very obvious next step. This involves an iterative approach to seek an answer to the question, If we redesign and replan the project to reduce capital cost by allowing operating costs (broadly defined) to increase, will there be a net saving over the holding period for the asset? Operating costs involve a cash flow, associated with costs like electricity for light (which may vary with design, for example), fuel for heating (which will vary with insulation specification, for example), painting and other routine maintenance, refurbishment, alterations associated with use changes, offsetting rental income, and so on. This cash flow needs to be considered over the life cycle of the asset of interest, or perhaps a planned holding period. Sale on completion by PROPS made the life cycle of interest to PROPS stop as soon as the completed project buyer was in place, but MEDS had to consider a much longer life cycle. A life cycle of many years means net present values must be used for comparison with capital cost at the same point in time. However, if this is not feasible for trigger contract purposes, it must be because there is a basic failure in the project planning process, or the project owners are in a position like PROPS/DABS before Ian came along. There has been a lot of attention given to whole life costing, but there is little evidence that trigger contracts of the kind suggested here have been used to deliver a balance between operating cost, capital cost and duration. Addressing these three criteria as outlined in this chapter is a 'minimalist' defensible position for most projects.

A first-pass estimate of the size of annual operating cost variations as a function of design might suggest that lighting efficiency, heating efficiency, the cost of adapting the layout to revised use, or some other component of operating cost is particularly important. In these cases it would be no more than common sense to pay particular attention to this component when seeking a preferred or optimum trade-off between capital cost and operating cost. For an office park built to rent out (at least in part), rentable values (income) may be usefully treated separately in considering possible trade-offs.

More generally, other performance criteria may be relevant in considering trade-offs. For example, in a railway system, air traffic control system, or road system, all the above performance measures may be relevant, plus new ones such as safety, reliability and availability. Each of these new criteria poses measurement difficulties, in terms of measures which can be compared directly to capital cost. Chapter 7 indicates how this could be done in relation to safety, and why there is no alternative if we want to consider safety properly in relation to competing demands on finite resources. Opportunity management in the sense of joint optimization with respect to all relevant criteria may require us to look at criteria which can only be evaluated indirectly, like safety, as well as criteria which can be measured directly, like capital cost, and intermediates like project duration.

It is important to appreciate that this search for an optimum trade-off applies to *each* performance measure and relevant components of concern to the buyer. That is, capital cost expenditure allocations need to be optimized at least approximately within any given total cost. This is largely a design issue linked to the operating cost aspects of design. Activity duration allocations also need to be optimized at least approximately within any given total project duration. This is a planning issue linked to design, and hence to capital and operating costs. These component optimization problems may be treated as separable to some extent, but they are certainly not independent.

The presence of uncertainty in costs and durations demands attention to risk-efficient trade-offs in relation to all performance measures. The only effective practical approach is to make the best guesses we can in all relevant dimensions, and then iteratively test the working assumptions involved in these best guesses. This is what opportunity management is about at its core – seeking risk efficiency (maximum performance with respect to all performance measures for a given level of risk). Most people understand this intuitively, but very few organizations pursue it in an effective, systematic way. Encouraging formal systematic pursuit of risk efficiency is at the heart of this book.

In developing a BIARS contract, appropriate contract performance criteria need to be selected, and the associated balanced incentive payments determined. If the project base plan has been optimized by addressing the above considerations, then the information required to complete these tasks will be available, in appropriate approximate terms.

Deciding on an appropriate level of risk sharing

The remaining consideration in developing a BIARS contract is determining the risk-sharing ratios for each contract performance criterion. Surprisingly perhaps, there is no clear-cut answer to the question of how much risk each of the parties to a BIARS contract should take. Often risk allocation is influenced by two conflicting rules of thumb:

- The party best able to manage the risk should take the risk
- The party best able to bear the risk should take the risk

Intuitively, this would seem to suggest that it should be in the best interests of both parties to put as much risk with the supplier as the supplier can reasonably bear at a price (for the risk transfer) which is profitable business for the supplier and value for money for the buyer in terms of creating sufficient supplier motivation. In most circumstances a risk-sharing rate below 10% taken by the supplier would fail this test. The best deal for both parties will be driven by their relative abilities to bear risk.

Formal analysis of optimal risk-sharing ratios can be pursued, and analysis of optimal risk sharing in relation to a single criterion (capital cost) can provide a useful starting point and conceptual framework (Ward and Chapman, 1994a, 1995). In the MEDS/DABS case it should be reasonably obvious to both parties where the optimal balance lies to the nearest 10%. Negotiations will be in terms of the increased fee necessary for agreement versus the risk-sharing ratio necessary for agreement, starting with a position like that outlined on page 187, where the buyer perceives the opening position as acceptable if it is acceptable to the supplier.

Capital cost is an obvious place to start, as a basic performance criterion. Starting with the premise that the supplier should take 50% of the risk associated with potential variations about a trigger cost seems a plausible place to start unless there are obvious reasons for more or less. The obvious next step is balancing this capital cost incentive with a duration incentive which reflects the actual and opportunity costs to the buyer of delay and early delivery. It is not clear what excuse could be given for failing to provide a balanced incentive, other than a lack of willingness to take the trouble to work out what these costs are. It is not clear why such an excuse should ever be acceptable.

Conclusion

This chapter introduced the PRAM process for project risk management as elaborated by Chapman and Ward (1997) and updated by subsequent papers. It also introduced the BIARS contract as a device for managing the differing motivations of parties to a project.

The PRAM process provides a widely accepted framework for best practice in project risk management. Other frameworks may be preferred because they are familiar, which is clearly acceptable provided all the best practice features associated with all available frameworks are embedded in whatever framework is adopted. Ian's tale provides a convenient vehicle for introducing an elaborated version of the PRAM process, and for highlighting the limitations in current common practice compared with appropriate application of the PRAM process. Most organizations need to manage their projects using the process outlined in this chapter or something very similar. A more detailed discussion of the PRAM process and practical issues in carrying out effective project risk management is given in Chapman and Ward (1997). In particular, the authors devote whole chapters to each of the nine phases, describe the generic project life cycle (PLC), and discuss the use of project risk management in relation to the various stages of the PLC. The ideas incorporated in the papers cited by Ian are incorporated directly in this book.

Ian's description of the PRAM process and related concepts is necessarily brief, but he does include some important features which facilitate uncertainty management:

- An iterative process is required because we do not know when we start what will turn out to be important. This is a key message in all chapters in this book.
- Stepping back from a detailed analysis is important (particularly if it is presented by another party to the project) to start with a broader overview. Failing to do this means critical features of the wood can be missed because we are distracted by the impressive number and variety of the trees. This involves using the 'define' and 'focus' phases to clarify both working and framing assumptions.
- The six Ws (the who, why, what, which way, wherewithal and when) that characterize a project are the basis of the roots of project uncertainty. The six Ws are interdependent and need joint consideration for effective management of uncertainty. Ian's tale highlights the central role of the who and the why in addressing uncertainty. For MEDS, much more critical than understanding the detailed activities proposed in the office park development was the need to appreciate the relationships between key parties to the project and their various objectives and motives.
- The F^3 scaling factor and its components F_b, F_k, and F_u capture views about the possible effect on estimates of bias, known unknowns and unknown unknowns. As both Thoms and Ian illustrate, such factors may be far more important than estimates of variability in project parameters. Consideration of F^3 factors is likely to be even more important where estimates prepared by one party are being relied on by another. Such situations are very common.

The PRAM process in Figure 5.1 is usefully seen as a generic version of Figure 1.1. Rather than embedding a specific process like that of Figure 3.12 in Figure 1.1, Figure 5.1 replaces Figure 1.1, for clarity and simplicity. The implications are the same as for Figure 1.1 plus Figure 3.12 in the sense that the core notion of a designed constructively simple process is involved in both. But there is a material difference in that the process of Figure 5.1 is generic rather than specific, in the sense that it is generic to all projects in all organizations. This means the focus phase must address tailoring generic best practice to the organization and the project in question. In a sense, generic processes are a halfway position between specific processes as illustrated in Martha's tale of Chapter 3 and the general process illustrated by Nicola's tale of Chapter 2. The minimalist estimation and evaluation process of Eddy's tale in Chapter 4 is a process module that could be embedded in a general, generic or specific process application. An important aspect of constructive simplicity is making use of all these ways to achieve an appropriate balance between simplicity and complexity, with effective and efficient use of both.

A central issue in this chapter was Ian's recognition that the construction contract being offered to MEDS did not motivate the contractor to perform in the best interests of MEDS. Part of Ian's concern was to demonstrate via a critique of the contractor's risk analysis the extent to which MEDS would be exposed if the offered contract was taken on. Ian then developed a BIARS contract to ensure the supplier PROPS/DABS performed in the best interests of the buyer MEDS. Subsequent discussion focused on the general principles underlying the design of an effective BIARS contract between any buyer and supplier. Not surprisingly, a key requirement to operate any form of BIARS contract is that the buyer must first be clear about their own objectives and performance criteria for the product or service they seek. Specifically, the buyer needs to:

- Identify pertinent performance criteria
- Develop a measure of the level of performance for each criterion
- Identify the most preferred (optimum) feasible combination of performance levels on each criterion
- Identify acceptable alternative combinations of performance levels on each criterion
- Identify the tradeoffs between performance criteria implied by these preferences

Adopting an iterative process may be the most effective way to complete these steps. The information gathered from these steps can then be used to formulate a BIARS contract by selecting some or all of the performance criteria for inclusion in the contract, developing payment scales which reflect the acceptable trade-offs, and negotiating acceptable risk-sharing ratios for each contract performance criterion with the supplier.

The BIARS form of contract is a generic form of contract capable of application in any buyer-supplier relationship. It can be applied in a very wide range of situations, including transactions between different units in the same organization, where one unit provides products or services to another. The tale in the next chapter provides an illustration of this generality.

The above steps are not just applicable to buyers contemplating a BIARS contract. They should be undertaken by any project owner, particularly in the early conception and design stages of a project. Undertaking these steps should be part of the process of understanding the relationships between the six Ws of the project, and managing uncertainty about project performance. The process of identifying and considering possible trade-offs between performance criteria is an opportunity to improve performance. It should enable a degree of optimization with respect to each performance measure, and it is an opportunity that needs to be seized.

6 Roger's tale: Assigning ownership of project uncertainty

Never put the bears in charge of the honey.

Introduction

The tale of this chapter is based on the way a UK-based oil major addressed ownership of project uncertainty for North Sea projects in the late 1970s. The initial focus of discussion is the ownership of uncertainty at a project manager's interface with corporate management and contributing units within the organization. One important aspect of this discussion is the need to distinguish between operational management responsibility for uncertainty and financial responsibility for uncertainty. Another is the impossibility of clear-cut simplistic delegation of responsibility. Effective management of responsibility for uncertainty requires an ongoing dialogue between project contributors. For example, unknown (unanticipated) extreme events may be realized. A prior assumption that such events are automatically the responsibility of the project manager or the board is inappropriate. The board and the project manager need a process in place to resolve associated expected cost adjustments. The legal contract relationship between a client (buyer) and a contractor (supplier) raises similar issues.

Ownership of uncertainty also has to address associated motivation to manage good luck as well as bad luck, otherwise the good luck will be wasted. To explore this issue the tale of this chapter looks at the design of an offshore pipeline by an internal design department, moving on to the procurement of pipe involving an in-house procurement department and a string of external suppliers and other subcontractors.

One important aspect of this tale is the management of the relationship between cost, duration and quality. A second is refinement of the basis for F^3 factors. A third is the need for internal trigger contracts to appropriately motivate internal suppliers of services like design. The use of trigger contracts internally, as well as externally, has implications in relation to capturing and managing good luck in an effective and efficient manner. Balanced incentive and risk sharing (BIARS) contracts can be seen as special cases of this 'trigger' contract concept.

A Corporate Understanding Of Uncertainty Ownership

The central character in this tale is Roger, an engineer working as a risk analyst in the London head office of the oil company. Roger's line boss was Barry, head of the company's risk management function. Barry reported to the board. At the time of our tale, Roger had been assigned to work for Paul, a senior project manager in charge of a £1000 million North Sea oil production project.

Within the company the general perception of project uncertainty ownership at the beginning of our tale could be characterized in terms of seven rules of conduct:

- The project manager was responsible for all project risk on behalf of the board of directors.
- Provisions for project risks (expected costs of project risks) were held by the project manager as part of the project's budget.
- The project budget agreed by the board should have enough contingency to give the project manager an 80% chance of completing within budget, a 20% chance of being overbudget, determined by estimating the probability distribution for project costs.
- The contingency sum defined by the difference between the project expected cost (best estimate of outturn costs) and the project budget cost was held by the project manager.
- The project manager would have to account to the board for any expenditure beyond the budget, but not for expenditure within the budget.
- The project budget cost was an 80% confidence estimate, not an expected value. It should not be used for overall corporate funding provision because it embodied a contingency sum which on average should not be needed. Corporate funding provision required an expected cost, with overall corporate expenditure variability and an associated contingency assessed in terms of all projects.
- Roger (as a risk analyst) reported to Paul (as a project manager) with respect to all issues associated with Paul's project. Roger also reported to Barry with respect to the technical quality of all his work, for which Barry was responsible to the board. Roger had to balance being a member of Paul's team, loyal to that team, with being an honest broker from the board's perspective.

At the time, this approach was seen as a very sophisticated and very sensible way to view uncertainty ownership and budget definition. Relative to earlier practice within Roger's company (and current practice in many organizations), this was a fair assessment. Underlying these seven rules of conduct were a number of important premises:

- A key reason for measuring uncertainty was giving the board confidence that exceeding budgets would become the exception that proved the rule, not the norm supported by earlier experience.
- The 80% confidence level chosen reflected an asymmetric penalty function for the organization as a whole, because exceeding a budget required additional funding and additional board involvement and an additional audit process, all of which were expensive and time-consuming. (The contingency this introduced is a buffer comparable to George's time contingency when travelling to Heathrow airport as assessed by Nicola in Chapter 2, and the choice of an 80% confidence level is testable in the same analysis framework.)
- The best way to control risks is to give them to those people most able to manage them, so the project manager should be given all project risks by the board.
- The project manager could pass risks on to staff working for him within the organization or to contractors working for the project.

This overall approach and all of these underlying premises may seem reasonable, but they involve ambiguity which Roger subsequently discovered, with widespread implications. When this ambiguity was stripped away, the overall approach described above and the underlying assumptions were revealed as rather naive.

Barry was widely held to be the initiator if not the author of the above prevailing corporate understanding of uncertainty, but it would be very unfair to suggest he was responsible for the naivety. Relative to previous practice the prevailing understanding represented a major step forward. However, the next step, which Roger was to develop, was even bigger. It would require a major shift in corporate mindset and practice.

Roger's Defining Moment

Roger's questioning of the company's approach to the ownership of project uncertainty arose from considering risks associated with a major element in Paul's project, the construction of a 200 km oil pipeline. This pipeline activity was similar to that addressed by Eddy and Charlie in Chapter 4. However, at this stage in the development of North Sea projects, the oil company Roger worked for took the view that pipe laying contractors did not have the experience or the financial base to undertake fixed price contracts. Roger's company employed pipe laying contractors on the basis of a fixed price per working day and a fixed price per idle day (bad weather day). The oil company took the risk in a hands-on manner and managed it directly. The lay barge operator working for the pipe laying contractor followed the oil company's instructions, apart from taking responsibility for deciding whether or not to work if the weather was marginal, for legal reasons related to safety.

Pipe laying involved lowering new sections of pipeline to the ocean floor in a smooth S shape from a lay barge as more pipe sections were welded to the pipeline on the barge, cranking forward on anchors out the other end of the barge for each new pipe section. The anchor lines were under significant tension, which could be difficult to control. As the barge approached an anchor, the tension was released, the anchor was picked up by a tug, carried out, dropped and retensioned. In this fashion the barge would crawl along on its anchors at about 3 km per day, weather permitting.

Roger's work concerned analysis of the time and cost involved in laying the pipeline. The nature of this analysis was similar to the more sophisticated versions Eddy was working towards. Roger's analysis employed Markovian process models with weather data to assess weather effects each month, and a more detailed source of uncertainty and response structure (e.g. Cooper and Chapman, 1987). One source of risk Roger had to deal with on Paul's project was a new one to all concerned. The new oil pipeline had to be laid across three existing pipelines. An obvious potential problem was that one (or more) of the anchors could damage one (or more) of the existing pipelines. The consequences of such damage could be 'serious bad news', as Roger would put it. Likely adverse consequences ordered according to increasing severity could include:

- Non-trivial direct costs of repairing any damaged pipeline
- Significant direct costs of cleaning up an oil spill
- Lawsuits for very significant compensation for loss of flow by the owners of the damaged pipeline
- Using the project's lay barge and other equipment to sort out the damaged pipeline before recommencing the new pipeline could cost a season, with knock-on costs that could be enormous
- A major oil spill would damage sales at pumps because adverse publicity associated with environmental damage has a direct impact on sales for oil companies and the cost of this could be colossal

Roger realized immediately that this new source of risk, with its associated potential extreme events, would need careful attention. What he did not realize was the extent to which it would trigger a reshaping of his thinking on a very wide range of issues. Uncovering this risk was a 'defining moment' for Roger, as he would later put it.

A Simple Analysis Of Anchor Risk

Roger was not familiar with Eddy's minimalist approach (it had not been developed yet), and he normally used more sophisticated first-pass approaches. However, for the anchor risk, Roger's engineering instincts led him to a simple first analysis.

Roger started by assuming that, only one anchor damage risk event scenario was involved. He called it anchor risk and he described it as follows: an anchor cuts an existing pipeline, causing a significant flow of oil into the sea. To assume that this risk event scenario either happens or does not happen is clearly a major simplification of a very complex set of possibilities. Minor damage to one pipeline with no release of oil is an optimistic possibility. A pessimistic possibility is a pipeline being completely severed during a major storm, with a failure of automatic shut-off systems and a prolonged period before the damage is realized, by which time a second or third pipeline is also severed, with a catastrophic set of consequences. There are a lot of intermediate possibilities. Roger then asked the engineers responsible for planning and costing this part of the project how much they thought such an event would cost. The collective answer was about £200 million: about £80million associated with direct and knock-on costs for the project which could be part of its budget, and about £120 million for costs the company would have to bear which could not be treated as part of the project's budget, like loss of sales. These numbers were clearly order of magnitude estimates, with significant associated uncertainty, much of it not worth resolving without a less ambiguous view of the associated scenarios and responses to mitigate their impact. Roger then asked the same group of engineers what they thought the probability of such a scenario occurring was. The answer was about 0.2, prior to detailed examination of how this risk might be minimized in terms of preventative measures. This probability estimate was also an order of magnitude value with significant associated uncertainty, much of it not worth resolving without a less ambiguous view of how the risk might be realized.

Roger then summarized his analysis as illustrated in Figure 6.1. One immediate consequence of this analysis was a significant interest in examining ways of reducing the probability of this risk occurring and reducing its impact if it occurred. At least halving the probability was thought to be feasible, with a target of reducing it by an order of magnitude. Whether or not this estimate of the scope for improvement was accurate, it was clearly worth spending time trying to reduce both the probability and the likely impact. A second immediate consequence of this analysis was a significant interest in examining the implications of the £80 million for the project's budget, and the appropriate home for the potential off-budget £120 million. This chapter is concerned with the second consequence. For the rest of this chapter, assume Figure 6.1 portrays anchor risk with all necessary precision.

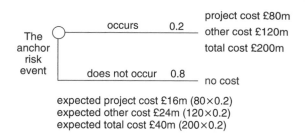

expected project cost £16m (80×0.2)
expected other cost £24m (120×0.2)
expected total cost £40m (200×0.2)

Figure 6.1—Simple event tree for anchor risk.

Distributing the Ownership Of Uncertainty

Anchor risk seemed to Roger a classic example of what he called explicit extreme events (triple Es). Ownership of such risks under existing company practices seemed to be somewhat problematic.

Explicit extreme events

Current company practice seemed to require that the £80 million possible cost and 0.2 probability associated with anchor risk be given to Paul as the project manager. However, doing so would involve giving Paul a provision of £16 million (the expected cost of the risk), plus a contingency (an additional amount, which on average should not be needed, to bring the chance of completing within budget up to 80%), say an extra £4 million, for a total of £20 million. An extreme event which happens or not with a single discrete consequence value makes the idea of a specific contingency problematic, but this is not an issue here. What is an issue here is the way giving Paul £20 million to live with anchor risk would put the board in what Roger considered to be a lose-lose situation.

If the anchor risk event occurs, Paul cannot cope if all he has is a provision plus contingency totalling £20 million . He will have to go back to the board for the £60 million (80 − 20) needed to deal with the risk event occurring. If the anchor risk event does not occur, the board does not want Paul to have £20 million to spend on other problems in a manner for which he is not accountable. The only sensible thing for the board to do is to accept responsibility for the risk in financial terms. The board can make Paul responsible for managing anchor risk in operational terms. Indeed, the board might make it clear that Paul will have to look elsewhere for employment if anchor risk occurs and anyone involved in the project is in any way culpable. But it does not make sense to give the project manager financial responsibility for this risk. It is too extreme in the low probability and high-impact sense; the key is the high possible impact value relative to the expected impact value.

Roger knew that insurance approaches to explicit extreme events had been considered by the company but rejected. Projects of this kind with £1000 million budgets could double in cost. This would be the case if, for example, the oil production platform sank on its way to being installed. While the replacement cost of the platform could be insured, the larger knock-on opportunity costs could not. As a consequence, the oil majors formed a consortium to self-insure against such losses. Forming such a consortium is expensive, in terms of bureaucracy costs. If a consortium is formed to withstand £1000 million losses, there is no point in not self-insuring most smaller losses. Exceptions might include liability for employee or public injury, when being directly involved in administering pay-offs might not be appropriate in public relations terms. Hence it soon became clear to Roger that some extreme event risks should be managed operationally by Paul as the project manager, but that it is appropriate for the board to own the associated financial risk, the £80 million part of anchor risk providing one example. It is in the board's best interest to own financially those risks which involve a large potential impact value relative to their expected impact value. The project manager does not have enough similar risks to effectively self-insure, and the board is in a much better position to self-insure, across its broader set of activities, or via consortium arrangements.

If the board cannot accommodate self-insurance in this way, it may be appropriate for the board to externally insure an appropriate part of the risk. The board is in business to take appropriate risk up to limits of its ability to do so. It should pass on risk (and expected profit) only when not to do so would increase the threat of corporate difficulties to an unacceptable level if a risk event were to occur. When transferring risk via external insurance, the board should be very selective. A common basis for such selectivity is only insuring losses above some acceptable threshold. That is, if £100 million is deemed the maximum event risk the company should run, a reinsurance approach to extreme event costs above £100 million should be used in conjunction with self-insurance of the first £100 million of any such event. With this line of reasoning as his basis, Roger argued, and both Paul and Barry agreed, that a board member acting on behalf of the board should be empowered to release to the project manager an estimate of the realized cost to the project of an anchor risk event should such an event occur, subject to a loss-adjusting process comparable to an insurance company paying a claim. That is, the board should explicitly recognize its corporate self-insurance role in the context of this kind of risk event, and arrange to manage it accordingly in a cost-effective manner.

The insight gained with respect to the £80 million aspect of anchor risk made it clear that the £120 million other costs possibility associated with anchor risk (expected value £24 million) had to be owned by the board in financial terms by default (there was no other place to put it). But this necessity could be viewed as a virtue, because the arguments that applied to the £80 million also applied to the

£120 million, whichever part of the organization managed prior prevention and mitigation and post-event mitigation. A crisis management unit (with substantial legal and public relations presence) might be charged with prior and post-event mitigation in relation to the £120 million, but they would clearly have to be exempt from financial responsibility. Insurance for the £120 million aspect of anchor risk was even more difficult and even less advantageous commercially than insurance for the £80 million component. Indeed, if any insurance looked sensible, it would probably address the £80 million component first. Hence it soon became clear that the financial risk which the board owned when it took on a risk like anchor risk was the full £200 million (expected cost £40 million). There was no point in making the £40 million (with or without extra contingency) part of the project budget. More generally, there were some explicit extreme event risks best owned by the board whether or not someone reporting to the project manager is responsible for the initiating events associated with realizing these risks. If these risks are not externally insured then they are by default self-insured, and such self-insurance should be explicit. Self-insurance does not mean ignoring such a risk. Self-insurance requires recognition of a self-insurance premium in the form of a provision for a loss. In particular, deciding to proceed with such a project or not requires explicit consideration of all such provisions.

The £80 million and the £120 million components of anchor risk are examples of Roger's triple E risks requiring self-insurance provisions or payment of external insurance premiums (provisions plus expected profits for insurance companies). Roger called these the triple E provisions and he associated them with a triple E adjustment factor, an uplift to the expected project cost to reflect the total of triple E provisions. On reflection it was agreed that the recommended size of the project's triple E adjustment factor ought to be based on an assessment by Roger reporting to both Paul and Barry. Paul was held to be directly responsible for all aspects of the identification, sizing and operational management of these risks because he owned them outright in operational management terms (with the exception of crisis mitigation issues). However, the board would be accepting the financial aspects of triple E risks, so Roger should report to the board through Barry with respect to the size of the triple E factor, in addition to reporting to Paul. The discussion of reporting structure that this issue triggered had further ramifications. A summary implication initially agreed was that Roger ought to report to Barry as well as Paul whenever the board ought to be involved in the details of uncertainty ownership or management.

Scope assumption provisions

After the excitement over the triple Es began to subside, it became clear that any unquantified risks associated with assumed project conditions were in effect risks owned by the board, whether or not the events were extreme. For example, the 'client route change' risk of Chapter 4, a late change in route because a collector system becomes desirable, is owned by the board, even if it is not useful to quantify it as a risk, and even if it is not an extreme event in any sense. Roger had identified about 20 such risks or conditions associated with the pipe laying activity. Recognition of this by the board would imply that the corporate expected project cost provisions should also include what Roger called a scope assumption provision (SAP), associated with a SAP adjustment factor. It was initially agreed that the size of this SAP factor had to be decision based on a recommendation from Roger reporting through Paul and Barry. Paul had to manage any scope changes in terms of their implications, but the board had to accept management responsibility for the approval of such scope changes. Both parties had some responsibility for their identification. The size of this board provision had to be based on the list of risks or conditions associated with the budget estimate, but not quantified as part of the budget. Most of these risks or conditions were scope assumptions, not risks in the usual sense, but this was not always the case. For example, scope assumption changes linked to regulatory changes might be anticipated, and they have most of the characteristics of other risks treated directly in the usual way.

Roger pre-empted negative reactions to the obvious derisory implications of the term SAP by pointing out that it was in both the board's best interests and the project manager's best interests to 'rise to the occasion', to ensure that neither was 'taken for a sap' in its determination. Humour of a sophisticated nature was not one of Roger's conspicuous strengths. However, the SAP label stuck, the SAP concept was accepted as sound, ambiguity about specific cases was accepted as reasonably easily resolved, and it was realized there would be no winners if SAPs were identified improperly. Any attempt by the project manager to pass risks to the board without good cause would put the provision for such risks and the control of release of funds to accommodate realization of such risks with the board, in addition to requiring the project manager to make a reasonable case for doing so. The project manager would be motivated to avoid doing this if it was feasible to do so. Conversely, any attempt by the board to pass risks to the project manager without good cause would force their quantification, and a corporate provision, as well as forcing a rationale for doing so. Neither party could benefit from inappropriate handling of SAPs.

It was accepted that board-level financial responsibility for conditions of a scope assumption nature was appropriate, subject to debate on some occasions. This was on the understanding that it was the responsibility of the project manager to bring such assumptions to the board's notice where the existence of such assumptions was most appropriately identified by the project. Where the board might be best placed to identify some major scope change assumptions, it had to accept responsibility. By implication, any scope assumptions or conditions not brought to the attention of the board would not be accepted by the board as part of the budget approval process unless it was clear the fault was theirs. From Paul's perspective, Roger's process for identifying scope assumptions was the basis of the project manager's process for passing appropriate risks to the board as part of the budget approval process. From Barry's perspective, Roger's process for identifying scope assumptions was the basis for the board's process for accepting appropriate SAP risks. Roger, Barry, Paul and the board had to work together on the details of the SAP issues, as for the triple Es. The key difference between triple E risks and SAP risks was the practice of quantifying some (not all) the triple E risks as quasi-insurable risks, because of their size, and never quantifying the SAP risks, because greater ambiguity made direct quantification more difficult, and quantification would not serve any useful purpose.

Paul and Barry agreed that it would be useful if a director acting on behalf of the board could release estimated additional actual costs associated with realized SAP risks to the project manager, the same director using the same review process that the board would entrust with the release of funds for a realized triple E risk owned by the board, without a formal budget review. For example, if a collector pipeline system to serve several offshore projects was agreed, adjustments to all relevant project budgets could be made without full budget reviews for all the projects. The director involved would be responsible for both corporate insurance and reinsurance (triple Es) and scope adjustments (SAPs), somewhat different issues usefully treated in a similar manner.

Provision for unknown unknowns

Triple E adjustments and SAP adjustments both involve what Roger referred to as 'the known unknown'. They were 'known' in the sense that they were identified. They were 'unknown' in the sense that they were not quantified in advance of a risk event in general, although some component triple Es might be quantified for reinsurance purposes. Recognition of the known unknown raised a further obvious question. What about unknown unknowns? And what about scope assumptions and other conditions like SAPs or risks like triple Es which are not identified? Should they be owned entirely by the project manager by default, by the board by default, or by some combination of the two? To begin with, there is no obvious way to assess an appropriate provision or contingency for unknown unknowns. The quality of a risk management process is a relevant clue, but not a clear-cut driver. From the perspective of a diligent project manager, it is clearly unreasonable to be made responsible for unknown unknowns by default, with no provision or contingency. From the perspective of the board, accepting responsibility for unknown unknowns by default is a clear case of leaving the bears in charge of the honey. However, depriving deserving bears of appropriate honey will encourage even moderately clever bears to take it by stealth, building fudge factors into estimates which build in ambiguity. Roger's proposed solution was to put the honey up a tree in a pot the board could keep an eye on, in what he called the provision for unknown unknowns. Roger soon dubbed it the PUU pot as in A.A. Milne's *Winnie the Pooh*; others called it the honeypot. Its purpose was to provide a budget provision to accommodate realized risks which were not anticipated. A director acting on behalf of the board would be empowered to release associated realized costs without a full budget review, provided that director was satisfied the project manager could not have been expected to identify the risk prior to budget determination.

The PUU factor would involve uncertainty ownership by the project manager and the board comparable to triple E or SAP risks, except that the case for release of additional funds had to be made after the risk event was realized, with responsibility for failure to identify it determined as part of the process. Roger argued, and everyone directly involved agreed, that a blame culture was to be avoided, but accountability was important, and learning from errors was important. Here is how he put it: 'Making use of the honey pot can involve a very visible sting for the project manager if the project manager should have identified the risk in advance, and a very embarrassing sting for the board if the board should have identified the risk in advance. These stings should be made sharp enough to motivate both the project manager and the board to ensure that honeypot dipping is minimal and appropriate.' As one colleague argued, Roger and Barry were not immune to stings either – any detectable failure in the uncertainty management process would be visible, and identified as such, whenever the honeypot was dipped.

Barry and Paul agreed that sizing the PUU factor had to involve the project manager and the board, and it had to involve Roger and Barry as stakeholders as well as advisors. In particular, Roger, Barry and Paul would have to argue for a large PUU pot to protect their own reputations if the quality of the uncertainty management process made a large PUU factor appropriate in their view. This could arise if the board wanted to rush a project, for example. Barry and Paul also agreed that the director acting on behalf of the board to manage triple Es and SAPs would need to deal with PUUs as well, determining which is which being part of the associated management process. Barry suggested the title 'projects director' for this director, recognizing that the company might wish to use a set of project directors reporting to one main board member in practice.

Bias in estimates

Roger recognized that the quality of estimates used in any analysis was a critical factor warranting explicit attention. In particular, he recognized that estimates provided by Paul's staff might be biased, in the sense that they might be systematically optimistic (usually the case) or pessimistic (occasionally the case), and it was crucial to identify an associated adjustment factor. Some of this bias might be conscious, because estimators were under pressure to provide low or high estimates, or there were benefits to them from producing low or high estimates. Some of this bias might be unconscious, for a range of reasons explored in depth in the psychology-based risk management literature (e.g. Chapman and Ward, 1997, Ch.

10). Roger recognized that bias in estimating was not necessarily stable over projects, and even if an average bias estimate was available, this might not be appropriate for Paul's current project. Roger also recognized that clues about the quality of estimates could be derived from the nature of estimating processes and the body language of the estimators, and the organizational position of the estimators. Roger took the view that bias was more difficult to think about than the unknown unknowns, and no easier to assess. Discussion made it clear that bias ought to be seen as jointly owned by the project manager, the board, and the risk management function (Roger and Barry). It was comparable to PUUs in some respects, although it also had aspects which could not be easily disentangled from appropriate provisions for triple Es and SAPs. The distinguishing features of bias in this context were that it could not be associated with a triple E or a SAP which had been overlooked (it was not a PUU). It might reflect systematic optimism or pessimism over a part or a whole of the project estimation process, which might not become clear until very late in the project, and might then be difficult to disentangle from good or bad luck. For the projects director responsible for triple Es, SAPs and PUUs, these features would make it difficult to deal with bias as a project proceeds. But this would not be resolved by ignoring bias.

A composite factor

Roger did not invent a label for bias comparable to the triple E, SAP or PUU. But he more than compensated for the omission when he put these factors together. He was well aware that a large number of separate adjustment factors requiring separate assessment might not be a good idea. So he proposed one composite factor, which he called the KUUUB factor, an acronym for known unknowns, unknown unknowns, and bias. KUUUB is pronounced 'cube'. Roger suggested that the short form KU^3B captured the idea nicely. His colleagues preferred F^3 for cube factor, and F_p^3 for project cube factor.

Roger pointed out that the expected cost for a project defined by financial responsibility attributed to the project manager (E_p) is a conditional expectation which does not embody the whole of the expected cost defined by financial responsibility attributed to the board (E_b). The difference is defined by the project cube factor F_p^3, where

$$E_b = F_p^3 E_p$$

For the organization to equate E_b and E_p, as currently was the case, F_p^3 had to be equated to 1 ± 0, corresponding to no known unknowns (triple Es and SAPs), no unknown unknowns, and no bias. In general F_p^3 will have an expected value greater than unity and a non-zero variance.

The three main components structure facilitates a graphical cube factor

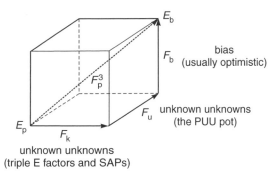

Figure 6.2—Project cube factor diagram.

diagram, as Roger was quick to observe. Figure 6.2 is Roger's version of Figure 4.6 from Eddy's tale. Roger's version predates Thomas's, and its rationale helps to underpin the general idea. The E_p expected project cost shown at the front, lower left of the cube is the estimated expected cost which embodies the risk provisions normally held by the project manager. The E_b expected project cost shown at the back, upper right of the cube is the estimated expected cost which embodies the additional provisions normally held by the board, defined by the vector F_p^3, made up of the three dimensions indicated. Roger argued the view, eventually accepted by Barry and Paul, that in most circumstances it might not be worth identifying the individual components, but F_p^3 always required explicit estimation.

Roger suggested that Paul and the project team might take an initial view on triple Es and SAPs with his help. The projects director might then take an extended view on behalf of the board of additional SAPs, unknown unknowns and bias, with his help. Barry would have oversight of both. Simple discrete value estimates of the form illustrated by Table 6.1 were suggested by Roger. The initial reaction by Barry and Paul to an expected uplift associated with F_p^3 of the order of 20% with the wide range indicated in Table 6.1 was hostile. It seemed to them that a very crude fudge factor was being applied to a comparatively rigorous and detailed estimate of E_p. However, a careful review by Roger of the kinds of issues

Table 6.1—Cube factor estimation (F_p^3)

Project cube factor F_p^3	Initial project estimate	Extended board estimate
1		0.1
1.1	0.2	0.2
1.2	0.5	0.3
1.3	0.3	0.2
1.4		0.1
1.5		0.1
Expected value	1.21	1.23

each component of F_p^3 had to capture, related to the experience of other similar projects, and the offer to break it down in a format like that of Figure 5.4 if they wished, convinced them both that this order of magnitude was itself probably biased on the optimistic side, at both the initial project level and the extended board level.

One colleague exposed to the discussion commented as follows. He had been instructed as a lad in the software industry that a 'best estimate', like E_p, should be multiplied by 3 to define the equivalent of E_b. He had later learned that π was a better multiplier, because it sounded scientific, and it was bigger. He supposed that F_p^3 was best thought of as a version of his π, much scaled down to reflect the very high quality formal risk analysis underlying E_p, and the comparatively certain nature of offshore projects relative to software projects. Was it really the case that the analysis underlying E_p was so good and offshore projects were so certain that $F_p^3 = 1.23$ was big enough? This comment left Barry and Paul convinced that $F_p^3 = 1.23$ probably was too small, but it was as big as they wished to make it on a first outing. Cube factors could be calibrated over time in relation to experience with the new risk management processes (later done). The critically important thing at this stage was to recognize that F_p^3 existed, that it probably had an expected value significantly greater than unity, that it had a significant variance, and that it mattered.

By the time the discussions leading to the identification of F_p^3 and the need for a projects director had run their course, Barry and Paul were convinced that Roger was moving things in the right direction from a corporate perspective. However, they were not entirely clear how the approach would work in practice, or how the board would react.

Roger's Simple Analysis of Distributed Uncertainty Ownership

'Extreme events' is a relative concept. A £200 million anchor risk event is an extreme event for a project worth £1000 million, but not for a board with a portfolio of £1000 million projects and consortium risk sharing. By the same token, £2 million may define an extreme event for someone with a £10 million budget reporting to a project manager. This implies that the triple Es examined on page 204 may have scaled-down equivalents in terms of the management hierarchy below the project manager. It is tempting to look at the interface between those who report to the project manager and the project manager in the same structure, assuming a cascading-down effect. However, some new issues are involved, which are best examined bottom-up. In particular, extreme events are not the initiating issue or the dominant issue at this level. The real driver at this level is most use-fully viewed in terms of who owns the uncertainty. Understanding who *should* own the uncertainty is in its turn driven by the need to distinguish between good luck and good management, bad luck and bad management, and bias. The key to successful management of good luck is avoiding ambiguous distributed ownership of uncertainty. The way uncertainty ownership is distributed needs to be explicit and very carefully designed. This section begins to explain why and how.

Roger uncovered the initiating driver of uncertainty ownership distribution considerations at the subproject level when addressing the five activities in Paul's project which precede the pipe laying activity. Table 6.2 portrays these activities in a variant of the Chapter 4 minimalist format. Table 6.2 assumes a discrete value uniform distribution between the minimum and the maximum duration for each activity, and it provides a nominal 80% value (excluding cube factor events), comparable to the project manager's budget. For example, activity A, 'design the pipeline', is assumed to have durations of 4, 5, 6, 7 or 8 weeks exactly, each with a probability of 0.2, implying a mean duration of 6 weeks, and an 80% chance of 7 weeks or less being required. Activities B to D are directly comparable apart from a scalar shift. Activity E involves only three possible outcomes, rounding up slightly to define the nominal 80% value.

'Design the pipe' was an in-house task for the engineering design staff in Roger's company. This task had an uncertain duration primarily because of the uncertain demand on design staff's time from other projects and other parts of the same project. The quality of the design staff allocated was also a factor. The project manager had limited control of design staff allocations, but some ability to exert pressure through in-house working relationships.

'Order the pipe' was an in-house task for the procurement staff in Roger's company. There were similar internal reasons for duration variability, plus poten-tial difficulties associated with suppliers. The project manager had even less control because of potential supplier difficulties, the ability of procurement staff to blame suppliers, whether or not they were the problem, and a strong 'separate empire' mindset among procurement staff.

Table 6.2—Simple sequential activity duration table

| Activity | Activity description | Duration (weeks) with no cube factor events | | | |
		minimum	mean	nominal 80%	maximum
A	Design the pipeline	4	6	7	8
B	Order the pipe	2	4	5	6
C	Deliver the pipe	8	10	11	12
D	Coat the pipe	5	7	8	9
E	Deliver the coated pipe	1	2	3	3
A–E	Design the pipeline and acquire coated pipe	20	29	34	38

'Deliver the pipe' was a task which the procurement staff were responsible for in so far as they let the contract, but its execution was in the hands of the company which manufactured the pipe and arranged for its shipping to the coating yard. The pipe manufacturing company might be on the other side of the globe (e.g. Japan), but the coating yard would be local (European).

'Coat the pipe' involved encasing the pipe with a concrete jacket and water-proofing material, to protect it and give it a slight negative buoyancy when full of air to facilitate laying. This work was contracted to a coating yard, with normal manufacturing process variabilities. The procurement staff in Roger's company were responsible for letting the contract, but its execution was in the hands of the coating yard.

'Deliver the coated pipe' would be contracted to one of the local (European) logistics companies which served the North Sea offshore industry. Roger's procurement department controlled letting the contract, and its execution was in the hands of the logistics company, but the project manager had some ability to influence matters through local working relationships.

Roger obtained the data used to define Table 6.2 by talking to appropriate staff from the project team, the design department and procurement department. The simple nature of the portrayal does not address uncertainty associated with the individual views of these staff or differences in view which Roger knew were important in practice. Nor does Table 6.2 address any extreme events. As indicated, Table 6.2 excludes the activity level equivalent of all project cube factor (F_p^3) events, what Roger later called activity cube factor (F_a^3) events. Roger wanted to begin by assuming Table 6.2 was a true and complete view of the uncertainty involved. Roger wanted to explore what could happen if Table 6.2 was used as the basis for managing uncertainty in the context of a situation where the project manager owns all the uncertainty not passed to the board, but with the exception of F_a^3 cube factor events which are not appropriately passed on to those reporting to him, he cascades this uncertainty on using a nominal 80% confidence level. That is, if Paul treats those reporting to him in the same way as the board treats him in terms of the use of 80% commitment values, what are the implications? To understand the implications of this starting point, Roger produced Figures 6.3 and 6.4.

Figure 6.3 is a simple probability tree which flows from Table 6.2 if it is assumed that each activity has a planned duration equal to the nominal 80% value, no activity ever finishes early in the useful sense that the following activity starts earlier than planned, and any delay can be accommodated without knock-on effects by all following activities. Durations for each activity sequence are added to provide a total duration for the summary activity A–E, 'design the pipeline and acquire coated pipe'. Associated probabilities are the product of the probabilities on each branch. The simplified tree of Figure 6.4 collects together the six ways of realizing a duration of 36, and the four ways of realizing a duration of 35 or 37, as well as showing the one way of achieving 34 or 38. The expected duration of 34.8 weeks is defined by the five possible outcomes weighted by their probabilities. The

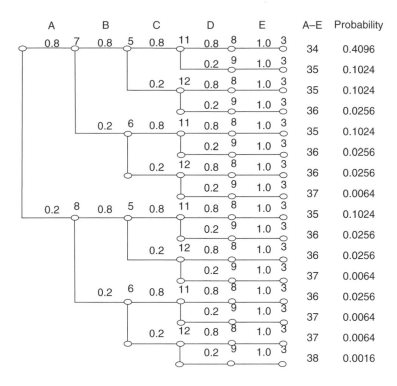

Figure 6.3—Simple sequential activity probability tree.

nominal 80% value of 35 weeks has an 82% chance of being achieved (0.4096 + 0.4096).

Having spent some time understanding what Table 6.2 and Figures 6.3 and 6.4 suggest, Roger prepared a presentation for Paul. He started by presenting Table 6.2 and Figures 6.3 and 6.4 as just outlined. He then began his interpretation as follows. Taking the model literally for the moment, without questioning the

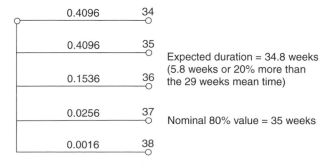

Figure 6.4—Simplified tree for 'design the pipeline and acquire coated pipe' (activity A–E).

validity of its assumptions, the mean duration of 29 weeks will never be achieved. The average duration will be 34.8 weeks, an increase relative to the mean of 5.8 weeks (20%). The nominal 80% value is 35 weeks, 6 weeks more than the mean. If we round the 34.8 weeks average duration to 35 weeks, the average duration and the nominal 80% value coincide. The reason for this in terms of the operational assumptions underlying Figures 6.3 and 6.4 is the truncation of the activity duration distributions on the low-duration side. The model assumes bad luck (delays) relative to the nominal 80% values are passed on to the following activity, but not good luck (time savings) relative to the nominal 80% values. The rationale which these assumptions illustrate is based on the understanding that those responsible for each activity have been given responsibility for the good luck relative to the nominal 80% values. As a consequence, those responsible for each activity are planning on the basis of 80% values for themselves and all other activities. When they realize they are going to take less time, there is no incentive to let anyone know and every incentive to keep quiet. If it is convenient to finish early, there is no incentive for a prior warning to the following activity, so the following activity is not going to be pulled forward. At least some of this truculence will be linked to the need to accommodate delays to earlier activities where there has been no allowance for knock-on effects. In effect, there are no swings and roundabouts, only swings. Put another way, all the good luck is wasted. Roger called it the wasted good luck syndrome.

Paul was incredulous at this revelation. His immediate reaction was, 'This must be a very pessimistic result because of inappropriate underlying assumptions.' Roger's response was, 'There are only two assumptions which are highly suspect in this model, and both are optimistic.' One is the assumption that there would be no direct knock-on effect associated with earlier delays, and no indirect knock-on effects in the sense that each activity owner would be prepared to accept a significant chance of delay imposed by earlier activities without padding their own estimate to help absorb it. The other is that each activity owner would be prepared to believe that all extreme events and other F_a^3 events have been transferred to the project manager, and if they happen there is no need for any further padding of their estimates. Given the optimistic nature of these two assumptions, it was very reasonable to assume that those responsible for each activity would make direct use of the available time defined by the 80% nominal values, allowing the work to expand to make use of the available time, a version of Parkinson's law (work expands to fill available time), or fail to pass on the effects of an early finish if one is achieved.

Paul, Barry and Roger spent some time exploring these and other assumptions which might modify the picture painted by Figure 6.4. As Roger expected, they eventually agreed that the inferences it provided were oversimplifications of a complex reality, but they were optimistic oversimplifications. The reality was much worse. Given a simple cascaded down version of the current or starting position approach outlined on page 200, activity owners would attempt to set the schedule using something approaching 80% values which incorporated extreme events and knock-on effects which were very important. In summary, an approach based on distributed ownership of uncertainty relative to nominal 80% values builds in a ratchet effect which accumulates the bad luck relative to the 80% values but dissipates the good luck relative to the 80% values. Ownership and control of the good luck is a crucial aspect of the more general issue of ownership and control of distributed uncertainty.

An Internal Trigger Contract to Manage Good Luck

What can we do to capture this wasted good luck? To begin answering this question, Roger suggested that the basis of the answer lay in who owns the luck, and whether or not those who control and make the luck are motivated to manage it in a manner congruent with the wishes of other interested parties. Roger suggested starting to explore what was involved with the specific case of the 'design the pipeline' activity. He proposed replacing the current approach with what he called an internal trigger contract.

Current practice within the company involved each project paying for design staff time allocated to the project at a fixed rate per hour, regardless of how many hours of design effort were involved, or how staff were allocated to the project. The nominal cost of a design activity was the sum of the recorded design hours used multiplied by a standard cost rate per hour. The cost rate per hour was company-wide and not negotiable, based on the average cost per chargeable hour for the design department. Recorded design hours used included a number of non-chargeable hours that designers did not wish to reveal. This arrangement resulted in the project manager giving the design activity duration good luck to the design department, via a base plan duration set at the 80% confidence level. It also had the undesirable effect of isolating the design department from the implications of that department's efficiency and effectiveness (or lack of it). Roger's position was that this current practice was not acceptable. The design department would have to accept a change in current practice or quite properly find itself outsourced (and probably out of work). However, if it changed in the way Roger was suggesting, this should be proof against any attempts to outsource design. Contracting the design to an external design company was feasible, but a case had to be made for doing so to Victor, the main board director responsible for the design department. Victor had a vested interest in supporting the design department.

In Roger's view, it was important to understand that uncertainty associated with design duration is driven by ambiguity about quality and cost and inefficient working practices. This needed to be managed, to reduce uncertainty, and to capture the benefits of managing the good luck, in the sense of the scope for low duration, high quality and low cost. This involves recognizing that the design department can make and share their luck to a significant extent if they are motivated to do so. The project manager cannot retain ownership of the associated good luck or efficiency and effectiveness issues. However, joint management of the good luck, efficiency and effectiveness is essential. This implies some form of internal contract between the design department and the project which encourages the design department to generate and deliver the good luck, efficiency and effectiveness with a minimum of uncertainty. As the design department is part of the same organization, a standard legal contract is not appropriate. However, a contract is still needed in the form of a memorandum of understanding, to formalize the agreement. Failure to formalize an internal contract in a context like this implies ambiguous psychological contracts for both parties, and they are unlikely to be effective. The ambiguity inherent in such contracts can only generate uncertainty which is highly divisive and quite unnecessary.

A core aspect of Roger's thinking was the need to move towards a significant change in corporate practice and culture, requiring the design department to contract on the basis of negotiated expected nominal hours as the basis for payment, rather than the realized nominal hours. If the design department takes fewer hours than expected, they should reap some rewards. Conversely, if the design department takes more hours than expected, they should not be able to charge for the extra time if the fault lies with them and scope changes are not involved. Once this core idea is accepted, providing bonus payments for quality improvements is a viable option, because the design department cannot compensate for low quality by charging for more hours. More important, it is essential to motivate high quality within a fixed, feasible number of hours assumed. This does not preclude additional non-chargeable hours being used by the design department if this time is needed or useful and it is available. Further, providing bonus payments for duration improvements is a viable option, because the design department cannot compensate for later durations by charging for more hours. It is essential to motivate low durations within a fixed number of chargeable hours. Again, non-chargeable hours can be used if needed or useful and available. Finally, eliciting accurate completion predictions for planning purposes is a viable option, because the design department can be put in a position where such predictions attract a useful formal bonus which is not tradable with other criteria. Put another way, the relationships between cost, duration, quality and uncertainty which Roger proposed to manage involves capturing and benefiting from good luck, but it also involves motivating associated efficiency and effectiveness to create good luck. We can literally 'make our luck' to some extent. But at a more fundamental level, much of the variability associated with good and bad luck is the product of ambiguity about the quality of the management process. Improving the quality of the management process is the best way to manage this uncertainty.

Building on these points, Roger pointed out that 'quality' was a standard term for measures of performance other than cost and duration, sometimes called 'performance'. Performance in a general sense is about value for money. Value for money is about the extent to which the project meets its objectives. Understanding the relationship between performance in this general sense and uncertainty is what is necessary. Internal contracts between departments and projects, and associated performance-related pay for individuals or groups of individuals, are all part of the same issue. The bottom line is being clear about what needs to be done, and motivating everyone to work towards congruent objectives, to maximize efficiency and effectiveness, and then minimize residual uncertainty associated with predicting completion. Most of the uncertainty associated with design department current practice can and should be eliminated, because it is the result of working practices which are inefficient and ineffective.

Roger and Paul discussed how this approach could be sold to Donald, head of the design department. It involved being completely open and frank about a partnership relationship across corporate boundaries for mutual benefit, akin to but stronger than a preferred supplier partnership. Possible performance-related pay implications of the proposed bonus payments would not be within Paul's gift, but Donald would be assured of Paul's support for appropriate change in this area. More important perhaps, Donald would be assured of Paul's support for a well-paid and highly motivated in-house design capability, and for resistance to current pressures to outsource design along with any other non-core activity.

Exploring performance capability

Roger suggested that Paul should start his discussions with Donald by reaching agreement on a probability distribution for activity duration conditional on current working practices and appropriate triple Es and SAPs, recognizing that associated factors plus PUU and bias factors might also be involved in the definition of an appropriate F_a^3. Assume that the activity A estimate in Table 6.2 is the result. Roger indicated that the design department could use a risk management process comparable to the first or later passes discussed in Chapter 4 to estimate this distribution, with Roger's support if they wished. For the purpose of defining the Table 6.2 distribution, the design department should think of themselves as an independent contractor. In the context of current practice they do not need to commit to a cost, and duration commitments are not enforceable. However, Roger suggested that they should be prepared to commit after a fashion for negotiating purposes to the nominal 80% duration value of 7 weeks (as per current practice), given agreement on triple Es and SAPs, as well as the 80% probability associated with Table 6.2. Roger suggested that Paul should use this duration distribution to define two key values, both conditional on the F_a^3 factor assumptions:

- The expected duration of 6 weeks
- The trigger duration of 7 weeks (the nominal 80% value)

Roger suggested that Paul should then reach agreement with Donald on the anticipated number of design hours given the expected duration, as indicated in Table 6.3. The duration 4 and 8 value rows were not required, except to make it clear that this distribution of nominal hours reflects the expected duration and the average realization of uncertainties associated with Table 6.2. Roger suggested that Table 6.3 should be associated with a simple uniform distribution 10–90 percentile range assumption for convenience (as in Chapter 4), with an expected value of 400 as indicated directly. Any distribution shape could be used to provide an expected value. Roger suggested that the expected number of design hours defined by Table 6.3 (400), multiplied by the standard design department rate per hour, should define the nominal cost for the design activity. Roger suggested this nominal cost should be the starting point for the internal trigger contract he proposed, an agreed best estimate of the hours that should be involved on average, excluding F_a^3 factor events, and given normal working practices.

Next Roger suggested that Paul should reach agreement with Donald on the anticipated quality of the design given the expected duration and nominal cost, as indicated in Table 6.4. The starting point would be defining what was meant by the mean (expected) 50% nominal quality. It would be defined in terms of a written description of what Donald viewed as the expected quality in terms of qualitative and quantitative measures specified by Paul with Donald's assistance. These would cover ease (cost) of manufacture and shipping as assessed by the manufacturer, ease (cost) of laying as assessed by the pipe laying contractor, ease (cost) of maintenance as assessed by the operations manager, and any other relevant design criteria. The next point of discussion would be what was meant by the 90% nominal quality value. It would be defined in terms of a written description of what Donald viewed as the 1 in 10 best quality outcome which was feasible in terms of the same qualitative and quantitative measures specified by Paul with Donald's assistance for the 50% level. This might involve weighting the different criteria if trade-offs were feasible, such as easier maintenance versus easier laying. The final point of discussion would be what was meant by the 10% nominal quality value. It would be defined on the same set of quantitative and qualitative measures as the 1 in 10 worst quality outcome which was still acceptable.

An honest broker (e.g. a quality department) would be involved in all post-

Table 6.3—'Design the pipeline' hours required distribution

| Duration | Nominal hours anticipated with no cube factor events | | |
	minimum	mean	maximum
4			
6	300	**400**	500
8			

Table 6.4—'Design the pipeline' quality distribution

Duration	Nominal quality anticipated with no cube factor events		
	minimum	mean	maximum
4 6 8	10% quality level	50% quality level	90% quality level

construction quality assessments of the score achieved in terms of agreed rules. Paul and Donald would agree the rules in the process of agreeing Table 6.4 (which is just a nominal scale) and all the associated quality definitions. For simplicity, quality would be judged to the nearest 10%. Roger acknowledged that this process would not be easy, and the resulting quality scale would be necessarily imprecise. Trade-offs between criteria would amplify assessment difficulties. However, it was crucial for Donald and Paul to reach a shared understanding of what was required of the design which could be measured approximately in a manner both saw as fair and appropriate for design. If this could not be done, the quality of the pipeline design would be a critical source of uncertainty which was completely out of Paul's control. If Paul could not reach a suitable agreement with Donald on this matter, Roger suggested that Paul should indicate he intended to approach external designers. However, Paul should make it very clear to Donald that this was a measure of last resort, and Paul should not even raise the issue unless it became necessary. This backstop position would apply to agreements associated with this scale as well as its definition at this stage.

Determining incentive, premium payments

Roger then suggested that Paul should negotiate an early completion premium payment rate of 5% of the nominal cost for each week the design department reduced the activity duration below the trigger duration of 7 weeks, the nominal 80% value, with negative premium payments for longer durations. That is, if the design department finished the design activity in 7 weeks, they would receive the nominal cost. If they took 8 weeks, they would receive the nominal cost less 5%. But if they took 6 weeks, the expected (average) duration, they would receive the nominal cost plus 5%. If they took 5 weeks, they would receive the nominal cost plus 10%; and if they took 4 weeks, they would receive the nominal cost plus 15%. Further, Paul should negotiate a correct completion prediction premium payment bonus of 5% of nominal cost if the design department correctly predicted the completion date 2 weeks in advance. For example, if at the end of week 3 they correctly predicted completion by the end of week 5, an additional 5% of the nominal cost would be paid as a bonus. Further still, Paul should negotiate a premium quality payment of 80% of the nominal cost for achievement of the 90% quality rating, on the understanding that the 10% quality rating will involve an 80% deduction. With post-project quality assessments working to the nearest 10%, this involves a 20% premium quality payment rate per 10% improvement in quality.

Having outlined these three premium payments structures, Roger then explained in some detail how they ought to work in the first instance, and how the basic idea ought to evolve in further internal contracts between the design department and projects. His starting point was explaining that a 5% early completion premium would be payable plus a 5% correct completion prediction premium if the design department took the expected duration of 6 weeks, advised this would be the case at the end of week 4, and a 50% (mean) quality rating was achieved. If the design department do what they expect to be able to do, they will receive 10% in premium payments. This starting position should be attractive to the design department. It is important that it is attractive.

His next point was that the premiums associated with design quality dominate the premiums associated with duration. If the design department achieved the minimum duration of 4 weeks, the 15% premium would not compensate for a drop in quality to 40% which would carry a 20% penalty. Further, the premiums associated with duration dominate the premium associated with correct prediction of duration. It is not worth adding a week to the predicted completion to be sure to obtain the bonus if completion a week earlier is feasible. These two levels of dominance imply that the design department should be motivated to treat quality as the first priority, duration as the second priority, and correct completion prediction as a third priority. Duration, cost, quality and uncertainty are not independent, and all four are functions of the motivation and priorities of those involved. The scheme provides a coordinated attack on all four performance criteria. If any subset is addressed without reference to the others, distortions will occur. For example, if quality is not addressed, it will tend to fall to the 10% level if motives to control duration, cost and uncertainty are introduced on their own. The premium rates suggested by Roger were selected to motivate high quality, low durations and minimal uncertainty without examining the true cost to the organization of variations in design duration or quality, or appropriate shadow prices or opportunity costs. One refinement of his scheme that could be pursued is assessing appropriate shadow prices or opportunity costs, explored in Ian's tale. A second refinement could be to allow external design companies to compete if quality, durations, completion predictions and average cost per design hours are not competitive. However, Roger suggested that this second refinement would be a symptom of failure in his view. Provided the design department managed a core of the organization's work in the way proposed, with the use of external designers controlled in a common quality and duration control and prediction framework, with external work to smooth troughs or maintain a cushion of capability, the loyalty and captured experience of in-house design should prove well worth preserving.

Implications of the trigger contract

Roger suggested that current normal working for the design department involved a significant level of multi-tasking, which impacted quality as well as duration, because keeping all the designers busy was the first priority, and keeping all the projects equally happy (or unhappy) was the second priority, subject to maintaining quality standards set by average past achievement within the acceptable range. The designers were all very quality oriented, but the work allocation approach led to unsatisfactory quality and duration because it was driven by keeping everyone busy. Nothing was optimized, apart from designer idle time minimization, because designer idle time was clearly visible to everyone within the design department, and nothing else was visible enough to optimize. The extent to which non-chargeable hours were buried or lost in someone's (anyone's) contract was not a big problem per se, but it was symptomatic of this idle time minimization mindset. With the internal contract Roger proposed, if Donald picked his best designers and avoided any multi-tasking, he could probably deliver 90% quality in 4 weeks, and predict completion correctly, with a 100% (80 + 15 + 5) premium payment. If this was not feasible, it would be duration that would suffer, with appropriate warning. The target duration for 'design the pipeline' would be the plausible minimum duration of four weeks. This target duration would be used for base planning purposes, including advising the procurement department when to assume the availability of a completed design for 'order the pipe' to begin. This is a core aspect of managing the good luck. The base plan assumes aggressive duration targets which allow all the duration good luck to be exploited.

In terms of the internal contract between the project and the design department, the trigger duration of 7 weeks for premium payments would be called a trigger duration. It would not be called a commitment duration, despite its 80% confidence level. There would be no commitment between Paul and Donald on design duration, although Paul and Donald's commitment in terms of having the design completed would be reflected in the incentive structure for Donald. A conventional commitment on duration is made redundant by Roger's internal trigger contract approach.

It could be argued that the expected duration, assessed assuming the current system, is not a relevant parameter for the new regime. A revised expected duration value should approach the target duration. However, Roger suggested that it would be unnecessarily complicated and confusing to estimate a revised expected duration in the short run. For similar reasons, Roger suggested no change to the nominal cost defined by the mean duration and the mean hours required distribution, or the mean quality assessment. However, he referred to these expected values as 'the internal contract' expected values, to reflect the fact that they were the basis of the contract and did not need to be taken literally by Paul or Donald for other purposes. Bearing this in mind, Roger indicated that the mean (expected) quality as assessed assuming the current system is the trigger quality level by definition. The expected cost in these terms is the nominal cost plus 10%. That is, the expected cost assumes the expected duration (6 weeks) and the expected quality (50%) with an accurate indication of completion at the end of week 4. Paul would need an F_a^3 to modify this expected cost for his budgeting purposes, the motivating effect of the contract being part of the bias to be accounted for, along with triple Es, SAPs and PUUs. Donald would normally need the same F_a^3 for his purposes, although more generally a different F_a^3 might be involved.

Roger indicated that in addition to no duration commitment in the usual sense, there should be no conventional commitment to a quality or cost. However, Paul and Donald's commitment on quality should be built into the incentive structure, and there should be a target quality of 90% and a target cost defined by the target duration and the target quality. This means that the target cost involves a 100% (15 + 5 + 80) premium on the nominal cost. The implications of this are very important. The target duration and quality should be achievable given no significant triple Es, SAPs or PUUs. However, they are very aggressive targets, and they would be recognized by all as such. Achieving both these targets should be good cause for celebration by everyone. Failing to meet both of them completely should involve understanding by all concerned. Variations on the downside are to be expected. Variation on the upside are conceivable but very unlikely. *The duration and quality targets are optimistic from everyone's perspective.* The target cost is really a price from Donald's perspective given the 'profit' element associated with premium payments. From the design department's perspective it is a very aggressive target price. Failing to meet it should involve understanding by all concerned. Variations on the downside are to be expected. Variations on the upside are conceivable but unlikely. Achieving the target cost (price) should be a good cause for celebration by the design department. *The target cost is optimistic from the design department's perspective.* From Paul's perspective, the target cost is 100% more than the nominal cost and 90% more than the contract expected cost. It is conceivable that it will cost more without F_a^3 issues, but very unlikely. Variations on the downside are to be expected, unless F_a^3 issues prove important. *The target cost is pessimistic from the project's perspective.*

From Paul's perspective, the target duration and quality are optimistic, the target cost is pessimistic. In terms of the management of expectations, this mix is interesting and useful. Departures from the cost target are negatively correlated with departures from the quality and duration targets. Disappointments related to quality and duration involve some compensation in relation to cost. Some of Paul's uncertainty is hedged, which means some of the organization's uncertainty associated with this project is hedged. From Donald's perspective all targets are optimistic, and there is no negative correlation. However, the design department is being paid a 100% premium for complete success, and partial success still involves a sizeable premium. Total failure could result in the design department owing the project money. However, this is unlikely, and it would probably mean outsourcing design from then on whatever form of internal contract was in place.

It would be generally understood that the design department have very strong incentives to do what the project wants of them, so there would be much less need for monitoring and attempts to control in the sense of interfering or bringing pressure. The design department would be motivated to generate and capture as much good luck as possible, and share the benefits. Having built in this motivation, there would be no point in attempting to exercise control in the 'chasing' sense. This is another win-win feature of the approach. Chasing is not a very enjoyable activity for project staff who are not natural bullies, and nobody enjoys being chased routinely. It was a matter of back them or sack them. Some control by Paul's staff would be essential to ensure that 'sack them' was not a relevant possibility, and very close control would be essential if 'sack them' emerged as a serious possibility, but the incentive structure should keep the design department motivated in a way which minimizes the need for normal direct control.

Roger suggested that Victor and the rest of the board should not object to doubling the cost of design, because it was a paper transfer from one part of the organization to another, used to motivate efficiency. If it worked, the average cost per hour of design should start to fall, and the profits generated by the design department could be shared by design staff and the rest of the organization. But more important, the 'quality' of design would lead to significant improvements in other costs. And allowing design staff to pursue quality in this way would start a virtuous circle, because it would be aligned with what motivated them to become designers in the first place. Roger suggested that other project managers and board members with their own interests at heart should not object to this change if all other projects could do the same, because it would force the design department to provide a similar high nominal cost but low duration and high-quality service for all projects, with further profits generated by efficiency gains shared by the design staff and the rest of the organization, and further improvements in other costs. If all projects did the same, the design department would have to drop most multi-tasking, take a lot more care over the timing and scheduling of all work, start fitting some holidays around work rather than the other way around, start looking at the use of external designers to manage peaks, start looking at the acquisition of external work for their designers to keep staff busy in troughs, and take more care recruiting and accepting top-quality designers. These changes could be motivated and facilitated by appropriate bonus payments associated with profits. The average cost per design hour ought to drop because of the increases in efficiency, but effectiveness in terms of the added value per pound of design time ought to increase at a much faster rate, both driven synergistically by the premium payments.

Roger emphasized the need to be careful about words used to describe sharing profits with the design department or making bonus payments to designers. On a scale of motivation by financial greed, ranging from stock market traders to volunteer charity workers, designers were closer to charity workers than market traders, and destroying their quality focus would be a serious mistake. Explicit design department profits might also be a mistake. However, Donald could manage this by simply promising and then delivering reasonable salary increases to his staff via standard annual reviews related to performance on projects which the individual was involved in, and some sharing in performance by the design department as a whole. Donald could agree with Victor that residual profit could be described as 'efficiency savings returned to the board', or other suitable phrases found to tell a version of the story people preferred to hear.

Roger and Paul discussed at some length the implications of agreeing a scope of work with the design department as a basis for the number of expected nominal hours. They recognized that this would establish a relationship between the design department and the project manager which was in part a cascaded version of the project manager's relationship with the board. Triple Es and SAPs became relevant, as did the known unknowns which are not embedded in the expected cost because it is inappropriate for the project manager to pass them on to the design department. Triple Es and SAPs which would not be accepted as part of the board's F_p^3 were a starting point. But in general, F_p^3 events at the project manager/board level are not the same as F_a^3 events at the design department/ project manager level. A major change in pipeline design because of a switch to a collector system is an example scope change which would impact both. However, if the project manager and the design department agree the expected nominal hours for design work assuming a given pipe operating pressure which later changes by 20%, the board will not wish to treat this level of scope change within their F_p^3. The board will expect the project manager to include this in his reported expected cost. This means that an expected cost at the design department/project manager level is generally conditional on a different set of conditions than that assumed at the project manager/board level.

Designing An External Trigger Contract

Roger next turned his attention to the remaining activities in Table 6.2: B (order the pipe), C (deliver the pipe), D (coat the pipe) and E (deliver the coated pipe). Roger began by suggesting Paul should refer to them collectively as activity B–E, 'acquire coated pipe'. He suggested Paul should see 'acquire coated pipe' as a subproject (or project within his programme) which he should subcontract as a whole to the procurement department. The head of the procurement department, Piers, should be persuaded to see activity B–E as his activity (project). The decomposition or separability of the component four activities was of some interest to Paul, and it would be of great interest to Piers, but it was useful to signify to the procurement department that activity B–E was their responsibility as a whole.

Current practice did not involve any payment by projects to the procurement department. The procurement department were an organizational overhead paid for indirectly, and there was no alternative to using the procurement department. At that time there was not a lot of warm feeling between project staff and procurement staff. When Roger asked people why, the answers were usually personal and uncomplimentary. However, Roger believed that the problem was organizational. In particular, from what Roger could see, procurement staff did the best they could despite the system. Given the system, their best was highly commendable, and their 'separate empire' mindset was to protect the professional self-esteem of procurement staff which made the system work as well as it did.

Roger suggested Paul should keep Piers informed of his discussions with Donald. As soon as the design department deal showed clear signs of being sorted and agreed within the company, Paul should persuade Piers (if it had not already occurred to him) to have the bright idea of inventing a comparable approach to managing activity B–E on behalf of the project, and take a sizeable share of the credit for the approach. The procurement department could not be bought with premiums like the design department, but they could be eased into a similar approach, driven by their professional concerns, and a potential enhancement of their status, in a partnership relationship based on mutual benefits. Rumours of enhanced pay because of enhanced status might provide an extra carrot, but performance-related pay which smacked of bribes or backhanders would clash with the desirable features of the procurement department culture.

Roger suggested that Paul might begin his discussion with Piers by agreeing activity definitions and details with duration estimates as portrayed in Table 6.2 for activities B to E (by way of an example). Once Table 6.2 was agreed with respect to activities B to E, Paul might indicate that the base plan completion date for activity A was determined by the minimum (4 week) duration, and that with something close to certainty, Paul would be able to give Piers an exact finish date 2 weeks in advance. An updated expected duration would be available prior to the 2 weeks notice. Paul would like Piers to plan to start activity B on the base plan start date, on the understanding there might be a delay with warning. Roger then suggested that like the design department, the procurement department could probably deliver the completion of activity B in the minimum duration, 2 weeks, if strongly motivated to demonstrate speed. For example, they could talk to the design department before the completion of design and obtain a preliminary working specification. They could talk to pipe suppliers in advance, based on this preliminary specification. In modelling terms, the B follows A precedence can be relaxed.

An important issue was providing the procurement department with motivation for speed, to capture this potential efficiency and effectiveness. However, the key issue was providing the procurement department with motivation to deliver quality. Under the current system Piers had no direct incentive for speed. But much more important, there were no mechanisms available to address quality. Roger suggested that quality should be directly defined in relation to Piers' department, given the design, in terms of the quality of the coated pipe delivered, the cost of the coated pipe delivered, and the duration of activity B–E as a whole. There is no cost associated with the procurement department's time from Paul's perspective, and the duration of activity B on its own is not a key issue. The key issue is quality as just defined. Paul should challenge Piers to deliver quality in this sense. Roger would help Piers to think through how to deliver it.

The contract with the pipe supplier would not raise the cost-plus difficulties associated with current design department arrangements. A fixed price for a given specification was common practice. However, if Piers was going to have his quality (given the design) assessed in terms which included the quality of the manu-factured pipe, the cost of the pipe manufacture, and the duration of activity B–E as a whole, it would be in Piers' interest to negotiate a contract which reflects these issues in terms of appropriate trade-offs. For example, consider activity C, 'deliver the pipe'. Piers might agree to a nominal cost for the pipe defined by a mean level of quality, and the nominal 80% (11 week) duration. Piers might agree to a 10% increase in cost (price) if the pipe supplier achieved an agreed 90% quality, a 10% decrease in cost (price) if the pipe supplier achieved a corresponding agreed 10% quality. Piers might agree to a 3% increase in price if the minimum duration of 8 weeks was achieved, 1% per week saved related to the 11 week trigger duration and a 1% penalty per week over 11 weeks. Piers might agree to a further 1% premium for 2 weeks notice of delivery.

A basic condition of the contract might be a base plan start date defined by activities A and B both taking the minimum duration, with 2 weeks notice of the actual date, and updated expected start dates prior to the 2 week notice. However, Piers might offer to compensate the pipe supplier for each week of delay by a 1% payment if the 2 week notice is correct, and a further 2% if the notice is incorrect. In this case the pipe supplier will achieve the nominal cost (price) plus a premium of 14% (the sum of 10 + 3 + 1) if nominal top-quality (90%) pipe is delivered in 8 weeks (the nominal minimum) after the notified (2 weeks in advance) start date and a 2 week accurate notice of completion of activity C is provided. And the supplier will receive additional payments if the base plan is delayed, with or without exact notice 2 weeks in advance.

Piers might agree to all these conditions by specifying the percentage premiums (and penalties) in advance for tendering purposes, along with the 10%, 50% and 90% quality definitions, requesting tenders on the basis of nominal cost (price) given these conditions. Alternatively and preferably, Piers might use these values as examples, and leave suppliers the option of adjusting these values to suit themselves, on the understanding that Paul and Piers can close down one degree of freedom. Assuming this, Piers can improve the effectiveness and efficiency of the choice of supplier. For example, supplier S might be able to deliver very high quality pipe at a low marginal cost relative to supplier T. If S and T are equal in all other respects, it would be worth contracting with S for a minimum 90% quality. If S wanted a larger 80% duration trigger for this quality, it might still be worth it, if the rest of activity B–E can be adjusted economically. Piers might use his example premiums and penalties to indicate the order of magnitude of the associated costs for his company. Piers could invite tendering companies to modify these example premiums and penalties to reflect their costs, on the understanding that the best overall package from Piers' company's perspective would be selected, usually leaving the selected contractor with only one real degree of freedom, normally duration. For example, if pipe quality is contracted at a minimum of the 90% level, the pipe supplier may take longer and lose duration premiums but a decrease in quality will not be allowed. This provides Piers with a very powerful way to discriminate between suppliers and reduce the uncertainty associated with what will be delivered. It allows alignment of the best interests of his company and the chosen supplier. Interests are aligned in advance when choosing a supplier, as well as in the face of uncertainty while the contract is being executed.

It should be clear that 'quality' as defined for the pipe supplier might be associated with premiums and penalties over more than one dimension. This would allow pipe suppliers to clarify their relative advantages and disadvantages, allowing Piers more discrimination when selecting the best overall package of quality, cost and delivery. To keep things simple, most quality measures might be assumed to be perfectly positively correlated, but important exceptions might be appropriate. For example, Piers might contract for 90% quality as a minimum on half a dozen measures, but only 50% on several, and only 10% on one, with duration the chosen degree of freedom. The quality levels selected by Piers' organization should not be chosen arbitrarily by the design department, and then allowed to vary within bounds in a manner which is unrelated to the best interests of Piers' organization. They should reflect the overall trade-offs within the project, and the feasible trade-offs within potential suppliers. Roger's approach allows these relationships to be addressed, pre and post bidding. Chapter 9 will consider conventional approaches to implementing this kind of analysis.

Careful pre-bidding specification of the appropriate quality measures is clearly of great importance once this route is adopted. The amount of effort involved is clearly significant. However, if this issue is not addressed, a large and important area of uncertainty is not being managed by the client, and it will be exploited by a competent contractor. Once this was understood, Roger suggested that the next step would be to fully embrace the idea of functional (rather than physical) specification by the design department, to the extent that this is feasible. Taken to its limit, this might embrace trade-offs with threats and opportunities over the whole life cycle of the project. For example, one supplier might propose a flexible pipe which made laying much easier and avoided the problem of buckles discussed in Chapter 4. However, this approach would have to be compared in terms of maintenance and other whole life cycle issues, as well as the cost of putting the pipeline in place. Expanding further on these ideas, Roger indicated that Piers might explicitly invite more than one bid from each supplier for all the activity B–E contents where options are available, including options which involve the management of risks associated with other project parties. For example, pipe coating yards might be invited to bid on the basis of a standard one-shift operation, with the option of two or three shifts, given a premium payment which might itself be a function of how much warning Piers can provide. As discussed in detail elsewhere (Chapman and Cooper, 1983a; Cooper and Chapman, 1987, Ch. 11), pipe coating multi-shift options might provide a cost-effective general response which could be used to manage collective residual delays over the whole of activity A–E. The focus of this earlier analysis is the collective (general response) management of downside risk (net of specific responses), but all the ideas involved could be focused on upside risk as well.

Roger made the point to Paul that it was important to avoid confusing people by going too far too fast with this contractual approach. If people were not allowed to see the ramifications of this approach unfold slowly, change would become an uphill struggle, and Paul might lose their confidence completely. However, by now Paul was getting quite excited. He needed calming down. His eyes were glazing over. He was picturing himself on the main board within a short space of time (Roger supporting him as his trusty lieutenant). While trying to calm Paul down, Roger turned the discussion to how they would sell these ideas to the procurement department, and all other interested parties. They would build on 'the success of the design department deal for the oil company as a whole'. They would sell this as an important partnership with the procurement department which was part of a new way of working for the company as a whole, giving fulsome credit to the procurement department's leadership. And if push came to shove, they would hint that subcontracting the whole pipeline, including 'design', 'deliver coated pipe' and 'lay the pipe', would be a way of achieving similar aims for the project within current corporate rules, albeit with more cost, less control and more risk than their preferred route. They would follow the maxim 'speak softly, but carry a big stick', a good uncertainty management rule of thumb. Changing organizational practice is a high-risk project in its own right, but very rewarding when successful, for the company and for individual careers.

Roger indicated that the approach to capturing and sharing the benefits of efficiency and effectiveness improvements and good luck they had developed for activities B–E should lead to a much lower expected cost. This impact could be much larger than that associated with activity A. The difference could be called the expected value of effectively managed good luck, and given suitable assumptions, it might be computed. However, Roger advised against even identifying it explicitly at present, to keep the discussion as simple as possible. At the end of these discussions Paul was convinced Roger's ideas were spot on. The principles were clear and he believed that they all made sense. However, he was well aware of the difficulties they would face in implementing them. At this point Roger turned his attention to the impact these ideas would have on the current corporate understanding of uncertainty ownership as outlined on page 200. He knew this current understanding would have to be revised in a way acceptable to Barry and Paul in the first instance, and to the board in the longer term.

A Revised Corporate Understanding Of Uncertainty Ownership

The discussion of page 201 was concerned with the ownership of high-impact, extreme events associated with Paul's pipe laying project. Roger's deliberations illustrated the important implications for uncertainty ownership at the boundary between project managers and the board. The discussion of page 217 was motivated by the dysfunctional implications of distributed ownership of uncertainty identified by Roger on page 212. Roger's proposals concerned the management of good luck, via trigger contracts, with important implications for uncertainty ownership at the boundary between a project manager, other internal uncertainty stakeholders like the design and procurement departments, and external uncertainty stakeholders like suppliers and subcontractors. Roger's proposals involve significant top-down and bottom-up changes in corporate practice, and a major shift in the corporate mindsets. Roger was aware of the need to bring these various proposals together, to provide a coherent and consistent view of the boundaries the project manager has to deal with in managing uncertainty. Roger explained to Barry and to Paul that this implied a need to rewrite the seven rules of conduct outlined on page 200. Roger proposed the following policy guidelines, using the same bullet point structure introduced on page 200:

Responsibilities for uncertainty

The project manager should be responsible for the operational management of all project uncertainty on behalf of the board of directors. This should include good luck as well as bad luck. Risk and opportunity management models and processes should be used as a basis to judge the project manager's performance in terms of good or bad management, distinguishing between good luck and good management, bad luck and bad management. The project manager's performance should not be measured in terms of outcomes directly. This would confuse luck and skill. The project manager should delegate partial operational responsibility for uncertainty, when appropriate, via trigger contracts, to the heads of departments within the organization like design and procurement. The head of the procurement department may further delegate partial operational responsibility for uncertainty, when appropriate, via trigger contracts, to external suppliers and subcontractors. As in the case of project managers, operational responsibility for uncertainty should include good luck as well as bad luck, and performance should be measured in terms of good or bad management, not the combination of good or bad management and good or bad luck associated with outcomes. A projects director should be responsible for the financial implications of all project uncertainty and the quality of performance of all associated corporate employees on behalf of the board of directors. The board of directors as a whole should review the quality of the projects director's performance, and if necessary the performance of other corporate employees, at a level dependent upon outcomes. Project uncertainty should be owned collectively by the organization, not any one party or group, although aspects of operational responsibility might be held by individuals and aspects of financial uncertainty might be held in trust by a particular party.

Provisions and expected values

Provisions for project risks (expected costs of project risks) and allowances for opportunities (expected benefits of opportunity management) should be held in trust by the project manager as part of the project's expected cost when quantification of identified risks and opportunities is appropriate and it is appropriate to give the project manager nominal financial responsibility for such risks and opportunities. 'In trust' in this case implies a light-touch audit by the projects director to make sure effective management of good or bad luck is planned and executed. There should be no budget in the usual sense, but the project expected cost E_p should serve some of the functions of a budget. The key distinction between E_p and a conventionally interpreted budget is that E_p is an expected outcome, which is expected to change over time according to the good and bad luck encountered, as well as changing to reflect the quality of the management. The way it changes and the reasons for these changes should be the basis of the measurement of performance of those responsible.

People should be rewarded for good management and punished for bad management. Good or bad luck should have a neutral effect, provided it is clearly good or bad luck. Clarifying the difference should be an important role of the uncertainty management process. So far as possible a project manager should use the trigger contract concept to manage good luck effectively, the expected costs associated with such contracts defining E_p. Target quality levels, durations and costs should be distinguished from trigger quality levels, durations and costs. Target quality levels and durations should be optimistic (aspirational). Target costs should be pessimistic, allowing for incentive payments to achieve minimum durations and maximum quality. There should be no attempt to aggregate target levels, durations or costs, with the possible exception of a base plan defined in terms of target durations for a sequence of activities with a collective (joint) 'float' provision at the end to reflect expected joint delay.

Probability distributions associated with expected values should be used to assess, monitor and control cost, duration and quality at all levels. Target quality levels, durations or costs should normally only be used in conjunction with probability distributions at the base level, with their aspirational nature in mind, and the expectation that they would not be met. In general, delay relative to target durations will be the norm, quality shortfalls relative to the target will be the norm, and cost savings relative to target costs will be the norm. There should be no commitments on cost and no associated cost contingency (buffer). There may well be implicit commitments on quality and durations, with buffers and associated asymmetries built into the incentive structure, but there should not be commitments in the fixed value sense. There should be a clear understanding, at all levels in the organization, of the difference between targets, expectations, triggers and commitments. An F_p^3 provision should be held in trust by the projects director, defined by $E_b - E_p$ where $E_b = F_p^3 E_p$ is the associated project expected cost from the board's perspective. This should reflect an aggregate (not fully decomposed by source) provision for triple Es, SAPs, PUUs and bias. 'In trust' in this case implies a light-touch review by the board to make sure effective management of associated uncertainty is planned and executed. E_b is an expected value and should not be confused with a budget or a target, and it should be expected to change over time.

Board involvement

The board should be kept informed of E_b, its associated probability distribution, and the expected values and associated probability distributions of its components in a top-down nested structure in appropriate detail, with a focus in detail on areas where significant changes occur. If board members wish to relate 80% confidence levels associated with E_b to past projects they are free to do so, but no other special meaning should be attached to any percentile value. The board should also be kept informed of the expected values for quality and duration plus associated probability distributions, with changes brought to their attention, and a top-down focus to the level of detail necessary on the reasons for changes. The board should also be kept informed of the quality of luck to date, and the quality of management to date, linked to changes in E_b and expected values for quality and duration. Staying within budget (time and quality) is not an appropriate measure of success for project managers. Demonstrating good management in terms of managing uncertainty as described in this chapter at all levels (projects director, project manager, head of design, head of procurement, etc.) is the performance objective.

Contingencies

The idea of a budget which implies ownership is inappropriate. The idea of a cost contingency, to reflect a buffer associated with asymmetric treatment of good luck and bad luck, is also inappropriate. Good luck management and bad luck management in relation to cost should both be subject to similar scrutiny, and positive or negative variations associated with luck treated equally. The idea of time or quality contingency, to reflect a buffer and trade-offs which are asymmetric is still appropriate, but it should be embedded in the trigger contract concept, rather than commitments in the usual sense.

Accountability for expenditures

The idea that expenditure within an agreed budget does not have to be accounted for is no longer applicable. In respect of E_p, the project manager should not need to seek prior sanction for any expenditures consistent with E_p, allowing for swings and roundabouts on individual items, but if E_p is beginning to look biased on the low side or the high side, early discussions with the projects director are mandatory. All members of the organization are accountable for all expenditure provisions held in trust, to ensure effective management of good luck as well as bad luck. The focus for accountability should be on changes in E_b and its associated probability distribution, and changes in expected duration and quality and their associated probability distributions. Evidence of opportunities missed should be looked for as well as evidence of threats realized. Key evidence of bad management should include sources of uncertainty missed (threats or opportunities), biased estimates of expected values or variability, unimaginative responses, poor management processes, ineffective contracts, and so on. Unwelcome outturns which could be explained in terms of bad luck in the face of good management are acceptable. Welcome outturns which could be attributed to good luck in the face of indifferent management are not acceptable. Judgements about the quality of a project's management should be available early in the project's life cycle, and action taken if necessary before problems get out of hand. A light-touch approach to audit and review should be maintained unless and until evidence of possibly inappropriate management quality is detected. Detection of possibly inappropriate management should trigger a succession of more detailed audits and reviews until an all clear or a need for management change is identified. The management of F_p^3 (the E_p and E_b differentiation) by the projects manager and the projects director should become part of this process, not a separate issue. A constructive tension in the relationship between a project manager and the projects director is to be expected, but destructive relationships should be seen as evidence of failure by both parties.

Corporate funding

At a corporate level, E_b should be used to plan the financing of all projects. Flexibility of financing should be recognized as more important than was formally acknowledged in the past, because of the use of E_b rather than budgets defined on the basis of a commitment. However, in practice properly estimated E_b values and effectively managed projects should make capital requirements more predictable. *Less commitment means more predictability, not less.*

The role of the risk analyst

The risk analyst should report to the project manager with respect to all the project manager's issues associated with the project. The risk analyst should also report to the projects director with respect to all his or her issues. The risk analyst should also report to the head of risk management (Barry) with respect to the technical quality of all his work. The risk analyst must balance being a member of the project management team, loyal to that team, with working for the project's directors team and being an honest broker from the board's perspective. The risk analyst's performance should be formally appraised by the project manager, the project director, and the head of risk management to ensure an appropriate balance, and to demonstrate the need for changes in performance measures. The quality of the risk analyst's work as judged by the head of risk management is important, but the usefulness of the risk analyst's work to the project manager and to the projects director is critical.

Roger takes a holiday

When Roger finished presenting these guidelines, Paul remained convinced that Roger was on the right track from a corporate perspective. However Paul was becoming more and more worried about the magnitude of the corporate culture change implications. Barry was distinctly nervous, because he did not understand how this was all going to work in practice, and he lacked Roger's fearless approach to new ideas and change. He was a prudent man, as he believed those in charge of risk management ought to be. Roger went on holiday, leaving Barry and Paul to think about how to take things forward when Roger returned.

Epilogue

Roger liked to call to himself a 'riskateer', with a self-image as a bold but effective risk taker. He fed this self-image a regular diet of rock climbing, mountain climbing, hang-gliding and other exciting but hazardous pastimes. Extreme sports like bungee jumping had not been invented, but this did not slow Roger down. According to the saying, there are old pilots, and there are bold pilots, but there are no old, bold pilots. Roger understood this notion, but he may have lost sight of it when he went rock climbing that fateful holiday. He may have been over-confident because of the high his discussions with Paul had engendered. Or he may have just been unlucky. We will never really know. But he came to an untimely early end when a shift in the weather on a Swiss mountain caught him unawares. All Roger's friends and colleagues missed him greatly. Paul was devastated. He was convinced Roger's ideas were the way forward and he was not lacking in courage or intelligence. But he felt very exposed as he contemplated taking them forward on his own.

Barry was very interested in Roger's latest ideas, especially when Paul explained them in much greater detail, but he had no feel for how to implement them. Nor did Richard, Roger's replacement. Perhaps more important, neither Barry nor Richard had any incentive to push for a high-risk change like this. Barry went so far as to counsel Paul to avoid being explicit about F_p^3 or F_a^3, to go public on the need to clarify who owns what risk in the triple E sense (page 204), but to keep the SAPs, PUUs and bias factor ideas to themselves, burying them in 'other' risks as used by Eddy in Chapter 4. Barry saw these ideas as very difficult to explain, and a clear threat to the image of scientific precision which the risk management process was acquiring. The basic notion that there is no such thing as an unconditional expectation was very upsetting to Barry.

Paul was persuaded to follow Barry's line of thinking, because he was not clear how he could do otherwise with a reasonable chance of success. Subsequently, Paul's project went very well. Recognizing the need to address F_p^3 and F_a^3 implicitly if not explicitly, he developed an effective approach to managing expectations upwards and downwards. He brought his project in early and under budget. Eventually Paul made the main board. However, an implication of Paul's failure to adopt Roger's ideas, which Roger had warned him of, haunted him. Within a decade, long before he got to the board, the design department was outsourced, as the company refocused on core business. Activities like acquiring pipe plus pipe laying were let directly on a fixed price basis, given the physical design specification of an external design company. The external design company did not understand either Paul's company's needs or the market in the sense Roger suggested design and procurement departments should. Cost variability associated with the result was dramatically reduced. But it was clear to Paul that the price paid was high. Uncertainty was neither reduced nor managed in the sense Roger had proposed. It was simply transferred to other organizations and managed by them in their interests. When Paul reached the board it was too late to recover the position, although he did manage a partial reversal.

Paul took some comfort from the fact that his organization was not the only one to go this way. He even allowed himself a private smile when Barry's risk management department was outsourced. However, he knew a massive mistake when he saw one, and he had the integrity to admit to himself that he might have prevented it.

Conclusion

Roger's ideas convinced Paul, but Barry and Richard were not able to implement them, and they were never tested in full. That is, the need to address triple Es and SAPs, PUUs and bias has been clear for some time, in a wide range of contexts, as has the need to manage good luck. Further, the need for boards to own the financial risks associated with triple Es and scope changes has been clear for some time. These issues were addressed in Chapman and Ward (1997) using different terms. However, explicit estimation of F_p^3 and F_a^3 was not addressed, or the distinction between $E_b = F_p^3 E_p$ and the project budget defined by E_p + project contingency. Nor was the distinction drawn between target and trigger contracts. Nor was the value of internal trigger contracts understood at a corporate level. Paul's feelings of guilt are acknowledged as a reflection of the authors' wish that these ideas had occurred earlier, as a matter of foresight rather than hindsight with respect to the trend to outsource departments providing design and other internal services, including risk management and operational research. There is no implied criticism of anyone in the organizations which served as a basis for this tale (or any other tale). The issue now is finding simple ways to implement the key concepts without undue complexity, and refining them via practice.

Some of the risk ownership ideas in this chapter build on published research noted earlier. Some of the good luck risk ownership ideas in this chapter were stimulated in part by Goldratt and Cox (1992) and Goldratt (1997), whose ideas are different in important ways, but complementary. Readers interested in this background may also wish to look at Steyn (2001) for a recent critical overview. The most important new ideas in this chapter fell out of an attempt to synthesize these various themes in a single practical context when writing the tale of this chapter. The way forward requires 'riskateers' with Roger's qualities, and appropriate stimulating real problems in organizations that are receptive to radical thinking. The basic concepts are not limited in their areas of application; for example, Chapters 5, 9 and 10 apply them in quite different contexts.

7 Sarah's tale: Facilitating the precautionary principle

The big question is not, How much risk is acceptable? It is, How do we frame the process for choosing the best decision option?
Adapted from S. Kaplan, 'The words of risk analysis'

Introduction

An important aspect of managing uncertainty concerns high-impact and low probability events which have only adverse consequences, such as earthquakes (acts of God) or accidents (unintentional errors of judgement or system failures). The insurance industry has traditionally classified such events as 'pure' risks, distinguishing them from 'speculative' risks which can have uncertain beneficial or adverse consequences. Most commercial decisions involve speculative risk as illustrated by all the other chapters in this book. This chapter is concerned with investment decisions to manage pure risks.

Possible approaches to managing pure risk include avoidance, transfer to another party, reducing the probability of an event occurring, reducing the size of the possible consequence either before or after the event, setting aside resources to provide a reactive ability to cope, and doing nothing. A hybrid strategy may incorporate more than one of these approaches. In simple terms a pure risk investment decision involves three interelated decisions:

- How much is it worth spending to reduce a risk?
- To what extent is it worth reducing a risk?
- Which responses provide the most cost-effective combination?

If a pure risk involves an expected cost of $£x$, then it will be worth spending up to $£x$ to eliminate that risk in risk efficiency terms, and it may be risk efficient to spend more in terms of the trade-off between expected value and associated risk in the sense of departure from expected values. For example, insurance in the form of an extended guarantee on a domestic appliance with a premium cost greater than the expected cost of not buying the extended guarantee (paying for repairs as and when the appliance fails) is not risk efficient, and it is a poor buy if the household can afford to meet the cost of occasional failures, unless the guarantee motivates the supplier to provide better reliability. However, household fire insurance is a good buy if the household cannot meet the price of rebuilding the house even if the premium exceeds the expected cost of fire risk, as it will on average if the insurance company is going to make a profit.

In pure risk contexts, fairly obvious sources of uncertainty include:

- Uncertainty about the likelihood of a risk event occurring
- Uncertainty about the possible consequences of a given event
- Uncertainty about valuing the cost of particular consequences
- Uncertainty about the range of responses available
- Uncertainty about the effect of a given response on the risk
- Uncertainty about appropriate trade-offs

The presence of high levels of uncertainty under some or all of these categories can make response selection decisions problematic. This is often the case in a wide variety of contexts involving high-profile potential hazards to public health, safety and the environment. Typical examples include the management of nuclear waste and other environmental pollutants, global warming, exposures to electromagnetic fields such as overhead power lines, safety in transport systems, the use of genetically engineered foods, and the treatment of diseases. A central dilemma is whether to take major protective actions promptly or whether to delay any significant action until uncertainties about the likelihood and possible extent of impacts are reduced or resolved (Graham, 2001). If the potential adverse impacts are high, irreversible, or long-lasting, significant immediate actions to reduce, prevent or avoid the risk may be justified, such as substantial controls on activities, banning activities which generate hazards, or large-scale investment in safety measures. However, delaying such action to reduce uncertainty about the likelihood and extent of impacts may suggest that a lower level of response would be more cost-effective.

A general guiding principle often applied to this type of decision is the so-called precautionary principle. Essentially this is a 'better safe than sorry' approach to risk management which suggests that action should be taken to avoid harm even when it is not certain to occur (Kheifet, Hester and Banerjee, 2001). Sadin (1999) reports 19 different definitions of the precautionary principle. These definitions vary in their precision and public policy implications, but the essence is captured by this version from the 1992 Earth Summit in Rio de Janeiro, albeit in an environmental context: 'Where there are threats of serious or irreversible damage, lack of full scientific certainty shall not be used as a reason for postponing cost-effective measures to prevent environmental degradation' (United Nations, 1992).

As a general policy guideline, Keeney and von Winterfeldt (2001) argue that 'the precautionary principle lacks a precise definition regarding what it means, where it is used, and how it should be implemented. . . . Its appropriateness often depends on assumptions about uncertainties and trade-offs. Without being clear about these assumptions, it is considered problematic to apply the precautionary principle without further analysis.' This further analysis needs to acknowledge two key issues. First, decisions must be made with less than complete information, sometimes when uncertainties are large. Second, decisions must balance conflicting objectives, including reducing costs, performance, intended risk reduction and unintended increases in risk associated with responses adopted. Consequentially the best alternative is not necessarily the one that produces the greatest intended reduction in risk. In the face of trade-offs and uncertainties, simple, cheap and adaptive measures may be preferable to complex, expensive and irreversible measures (Keeney and von Winterfeldt, 2001).

The tale in this chapter illustrates the above issues, and addresses them in terms of a practical operational approach. The context chosen is safety in a railway system, but the conceptual features of the situation explored in the tale are common to a wide range of pure risk management problems, whether or not the precautionary principle is relevant, in an obvious way. The authors would like to stress that we make critical observations about conventional approaches to safety analysis, but no criticisms particular to the Railway Group (the UK railway industry) are made or implied. The tale focuses on assessing uncertainty about the likelihood and possible consequences of a particular risk event. This assessment uses a basic analytical approach which is similar to that employed in previous chapters. The analysis then considers the importance of trade-offs between cost and benefits in adopting an efficient risk management strategy. This leads into a discussion of ambiguities that can be present in evaluations of the benefits of reducing levels of risk, how these ambiguities should be treated, and a possible role for a mandatory insurance-based approach.

Some people argue that the distinction between pure risk and speculative risk adopted by the insurance industry is old-fashioned and redundant, for two reasons. One is because people take pure risks or impose pure risks on others for benefits, so there is always a speculative risk aspect to decisions involving pure risks. The other is because insurance needs to address both pure and speculative risks jointly, and separability is not a useful working assumption. The tale in this chapter accommodates this perspective. The purity of the risks is not an issue. The key issues are the low probability and high impact of the risks, the uncertainties associated with probabilities and consequences, and the different perspectives of the different parties involved. These are the issues which make the precautionary principle relevant and motivate the approach to facilitating its effective application outlined in this chapter.

The Rail Passenger Safety Trust

On 5 October 1999 the UK's worst train accident for 11 years took place, at Ladbroke Grove, referred to as the 'Paddington crash' by the press. A Thames turbo train leaving Paddington collided head on with a London-bound Great Western express. Thirty-one people were killed, including both drivers, and 160 were injured, some very seriously.

Very soon after afterwards, Wynn, a seriously affluent and influential City executive whose son was killed in the Paddington crash, established the Rail Passenger Safety Trust, a charitable trust dedicated to supporting the interests of existing train user organizations by undertaking independent research into railway safety from a train passenger perspective. Wynn travelled into London by train every day himself, on another line. He was haunted by his son's death every time he got on a train, and he wanted to do something positive to ease the pain. Wynn knew that the Chinese wall separating the Railtrack Safety and Standards Directorate from the rest of the Railway Group (the UK railway industry) was a fragile device to resist the commercial and political pressures on the railway industry since privatization. He viewed all those involved in safety in the railway industry as honourable men and women, but he did not trust the restructuring of the railway system after the privatization of British Rail to deliver a level of safety (or a level of service more generally) which was in the best interests of railway passengers. He was a confirmed capitalist, but he thought the current structure was a serious political mistake. In an age of single-interest politics and self-regulation driven by public pressure generated by open information flows, he thought the existing groups looking after the best interests of train passengers needed more professional help – 'some sharper teeth to bite' and 'a much more assertive bark', as he put it to his friends and acquaintances. Within weeks, the very generous initial gift Wynn made to the Rail Passenger Safety Trust was scaled up by several orders of magnitude, he had a board of trustees, and the trust was advertising for research staff. Soon after this Wynn recruited two research staff, Sarah and Eric.

Sarah's father is a fireman. Sarah's mother is a nurse. This may explain in part Sarah's long-standing desire to find a career which reflects the safeguarding and caring nature of her parents' occupations. Sarah is bright and ambitious. She is also pragmatic and sensible. At school her target career was to be a serious player in an organization like Greenpeace by the time she was 30 or so, but she knew this did not involve a well-defined or structured career path. Sarah chose to study engineering at university, because her careers adviser had suggested in jest that she couldn't spell but she was good at mathematics, so engineering was the obvious choice, and she didn't receive any other advice which was more convincing. By the time Sarah was approaching graduation, she was pleased that she had acquired an education which included engineering, but she was convinced she needed an MSc which would give her a better chance to get her career started in a direction that was reasonably likely to lead to the destinations which interested her. She decided to take an MSc in risk management with a philosophy aligned to this book, and a broad scope. When she finished her course in the autumn of 1999, she had an extended holiday and then started looking for a job. She knew she could not put off making a commitment to a specific line of career development any longer.

Eric is a former British Rail safety systems engineer, who had just retired early from a train operating company. His niece was seriously injured in the Paddington crash.

Wynn had no difficulty persuading the board of trustees that Sarah and Eric were an ideal pair. Both were strongly motivated. Sarah had a broadly based, leading-edge risk management training, including research training, which would let them take a fresh view and break new ground, which Wynn considered essential. Eric had deep and up-to-date knowledge of how the UK railway industry addressed safety, an ideal 'gamekeeper turned poacher' as Wynn put it to the board of trustees. Eric preferred the original, 'poacher turned gamekeeper', which clearly indicated the new loyalties underlying his changed mindset.

Sarah's first few weeks with the trust involved substantial background reading of the library which Eric assembled. It also involved numerous tutorials with Eric, as he explained the perspectives and rationale which underlay the approaches adopted in the considerable volume of publicly available material produced by the railway industry. Eric was the tutor initially, but not for long. He remained the mentor, but Sarah and Eric soon worked as equal partners with complementary skills and knowledge.

A Conventional Analysis of Railway Buffer Events

The starting point for the development of a partnership between Sarah and Eric was a review of the models used to consider buffer events – when a fatality occurs because a train runs into buffer stops at a station where the tracks end, or into another stationary train at a station. Buffer events might be defined to include accidents when no one is killed, and accidents when no one is injured, but a common more restrictive definition was adopted to simplify their analysis, ignoring incidents which do not result in fatalities. Buffer events defined in this way are examples of very low frequency and very high impact events which cause particularly obvious difficulties for safety analysis. They were chosen by Eric and Sarah as a starting point for analysis because they had the necessary low-frequency and high-impact characteristics of the Paddington crash, but they were a reasonably simple place to start, and they were free of the immediate emotive connotations of collisions involving two moving trains. The idea was to start with a clear mutual understanding of how the railway industry viewed buffer events, and then to develop an appropriate alternative view for the trust. The trust's view should not be constrained by conventional railway safety thinking, or conventional safety thinking more generally. It would, however, have to be linked to conventional railway safety thinking, to demonstrate flaws or bias in that thinking, and to argue for changes or reinterpretation of that thinking.

The obvious place for Eric and Sarah to start was a publicly available analysis of buffer events. Eric suggested they use *Railway Safety Case Version 22*, Volume 2, section 4.18, pages 138 and 139 (Railtrack Safety and Standards Directorate, 1999). Whatever Eric and Sarah produced would have to be related to this kind of analysis for benchmarking purposes. Eric was familiar with this report, and explained the relevant section to Sarah. Two buffer events were listed as the database for the analysis. One was a buffer event in 1975 at Moorgate Station which caused 50 equivalent fatalities. The second was a buffer event in 1991 at Cannon Street Station which caused 3 equivalent fatalities. An equivalent fatality (ef) equates one actual fatality to a number of people seriously injured (10) and a larger number of people receiving minor injuries (200). This equation raises issues addressed on page 262. For the moment, equivalent fatalities seemed a reasonable enough approach to both Eric and Sarah. To manage safety across the railway system, an equivalent fatality has to be equated with a notional monetary value – the price of a life (this is known as the value of a prevented fatality, or VPF, in standard railway terminology). Eric explained that this price of a life is usually interpreted as a willingness-to-pay evaluation – what the relevant public consider it is just worth paying, or not (a point of indifference at the margin) to improve safety enough to save one life. Alternatively it can be regarded as the cost of one ef at the margin, defined to include material damage, third-party liability and business interruption costs. Eric added that the current notional price of a life in the UK railway industry was about £2 million. The respective figures for road and air travel were about £1 million and £10 million. Price of a life is affected by several factors:

- The extent to which the relevant public have control over safety; there is a lower rate for roads because drivers feel more in charge than train passengers.
- The extent to which large numbers of people are killed at one time; an air crash killing 300 is deemed very much more serious than 100 car crashes each killing 3 people, because of the horror of the large number involved in one incident.
- The quality of the death; being irradiated to death by a nuclear accident is usually deemed less desirable than being killed in an air crash.
- Choice about being involved; there are lower values for voluntary exposure.
- Income; higher incomes mean higher valuations.

Sarah understood these death (or life) valuations and equivalent fatality issues. They were common safety industry ideas she had been exposed to on her MSc.

However, she appreciated being reminded by Eric of current industry parameter values and comparisons.

Eric explained that the Railtrack report notes that there is very little evidence on which to base frequency estimates for very high consequence events in general, and only two UK observations for buffer events. Further, the evidence on which consequence estimates could be based is also very limited and, in the context of consequence assessment, the Railtrack report effectively dismisses the Moorgate event as 'an unrepresentative sample' (an outlier) because 'it involved a full speed collision of an LUL (London Underground) train without precedent in the UK'. The Railtrack report then assumes that one collision equivalent to Cannon Street (with 3 equivalent fatalities) every 12 years is an appropriate frequency and consequence estimate, justified in terms of 'a manual adjustment to the performance data to take account of these infrequent, high consequence accidents', linked to a 12 year safety case data period. That is, the Moorgate incident is, in effect, included for assessment of frequency purposes but ignored for assessment of consequence purposes. Eric indicated that Railtrack could use the 12 year return period, the £2 million price of a life, and the 3 equivalent fatalities per buffer event to compute an expected cost of £0.5 million per year ($3 \times 2/12$). In simple terms, this implies that it would be worth spending up to about £0.5 million per year to eliminate this risk, about £0.17 million per annum (0.5/3) for each life saved, but no more. If there is no feasible way of doing this, the system could be deemed 'safe enough' in terms of buffer events. This is what is known in the trade as an ALARP (as low as reasonably practical) approach to safety analysis. Eric could see why this analysis was easy to attack, but he thought the Railtrack staff involved were being quite reasonable and conservative. The Moorgate event clearly was very extreme, it happened 25 years ago, it was not really representative of the mainline railways Railtrack was concerned with, and a 12 year return period (implying 1/12 = 0.083 events per year) was more pessimistic than the 2 events in 25 years (or more) which the data suggested. Given this limited data, he did not see how anything else could be done without distorting the analysis in counterproductive ways. For example, if the 50 equivalent fatalities for Moorgate and the 3 equivalent fatalities for Cannon Street were just averaged to obtain 26.5 equivalent fatalities per event (($50 + 3)/2$), the result would be 2.2 equivalent fatalities (26.5 × 0.083, an average cost of £4.4 million per year) instead of 0.25 equivalent fatalities (3 × 0.083, an average cost of £0.5 million per year). This order of magnitude increase would imply the need for much more money to be spent by the Railway Group to prevent such accidents. But 26.5 equivalent fatalities per event was clearly a serious overestimate of the average event, and a large unwarranted increase in expenditure on the prevention of this kind of potential accident would have a detrimental effect on more pressing safety scenarios, like collisions between trains moving in opposite directions or at different speeds on the same track.

Sarah expressed some sympathy for Eric's views, and the Railway Group's dilemma. However, Sarah pointed out that the dilemma was largely caused by the framing assumptions implicit in the Railtrack analysis. Tending to think in terms of an average event was a core problem for the safety industry as a whole. If these assumptions were relaxed in line with current thinking outside the world of UK railway safety, it might be possible to portray Eric's concerns in a more defensible manner. The problem was not the safety of the system in terms of the aspect being examined, it was the perceived safety given the approach to analysis. Eric asked for an immediate explanation of this observation, but Sarah suggested it might be better if she spent the weekend putting her thoughts in order, for a discussion first thing Monday morning. It was mid-afternoon on Friday, and an early train home from their London office suited them both. They agreed to call it a day and reconvene on the following Monday.

A Simple Scenario Analysis of Buffer Events

On Monday morning Sarah explained there was a need to capture uncertainty about the frequency of a buffer event, the possible consequences in directly measurable terms, and the implications, using assumptions like the value of a life. As a basis for discussion, Sarah suggested they start with an illustrative version of the simple scenario approach she had learned about at university in the context of project risk management (Chapman and Ward, 1997, Ch. 10).

Estimating buffer event frequency

Sarah began by asking Eric to consider uncertainty about the frequency of a buffer event. Given the Railway Group data and in terms of the trust's perspective, she asked Eric to identify a plausible minimum return period for a buffer event; by 'plausible minimum' she meant a 10 percentile value of the probability distribution for the true return period in order of magnitude terms. Eric's estimate was 10 years (1/10 = 0.1 events per year). That is, he thought there was about a 1 in 10 chance that the true return period was less than 10 years, and he thought there was about a 9 in 10 chance that the true return period was greater than 10 years. Sarah then asked Eric for a comparable plausible maximum return period for a buffer event, a 90 percentile value of the same probability distribution. Eric's estimate was 50 years (1/50 = 0.02 events per year). Eric explained his responses to Sarah as follows. Because he was estimating an 80% confidence range in order of magnitude terms, he could infer that both observations (Moorgate and Cannon Street) might be relevant, and they might constitute an optimistic (lucky) sample of what might happen over a longer period, which would be consistent with a 10 year return period. However, neither might be strictly relevant, or they might constitute a pessimistic (unlucky) sample, which would suggest a 50 year return period might be more appropriate. He had no basis for suggesting a 100 year return period might be more appropriate still, so he opted for 50 on the grounds that a conservative assumption was more appropriate unless there was evidence to the contrary.

Even as Eric was thinking this through to explain it to Sarah, he could see merit in Sarah's approach, and where it was leading them. The traditional approach assumed a single value for the return period. This forced a conservative (pessimistic) low estimate of the return period, to make the estimate defensible. Sarah's approach acknowledged that the return period and corresponding probability per annum were not known. Indeed, Sarah's approach started from the premise that it was not possible to know the return period. This allowed plausible extreme positions to be explored, both optimistic and pessimistic. Railtrack's 12 year return period was embraced by the 10–50 year range, but it was at the bottom end, reflecting its somewhat conservative (pessimistic) nature. Eric explained this to Sarah. Sarah's response was to build on this idea in more general terms. She pointed out that the past may not reflect the future. The future may be better than the past, or it may be worse, but it is almost certain to be different. Growing traffic intensity or financial pressures might suggest it would get worse. More sophisticated control systems might suggest it would get better. The net balance might be difficult to judge. What was crucial was the understanding that we do not have to know the true value of probabilities, or assume (even pretend) that we know them. However, we do have to take a view about the likely value of probabilities, based on data and other factors, like the relevance of the data. If we do not, we will make judgements which are inconsistent with our beliefs.

Eric warmed to this. He pointed out that he had a passing familiarity with safety statistics for railways outside the UK – he had drawn on this implicitly to give his subjective estimates – and Sarah's perspective clearly implied that it was important to recognize that data associated with systems outside the UK could be relevant, perhaps much more relevant than the UK data. Subsequent analysis could address this issue. They could show international comparisons of relevant events, by railway type in some cases, and selectively weight and adjust all sources of data to reflect its relevance. This would not only provide a better database for estimation, it would provide benchmark comparisons to form the basis for arguments about the need for the Railway Group to change. Sarah agreed that this was of course correct, and important. Further, there was no need to spend the time and effort on this kind of data collection and analysis until they had identified an area of concern. They could rely on Eric's experience and subjective estimates to get started, to take a first pass at all aspects of the railway system's safety, just as the book she was drawing on (Chapman and Ward, 1997) used the simple scenario approach to take a first pass at assessing the risk for all aspects of a project. They could use a first pass to size the problem, and locate the critical areas. They could then use a second pass, drawing on readily available data, to confirm or revise, as appropriate, inferences based on the first pass. They could then use subsequent passes to suggest actions and attempt to validate those actions. A thorough analysis of worldwide buffer events could await the later passes if buffer events proved important. The current concern was the first pass.

Next Sarah suggested they consider the 80% confidence bound on the frequency of buffer events in events per year format, adding a nominal midpoint, to produce a three-value 'default' simple scenario form. That is, she suggested the following three assumptions, associated with Figure 7.1:

- 0.02 events per year, probability 0.2
- 0.06 events per year, probability 0.6
- 0.10 events per year, probability 0.2

The 0.2 probability associated with 0.02 events per year is related to a uniform probability distribution over the interval 0.00 to 0.04 events per year, which corresponds to a 10% chance of a return period of more than 50 years (fewer than 0.02 events per year). Similarly, the 0.2 probability associated with 0.10 events per year is related to a uniform probability distribution over the interval 0.08 to 0.12 events per year, which corresponds to a 10% chance of a return period less than 10 years (more than 0.10 events per year). The 0.6 probability associated with 0.06 events per year is simply the residual probability $(1 - 0.2 - 0.2 = 0.6)$ associated with a convenient midpoint value $((0.02 + 0.10)/2 = 0.06)$. The simple linear segment cumulative probability distribution of Figure 7.1 is easy to use, and it emphasizes

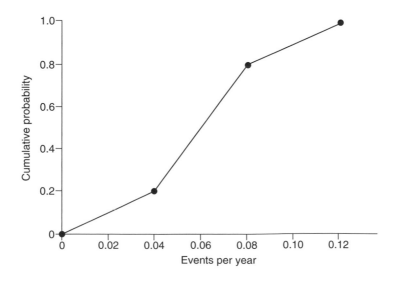

Figure 7.1—Events per year: cumulative probability distribution.

the approximations involved. Its rectangular density function equivalent is also easy to use. The simple scenario approach is slightly more demanding than the minimalist approach of Chapter 4, which might have been used instead. However, in the present context, Sarah was not under the same pressures for simplicity as Eddy in Chapter 4, and she needed more sophistication for reasons which will reveal themselves shortly.

The expected value of the Figure 7.1 probability distribution is clearly 0.06 events per year, as a result of the assumed symmetric distribution. This is 28% lower than the 0.083 Railtrack estimate. If an asymmetric result is required, simple variants of the default simple scenario approach could be used. This would probably lower the expected value; 0.06 was probably a conservative (pessimistic) estimate.

Estimating the possible consequences

Sarah next suggested an asymmetric variant of the simple scenario approach just employed to deal with the possible consequences in terms of equivalent fatalities (ef) if an event occurs, as follows, associated with Figure 7.2.

	Equivalent fatalities (range)	Probability
Plausible minimum	3 (1–5)	0.9
Intermediate value	10 (5–15)	0.09
Intermediate value	30 (15–45)	0.009
Plausible maximum	100 (45–155)	0.0001

That is, a plausible minimum ef scenario might be 3 equivalent fatalities (as for Cannon Street), associated with a range 1–5, with a 90% chance that the outcome would lie in this range. A plausible maximum ef scenario might be 100, associated with a range 45–155, with a 0.0001 probability that the outcome would lie in this range. Two intermediate scenarios might be used to complete a rectangular histogram or linear segment cumulative distribution approximation to a negative exponential distribution, a form of distribution often found to approximate to the reality of extreme events like this. The Moorgate 50 ef event is part of the very low probability (0.0001) plausible maximum scenario (45–155). A number not greater than the maximum number of people involved in such a crash clearly defines an absolute upper limit.

Sarah emphasized that the approximate nature of Figure 7.2 indicates that refinement is possible if warranted. Sarah reminded Eric that the current Railtrack approach in effect approximates Figure 7.2 by assuming that 3 equivalent fatalities (their average consequence) occur each time, because it does not explore

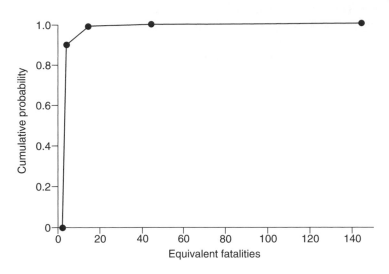

Figure 7.2—Equivalent fatalities per event: cumulative probability distribution.

the implications of alternative levels of ef. In respect of Figure 7.2, the expected value of equivalent fatalities per buffer event is

3×0.9	=	2.70
10×0.09	=	0.90
30×0.009	=	0.27
100×0.0001	=	<u>0.01</u>
		3.88

This is 30% higher than the Railtrack assumption of 3 ef for each buffer event. Sarah also reminded Eric that the current Railtrack approach in effect approximates Figure 7.1 by assuming that the probability of a buffer event per year is known, and equal to 0.083. In both cases Sarah's approach is a generalization which reflects the obvious uncertainty associated with reality, and the Railtrack approach is a special case which assumes away this uncertainty. (The authors have been advised that Railway Safety, the body which replaced the Railtrack Safety and Standards Directorate in 2001, now uses a form of analysis that reflects departures from an average.)

Justification of a consequence distribution like that of Figure 7.2 could consider data from other railway systems to even greater effect than the events per year distribution, with appropriate reference to differences in what is being compared in both cases. In respect of events per year, differences in operating conditions and safety systems would have to be considered. In respect of equivalent fatalities per event, the number of carriages, carriage configurations, speeds, and so on, would have to be considered. Both these sets of differences would be important, but there is probably more commonality in the second set.

Sarah pointed out that the expected values for the frequency and consequences distributions could be used to compute a simple estimate of the expected number of equivalent fatalities per year of $0.06 \times 3.88 = 0.23$. This is 8% less than the Railtrack figure of 0.25, but the same order of magnitude. It implies an associated expected cost per year of about £0.46 million using a £2 million price per equivalent fatality (0.23×2), compared with £0.50 million using the Railtrack figure of 0.25. Taken simply and literally, this implies it would be worth spending up to about £0.5 million per year to eliminate the risk of all buffer equivalent fatalities, but no more, as in the Railtrack analysis case. If there is no feasible way of doing this, the system would seem to be 'safe enough'.

A probability tree presentation

Sarah pointed out that the basic approach used by Railtrack does not deal with the perception that one big accident which kills 100 people is not equivalent to 100 single fatalities. Nor does it deal with the potential variability about the expected cost of equivalent fatalities, some of which is geared to uncertainty about the number of people who would be killed or injured, some of which is due to uncertainty associated with the low probability event nature of the phenomenon, some of which is due to lack of data and uncertainty about the relevance of what there is, and some of which is due to uncertainty about the modelling assumptions being used. Eric indicated that Railtrack does increase the £2 million price per equivalent fatality to assess large accident scenarios, and reduces it to assess small accident scenarios, although Railtrack does not systematically vary the £2 million figure in an embedded manner in a given analysis. Sarah suggested that she and Eric had to be consistent and systematic about this. To illustrate why, and the impact of doing so, Sarah produced for Eric the probability tree in Figure 7.3.

Sarah explained Figure 7.3 to Eric as follows. The top branch associated with a buffer event not occurring has an expected probability of 0.94 as indicated ($1 - 0.06$), and the 'occurs' branch has an expected probability of 0.06, the expected value from Figure 7.1. However, all the probability tree calculations are conditional on a buffer event occurring. This is because Sarah wanted to highlight the variability associated with the scenario 'when a buffer event occurs' and exclude the variability associated with the 0.06 probability of a buffer event occurring *for the moment*.

The first node on the 'occurs' branch has four branches, each characterized by one of the ef outcome scenarios underlying Figure 7.2. The probabilities are shown on top of each branch, the corresponding ef values at the next node. The second set of nodes on the 'occurs' branch each have three branches, characterizing the uncertainty about appropriate financial equivalence or transformation values for

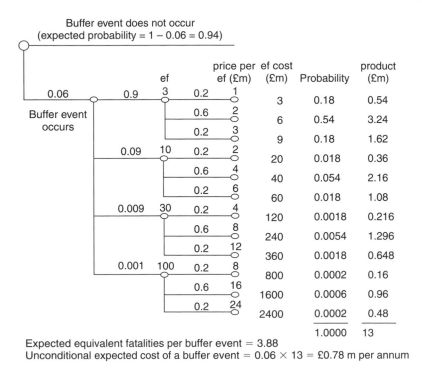

Expected equivalent fatalities per buffer event = 3.88
Unconditional expected cost of a buffer event = 0.06 × 13 = £0.78 m per annum

Figure 7.3—Probability tree for the cost of a buffer event.

each ef. They use a simple symmetric probability distribution like that underlying Figure 7.1. However, these possible financial values are conditional on the associated ef numbers.

For 3 ef, the possible price per ef values are £1 million, £2 million or £3 million: a mean of £2 million per ef for 1–5 equivalent fatalities, which corresponds to the £2 million with the possibility of significantly higher or lower values. For 10 ef, the possible price per ef values are £2 million, £4 million or £6 million: a mean of £4 million per ef, consistent with Railtrack practice of using large values when more equivalent fatalities are involved, giving this practice an explicit functional form. When the ef number triples (plus a bit), the price per ef doubles. For example, when the centre branch 3 ef becomes 10 ef, the price per ef changes from £2 million to £4 million. For 30 ef, the possible price per ef values are £4 million, £8 million or £12 million, still consistent with Railtrack practice, extending the same explicit functional form. When the ef number triples again, the price per ef doubles again. For 100 ef, the possible price per ef values are £8 million, £16 million or £24 million, further extending the same explicit functional form. When the ef number triples again (plus a bit), the price per ef doubles again.

The 'ef cost' column shows the product of the ef and the price per ef values: 3 × 1 = 3 through to 100 × 24 = 2400, the net effect of going down each branch described in terms of a monetary evaluation of the consequences. The 'probability' column shows the product of the associated probability values: $0.9 \times 0.2 = 0.18$ through to $0.001 \times 0.2 = 0.0002$, the probability of going down to each branch endpoint. The 'product' column shows the product of the two preceeding column entries: $3 \times 0.18 = 0.54$ through to $2400 \times 0.0002 = 0.48$, the contribution to the expected value of each branch endpoint.

Interpretation of the probability tree

Scrutiny of the probability tree reveals some useful results:

- The sum of the 'product' column is £13 million, the expected cost of the consequences given that a buffer event occurs. The unconditional expected cost per annum is £0.78 million (obtained by 0.06×13). This provides a direct comparison with the simple product of expected values approach, which yielded £0.46 million (£0.50 million using Railtrack's 0.25 instead of 0.23). The probability tree presentation indicates a 70% increase in the expected cost of the consequences per annum because of the increase in price per ef as ef increases assumed in Figure 7.3. That is, even if expected cost per annum were the only concern, modelling the relationship between ef and price per ef is clearly very important.
- The expected return period for a buffer event is 17 years (1 / 0.06), so on average 16 out of 17 years will involve no buffer event, and when a buffer event occurs the expected cost is £13 million. This emphasizes the infrequent event implications: longish periods with no events, followed by an event which on average is 17 times the annual average size.
- The 'ef cost' column implies that the amount the relevant public would consider it worth paying to eliminate fatalities from buffer events is a function of the ef number over the range £3 million to £2400 million. A £3 million buffer event and a £2400m buffer event are very different animals, and an average of £13 million per event obscures the fact that any event approaching a £2400 million event could change the future of the railways in the UK.
- If a buffer event occurs, the probabilities of the cost exceeding £10 million, £100 million and £1000 million are respectively about 0.1, 0.01 and 0.001.

Sarah pointed out that Figure 7.3 provides a much clearer picture of what buffer events involve than the Railtrack average cost per year figure of £0.5 million. As a measure of risk, £0.5 million per year is not very illuminating. In Sarah's view the £0.5 million per year is not a measure of risk at all – it is purely and simply a very crude estimate of expected value, conditional upon the validity of obviously defective framing assumptions. This was the consequence of a safety industry definition of risk as 'probability times impact', not unique to Railtrack.

Part of the additional insight in Figure 7.3 comes from recognizing that a buffer event can occur or not in any given year. However, of much greater importance is the recognition that each buffer event can vary widely in terms of equivalent fatality consequences. Further, the impact of this wide variability is amplified, when large numbers are involved, by the relationship between ef and price per ef. It is this amplification which lifts the average annual cost to £0.78 million from £0.46 million, even though an average price of £2 million or less per ef is assumed in about 74% of buffer events in Figure 7.3. In Sarah's view, risk is about the implications of departures from expectations, not the expectations themselves, and it is extreme departures from expectations that define the most important risks. The ef and the price per ef relationship assumed is subject to uncertainty, but it is much closer to the truth than an assumed price of £2 million per ef regardless of the size of ef, and if the relationship proves crucial, it can be reconsidered, like any of the probability assessments, although this may involve even more uncertainty.

By the time Sarah and Eric had finished discussing the implications of Figure 7.3, Eric was convinced that Sarah had captured the critical essence of what they needed to get started looking at the whole railway system. That is, the kind of model Sarah had outlined could be applied to all aspects of the railway system to look at comparative safety levels. Eric was aware that Figure 7.3 would need development and refinement before he and Sarah could show it to others with a view to making a public case. However, that refinement could wait. He had picked up the spirit of a multiple-pass approach with a first pass designed to quickly indicate what mattered and what did not matter, a core idea in this book.

Risk Efficiency For A Railway System

Eric and Sarah now looked at the rest of the railway system in a comparable manner. That is, they looked at collisions resulting in fatalities involving two trains travelling in the same direction on the same track at different speeds, two trains on the same track travelling in opposite directions, two trains on adjacent tracks when one is derailed, and so on. The top-level building block to view the system as Eric described it was an event category. Event categories allowed the safety of the system to be assessed in terms of different kinds of events. Sarah and Eric agreed at the outset that there were two lines of thinking behind this approach which could be exploited. First, this structure would allow them to examine safety data for the UK mainline rail system in comparison with other similar railway systems worldwide. It would allow comprehensive benchmarking, in addition to refinement of Railtrack estimates, as discussed earlier. Second, it could allow them to examine event-specific risk efficiency and related system-wide risk efficiency. A concern for event-specific risk efficiency is implicit in the estimation of the value of preventing an additional death at the margin. For example, suppose £13 million is the expected cost of buffer events over the return period as calculated in Figure 7.3, but the estimated expected incremental cost of saving all equivalent fatalities related to buffer events over this period is more than twice as much, say, £26 million. The railway system might already seem to be safer than it needs to be with respect to buffer events. More accurately, if the expected cost per annum per ef is £0.20 million (0.78/3.88), but the estimated expected incremental cost per annum of saving one ef is £0.40 million, then the railway system might seem to be safer that it needs to be (robustly ALARP). However, this depends on the assumption that the most efficient way of eliminating equivalent fatalities resulting from buffer events has been identified and has been used to estimate the incremental costs of £26 million and £0.40 million.

A concern for system-wide risk efficiency is usually the explicit concern when estimating the cost of preventing an additional death at the margin. Suppose £4.9 million is the expected cost per annum of equivalent fatalities arising from head-on collision events, but £5.0 million is the estimated incremental cost per annum of saving these quivalent fatalities in terms of managing head-on collisions. The system might seem to be just safe enough (marginally ALARP) with respect to head-on collision events, assuming the most efficient way of eliminating equivalent fatalities from head-on collision has been identified and used to estimate the incremental cost of £5 million per annum. If it were possible to reallocate funds from preventing buffer events to preventing head-on collisions, the system as a whole might be deemed more efficient in risk reduction terms, because its safety is better balanced. What is involved here is relative risk-efficient trade-offs, risk-efficient trade-offs for one event in relation to another. In practice it is not usually possible to manage risk by transferring funding in this way. However, it is possible to focus new funding on areas where the relative risk-efficient trade-offs suggest it would do the most good, such as head-on collisions in the example just given. The pursuit of relative risk-efficient trade-offs in this sense is clearly important in terms of the risk efficiency of the system as a whole.

If it were possible to reduce the expected incremental cost of saving a life in terms of buffer events from £0.4 million per annum to say £0.1 million per annum, this would imply that the safety of the system in relation to buffer events was not risk efficient. For relative risk-efficient trade-offs to mean anything useful, we have to ensure that event-specific risk efficiency is obtained via the assessment of ways to improve safety for all specific event types. We need to be basing investments decisions on thc least-cost ways of improving the system's safety with respect to all types of events. Responses to reduce risk may be event-specific or they may be system-wide. All feasible responses need to be considered when assessing event-specific risk efficiency, recognizing that separate treatment of events may be convenient but inappropriate. For example, if driver error is a contributing cause for all risks, and better training, reduced working hours or better driver's cabin design reduces the chance of driver error, the system-wide effect of those responses needs to be addressed.

A risk-efficient railway system requires event-specific risk efficiency, coupled to event-specific and system-wide response management, as well as a balance in the relative risk-efficient trade-offs involved. Risk efficiency in this sense can be usefully explored using the top-level building block view of the system provided by event categories. However, on its own this top-down view of the system is not an effective perspective for checking for risk efficiency, or for managing changes in safety more generally, or for understanding the safety issues which need to be managed. It needs to be linked to a bottom-up view with more operational content. The safety industry usually employs two tools to provide this operational content: event trees and fault trees. Both are ways of elaborating on the simple probability tree of Figure 7.3, using specialized forms of probability tree. Sarah was convinced that risk-response diagrams developed to portray risk-response sequences in a project management context, linked to examples like those in Chapman and Ward (1997) and Cooper and Chapman (1987), might be preferable to basic fault trees and event trees. She argued that they were derived from early fault tree and event tree models, but they were given a decision tree content to allow a focus on suitable response generation to manage the risk. For example, she suggested that advanced train protection (ATP), a system designed to automatically stop trains which run through a red light, was a response which would deal with many kinds of train collision accidents, but by no means all accidents. It was very important to see clearly the effect of possible general responses and other very specific responses, in her view. Eric argued that decisions (responses) were implicit in fault trees and event trees as he had used them for railway safety analysis, and ATP-type general responses were very clearly analysed. He was not convinced a new model form was needed, but he was willing to try out new models and compare the results. However, Eric could see clearly that accommodating uncertainty about uncertainty was going to be an enormous asset, and uncertainty about responses and different types of responses might also be an asset. He warmed even further to this idea when Sarah explained how the minimalist approach (Chapter 4) might be used for some exploratory analysis.

Eric and Sarah both agreed that they had to work towards models in all the areas that mattered which could be used to judge relative and overall risk efficiency for the system. The exact form of these models might be a matter of modelling taste and judgement. However, they should be able to capture the judgement and experience of those who understood railway safety in an internally consistent, comprehensive and easily understood manner. Hard data to verify probabilities was not the issue. The issue was a plausible understanding of the relationships between issues which was consistent with whatever limited data was to hand and useful in terms of improving safety in a manner which provided reasonable confidence that the key issues were understood.

Sarah explained to Eric the idea of cube factors (F^3) related to particular assumed conditions, as developed in Chapter 4. They both agreed that they should aim to produce top-level probabilities which did not need such factors, linked to appropriate lower-level probability structures which were internally consistent. They took this view because they believed that conditions associated with safety statistics would be unethical, and would be equivalent to giving a high safety rating subject to small print which was full of let-out clauses, a form of conditional estimate cop-out. They observed that avoiding the use of F^3 as proposed was consistent with the top-level statistics provided by Railtrack safety reports, but it had profound implications for the way lower-level models were linked to such top-level statistics. That is, fault tree models and event tree models, and any risk-response diagram variants they might care to use, involve simplifications which tend to generate bias. If formal F^3 factors are not used, comparable devices have to be found to reflect this bias. The use of an informal F^3 factor as a lens to look at this issue was their assumed way forward.

Sarah and Eric discussed how they could consider risk efficiency at length, but eventually agreed this kind of analysis was not an immediate concern. It was something they could address in critical areas once those critical areas were identified. Sarah and Eric agreed that their first priority was identification of critical areas. This required an understanding of more than just risk efficiency. They had to be clear about an appropriate risk-reward balance, and address the question, How safe is safe enough?

Risk-Reward Balance: How Safe is Safe Enough?

Obtaining risk efficiency was seen by Eric and Sarah as a technical railway management issue which is probably best entrusted to the railway industry, subject to audit and regulation, with focused attention by regulators on any hot spots that emerged later, although they might wish to audit this. How safe is safe enough? was seen by Eric and Sarah as a different question altogether. That is, should the price per ef scale of Figure 7.3 be used, or should this scale be multiplied by 2, or should it be made to rise more quickly as ef increases? These were questions which Eric and Sarah believed ought to be answered by railway passengers. When Eric asked, 'How do we let passengers decide?' Sarah had a simple reply, 'Ask them.' She suggested they could use a simple survey questionnaire for a large sample of railway passengers which put appropriate questions in context along the following lines.

In 1998/99 the number of accidental passenger fatalities on Railway Group services per 100 million passenger journeys was 2.98. In 1999/00 this statistic rose to 4.42, the Ladbroke Grove (Paddington) accident (with 31 fatalities) having a serious impact. The Railway Group Safety Plan for 1999/00 involves a target for 2008/09 of 1. To ensure that money to do what is necessary to achieve improvements on this scale is found, the Rail Passenger Safety Trust would like to know how much money passengers believe ought to be spent, recognizing that much of it may have to be found via fare increases.

You might like to know that the UK transport industry uses figures which range from about £1 million to £10 million as the nominal monetary price of a life, assumed to reflect the amount that the relevant population would be prepared to spend to prevent one death at the margin. One reason it is assumed there are differences between modes of travel is because people are more concerned about accidents in which there are large numbers of fatalities. The two questions which follow are designed to seek your views on this issue in terms of railway accidents.

Given this background, please answer as best you can the following two questions:

(1) If the chance of another accident like Ladbroke Grove with 31 fatalities could be halved by increasing passenger fares, what is the maximum percentage increase in rail fares you believe would be appropriate?

(2) If the average number of individual passenger fatalities per annum, involving accidents like falls from train doors, could be halved by increasing passenger fares, what is the maximum percentage increase in rail fares you believe would be appropriate?

Sarah acknowledged that such questionnaires have a wide range of obvious and not so obvious problems. She suggested that professional survey design help could be used to minimize those difficulties. The results could provide a useful basis for validating a scale like that used in Figure 7.3. Such validation was crucial. Sarah argued that if the trust could establish the validity of a scale like that used in Figure 7.3, in the sense that it reflected on average what railway passengers want and are prepared to pay for, with associated variability measuring uncertainty about consequences, surely the railway industry would want to use it. Further, surely the relevant railway regulators and the government would insist that it be used. Further still, surely they would want to try to reduce the uncertainty associated with consequences via further survey work.

It would be important for the trust to undertake one or more pilot surveys, to iron out difficulties. It would be very important to take professional advice about surveys, and minimize the scope for criticism. It would be important to survey as many passengers as possible. Indeed, the survey questionnaire could be used as an invitation to join the trust, and participants who paid a small nominal fee to join (with optional additional donations) could be offered a free copy of a summary analysis, to further lever the clout provided by the survey.

Eric agreed the survey would be a good idea, although he had reservations about how it would be accepted. They both went to Wynn to discuss necessary funding. Wynn immediately saw the implications of the ef and price per ef relationship in Figure 7.3. He was very enthusiastic about proceeding with the survey, and he said he would organize the money if Sarah and Eric could define a suitable budget. However, Wynn indicated that results which upset current plans would probably be resisted by any party whose current plans were upset. This might be at several levels: Railway Group, regulator or government.

Wynn suggested that Sarah and Eric should pursue their survey-based line of attack. Meanwhile he would take another line. He would try to ensure that the Railway Group felt 'the pain' associated with any changes in passenger safety in terms which reflected the scale of Figure 7.3 as confirmed or adjusted by the survey. Wynn had in mind a programme of legal advice and support for any passengers or relatives of passengers wishing to sue for damages. This would involve a coordinated public information programme which 'took the gloves off' when attacking any investment decisions which might be interpreted as conflicting with passenger interests, and support for the corporate manslaughter pressure group, who wanted to see all company directors face criminal charges if their organizations overlooked legitimate safety concerns with fatal consequences. Wynn argued that any organization, be it a member of the Railway Group, a regulator or government, could ultimately be counted on to make decisions in what they perceived to be the best interests of the public, coloured by its own interests. The trust would have to make it in the best interests of all the organizations involved to do what the trust wanted them to do, to the extent this was politically feasible. Sarah and Eric's analysis could provide very effective 'sticks', which could be employed like a 'carrot' to some extent, depending on the organization. For example, if a suitable regulatory body financially linked to the Treasury fined the Railway Group the agreed price per ef every time an accident occurred and then met in full compensation claims from passengers and their families, this body could operate in the best interest of rail passengers in terms of ensuring that the Railway Group behaved the way train passengers wanted it to behave. Sarah was visibly taken aback by this view. Eric just smiled.

Wynn then tried to explain his approach to Sarah in slightly different terms. He said that if the Railway Group accepted Sarah and Eric's survey results and used them directly, there would not be a problem, but he did not think this would be the group's natural inclination, at least initially. Personal pride and inertia would lead to a natural and understandable reluctance to change anything which did not have to be changed. What he would be doing is harassing the Railway Group until it decided it was in its interests to change to Sarah and Eric's price per ef scale, or until it behaved as if it had changed to this scale. The trust had to make the Railway Group perceive as its problem what Sarah and Eric defined as the trust's problem before the Railway Group would warm to the trust's solution. What mattered at the end of the day was whether or not the Railway Group acted as if it believed the appropriate version of Figure 7.3. Whether or not the group actually used Figure 7.3 did not really matter to him, although he appreciated that it mattered very much to Sarah. Wynn also explained that although he wanted to use Sarah and Eric's questionnaire as a stick and a carrot, it was important to him that Sarah and Eric were comfortable with it as a fair and reasonable picture. Their professional integrity was important to the trust, not just because he knew that Sarah and Eric would not be prepared to operate in a context they saw as unethical, but because the trust wanted all its analysis to be deemed beyond criticism in terms of impropriety or wilful bias. Sarah was greatly relieved by this, and Eric saw it as reassuring confirmation of what he expected.

Ambiguities In 'The Relevant Public'

The concept of risk efficiency discussed in Section 7.5 did not seem to raise any ethical issues for Sarah or Eric. However, thinking about its application across all kinds of events did. British Rail, as a state-owned railway prior to privatization, addressed safety from the perspective of the state. An aspect of this was that the monetary value of a life for railway system safety purposes, interpreted as 'what the relevant public are willing to pay at the margin to improve safety enough to save one life', could be related to a 'relevant public' equated to the UK population as a whole. All people might not be treated as equal in many circumstances, but British Rail could treat them as if they were equal for these purposes, on the assumption that the state (the population at large) would wish to do this. The Railway Group had largely followed this tradition, implicitly if not explicitly. However, it was soon clear to Sarah and Eric that this was not necessarily appropriate from the perspective of the trust. For example, in 1998/99, there were 11 level crossing user fatalities, 8 involving pedestrians, 3 involving vehicles (Railtrack Safety and Standards Directorate, 2000). This makes level crossing events more than an order of magnitude more important than buffer events in terms of the expected equivalent fatality cost per annum. However, as indicated in the same report (pages 71–72), in the period 1993–2000, 74% of road user fatalities and 40% of pedestrian fatalities involved behaviour that was not legitimate. If railway safety is predominantly funded by railway passengers, should the value attributed to fatalities associated with improper use of a level crossing be the same as that attributed to fatalities associated with being a train passenger, from the perspective of the train passengers? Eric was convinced that the obvious answer was no. If road safety is assessed for all road users and pedestrians using a price of £1 million per equivalent fatality, then £1 million clearly ought to be an upper limit for road users who get involved in a level crossing accidents, in Eric's view. He believed there was a moral case for lower price per ef values associated with improper use of level crossings. Sarah agreed that this seemed to make good sense, but pointed out that the same source noted more than a third of level crossing fatalities occur to people with impaired competence, usually through age or disability, rather than alcohol. It would be unethical in her view to discriminate against such people in favour of railway passengers, especially as many might not use the railway. These people had a railway system imposed on them in a sense, and discriminating against them further in relation to safety would not be ethical.

After some discussion Sarah and Eric agreed that distinguishing different groups of the population would open a Pandora's box. For example, railway staff are a separate population from passengers, who would also warrant very complex separate treatment. In principle, railway staff could be given a questionnaire like passengers, with increased safety levels traded off against reduced pay. However, drivers travel on the same trains as passengers, they travel much more often, and they are much more likely to be killed in a crash. Conductors and other staff travelling on trains also have higher risk exposure than passengers. These people had a choice, to take their job or not, but there was no obvious ethical argument for treating them differently to passengers.

Eric and Sarah eventually agreed that it would not be appropriate to vary the price per ef scale used in Figure 7.3 depending upon the type of event or the people involved, but the fact that they were using a price per ef which increased as ef increased would, in itself, shift the priorities, away from level crossing and other incidents which involved small numbers of fatalities, towards train collisions involving large numbers of fatalities. This shift was consistent with the purpose of the trust, and it was useful to recognize that this shift could be achieved via the Figure 7.3 approach without direct discrimination in favour of railway passengers at the expense of others. There was strong evidence that people in general viewed one accident killing 300 people as more than 100 times worse than an accident killing 3 people. So it was ethically sound to reflect this view. However, any rising scale, like that used in Figure 7.3, necessarily discriminates against those killed in frequent small accidents and in favour of those killed in infrequent large accidents, relative to a flat rate. Indeed, a failure to properly reflect this, by using a flat rate for example, necessarily discriminates in a converse fashion. Any model assumption of this kind discriminates, implicitly if not explicitly. The implications of this were very disturbing to Sarah. Her basic model had ethical implications or moral content; there are winners and losers by definition, whether she liked it or not. In effect, any assumption will favour some people relative to others, and any change in assumptions will simply change the discrimination. Such discrimination cannot be eliminated. It is inherent in any set of assumptions. Sarah raised this with her then boyfriend Larry, who was a newly qualified lawyer. Larry suggested that Sarah had no business worrying about level crossing fatalities, because her role was to look after the best interests of railway passengers, like him. He used as an analogy someone charged with murder he had to defend. It was up to the court to decide innocence or guilt. His role was to make the best case he could on behalf of the accused. British justice demanded this of him, whether or not he thought the accused was innocent or guilty. It was part of a citizen's right to a fair trial and the notion of being innocent until proven guilty. It would be improper of him to weaken his defence because he suspected guilt. Similarly, the British political system allowed railway passengers to campaign for their interests, and level crossing users to campaign for theirs. It was up to the level crossing users to provide arguments to be balanced against those of railway passengers. It would be improper of Sarah to weaken her case for railway passengers because she thought this might discriminate against others.

Sarah was even more disturbed by this line of argument, and by Larry. In fact, it was the beginning of the end of their relationship. However, it was the beginning of the beginning of her growing understanding of the importance of ethics in practice. Actually, there was more than a grain of truth in Larry's argument. As a professional hired by the trust to look after railway passengers' interests, Sarah had a duty of trust to those passengers. If she thought they were getting more consideration relative to others than they should, she had the option to change her employer. But to deliberately sabotage their case would be unprofessional. Indeed, so long as Sarah believed they were getting a raw deal, it might be both proper and ethical to ensure that she made relatively few assumptions which biased the argument against their case, by implication making relatively more assumptions which biased the argument for their case, all such assumptions being reasonable in the sense that they were defensible approximations to a reality too complex to address directly. It would be naive as well as unprofessional and unethical to be overtly biased. However, it would be effective as well as professional and ethical to push the argument in the right direction in a credible manner. It was not a question of the ends justifying the means. It was a question of recognizing and living with the ethical implications of her actions in a wider framework than she had used previously.

Ambiguities in Equivalent Fatalities

Sarah discussed her concerns with Eric, including her conversation with Larry. Eric later indicated that these discussions had triggered attempts to clarify long-standing concerns he had about the equivalent fatalities concept. Previously, British Rail had been able to make a judgement about the relative weight to give to people killed and people injured to various degrees because it was attempting to act in the best interests of the whole population, and it was not making decisions involving trade-offs like killing a few more people in order to injure few less. The Railway Group was implicitly attempting to carry on this tradition, but the situation had changed. The Paddington crash had driven home the political reality that large numbers of people killed in one event have important political and economic consequences for the railway industry, out of all proportion to the implications of a flat rate price of £2 million per ef. The railway industry would be forced to improve safety to an extent that a larger number of smaller accidents would not even approximate. The economic costs to the Railway Group would involve a price per ef relationship with ef like that illustrated by Figure 7.3 because the politics of the regulatory approach to safety would drive it in that direction. Indeed, as noted earlier, it was very much Eric and Sarah's business to help ensure that political and regulatory pressure on the railway industry made the Railway Group behave in a way that reflected the views of railway passengers. At the end of the day, the Railway Group made the safety decisions, subject to audit, with criteria which were financially driven. As Wynn had indicated, the Railway Group had to be made to feel pain in proportion to the pain inflicted, to make them behave in an appropriate manner. However, if when 30 people are killed the price per ef rises to a mean value of £8 million as indicated in Figure 7.3, is it defensible to use the same ef conversion proportions for injuries? Indeed, is it ever ethical to equate one fatality to x severed limbs, or y broken legs or z cases of trauma? Surely the answer was no, unless a sample of passenger opinions, along the lines discussed on page 257, provided average rates, in which case associated variability ought to be treated as part of the overall uncertainty. Sarah did not know how to respond to this. She and Eric agreed to raise it with Wynn. Wynn's considered response – he insisted on time for consideration – was as follows.

Wynn's personal goal was to use the trust to drive Railway Group safety towards the much higher levels he believed were appropriate, in part by allocating their safety money more effectively, in part by spending more money on safety. Wynn thought the use of a price per ef scale like Figure 7.3 and associated surveys was a key part of the best way to achieve this, because it took well-established concepts and restated them in a way that supported the direction of movement he wanted to stimulate. That is, a price per ef was standard practice, and the notion of a larger price per ef when more people were involved was part of conventional wisdom. Putting these ideas together in a functional relationship like that provided by Figure 7.3 was not standard practice, but it made sense in terms of conventional wisdom. And it moved the trust's case in the right direction. Wynn thought that getting involved in disputes about equivalent fatality relationships would just muddy the water. Indeed, he had in mind using the trust to greatly increase the awards for compensation paid to those injured, to US levels if possible, via both court action and political lobbying. If he was successful in this, £8 million per fatality for 30 fatalities might look very inexpensive in terms of the injury claims and the associated legal costs. This would mean high injury claims could be used to lever up associated equivalent fatality costs if a scale was in place which had not been challenged in terms of credibility. Sarah and Eric should let ambiguity persist in this area and concentrate on the immediate implications of Figure 7.3.

Wynn did not wish to muddy the water further with Sarah at this stage, but he might have indicated that even if injuries were not an ambiguous issue in the ef concept, the use of an average price per ef was. Statistically speaking, if x is the average amount which people would be prepared to spend to prevent a marginal death, then y percent would be prepared to spend more, and $100 - y$ percent would only be prepared to spend something less, with y approaching 50% if the distribution is symmetric. Those who wish to see more spent may complain the system is not safe enough for them. Those who feel too much is being spent may complain about this. Both groups may avoid rail travel and drive instead, imposing even greater risks on themselves and others. The government may wish to impose a high value for x as a policy parameter to encourage rail travel with safety and other objectives in mind. For example, encouraging rail travel might be a way of avoiding spending more money on roads. Pandora's box can be opened if framing assumptions are examined closely. More generally, ambiguity was not all bad in Wynn's view, and some desirable ambiguities are best left alone. The trick was knowing which ambiguities are usefully resolved with a view to furthering one's own interests, recognizing that others have interests which may be served by developing understanding about other ambiguities. Turning over a stone may reveal more than you wish to see.

Regulation Via Mandatory Insurance

One member of the trust's board, Ivor, is an actuary in the insurance industry. When Wynn explained the issues discussed in earlier sections as part of his report to the board, Ivor suggested that Wynn's notion of a regulator fining the Railway Group on an ef scale every time an accident occurred, or trust-supported legal action attempting to perform a similar role, might be usefully developed into a form of mandatory insurance-based regulation. Here is his preliminary view of how an insurer/regulator would operate such a notion.

The insurer/regulator would use ef scales assessed in Eric and Sarah's framework, and an independent evaluation of Railway Group safety risk in Eric and Sarah's framework, to compute an annual insurance premium to carry this risk. The Railway Group would be required by law to carry this insurance for the same basic reason that all motor vehicle drivers in the UK are required to carry liability insurance. How the Railway Group allocated the premium to the various companies would be up to the Railway Group or an overseeing body like the Strategic Rail Authority, but they would have full access to the details of the assessment process to help. If they could reorganize to improve overall safety, they would immediately benefit collectively from lower premiums. If, as many people think, the current structure could not deliver safety effectively, there would be direct commercial pressure to change the structure, perhaps to the single controlling body which many think is essential. Every time an accident occurred, the insurer/

regulator would act as a mutual fund, working on behalf of rail passengers, making full use of the available premium income and ef scales as guidelines to meet all claims as quickly as possible. If a major event like Paddington occurred, Treasury funding would fill the gap between premiums and claims, with Treasury access to favourable gaps when no serious events occur, unless and until reserves are built up. A long-run neutral net balance would be sought.

Relative to letting a regulator or the courts punish the Railway Group as and when accidents occurred, Ivor argued the following advantages:

- The present situation involves implicit self-insurance by each player within the Railway Group for liabilities beyond regulatory limits for public liability insurance policies, with each player determined to pass the cost of preventative measures and claims onto another player as far as possible, for obvious commercial reasons, and no direct collective management of overall insurance arrangements. The incentive to collaborate or face being bought out by a single organization which could effectively pull things together is not there. Ivor's scheme could provide a carrot to stimulate collaboration within the current structure. It could also provide a stick in terms of the threat of hostile takeover to impose a revised structure if current Railway Group players did not collaborate effectively. Ivor indicated that the required unity of command could be restored by renationalization, or other direct government interventions, but he did not think this was likely, for a variety of reasons. His approach could fill the political vacuum.
- A safety culture was another key requirement for the safe system which the trust wanted to achieve, which was currently not being achieved. For example, central recording of near-miss incidents in a no-blame culture as a means of improving system safety is essential, but not feasible in an organizational structure which makes it a key issue to blame the company for an accident. Ivor's approach to providing unity of command would meet a necessary condition for a safety culture by letting the Railtrack Safety and Standards Directorate change its role to a Railway Group interface with the insurer/regulator, acting directly and explicitly on behalf of the railway industry as a whole. Its current ambiguous role and positioning could be clarified and enhanced.
- When the railway industry has an unlucky year, this would not be as likely to force immediate radical change that might not be justified. Conversely, when the railway industry has a series of lucky years, this would not be as likely to lead to complacency.
- Net subsidies for the railway industry by the government might be involved, but it would become clear to the population at large what portion of these subsidies was insurance and what was not. Subsidies related to insurance might be disallowed, to improve the incentive effect. Unreasonable expectations about safety would be easier to deal with. Coordinated government transport policy concerned with all modes of travel would be facilitated.

- The risk of one player in the Railway Group causing a major accident through proven negligence and simply going broke in the face of resulting claims, leaving large numbers of people without compensation, would be eliminated. The UK government would not allow a road haulage operator to operate on a liability self-insurance basis. Why should it allow a similar risk with Railway Group companies? If it is clearly pointed out to the government that this risk is currently being run, and the party in power takes no notice, when (not if) such an incident occurs at some time in the future, that party will have no place to hide. Trust publicity ought to be able to make this clear to the government, and the population at large. This reason did not depend on subtle analysis of complex issues. It could be publicized in simple terms anyone could understand. It could be sold as a sufficient reason on its own, with the other four expressed as further benefits associated with meeting this fundamental concern.

Wynn's reaction to Ivor's argument was cautious optimism. He encouraged Ivor to develop and promote his ideas through the Institute of Actuaries and in related professional forums, before the trust openly backed it. He was hopeful and positive about it, but concerned that it might seem too radical for the present situation.

Conclusion

Kaplan (1997) suggests, 'We are asking the wrong question. . . . The question is not how much risk is acceptable? The question is what is the best decision option?' Dowie (1999) develops this idea from a Bayesian decision theory perspective in the context of a case for avoiding the use of the word 'risk'. The epigraph at the start of this chapter revises Kaplan's question to, How do we frame the process for choosing the best decision option? and emphasizes it is the *big* question, how much risk is acceptable remaining a component question. The short answer is to use a constructively simple decision process. Sarah's contribution was a starting position which embraces current safety models as special cases but allows substantial generalization for new insights, drawing on input from people with experience like Eric and a much wider set of data. However, Wynn could interpret the results of the process developed by Sarah and Eric in a still wider framework which included the politics, the legal system and the economics of the industry. And Ivor proposed mandatory insurance to make all these issues a formal part of the framing assumptions addressed by the process. In this context as in all other contexts, it matters *how we frame the process to choose*.

It seems only a matter of time before the approach adopted by Wynn, Sarah and Eric is taken up by other charitable organizations who seek to increase their power and influence concerned with safety management or environmental issues with comparable implications in other contexts. And sooner or later Ivor's idea should find a shape and time to become a central part of received wisdom, perhaps in other contexts, like that explored in Chapter 11. Applying the ideas developed in this chapter elsewhere might prove the biggest opportunity offered by this book, but uncertainty about how best to proceed is proportionately scaled, and addressing it is beyond the scope of this book.

Most of the key issues raised in this chapter are best viewed in relation to key issues in earlier chapters. That is, what ideas generalize or carry over, and what is different?

Analytical approach

Sarah's use of a simple scenario approach is constructively simple in the terms used to define constructively simple probabilities in Chapter 4. That is, the additional complexity associated with Figures 7.1 to 7.3 relative to Eddy's minimalist approach are good examples of constructive complexity that is worthwhile on the first pass, because the added insight is more than worth the added effort. A key common theme is the idea that any important source of uncertainty which has a form that can be quantified should be quantified if quantification is useful, recognizing the importance of uncertainty about uncertainty. That is, it is useful to define a relationship between ef and price per ef as in Figure 7.3, and to recognize the associated uncertainty in that relationship. The form of Figure 7.3 can be interpreted as a probability tree incorporating statistical dependence, but the ef and price per ef expected value relationship can be given a causal regression function interpretation too. A corollary is not attempting to quantify when it would not be useful to do so, as when developing the concept of equivalent fatality.

The idea of uncertain probabilities associated with events, as well as uncertain outcomes, was a key idea developed earlier. Extending this to uncertain outcome conversions (fatalities to monetary values) is an important generalization of this basic theme. Anything which is uncertain should be addressed by recognizing that uncertainty explicitly, provided this is useful. If we do so, we get a much richer picture of what we are dealing with, and one which can draw out important ambiguities associated with assuming certainty where it does not exist. In this sense Figure 7.3 compares very favourably to the implicit model which says 'if a buffer event occurs the mean outcome is 3 fatalities, full stop'. However, adding further complexity involves costs which may outweigh the benefits.

The need for analysis on early passes to focus on identifying what matters, and what does not, is another common theme, as is the related need for creative leaps, illustrated by Wynn's plans to exploit the questionnaire approach. An important notion, not discussed earlier, is the use of data that is relevant but outside the usual data set. This has implications beyond safety. It has received attention by others in a safety context (Toft and Renolds, 1997) in terms of an 'isomorphic approach' which may have value beyond safety. The use of non-UK data to address UK Rail Group buffer events is a usefully simple illustration of some of the key issues. Other relevant references for those interested in this area include Turner and Pidgeon (1997) and Hood and Jones (1996).

Subjective probabilities, ambiguity and bias

The idea of a subjective probability distribution being used to assess the probability of an event, a probability distribution for probabilities, was introduced in Eddy's tale of Chapter 4, under the concept of constructively simple probability.

Low-probability events by definition offer little chance of appropriate data. However, the safety industry tends to have a very 'hard science' perspective which is very uncomfortable with subjective probabilities. If those who produce statistics like those assessed on page 244 are not prepared to change, those who interpret them must explicitly address these shortcomings. This might be done by considering associated cube (F^3) factors, as discussed in Chapter 4. If the users of such probabilities do not have the expertise which Eric supplied on page 246, the associated F^3 distribution ought to be wider than Eric's. Taking this line a little further, when assessing the safety of British beef or new drugs, many scientists pronounce things 'safe' when what they mean is 'there is no hard scientific evidence that it is not safe', which common sense recognizes is something quite different. Popular mistrust of science will continue to be well founded so long as scientists who are employed to protect specific interests are prepared to persist with this type of ambiguity and allowed to get away with it.

It would have been interesting to tackle these kinds of questions here in some detail. More modest aims were essential to ensure the purposes of this chapter were achieved without undue complexity or diversion. However, it is perhaps worth noting that one response is to apply an F^3 factor to all such statements, recognizing that addressing ambiguity arising from responding to one question with the answer to a different question is the starting point. If enough people did this publicly and forcibly enough, some progress might be possible. However, it would be unwise to underestimate scientific communities' unwillingness to change unless they are forced to do so. Anyone outside the trust might wish to apply an F^3 factor to results produced by Sarah and Eric. However, the approach used by Sarah and Eric attempts to avoid the need to do so. They might measure their own success to some extent by the lack of need for such an adjustment. Others might follow this example.

Bias was an important F^3 issue in the context of Chapters 5 and 6, along with other F^3 factors which have a comparable effect if not identified. For example, those who want a project to proceed because it would be interesting to work on it, or their livelihood depends on it, can be expected to perceive issues differently from those who do not want the money spent because they do not think the organization should be doing what is proposed. The rationale for developing the F^3 factor was driven in part by these very important concerns.

This chapter did not use a formal F^3 factor, and the idea that Sarah and Eric were attempting to avoid the need for one is important. However, the political motivation associated with the kinds of issues addressed in this chapter means everyone will in effect be putting an F^3 factor in front of everything everybody else says. And so they should. That is, the Railway Group is not going to deliberately bias its assessment of its safety on the pessimistic side, and it would be silly to expect it to do so in the context of measures which are uncertain. Nor is Wynn going to attempt to change things the way he wants to change things with statistics which understate his case. 'There are lies, damned lies and statistics' is a timeless and often apt quote for good reason. The reason statistics are often deemed worse than 'damned lies' is because those who produce them or purvey them seem to see them as the truth, and those who are at the receiving end do not have a suitably constructed F^3 factor. An important message from this chapter is the need to use an informal F^3 factor as a lens to interpret our own statistics if we are consciously trying to make sure that such a factor is not necessary. An equally important message is the value of an informal F^3 factor to interpret statistics produced by anyone else, with a keen eye to the motivation behind the production of those statistics. There is no such thing as an objective statistic free of bias for any intended use, and any 'scientist' who argues there is doesn't understand the issues.

The ambiguities implicit in cost-benefit analysis which are replaced by difficult political and ethical issues when a 'single-issue politics' lens is used is very important in the authors' view. In the real world of decision making on public issues, 'the gloves are coming off', as Wynn would say. Interests which are not skilfully defended with bare knuckles may not survive. Some single-interest groups which are alarmingly successful put themselves beyond the law, and the law is increasingly tested beyond its design and found wanting. Those who care about the processes used to make decisions involving the public interest have a major challenge on their hands.

Risk efficiency and trade-offs between objectives

Risk efficiency was addressed briefly in this chapter to clarify the relationship between local risk efficiency which is event-specific and global risk efficiency which embraces the whole system. Risk efficiency here means 'a minimum level of expected equivalent fatalities (or ef cost) for a given level of system safety cost'. The trade-offs here are between expected equivalent fatalities and expected system safety cost. In previous chapters similar trade-offs and risk efficiency issues were considered between cost, duration and quality. Seeking risk efficiency in a multiple-attribute or multiple-criterion context means ensuring that we cannot do better in terms of one attribute or criterion without doing worse in terms of a second attribute or criterion. From a multiple-attribute or multiple-criterion perspective it might be argued that the relationship between ef and price per ef modelled by Figure 7.3 is an irrational prior expression of priorities which values frequent small numbers of fatalities less than the same number of people killed all at once. However, this argument implicitly uses rationality concepts based on assumptions which are not appropriate. The trade-offs here are qualitatively different from simple financial risk/reward trade-offs. People are entitled to a horror of large numbers of people killed all at once, and if that is the way they feel, they are entitled to demand that these preferences are taken into account. There is no need to explain it in terms of financial risk aversion or any other analogy. It is a simple fact of life we ought to accommodate.

The price of a life as a shadow price

Another key common theme from previous chapters is the importance of opportunity costs (valuations based on best alternative uses for scarce resources if we do not commit them to a use being considered) and shadow prices (valuations based on the increased achievement of overall objectives if a constraint can be relaxed). Opportunity costs and shadow prices are closely related ideas, both defined in terms of resource constraints, expressed in a different form.

The price of a life should be viewed as a shadow price. That is, assuming a railway system is 'risk efficient' in the sense discussed on page 254, the price of a life should equate to the additional expenditure that would be necessary to reduce the expected number of fatalities by one. The shadow price that is the price of a life is a property of a system, arising from the constraints on the expenditure necessary to make the system safer. Implicitly, if nothing is done, the relevant population are saying they are not prepared to spend this amount. However, most of the time nobody asks them. To take the price of a life and make it the amount at the margin the relevant population is (or is not) prepared to spend to reduce the number of deaths by one, we have to ask them. If we suppose (assume) we know, and we do not, this is a crucial source of ambiguity in any associated analysis.

There was a time (only a few decades ago) when economists and others attempted to value a life in economic terms based on lifetime earnings, the cost of supporting dependants, and so on. In some legal contexts this is still common practice. Such calculations may be useful background in some cases, but they cannot be more than background. Such calculations should never be confused with the price of a life in shadow price terms as used here, in anything other than very restrictive terms. 'They know the price of everything, the value of nothing,' a quote usually attributed to Oscar Wilde, is very apt if anyone attempts to put a value on life, death, injury or environmental damage which does not have the very clear restrictive meaning of a shadow price. Key factors in the way people price life in this sense, if asked, are their income, their degree of control and choice, the number of people involved in an incident, and the quality of the death, as indicated earlier. There is nothing 'irrational' about this, in the plain English sense of the word, although some people argue it is irrational in terms of constructed scientific (axiomatic) views of rationality which they wish to employ. Those axiomatic approaches introduce ambiguity, as do associate claims of irrationality. They do not resolve the ambiguity inherent in people's perceptions. There is no moral content per se in a shadow price valuation of the price of a life associated with a system. However, there are ethical issues about the way such values are interpreted and used. These ethical issues are inescapable and they may be extremely important.

The need to work with a shadow price equated with the price of a life is clearly something very different about this chapter relative to earlier chapters. We took the view that it was important to include this chapter because it was important to make the connection to issues like this via shadow prices. But we resisted the temptation to develop these links further in terms of environmental issues – the value of cleaner water in our rivers, the value of less carbon dioxide in our atmosphere, etc.– apart from a modest contribution in Chapter 11. The same kind of shadow price links can be used, and such issues are addressed as part of the approach to Chapter 11, but it did not seem appropriate to take this discussion any further here. It would soon get beyond our competence, and the interests of most target readers. That said, the ability to connect in this way with these issues is very important.

The concept of equivalent fatality is best viewed as a development of 'the price of a life' shadow price which does not necessarily work. That is, if shadow prices for very serious and less serious injuries could be identified in terms of system improvement costs, they may not relate to the price of a life in the 'scale of misery' way implicitly assumed, and asking the relevant population what they would pay to avoid a scale of misery may compound the ambiguities. Apart from confirming Wynn's stance, this explains in part our caution about moving too far into these issues.

The effects of luck

The overwhelming and quite fundamental flaw in most conventional safety industry thinking is an 'expected value' limitation of the risk concept, because 'risk' is defined and measured as probability times impact. This does not allow for good or bad luck. It is analogous to an approach to budgeting which uses provisions (estimates of what should happen on average) to set budgets but ignores contingencies (buffers to reduce the probability of exceeding average values when asymmetric penalties are involved) and fails to manage expectations about exceeding budgets. As a consequence, some reasonably safe industries or enterprises may be punished as a result of bad luck, while some unsafe ones may get away with being unsafe for decades. More important, both kinds of industry or enterprise are going to manage safety ineffectively. The lower the probability of relevant risks in a given system, the greater the importance of luck. Luck is a particularly important factor with low-probability and high-impact risks.

A particular issue is the problem of fine tuning (Starbuck and Milliken, 1988). Lengthy periods without failure can motivate engineers and managers to fine-tune systems to render them less redundant, more efficient, cheaper or more profitable. An example of fine tuning is the incremental reduction in safety margins. As the period without failure increases, safey margins may look more and more unnecessary and therefore reducible. 'We can reduce margins a bit because we got away with it last time' is the rationale. However, such fine tuning can actually make future failure more likely. If managers attribute the absence of failure to their control systems, rather than possible good luck, managers may become complacent and overconfident about the possibility of failures in performance. It may be increasingly assumed that existing procedures are adequate to prevent failures or flag developing problems when in fact they are not, future risks are underestimated, and further fine tuning is encouraged. The concern is that in a continuing absence of failures, managers will continue to fine-tune systems until safety margins become inadequate and something breaks. The concept of excessive fine tuning has relevance beyond safety management, to contingency allowances and a variety of forms of organizational slack which provide a general ability to cope with uncertain operating conditions. In addition to safety margins and procedures, back-up systems, spare capacity, long lead times, a third shift capability, additions to cost and time budgets, and financial reserves all represent subjects for (excessive) fine tuning. Ivor's mandatory insurance approach addresses this issue in part, but it is a widespread issue, and Ivor may not succeed.

This suggests that risk management in a safety context should recognize that luck matters, and so include efforts to identify and share the benefits of good luck as well as identify and reduce the potential for bad luck. Where appropriate, suitable incentive or trigger contracts to provide the necessary motivation could be introduced between customers or regulators and suppliers along the lines outlined by Roger in Chapter 6. The significance of luck should not be underestimated. For example, in August 2000 Concorde supersonic aircraft were grounded after the disastrous Paris crash of a Concorde attempting take-off. The UK Civil Aircraft Authority (CAA) reasoning as reported on television was in effect 'a tyre failure should not lead to fuel tank rupture, but the Paris crash showed this could happen'. However, Concorde had operated for decades without this happening. Were those involved just lucky for decades? Or were those involved just unlucky that a piece of metal on the runway led to tyre failure on take-off on this occasion? The answer is not clear. A pertinent question is does this kind of safety decision have to depend upon horses bolting before stables doors are shut?

The precautionary principle in more generalized operational forms

The kind of analysis essential to make the precautionary principle operational in an effective form is explored in the context of rail safety in this chapter. In the context of rail safety, many of the general issues the authors are aware of are touched on, and we believe some important ones are resolved. However, the authors make no claim to have considered all the relevant issues in a rail context or any other context. Further, as indicated earlier in other contexts, appropriate forms of analysis have to be significantly adapted to the particular circumstances addressed. This chapter just scratches the surface of the full set of approaches necessary to make the precautionary principle effective in any circumstances in terms of all reasonable views of what the precautionary principle ought to address.

The authors believe it is important to take a modest view of what this chapter achieves in terms of making the precautionary principle operational in general terms, and a conservative or pessimistic view of how much more needs to be done, because we are very uncertain about the scope of what remains. However, we are optimistic about the validity of the direction taken here. The analysis features developed in this chapter are unlikely to prove sufficient, but they are necessary. They may seem radical to some, especially those who suffer from irrational objectivity as explored in Chapter 4. However, they embrace conventional analysis approaches as special cases, and clarify the limitations of the framing assumptions which these approaches rest on in a clear manner. Pushing back the limitations of framing assumptions in this way is the only way forward. Exactly where this will take us, and exactly how to proceed, remains ambiguous. But that is why the journey looks so interesting. Building a bridge between science and social science perspectives is a grand overview of the generality we need. Getting ropes across the chasm one at a time to resolve specific issues in an internally consistent form which can be generalized is the way forward the authors favour.

8 Norman's tale: Discounting future performance measures

A bird in the hand is worth two in the bush.

Introduction

This chapter is about the financial valuation of projects when key aspects are characterized as future performance measures, in particular as cash flows in future time periods. The basic net present value (NPV) model converts future cash flows into an equivalent sum via a discounting process. NPV and all associated discounted cash flow (DCF) approaches, like internal rate of return (IRR), recognize that £1 in the future is usually worth less than £1 now. Table 8.1 shows the usual notation and decision rules when project cash flows, horizons and discount rates are assumed to be known with certainty.

Putting aside the issue of uncertainty for the moment, correctly evaluating the Table 8.1 parameters involves issues often overlooked. Relevant cash flows are *incremental* cash flows, so project boundaries have to be clearly and appropriately

Table 8.1—Decision rules for valuing project discounted cash flows

Conventional basic notation

n is the number of time periods (years usually) in the planning horizon
X_t is the net cash flow inwards at the end of period $t = 0, 1, \ldots, n$
D is an appropriate discount rate (usually a hurdle rate)

Conventional net present value (NPV) decision rule

$$NPV - \sum_{t=0}^{n} X_t/(1 + D/100)^n$$

Accept the project if NPV is greater than zero, otherwise reject

Internal rate of return (IRR) approach

The internal rate of return of a project, d, is given by the value of D when NPV = 0
Accept the project if d is greater than the hurdle rate, otherwise reject

defined. Important interdependencies between projects may have to be taken into account. In addition, we need to ensure that inflation, taxation, depreciation and interest payments on loans are correctly treated. A common error, for example, is to use a discount rate incorporating inflation, but fail to adjust cash flows for inflation (Van Horne, 1971). In practice it is usually easier to let general inflation cancel out when considering economic desirability in terms of NPV, addressing only escalation (differential inflation), of non-renewable fuel prices for example (Chapman and Cooper, 1983b). It is well-established common practice (Joy and Bradley, 1973) but not appropriate to compare two projects in terms of their internal rates of return, and d values must always be given a parametric analysis interpretation (Hawkins and Pearce, 1971). However, any pair of mutually exclusive possibilities can be compared in parametric terms using the IRR rate if a differential cash flow is defined directly, generally a useful simplification for any DCF approach (Brealey and Myers, 1996). Financial feasibility and project timing decisions should consider inflation (Chapman and Cooper, 1985).

In addition to these definitional problems, we also need to address several kinds of uncertainty associated with project cash flows:

- The duration of project cash flows defined by n, often project life
- The total and the timing of expected cash flows over the duration of the project, the X_t
- The range (variability) of possible cash flows at particular points in time
- The possibility that very different revised estimates of expected cash flows will occur during the life of the project
- The possibility that the appropriate D will vary over the life of the project

When faced with the need to evaluate investment proposals whose future cash flows are uncertain, project evaluators are often unclear how to proceed within a DCF framework. A common procedure is to discount best estimates of project cash flows at a hurdle rate which is assumed to correspond to the firm's cost of capital. If the NPV of project cash flows discounted at the hurdle rate is positive, then the project is assumed to be acceptable. Uncertainty about cash flows may then be examined in an ad hoc way using sensitivity analysis on a few key variables.

Compared to identifying and quantifying cash flows, the problem of choosing an appropriate discount rate is often regarded as a minor one of fine tuning a reasonable base estimate. Analysts and client managers are usually aware that the size of the discount rate can materially affect project evaluation, but are frequently content to employ a single ballpark hurdle discount rate for all projects. Many evaluators postpone the problem of identifying an appropriate rate for a project by calculating the IRR for the future stream of best-estimate cash flows. This leaves the problem of identifying the appropriate rate for a particular project with the decision maker. Often the decision maker is pleased to have information about project profitability in this form, because he or she is used to thinking in terms of rates of return and comparing potential investments in this way, but it may encourage the view that precise assessment of the relevant rate is unnecessary. Some attribute the continuing popularity of IRR incorrectly used to compare projects without differential cash flows to this feature of IRR.

The financial valuation of an investment project is a conceptually difficult problem because it involves taking into account the timing of cash flows and the level of uncertainty associated with cash flows at different points in time. Table 8.2 lists the basic evaluation approaches available along with the format of cash flow data required to apply each one. All the approaches listed in Table 8.2 attempt to summarize the complex pattern of uncertain project cash flows in a form convenient for making comparisons with other investment opportunities.

Conceptually the simplest approaches are those which combine all uncertainties about project cash flows into a probability distribution for the project as a whole. For example, Monte Carlo simulation can provide a complete NPV distribution, analytical approaches can deduce the mean and variance of the underlying distribution, and sensitivity analysis can give a partial picture of overall project NPV variability. These approaches imply a two-dimensional assessment of projects based on the expected value and variance or variability of the NPV as an assessment of the financial risk. Use of a mean–variance criterion, or first- and second-order stochastic dominance, allows projects which are not preferred by any risk averse investors to be identified and rejected. Any further reduction in the remaining preferred (efficient) set of alternative investments requires further

Table 8.2—Basic approaches to valuing variability in project cash flows

Basic approaches	Format of cash flow data required
Ad hoc sensitivity analysis of the main variables compared with the 'best estimate' valuation	'Best estimate' cash flows
Analytical derivation of NPV distribution (Hillier, 1963; Weiss, 1987)	Means and variances of cash flows, preferably serially independent cash flows
Monte Carlo simulation to deduce NPV or IRR distribution (Hertz, 1964)	Probability distributions for component cash flows, interdependencies specified
Risk-adjusted discount rate derived from the capital asset pricing model applied to mean cash flows (Sharpe, 1964)	Estimation of covariance of cash flows with market portfolio, plus mean cash flows
Certainty equivalence or risk-adjusted discount rate applied to mean values of cash flows	Mean values plus subjective estimation of variability
Certainty equivalence using an exponential utility function (Bernhard, 1984)	Time-state series or cash flows with estimated probabilities for each state in each time period

input in the form of an individual's preference function or, in the case of a group decision, at least an informed debate among individuals.

The certainty equivalence approach requires a specification of the investor's preference function for monetary outcomes in each time period of the project's duration. For risk-averse investors, risk is evaluated in terms of a deduction applied to expected cash flows in each period. The information required about the investor's preferences is more onerous as a consequence, and assumptions become embedded in the analysis which are difficult to assess in terms of robustness. Nevertheless, the perspective is still one of a managerial decision maker considering the total variability of project cash flows.

Probability distribution approaches treat risk *after* discounting. The certainty equivalence approach takes risk into account *before* discounting, and it implies a hurdle discount rate equal to the rate of interest on risk-free investments. Managers used to comparing the rates of return of different investments are often uncomfortable with this. Many require convincing that risk is adequately treated elsewhere. The risk-adjusted discount rate (RADR) approach is more satisfactory in this respect for some, because the size of the hurdle (discount) rate reflects the riskiness of project cash flows. The positive relationship between risk and the rate of return required by investors is incorporated directly. The associated capital asset pricing model (CAPM) provides a market-based rationale for determining the level of RADR required (Sharpe, 1964).

In any given context the choice of valuation approach from these alternatives is not clear-cut. The modelling assumptions and information requirements of the certainty equivalent and RADR approaches are considerable, and the validity of assumptions associated with the theory used is difficult to verify (Ward, Chapman, and Klein, 1991). As a practical matter, the choice of evaluation approach employed is likely to be influenced by the expertise of analysts and decision makers, and the level of effort injected into the evaluation process. Faced with high uncertainty about the size and timing of future cash flows, most decision makers welcome a constructively simple approach to project evaluation. As the tale in this chapter illustrates, a multiple-pass approach starting from a simple parametric sensitivity analysis facilitates much more than just a valuation of an investment proposal.

The protagonist of the tale of this chapter is Norman. In the mid 1990s Norman was working on a proposal for the permanent disposal of the UK's intermediate-level nuclear waste. Norman shared the views of many who have dedicated a career to nuclear power. He saw nuclear power as a low-risk, clean, effective, and efficient way to generate electricity. He saw it as seriously misunderstood and widely misrepresented, needing protection from its many detractors. This chapter neither supports nor tests this perspective, and the authors' stance is neutral. However, Norman's perspective on the nuclear industry is a key aspect of the context which motivates the analysis undertaken in the tale. The reader needs to temporarily suspend any disbelief about the appropriateness of Norman's views on nuclear power to understand the issues Norman explores in relation to discounting models. The implications are wide enough to make this worthwhile, and the reader need have no interest in nuclear power for Norman's tale to be of interest.

Norman's Situation

Norman saw the future of the nuclear industry as dependent upon a satisfactory resolution of the problem of nuclear waste disposal. That is, if the UK nuclear industry could not find a safe, permanent solution to the growing volumes of nuclear waste, Norman believed it would be shut down, a bit at a time over several decades, if not directly. Norman was very aware that even if the nuclear industry was shut down, a solution for permanent disposal of existing nuclear waste would have to be found. This was an issue that was not going to go away without positive action, and Norman believed it required action sooner rather than later.

International agreements had made dumping nuclear waste at sea illegal. The only viable alternative, by common consent internationally, was deep mine repository disposal. The proposed UK site was the preferred site by common consent within the UK nuclear industry, although it was not free of problems or adversaries. The plans being considered involved four phases:

- **Initial construction** involved the construction of a deep mine and associated laboratory facilities near a site of substantial current nuclear industry reprocessing and surface storage of nuclear waste.
- **Intermediate experimentation** involved extensive research based on experiments located in the laboratory facilities to prove the safety of the mine as a site for permanent disposal of intermediate-level nuclear waste.
- **Further construction** involved enlargement of the mine to form a repository.
- **Permanent disposal** of waste material in the repository until it becomes full.

Substantial sums of money were involved, and the time frames being considered were long. Norman's particular concern was obtaining permission to proceed from the national government, in terms of Department of Environment (DoE) and Treasury approval in particular. The Treasury was known to be keen to defer the project, and a DoE report had recommended deferral for 50 years, relying on surface storage in the meantime (DoE, 1994).

A first attempt to define the cost of a deep mine project in NPV terms had been made, and incorporated in the DoE report. It was based on outline plans developed over several years for the two construction phases, the intermediate experimentation phase, and all associated activities. A first attempt to define the cost of the surface storage alternative had also been made, and incorporated in the DoE report. Some analysis of uncertainty and risk associated with these calculations had been made, with input from Norman. However, the adverse recommendation in the DoE report, for a 50 year deferral of the project, prompted a rethink on Norman's part. Norman wanted to re-examine the DoE (1994) analysis from first principles, to explain everything very carefully to himself and his boss, Nigel, as a basis for rethinking their strategy with the DoE and the Treasury.

A First-Pass Model And Parametric Analysis

Norman started his rethink of the DoE NPV modelling process with the working assumption that all aspects of his initial model should be very simple, but easy to make more complex, as and when a rationale for introducing complexity emerged. Norman recognized that differential cash flows would be appropriate. For consistency with the DoE (1994) he decided to assess the NPV of deferring the project for 50 years relative to proceeding now (1995). A positive NPV would imply it was more expensive to proceed now, and deferral was the preferred decision. He was looking for a negative NPV, indicating that proceeding now is the preferred choice.

Norman then aggregated the time periods involved in the two construction phases and the intermediate experimentation phase, expected to take about 15 years. That is, Norman defined $X_0 = C_0$ as the net cash inflow defined by the capital cost of deferral less the capital cost of proceeding now, with $t = 0$ corresponding to 2010, the expected end date of the second phase of construction if the project as a whole began in 1995. Formally, locating C_0 in 2010 to simplify the initial cost parameter involved assuming the use of an interest rate during construction calculation which should be linked to D. Norman recognized that this could be a potential source of inconsistency associated with sensitivity analysis which varies one parameter at a time, and a source of inconsistency which the differential cash flow approach normally attempts to avoid. However, an interest rate during construction which does not equate to D may be appropriate, and it was sensible to be explicit about this possibility. The simple structure of C_0 was vital, but it was equally vital to avoid ambiguity about what C_0 involved, or its location in time. To quantify C_0, Norman used 1994 money as for the DoE estimate, and the same assumed pattern of expenditure during construction. Relative to DoE models, this collapsed a complex 15 year construction period profile into a single value in one year, without changing its basis. From the earlier DoE analysis, the expected value estimate of C_0 was £2500 million, rounded to reflect appropriate precision. C_0 was the first of five basic parameters Norman defined. The second was n.

The planning horizon n was just the number of years (time periods) of commitment to the implications of the two choices. Norman assumed $n = 50$ years for consistency with the DoE, but noted that this value was arbitrary: $n = 1, 10, 25$, or 100 years were other options for the planning horizon.

In general, when comparing two investment alternatives for $t = 1, \ldots, n - 1$, the differential cash flow X_t might be the difference in revenues from each alternative, net of operating costs. In this case it was just 'minus the annual storage cost' associated with keeping the nuclear waste safe on the surface, $X_t = -S_t$. Norman knew S_t had a very complex expected pattern, but for simplicity he equated all S_t to S, assumed to be constant over the planning horizon. S was estimated by averaging available estimates of S_t over the planning period. From the earlier DoE analysis, the expected value of S was £135 million in 1994 money, suitably rounded.

The capital cost associated with deferral, C_n, where $X_n = -S - C_n$, was the fourth parameter of concern for Norman, to complement C_0. In general when comparing two choices, X_n might reflect the difference in terminal scrap values, or terminal market values of ongoing opportunities, but in this case it was predominantly the capital cost of deferred construction, located in a single time period (akin to C_0) 50 years from year 0. From the earlier DoE analysis, the expected value estimate of C_n was £5000 million in 1994 money, rounded appropriately. This doubling of expected capital cost reflected a high probability of having to use another site if a 50 year delay occurred. According to the DoE report, the probability of having to use another site was at least 80% (the implications of this are explored later).

The fifth parameter Norman identified was the appropriate real discount rate, D. Using a real discount rate (net of inflation) meant that inflation could be ignored. The DoE used $D = 6\%$, as a matter of Treasury policy. Norman also assumed $D = 6\%$ for consistency.

Using these five basic parameters and estimated values to get started, Norman defined the NPV of the decision to defer relative to the decision to proceed now as V, where

$$V = C_0 - S \sum_{t=1}^{n} r^t - C_n r^n$$

where

$C_0 = $ £2500 million, the expected initial capital cost
$C_n = $ £5000 million, the expected deferral capital cost
$S = $ £135 million, the expected annual storage cost
$r = 1/(1 + D/100)$, the discount factor for one year
$D = 6\%$, the real discount rate
$n = 50$, the number of years in the planning horizon

This involves only five base-level parameters, simplification achieved by aggregation (C_0 and C_n), averaging (S) and decomposition ($X_n = -S - C_n$).

Norman then defined a nested composite parameter structure to further simplify interpretation of this basic model:

$$R = \sum_{t=1}^{n} r^t, \text{ a composite discount factor}$$

$T = C_n \, r^n$, the present value of deferral capital cost
$N = C_0 - T$, the present value of the capital cost saving

Substituting these composite parameters reduces the definition of V to

$$V = N - SR$$

The basic NPV decision criterion for preferring deferral is $V > 0$.

Using the parameter values given above, $V = 100$. This value of V and the associated parameters were all consistent with the DoE (1994) report. Since $V = 100 > 0$, deferral is the preferred alternative.

As noted in Table 8.1, an IRR approach adopts the condition $V = N - SR = 0$, and determines d given expected values for all the other parameters by solving this equation for D. This is most appropriately interpretted as a parametric analysis in relation to D. A comparable discounted payback approach determines the minimum value of n which yields $V = 0$, given expected values for all other parameters. An alternative way of expressing the NPV criterion is the annualized average cost approach, which rewrites the NPV criterion in the form $S < N/R$. This can be interpreted as a parametric analysis basis for S. Another alternative is to express the NPV criterion as a condition on the minimum value for N, $SR < N$, a basis for parametric analysis of N. Norman's intention was to choose from all of these approaches the form of presentation most suited to the situation, once he understood it more clearly, proceeding via a sequence of steps designed to facilitate the development of understanding (Chapman and Cooper, 1983b).

Estimating plausible ranges

Norman's next step was to consider the effect of plausible ranges for composite and basic parameters, one at a time. A precise probabilistic interpretation of these plausible ranges (like a 90% confidence band) was not required, but consistency was.

In view of the lengthy planning horizon, the size of the parameter D was of particular interest. Small changes in D would induce large changes in R and N. High values for D would increase the value of V via both N and R, and favour deferral. Low values for D would reduce the attraction of deferral. To get started, Norman used 0% to 8% as the plausible range for D. Norman's rationale for selecting 8% was simply that the DoE had used $6 \pm 2\%$ as sensitivity analysis limits around their 6% policy figure (DoE, 1994), and he wanted to link his plausible range to their range. Norman's rationale for selecting 0% was that it was roughly as plausible as 8%. The associated arguments are complex, but Norman carefully crafted an explanation of appropriate D values in general for his boss Nigel along the following lines.

The simplest way to interpret the discounting process and the appropriate value for D involves assuming any amount of money can be borrowed or lent at the rate D compounded annually. This implies we should be indifferent to an amount of money Z now, or an amount of money $Z(1 + D/100)^t$ after t years in terms of basic utility theory as employed by economists. If we have an amount of money Z now we can invest it at the rate D and have an amount $Z(1 + D/100)^t$ in t years time. Alternatively, if we have $Z(1 + D/100)^t$ coming to us t years hence, we can borrow Z now and repay our loan when the money arrives. Whatever our current or future needs for money, we should be indifferent to Z now or $Z(1 + D/100)^t$ in t years time. The basic NPV formula follows for a multi-year (or other period) cash flow, equating all future cash flows to a present value equivalent. This formula depends upon the basic arithmetic of compound interest rates, known cash flows, and the ability to borrow or lend at rate D. No other assumptions are required apart from rational indifference curves which seem obviously sensible. In practice, borrowing and lending invariably involve different rates. However, individuals can still use this interpretation if they are predominantly borrowers or lenders, if they can predict a suitable expected borrowing or lending rate over the appropriate period, and if they can predict the cash flow expected values, all assumptions clearly involving some uncertainty.

For publicly quoted companies (PLCs), appropriate assumptions in relation to values for D become more complex. What they can be boiled down to is that D ought to reflect the rate of return which shareholders can reasonably expect from the industrial sector the PLC is investing in over the period of the investment. We have to use a utility theory interpretation of the discounting process where the relevant utility evaluations are attributed to shareholders. Statistical analysis of past rates of return in this industry can be used, but appropriate expected future values are what we need. The uncertainty involved is clearly even more difficult to address in a satisfactory manner than for individuals. The attractiveness of an IRR approach can be interpreted as a reaction to these difficulties. However, PLCs should have a reasonable notion of what an appropriate D value is. The difficulties are tractable, and they need to be faced.

For governments appropriate assumptions in relation to values for D become still more difficult. Market-based rates for government bonds can be used as a starting point, but there are important additional utility theory and opportunity cost or shadow price arguments which have to be addressed. For example, in the UK the long-term (over a hundred years) average real cost of capital for the government as measured by the real rate of return (net of inflation) paid on government bonds is a good place to start. This rate has been about 3% over the past 100 years or so. One line of argument for using a rate above 3% is based on capital rationing and opportunity costs or shadow prices. The government does not wish to borrow all the money needed to finance all the worthwhile projects the government might undertake on our behalf. This constraint means that the expected rate of return on the best rejected project is our best estimate of the appropriate D. (Norman's argument here is comparable to the value of a life argument in Chapter 7, and the value of Dave's time argument in Chapter 2.) In this case D is a function of investments which could have been made if it were appropriate and politically feasible for the government to borrow more money. A second line of argument for using a rate above 3% is based on 'social time preference' for consumption now, rather than consumption in the future, arising from the reasoning that because we will be richer in the future, the marginal value of consumption in the future will drop. This involves an important framing assumption – we will all go on getting richer.

The DoE/Treasury real discount rate of 6% is based on both the above arguments (HMSO, 1991). This 6% discount rate is a policy parameter for the Treasury, in the sense that the Treasury assumes it is acting on behalf of all UK citizens, subject to guidance on this from the government of the day, and the Treasury must determine D as a matter of policy, with no implicit or explicit error. Another way to look at this is that all citizens in the UK are shareholders in UK plc, and they expect a 6% real return on government investment for the foreseeable future. Treasury policy simply reflects a Treasury estimate of this public expectation, comparable to the estimation of an appropriate D by the finance director of a PLC on behalf of shareholders. A comprehensive role for private finance initiative (PFI) funding of public projects makes this an attractive alternative perspective.

Either of the above perspectives involves expectations which may prove unfounded. If the UK economy takes a serious nosedive, or a massive long-term boom occurs, we may find the 'wrong' (non-optimal) investments have been made on our behalf. The Treasury will not have been wrong because what is realized is not what we all expected. However, the Treasury will be wrong if 6% does not reflect reasonable expectations. Proving the Treasury is right or wrong may seem nigh on impossible, which may explain in part the Treasury's unwillingness to even admit the possibility. The issue for any industry which is unhappy with the implications of a Treasury-imposed real discount rate of 6% effectively reduces to special case pleading.

In the case of nuclear waste disposal, one line of argument for using a rate below 6%, 0% for example, is based on the fact that a high D value inevitably means postponing resolving the issue of permanent disposal of nuclear waste. An argument which follows this fact is based on the notion that such an outcome is unethical. That is, it is not ethical to enjoy 'cheap' nuclear electric power today and leave the legacy of clearing up to our grandchildren, given we cannot be sure the money will be in the bank to pay for cleaning up, because the government has not made separate provisions to do so. Such a view will be proven right if the economy does not continue to grow as assumed by the Treasury, we are subsequently unable to afford permanent storage in the future, and it becomes clear we should have afforded it now.

Hence, going back to the plausibility of the 0% to 8% range, 8% is a plausible optimistic value if there is a plausible argument for the possibility of a sustained long-term (50−100 year) boom in the UK economy (above current expected growth rates). That is, we all go on getting richer and richer at an even faster rate than over the past 50−100 years, and the government is still subject to capital rationing. However, 0% is an equally plausible pessimistic value if there is a plausible argument for the possibility of a sustained long-term decline in the UK economy, and that given this possibility, there is a need to take an ethical position with respect to future generations. The asymmetry of the 0% to 8% range relative to the 6% Treasury policy value is very important.

Sensitivity analysis with the discount rate

Norman felt that his arguments for considering discount rates over the range 0% to 8% were convincing. He now needed to examine the effect of different discount rates in terms of influencing the V, using the expected values for other parameters.

Table 8.3 and Figure 8.1 show the results of Norman's calculations. Table 8.3 portrays the implications as D changes from 0% to 8% using 2% increments, showing 6% (the expected value) in bold. The summary implication is the value of V in the extreme right-hand column. The bold 6% D value shows a V of £100 million, the base case DoE valuation as noted earlier. This positive NPV, favouring deferral, increases to £740 million if D is 8%. It becomes −£1110 million if D is 4%, and −£9250 million if D is 0%. Figure 8.1 plots these V values as a function of D. Figure 8.1 shows the value D = 5.7% where V flips from positive to negative. If all the other expectations are unbiased estimates, and if an unbiased estimate of D is greater than 5.7%, then deferral is the best choice ignoring risk, otherwise

Table 8.3—Composite parameter changes as the real discount rate (D) changes

D	$T = C_n r^n$	$N = C_0 - T$	$R = \sum_{t=1}^{n} r^t$	N/R	$N/R - S$	$V = N - SR$
0	5000	−2500	50.00	−50	−185	−9250
2	1860	640	31.42	20	−115	−3600
4	710	1790	21.48	83	−52	−1110
6	**270**	**2230**	**15.76**	**141**	**6**	**100**
8	110	2390	12.23	195	40	740

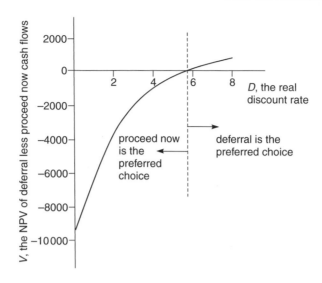

Figure 8.1—Plotting V as a function of D (from Table 8.1).

proceeding now is the best choice. $D = 5.7\%$ is a decision flip-point, and this flip-point is very close to the assumed expected value, $D = 6\%$.

The asymmetry of the range for V, driven by the asymmetry of the range for D and the way the NPV formula works, is very important, in terms of risk and in terms of a proper understanding of expected values for D and V. In terms of risk, for example, the asymmetry means that a true D of 0% when deferral was the choice involves a mistake with an opportunity cost of more than £9000 million, while a true D of 8% when proceed now was the choice involves a mistake with an opportunity cost of only £700 million. Betting on a discount rate greater than 5.7% (and deferral), is a very high risk gamble relative to betting on a discount rate less than 5.7% (and proceed now), with a plausible maximum 'mistake' cost that is greater by a factor of 13.

Norman explained all this to Nigel when they met to review his analysis. It was tempting to conclude that the large asymmetry in cost of error, together with the precautionary principle (Chapter 7), suggested that proceed now is the obvious choice, end of story. He indicated that an even stronger case could be made, but before he got to this even stronger case it was worth using the intermediate columns of Table 8.1 to understand what was going on, starting with the first row. With $D = 0$, T (the present value of C_n) is the full £5000 million, and N (the present value of the capital cost saving resulting from deferral) is −£2500 million. R is simply 50, so the annualized capital cost saving associated with deferral (N/R) is −£50 million, (−2500/50). Given the annual storage cost (S) of £135 million, this implies a net annualized cost saving associated with deferral ($N/R−S$) of −£185 million (−50 − 135). Over the 50 year planning horizon, −£185 million per year sums to a total V

of $-£9250$ million. With $D = 2$, T (the present value of C_n) is only £1860 million, and N (the present value of the capital cost saving resulting from deferral) is £640 million (2500 − 1860); this 'saving' becomes positive in the range $D = 1$ to 2. R has now reduced to 31.42, so $N/R = £20$ million (the annualized capital cost saving associated with deferral). This in turn implies $N/R - S = -£115$ million, and $V = -£3600$ million. With $D = 4, 6$ and 8 these changes continue. By $D = 6$ the values of $N/R - S$ and V have become positive at £6 million and £100 million respectively.

In summary, with $D = 0$ there is a massive NPV advantage associated with proceed now relative to a 50 year deferral option, because all of the surface storage costs and the doubling of the capital cost (from C_0 to C_n) are saved. As D moves from 1 to 2, the capital cost saving associated with deferral in discounted terms (N) becomes positive, but in annualized terms (N/R) it is still small relative to the annual storage cost (S), so the net annualized cost difference ($N/R - S$) remains negative ($-£115$ million at $D = 2$). Only when D reaches 5.7 does $N/R - S$ become positive, with V becoming positive as a consequence. In other words, $D = 5.7$ can be given an IRR interpretation, but the annualized average cost interpretation embedded in Table 8.3 is the most useful way to understand what is going on as D changes and the implications of the asymmetric D range.

Sensitivity of other parameters

The $D = 6$ row of Table 8.3 is also a useful basis for understanding the relative sensitivity of other basic and composite parameters, by considering associated flip-points. For example, V goes to zero if $N/R - S$ goes to zero. This would occur if S were equal to £141 million (N/R), or if N were equal to £2127 million, (135 × 15.76). N equal to £2127 million corresponds to C_0 equal to £2397 million (2127 + 270), or T equal to £373 million (2500 − 2127). T equal to £373 million corresponds to C_n equal to £6907 million (5000 − 373/270). These flip-points, given expected values for the other parameters, are summarized in Table 8.4.

Table 8.4 shows that small (4%) swings in the value of S and C_0 take V to the flip-point, comparable to the 5% swing in D needed to flip the decision. A large (38%) swing in the value of C_n is needed to take V to the flip-point, because of the discounting effect with $D = 6$. This clearly indicates that plausible S and C_0

Table 8.4—Flip values for parameters and associated swings

Parameter	Expected value	Flip value	Percent swing flip value
D	6	5.7	−5
S	135	141	−4.4
C_0	2500	2397	−4.1
C_n	5000	6907	38

variations could flip the decision, as could less plausible C_n variations. Norman prepared the equivalent of Table 8.3 and Figure 8.1 for S, C_0 and C_n to illustrate what was involved. However, they are not provided here, and it should be clear that they would indicate that D is the most sensitive parameter relative to its plausible range. It is the change in expected value required to cause a decision to flip relative to the plausible range which determines the relative sensitivity and the relative 'cost of being wrong' when making a decision choice, and it is the relative sensitivity in these terms which is the key concern at this stage in the analysis.

Norman might have produced a version of what some people call a cat's whisker diagram, by converting the V and D scales of Figure 8.1 to percentage variation terms, and superimposing the equivalent curves for V and S, V and C_0, V and C_n. The curves would all intersect at the expected parameter values for D, S, C_0 and C_n. The extent to which each curve straddled the $V = 0$ line would indicate the relative sensitivity of that parameter. However, Norman preferred separate Figures like 8.1 with underlying tables like Table 8.3 for all the parameters which mattered, to keep each diagram simple, to make sure he and Nigel understood the comparative importance and what drove it for all the parameters.

Probabilistic Analysis To Support The First Pass

Norman regarded the simple parametric analysis just discussed as an appropriate first-pass analysis, without any formal requirement for probabilistic analysis, but he recognized that it might be easier to obtain unbiased expected values for parameters and a feel for associated ranges if simple probabilistic models were used. For this reason he had used probabilistic approaches to produce all of the expected values associated with the DoE report. In most cases the benefits went beyond reducing bias for expected values, increasing confidence in the estimates being of particular importance. For example, when estimating annual surface storage costs, the engineers involved found it very useful to employ a decision tree/Markov process approach. They could usefully model the notion that after 5 years current surface-stored material might still be safe as is, but there was a chance money would have to be spent making it safe, and if it was made safe, the chance that more money would have to be spent after 10 years was much lower. Such modelling corresponded to, and replicated, the decision process coupled to the storage management processes which would take place in practice. Making these processes explicit helped the engineers involved to estimate the $S = £135$ million with confidence, recognizing that the actual cost per year would vary substantially around the average (expected) value. It reduced the potential for bias in their estimates, and it clarified the distinction between variability in S_t and potential error for S.

The DoE had also used probabilistic approaches to produce some of the expected values associated with its report, to clarify what was involved, make the process more realistic, reduce potential bias, and clarify the associate range. When estimating C_n, a probability greater than 0.8 that a change in site would be required underlay the C_n = £5000 million figure, as noted earlier. For example, a 0.83 probability of a deferred capital cost of £5500 million and a 0.17 probability $(1 - 0.83)$ of a deferred capital cost of £2500 million would correspond to the £5000 million expected value. If C_n had been critical, Norman was convinced that it might have been interesting to explore the probability of the loss of the current site associated with further increases in expected capital cost. Norman was interested in the politics behind this. It involved assuming that deferral would probably lead to a collapse of the UK nuclear industry located in the area of the proposed repository, and this would lead to a hostile reaction to plans for a deferred repository in the area (couched in terms of a withdrawal of the presumed favourable view currently), which would necessitate a much more expensive alternative site with associated transport costs. Norman had helped to start this particular rabbit running in his earlier analysis as input to the DoE. His awareness of this risk grew out of his concern for the future of the nuclear industry if permanent storage was deferred. However, his present first-pass analysis was telling him that if he wanted to serve the UK nuclear industry, arguing for a higher value of C_n was not going to do the trick, given the other expected values.

A Second-Pass Probabilistic Analysis

Nigel was impressed with Norman's first-pass analysis and was happy to agree with Norman's conclusion that D was a critical parameter. The high (6%) value of D used by the DoE as a matter of Treasury policy was driving the decision to defer disposal. In terms of developing their understanding of the associated uncertainty, D was the parameter they should home in on first. To preserve the nuclear industry by successfully arguing for permanent disposal of intermediate nuclear waste now, Norman had to make a convincing case for a D value of less than 6%.

Norman was of the view that more detailed probabilistic analysis focused on D would provide a useful second-pass approach. The idea was to explore the uncertainty associated with expected values and plausible ranges in more detail, including the impact of embedding uncertainty over the plausible range in the $V = N - SR$ relationship. Probabilistic analysis of discount rates is not normally undertaken, and it might seem to be expressly excluded by the Treasury view that D was a Treasury policy variable. However, Norman was prepared to challenge the DoE and the Treasury on this issue. In his view it was the most uncertain variable as well as the most critical, for reasons already discussed in relation to the plausible range. The key issue was finding a way to demonstrate that 6% was a biased estimate, and that using this expected value in a deterministic version of the $V = N - SR$ relationship induced further bias.

Norman started with a variant of the simple scenario approach (Chapman and Ward, 1997), using a very simple first-order model of the uncertainty underlying the DoE's 6% ± 2% range. This involved three possible discrete outcomes – 4%, 6% and 8% – with associated probabilities which sum to one. A very simple first-order estimate of the associated probabilities was 1/3 each, with an expected value of 6%. A continuous variable second-order interpretation is then obtained by interpreting 4% as the expected value of a uniform probability distribution between 3% and 5%, and a similar interpretation for 6% and 8%. Using Table 8.3, this yields an expected NPV of −£90 million (obtained by $(-1100 + 100 + 740)/3$). This result is consistent with DoE use of 6% ± 2% and a plausible probabilistic interpretation of what this means, but it is entirely *inconsistent* with the DoE report's bottom line:

> The conclusion was that allowance for data shortcomings and uncertainties for other factors did not significantly affect the balance of benefits and costs as summarised in Paragraph 11 above, with the impact of factors leading to increase the benefit of delay being broadly offset by those operating in the opposite direction. In particular, it was concluded that the outcome for a 50 year delay, as reported in Paragraph 11, provided a broadly reasonable indication of the economic case for a repository delay at a 6% discount rate. (DoE, 1994, Annex C, para 21)

That is, even if 6% is the expected value of D in a symmetric distribution involving 6% ± 2% as just described, the expected value of V is −£90 million, not £100 million, an 'error' of £190 million. This error is attributable to ignoring the variability (uncertainty) associated with D in the context of the inherently asymmetric relationship between D and V associated with $V = N - SR$, as indicated in Table 8.3 and Figure 8.1 over the range $D = 4\%$ to 8%. Uncertainty associated with D matters because of this asymmetric relationship, even if D involves a symmetric distribution over the range 4% to 8%. Norman acknowledged that if the 1/3 probabilities for each of the 4, 6 and 8 values was changed to allow a higher value for the probability of 6, the £190 million error would be smaller. But this error would not approach zero until the probability of a 6% discount rate approached unity. Norman then put his case a bit differently. He used a form of parametric analysis on his first-order probability model. He asked the question:

> If $P(D = 6) = 0.5$, the probability $D = 6$ is 0.5, what do the values of $P(D = 4)$ and $P(D = 8)$ have to be for $V = 100$, the NPV of 100 assumed by the DoE? Using the equation implied by the above and $P(D = 4) + P(D = 6) + P(D = 8) = 1$ yields

$$P(D = 4) = 0.17 \qquad P(D = 6) = 0.50 \qquad P(D = 8) = 0.33$$

Norman argued that both the high value of $P(D = 8)$ and the asymmetry were not credible. $P(D = 8) = 0.33$, high, and $P(D = 4) = 0.17$, only half the size. Further, altering the assumed $P(D = 6)$ over a credible range does not significantly affect this argument. These two simple interpretations of the DoE bottom line both demonstrated conclusively that DoE conclusions were not credible, purely in terms of the importance of the uncertainty associated with D because of the asymmetric way D drives V in terms of the ± 2% bounds used by the DoE and the expected values of all the other parameters adopted by the DoE.

Norman then argued that a much more credible first-order probability model is $P(D) = 0.2$ for $D = 0, 2, 4, 6$ and 8. This yields $V = -£2624$ million (obtained by $(-9250 - 3600 - 1110 + 100 + 740) \times 0.2$), implying a DoE error of £2724 million (obtained by 2624 + 100). This result is alarmingly inconsistent with DoE paragraph 21 cited above. The associated probability distribution is debatable, but the alarm is credible.

Norman reiterated that it was the asymmetric relationship between V and D which was driving this, given expected values for all the other parameters as assumed by the DoE, but the asymmetric range for D of 0% to 8% was amplifying this effect. All he was doing which was different to the DoE approach was embedding the probability distribution which portrayed the uncertainty about D over a plausible range in the calculation of V, to capture the impact of that uncertainty on the expected value of V. The asymmetry of the D range was important, but the asymmetry in the V and D relationship defined by $V = N - SR$ was also very important and more fundamental. The second-pass probabilistic analysis was concerned with embedding a simple parameter distribution into the calculation of V, given expected values of all the other parameters. It was not a general simulation of uncertainty. It was focused on what mattered as identified by the first pass.

Nigel was very impressed by this analysis. He was convinced they were on the right track. However, he knew that scrutiny by the DoE and the Treasury of any analysis which criticized their position in this way would be rigorous, to say the least. He asked Norman to think about how they could take Norman's second pass further, to substantiate its conclusions.

A Third-Pass Probabilistic Analysis

Over the next few weeks Norman spent some time considering how to develop his analysis. If the size of D was important, so was the length of the planning horizon, n, set rather arbitrarily at 50 years. Circumstances could change during this period, and deep storage might be reconsidered, particularly if new options became available. This line of thought reminded Norman of the current fad in the capital investment decision advice industry for the concept of 'real options', promoted by the financial economics community. Treasury economists would probably be partial to the real options lobby, so Norman and Nigel would have to show awareness of this approach, and counter its claims to provide a preferable alternative route to sophistication.

Considering a real options perspective

As Norman saw it, the thrust of a real options approach to the storage question which the DoE/Treasury might wish to promote would be based on the notion that permanent storage now foreclosed on future options to store later, and options to store later had value which a traditional NPV framework overlooked. For example, a real options approach might assume that if disposal is deferred, nominally for 50 years, disposal after 25 years was a real option, with a value which should be deducted from the NPV of disposal now because it was pre-empted by a decision to proceed now. NPV models locked in decisions on options which 'real options' approaches could recognise.

Norman's objection to the real options approach was its basis in expected utility theory and the additional complex assumptions it required which were clearly not true and difficult to assess in terms of robustness analysis. Norman decided to discuss the idea of applying an options pricing approach with his friend Franz, a finance PhD student. As Norman anticipated, Franz was enthusiastic and optimistic about the contribution a real options approach could make to Norman's problem. In short order Franz suggested an options pricing framework which involved working with all the expected values and other assumptions of the DoE analysis as embedded in Norman's first-pass parametric analysis on page 280, together with the following assumptions:

- The risk-free interest rate is 5%, its term structure is flat, and it is constant for the next 50 years.
- S_t is the annual storage cost of the nuclear waste; $S_1 = £135$ million; S_t, $t = 2$ to 50, follows a stochastic binomial process with yearly jumps and an estimated (guessed) volatility defined as the standard deviation of $n(S_{t+1}/S_t)$ equal to 30%.
- There is a twin-stock security, traded in the market, whose value at time t is Y_t; Y_t has the same probability distribution as S_t and the correlation coefficient between Y_t and S_t is 1.

In effect, Franz proposed to treat the liability to safely store nuclear waste on the surface indefinitely as if it were a floated security option, in a form like a European call option.

Shortly after speaking to Franz, Norman suggested to Nigel that they ought to give a contract to Franz to explore this kind of option pricing analysis thoroughly, to see if it would produce any useful insights. Norman was primarily concerned to ensure they could counter any DoE/Treasury assertions that they had inappropriately ignored a real options approach to adding sophistication. He was confident that Franz could fulfil the second objective, less sanguine about the first. If this first contract bore fruit, Norman suggested they could give a follow-on contract to Franz, to explore the link between real option modelling of this kind and comparable decision tree modelling. (Directly related decision tree modelling will be explored in Chapter 9, linked decision tree modelling in Chapter 11.) The kind of models Norman had in mind would value deferral in terms of the range of changes in parameter values that might occur over time and which might make us pleased that deferral for a nominal 50 years was the decision taken. These models would also compare this value with the costs of deferral associated with interim storage costs plus an increase in the probability that the current proposed site could not be used and other changes over time which might make us regret deferral. Norman was confident that the value of the flexibility associated with deferral would not provide a convincing argument for deferral, but he believed a case made by Franz in both real options and directly comparable decision tree terms would be a worthwhile investment for the UK nuclear industry.

Decomposing variability and ambiguity looking for trends

Norman was convinced that a real options approach or an equivalent decision tree based approach would not suggest significant new insights unless they portrayed the impact of persistent trends in changes in the expected values of the basic NPV calculation parameters if deferral occurs. Norman suggested to Nigel that the best way to address this involved a blend of conventional current project risk management thinking and conventional futures forecasting or scenario planning (e.g. Kahn and Wiener, 1967; MacNulty, 1977; Bunn and Sato, 1993). For example, they might begin by addressing variability associated with D, and ask the question, What kinds of underlying long-term changes in the UK economic and political situation might lead to an expected value for D of 8% in 25 years time, defining a pessimistic scenario from a current nuclear industry perspective, an optimistic scenario from most other points of view, referred to as the '8% scenario' for neutrality? Answers, Norman suggested, would include alternative low-cost energy sources, a thriving economy, low taxes and limited public investment spending, lots of alternative productive government investments, and other similar statements consistent with a very upbeat view of the future in economic terms, although it might also be linked to a new cold war or other undesirable political developments.

Next they might ask the question, What would define a comparable '0% scenario' in terms of the appropriate D for this particular decision? Answers, Norman suggested, would include: declining stocks of non-renewable energy sources and no new inexpensive renewable sources of energy, a collapsed economy, high taxes and associated public investment spending, few alternative productive government investments, a moral outrage based on the enjoyment of low-cost electric power by the previous generation who had not paid to clean up their own mess, something which the current generation was not prepared to pass on to their children in the face of long-term prospects for the UK which looked forbidding.

Norman suggested these two scenarios might be developed to clarify the expected value of D now and the plausible bounds now. Sources of variability which will tend to cancel out because they are independent would be listed, but not embodied in the scenario definitions. What is involved is scenario building in relation to the key parameter identified in the earlier phase of analysis. Next they might address similar questions related to each of the other basic parameters S, C_0 and C_n. Then they might ask the question, What degree of causal and statistical dependence exists between the parameter probability distributions associated with the scenario ranges? For example, to what extent are the factors underlying a $D = 8\%$ scenario likely to occur with high or low scenario values of S, C_0 and C_n, and does this suggest a coefficient of correlation in a range like 0.6 to 0.4, a higher or a lower degree of correlation?

Finally, using these causal or statistical dependence estimates, and simple scenario or minimalist probability distributions for each parameter's probability distribution, they might run a Monte Carlo simulation to determine an expected value and associated probability distribution for V. Norman was convinced this kind of approach was the best way forward, and its insights could be used to derive the form of alternative models they might have to confront, be they based on real options, decision trees, or any other approach. The basis of risk in a decision like this was a future which revealed outcomes and assumptions, implicit as well as explicit, which were not anticipated, which would have changed the decision if they had been anticipated at an appropriate level of likelihood. Additionally, it was important to recognize that we do not have to passively accept alternative futures which may occur. We can design alternative futures we want, and then manage our way towards these desirable futures. At a more pedestrian level, we can consider both preventative and mitigating responses to identified risks, and select a portfolio of responses to manage uncertainty as effectively as possible. This is the basis of current project risk management, and it has long been the basis of safety management.

A Sudden Flash of Hindsight

Just after Norman made his presentation to Nigel, local authority planning approval for the first phase of construction was turned down. Disaster had struck from an unexpected quarter. The current 'proceed now' proposal was dead. Permanent disposal of intermediate-level nuclear waste would have to be somewhere else. As Nigel put it, there were three scenarios people might be betting on. One, the DoE or the Treasury had nobbled the local authority planning approval process to get their way. Two, the local authority planning approval people knew that the UK nuclear industry was a political liability for the national government, the UK nuclear industry would be allowed to die whether or not permanent disposal of waste proceeded, and the planning authority ought to do whatever they had to in order to ensure that the corpse ended up somewhere else. Three, there were no conspiracies, just the usual cock-ups. Nigel was betting on the third.

As Nigel contemplated early retirement, and Norman started looking for a new job to pre-empt redundancy, they did a bit of retrospective, hindsight reflection. Norman started by suggesting C_0 was now equal to C_n, adding more than £2500 million to V at a stroke, so there was no way permanent storage was going to proceed without a massive change in the perceived economics or politics of the situation. For example, Table 8.3 showed that a D less than 3% would be required to favour deferral. Nuclear waste 'temporarily' stored on the surface was here to stay as a permanent feature of the geographic and political landscape. Nigel's response was that if one believed permanent storage was the right decision, the mid 1990s was too late to commit to it. The commitment should have been made in the 1980s or earlier. What a real options perspective did was focus on the value of flexibility in the future. What mattered here was the loss of flexibility which waiting had imposed. Waiting was a two-edged sword, with costs as well as benefits. Norman observed that long-term storage of nuclear waste on the surface by a country with no nuclear industry was a clear lose-lose situation for everybody. In time the nuclear expertise to look after it would be lost. No other country would want it. No region in this country would want it. It would become an albatross, haunting them forever. This was too ridiculous, too silly, and too awful to contemplate.

Nigel's response was that it all depended on your perspective and framing assumptions. If you were Greenpeace, for example, the most effective way to kill the nuclear industry was the current outcome. If they had any part in it, which he doubted, they couldn't have managed it better. Once the nuclear industry's body was visually decomposing, public outcry would ensure proper burial somewhere. If the same scenario occurred in enough countries, he would bet on a relaxation of international agreements about burial at sea. He and many other nuclear experts believed deep sea burial was the best solution anyway, provided you were talking about a limited amount, as distinct from an ongoing situation. Sooner or later it was all going to leach into the sea in any event. Norman was visually shocked by this view coming from Nigel, although the associated technical arguments were familiar. However, it triggered thoughts linked to a 'planning a desirable future' approach to futures analysis scenario planning. If the future as they now understood it was 'nuclear power free with ongoing temporary surface storage of nuclear waste', should this future be publicized now, not to provide a forecast per se, but to provide a straw man which would have to be knocked down before it was too late. One outcome of confronting this straw man might be a proper wind-down of the nuclear industry. Another might be a decision to sustain it, perhaps at a lower level, with appropriate ongoing provision for waste. Publication of their views would be in the spirit of a self-rejecting prophecy, a forecast used to mobilize a reaction to prevent its realization while there was still time. In other words, using a forecast which portrays what will happen if nothing is done in order to motivate others to do something to ensure the forecast does not happen. Nigel was impressed by Norman's grit and perseverence, and cunning he did not realize Norman possessed, but he pointed out as kindly as he could that the current politics of the nuclear industry would not allow this kind of argument to be promoted by the industry itself. What motivated the relevant movers and shakers was not the same as what motivated Norman, and their incentives would take them in a very different direction.

Nigel then pointed out that this kind of outcome from a DCF process was not unique to nuclear waste. For example, he had a friend who specialized in irrigation and land drainage schemes in less developed countries. A common problem involved the approval of irrigation schemes and associated use of fertilisers which poisoned the soil with residual salts over a period of 30 or 40 years because the cost of preventing this could never be met by the value of future crops 30 or 40 years hence, given the discount rates required by the international lending author-ities. Similar problems arose for forestry decisions. The UK Treasury recognized this problem in their guidelines (HMSO, 1991). They allowed for reduced discount rates to be used in special circumstances like forestry decisions. It is important to appreciate that the need for special cases of this kind is a clear indica-tion of underlying ambiguity which has to be confronted as part of the uncertainty associated with any DCF assessment. It implies issues which are not considered directly in the X_t or D values. For example, it might be argued that the nuclear industry and associated waste disposal should not be a special case so long as nuclear electric power generation is viewed as a potentially profitable candidate for privatization, but if the 'commercial' nuclear industry dies, a totally different perspective is appropriate. If society prefers more trees and less nuclear waste to more roads, associated D values may be adjusted to produce the desired outcome, by the Treasury and other government agencies.

In conclusion, Norman and Nigel agreed it was far too early to give up. There were ways to rescue the situation. It was a matter of searching for the most promising strategies and developing a portfolio of possibilities, hoping one or more would pay-off.

Is A Real Options Approach Really Useful?

Norman was sceptical about the usefulness of a real options approach to valuing projects, although he was prepared to invest effort to explore its potential. The concept of the options associated with a project having value is a different matter, long recognized by project managers, usefully addressed using some of the language of real options, possibly including these three terms:

- **Timing options** Decision makers can accept or reject a project. They can also delay deciding, or accept provisionally but delay implementation, waiting on events.
- **Project management options** Management has discretion to respond in a flexible manner to events as they unfold, or as uncertainties are resolved, throughout the duration of the project.
- **Growth options** Implementing a project usually gives rise to further investment opportunities (growth options) which would not have otherwise been available. Such opportunities may or may not be profitable, but management has discretion on whether or not to invest in these opportunities when they arise. Examples of spin-off or consequential growth opportunities include the conversion of by-products to saleable goods, and the development of complementary products to fill out a line. An extreme example is R&D activity whose only source of value is the set of options created to undertake other projects.

Each of these types of option contributes in different ways to the flexibility and value of a project, yet their potential impact on project evaluation is ignored in conventional DCF analysis. By neglecting option components inherent in many projects, conventional DCF is likely to significantly underestimate the value of such projects. However, for some projects, a conventional DCF analysis may *over-estimate* project value by failing to recognize losses in flexibility to the firm resulting from their implementation. For example, a project to reduce unit costs through increased economies of scale may significantly reduce a firm's flexibility to respond to changing markets.

This section considers how project-related options might be brought into the evaluation process. For convenience, managerial discretion to vary actions during the life of a project will be considered first.

Project management options

A serious shortcoming of conventional DCF analysis is that the pattern of activities constituting the project is assumed to be predetermined from the outset. No allowance is made for flexibility in managerial action during the life of the project which allows managers to respond to uncertainty as the project progresses. In practice, decisions may be made over the life of a project to change production levels, expand or close facilities, or even abandon the project altogether. The existence of such flexibility can contribute significantly to the value of a project because it allows avoidance or mitigation of undesirable developments and additional exploitation of desirable developments. Explicit recognition of flexibility to vary production levels is particularly important when choosing among alternative technologies with different ratios of variable to fixed costs.

To some extent the failure of the conventional DCF approach to consider project options can be overcome by employing a simulation or decision tree approach incorporating different project scenarios explicitly. For example, such approaches could be used to evaluate projects where there is an ongoing option to abandon the project. In this type of project, the project should be abandoned at the moment when its abandonment value exceeds the NPV of the project's subsequent expected future cash flows. Robichek and Van Horne (1967) used a Monte Carlo simulation to illustrate the value of such an abandonment option. Their example shows a clear increase in project NPV and a reduction in project risk with the abandonment option over the same project without an abandonment option.

Even if a simulation approach is employed, there are always potential managerial responses to contingencies that are not included in the simulation model. This is especially likely when the model does not incorporate particular risks, through ignorance, oversight or design, as in the case of high-consequence and low-probability events. It follows that the tails of output distributions will be unreliable because the model will have failed to incorporate likely changes in project strategy which management would in practice implement under these extreme conditions. It can be argued that it may be best to ignore tails of output distributions altogether, and focus on the range of values covered by the central 80% of the probability density function (Myers, 1976). But this is debatable.

Valuing growth options

To see how growth options associated with a project might be valued, it may be useful to think of growth options as analogous to traded call options on financial securities (Kester, 1984; Myers, 1984). A traded call option gives the investor the right (as distinct from the obligation) to buy the associated security at a fixed, predetermined price (the exercise price) on or before some fixed date (the maturity date). The exercise price of a growth option is the investment required to implement the project. The value of the option is the present value of expected cash flows (plus the value of any further growth opportunities that may subsequently arise as a result of undertaking the investment, and so on). The time to maturity is the amount of time available before the opportunity disappears (Kester, 1984). Investing in a project A at time t purchases an intangible asset, a series of call options on further investment opportunities, B. Even if A has a negative NPV, it may still be justified if the present value of the growth options generated is large enough. This may explain why managers sometimes accept low-NPV projects for strategic reasons.

The theory of option valuation is well developed for traded securities such as call and put options, warrants, and convertible bonds. However, very little progress has been made in applying these techniques to project-related growth options. In comparison with traded options, growth options are more complex, with implied rather than explicit 'contract terms' (Myers, 1984). A particular difficulty is that the exercise price of a growth option is not determined in advance. Although it is not clear that the techniques used to evaluate traded options will carry over to growth options, it is possible to identify some common considerations. In the case of a call option on a particular financial stock, option prices vary directly with an option's term to maturity and the volatility of the underlying stock price (Black and Scholes, 1973). Drawing on the analogy between call options and growth options, Kester (1984) argues that the length of time an investment can be deferred can enhance the value of the related growth options. The ability to delay the decision to start a project gives the decision maker the opportunity to wait on events and avoid costly errors if unfavourable developments occur. Kester argues that this delay provides an interval during which a positive turn of events may make a project more profitable, and that the longer the interval, the more likely this will happen. However, this assumes there are no significant costs of delay. In the case of call options on stocks, extending time to maturity is valuable because the exercise price is fixed, and there is more potential for stock prices to rise during the maturity period. This is not the situation with a growth option. A key factor in the case of growth options is the extent to which a firm's right to exercise the option (implement a new project) is proprietary. Growth options which are proprietary may result from patents, for example, which can be extremely valuable. On the other hand, growth options which can be emulated by competitors are less valuable because counter-investments by competitors can erode or even pre-empt a project's profitability. Nevertheless, such a shared option may still have option-related value to a firm, if the firm is a market leader in the industry.

Kester (1984) also argues that project risk can have a positive effect on project valuation in the same way that traded call option prices vary directly with the volatility of the underlying stock price. In the case of traded call options, greater price volatility of the associated stock increases the chance that the option will become more valuable during the period to maturity. For a given expected increase in the price of a stock during the period to maturity, the more uncertain the price of the stock, the greater the potential of the call option for providing downside risk protection and upside risk gains. In likening growth options to call options, Kester argues: 'If two investment opportunities have identical expected present values and can be deferred for the same amount of time, the riskier of the two will be a more valuable growth option. Thus high risk increases the chance of eventually realising a large gain without equally increasing the chance of a large loss.' The implication is that if two projects have associated growth options, the project with the more risky (uncertain) growth options ought to be preferred, other things being equal. This assumes of course that downside risk associated with a growth option will decrease (and that the upside risk will not decrease) as time passes during the period to maturity.

In practice most firms do not choose projects on a stand-alone basis, because projects should be consistent with the corporate strategy of the firm. However, often strategic and financial analyses are not reconciled, even when the analyses are of the same project. Any commitment of resources to a particular line of business is an investment project, so if management invests in a strategy, there must be an implicit estimate of net present values. Yet most strategic planners are not guided by the tools of modern finance (Myers, 1984), and the strategic planning literature shows little interest in financial theory. Rather it considers techniques for identifying strategies with sustainable competitive advantage in a complex and highly uncertain business environment. Often two sides develop – the strategists who look at what a project might accomplish are pitted against financial analysts who focus on what it will cost (Kester, 1984). Faced with a DCF appraisal of a project, strategically aware managers in a commercial context will apply the following check according to Myers (1984): 'All projects have zero NPV in long-run competitive equilibrium. Therefore, a positive NPV must be explained by a short-run deviation from equilibrium or by some permanent competitive advantage. If neither explanation applies, the positive NPV is suspect. Conversely, a negative NPV is suspect if a competitive advantage or short-run deviation from equilibrium favours the project.' This might be taken to explain why low-NPV projects are sometimes acceptable for strategic reasons. The financial analysis may incorporate errors, or may have failed to capture some important strategic features of the project. However, strategic analyses may also be subject to random errors, so Myers argues that strategic and financial analyses ought to be explicitly reconciled when evaluating major projects. An example of the value of DCF analysis in this context is Reinhardt's (1973) break-even analysis for Lockheed's TriStar. Reinhardt was able to piece together enough data from records of congressional hearings and other public sources to calculate the NPV of the TriStar program to Lockheed. His analysis was based not on hindsight, but on information available to Lockheed at the time the programme was launched. Reinhardt's analysis showed that the programme had a negative NPV even under the most optimistic assumptions about demand, costs, and the opportunity cost of capital. It seemed that Lockheed's decision to go ahead with TriStar was based on a failure to take into account the opportunity cost of capital invested in the project (erroneous analysis), plus perhaps strategic considerations such as viewing TriStar as a loss-leader designed to re-establish the company in the commercial aircraft market. If so, Reinhardt argued that the project ought not to have been evaluated in isolation, but instead as an integral part of a much longer-range investment strategy aimed at developing a more diversified set of business activities. DCF analysis *can* provide valuable quantitative verification of the potential profitability of major strategic initiatives. However, to do this something more is required than the procedures typically used to evaluate risky projects described earlier.

Timing options

Conventional DCF analysis assumes that projects will be initiated according to some predetermined schedule and a specific start point. However, management always has the option to choose when to initiate a project, and this option can be valuable. For example, by waiting on events, a firm can avoid uncertainty about which of several technologies for a new product will become adopted as the standard by the industry. Such holding periods, in which technological and political uncertainties become resolved, are frequently of long duration.

The exercise of proprietary and shared growth options is clearly applicable to the initiation of project A discussed earlier. For growth options, the purchase price of the option is the implementation of project A. For project A itself, the purchase price of the option to initiate A will often be a sunk cost associated with existing corporate activities and resources. In other cases the option to initiate a project rapidly may be acquired, or secured from competitors by undertaking an initial, smaller investment in recruiting specialized staff or undertaking pilot studies. The purchase of offshore oil leases is an example. A significant part of the price paid for a lease may be due to explicit recognition of the proprietary timing of the development option acquired.

The existence of timing options is a further argument for the need to reconcile financial and strategic analyses. Not only may the option be valuable in itself, but variations in the timing of projects can clearly influence the pattern of future project cash flows. It follows that sensitivity analysis of project cash flows should include variations in the start-up date where strategic considerations make this a significant factor.

Norman's approach

Norman's approach implicitly acknowledges the existence of the above kinds of options, using a discrete form of analysis which highlights the importance of such options. Core reasons for Norman's discrete form of analysis are the preservation of simplicity, clarity, lack of ambiguity, and all the other characteristics of effective and efficient management of uncertainty espoused in the other tales of this book. Avoiding inconsistent sensitivity analysis is a more particular reason. The importance of this should be clarified by earlier discussion. We have to address the way available options change in character and availability, as well as the value of such options. To address one without the other is an obviously unacceptable source of bias. It is not clear to the authors how both can be addressed in an effective manner in a real options pricing framework. More generally, we favour the practical decision analysis approach of Chapter 9 for the implementation of the options concepts discussed in this chapter.

The arbitrary nature of the $n = 50$ value and the intermediate 25 years used in the real options discussion may be addressed by the use of a table/figure combination comparable to Table 8.3 and Figure 8.1 with V defined as a function of n rather than D, given expected values of all the other parameters. Norman prepared these as part of his parametric analysis. However, using this table/figure combination requires attention to consistency of sensitivity analysis assumptions. In particular, the probability of needing a more expensive alternative site is a major driver of the size of C_n, but it is not independent of the choice of n, as earlier discussion clearly demonstrates. This means that the only sensible way to consider alternative values of n is via separate discrete alternative analyses for each of a representative set, like $n = 1, 5, 10, 25$ and 50. Further, separate analysis of this kind compared to deferred decisions at these points in time is a better way to address the value of deferred decisions than a real options approach.

The focus of the real options approach outlined on page 292 is the variability over time of surface storage costs, averaged out to S in Norman's approach, and the use of a 50 year average value for surface storage cost is clearly a significant simplification. The thrust of Norman's argument for using an average value is that annual variations underlying S do not really matter when trying to decide whether or not deferral for 50 years is a good idea, unless there is evidence of a long-term trend. However, cycles would matter when timing a decision to proceed, to avoid the obvious waste of money associated with making waste safe for a further 10 or 20 years and then disposing of it the following year. This distinction between basic strategic choices and timing of the implementation of components will be developed further in Chapter 11.

Conclusion

A bird in the hand is worth two in the bush; this time-honoured wisdom recognizes the risk associated with giving up the bird in hand for the uncertain opportunity of catching two in the bush. Its focus is the uncertainty involved, not the time it takes to catch two birds in a bush. Standard NPV analysis concentrates on the time it takes, and the value of a bird today versus a bird next year, but it forgets about the uncertainty associated with catching the future birds. The time is important, but so is the uncertainty. Both are addressed in this chapter, as separable but interdependent issues.

One of the earliest published approaches to risk analysis in a discounting model framework is a very early example of the use of Monte Carlo simulation (Hertz, 1964). The approach recommended by Hertz (1964) and later by Hertz and Thomas (1983), and adopted by many who followed this lead, does not simplify the parameter structure, or compose it, or use parametric analysis, or use scenario analysis. It goes straight to the estimation of probability distributions for all the relevant parameters, followed by simulation to estimate a probability distribution for NPV. We have outlined the intermediate steps and we hope their value is clear. The core message is the advantage of an iterative approach which starts simply and adds complexity as appropriate.

Starting by simplifying the cash flow definition, to $V = N - SR$, is a key first step, involving aggregation to define C_0 and C_n, averaging to define S, decomposition to define $X_n = -S - C_n$, and composition to define R, T and N. This structural simplification will involve different forms and notation depending on the context, but all contexts benefit from this step. The contexts which led to the parametric approach of page 280 came from Chapman and Cooper (1983b). This paper compared a proposed hydroelectric project to a coal-fired electricity alternative in Alaska; it also considered an illustrative decision on whether or not to insulate the walls of a house in the UK. Both these contexts are illuminated by this first step in a comparable way to the first-pass model in this chapter. Once this basic simplification is in place, parametric analysis is clearly a very useful second step, as is the linked flexibility to choose a DCF framework which best suits the results of parametric analysis. For example, Norman's analysis led to a focus on D in an NPV framework, but the Alaska hydro example led to a focus on the value at the 40 year planning horizon (defined by the life of coal-fired power stations) of a hydroelectric facility (which might be more than it cost to build, if non-renewable fuels are very scarce and expensive, or zero if the dam silts up), and the UK house insulation example led to a focus on how long the decision maker would live in the house (a discounted payback period framework).

Once it is clear which composite or aggregate parameters are most important, all the constructively simple analysis ideas of Chapters 2 to 7, and those to come, can be applied. For example, C_0 or C_n are project costs as addressed in Chapters 3 to 6, and S is an operating cost with obvious links to Sarah's tale of Chapter 7. Norman's approach to the probabilistic analyses should be seen as illustrative of the way some of these common ideas can be embedded in the relevant aspects of $V = N - SR$ equivalents, without excluding others, like Eddy's approach to sources of uncertainty for example. Indeed, Norman treated uncertainty about the size of the storage facility needed (a major uncertainty discussed briefly in Martha's tale) as a condition, because its ownership was passed to other parties.

The need to see project evaluation in DCF terms in relation to operations and strategic management issues is demonstrated by this tale and is important to remember. It involves ambiguity about project boundaries and strategic impacts ambiguously linked to D as well as through life issues.

Approaches like risk-adjusted discount rates and certainty equivalents noted with some references in Table 8.1 were not pursued by Norman because they do not meet constructive simplicity requirements. Real options approaches are rejected for the same reason, although the kinds of options they illustrate do need attention, via constructively simple models. Chapter 9 addresses how to make practical use of real options ideas.

Constructive complexity can make very effective use of additional analysis effort. Analysis which relaxes key framing assumptions should be the focus. But important political issues often shape the allowable framing assumptions. Page 295 attempts to illustrate their nature and impact.

The cash flow nature of the $X_0, X_1, \ldots, X_n$ framework in Table 8.1 implies all future performance measures must be reduced to monetary terms to facilitate discounting. Sarah's tale illustrates how safety issues can be put into monetary terms, and cost-benefit analysis techniques can be used to further widen the set of performance measures considered. However, the ethical issues associated with D values and related intergenerational transfers of wealth or environmental problems which Norman addressed sound a warning, as do the limitations addressed by Nigel on page 295, and issues discussed in Chapter 7.

The current move to resolve those difficulties in the larger context of linking financial and strategic management is largely focused on the use of a balanced scorecard approach. In effect, the balanced scorecard approach is a multiple-attribute approach which treats financial considerations via DCF approaches as one attribute, driven by (causally dependent upon) other attributes, providing a simple framework for managing all relevant attributes. As Mooraj, Oyon and Hostettler (1999) put it, 'Financial results are a consequence of strategic initiatives, and not in themselves the driving force for superior performance.' The authors have worked with one organization which implemented a very successful 'benefit risk management' approach built on a synthesis of a balanced scorecard approach and the PRAM process outlined in Chapter 5, which looks a very sound way to go. Useful references to the balanced scorecard literature include Kaplan and Norton (1992, 1993a, 1996a), Olve, Roy and Wetter (1999), Frigo and Krumwiede (2000) and Norreklit (2000).

This chapter is based on Chapman and Howden (1997) and Chapman (2000a), which may be useful references in terms of their focus on the process sequence. New material in this chapter includes the real options discussion. Further development of the process sequence, into a p-pass process, $p = 1, \ldots, p^*$, might start with a synthesis of those references, this chapter, Eddy's tale, Tess's tale (Chapter 9) and the balanced scorecard literature. For example, the first pass might use a minimalist approach directly, the second might equate to the first pass in this chapter, later passes might address different types of options as discussed on page 297 and in Chapter 9, and final passes might include balanced scorecard ideas to integrate implementation and a holistic approach to strategy.

9 Tess's tale: Making decision analysis practical

If I wanted to go there, I wouldn't start from here.

Introduction

One of the simplest ways to set out a decision problem is in the form of a decision matrix, usually known as a pay-off matrix. A pay-off matrix characterizes the situation as a single-stage action choice, with each choice involving a common set of outcome events, with pay-offs dependent on each action/event combination. Basic textbook decision analysis or decision theory usually starts with this characterization of decision choices. Alternatively, the same situation can be portrayed in terms of a single-stage decision tree. This provides additional clarity and flexibility. More complex multiple-stage decision trees provide further flexibility, to consider issues like the possible purchase of additional information, responses to first-stage action choices which require contingency plans if downside risk is realized, and responses to first-stage action choices which require options to be taken up to realize potential opportunities. These decision analysis models are familiar to most decision makers. They are part of the basic tool kit that most decision makers use, intuitively if not explicitly. Their use is embedded in the approaches of many other chapters of this book. Unfortunately, the simplicity that these models provide is not always constructive simplicity, and such models can be the wrong place to start. Further, some of the textbook ideas about their use are extremely confusing and misleading.

This chapter illustrates the practical use of basic textbook decision analysis ideas, and considers their limitations. In particular, it considers sources of confusion associated with basic framing assumptions, like mutually exclusive choices, predefined choice sets, and discrete outcome events. This chapter also explores sources of possible confusion associated with decision alternatives having more than one attribute (characteristic quality), and analytical approaches involving more than one criterion (principle or standard that a thing is judged by). The tale begins with what looks like a simple machine selection problem, a standard variant of a classic textbook decision analysis problem.

A Machine Selection Problem

Tess took the same mechanical engineering university course as Nicola, the central character of Chapter 2, but a decade later. Tess and Nicola had more in common than the same university education, but Tess did not have an Uncle George to provide her first job. Shortly after graduating Tess returned to her family home in a Yorkshire village and looked for local employment. Tess soon found a post with a firm which manufactured injection-moulded plastic point-of-sale displays. Some of her work was technical engineering, helping to develop new ways to produce new kinds of displays. Some of her work was sales, helping sales staff to finalize agreement with clients on product specifications. Not long after Tess was established in this role, and getting to know a bit about the business more generally, Stan, the sole proprietor (owner) of the firm, asked Tess for assistance analysing a decision he had to make. Stan was a very practical man, who put great store on practical experience. Tess was the only employee he had with recent formal exposure to management theory. As Stan would put it, 'Why keep a dog and do the barking yourself?'

Stan had learned that a new type of injection moulding machine had become available which could fabricate a completely different kind of display product. The new products might compete with Stan's existing products, but they would probably complement them, and manufacturing them would probably strengthen Stan's overall marketing position. Three different sizes of machine in terms of production rate capacity were available. All were highly automated, sophisticated, and expensive. There were differences in associated technologies, but Stan did not see these as important. All of them would fit into the existing space for manufacturing facilities, so space was not a problem. Manufacturing staff would need some new skills, but the same staff could be used, and the impact on the number of manufacturing staff required could be negligible. Borrowing the necessary money to finance the purchase was not a problem, other than the cost. The decision, as Stan saw it, and as he explained it to Tess, was a machine selection problem which involved matching the size of the machine purchased to the size of the market. Stan was having serious difficulty deciding what to do because he was very uncertain about the size of the market for the new products and he believed that it would be very inefficient to mismatch machine size to market size. Stan also believed that if he could meet all the local demand quickly, he could effectively establish a local monopoly for the new products. However, any delay would weaken this position, and significant delay could lead to the emergence of a local competitor, which could be disastrous for existing business as well as the potential new business.

Stan asked Tess to help him put together an analysis, starting with a brief tutorial on how she believed they should proceed, as soon as possible. Tess put together her tutorial by adapting a textbook decision analysis example she was familiar with. She was ready the next morning, and Stan was able to make the time available.

A Basic Model And First-Pass Analysis

Tess began by explaining that what Stan had described was a classic textbook decision analysis problem. However, the practical difficulties and the drawbacks of some textbook theory had to be clearly understood to make effective use of the ideas. She would start with the textbook basics, then deal with the complications practice required. She would use numbers based on a very similar example from her undergraduate textbook *Management for Engineers* (Chapman, Cooper and Page, 1987, Ch. 23) to illustrate the issues. Stan and Tess could estimate more appropriate real numbers once Stan was comfortable with the framework of the approach and they had refined the structure to suit Stan's concerns. Tess then explained they would start by identifying a small number of potential actions, sometimes called strategies, consisting of a disjoint and exhaustive set of alternative decision choices which represented the full range of basic options of interest. Tess suggested that for Stan's problem these actions were: no machine, a small machine, a medium machine, and a large machine, with these machine sizes defined by the production rates of the choices available.

Tess suggested they could then identify a disjoint and exhaustive set of possible futures, usually known as events, sometimes known as states of nature: a disjoint and exhaustive set of possible market growth patterns. Tess indicated that the four actions just defined were discrete alternatives because of the limited choice of machines available. To keep the analysis simple, Stan needed to select a similar number of product market scenarios from a virtually infinite set of possibilities. For convenience she had chosen four market scenarios: good, moderate, poor and zero. They would have to spend some time defining what they meant by these (or similar) event labels, in terms of an expected sales or profit growth profile and associated bounds. For example, 'poor' might mean a sales level of £200 000 in year 1, £400 000 in year 2, £500 000 in year 3 and thereafter, plus or minus £200 000 with respect to the ongoing level, or a net present value (NPV) of additional profit equivalent. 'Moderate' might mean a sales level of £1 500 000 plus or minus £500 000 from year 3 onwards, or an NPV of additional profit equivalent, with a proportionate growth rate in years 1 and 2. There was no need for a linear scale, and it would be useful to match market event definitions to the different machine capacities. For example, a moderate market could be defined as the ideal event if a medium machine is the action chosen.

Tess then suggested they need to identify a suitable pay-off criterion, and each action/event combination would have to be assessed in terms of a value for this criterion. A classic criterion was the NPV of additional profit. Tess recommended this choice, and presented Table 9.1 as an example pay-off matrix this approach might define. She explained the numbers assumed that pay-offs on the diagonal presented the best choices given the market outturn. The best choice if the market was good was the large machine, the best choice if the market was moderate was the medium machine, and so on. If a medium machine was purchased and the market was small, the payoff dropped from 5 to 2 because fixed costs would have to be written off with a lower sales volume. If a medium machine was purchased and the market was good, the pay-off dropped from 5 to 2 because a competitor would take up the slack in the local market and drive down prices. Similar arguments applied to all the other off-diagonal non-optimal action/event combinations. Tess pointed out that this pay-off pattern implied that none of the actions was dominated; that is, no action was clearly inferior to another action for all events. If any actions were dominated, they could be eliminated from further consideration.

Tess indicated that aligning each event definition to an ideal outcome, given one of the actions, automatically avoided rejecting options due to spurious dominance. If only two events had been used, one or two actions might have been rejected as dominated simply because of the event definitions chosen. If four events had been used but the poor market scenario was ideal for the 'large' machine, the lack of granularity in the zero to poor range of market scenarios could have a similar effect. Using more than four event scenarios, ten say, could provide more granularity than necessary and increase the analytical effort without increasing the quality of the decisions. Subjective judgements about what constituted appropriate ideal market event scenarios for each action choice were important, and she and Stan would have to make these judgements with some care.

Tess then showed Stan Table 9.2. Tess explained that Stan needed to estimate subjective probabilities for each event, so she could compute related expected

Table 9.1—Basic pay-off matrix in terms of NPV of additional profit

Action: size of machine	Event: market growth (£100 000)			
	Zero	Poor	Moderate	Good
No machine	0	0	0	0
Small	−1	3	2	1
Medium	−2	2	5	2
Large	−4	−2	2	8

Table 9.2—Action choice maximizing expected pay-off

| Action: | Event: market growth | | | | Criterion: |
size of machine	Zero	Poor	Moderate	Good	expected payoff
No machine	0	0	0	0	0.0
Small	−1	3	2	1	1.6
Medium	−2	2	5	2	2.1*
Large	−4	−2	2	8	0.3
Probabilities	0.20	0.35	0.30	0.15	

*Maximum value of expected pay-off, preferred action.

pay-offs for each action, and identify the action which maximized expected pay-off, as illustrated by Table 9.2.

Tess explained that subjective probabilities did not need to be linked to appropriate hard data. They could be defined in terms of relative likelihood as perceived by Stan using his purely intuitive understanding of what was involved. As such they might not be correct, in the sense that they were unbiased estimates of a true underlying probability. Their purpose was to allow Stan to make decisions which were consistent with his beliefs. If his beliefs were incorrect, his decisions would be incorrect. However, on average, making decisions which were consistent with his beliefs ought to be more effective than making decisions which were not consistent with his beliefs. Internal consistency was the goal, a form of procedural rationality, on the grounds that a lack of internal consistency would impair effective decision taking. Stan could use equal probabilities for each event as a starting point (0.25), and adjust them (or not) until he felt comfortable with the implied relative likelihoods. For example, Table 9.2 implies the moderate market is twice as likely as the good market, the poor market is a bit more likely than the moderate market, and the zero market is more likely than the good market but less likely than the poor or moderate markets. It was pointless trying to define such probability estimates to more precision than two significant figures, and working to the nearest 0.05 in Table 9.2 made it easier to ensure Stan was comfortable with relative probabilities which added to 1.0, a property of probabilities required for expected value interpretation.

Tess also explained that maximizing expected pay-off could be shown to be rational in the sense that it was the optimal (best) decision criterion in the long term, *provided* risk in the sense of seriously bad outcomes which might occur was not an issue. That is, if Stan always maximizes expected pay-off, in the long term this will maximize actual pay-off, provided Stan does not sustain a loss which alters his ability to carry on. For example, if the probabilities in Table 9.2 were subjective probabilities of pay-offs estimated by Stan, the medium machine would be the best choice, with an expected payoff of 2.1, *provided* Stan could live with the 0.20 probability of no market and an associated payoff of −2.

Still following the recommended approach in her textbook, Tess then presented Table 9.3 to show how Stan could consider the uncertainty associated with a decision based on maximizing expected pay-off, and the robustness of this decision. This approach assumes that pay-off in terms of additional profit as measured in NPV terms in Table 9.1 is the only attribute of interest, but that a multiple-criterion approach is appropriate. The primary criterion is expected pay-off. A secondary criterion is the standard deviation (square root of the variance) associated with the expected pay-off, following a Markowitz mean–variance approach. To cater for other measures of risk in the threat sense, Table 9.3 also shows the probability of a loss. To cater for other measures of risk in the opportunity sense, Table 9.3 shows the probability of a gain of 2 or more.

Although the medium machine produces the highest expected pay-off, 2.1, this is associated with considerable variability, crudely measured by its standard deviation of 2.4, in this case $(-2 - 2.1)^2 \times 0.20 + (2 - 2.1)^2 \times 0.35 + (5 - 2.1)^2 \times 0.30 + (2 - 2.1)^2 \times 0.15)$. If risk is measured by the chance of a loss, a 0.20 probability is involved. If opportunity is measured by the chance of a gain of 2 or more, a 0.80 probability is involved. By comparison, choosing the large machine involves an expected pay-off of only 0.3, associated with more variability (a standard deviation of 3.9) and more risk (a 0.55 probability of a loss). Assuming Stan prefers more pay-off to less, but less variability to more, the medium machine is better on both counts. The large machine is a risk-inefficient choice, dominated by the medium machine in risk efficiency terms.

Choosing the small machine involves an expected pay-off of only 1.6 (0.5 less than the medium machine's 2.1), but a reduced standard deviation (1.5 compared with the medium machine's 2.4), so it is a potentially attractive alternative to the medium machine. Although the same probability of loss is involved (0.20 for the small and medium machines), the size of the potential loss is larger for the medium machine. The medium and small machines both offer potentially acceptable trade-offs between expected cost and variability. They are both risk-efficient actions. The 'no machine' action is also risk efficient, but it involves no opportunity as well as no risk.

Tess explained that Stan needed to think about all these implications, using additional forms of presentation if appropriate, considering other issues which the

Table 9.3—Additional criteria table

Action: size of machine	Criteria			
	Expected pay-off	Standard deviation	Probability of a loss	Probability of two or more
No machine	0	0	0	0
Small	1.6	1.5	0.2	0.65
Medium	2.1	2.4	0.2	0.80
Large	0.3	3.9	0.55	0.45

model does not capture if appropriate, and then he should make a choice. For example, if Stan thought he could fund the small machine himself, but the medium machine would require borrowed capital which made him nervous, this would be a relevant concern to factor into the choice, perhaps tipping the balance if it was a close call otherwise.

Exploring The Value Of More Information

Tess suggested that an obvious question for Stan to ask was, would it be desirable to acquire more information before making a machine size decision? In particular, what would it be worth to get more information about possible levels of market growth? This took them into the 'value of information' area that early use of decision trees and many textbook examples focus on.

Tess indicated that the value of perfect information could be defined using Table 9.2. If someone could tell Stan in advance of his machine size decision which market was going to be realized, he could always choose the optimal action for each event. His pay-offs would be defined by the diagonal of optimal choices, with the probabilities of those events as defined by Table 9.2. This means an expected payoff given *perfect* information of 3.75 (in this case $0 \times 0.20 + 3 \times 0.35 + 5 \times 0.30 + 8 \times 0.15$) using pay-offs on the diagonal and probabilities from the bottom line. The expected payoff given *imperfect* information is the 2.1 computed using the medium machine row pay-offs and the bottom line probabilities in Table 9.2. This implies the expected value of perfect information is 1.65 (obtained by $3.75 - 2.1$). Tess explained that this concept of perfect information illustrated four key ideas:

- The potential value of information is very high. Perfect information would allow Stan to increase his expected pay-off by 80%, from 2.1 to 3.75.
- The value of information depends on the decision criterion and the degree of risk aversion where trade-offs are involved. For example, in the context of imperfect information, if Stan felt constrained to choose the small machine because of risk trade-offs associated with the use of Table 9.3, his value of perfect information would rise to 2.15 (obtained by $3.75 - 1.6$). The more risk averse Stan is, the more information is worth to him.
- It is very misleading to suggest, as some texts do, that a decision maker should be prepared to pay up to the expected value of perfect information in order to acquire the information, because buying information involves risk. For example, if Stan felt constrained to choose the small machine because of the risk trade-offs when using Table 9.3, the value of perfect information is 2.15 as just pointed out. However, if he paid 2.15 for perfect information and was then

told the market would be zero, he would have lost more than if he had just gone ahead with the medium machine, with the same probability of a similar loss being realized. Paying 2.15 for perfect information would not be risk efficient.

- Short of bribery in some very special circumstances, perfect information is not a practical proposition, and we generally have to settle for imperfect information.

All of these ideas can be addressed by using decision trees to model the possible acquisition of further imperfect information. Still using her textbook examples directly, Tess now showed Stan Figure 9.1, portraying the two key Table 9.2 actions in tree format, assuming that dropping the risk-inefficient large machine option and the zero-opportunity no plant option are filtering decisions Stan might be comfortable with after the first pass. Tess explained that square nodes are the convention for decisions, circular nodes are the convention for chance events, and the rest of Figure 9.1 is related to Tables 9.2 and 9.3 in a fairly obvious way. Tess suggested that in practice the Figure 9.1 format was preferable to the tabular decision matrix format of Table 9.2. Among other advantages, it did not require event probabilities to be the same for all the actions. For example, a medium machine may involve a higher probability of a moderate market than a small machine because of economies of scale and lower prices: to some extent machine choices may involve self-fulfilling forecasts about market size. The decision tree format also provides a more convenient way to examine multi-stage decisions, incorporating for example, the possible acquisition of further information.

Tess suggested that Stan might be able to commission a consultant to undertake a market survey. Say Stan did this, the consultant agreed to provide an estimate of the probability of events as defined by Stan, the consultant guaranteed to be within one event class, and the consultant revealed indirectly that he might deliberately bias his forecasts on the low side to reflect the penalties to him for getting it

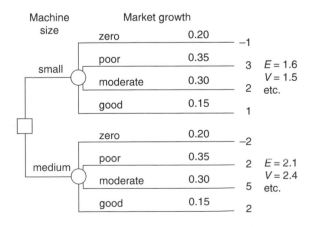

Figure 9.1—Decision tree for a reduced action set.

wrong, in particular never forecasting a good market. Tess suggested that the possible commissioning of the consultant could be modelled as a decision tree defined by Figure 9.2. Tess explained that Figure 9.2 was a two-level decision tree, each decision level being associated with uncertainty, resulting in four branch levels in total (two levels of square decision nodes, and two levels of round chance nodes).

To analyse the implications of the decision tree, Tess explained that lower-level decisions have to be made first, before rolling back to higher-level decisions. For example, the underlined expected pay-off $E = 1.4$ and the lack of underlining for the $E = 0.4$ implies that a zero growth forecast would lead to a small machine decision with an expected pay-off of 1.4. This conditional decision might be the first examined. In a similar way, the decisions implied by poor and moderate growth forecasts might be examined next, the underlining implying conditional decisions to buy a medium machine. These lowest-level decisions could be associated with simply maximizing E, subject to robustness testing in the spirit of Table 9.3. Once they were made, the expected pay-off associated with employing a consultant is calculated as 2.16 (obtained by $0.4 \times 1.4 + 0.4 \times 2.4 + 0.2 \times 3.2$), using the lower-level decisions as input assumptions. Comparing the Figure 9.2 expected pay-off of 2.16 with the Figure 9.1 expected pay-off of 2.1 for a medium

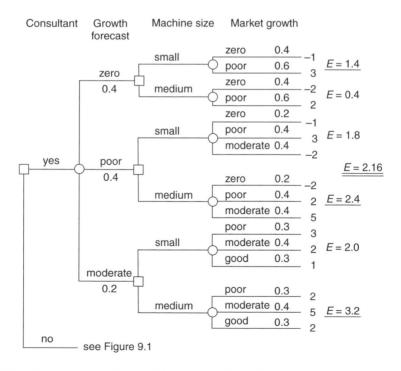

Figure 9.2—Decision tree with possible further information.

machine suggests that employing the consultant looks like a good idea, subject to robustness tests in the spirit of Table 9.3, including a comparison of the probability of a loss, and an assessment of the cost of the consultant's fee. Tess explained that this fee should be deducted from all the pay-offs in Figure 9.2.

Tess pointed out that making Figure 9.2 operational required market growth forecast probabilities which would be Stan's estimates prior to the market survey of what the consultant's forecast would be. For example, Figure 9.2 indicates a 0.4 probability the consultant will forecast zero growth, as assessed by Stan before commissioning the report. Tess explained that making Figure 9.2 operational also required Stan to estimate, prior to the market survey, what the market growth probabilities would be given the various consultant's forecasts. For example, the top branch zero market growth probability of 0.4 is the probability of a zero market *given* a zero market forecast. Tess also explained that the probabilities associated with the consultant's growth forecasts should correspond to Stan's estimates of probabilities if Stan believes both are unbiased. However, in general this might not be the case. Tess further explained that unconditional probabilities for each event associated with Figure 9.2 should be calculated for comparison with those of Figure 9.1. They should be the same for internal consistency, although this is not the case here. For example, the probability of a zero market in Figure 9.2 is 0.24 (obtained by $0.4 \times 0.4 + 0.4 \times 0.2$) while in Figure 9.1 it is 0.20. One or the other should be revised to obtain consistency. Such internal consistency checks are an important part of the modelling process, which provides insight as well as more confidence in the model.

Tess explained that buying imperfect information need not involve a consultant. It might involve various forms of market testing. She also explained that there was no need for a single-stage information-gathering process. An initial phase of analysis could be used to ascertain whether or not more information was required, a second phase could elaborate the test before committing to a major exercise, and so on. It was important to keep the model simple enough to make it manageable. However, it was also important to reduce uncertainty to a cost-effective level if appropriate.

Difficulties With The Model

By the time Tess had finished this part of her tutorial, Stan could see how decision trees were a potentially useful tool to evaluate a possible acquisition of additional information. However, he was worried about the cost of this information-gathering process in terms of delay and a potentially deteriorating local market advantage. He raised this issue with Tess, vigorously, having sat fairly passively throughout her tutorial. Tess was badly taken aback. She indicated that her text-book did not explain how to cope with the potential market position deterioration issue. She would have to think about it and get back to him. Stan did not like the thought that he had upset Tess. He was even more concerned by the thought that she might not have a satisfactory response to this key issue. However, he had other things to do and he was grateful for the chance to get out of school. They agreed to meet again early the following week.

Tess immediately started to review her analysis. She began by recognizing that Figure 9.2 explicitly modelled the impact of additional information, but it also *implicitly* modelled all other changes in the situation resulting from the use of a consultant, including the implications of a decision delay. In principle the impli-cations of delay might be captured by just adjusting the market growth prob-abilities associated with both more information and delays. For example, the Figure 9.2 zero growth forecast associated with a small machine choice might involve a 0.5 probability of zero market growth rather than 0.4, with a corre-sponding decrease in the poor market probability from 0.6 to 0.5, lowering the expected pay-off for this bottom-level branch from 1.4 to 1 (obtained by $-1 \times 0.5 + 3 \times 0.5$). Similar effects could be modelled for all the other lowest-level prob-ability branches. For clarity, the incremental effect of these probability changes could be separately identified, and adjusted for different assumptions about the time a report would take to prepare. Further, Figure 9.2 could be retitled 'decision tree associated with delay'.

However, when Tess tried to think through the implications of this kind of adjustment to the probabilities, she became very unhappy with the meaning of the market event scenarios as she had defined them. She did not believe they were transparent and robust representations of the actual situations Stan would have to deal with, or ought to deal with, whether or not market position deterioration was an issue. A particular concern was relationships between the new markets and existing markets. Further, once the very large can of worms associated with event definitions was opened up, other concerns associated with action definitions surfaced. For example, it was clear that Stan had a wide range of options to exit from an unsatisfactory initial decision, including taking a machine that was too small and trading it in for a larger one. More seriously, the decision tree structure assumed that the actions identified were mutually exclusive and exhaustive. Clearly they were not, and this restricted Stan's options in a seriously non-optimal way.

In short, the event concept and the action concept in the context of a two- or three-level decision tree structure did not look like an appropriate way to struc-ture the issues Stan needed to address. Tess had started working on a revision to her decision tree model about noon on a rainy Friday. By the end of Friday afternoon she had convinced herself that the whole approach was unworkable. Her starting position had unravelled. Her mood was as miserable as the weather.

A Project Portfolio Perspective

Tess spent a dry but windy weekend rambling in the Yorkshire dales with her partner Paul. As they rambled, Tess kept thinking about her decision tree problem. Repeatedly she found herself pondering the advice in almost every chapter of her textbook, particularly strident in the decision analysis chapter, that real management problems required a mixture of basic tools, with the nature of mix determined by the most important characteristics of the individual situations. Consequently, on the following Monday morning she started to test some alternative starting places, and explore their ramifications. This led to a sensible way forward, in her view, which she explained to Stan on Monday afternoon.

What her revised starting position boiled down to was replacing the notion of alternative, mutually exclusive and exhaustive base level actions associated with dependent events by a portfolio of potential projects. Some of these projects might start together and run in parallel, but some might be deferred. Some of those started might be put on hold or dropped when they became dominated by preferable projects. New projects might be defined as new ideas occurred, or previous ideas were merged. Three key parallel initial projects were used to explain the idea, which Tess dubbed P1, P2, and P3:

- **P1** do not buy a machine, but engage in the development of the potential new market and protection of the existing market by subcontracting new product manufacture.
- **P2** buy a small machine as soon as it looks like the expected loss if it has to be disposed of is acceptable given the expected benefits of in-house manufacture.
- **P3** buy a medium machine as soon as it looks like the expected loss if it has to be disposed of is acceptable given the expected benefits of this approach.

Tess explained that in this conceptual framework everything that was known about good project risk and opportunity management and associated programme management could be brought to bear, together with broader corporate strategy formulation and implementation ideas. Decision trees could be embedded in the associated analysis, but in the form of responses to identified threats and opportunities. The threat and opportunity identification process would in turn be preceded by initial attention to the roots of project uncertainty associated with the who, why, what, which way, wherewithal and when. At this point Tess briefly explained what these six Ws and the rest of the project risk management process involved, providing a summary of relevant ideas from Chapter 5.

To define project P1, Tess suggested that Stan might start by identifying the who (the parties) as himself, his production staff, his sales staff, his existing customer base, his potential new customer base, potential manufacturing subcontractors, potential competitors. Stan might identify the why in terms of relevant motives for himself and his sales staff, like 'ensuring no room for local competitors', linked to an attempt to clarify what would motivate potential competitors to start a new local operation on Stan's patch. He might identify relevant motives for potential manufacturing subcontractors like 'spare capacity on a new machine for a business similar to Stan's which is too geographically remote to attack Stan's local customer base'. Stan might identify potential motives for existing customers in terms of why they might wish to switch product types, which might or might not link to potential new customers. Stan might identify the what in terms of an effective new products marketing operation for an initial period of six months based on existing sales staff, existing customers, and two or three manufacturing subcontractors. The which way (activities), when (timing) and wherewithal (capital investment and other resources) would require a base plan and associated estimates capturing associated uncertainty in minimalist terms. Collectively, these six Ws in a P1 context might describe a modest investment which might serve purely as insurance to forestall new local competitors, but which might take off and trigger full pursuit of P2, P3 or more ambitious projects.

Threats associated with P1 would include issues like customers persuaded to buy the new products whose demands could not then be met, manufacturing subcontractors who attempt to steal Stan's customers, sales staff not fully versed in the new products, and so on. Opportunities associated with P1 would include issues like customers who could help Stan's staff define new kinds of products in joint development partnerships, other firms considered as manufacturing subcontractors which were good candidates for a takeover, other firm's staff who could be hired by Stan's firm, and so on. Responses to these threats and opportunities could include actions like accelerating P2, partnering contracts with customers and other manufacturers, takeovers, and so on.

To define project P2, Stan might start with the same who (the parties) as P1 apart from 'the vendor of the small machine' replacing in part 'potential manufacturing subcontractors'. Possible motives to be explored for 'the vendor of the small machine' would include 'a desire for early market penetration', perhaps suggesting possible favourable terms or partnering links, perhaps even using Stan's firm as a demonstration site and a collaborative approach to new product development. New aspects of the rest of the six Ws and the rest of the project plans would flow from these changes.

To define project P3 Stan might adjust P2 to include 'potential wholesale buyers of spare capacity', including geographically remote operations like Stan's which might like to operate a P1 approach based on Stan's manufacturing capability. New aspects of the rest of the six Ws and the rest of the project plans would flow from these changes.

Tess made the point that if a number of particularly suitable potential subcontractors were identified, P1 might lead to Stan never buying a machine himself. On the other hand, P1 might use a single, not particularly suitable subcontractor for a few months to allow Stan to test the market, order and take delivery of a suitable machine, and train his staff. The shape of P1 would depend on what its development uncovered in its early stages. P1 was in effect a way for Stan to keep his options open, immediately grasping most of the benefits of owning a new machine without the risk associated with a purchase. Similarly, project P1 might give way to P3 rather than P2 because the firm making or selling the medium machine might offer better terms, put him in contact with potential buyers of his spare capacity, and so on. This kind of approach could redefine Stan's decision problem so that no risks which he could not afford to address in expected profit terms would be involved, tested by robustness analysis. This would simplify the decision criteria used, as well as giving Stan more comfort about his decisions. Tess acknowledged that in all other respects the 'portfolio of projects' framework suggested was apparently more complex and more ambiguous than the 'decision analysis decision tree' framework as a top-level lens to view what was involved. However, she suggested this complexity and its associated ambiguity was clearly useful in practical terms. It was constructive complexity. The ambiguity would have to be managed to reduce it to an acceptable level, and the complexity would have to be managed as well. All this complexity, and the associated ambiguity, was implicit in the decision tree structure, but it was unidentified and unmanaged. It was not constructive to leave it unidentified and unmanaged. Tess's 'portfolio of projects' approach was an attempt to make explicit and practical the resolution of ambiguity as well as the management of variability. It was designed as a more powerful and robust approach to what appeared to be a classical decision analysis situation. It raised more questions than it answered. Indeed, it was a process concerned with asking the right questions before providing a basis for answering them. However, in Tess's view this was the kind of approach Stan needed.

Stan was impressed with Tess's alternative approach. He did not recognize some of her project risk management terminology, but he was attracted by what he saw as the common sense of the approach, and the way it generated lateral thinking. His major concern was the way Tess kept attaching his name to judgements and other actions. Stan asked for considerable clarification, and effectively started the P1, P2 and P3 project definition process. Stan then suggested Tess should regard herself as 'the new production process and market development programme director', reporting to him as appropriate, and get on with it as quickly as possible. Tess spent the rest of that week 'getting on with it'. She was very pleased with herself, and her confidence grew as her P1, P2 and P3 projects started to take shape. Nevertheless, Tess remained concerned about the blind alley she had found herself in using a decision analysis approach to what had seemed to be a classic decision analysis problem. Was it appropriate to conclude that decision analysis incorporating decision trees was only useful in very special circumstances which did not commonly occur in real decision problems? This seemed hard to accept given that her basic model and initial decision tree formulation had induced some useful thoughts about the value of additional information. Why was her application of conventional decision analysis inadequate? Was it possible to modify and augment the approach to remove the shortcomings she had experienced? While Tess was pleased with her concept of a portfolio of potential projects, it seemed to be a rather ad hoc approach. And it left open questions about how alternative courses of action might be developed, evaluated and selected in future decision situations.

Abandoning A Common Set Of Discrete Events With Certain Pay-offs

As recognized by Tess, Table 9.2 presented a very simple view of uncertainty, by characterizing the future in terms of a small number of discrete events, each with certain pay-offs. Some events are discrete in nature, but most are not. The market size events of Table 9.2 are discrete approximations to a multidimensional set of continuous variables defining demand growth patterns. Each of these patterns can generate a range of NPV pay-offs rather than particular single-value pay-offs like those shown in Table 9.2. Leaving aside for the present the multidimensional nature of the market size variables, consider a simple interpretation of Table 9.2 pay-offs in continuous variable terms based on Table 9.4 and Figure 9.3.

For the large machine the pay-off 'class mark' column in Table 9.4 simply notes the pay-offs indicated in Table 9.2 for zero, poor, moderate and good markets. The adjacent pay-off 'range' estimates of Table 9.4 associate a payoff class mark of

Table 9.4—Continuous variable interpretation of Table 9.2 information

Action: size of machine	Pay-off Class mark		Range	Probability Initial allocations	Collected	Cumulative
Large	−4		−5 to −3	0.20	0.20	0.20
	−2		−3 to −1	0.35	0.35	0.55
	2		−1 to 5	0.30	0.30	0.85
	8		5 to 11	0.15	0.15	1.00
Medium	−2		−4 to 0	0.20	0.20	0.20
	2		0 to 4	0.35	0.50	0.70
	5		4 to 6	0.30	0.30	1.00
	2		0 to 4	0.15		
Small	−1	−2	−4.5 to 0.5	0.2 0.14	0.14	0.14
		1	0.5 to 1.5	0.03	0.18	0.32
		2	1.5 to 2.5	0.03	0.33	0.65
	3		2.5 to 3.5	0.35	0.35	1.00
	2		1.5 to 2.5	0.30		
	1		0.5 to 1.5	0.15		
No machine	0		0 to 0	1.0	1.0	1.0

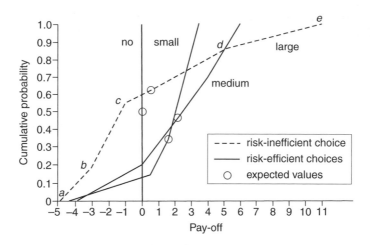

Figure 9.3—Plotting the cumulative distributions from Table 9.4.

−4 with a payoff range of −5 to −3, a class mark of −2 with a range of −3 to −1, and so on. Class mark values are central to all the ranges; range definitions were selected to ensure this is the case. The corresponding probabilities are associated with a rectangular histogram in density form. For example, the 0.20 probability associated with a pay-off class mark of −4 is assumed to be uniformly distributed over the interval −5 to −3, while a probability of 0.35 is assumed to be uniformly distributed over the range −3 to −1. The rectangular density function assumption with central class mark values means that the certain (known with certainty) pay-offs assumed in Table 9.2 now correspond to conditional expected values in a range, which makes this generalization easy to interpret. That is, analysis of Table 9.2 so far has assumed that if the large machine is chosen and the zero market occurs, the payoff is −4 *with certainty*. The Table 9.4 representation reinterprets this, assuming that if the large machine is chosen and the zero market occurs, the pay-off has an expected value of −4 associated with a uniform distribution over the range −5 to −3. This clearly approximates a more complex underlying situation, but it does so in a constructively simple way. A similar generalization applies to all the other 'certain' pay-offs in Table 9.2.

For the large machine, the probability initial allocations of Table 9.4 are just the probability values from Table 9.2, and the adjacent probability 'collected' entries are a simple special case repeat. The cumulative probability is derived directly from the collected probability column. The cumulative probabilities and the range limits can then be used to plot the cumulative probability curves for the large machine as shown in Figure 9.3, the rectangular density function assumption making the cumulative form piecewise linear as shown. That is, the lowest feasible pay-off value is −5, with zero probability of a lower value, letting us plot point *a*. The cumulative probability of 0.20 associated with this class (−5 to −3) lets us plot point *b*: the probability of a pay-off less than −3 is 0.20. The cumulative probability of 0.55 associated with the next class (−3 to −1) lets us plot point *c*: the probability of a pay-off less than −1 is 0.55. Points *d* and *e* are plotted following the same process as point *c*.

For the medium machine, the Table 9.4 pay-off class marks, ranges and probability initial allocations are all produced in the same way. However, this time the pay-off class mark value 2 with an associated range 0 to 4 occurs twice (once when the medium machine is too big, once when it is too small). The collected probability column collects both these probability values together, and simply repeats the other entries. The cumulative probability column is derived directly from the collected column, and the cumulative probability curve for the medium machine curve is plotted in Figure 9.3 in the same manner as for the large machine curve.

For the small machine, the Table 9.4 pay-off class marks and ranges became more complicated. A class mark of −1 might be associated with the range −4.5 to 2.5, followed by entries for 3 (2.5 to 3.5), 2 (1.5 to 2.5), and 1 (0.5 to 1.5). However, the last two need to be collected with part of the −1 (−4.5 to 2.5) entry. To facilitate this, the range −4.5 to 2.5 has been decomposed into −4.5 to 0.5, 0.5 to 1.5 and 1.5 to 2.5, associated with mid-range class marks of −2, 1 and 2 respectively. The initial allocation apportions the 0.2 probability according to the uniform distribution assumption over the range −4.5 to 2.5, yielding the 0.14, 0.03 and 0.03 entries. The collected column can then use the same process. The 0.18 probability associated with a pay-off of 1 (0.5 to 1.5) is defined by 0.03 + 0.15, the 0.33 probability associated with a pay-off of 2 (1.5 to 2.5) is defined by 0.03 + 0.30, and the other collected probability entries are simply initial allocations transferred across. While this is more complicated, it allows a simple cumulative distribution calculation and a plot on Figure 9.3 as for the other machine choices.

As indicated in Chapter 3, using simpler forms of cumulative probability graphs defined in cost terms, a cumulative probability distribution comparison provides a simple visual test for risk efficiency when making a choice between alternatives in terms of a single measured criterion involving uncertainty. Inspection of the medium and large machine curves in Figure 9.3 shows that the large machine choice is risk inefficient. It is dominated by the medium machine, and should be rejected. Its expected value is lower (0.3 verses 2.1), and it has a higher cumulative probability for any pay-off up to 5 (the curves do not cross until a pay-off of 5). Comparing the medium and small machine plots in Figure 9.3 reveals that neither are clearly risk inefficient. The small machine has a lower expected value (1.6 versus 2.1), but less downside risk over the pay-off range −3.3 to 1.9 (a smaller cumulative probability for pay-offs in this range). The class range assumptions used to plot these two curves means that they cross twice, with the small machine exhibiting more risk over the range −3.3 to −4.5. If these curves can be taken literally (deemed true) and it is pay-offs below −3.3 that define risk, rejecting the small machine as risk inefficient could be considered. However, the piecewise linear curves on Figure 9.3 are clearly approximations to smooth underlying 'true' curves, and do not have enough precision to indicate rejection of the small machine choice in terms of risk inefficiency, even if concern is focused on pay-offs below -3.3.

The 'no machine' choice is a simple special case in Table 9.4 and Figure 9.3, and a risk-efficient choice, if somewhat lacking in opportunity.

A multiple-criterion perspective

Tess's approach using Table 9.3 to compare machines is a multiple-criterion approach based on a mean–variance approach as developed by Markowitz in terms of portfolio theory, using expected values and standard deviations in this case. A single attribute is involved, profit as measured by NPV, but two basic criteria are used, expected value and standard deviation (variance), plus additional risk criteria to reflect the shortcomings of standard deviation as a sole measure of risk. The cumulative probability curve approach of Figure 9.3 generalizes this multiple-criterion approach so that expected values can be traded off, with risk defined in terms of complete probability distributions, not just variance or standard deviation measures. Any number of higher moments of distributions which are relevant can be considered indirectly, reflecting skew (measured by a third moment), kurtosis (peakedness, measured by the fourth moment), and so on. And this is done (must be done) considering those moments in a non-separable way. Variance is not a measure of risk without knowing the expected values, for example. That is, an approach in terms of figures like Figure 9.3 is a multiple-criterion approach with non-separable criteria. It requires attention to the shape of the whole probability distribution if all the curves do not have the same skewness and peakedness. Even if all the distributions are Normal, two non-separable criteria, mean and variance, are involved, risk-inefficient solutions need to be rejected, and risk-efficient trade-off choices need to be made. Tess's use of Table 9.3 was implicitly attempting the same approach, but it was inhibited by the discrete outcome structure of a basic decision theory approach. The continuous variable framework of Figure 9.3 is much more illuminating than Table 9.3. Figure 9.3 makes it clear that:

- The pay-off expected values (small machine 1.6, and medium machine 2.1) favour the medium machine by 0.5.
- This advantage needs to be traded off with the risk associated with the two downside distribution tails.
- The chances of a loss are marginally higher for the medium machine (about 0.2 versus 0.13).
- The ultimate or maximum downside in both cases is roughly the same for all practical purposes, approximately -4.

So the key question is, Is it worth giving up an expected pay-off of about 0.5 in order to reduce the probability of a loss from about 0.2 to about 0.13 with no change to the ultimate downside exposure of about −4? This is a fairly clear choice, even if some other informal considerations are involved. It is a much clearer choice than Table 9.3 suggests. It is clearer because we can see both the expected values and the complete associated cumulative probability distribution.

The risk efficiency approach to dealing with a single attribute is best served by a continuous variable representation in Figure 9.3 format. By and large we live in a continuous variable world. If we work directly with continuous variables, the risk efficiency perspective based on a Figure 9.3 format will serve us well, unless there are good reasons to do otherwise. Discrete scenario representations of ranges for underlying continuous variables can be very useful, but a framing assumption that suggests events are always discrete is a serious handicap if we accept a risk efficiency perspective as the appropriate perspective. Making choices in the framework of Figure 9.3 allows us to address expected value differences and differences in risk as defined by complete cumulative probability distributions without any need for the standard deviation (variance) plus other risk measures approach of Table 9.3. We can deal with any probability distribution shapes without any restrictive assumptions, a classic use of Occam's razor. If there is only one relevant attribute (pay-off in NPV terms for Stan's example), risk-efficient choices can be made without difficulty or ambiguity.

A flexible basis for estimating pay-offs

The route to Figure 9.3 via Table 9.2 and then Table 9.4 is rather complex, and it is not practical as a basic analytical approach. However, the complexity of this route was a consequence of accepting the framing assumption that a *common* set of discrete events with *certain pay-offs* was necessary to define Table 9.2. In practice, if events are used in scenario terms to define curves like those of Figure 9.3, *they do not need to be certain or common* to all or even some of the identified possible actions. The probability distributions for a Figure 9.3 representation could be estimated *directly* using a *different* set of events for each action. Further, *any* approach to estimation can be used, and associated ranges can overlap as appropriate.

The 'common set of discrete events with certain payoffs' assumptions which underlines most (not all) modern decision analysis is not consistent with constructive simplicity. It is destructive simplicity. Direct estimation of curves like those of Figure 9.3 is constructively simple, and it facilitates subsequent constructive complexity. For example, a first-pass approach could be based on a plausible maximum and minimum pay-off for each action, assuming a simple uniform probability density function and linear cumulative probability distribution for each, providing graphs like Figure 3.2. Alternatively, such plausible maximum and minimum values could be interpreted as 10 and 90 percentile values. This would facilitate the use of the minimalist first-pass basis of Chapter 4, with further passes developing more detail, as and where appropriate, via the approach outlined in Chapter 4.

Although a single-level decision tree does not need events, common or otherwise, multiple decision levels will need events in relation to dependent decisions points. However, these events are subjectively defined, not objectively determined states of nature. They can be chosen to suit the analysis, and defined in terms of possible responses. For example, the Figure 9.2 example of a decision tree associated with possible further information in the form of a consultant's report could be revised to define 'events' in terms of decisions to acquire specific machines, in the limit using the parametric analysis approaches of Norman's tale (Chapter 8).

An Explicit Threat And Opportunity Management Structure

Although the action (machine) choices of Table 9.4 could each be directly associated with an estimated pay-off probability distribution, without any linking analysis involving the redundant alternative discrete market size events structure, this might not be advisable. Market size variability is important, and related key threats and opportunities should be worth exploring. One way to do this is by considering an exploratory tree structure like Table 9.5. Here the linkage between the basic action choices (different sizes of machine) and the consequences of each choice (total pay-off) is considered in terms of five intermediate parameters: market size, the number of local competitors, the mark-up (pricing policy) employed, and the direct and indirect pay-offs.

Tess might start by addressing the large machine action, defining a plausible range for the market size given that machine. As indicated earlier, market size might be defined in terms of an annual sales volume in three years time with a particular assumed growth pattern (or a comparable pattern), avoiding the complexities that a wide range of alternative growth patterns might raise. Then for each market size, Tess might consider how many local competitors it is plausible to anticipate in the first three years. Table 9.5 suggests that the answer is none if the market size is less than X_{12}, where X_{11} is the minimum plausible market size; possibly none but possibly one if the market size is X_{12} to X_{13}; and possibly none, one or two if the market size is X_{13} to X_{14}, where X_{14} is the maximum plausible market size. Tess might start the construction of Table 9.5 by defining X_{11} to X_{14}, the plausible market size range, given a large machine, but link this to a plausible

Table 9.5—Exploratory tree structure

Action: size of machine	Market size (given machine)	Local competitors (given machine and market)	Mark-up (given ...)	Direct pay-off	Indirect pay-off	Total pay-off
Large	X_{11} to X_{12}	0	Y_{11} to Y_{12}			Z_{11} to Z_{12}
	X_{12} to X_{13}	0	Y_{13} to Y_{14}			.
		1	Y_{15} to Y_{16}			.
	X_{13} to X_{14}	0	Y_{17} to Y_{18}			.
		1	.			
		2	.			
	.		.			
	.					
No machine	X_{41} to X_{42}	0				
	X_{42} to X_{43}	0				
		1				
	X_{43} to X_{44}	0				
		1				
		2				
	X_{44} to X_{45}	0				
		1				
		2				
		3				
	.					
	.					
	.					

Conclusion: we need to satisfy most of the local market, whatever its size, and price to keep out local competitors.

range for the number of local competitors, for example the 0 to 2 assumed here, and define the conditional probability tree structure which links them. If the market is very small, local competitors are not very likely. But if the market is very big, more than one local competitor may become plausible, even if Stan has the large machine, with one intermediate case in this example. If the plausible number of competitors is a small discrete number, discrete events can be used, but ranges could be employed if a small number range was appropriate rather than 0, and a large number range was appropriate rather than 2.

As indicated in Table 9.5, Tess might then look at plausible pricing options in terms of average mark-up ranges given the machine size, market size, and number of local competitors. For example, if the market size were X_{12} to X_{13} with 0 competitors, Tess might anticipate high prices (a seller's market), but if the market size were X_{12} to X_{13} with 1 competitor, Tess might anticipate low prices (a buyer's market). However, Tess might be more prudent to examine this question the other way around: What sort of prices could be charged with reasonable expectations of keeping out all local competitors and a small chance of no more than one local competitor? That is, the dependency (causality) structure might operate in both directions, with the mark-ups Y_{13} to Y_{14} and Y_{15} to Y_{16} chosen to reflect a suitably low probability of 1 local competitor and no more, given a market size of X_{12} to X_{13} and a large machine. Tess might then look at the direct pay-off (as captured in Table 9.2), and the indirect pay-off in terms of impact on current sales of other products (not captured in Table 9.2), using both to define the total pay-off, Z_{11} to Z_{12}, and so on in Table 9.5.

Tess might then use this structure to look at the actions medium, small and no machine. If Tess did this, what might become obvious early on is the ability to constrain the number of possible competitors to 1 or 2 with a low probability of any competitors given a suitable machine and an aggressive pricing policy. Similarly, it might become clear that there would be a serious risk of multiple competitors if 'no machine' is the action choice, with associated large negative indirect pay-offs. Indeed, the importance of satisfying most of the local market whatever its size, and setting prices to keep out local competitors, might emerge as key conclusions once the shape of Table 9.5 started to clarify itself *without any need for probability estimates*.

The point of the exploratory tree structure of Table 9.5 is transparent linking of basic action choices to outcomes via a threat and opportunity management structure which clarifies what is involved and how best to manage it. These threats and opportunities can include all the issues addressed by real options and further information as well as the risk management issues explored in project risk management and other contexts. In this particular case the key threat identified explicitly is the number of competitors, and the key response identified explicitly is aggressive pricing policy. The focus is this: Given each basic action choice (machine size), what can vary, and in terms of a key driver of this variability (number of competitors), what can Tess do about it? (price aggressively)? Moving from Table 9.5 to the approach Tess adopted on page 316 still involves a significant leap. However, the exploratory tree structure of Table 9.5 looks much more useful than Table 9.2, with or without extensions like that of Figure 9.2.

Important questions which the exploratory tree approach raises are the treatment of the two-way dependencies between mark-up and local competitor numbers, and the management of these dependencies. In terms of deeper analysis in later passes, this is an entry point for the use of demand analysis to link pricing policy to sales given no local competitors, supply analysis to link numbers of competitors to market prices, and game theory to link gaming behaviour to issues like competitor entry, if such complexity is constructive. The more sophisticated forms of competitor analysis discussed in Martha's tale could be recast to address these issues, as could the consumer behaviour analysis aspects of Chapter 10. Table 9.5 clearly allows the impact of machine size on market size to be considered directly, through mark-up and price, and this structure can be used to encourage considerations like this. What Table 9.5 does not encourage to the necessary extent is the evolution or shaping of action choices. A key reason for this shortcoming, and an underlying defect of considerable general practical importance, is the focus on a single attribute – pay-off measured in NPV terms. This single-attribute framework forces ambiguity about the underlying assumptions into the analysis, which is counterproductive.

An Explicit Multiple-Attribute Structure

To illustrate the significance of considering multiple attributes of option choices, consider Table 9.6. This shows an exploratory, three-level attribute structure for the purchase of a large machine, and associated events from Table 9.5: a market size X_{11} to X_{12}, and an average markup Y_{11} to Y_{12} to ensure no local competition.

Table 9.6—Exploratory attribute structure: part 1

Large machine, year 3 market size X_{11} to X_{12} units, year 3 average unit markup Y_{11} to Y_{12}

	Attributes at levels 1 to 3			Level 3 estimates, other indicators or judgements
Level 1	Level 2	Level 3		
Profit	Annual revenue	Annual sales year	1	range
			2	range
			3	X_{11} to X_{12}
		Average unit price year	1	range
			2	range
			3	Y_{11} to Y_{12}
	Annual fixed cost	Capital cost		range
		Value after year	1	range
			2	range
			3	range
	Variable cost per unit	Annual maintenance		range
		Materials, labour, etc.		range

Average annualized additional contribution to profit assuming operation for						Given a discount rate of	Associated percentile value
1 year	2 years	3 years	5 years	10 years	20 years		
range	range	range	range	range	range	12	10
range	range	range	range	range	range	10	50
range	range	range	range	range	range	8	

Each numeric estimate labelled 'range' in the right-hand column of the top part of Table 9.6 could be a plausible minimum to maximum range, or a 10 to 90 percentile range estimate in approximate terms, for each level 3 attribute. The X_{11} to X_{12} and Y_{11} to Y_{12} estimates would be special cases of these 'range' estimates, the year 3 assumptions as discussed earlier in relation to NPV pay-off assessment. The estimates for years 1 to 3 might assume a simple linear growth pattern and a steady-state pricing policy as assumed earlier in relation to NPV pay-off assessments, but they could reflect whatever information was available about likely market growth and pricing patterns. Constant demand and prices after year 3 could be assumed, as discussed earlier in relation to NPV pay-off assessment. More than 3 years of estimates could be employed if growth or decline in demand or fluctuating prices after 3 years was an issue, perhaps at 2 year intervals, to keep it simple. The purpose of the top part of Table 9.6 is to make all the key basic parameter assumptions transparent, and avoid any other assumptions with unclear implications, like the impact of specific growth or pricing patterns, the horizon over which variations are considered, or the effect of discounting assumptions used to produce NPV estimates.

The purpose of the bottom part of Table 9.6 is maintaining transparency, but providing simple summary attribute measures comparable to NPV, without imposing specific horizon or discount rate assumptions. Annualized figures correspond to NPV values, but they are easier to compare in this context. In this case the range estimates could reflect a simple perfect positive correlation assumption in relation to the top portion, all the top portion 10 percentile values being used to complete a 10 percentile result, with a similar approach to 50 and 90 percentile values. The 'years of operation' dimension of the table could be reduced to 10, 50 and 90 percentile values too. The format chosen avoids any need for specific probability distribution assumptions with regard to the number of years of operation. Similarly, the discount rate values could simply define a plausible scale but take advantage of a likely feel for an appropriate 50 percentile discount rate to define an associated range, to provide central (expected) estimate profit values on the 50 percentile line, with associated profit range estimates above and below. If the annualized figures are converted to NPV equivalents, and 3 years to 10 years operation corresponds to 10 and 90 percentile operating period values, the 3 years 10 percentile annualized profit value using a discount rate of 12 per cent, and the 10 years 90 percentile annualized value discount rate of 8 per cent, provide a direct estimate of Z_{11} to Z_{12} (the NPV range) on Table 9.5. This in turn corresponds to the large machine pay-off curve of Figure 9.3, or the Table 9.2 discrete value equivalents.

Table 9.6 would give Tess and Stan a much better feel for pay-off-related uncertainty than the pay-off values in Table 9.2. This is a multiple-attribute perspective which decomposes NPV in a more convenient and digestible multiple-attribute annualized average profit framework, leaving the time horizon and discount rate assumptions open. Table 9.6 provides a useful multiple-attribute perspective, even though collapsing these attributes into a single attribute like NPV (or annualized average profit) is commonplace, and it does not involve assumptions which are controversial.

Table 9.7 extends the range of attributes that might be considered in a Table 9.6 format by introducing new level 1 attributes, and three additional level 2 attributes influencing profit: machine flexibility, machine reliability, and product quality. 'Machine flexibility' is an example of an attribute which might be measured directly in terms of an opportunity cost for compatibility with Table 9.6 measures, but the 'opportunity' (lost revenue) implications will not be straightforward. At an early stage of an analysis Stan would probably find it more useful if Tess were simply to indicate the ranges for the level 3 'set-up time' and 'start-stop' attributes, explicitly introducing new measurement scales. 'Machine reliability' takes this line of thinking further, with additional new attribute measures. 'Product quality' goes further still, with qualitative judgements rather than numeric estimates: excellent and good for level 3 attributes like 'finish' and 'durability'.

Table 9.7—Exploratory attribute structure: part 2

Large machine, year 3 market size X_{11} to X_{12} units, year 3 average unit price Y_{11} to Y_{12}

Additional attributes at levels 1 to 3			Level 3 estimates, other indicator or judgements
Level 1	Level 2	Level 3	
Profit (continued)	Machine flexibility	Set-up time (min)	range
		Stop-start (min)	range
	Machine reliability	Routine lost time (%)	range
		Catastrophic failure probability	range
	Product quality	Defects (%)	range
		Finish	excellent
		Durability	good
Respect	Many of the above + operator preference	Noise level	first choice
		Ease of operation, etc.	first choice
	Visual impression	Colour	yellow
		Size	big
		Bells and whistles	lots
		Style	excellent
	Number of competitors	Locally	0 likely
		Nationally	range
		Internationally	range
Fun	Many of the above ++		
Passion	Many of the above ++		

These additional attributes could have very important impacts on profit, and an explicit multiple-attribute approach to 'profit' will encourage the identification and consideration of all relevant criteria, even if they are associated with non-numeric measures or judgements. Comprehensiveness is critical at this stage, to ensure that important performance criteria are not overlooked. Given the point-of-sale display nature of Stan's products, the quality of 'product finish' might be absolutely critical, and anything less than excellent might be unacceptable.

Like many manufacturers, Stan may be concerned about attributes other than those related to 'profit', such as 'respect' in a broad sense, to cover self-respect through to reputation in the brand reputation sense. 'Respect' may be affected by 'machine reliability' and 'product quality' in ways which may concern Stan directly, over and above profit effects. Pride in his products may be very important to Stan, and pride in smooth uninterrupted production may also be of direct importance to Stan. Smooth production may also be important to Stan because it is important to his staff. 'Respect' may include this aspect, and identifying this issue may suggest further attributes like those associated with 'operator preferences': 'noise level', 'ease of operation', and so on.

Visual impression may involve a feel-good factor for Stan, directly, or the implications for Stan of a feel-good factor for his staff. Explicit identification and discussion of visual impression with Stan might lead to excluding this feature on the grounds that it is irrelevant. However, a failure to identify it explicitly might lead to important unconscious bias if Stan loves bells and whistles and big yellow machines, and a failure to explicitly cater for both Stan's feelings and the rest of his staff's feelings about such issues could be a serious mistake. Including it explicitly, and suggesting that Stan might discuss it with his staff, does not mean it has to be judged very important. It simply acknowledges that it might be of interest, and it might serve to root out other attributes not yet identified which are of even more interest.

'Number of competitors' is an example of a 'respect' attribute which might be triggered by the 'visual impression' discussion. If pushed, Stan might admit, to himself if not to Tess, that lack of a local competitor was important to him in terms of his public image at the local Rotary or sailing club. Thinking about a rationale to justify this to himself, he might see the wider national competition issue as different but possibly of importance too, although he had not previously thought so in the context of an NPV focus. Indeed, a discussion of the importance of local/national competitors might trigger an interest in possible international competition issues, even if this was for no other reason than he would like to be seen locally as an 'international player', with sales across the EU. 'Number of competitors' may have quite important implications which include 'profit' but go well beyond profit, and for both profit and non-profit purposes it may be useful to recognize that local competitors are not the only issue.

To take this notion to its logical conclusion suggests always including two more level 1 attributes to a Table 9.7 assessment: 'fun' and 'passion', to give four level 1 attributes:

- 'Passion' is what makes you want to get up in the morning
- 'Fun' is why you enjoy the day
- 'Respect' is what lets you sleep easily
- 'Profit' is what makes passion, fun and respect feasible

All potentially relevant attributes can be captured within these basic four attributes at level 1. In practice many corporate ventures, never mind sole-proprietor ventures like Stan's, are driven by passion, fun, respect and profit in that order of priority. Stan would do well to think on that. Most great entrepreneurs do, and it is perhaps the test of a rational person that they do not omit such considerations. Will a decision being considered excite the imagination of those involved, and will it be a fun thing to do? Indeed, in some matters profit may not be the issue at all, and any general rational approach to decision analysis has to be able to address the really important questions in life, like where to live and who to live with. This is a test which conventional textbook decision analysis clearly fails.

A key point is that once an explicit multiple-attribute framework is established, it facilitates and generates consideration of a wide range of directly relevant issues which otherwise tend to get overlooked if the focus is a single attribute like 'profit' measured in terms of a single attribute like NPV. In particular, an explicit multiple-attribute approach promotes consideration of alternative objectives, which in turn helps to clarify why Stan should make one choice rather than another. Explicit consideration of potentially relevant attributes may also be important in terms of shaping options, before seeking to evaluate options in terms of these attributes. Where this is likely to be the case, a list of key attributes for initially identified options should be developed and reflected on before proceeding to structuring and estimating the various attributes. Recall that a similar sequence in respect of project issues is advocated in Figure 5.1. Thus Stan and Tess should start with an unstructured, preliminary list of machine attributes such as Table 9.8 – part 0 of an attribute exploration process – before developing parts 1 and 2 in the format of Tables 9.6 and 9.7.

The ten attributes for each machine option listed in Table 9.8 illustrate the best kind of simple multiple-attribute approach to start with. The only directly measured attributes are 8 and 9, and they are simple to determine but very telling. They immediately suggest that other things being equal, the large machine looks the best bet if it can be used to its full capacity. Attribute 7 reinforces this in terms of a way out if high demand cannot be sustained, a flexible attribute in terms of exit options which need to be explored. Attribute 10 reinforces the notion that this looks like the way to go if the opportunities and threats can be managed effectively. But attributes 1 to 6 are keys to shaping the sort of proposition which Stan might develop. For example, Stan might take the view that an immediate deal to purchase a large machine, and acquire the UK franchise for sale of these machines, would guarantee his dominance of the local market for point-of-sale displays, his initial objective, but it would do much more as well. It would put him in a very strong position in the UK 'large machine' sales market. He could

Table 9.8—Exploratory attribute structure: part 0, key attributes for initial shaping

Large machine
1. Very advanced leading-edge technology
2. Patents in place will protect technology
3. Excellent performance with guarantees
4. Very high reputation manufacturer
5. Non-EU manufacturer
6. Manufacturer has no UK sales presence
7. High resale value / low depreciation likely
8. Low variable cost per unit produced ($£C_{11}$)
9. Low purchase cost per unit production capability ($£C_{12}$)
10. A fun machine

Medium machine
1. Very old-fashioned technology
2. No patents to protect technology
3. Moderate performance expected, but no guarantees
4. Manufacturer has a debatable track record
5. UK manufacturer
6. Aggressive UK sales presence
7. Low resale / high depreciation likely
8. High variable cost per unit produced ($£C_{21}$)
9. Low purchase cost per unit production capability ($£C_{22}$)
10. An ugly machine

Small machine
1. Intermediate technology relative to above
2. Patent in place will protect technology
3. Good performance with guarantees
4. Manufacturer has a good reputation
5. EU manufacturer (not UK)
6. No UK sales presence
7. Moderate resale value / depreciation likely
8. Medium variable cost per unit produced ($£C_{31}$)
9. High purchase cost per unit produced ($£C_{32}$)
10. A boring machine

demonstrate its use, use some of his production staff as support marketeers and trainers (which they would enjoy), provide backup production capability guarantees, savage the 'medium machine' opposition in the UK (which Stan would enjoy), and keep the 'small machine' opposition on the other side of the Channel, with occasional successful attacks on their territory (which Stan would enjoy even more). Based on this strategy he should be able to offer the 'large machine' manufacturers a desirable proposition. This would be a 'fun' business venture, built around a 'fun' machine. The shape of this venture is quite different to that developed by Tess and Stan earlier.

The multiple-attribute framework provided in this section is the basis of the missing link that Tess needed to build a conceptual bridge between decision analysis and project risk management. Rather than proceed directly with her P1, P2, P3 project portfolio as outlined on page 316, Tess needed to step back from her earlier analysis and use something like Table 9.8 to make sure she had started off the initial shaping exercise in an appropriate direction.

Explicit Analysis Of Multiple-Attribute Trade-offs

Assuming Tess and Stan make use of a multiple-attribute approach to shaping their choices, there is an obvious need to consider trade-offs between different option attributes that may be implied in choosing one option over another. Most of the time easy choices are involved, and implicit trade-offs are not difficult. However, the 1 in 10 exceptions involving difficult choices are important.

Multiple-attribute value theory

The most popular standard way to tackle explicit formal analysis of multiple-attribute trade-offs is a multiple-attribute value theory (MAVT) approach (Belton, 1990; French, 1991; Stewart, 1992). Conventional MAVT approaches usually suggest attempting direct estimation of multiple-attribute value functions. For example, a quadratic form of two-attribute value function is

$$V_{12} = b_0 + b_{11}Q_1 + b_{12}Q_1^2 + b_{21}Q_2 + b_{22}Q_2^2 + b_3Q_1Q_2 \qquad [9.1]$$

where the b_i are constants, and Q_1 and Q_2 are amounts of attributes 1 and 2 respectively associated with a particular decision alternative. If $b_3 = 0$ this function is separable into the sum of a function of Q_1 and a function of Q_2. For convenience this assumption is usually made. If a value function of the form V_{12} were employed, it would also be usual to assume $b_0 = 0$. Standard practice would then involve attempting to estimate b_{11}, b_{12}, b_{21} and b_{22} via direct comparison questions to the decision maker couched in terms of possible Q_1 and Q_2 bundles. More generally, for n attributes, $i = 1, \ldots, n$, it is usually assumed that a value function V is separable into a sum of functions in each Q_i of the form

$$V = V_1(Q_1) + V_2(Q_2) + \cdots + V_n(Q_n) \qquad [9.2]$$

with

$$V_i = b_{i1}Q_i + b_{i2}Q_i^2 \qquad [9.3]$$

Each V_i defines a curve like that illustrated by Figure 9.4, with the b_{i1} and b_{i2} parameters sized appropriately in relation to the other attribute value functions.

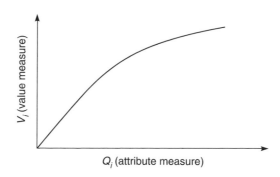

Figure 9.4—An example separable value function component.

For example, if $b_{11} = b_{21} = 1$, but $b_{12} = -0.002$ and $b_{22} = -0.001$, this implies that low values of Q_1 or Q_2 have approximately equal value, but as Q_1 or Q_2 increase, the decline in marginal value is faster for Q_1 than it is for Q_2. Questions about a decision maker's indifference between bundles of Q_1 and Q_2 values can be used to define $b_{11}, b_{12}, b_{21},$ and b_{22}. Similar questions can then link these preferences to Q_3, Q_4, and so on. Once the V_i value functions have been determined, the value V of a particular decision option is readily obtained by adding the contributions to value from each attribute of the decision option. The preferred option is the one with the largest value of V. The MAVT approach provides a method of comparing different options where the amounts of each attribute associated with each option are assumed to be known with certainty. The approach does not address uncertainty about the amounts of attribute Q_i, or about the parameters or form of the value function.

Multiple-attribute utility theory

One standard way to tackle uncertainty about the amounts of attribute Q_i is to employ a multiple-attribute utility theory (MAUT) approach. For an introduction linked to MAVT see Goodwin and Wright (1998). Like MAVT, MAUT discussions usually assume separability. A standard approach involves a multiple-attribute utility function U which is separable into a sum of utility functions U_i in each Q_i. For an option with an uncertain Q_i, the contribution to value of the uncertain Q_i is determined by calculating the expected utility of Q_i, defined as E_i, where

$$E_i = \int P(Q_i) \, U_i(Q_i) \, dQ_i \qquad [9.4]$$

$P(Q_i)$ is the probability density function for Q_i and the integral is over all possible values of Q_i. Alternatively, for discrete values of Q_i, Q_{ij} where $j = 1, \ldots, m$ we have

$$E_i = \sum_{j=1}^{m} P(Q_{ij})\, U_i(Q_{ij}) \qquad [9.5]$$

where $P(Q_{ij})$ is the probability of the amount Q_{ij} and the sum is over all m discrete values of Q_i.

There are several ways of interpreting and implementing the MAUT approach, none easily grasped or applied. Tess's textbook offers one way, designed to clarify why it is not a good idea to go down this route. Here we provide a brief summary linked to the use of Figure 9.3 variants.

Each single-attribute utility function $U_i(Q_i)$ is determined by asking the decision maker to value a series of hypothetical lotteries. For example, working with Table 9.2, considering a single attribute, 'pay-off', we can drop the i subscript in equations [9.4] or [9.5] and consider $U(Q)$, a single-attribute special case of an expected utility approach. In this case the maximum pay-off in the Table 9.2 matrix (8) is designated S_{max}, and assigned a utility of unity, the minimum pay-off in the matrix (-4), is designated S_{min}, and assigned a utility of zero. The utility of any *certain* pay-off between S_{min} and S_{max} is then determined by asking questions designed to seek a point of indifference between *an outcome with certainty Q*, and a lottery with probability P of winning S_{max} and probability $1-P$ of losing and obtaining S_{min}. Setting P or Q to different values allows $U(Q)$ values to be determined directly and intermediate U values to be obtained by interpolation so that $U(Q) = PU(S_{max}) + (1-P)\, U(S_{min}) = P$. For example, in the context of Table 9.2, Stan might reveal that he is indifferent to a *certain* pay-off of 2 and the lottery just described with $P = 0.8$, imputing a utility of 0.8 to a pay-off of 2. Note that the expected pay-off of this lottery is $0.8\,(S_{max} = 8) + (1 - 0.8)\,(S_{min} = -4) = 5.6$, which is rather more than the certain pay-off of 2. This gap is a measure of Stan's risk-averse behaviour. A risk-neutral decision maker would define a point of indifference when the pay-off with certainty and the expected pay-off of the lottery were equal. For example, a risk-neutral decision maker would be indifferent between a *certain* pay-off of 2 and the lottery with $P = 0.5$, which yields an expected pay-off of $0.5\,(S_{max} = 8) + (1 - 0.5)\,(S_{min} = -4) = 2$.

Once each $U_i(Q_i)$ function is determined in this way, a multiple-attribute utility function can be defined of the form

$$E = w_1 E_1 + w_2 E_2 + \cdots + w_n E_n \qquad [9.6]$$

for n attributes. The w_i $(i = 1, \ldots, n)$ are the weights which define the relative importance of the n attributes. The preferred option from a set of options is the one with the largest value of E.

The MAUT equation [9.6] resembles the MAVT equation [9.2] closely if quadratic forms are used for both. The weighting factors in equation [9.2] are incorporated via the relative sizing of the coefficients b_{i1} and b_{i2} in equation [9.3]. The essential difference is that the MAUT approach has incorporated consideration of uncertainty about outcomes in terms of each attribute via a single criterion, expected utility. For a risk-neutral decision maker, the MAUT approach and the MAVT approach using expected values are identical if both use quatratic forms. Whether or not the decision maker is risk neutral, risk efficiency and risk/expected pay-off considerations are not involved in an explicit way. There are no risk-inefficient options to eliminate, or trade-offs between efficient options to consider. Maximization of the single criterion, expected utility, yields preferred choices, subject to sensitivity analysis about the location of the U_i curves and selection of appropriate values for the w_i.

Difficulties with MAUT

The MAUT approach has many supporters, but it also has as many opponents. Supporters of MAUT see it as an axiomatic, rational basis for normative analysis (what people should do). Opponents point to a number of conceptual and practical problems with the MAUT approach. We begin with some well-known problems.

The need to deduce utility functions for each attribute prior to considering choices gives rise to both conceptual and practical difficulties:

- Deducing a decision maker's utility function for a particular attribute can be time-consuming, context dependent, and necessitate cross-checking to ensure consistency in responses to lottery comparison questions (Hershey, Kunreuther and Schoemaker, 1988, Kahneman and Tversky, 1979).
- Interpolation is necessary to define utility values for all possible attribute values.
- The calculation of expected utility for a continuous range of possible attribute values, as in equation [9.4], is not practicable unless a convenient analytical form is assumed for the U_i.
- If the expected utility difference between two options is small, the preferred choice will be very sensitive to the assumed utility curve, but it will not be clear how it is sensitive. Sensitivity analysis associated with a deduced utility function is problematic.
- Maximization of expected utility (in respect of a single attribute) can be shown to be a reasonable interpretation of a decision maker's preferences involving uncertainty only under certain assumptions about the way the decision maker chooses between alternative options (e.g. Smith, 1988; French, 1988). There is substantial evidence to suggest that these assumptions are not valid in general (Einhorn and Hogarth, 1981). For example, decision makers are often 'risk averse' in respect of potential uncertain gains, but inclined to prefer risky options in respect of choices between options which involve potential losses. There is some evidence – for an introductory summary see Wright (1984) – that

some decision-makers want to consider characteristics of pay-off distributions such as variance, skew, and probability of loss, and they are prepared to defend choices made using these characteristics, even if they are inconsistent with choices based on agreed utility curves. Some decision makers do not behave as if they were utility function maximizers and they do not wish to do so. Most supporters of utility theory decision analysis (such as Wright) argue that utility theory can remain a basis for normative analysis even if it is not valid for descriptive analysis (what people actually do and wish to go on doing). The authors of this book are sceptical.

A further well-known difficulty, related to the combining of expected utilities for individual attributes in equation [9.6], is arriving at appropriate attribute weights (w_i) to indicate the relative values placed on quantities of each attribute. Various approaches to obtaining weights have been proposed, including swing weights (Goodwin and Wright, 1998) and the analytical hierarchy process (Saaty, 1980, 1990a, 1990b). Given uncertainty about the most appropriate weights (w_i) to use, sensitivity analysis in respect of the w_i used in any given option comparison is usually necessary.

All the above difficulties are compounded when more than one person is involved in the evaluation and selection of a preferred decision option. In an organizational context this applies to the majority of significant decisions. In our view all these difficulties with expected utility and associated MAUT approaches constitute a compelling case for abandoning this approach altogether. However, from a constructive simplicity perspective, a further somewhat different argument is involved. The use of Figure 9.3 variants estimated directly for each action choice without common event structures, as discussed on page 323, facilitates a practical and easily applied multiple-criterion approach to a single attribute like pay-off. This generalizes a Markowitz mean–variance approach in a clear and unambiguous manner. Viewed from within this framework, the MAUT E_i values are each attempting to collapse the multiple criteria associated with mean, variance and further higher moments into a single composite criterion, expected utility. If Normal distributions for Q_i or risk-neutral $U_i(Q_i)$ are assumed, equivalence can be shown, but even then the relationship is not transparent. Essentially, an expected utility approach involves implicit restrictive assumptions being used to reduce a multiple-criterion problem (transparently addressed via Figure 9.3 equivalents) to a single-criterion problem obscurely addressed via E_i functions. This is an example of destructive subjectivity, a form of destructive complexity, which is not consistent with constructive simplicity. Transparency is lost. Flexibility is lost. Clarity is lost. From a constructive simplicity perspective, expected utility and MAUT suggest three principles for model building. The first principle is never use a restrictive assumption to embed a subjective judgement into a model unless it is clearly constructive. The second is embed subjective judgements into models at as late a stage or as high a level as possible. The third is *never, ever* assume all relevant aspects of a decision can be quantified in a single, subjectively based index. Instead of the MAUT approach, decision makers like Stan need a constructively simple approach.

A recommended multiple-attribute approach for discrete choices

Well-known good advice when using a MAVT approach is choose an approach which suits the context – there is no one approach which is best for all contexts. This advice applies to constructively simple approaches as well. A fundamental characterization of the context is discrete choices (like Stan choosing between two machines), and portfolio choices (addressed in Chapter 10). The focus here is discrete choices.

The starting point given a discrete choice context has to be the design of a constructively simple first pass, evolving later passes which add complexity constructively, in a simplicity-efficient manner. For example, if Stan can use tables like Tables 9.6 to 9.8 to make decisions without formal explicit analysis of attribute trade-offs, he should do so. Figuratively speaking, this should be the case 9 times out of 10. But suppose this is not the case, and Stan's choice between two options involves half a dozen measurable attributes, and one or two non-measurable attributes (like the extent of the fun and passion involved). For the half-dozen measurable attributes, directly estimated variants of Figure 9.3 could be prepared, one figure for each attribute, each figure showing two cumulative probability curves, one for each choice. Even if these figures do not all show one choice dominating the other, the process of preparing the figures may produce enough insight to make the preferred choice clear. Figuratively speaking, this should be the case 9 times out of 100. If this is not the case, a reasonable next pass might involve asking Stan to value the difference between the two curves for each attribute's Figure 9.3 variant in money terms, add up these valuations, and then ask Stan if the resulting net advantage in money terms for one option is worth the non-measured attribute advantages for the other. Figuratively speaking, this might do the trick 9 times out of 1000.

A really difficult case may have to take the analysis much deeper still. However, the quest must remain insight, not ever more complex multiple-attribute models per se. For example, Chapman *et al.* (1985) describe a very large-scale study addressing how best to take a proposed major gas pipeline across the Yukon River. A formal multiple-attribute methodology was essential, to trade off issues like national security, pollution of the Yukon River, loss of gas supply revenue, and so on. However, it was clear that separability was not an appropriate assumption, and responsibility for sources of risk and the state of the nation in terms of war or peace were among the reasons. For example, pollution of the river would be of critical importance in a time of peace and plenty in the context of gas pipeline operator failures, but national security would be far more important in a time of war and scarce resources in the context of sabotage. Estimating Figure 9.3

variants based on a careful decomposition of sources of risk and responses provided constructive complexity which yielded the insight to make a clear recommendation without resorting to the formalization of values or utility functions. Had this not been the case, dollar value transformations of attributes would have been used, but these would have required explicit consideration of uncertainty and interdependencies. The ultimate use of such transformations involves a special case of utility theory as used by economists for a wide range of applications, like consumer behaviour theory (e.g. Green, 1970). Special assumptions are necessary to aggregate preferences across the relevant population as well as to use a cardinal dollar value scale. However, such preferences can be considered in terms of Figure 9.3 variants, directly and explicitly considering uncertainty in relation to the Q_i via complete probability distributions without resorting to expected utility functions. Further, such approaches can use what economists call revealed preference functions, which describe directly how people seem to operate without presuming they actually employ utility functions which can be aggregated. Further still, such functions can address uncertainty associated with the errors generated by parameter and functional form assumptions in an integrated manner. Finally, such approaches can use separability in very powerful but simple ways via what Pearce (1964) called neutral want association, a pairwise form of separability explored briefly in Chapter 10.

Conclusion

A principal conclusion of this chapter is that a constructively simple approach to practical decision analysis needs to begin with opportunity analysis in a multiple-attribute framework like Table 9.8. It then moves on to project formulation and development with associated risk analysis, which embeds more conventional decision analysis in it, using diagrams like Figure 9.3 to make risk-efficient choices in terms of all relevant attributes at all levels of decision making. This approach intersects effectively with the project risk management process Tess had quite correctly identified (page 316) as the process needed to identify an effective portfolio of projects. A key difference between the approach taken by Tess on page 316 and practical decision analysis is the opportunistic nature of the suggestions which flow from a consideration of option attributes, and the favourable light these shine on the large machine to illustrate the differences. In practice the large machine might not be the best choice, and Stan might have previously picked up the extent of such advantages if they were real. However, Tess needed to explicitly ensure that she and Stan addressed opportunities via a rich set of attributes at the outset.

Despite Tess's difficulties with the limitations of decision tree models, they can be very useful. They underlie most effective decision-taking processes, and many of the other chapters in this book. A polished ability to conceptualize decisions in terms of decision trees is an important decision-making skill. Studying decision analysis case studies which emphasize the model development and reflection aspects of the use of decision trees, like Phillips (1982) and Moore and Thomas (1973), involves time well spent. It is also important to understand the sensitivity analysis aspects discussed in standard decision analysis texts. When decision trees are used in a real decision context, considerable care needs to be exercised when choosing event definitions, identifying sources of uncertainty, thinking about causality, and modelling structure in general. For this reason decision trees are not the model to use to start thinking about a decision.

Table 9.8 illustrates a set of initial attributes for the three machines considered in Tess's tale. As a suggested starting point, Table 9.8 is simple but not simplistic. It is a set of comparative lists, not a model in the usual decision analysis model sense. However, it reflects the need to consider multiple attributes at the outset, to start by addressing why some choices may be better than others. It also reflects the need to focus on shaping the obvious options, and generating new ones in the process, before considering the choice of options. Table 9.8 is not suggested as a starting point for all decision analysis problems, it is simply illustrative of the kind of framework that needs to be addressed early in the process. Tables 9.6 and 9.7 illustrate how an exploratory attribute structure might be developed to clarify profit and other attribute implications of choices as a decision analysis progresses. Table 9.5 illustrates how an exploratory tree structure might be developed to explore a key risk (local competitors) via a key criterion (profit) as a decision analysis progresses further. Again the intention is to illustrate the kind of framework that needs to be addressed at this stage of the process, rather than to define a universal tool. Page 316 illustrates where this might lead, viewing the emerging decision options as a portfolio of projects which need to be managed using risk and value management approaches. At its simplest this approach could lead directly to a choice between discrete alternative actions, but even then the framework would be a development of Figure 9.3, not a variant of Table 9.3. Where any decision analysis starts will have a major influence on where the process gets to. Tess's tale is very concerned about starting in the right place.

The value of decision trees

Decision trees are very effective tools at a tactical level. They should be a natural part of many forms of analysis. But in general, practical decision analysis should not start the problem formulation and model definition process with defining decision trees in mind. Tess's presumption that a conventional decision analysis model approach was an appropriate approach was her basic mistake. Explicitly linking Tess's situation back to Nicola's in Chapter 2 may be useful. Nicola's general approach, as characterized by Figure 1.1, is what Tess needed to apply at the outset. Defining objectives, defining options, and shaping options, all come earlier than decision tree models. Understanding threats and opportunities, and how to manage them, also comes earlier. If people see decision analysis in general terms as a process built around conventional decision trees, they will be training themselves to play chequers as preparation for a lifetime of chess.

If decision tree representations are to be useful, their limitations and the assumptions employed need to be very clearly understood. The idea of a *common* set of discrete events with certain pay-offs which relates to all actions needs to be firmly rejected. Continuous variable evaluation of pay-offs for each action using the format of Figure 9.3 is preferable, with or without associated event sets which are different for each action. This facilitates a very simple view of departures from expected values which rests on a general non-separable multiple-criterion approach if only one attribute (such as profit) is involved. This involves a standard project risk management perspective. It is not a new idea.

The tree structure needs to explore the reasons for variations from expected value for each action, and the ways such variations can be managed in a favourable direction. Sources of uncertainty are relevant. So are preventative and reactive responses, including the availability of options in a real options sense as opposed to a financial options sense, and the acquisition of information in the decision theory sense. Understanding the sources of uncertainty is a sensible first step, as effective responses are often conditional on the sources of uncertainty. For example, Stan's pricing policy is a source of uncertainty about demand, and an aggressive pricing policy is the obvious instrument of control.

The relevance of utility theory

An important observation in this chapter is that expected utility theory and the MAUT approach have no place in practical decision analysis. These approaches waste time better spent on other forms of analysis. Many MAUT advocates argue for clarity, transparency, simplicity and other key constructively simple attributes (e.g. Stewart, 1992), which suggest their heart is in the right place, but they have been seduced by the mathematical elegance of MAUT, which has led them to start their analysis process in a place which is not simplicity efficient and take it in a direction which is not simplicity efficient.

It is most unfortunate that advocates of MAUT attempt to stake a proprietorial claim on the term 'utility theory', and that advocates of MAVT seem to acknowledge this claim. Their perspective on utility is very different from, and not as useful as, the utility theory employed for demand analysis and other aspects of economic analysis. However, this is consistent with an associated proprietorial claim on the terms 'decision theory' and 'decision analysis', very general terms which they address in terms of discrete exhaustive sets of predefined choices, in basic terms with discrete event certain outcomes, the only uncertainty being associated with which outcome events will occur. It is also consistent with their use of the term 'risk analysis' as a subset of 'decision analysis', rather than the other way around, with a quite different meaning to that adapted by others. Utility theory ought to be useful, as the term suggests. There are many forms which are extremely useful, MAVT to name but one, but especially utility theory in the forms developed for consumer behaviour theory, like revealed preference theory. This consumer behaviour theory perspective on utility theory is highly developed and very powerful. Nevertheless, this theory is rarely linked to mainstream MAVT or MAUT perspectives. Utility theory more generally defined, in revealed preference or axiomatic preference theory forms, has an important place in practical decision analysis. If multiple-attribute and multiple-criterion considerations require formal analysis, a sound understanding of general utility theory notions is desirable to make effective choices from available simple practical tools to suit the situation. The works of Arrow (1961), Gorman (1959, 1963, 1968) and Strotz (1957) are early examples of a vast relevant literature.

There is the need to view practical decision analysis in a very much wider framework than is normally provided. If a reader does not understand the finer points of separable versus non-separable utility functions, this should not matter most of the time. But it will matter if the simple and practical starting point illustrated by Table 9.8 is a frequently used approach and a decision involving difficult and important trade-offs is encountered. And it will matter if the events of interest involve managing the motivation of others which could be examined in terms of market models or other formal frameworks for considering competitive choices. Understanding how all the parties involved may behave, including market behaviour and other competitive responses, may be very important. Utility theory generally defined, agency theory, and game theory may all be relevant. But sensitivity to the importance of motivation for all relevant parties and common sense is the key.

The way forward

A recent paper (Chelst and Bodily, 2000) observes that the risk management literature (defining the term as used outside decision analysis) makes frequent references to the decision analysis literature, but not vice versa. They go on to suggest that risk analysis processes can greatly enrich decision analysis education, and make specific suggestions. Our view is that this is not the way forward, and in the longer term all the decision analysis books noted in this chapter, and all associated university courses, need to be rewritten from a perspective more like that presented in this chapter. They all start in the wrong place to some extent, some more than others. In the meantime they still provide a useful account of valuable journeys, but it is not just a quick fix to a conventional modern decision analysis framework that is needed. 'Practical' decision analysis as espoused here needs to be developed in a manner which is free of conventional modern textbook decision analysis baggage. In particular, it needs to link the decisions which are responses to sources of uncertainty to an understanding of that uncertainty, along the lines of the approaches discussed in Ian's tale (Chapter 5), among others. Modern textbook decision analysis based on expected utility largely replaced classical decision analysis based on Knight's (1921) decisions under 'risk' and 'uncertainty' distinctions over the last half of the 1900s (for a clarification of the reasons see Tess's textbook). Some pockets of resistance continue to defend classical decision analysis, and it may take a similar period to even partially replace modern decision analysis with practical decision analysis, because MAUT enthusiasts are unlikely to give up easily. However, this need not hold back those who understand the implications of a constructively simple perspective, whether or not they sympathize with the well-established campaign against expected utility (e.g. Tocher, 1977).

This chapter has not explicitly considered balanced scorecard approaches. In contexts more complex than that faced by Stan and Tess, it may be very useful to see these approaches as a form of MAVT, and apply an extension of the thinking discussed here in conjunction with ideas outlined at the end of Chapter 8 and further ideas to come in Chapter 11. The frontiers of best practice will be about this kind of interface in our view. Standard MAVT and balanced scorecard approaches involve significant differences, but if MAVT is interpreted in general terms, a wide range of approaches are available, some of which approach multiple-attribute decision making from quite different angles. Goal programming (a variant of linear programming), for example, portrays multiple criteria or attributes as constraints, with shadow prices used to consider trade-offs, a very useful conceptual framework. And Chapters 5 and 6 approached MAVT in terms of quality, time and cost trade-offs somewhat differently.

This chapter should clarify how options as identified by the real options literature and discussed in Chapter 8 can be considered in a practical decision analysis framework, along with other forms of options. Dependence on an expected utility basis is part of the problem with real options used directly, but this is just the tip of the iceberg.

In summary, if examining discrete decision option choices is where you want to go, avoid starting with a conventional decision analysis framework, use real options concepts but not the models, along with other forms of options, and give MAUT a complete miss. Start with a practical (constructively simple) approach in the spirit outlined in this chapter, drawing on a range of compatible and complementary ideas as appropriate.

10 Sam's tale: Concepts and issues in portfolio management

The boldest measures are the safest.
Motto of the Chindits

Introduction

Portfolio management is concerned with allocating resources to a number of different possible contemporaneous uses. The term 'portfolio' is most commonly applied to a set of financial investments where the problem is to decide whether to hold or sell existing investments and how much money to invest in new additions to the portfolio. However, portfolio management problems can take many other forms, such as: allocating resources to business units, research projects, or activities in a project; determining the size of product ranges; allocating marketing expenditure to different products; selection of personal skills and knowledge required to build a career; personal time management; and so on.

Portfolio management decisions usually involve significant uncertainty and associated risk and opportunity related to each alternative use of resources, and to limitations on the amount and type of resource that can be brought to bear. All available resources might be allocated to a single possible use, but this is not always the best course of action, or even practicable. As with most decision choices, trade-offs have to be made between potential benefits and potential costs. In terms of risk and opportunity management, a key issue is understanding the correlation of uncertainty associated with each alternative use of resources, because this is an important driver of the overall level of risk and opportunity. Portfolio analysis intended to assist effective management must address this correlation, along with all other relevant issues.

Most other chapters in this book draw on portfolio analysis ideas, even if portfolio analysis is not involved directly. For example, Chapters 3 to 6 view the way uncertainty is aggregated across project activities, and the way it is managed for the project as a whole, in portfolio analysis terms. Chapter 11 considers strategic planning for an electric utility, investment in alternative forms of generating capacity (hydro, nuclear, gas, oil, etc.) requiring a portfolio perspective. To explore the concepts and issues involved in portfolio analysis, this chapter focuses on a common stocks portfolio context. However, the reader needs no special interest in this particular application area to find most of the ideas relevant to other kinds of portfolio.

Stocks and shares make a useful starting context because they make the analysis comparatively simple. As a working assumption to begin with, we assume investing in securities is purely for short-term financial gain, relatively simply defined in terms of security market prices and dividends. An obvious focus of attention is the uncertainty about future security prices and dividends, but the reader may be surprised at the extent to which other sources of uncertainty require and receive attention in this chapter. What may also come as a surprise is the extent of the complexity which needs to be addressed, even in this comparatively simple context for portfolio analysis.

As with previous chapters, a key concern is to keep the whole of the discussion simple without losing sight of important complexities which cannot be ignored. A key device employed to achieve this is separability. Separability is a concept of direct operational importance as well. Its uses are not restricted to portfolio analysis. It is a core concept for analysis in general. It is the basis of decomposing a complex whole into parts, whose joint operation defines how the system as a whole works. Assuming that designated parts operate independently of one another is a very strong and rather obvious special case. Separability which does not involve independence is the focus of this chapter. A thorough and deep technical treatment is not attempted, but key insights associated with sophisticated forms of separability are provided, and the technically inclined can use this chapter as a starting point for further reading.

Statistical dependence is a related but quite different core concept explored in this chapter. Understanding uncertainty in any context demands an understanding of the implications of statistical dependence. As with separability, a thorough and deep technical treatment of statistical dependence is not attempted here, but key insights associated with basic forms of dependence are provided, and the technically inclined can use this chapter as a starting point for further reading.

The previous chapter provided a practical (constructively simple) decision analysis framework for discrete choices which incorporates a generalization of perspectives drawn from portfolio theory and risk management broadly defined. This chapter embeds a decision analysis and broadly defined risk management perspective into a portfolio analysis framework, integrating decision analysis and portfolio theory from the other direction. Portfolio analysis and decision analysis involve quite different starting positions, but they should not be regarded as independent frameworks, and they both have important links with project risk management and other forms of risk management.

Sam's Assignment

Sam liked to think of himself as something of a creative thinker interested in new ideas, and willing to reflect critically on established ways of doing things. It was perhaps these traits that had led him to choose, from several attractive offers, a job in new product development with a rapidly growing information systems firm, International Business Systems (IBS). Following a first degree in management science and finance, Sam had joined a firm of accountants to begin training as a chartered accountant. However, a year after completing his training, Sam had decided accountancy was not for him, and he had taken a one year MSc course in information systems, graduating in 2000. Sam had enjoyed the wide-ranging course and, exploiting previous job contacts, had undertaken his MSc project on the management of uncertainty in control systems.

Sam reported to Naomi, the 'new products' director of IBS, based in London. Naomi's background was computer science, with extensive experience as a systems designer and project manager. She had a good grasp of what marketing was about, a key aspect of her current position. IBS specialized in operations management systems for retail and manufacturing organizations, and to date Naomi's new products development experience had been based on production planning and inventory control systems. She had made her reputation by seeing market opportunities in terms of new approaches to systems which a client would fund development of to meet their needs. Such development work provided only modest returns for IBS, but the expertise developed could then be resold in other variants to other clients at premium profit rates.

Following Sam's induction into IBS, Naomi explained to Sam that she was looking for a way into the financial services sector, and security portfolio management in particular. Her partner was a well-established stock broker, and her brother was IT director for a stockbroking firm, so she had informal access to security industry knowledge and contacts. However, she was well aware of the difficulties associated with taking her firm into any new market, and the particularly serious barriers to entry in this market. Naomi explained she was looking for ideas which would allow her to position the role of the new systems IBS would build alongside the wide range of approaches to security holding and trading various firms adopted, adding value without necessarily altering or replacing any existing information systems or their functions. She was keen to accommodate the growing activities of financial engineers and sophisticated finance theory driven approaches, and the concerns associated with risks generated by systems built on these approaches, rogue traders, and developments in corporate governance. Ensuring another Barings couldn't happen to your organization was the opening sales pitch Naomi had in mind, later extended to include the Allied Irish Bank incident in 2002.

In view of Sam's educational background at both undergraduate and postgraduate level, Naomi thought Sam might have some ideas which could act as a catalyst. In fact, this had been one of the reasons why Naomi had recruited Sam. Naomi asked Sam to prepare a presentation which would brief her on the relevant general issues with suggestions for areas of potential development. So began several very intense weeks of work for Sam, developing ideas based on the basics of portfolio theory and a concern for constructive simplicity. The sections that follow describe the presentation Sam prepared for Naomi.

A Basic Markowitz Mean–Variance Model

Sam began by explaining that he proposed to start his exploration with a simple two-security portfolio, using a basic Markowitz (1959) mean–variance model to define the portfolio selection problem. This would enable them to focus on the basic issues in portfolio investment decisions, before considering an associated information system that would aid decision making and management control. For convenient future reference, Sam presented Naomi with Table 10.1 which set out a basic Markowitz model. The assumptions were designed to keep the discussion as simple as possible, and all were amenable to later relaxation.

Sam then asked Naomi to imagine that she was responsible for a portfolio of two securities. Naomi's portfolio selection problem is to determine the amounts X_1 and X_2 to invest in securities 1 and 2 respectively, which maximise $E - kV^2$ for a given total investment X. As indicated in Table 10.1, k is a behavioural constant, varying between 0 and ∞, defining the investor's preferred trade-off rate between expected return E and variance V^2. That is, E is one criterion, to be maximized, and V^2 is a second criterion, to be minimized. E is a direct measure of a value of interest. E is Naomi's best estimate of what should happen on average. If Naomi maximizes E, on average she will maximize A, actual returns. V^2 is a surrogate for downside risk (like the unemployment rate is a surrogate for unemployment). It is not a direct measure of downside risk. Given the assumption that A_1 and A_2 are Normally distributed, for a given value of E, the bigger V^2 is, the greater the risk, where risk is associated with the chance of returns less than that expected.

Knowing that Naomi might be familiar with the Normal probability distribution, but she might not, Sam pointed out that for the present she really needed only four ideas:

- The Normal distribution is a two-parameter distribution, defined by its expected value and its variance, its standard deviation being the square root of the variance. Assuming future returns are Normally distributed means that uncertainty about returns can be fully described by the mean and variance of B_s and B.

Table 10.1—A basic two-security model

The decision problem is to select a suitable combination of two common stocks to purchase now and hold for one year. Holdings involving fractions of a share are not a problem. Transaction costs and taxes are not an issue.

For **two securities**, $s = 1$ and 2, define the following terms:

B_s = the currently uncertain value at the planning horizon of £1 invested now in security s, including dividend payments reinvested at a standard rate of return. The B_s are assumed to be Normally distributed

E_s = the current estimated expected value of B_s

V_s = the current estimated standard deviation of B_s

X_s = the amount to be invested now in security s, the key decision variable

R_{12} = the coefficient of correlation between security 1 and security 2. R_{12} is the sum over all possible combinations of B_1 and B_2 of $(B_1 - E_1)(B_2 - E_2)/V_1 V_2$, and $R_{12} = R_{21}$

A_s = the actual value at the planning horizon of £1 invested now in security s, including dividend payments reinvested at a standard rate of return

For the **portfolio** of securities 1 and 2 define the following terms:

X = the amount invested now in the portfolio, given by

$$X = X_1 + X_2 \qquad [10.1]$$

B = the currently uncertain value at the planning horizon of £1 invested now in the portfolio, given by

$$B = (B_1 X_1 + B_2 X_2) / X \qquad [10.2]$$

E = the current estimated expected value of B, given by

$$E = (E_1 X_1 + E_2 X_2) / X \qquad [10.3]$$

V^2 = the current estimated variance of B, given by

$$V^2 = (V_1^2 X_1^2 + V_2^2 X_2^2 + 2R_{12} V_1 V_2 X_1 X_2) / X^2 \qquad [10.4]$$

A = the actual value at the planning horizon of £1 invested now in the portfolio, given by

$$A = (A_1 X_1 + A_2 X_2) / X \qquad [10.5]$$

If B_1 and B_2 are Normally distributed, B is also Normally distributed, that distribution being completely defined by E and V^2.

The portfolio selection problem is to determine the values of X_1 and X_2 which maximize $E - kV^2$ for a given value of X where k is a predetermined behavioural constant defining the decision maker's preferred trade-off between E and V^2, $0 < k < \infty$.

- The Normal distribution is a symmetric distribution, with a bell shape in its density form, a tilted S shape in its cumulative form.
- The cumulative form of the Normal distribution shows a 67% chance of values within one standard deviation of the mean, a 95% chance of values within two standard deviations of the mean, a 99% chance of values within three standard

deviations of the mean. This is a useful rule of thumb for interpreting the standard deviation (or variance).
- The central limit theorem shows that if a reasonably large sum of independently distributed random effects determine the size of a variable of interest, that variable can safely be assumed to be Normally distributed. This provides a rationale for assuming Normality. The key to the operation of the central limit theorem is the independence of the effects driving the variability of interest. Applying this theorem to Normality for the B_s is dubious.

In a similar spirit, Sam reminded Naomi that the coefficient of correlation R_{12} was an important parameter in the definition of portfolio variance V^2. R_{12} defines the level of correlation between security 1 and security 2. R_{12} can take any value between -1 and $+1$:

- $R_{12} = 0$ would imply statistical independence; knowing B_1 would tell her nothing about B_2, and vice versa.
- $R_{12} = 1$ would imply perfect positive correlation; knowing B_1 would determine B_2 exactly as they always move up and down together in a known relationship.
- $R_{12} = -1$ would imply perfect negative correlation; knowing B_1 would imply knowing B_2 exactly as they always move in opposite directions according to a known relationship.
- $R_{12} = 0.5$ reflects a midway position between $R_{12} = 0$ and 1, representative of typical relationships for securities associated with quite different sectors.

Sam explained that an $R_{12} = 0.5$ assumption could be interpreted in terms of some variability which relates to the stock market as a whole (perfectly positively dependent or $R_{12} = 1$ effects), and some variability associated with B_1 and B_2 which relates to the specifics of these individual firms and their market sectors (independent or $R_{12} = 0$ effects). To illustrate what the basic Markowitz model implies, Sam defined two example securities:

- Security 1 is a high-performance common stock, of a progressive high-technology company for example, with $E_1 = 1.25$ and $V_1 = 0.4$.
- Security 2 is a moderate-performance common stock, of a national retailer for example, with $E_2 = 1.15$ and $V_2 = 0.2$.

In addition, he assumed $R_{12} = 0.5$ and $X = X_1 + X_2 = 100$.

Relative to security 1, security 2 is a comparatively low-yield 'safe' security. Given the assumption that B_2 is Normally distributed, the range $E_2 \pm 3V_2 = 1.15 \pm 3 \times 0.2$, 0.55 to 1.75, should capture the realized value A_2 99% of the time, while the corresponding 99% confidence band for A_1 is wider, and given by $E_1 \pm 3V_1 = 1.25 \pm 3 \times 0.4$, 0.05 to 2.45. Using these parameter values, Sam presented Naomi with two tables and associated graphs showing the effect of varying X_1 and X_2 with

Table 10.2—Two-security illustration showing the expected value and variance for different mixes of two securities

X_1	E	$X_1^2 V_1^2$	$X_2^2 V_2^2$	$2R_{12}X_1X_2V_1V_2$	V^2	V
100	1.25	0.1600	0	0	0.1600	0.400
90	1.24	0.1296	0.0004	0.0072	0.1372	0.370
80	1.23	0.1024	0.0016	0.0128	0.1168	0.342
70	1.22	0.0784	0.0036	0.0168	0.0988	0.314
60	1.21	0.0576	0.0064	0.0192	0.0832	0.288
50	1.20	0.0400	0.0100	0.0200	0.0700	0.265
40	1.19	0.0256	0.0144	0.0192	0.0592	0.243
30	1.18	0.0144	0.0196	0.0168	0.0508	0.225
20	1.17	0.0064	0.0256	0.0128	0.0448	0.212
10	1.16	0.0016	0.0324	0.0072	0.0412	0.203
0	1.15	0	0.0400	0	0.0400	0.200

$E_1 = 1.25$ $V_1^2 = 0.16$ $V_1 = 0.4$ $R_{12} = 0.5$ $X_2 = 100 - X_1$
$E_2 = 1.15$ $V_2^2 = 0.04$ $V_2 = 0.2$

X set at 100, so that values for X_1 and X_2 could be read as percentages of the total portfolio.

Sam spent some time explaining these tables and figures to Naomi, to make sure she understood what they implied. Sam started with Table 10.2, which tabulates the computation of E and V at £10 intervals for $X_1 = 100$ to 0, showing the components of V^2. He pointed out that $X_1 = 100$ is clearly the highest E (and V) portfolio, which makes it a good place to start. E and V are simply E_1 and V_1. $X_1 = 0$ is clearly the lowest V (and E) portfolio, when V and E are simply V_2 and E_2. Intermediate portfolios involve a linear combination of E_1 and E_2 to define E. Intermediate portfolios involve a non-linear scaling of V_1 and V_2, incorporating a covariance term $2R_{12}X_1X_2V_1V_2$ which is a maximum when $X_1 = X_2 = 50$.

Sam then considered Table 10.3, which shows the sensitivity of the Table 10.2 calculations to the R_{12} assumption. He indicated that the coefficient of correlation between returns on the two securities R_{12} is the key to understanding the diversification effect of a lack of perfect positive correlation, and this diversification effect is a key concept associated with portfolio analysis. The $R_{12} = 0.5$ column simply replicates the final column of Table 10.2, the other columns scaling and in some cases changing the sign of the effect of the $2R_{12}X_1X_2V_1V_2$ column of Table 10.2. When $R_{12} = 1$, equation [10.4] simplifies to

$$V = (V_1X_1 + V_2X_2)/X \qquad [10.6]$$

and V is simply a linear combination of V_1 and V_2, corresponding to a zero diversification effect. By way of comparison, $R_{12} = 0.5$ involves a partial diversification effect which means that V decreases more rapidly as X_1 decreases from 100 to 90, this initial decline in V slowing as X_1 approaches 0. $R_{12} = 0$ increases this

Table 10.3—Two-security illustration showing sensitivity of portfolio
standard deviation V for different levels of correlation R_{12}

	Portfolio standard deviation V, given $R_{12} =$				
X_1	1.000	0.500	0.000	−0.500	−1.000
100	0.400	0.400	0.400	0.400	0.400
90	0.380	0.370	0.361	0.350	0.340
80	0.360	0.342	0.322	0.302	0.280
70	0.340	0.314	0.286	0.255	0.220
60	0.320	0.288	0.253	0.212	0.160
50	0.300	0.265	0.224	0.173	0.100
40	0.280	0.243	0.200	0.144	0.040
30	0.260	0.225	0.184	**0.131**	**0.020**
20	0.240	0.212	**0.179**	0.139	0.080
10	0.220	0.203	0.184	0.164	0.140
0	**0.200**	**0.200**	0.200	0.200	0.200

$X_2 = 100 - X_1$. Italics indicate the base case from Table 10.1; values in
bold indicate a minimum V; boxed values indicate inefficient choices.

diversification effect, to the extent that a minimum value for V involves $X_1 = 20$
and $X_2 = 80$. This implies that the proportions (10,90) and (0,100) of X_1 and X_2 are
risk-inefficient (variance-inefficient) choices. They involve less E and more V than
$X_1 = 20$ and $X_2 = 80$. No rational decision maker should choose these proportions
of X_1 and X_2. Sam explained that the pursuit of risk efficiency is a fundamental
aspect of effective uncertainty management, and a key consideration in portfolio
decisions. Sam pointed out that $R_{12} = -0.5$ further increases the diversification
effect. The portfolio $X_1 = 30$ and $X_2 = 70$ now provides the minimum V solution.
The set of risk-inefficient portfolios includes those with $X_1 = 20$ as well as $X_1 = 10$
and $X_1 = 0$. Interpolating by inspection, the minimum V portfolio is obtained by
selecting X_1 between 30 and 40. $R_{12} = -1$ increases the diversification effect
further. By inspection the minimum V portfolio is obtained with X_1 between 30
and 40 (when $V = 0$ can be achieved, the perfect hedge).

Sam then considered Figure 10.1, which plots the key relationships portrayed
by Table 10.3. He indicated that the diversification effect associated with $R_{12} = 0.5$
relative to $R_{12} = 1$ is now clearly visible. It involves a steeper decline in V as X_1
decreases from 100 to 90, this faster initial decline slowing as X_1 approaches zero.
Over the range $X_1 = 100$ to 50 the $R_{12} = 1$ and $R_{12} = 0.5$ lines spread out at a near
linear rate as X_1 is decreased. Only in the range $X_1 = 20$ to 0 does the $R_{12} = 0.5$ curve
flatten to a marked extent. The $R_{12} = 0$ curve shows clearly the increased diversification effect for all values of X_1, with X_1 in the range 100 to 50 involving a near

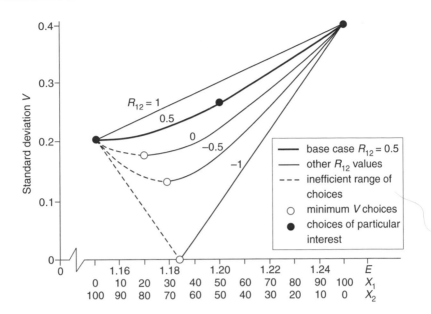

Figure 10.1—Standard deviations (V) for different correlation coefficients (R_{12}) and different proportions (X_1 and X_2).

linear divergence relative to the $R_{12} = 1$ line. The risk inefficiency of portfolios with X_1 in the range 20 to 0 is also clear. The $R_{12} = -0.5$ curve in Figure 10.1 shows clearly the further increased diversification effect. The risk inefficiency of portfolios with X_1 in a wider range is now clear. A flat curve in the narrower range $X_1 = 55$ to 25 is also clear. So is a near linear divergence relative to the $R_{12} = 1$ line in the range $X_1 = 100$ to 50. The $R_{12} = -1$ line shows clearly the maximum feasible increase in the diversification effect. The risk inefficiency of portfolios for a still wider range of X_1 values is now clear. Also clear is the lack of a flat region – the perfect hedge, with $V = 0$, requires precise definition. The divergence relative to the $R_{12} = 1$ line increases linearly with X_1 over the range $X_1 = 100$ to 33.

Sam explained to Naomi that the R_{12} sensitivity analysis of Table 10.3 and Figure 10.1 clarified the importance of diversification as R_{12} ranges from 1 to -1. In the range $R_{12} = 1$ to 0.5, a diversification strategy may buy relatively little overall risk (V^2) reduction for the quite large reductions in E which may be required. In the range $R_{12} = 0.5$ to -0.5, a diversification strategy may buy significant risk reduction for a modest reduction in E. In the range $R_{12} = -0.5$ to -1, a diversification strategy may buy substantial overall risk reduction for a comparatively small reduction in E. Sam indicated that an understanding of these differential effects was crucial to understanding his later ideas, and uncertainty management more generally.

In Figure 10.1 the assumed base case V curve with $R_{12} = 0.5$ is also useful to show how the optimal portfolio in terms of maximizing $E - kV^2$ varies with different choices for k. If k is approaching zero, the optimal portfolio is $X_1 = 100$, $X_2 = 0$. If k is approaching infinity, the optimal portfolio is $X_1 = 0$, $X_2 = 100$. A range of k values in between would yield intermediate solutions. However, Figure 10.1 is not a convenient operational framework for making portfolio choices, with or without the R_{12} sensitivity analysis. Sam indicated that a better way of selecting a preferred portfolio from a number of choices is to compare cumulative probability distributions for each possible choice as advocated in previous chapters. To illustrate this, Sam showed Naomi Figure 10.2, which portrays the cumulative probability distribution of B, the value at the planning horizon of the example two-security portfolio, for three possible portfolios given by $X_1 = 0$, 50 and 100 (and $X_2 = 100 - X_1$). In Figure 10.2 the $X_1 = 50$ curve might be interpreted as a nominal base case choice, with the other two curves bounding the set of all choices between $X_1 = 100$ and 0, as well as providing ±50 bounds for the nominal base case choice. Sam suggested that Naomi might use Figure 10.2 to address the question, Do I prefer a portfolio with X_1 in the range 100 to 50, or X_1 in the range 50 to 0? If she prefers X_1 in the range 100 to 50 (a reasonable surmise, because by $X_1 = 50$ most of the downside variability is eliminated) then the $X_1 = 0$ curve can be dropped and replaced by a new nominal choice base case of $X_1 = 75$. A similar question can then be addressed, Do I prefer X_1 in the range 100 to 75, or in the range 75 to 50? In this way, simple consecutive choices can lead to decisions with whatever degree of precision is appropriate. Keeping such diagrams and associated choices simple is of practical importance.

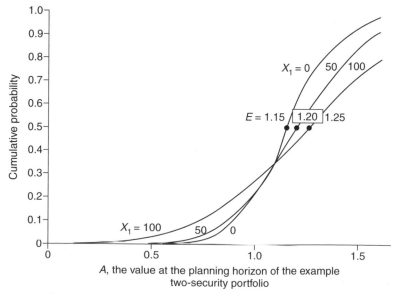

Figure 10.2—Cumulative probability distributions for the three alternative portfolios.

Extending The Basic Markowitz Model

When Naomi was comfortable with the implications of Tables 10.1 and 10.2 plus Figures 10.1 and 10.2, Sam briefly outlined several ways the basic Markowitz model could be extended. Sam first explained that generalizing to three or more securities involved defining X_s, B_s, E_s, V_s and B_s as in Table 10.1, but with $s = 1, \ldots, S$. In addition, define R_{s1s2} to be the coefficient of correlation between security $s1$ and security $s2$, with $s1$ and $s2 = 1, \ldots, S$, $s1 \neq s2$. For S securities there will be $S(S-1)/2$ correlation coefficients. Then for the portfolio X, B, E, V^2 and A are given by

$$X = \sum_{s=1}^{S} X_s \qquad\qquad [10.7]$$

$$B = \sum_{s=1}^{S} B_s X_s \qquad\qquad [10.8]$$

$$E = \sum_{s=1}^{S} E_s X_s \qquad\qquad [10.9]$$

$$V^2 = \left(\sum_{s=1}^{S} V_s^2 X_s^2 + \sum_{s1,s2}^{S} R_{s1s2} V_{s1} V_{s2} X_{s1} X_{s2} \right) / X^2 \qquad\qquad [10.10]$$

$$A = \sum_{s=1}^{S} A_s X_s / X \qquad\qquad [10.11]$$

If $R_{s1s2} = 0$, it is easy to show from equation [10.10] that the larger S becomes, the smaller V becomes. That is, if returns on each security are independent, the effect of diversification with $S > 2$ is extremely significant. This is the key to the pricing of retail insurance premiums. The effect of $S > 2$ is unimportant if $R_{12} = 1$ or -1, while intermediate values of R_{s1s2} have intermediate implications.

The portfolio selection problem with S securities involves determining the values of X_s which maximize $E - kV^2$ for a given value of X and a specified value for k as for the simpler two-security case. This is a quadratic programming problem: a quadratic objective function to be maximized (or minimized) subject to linear constraints. Quadratic programming was developed to provide solutions to this Markowitz model (Hadley, 1964). Quadratic programming algorithms are comparable to linear programming algorithms in terms of efficiency, unlike most non-linear problems. Quite large problems in terms of the size of S are tractable, with reasonable solution times. As a consequence, it was widely assumed when quadratic programming algorithms were developed that everyone would use them directly to manage their security portfolios. This would be done by first estimating all the E_s, V_s^2 and R_{s1s2} values, then using a quadratic programming algorithm to identify the values for the X_s that maximize $E - kV^2$ for a set of assumed values for k.

Given the assumption of Normal distributions for all B_s, and hence for B, the distribution of B for each feasible portfolio (selection of X_s values) can be described by the corresponding values for E and V (or V^2). In Figure 10.3 the shaded area represents the set of all feasible portfolios. Maximizing $E - kV^2$ for a specified value of k identifies an optimal portfolio (selection of X_s values) which is risk efficient (lying on the boundary of the feasible solution area as shown in Figure 10.3). Different points on the risk-efficient boundary correspond to optimal portfolios for different values of k.

The risk-efficient boundary of Figure 10.3 is a generalization of the risk-efficient X_1 and X_2 combinations identified in Figure 10.1. Each E value on the curves of Figure 10.1 can be associated with a unique combination of X_1 and X_2 values, some of which are efficient. For a given E value, a point on the risk-efficient boundary of Figure 10.3 is associated with a unique set of values for $X_1, \ldots, X_S$ which minimizes V^2 (and V). Other points in the shaded feasible solution area above that E value are risk-inefficient portfolios comparable to the inefficient combinations identified in Figure 10.1. Each point or portfolio on the risk-efficient boundary could be presented to Naomi in cumulative probability distribution form, with two or three curves overlaid on the same graph to facilitate comparisons between alternative portfolios, as illustrated in Figure 10.2. This formulation and portrayal remains a very important conceptual model, usefully understood as a direct generalization of the $S = 2$ special case. However, direct use of quadratic programming to make real-time investment selection decisions in this framework

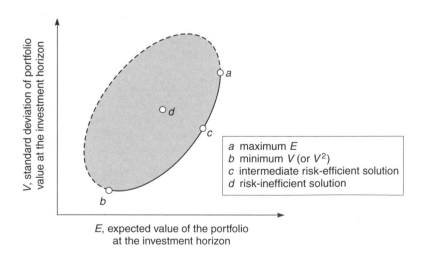

a maximum E
b minimum V (or V^2)
c intermediate risk-efficient solution
d risk-inefficient solution

V, standard deviation of portfolio value at the investment horizon

E, expected value of the portfolio at the investment horizon

Figure 10.3—Risk-efficient boundary diagram.

is not widespread. Some successful applications have been claimed, but real-time security selection is not generally amenable to effective direct use of this model. Some of the reasons for this will become clear in the next section.

Varying the size of the portfolio

Sam indicated that most finance texts make use of one 'zero-risk' security, usually taken to be a government bond, for a number of purposes, one being to allow the inclusion of a zero-risk portfolio in the risk-efficient set. Sam explained that it was useful to consider this possibility here for reasons which will become clear later. Assume security S is the risk-free security, as a simple convention. The immediate impact is that Figure 10.3 can be redrawn with the feasible solution space extended downwards so that the minimum risk point b lies on the E axis. Sam indicated that it is also sometimes convenient to allow X to vary, to allow borrowing of additional funds to invest with an associated average cost of capital C per pound. In general, C gets bigger as X increases. Borrowing in itself can be assumed to be risk free for the borrower, but borrowing does involve gearing up risk for the borrower in terms of the investment consequences. The portfolio decision problem now becomes: identify the values of X_s and X which maximize $E - C - kV^2$, where C is defined in terms of a curve like that of Figure 10.4.

Figure 10.4 illustrates the piecewise linear increasing incremental rate approach often used in conjunction with linear and quadratic programming models. This is a conceptually and operationally convenient form. The L_1 ... and C_1 ... values

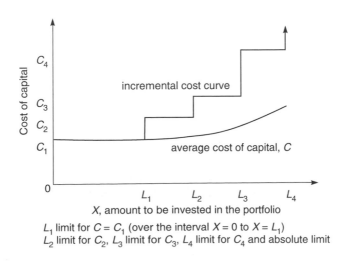

L_1 limit for $C = C_1$ (over the interval $X = 0$ to $X = L_1$)
L_2 limit for C_2, L_3 limit for C_3, L_4 limit for C_4 and absolute limit

Figure 10.4—Average cost of capital relationship with portfolio size.

can represent alternative sources of finance, or simply a computational device to approximate a non-linear function defined in any appropriate manner. The L_1 ... values can be used as discrete alternative X values to be tested in order to select the most appropriate X in terms of associated E and V^2 values, comparing choices in the Figure 10.2 format. The selected value of X, and its associated C, has behavioural implications akin to k and related to k. However, if Naomi selects her preferred portfolio given $X = L_1$, then her preferred portfolio given $X = L_2$ and $X = L_3$, she can choose between the three portfolios using a Figure 10.2 format without considering k directly. She will then need to refine her choice of X to a suitable degree using the same approach applied to the Figure 10.2 format earlier. The reason this extension is important will become clear. Its immediate impact is that Figure 10.3 might be redrawn with the E axis replaced by $(E - C)$ for assumed values of X and C, shifting the feasible solution space to the left.

Sam's Basic System

Sam was now in a position to outline his ideas for a basic securities information and control system. Mindful of Naomi's commercial agenda, Sam indicated that the acronym SINCOS (securities information and control system) might be a useful working name for the system he was proposing.

Sam indicated that security market conditions are clearly the source of part of the risk associated with managing an organization which invested on a large scale in the securities market. However, much of the risk for the investing organization lies in the systems for distinguishing between risk and opportunity, motivating staff, selecting/deselecting and training staff, ensuring effective communication, and providing sound control without distorting behaviour. SINCOS was concerned with all these sources of risk. Working alongside existing systems, SINCOS was designed to enhance opportunity management, motivation, communication and control. To achieve this, the basic system needed to extract a minimal amount of additional information from all levels of this management structure. Most of this additional information was implicit in existing systems, and some of it was explicit in existing systems, but it was usually not captured, analysed and integrated in the way he proposed. Sam suggested to Naomi that she should imagine she was the managing director of her target first client, the organization that would help to fund the first version of her new securities information and control system. In this imagined role, Naomi is not going to make individual investment decisions herself. She will manage a group of directors, each of whom manages a group of managers, who in turn manage a group of traders that make the minute-to-minute security buy and sell decisions.

Some working assumptions

Sam indicated that a number of working assumptions would be useful to simplify the introductory description of his system for Naomi. Naomi would also wish to use these assumptions when explaining SINCOS to her target organization. Relaxing them is addressed later. Here are some of these working assumptions:

- Only simple 'purchase to hold' decisions in respect of common stocks are involved, and transaction costs and taxes are not an issue.
- Each trader manages a portfolio of securities which does not overlap with the portfolios of other traders. Traders are empowered with a maximum level of autonomy within their security sector.
- Each manager manages a group of traders (a portfolio) which does not overlap with the portfolios of other managers. Managers are empowered with a maximum level of autonomy within their security and personnel management sectors.
- Each director manages a group of managers, a portfolio; each portfolio does not overlap with the other portfolios. Directors are empowered with a maximum level of autonomy within their security and personnel management sectors.
- The managing director (Naomi) manages the directors. She also manages the support staff, who provide corporate support for personnel selection/ deselection and training, security market intelligence, computer information systems support, and so on.
- There are D directors designated $d = 1, ..., D$, M_d managers under director d, designated $m = 1, ..., M_d$, and T_m traders under manager m, designated $t = 1 ... T_m$. Each trader t is responsible for trading in S_t securities, designated $s = 1, ..., S_t$. This means each individual security can be associated with and identified by s, t, m and d indices. However, the strong autonomy empowerment assumption means we can work separately with one index at a time. This simplifies matters greatly.

Sam indicated that other working assumptions would be made as he proceeded, which would also require revisiting later. The following sections outline the ideas Sam put to Naomi.

Phase 1: the traders' system

The idea of the system at this level is to encourage traders to act in their own best interests in a manner which means they act in the best interests of the organization as a whole, giving them the feedback and the financial incentive they need to do this, while capturing the information needed higher up the management structure for both control and higher-level strategy.

A key piece of information needed for SINCOS was E_s for each security (as defined in Table 10.1). When a trader makes a buy on security s, the expected return or spread over a relevant planning horizon that the trader had in mind when making a buy is not usually recorded. Sam's system would require the capture of this information as part of each buy transaction. To make this as easy as possible for the traders, a nominal planning horizon used as a default horizon, and simple percentage return choices over the default horizon, with a nominal return used as a default option, would be employed for most transactions. All the traders forming a manager's group would be encouraged to work within a limited set of standardized alternatives as far as possible. It would be up to each manager and his group of traders to select planning horizons and return scales suitable to their needs, with a range of alternatives they were comfortable with. For example, one group of traders and their manager might agree that most buys involved a nominal planning horizon of 1 day, but it might be useful on occasion to be able to specify any horizon, covering for example just part of a day or several days. This group might also agree that when one day was the nominal planning horizon, about 0.5% was the usual expected spread, on a five-point scale specified as follows: point 1 is 0.25; point 2 is 0.50, the expected spread percentage; point 3 is 0.75; point 4 is 1.00; and point 5 is 1.25. Similar five-point scales might be specified for 1 hour and 1 week nominal planning horizons. An absence of additional information after the trader initiated a buy on his or her terminal might indicate a default 1 day nominal horizon and a point 2 (0.50%) expected spread. If a trader was happy with a 1 day horizon for a particular buy, but had a point 4 (1%) increase in mind, he or she might keystroke 'p4' after the buy instruction. If a trader wanted to use a 1 day horizon but had a 0.1% increase in mind, he or she might keystroke 'p0, 0.1', the 'p0' designating point 0, indicating a free definition scale would be used, the 0.1 indicating percentage change to whatever precision is deemed appropriate, within or beyond the range covered by spread points 1 to 5. If a trader wanted a one hour or a one week horizon, 'h1' or 'h2' for alternative horizon 1 or 2 might be keyed in prior to 'p1-p5' for appropriate agreed points on scales defined for these horizons, or 'p0' for a free definition scale followed by a percentage increase. A completely free definition entry might be initiated by 'h0' horizon, zero indicating a completely free definition. A modest amount of prior discussion between each manager and his or her group of traders would allow them to select an appropriate near minimal effort way of capturing E_s information for all buys. Experience using this system would allow them to adjust it to make it become a minimal input effort way of capturing E_s values.

What return a trader actually achieves in relation to each sale, A_s, is not usually recorded in conjunction with the associated E_s for the period the security was held. SINCOS would require the capture of this information as part of each sell transaction. The system would then redefine these E_s, A_s couplets for the nominal horizon, to provide a standard basis for comparison. A first-in first-out inventory management assumption would be used in relation to units of each security in each trader's portfolio. For example, if a trader made security s buys of 1000 shares on Monday, 4000 on Tuesday, 10 000 on Wednesday, and sold 12 000 on Thursday and 3000 on Friday, this would produce E_s, A_s couplets for

1000	Monday–Thursday
4000	Tuesday–Thursday
7000	Wednesday–Thursday
3000	Wednesday–Friday

all presented on a nominal 1 day horizon basis for easy comparison. These E_s, A_s couplets for each trader's sell transactions are a key source of information SINCOS would build on.

Performance feedback to traders

Feedback would initially start with a focus on designing feedback formats which the traders found useful, presenting them with alternatives to choose from and involving them in the design process. Structure for this feedback could be provided by V_s values, calculated from the growing database of previous E_s, A_s couplets. Defining $j = 1, \ldots, J_s$ as the relevant available data set of actual value E_s, A_s couplets, Sam reminded Naomi that V_s values would be defined by

$$V_s^2 = \sum_{j=1}^{J_s} (A_{js} - E_{js})^2 / J_s \qquad [10.12]$$

That is, V_s^2 is the mean (average) squared error, treating $A_{js} - E_{js}$ as an error in the sense that E_{js} was the prediction, A_{js} the corresponding actual value. If a Normal distribution is assumed for the observed A_{js} values, V_s provides a confidence bound structure as described earlier. For example, traders might get a report at the end of each day for their trading that day. The first part of the report might be about realized performance that day, based on sales. For each security sale by that trader on that day, this report might list (or plot on a scatter diagram) each E_{js}, A_{js} couplet generated that day, showing E_{js}, A_{js}, and the error $(A_{js} - E_{js})$. It might show the V_s values using all observations for that day, and separate V_s values using all relevant observations in a database which dates back to the start of this trader's sales on the system. The report might highlight, or list separately, all E_{js}, A_{js} couplets which are outside a 95% confidence bound generated by the V_s defined by all relevant data. In addition, it might show the total value of shares sold that day, the cost of buying these shares, and the rate of return. A second part of the report might be about the trader's portfolio position at the end of the day, based on purchases not yet sold. This might show, for each security in the trader's portfolio, X_s, E_s couplets on a 1 day forward basis, and notional associated A_s values assuming disposal at close-of-trading prices. It might also show associated summary measures for the S_t securities traded by trader t:

- The purchase value of the current portfolio:

$$X_t = \sum_{s=1}^{S_t} X_s \qquad [10.13]$$

- The valuation of the current portfolio per pound invested in the terms of close-of-trading prices that day:

$$A_t = \sum_{s=1}^{S_t} A_s X_s / X_t \qquad [10.14]$$

- The valuation of the current portfolio per pound invested in terms of prices expected on disposal:

$$E_t = \sum_{s=1}^{S_t} E_s X_s / X_t \qquad [10.15]$$

This part of the report might also use the V_s defined by all relevant data, and associated R_{s1s2}, to compute V_t, akin to V at the trader level for the Markowitz model defined in the previous section. And it might show comparative V_t values for previous days that week, an average for last week, an average for last month, and so on.

Decisions involving traders, their managers, and systems developers would initially focus on the value of this information to traders to help them manage their own portfolios. Discussion would then move on to generating information for communication from traders to managers. For example, each team might agree that it would be reasonable for traders to provide their managers at the end of each day with a brief note as to why values for a security s occurred beyond previously estimated 99% confidence bounds for A_s (in terms of actual sales or close-of-trading valuations). Such information might help managers to deal with their directors, the 99% bound level being negotiable. The system could identify the relevant cases and ask for information when the traders were ready and able to provide it, at the close of each day's trading for example, as part of the daily report. Additional aspects of control and motivation would then be addressed.

Trader remuneration and motivation

In practice a key risk is a financial motivation system for traders which does not encourage them to behave in the best interests of the organization. A key aspect of this is a failure to distinguish between good luck and good management, or bad luck and bad management. Sam explained that SINCOS would provide the basis for addressing this. It would allow an organization to tune its payment system to enhance rewards for good judgement and diminish rewards for general good luck.

Each trader would have a risk-free cash balance associated with security S_t, with an $E_{S_t} = A_{S_t}$ determined by the manager (a risk-free return option). Each trader would have a portfolio size X_t, an associated average cost per pound of capital C_t, determined by a relationship of the form in Figure 10.4, set by his or her manager. The basis for a trader's remuneration might be determined as a percentage of that trader's net profits realized from sales, a direct function of the $A_s X_s$ on disposal, net of $C_t X_t$.

One very important downward adjustment to this basis might be a direct function of $V_t X_t$: the larger a trader's error, the less his or her remuneration. At one level this might be designed to encourage unbiased estimation of the E_s. However, at a deeper level of understanding, its purpose might be to address a corporate concern for distinguishing between good luck and good judgement (or bad luck and bad judgement), through encouraging and rewarding good judgement by subtracting a surrogate function of good and bad luck.

Another very important downward adjustment to reflect the difference between good luck and good judgement (or bad luck and bad judgement) might be a direct function of AX, the actual return on the organization's portfolio as a whole. That is, when the market as a whole does *well*, every trader's remuneration might be *reduced* so a trader does not benefit from general good luck, just the extent to which he or she beats the market in terms of their achieved X_s, A_s values. Conversely, when the market as a whole does *badly*, every trader's remuneration might be *increased*, so that traders are not too exposed to general bad luck.

Providing short-term motivation to reduce corporate exposure in a trader's area might be managed by manipulating C_t or E_{S_t} upwards. Providing short-term motivation to increase corporate exposure in a trader's area might be managed by manipulating C_t or E_{S_t} downwards. The differential effect on a trader's income associated with C_t and E_{S_t} could be used to preserve 'fair' rewards and morale in the face of major shifts in position. Good performance might be motivated by a lower C_t or a higher E_{S_t} or a larger X_t or some combination of all three, in terms of a review cycle with intervals like once a month.

It would be naive to assume that the primary motivation of traders was anything other than maximizing their own incomes. However, they will perform at their best if the system they work within is seen to be fair, and more generally it maximizes the dignity of the individual as well as building on the positive aspects of teamworking. Rivalry and team spirit might be managed, for example, by publicized special bonus payments for realized returns outside the average upside confidence bounds defined by the group of T_m traders, 50% for the trader involved and 50% of the rest of the group, with private penalties for realized returns outside the average downside confidence bounds defined by the group, 100% incurred by the trader involved. This approach could be tuned to pay stars enough to stay, and ensure poor performers were encouraged to move elsewhere without any need to terminate individual trader contracts in most cases. Support staff involved in personnel and training as well as technical market support could be involved to improve trader judgement where possible. The ability to distinguish operationally between good luck and good judgement (or bad luck and bad judgement) could be treated as the key to minimizing risk associated with employing the poor traders and failing to provide effective training and support for all traders retained. Further, selection could be approached on a trial basis, with individual performance monitored even more closely than for established traders.

All these motivation issues are part of the broader issue of ensuring an information and control system that aligns the best interests of the organization with the best interests of the individuals within it, in addition to ensuring that appropriate controls are exercised. SINCOS is designed to allow this kind of tuning. Any system which lacks the key controls for such tuning will involve significant risk associated with conflicts of interest, in addition to those associated with inappropriate control mechanisms. For example, a trader who loses a lot of money may be encouraged to take a flyer on the grounds they might as well be hung for a sheep as a lamb. Serial behaviour of this kind which is not designed out or picked up quickly can be seriously damaging to an organization's health. Designing it out in so far as feasible, but monitoring it anyway, is the most effective response, and the rationale of SINCOS.

Risk efficiency in trader portfolios

Diversification is not an issue of importance for individual traders. In terms of Figure 10.1, we are in the $R_{s1s2} = 1$ to 0.5 range most of the time, and the level of exposure to market risk in corporate terms is limited. Risk efficiency is an issue, but effectively it is about maximizing E_s values, not trade-offs involving V_s. Quadratic programming is not used to select X_s, but the V_s and V_t are measured retrospectively. Support staff could use each trader's daily close-of-trading X_s, E_s, the V_s defined by all available data and associated R_{s1s2}, to test the risk efficiency of traders. That is, they could relate actual portfolio positions of trader t to maximizing $E_t - k_t V_t^2$ with k_t approaching zero. Feedback based on this, interpreted by support staff, could be treated as a learning process, as well as a way of moving a trader's portfolio towards an improved position the next day. If the Markowitz models were run overnight, this feedback could be provided before the start of trading the next day.

In summary, phase 1 of SINCOS introduction would start with the capture of these E_s, A_s couplets. As part of phase 1, traders and managers would be made comfortable with the system for E_s capture, and feedback about E_s, A_s couplets. In practice it would be useful to implement this first as a pilot with a carefully selected subset of the traders and managers, before going live with the rest of the traders and managers.

Phase 2 : the managers' system

A manager's job is more complex than a trader's job. It needs to be defined in terms of two primary tasks. The first is ensuring that all their traders are under control, and each trader is as close as possible to maximizing $E_t - k_t V_t^2$ with k_t approaching zero. To do this, a manager needs to review all their trader's feedback from the system on an exception basis, together with associated risk-efficiency advice from support staff. The second primary task for managers is treating their trader's X_t, $t = 1, \ldots, T_m$, as indirect primary decision variables in terms of the manager's portfolio problem which involves maximizing $E_m - k_m V_m^2$ where:

- A suitable measure of V_m^2 for managers, akin to V^2 in the Markowitz model of the last section, is taken to be a function defined in terms of V_t and R_{t1t2}.
- An appropriate trade-off rate for managers is k_m; assuming a limited interest in diversification at this level, k_m will be close to zero.
- The value of the manager's portfolio in terms of prices expected on disposal per pound invested is

$$E_m = \sum_{t=1}^{T_m} E_t X_t / X_m \qquad [10.16]$$

- The purchase value of the managers portfolio is

$$X_m = \sum_{t=1}^{T_m} X_t \qquad [10.17]$$

- The valuation of close of trading that day for the managers portfolio per pound involved is

$$A_m = \sum_{t=1}^{T_m} A_t X_t / X_m \qquad [10.18]$$

Overnight use of Markowitz models by support staff could allow managers to address their position in the above terms as part of a process of dialogue with their traders. In particular, where they form a view that a trader's position needs adjustment, in addition to providing advice, they can adjust their instruments of control: E_{S_t}, the zero risk rate of return on X_{S_t} for each trader; and C_t, the average cost of capital for each trader. Each manager would have to link these instruments of control to analogous instruments used by their director to control them.

Phase 2 might involve managers, directors and system designers working together with agendas at this level comparable to all those discussed in phase 1.

The initial focus might be reports useful to managers, moving on later to reports useful to directors, and remuneration definitions for managers which aligned their best interests with the organization's best interests. Extending the income definition approach for traders, a manager's remuneration might be a direct function of their traders $A_t X_t$, an inverse function of V_t, and an inverse function of A_m. However, a simpler and more direct way to capture the desired effects could be to make each manager's remuneration a direct function of their traders' incomes, weighted by the X_t. This makes it crystal clear that what benefits good traders benefits good managers, and vice versa, providing an incentive for discriminating teamwork.

Provided SINCOS is properly defined, manager jobs can be defined in terms of each manager maximizing their remuneration by maximizing the effectiveness of individual traders, and leveraging the most effective traders' activities while reducing the impact of the least effective traders, encouraging them to leave if it is a matter of bad judgement, within the rules defined by the system.

Phase 3: the directors' system

A director's job is more complex still. It needs to be defined in terms of three primary tasks: controlling managers, managing the director's portfolio, and taking a longer view of trading and diversification. The first task is to ensure that all their managers are under control, and that each manager is as close as possible to maximizing $E_m - k_m V_m^2$ with a k_m approaching zero. A second task is to treat the size of each of their manager's portfolios X_m, $m = 1, \ldots, M_d$, as indirect primary decision variables in terms of a portfolio problem associated with maximizing $E_d - k_d V_d^2$, where:

- A suitable measure of V_d^2 for directors, akin to V^2 in the Markowitz model of the last section, is taken to be a function defined in terms of V_m and R_{m1m2}
- An appropriate trade-off for directors is k_d, also assumed to be near zero for reasons noted earlier.
- The value of the director's portfolio in terms of prices expected on disposal per pound invested is

$$E_d = \sum_{m=1}^{M_d} E_m X_m / X_d \qquad [10.19]$$

- The purchase value of the director's portfolio is

$$X_d = \sum_{m=1}^{M_d} X_m \qquad [10.20]$$

- The valuation at close of day for the director's portfolio per pound invested is

$$A_d = \sum_{m=1}^{M_d} A_m X_m / X_d \qquad\qquad [10.21]$$

Both these primary tasks might attract comments and treatment analogous to those for the directly comparable managers' tasks. In this case a director's formal instruments of control with respect to managers are E_{T_m}, the zero risk rate of return on X_{T_m} for each manager; and C_m, the average percentage cost of capital charge for each manager. In a manner analogous to managers, directors would have a significant part of their remuneration defined as a direct function of their managers' remuneration. Analogous to managers' tasks, directors could see these two tasks in terms of maximizing the effectiveness of individual managers, and leveraging the most effective managers' activities while reducing the impact of the least effective, encouraging them to leave if it is a matter of bad judgement, within the rules defined by the system. This coincides with maximizing their own remuneration.

The third primary task for directors is to take a longer view of trading (say a week rather than a day), to take a wider view of the factors affecting the markets, and to take a careful look at diversification beyond that achieved by having a large set of directors, managers and traders. To start this process, computer software associated with SINCOS might produce E_{db} and V_{db} values, based on the one day E_d and V_d just defined, but transformed to reflect a week rather than a day. In the case of E_{db}, the 'b' stands for 'bottom-up', to indicate that it aggregates trader views. In the case of V_{db}, the 'b' stands for bottom-up and 'backward looking', to indicate it involves looking back at available relevant data on a bottom-up basis, aggregating observable trader errors in the sense defined earlier. Sam suggested that a key issue in SINCOS is adjusting these E_{db} and V_{db} estimates to reflect directors' forward views, explicitly defined to extend beyond the planning horizon of managers and traders. In principle, directors might define a single forward-looking adjustment factor F_d to be applied to both E_{db} and V_{db} values to arrive at forward-looking estimates of expected return and standard deviation, E_{df} and V_{df} respectively, given by

$$E_{df} = F_d E_{db} \qquad\qquad [10.22]$$

$$V_{df} = F_d V_{db} \qquad\qquad [10.23]$$

This adjustment embraces the bottom-up backward-looking estimation process plus forward-looking adjustments, an upside adjustment (possible opportunities not embodied in traders' E_s assessments or the associated V_s data) and a downside adjustment (possible threats not embodied in traders' E_s assessments or the associated V_s data). For a given securities sector d, this adjustment ought to incorporate an adjustment for uncertainty about whole-market price movements, as well as an adjustment for uncertainty about sector-specific price movements.

Estimating adjustment factors

Sam reminded Naomi that traders and their managers had to get together to design initially and then refine a set of simple scales and default options to minimize trader effort when capturing E_s values. Once that refinement took place, data capture would be very efficient. A similar issue was involved here in determining the F_d factors. Directors would have to get together with their managing director to design initially and subsequently refine a simple set of scales and default options to minimize director effort in determining F_d values. To capture both all-market uncertainty and sector-specific uncertainty, Sam suggested that the simplest framework for estimating the F_d factors would be a two-level probability tree structure like Figure 10.5. This portrays possible all-market adjustment factors F_i, $i = 1, \ldots, 3$, and sector-specific adjustment factors F_{ijd}, $j = 1, \ldots, 3$ and $d = 1, \ldots, D$, which scale the E_{db} and V_{db} values to reflect upside and downside scenarios not embodied in trader's E_s assessments or the associated

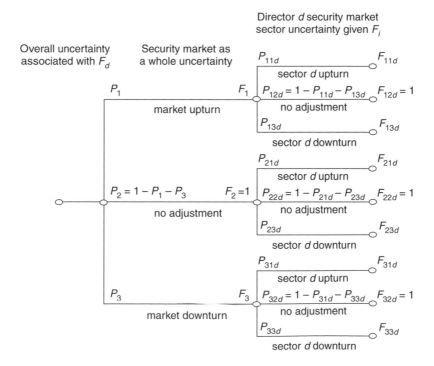

Figure 10.5—Simple forward-looking factor tree.

V_s data. The P_i, $i = 1, \ldots, 3$, and P_{ijd}, $j = 1, \ldots, 3$ and $d = 1, \ldots, D$, are forward-looking factor probabilities, to capture the likelihood of these upside and downside scenarios.

F_1 scales the implications of a significant growth in the return on all market securities, perhaps due to a significant upturn in global economics and politics and other general market factors, beyond what could be associated with E_{db} and V_{db}. For example, $F_1 = 1.2$ would be interpreted as a 20% increase in E_{db} and V_{db} if such a favourable scenario occurred, and $P_1 = 0.1$ would be interpreted as a 10% chance of such a shift over the next week. F_3 scales the implications of a significant downturn in the return on all securities, perhaps due to a significant downturn in global economics and politics and other general market factors, beyond what could be associated with E_{db} and V_{db}. For example, $F_3 = 0.6$ would be interpreted as a 40% decrease in E_{db} and V_{db} if such an unfavourable scenario occurred, and $P_3 = 0.1$ would be interpreted as a 10% chance of such a shift over the next week. F_2 is the middle ground or default case, corresponding to global economics and politics and other general market factors remaining as implicitly assumed (as they were) in E_{db} and V_{db}. $F_2 = 1$ by definition, and $P_2 = 1 - P_1 - P_3$ by definition, $P_2 = 1 - 0.1 - 0.1 = 0.8$ for our example.

The four general market shift degrees of freedom, the four instruments for portraying potential departures from E_{db} and V_{db} in terms of general market shifts, are F_1, P_1, F_3 and P_3. All the directors, including the managing director, need to agree these four market-level parameters. They will need support staff, and they may want to involve managers and traders. In a formal full-devolution context, the managing director might take responsibility for these four parameters. However, Sam suggested collective responsibility by all the directors. In a similar way, the 12 parameters for portraying potential departures from E_{db} and V_{db} in terms of shifts within each director's market sector are F_{11d}, P_{11d}, F_{13d}, P_{13d}, F_{21d}, P_{21d}, F_{23d}, P_{23d}, F_{31d}, P_{31d}, F_{33d}, and P_{33d}.

In Figure 10.5, $F_3 \times F_{33d}$ scales the implications of a significant decline in the return on all securities because of overall market factors, the F_3 scenario, plus a significant downturn in growth within the market sector d given the F_3 scenario, possibly due to the collapse of takeover activity, unfavourable dividend announcements, unfavourable regulatory decisions, and other market sector d factors. For example, $F_{33d} = 0.8$ would be interpreted as a 20% decrease in E_{db} and V_{db} beyond the F_3 effect if such an unfavourable scenario occurred, and $P_{33d} = 0.1$ would be interpreted as a 1% chance of such a shift over the next week. The example joint F_3F_{33d} factor is $0.6 \times 0.8 = 0.48$ and the associated joint probability P_1P_{11d} is $0.1 \times 0.1 = 0.01$.

Alternatively, $F_3 \times F_{31d}$ scales the implications of a significant decline in the return on all securities because of overall market factors, the F_3 scenario, but a significant upturn within the director d security market sector, possibly due to new takeover approaches, favourable dividend announcements, favourable regulation decisions, and other market sector d factors. An $F_{31d} = 1.1$ would be interpreted as a 10% increase in E_{db} and V_{db} if such a favourable scenario occurred, relative to and partially cancelling out the 40% decrease associated with $F_3 = 0.6$. In this case the joint $F_3 F_{31d}$ factor is $0.6 \times 1.1 = 0.66$ and the associated joint probability $P_3 P_{31d}$ is $0.1 \times 0.1 = 0.01$.

F_{32d} is the middle ground or default case in terms of F_3, corresponding to a downside general market but an unadjusted market sector d. Similar comments apply to $F_{21d}, F_{22d}, F_{23d}$ and $F_{11d}, F_{12d}, F_{13d}$.

Each of the directors needs to decide upon the 12 market sector parameters for their sector. They will need support staff, and they may want to involve traders and managers. In a formal full-devolution context, the directors could each take full responsibility for their 12 parameters. However, they might be wise to do so in the context of a weekly meeting with their managers, when managers offer advice drawing on their support staff and traders. Such a meeting might be the appropriate forum for directors to seek advice on the P_i and F_i as well as the P_{ijd} and F_{ijd}. Once the 4 market parameters and 12 sector parameters have been defined for sector d, then the adjustment factor for E_{db} and V_{db} is

$$F_d = \sum_i F_i P_i \sum_j F_{ijd} P_{ijd} \qquad [10.24]$$

It could be argued that conventions should be used to simplify estimation of these parameters. For example, all P_i and P_{ijd} might be set equal to 0.1 or 0.05. Should this prove an operational convenience, it is clearly allowable, but it would seem unwise to assume this in advance. On a weekly basis it might be preferable to have stable F_i and F_{ijd} with P_i and P_{ijd} that fluctuate; then F_i and F_{ijd} could be reappraised monthly, for example. An obvious simplification would be to assume that $P_2 = 1$ and $P_{22d} = 1$ for all d, so that all other P_i and $P_{ijd} = 0$, and $F_d = 1$. However, this would be equivalent to assuming that the foreseeable future will be 100% consistent with a backside look at available data. This is so naive as to render elegant Markowitz model optimization using E_d and V_d values akin to rearranging deckchairs on the Titanic.

An alternative approach to estimating the P and F parameters would be to adopt a minimalist approach (Chapter 4), recognizing that estimates of each P_i, F_i, P_{ijd} and F_{ijd} are themselves uncertain, particularly for the extreme scenarios of Figure 10.5. For example, individual directors might start with estimates like $P_3 = 0$ to 0.05, $P_{33d} = 0$ to 0.05, $F_3 = 0.2$ to 0.8, and $F_{33d} = 0.5$ to 0.9, assuming all these interval distribution specifications are uniform (constant probability over the interval) to reflect uncertainty about uncertainty in a simple and convenient form. Other sources of expertise might be tapped in a similar format. Support staff might then combine all these views, highlighting the extent to which there is uncertainty about the uncertainty about uncertainty, which can be reduced by dialogue and further analysis where it matters to the extent that it matters. The idea is to be explicit and clear in relation to uncertainty about uncertainty, because it is important in terms of determining where we need to spend more time thinking about uncertainty.

This approach need not be taken too far before it becomes important to understand where uncertainty is coming from, in terms of identifiable key sources, and to model these sources separately if appropriate. For example, it might be very useful to start with a list of key reasons why P_3, F_3 and P_{33d}, F_{33d} might vary, and the contribution each reason makes. Once this door is opened, large parts of processes designed to understand somewhat different opportunity and risk structures, like Chapman and Ward (1997), become directly relevant. For example, it becomes feasible to use different experts to assess uncertainty associated with different reasons why the securities market might decline, in general and in specific areas. This kind of thinking is approached in a somewhat different way in the area of scenario building (e.g. Schoemaker, 1995), also clearly relevant once the door is opened by the structure of Figure 10.5, and particularly relevant in terms of the P_i or F_i as distinct from the $P_{ijd} F_{ijd}$. When this thinking is properly developed in an operational form, further benefits become clear. For example, the V_s underlying the V_{db} concept can be redefined in terms of normal market variation. Associated A_s outside an agreed confidence bound (e.g. 95%) can be flagged within SINCOS for examination retrospectively for 'abnormal variation'. When an A_s observation which is outside normal market variations is identified by this sort of screening, or directly by the responsible manager or director or support staff, it can be taken out of the V_s and V_{db} estimation process (identified as an outlier) and fed into an appropriate 'source of risk for V_s and V_{df} estimation' process.

This could be part of a process which embraces V_t and V_m as well. That is, at the base level of the portfolio management process, the E_s, A_s couplets could be used to define V_s and V_t with a 'normal market variations' interpretation. Explanations for values outside agreed confidence bounds (like 95%), and other volunteered explanations, could be used to remove outliers for consideration as part of separate assessment of V_{df} by source of variation. This approach could also be used at the manager level and the director level in an integrated manner. In the context of SINCOS, the key to keeping all the directors on their toes is to ensure that any realized scenarios outside the F_i or F_{ijd} adjustments, or any reasonable grounds for suspecting misleading P_i or P_{ijd}, is a good reason for reducing their remuneration, to zero in extreme cases, no matter how good their managers and traders are, with contracts that spell this out. That is, taking informed risks is encouraged, but surprises are not, and over the longer term P_i and P_{ijd} would be related to outcomes, to test their validity.

It could be argued that E_{db} and V_{db} factors should not be the same. Generalizing to separate factors is clearly a possibility which could be explored as part of a more general process of assumption testing. This is discussed later. Twelve parameters might be an acceptable first-cut basic model for introductory discussion purposes, but there is nothing sacred about this level of complexity.

Naomi could see that Sam's concept of adjustment factors and structures like Figure 10.5 could also be used in principle at manager and trader levels, or in an integrated way at more than one level. Sam agreed, but did not think this was a priority in any development of his system. He was concerned to keep things constructively simple, only adding complexity where it was clearly beneficial. For this reason it made sense to introduce the idea of adjustment factors at the director level where such adjustments were clearly important and comparatively simple to introduce. If their use at this level were to suggest benefits from lower-level application and more detail, then exploring more sophisticated alternatives should follow. But learning to walk before attempting to run, and introducing complications in a manner which allows assessment of the benefits in an effective manner, was a key consideration in Sam's view.

Phase 4: the managing director's system

Once the E_{df} and V_{df} values for $d = 1, \ldots, D$ have been determined, support staff could use these values to run a Markowitz model to help the managing director maximize $E_f - kV_f^2$ where:

- A suitable measure of V_f^2 at this level is taken to be a function of the V_{df} and associated R_{df1df2}
- k is a very carefully considered appropriate trade-off at the overall portfolio level.
- The value of the portfolio as a whole in terms of prices expected on disposal per pound involved is

$$E_f = \sum_{d=1}^{D} E_{df} X_d / X \qquad [10.25]$$

- The purchase value of the overall portfolio is

$$X = \sum_{d=1}^{D} X_d \qquad [10.26]$$

- The valuation of the close of day for the overall portfolio per pound involved is

$$A = \sum_{d=1}^{D} A_d X_d / X \qquad [10.27]$$

Ensuring appropriate selection of this overall portfolio could be interpreted as the number one primary task for the managing director, monitored (in control terms) by all the other directors, including non-executive directors. Linked to this, the number two primary task for the managing director could be interpreted as leveraging the most effective directors' activities, $d = 1, \ldots, D$, while reducing the impact of the least effective, exposing all these directors to a review of this by all their fellow directors. Linked to this, the number three primary task could be interpreted as maximizing the effectiveness of directors $d = D + 1$, and so on, responsible for support, personnel, and so on.

The managing director's formal instruments of control for directors $d = 1, \ldots, D$ are: E_{M_d}, the zero-risk rate of return on X_{M_d} for each director; and C_d, the average cost of capital rate for each director. The managing director's remuneration could be largely defined as a direct function of traders, managers and directors. This approach could separate out to a significant extent the good luck and the good management (plus the bad luck and the bad management) which the managing director is responsible for, as for all those reporting to the managing director. At the managing director level, the extent to which V_f actually captures all outturn events might take on even more significance than it would for other directors. That is, V_f might be seen as the managing director's perception of future risk for the portfolio as a whole, and his or her ultimate responsibility. The extent to which V_f fails to bound what subsequently happens could be seen as a direct measure of the managing director's failure to understand the possibilities. At this level, shareholders of the organization have an important role with respect to directors' remuneration, in principle if not in practice. Whatever current practice, successful use of such an approach by one major fund manager could have a big impact on the others.

Further Considerations With A Simplified Portfolio

Sam was very aware that Naomi might be somewhat daunted by the complexity of his system, even in the early basic forms. Sam had recognized this was a risk, but he had wanted to demonstrate the potential benefits SINCOS offered in a hierarchical context related to a bold approach to security trading, control, staff motivation, and alignment of objectives between staff and organization. In fact, Sam had some more ideas for developing his hierarchical system, but rather than incorporate them directly, Sam thought it would be easier to discuss them first in a simpler context.

Sam knew that if he built further complexity directly onto the system just discussed, it would not be clear that this complexity could be tailored to the complexity of reality in a flexible manner. Sam recalled the advice of his MSc project supervisor: 'Making a model more complex should always provide a net improvement in effectiveness if it is going to be sustainable in terms of direct practical usefulness. As a consequence, it is important to understand the extent to which some features of complexity are separable, while others are not.' In any case, Sam wanted to show Naomi how SINCOS could be greatly simplified, and the underlying concepts used to advantage, even with no computer support and analysis that stopped short of a formal Markowitz model.

The obvious simplification was to consider a single decision maker and a small number of securities, say half a dozen for illustrative purposes. In this simple context, the trader–manager–director–managing director hierarchy in SINCOS is eliminated, but most of the associated ideas can still be applied. In the absence of a hierarchy, the indices t, m and d are all redundant, and the indices $s = 1,. . ., S$ equate to $s = 1, . . ., S_t$, $t = 1, . . ., T_m$, $m = 1, . . ., M_d$, $d = 1, . . ., D$. Adopting this approach, it was easy to see that issues arising in the hierarchical system, such as the identification of forward-looking adjustment factors, could still be applied if desired, to a small portfolio. At this point Sam reminded Naomi that his system was not just concerned with identifying optimal portfolios as the Markowitz model was. It was also an information and control system concerned with the practicalities of capture and effective use of performance data to assess the quality of past decisions and inform current investment decisions.

Recording E_s values

The Markowitz model does not concern itself with recording E_s values, although it assumes they are known. Sam argued that recording E_s values is important as a way of ensuring E_s values are explicitly addressed, as a form of self-discipline, to avoid decisions to buy merely because a security is deemed a good thing, without explicit separate consideration of expected return and risk. SINCOS provides a mechanism for recording E_s values that is as simple to use as possible for security investment professionals using computer-based systems. Even if Naomi wanted to manage a personal portfolio on her own on a computer-free (manual) basis, this feature of SINCOS would be worth adopting in a suitable investment diary form. Recording what return she thought she was going to obtain when she made investment decisions is recommended as a minimal aspect of any formalization of the security investment process.

Estimating expected returns

The Markowitz model assumes estimates of future expected returns are known, but it does not concern itself with how they are estimated. Previous E_s, A_s couplets provide a sound data basis for estimates of expected returns associated with new buys. That is, apart from using E_s, A_s couplets to observe persistent general estimation bias, the pattern of past E_s, A_s couplets can be used to estimate an E_{sb} (adjusted to reflect an appropriate planning horizon), which is a reasonable basis for a partial view of what might happen in the future. For example, seasonal effects might be formally identified and modelled. SINCOS builds in this kind of capability with minimal additional effort required from security investment professionals using computer-based systems. Even if Naomi wanted to manage a portfolio on her own, on a computer-free basis, this feature of SINCOS would also be worth adopting in a suitable investment diary form. It need not even approach the complexities of a chartist approach to analysis of past performance, but it should embody some basic understanding of the impact of common seasonal effects, post-dividend effects, end of the financial year effects, and so on (e.g. see Keasey, Hudson and Littler, 1998).

Forward-looking adjustments

When estimating expected returns, an E_{sb} estimate is a reasonable place to start but some adjustment to reflect views about the future is generally appropriate. The E_{sf} approach is a simple way to achieve this, where $E_{sf} = F_s E_{sb}$, and F_s is based on an adjustment factor tree like Figure 10.5. This tree structure is essential to address the investor's view of the chances of a general market upturn or downturn (P_1 or P_3), and the investor's view of an upturn or downturn specific to the security in question (P_{i1s} or P_{i3s}, the s index replacing the d), in relation to an ongoing situation based on E_{sb}. Even if all these P_i and P_{ijs} are of order 0.1, as used in Sam's basic system, the asymmetry of associated F_i and F_{ij} can have important implications. For example, if $F_1 \times F_{11s} = 1.2 \times 1.1 = 1.32$, but $F_3 \times F_{33s} = 0.6 \times 0.8 = 0.48$, the average factor is $(1.32 + 0.48)/2 = 0.9$. If this is a starting position with reasonably symmetric probabilities, but a change in the potential for a market downturn suggests $P_3 = 0.1$ should change to $P_3 = 0.2$, the downward swing in E_s relative to a risk-free option will be significant. That is, Naomi or any other single-person investing organization could usefully start with an estimate E_{sb} of expected return based on past experience, and use a simple standardized tree like Figure 10.5 to reflect on the effect of asymmetries in P_i, P_{ijs}, F_i and F_{ijs}. The investor could readdress this tree periodically to assess the effects on the E_{sb} if there is any significant shift in their perception of the likelihood of upturns or downturns in the market as a whole, or in particular security sectors. Sam suggested that any serious investors should go through this kind of exercise a few times to see if it matters. If it doesn't matter, they can stop. If it matters, but only a little bit, they can simplify the process. If it matters a lot, they can make it more sophisticated. If they never ask the question, they are taking a very big risk associated with an important source of ignorance which is resolvable with simple pencil and paper models.

Estimating variance and correlation

The Markowitz model assumes V_s and R_{s1s2} values are known, but it does not concern itself with how they are estimated. If previous E_s, A_s couplets are captured, then appropriate estimates of V_s and R_{s1s2} can be computed. Further, if a forward looking factor tree like Figure 10.5 is available, these V_s and R_{s1s2} estimates can be given a V_{sf} transformation. This would allow direct observation of basic measures of risk, which would be useful to reflect upon, even if a Markowitz model is not going to be used in any form. As in relation to the use of Figure 10.5 to estimate E_{sf}, Sam suggested that any serious investor should go through this kind of exercise a few times to see if it matters. If it doesn't matter, they can stop and carry on using whatever rules of thumb they use to assess risk given appropriate E_{sf} values. If it matters, but only a little bit, they can simplify the process. If it matters a lot, they can make it more sophisticated. If they never ask the question, they are taking a very big risk associated with an important source of ignorance. In this case, resolving the ignorance involved needs sufficient statistical analysis to take it a little (but not much) beyond simple pencil and paper analysis. However, Sam made the point that he was not talking about rocket science, and in the context of professional investors, this analysis could be provided automatically given the recording of information noted earlier.

Using a Markowitz model

Sam's approach envisaged using a Markowitz model analysis as a retrospective assessment of the effectiveness of investment decisions. If all the information required to use a Markowitz model formally is available, because it is useful in itself, even Naomi working on her own might find it useful to try out a Markowitz model analysis to assess her investment effectiveness. However, for half a dozen securities managed by herself, Sam acknowledged that Naomi might not be convinced of the need to use a Markowitz model at all, even for a retrospective analysis of her investment effectiveness. He suggested that there were some good reasons for not using a Markowitz model which he proposed to address in the next three sections.

A modular decision analysis approach

First Sam wanted to show Naomi a computer-free process that she might find useful for a small portfolio of, say, half a dozen securities. In fact, this amounted to a restricted version of the Markowitz model, and an explanation of this would facilitate some important generalizations of the Markowitz model which Sam wanted to address later. To explain how this restricted version could work, Sam suggested Naomi consider a personal portfolio of six securities defined as follows, with all the simplifying working assumptions of page 348:

- **Security 1** is the high-performance common stock discussed on page 350, now explicitly associated with a UK-based organization.

- **Security 2** is the moderate-performance common stock discussed on page 350, also explicitly associated with a UK-based organization.
- **Security 3** is a high-performance common stock for a US-based organization in a field different to security 1.
- **Security 4** is a moderate-performance common stock for a US-based organization in a field different to security 2.
- **Security 5** is an unrestricted access UK-based investment account.
- **Security 6** is a UK government bond which serves as a risk-free choice over the horizon chosen.

Sam suggested that Naomi might start by taking a view on the E_s, V_s and R_{s1s2} using the E_{sf} and V_{sf} perspective based on an F_s factor tree like Figure 10.5 whether or not E_s, A_s data couplets were available, following the line of thinking developed in the last section. Sam suggested that Naomi might then use the R_{s1s2} to guide the definition of a pairwise decision root like that of Figure 10.6.

Sam next suggested that Naomi used this decision root to start a bottom-up, pairwise composition process by looking at $s = 1$ and 2 together as a new composite security $s = 7$, called 'UK common stocks', working with a diagram of the form of Figure 10.7.

Figure 10.7 recasts the information of Table 10.2 used to define the $R_{12} = 0.5$ curve of Figure 10.1. The axes are X_1 and X_2, and a constant X_7 line is drawn for

$$X_7 = X_1 + X_2 = 100 \qquad\qquad [10.28]$$

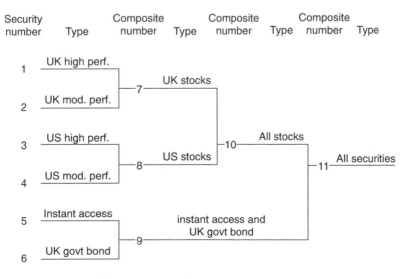

Figure 10.6—Pairwise decision root example.

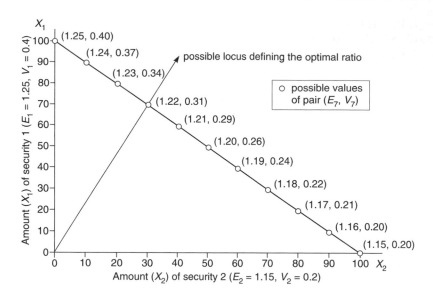

Figure 10.7—Example of neutral covariance presentation using the Table 10.1 pair of securities.

Representative combinations of X_1 and X_2 (at £10 intervals) identify points on this constant $X_7 = 100$ line. Each is associated with an E_7 and V_7 value, where

$$E_7 = (E_1 X_1 + E_2 X_2)/X_7 \qquad [10.29]$$

$$V_7^2 = (V_1^2 X_1^2 + V_2^2 X_2^2 + 2R_{12} X_1 X_2 V_1 V_2)/X_7^2 \qquad [10.30]$$

Naomi chooses her preferred combination of X_1 and X_2 in terms of the trade-off between E_7 and V_7 as X_1 declines from 100 to zero, using the E_7, V_7 scales with the assistance of cumulative probability distributions like those of Figure 10.2. Figure 10.7 assumes $X_1 = 70$ and $X_2 = 30$ is the selected optimal combination, with $E_7 = 1.22$ and $V_7 = 0.31$. The rationale for Naomi choosing this point might be that the decline in the rate of reduction of V_7 as X_1 runs through 100, 90, 80, 70 and 60 drops at this point from 0.03 to 0.02 (working to two significant figures). In other words, Naomi believes diversification to the extent of a 70:30 combination is as far as she wants to go. Going further involves the same rate of decline in E_7, but a smaller decline in V_7. This implies that Naomi's k is defined in terms of an optimal trade-off between E_7 and V_7 in the region 0.03 to 0.02. A line from the origin through the selected point is then drawn to define a linear locus of optimal combinations for all values of X_7 as shown. This corresponds to the assumption that Naomi is happy to regard the 70:30 combination of X_1 and X_2 as the optimal ratio whatever the value of X_7. She does not yet know what the value of X_7 is, but she can define the optimal ratio of X_1 and X_2. This straight line defines a composite security, $s = 7$, with $E_7 = 1.22$ and $V_7 = 0.31$. This composite security can be treated as a base-level security for most purposes because it is uniquely defined. It is not an unspecified aggregate security of uncertain make-up.

Naomi then moves on to consider X_3 and X_4, defining the composite security $s = 8$ in the same way. A similar process is repeated for $s = 9$, 10 and 11. At the levels $s = 10$ and 11, component securities are composites as well as the combination. For S securities this implies $S - 1$ diagrams like Figure 10.7. Once the preferred (optimal) ratio of X_9 to X_{10} is determined, defining the composite X_{11}, a known value of X_{11} means optimal values of X_9 and X_{10} are determined. These values can be used to determine optimal values of X_8, X_7, X_6 and X_5. Optimal values of X_8 and X_7 can then be used to determine optimal values of X_4, X_3, X_2 and X_1. To be consistent, each optimal trade-off for $s = 7, \ldots, 11$ should involve the same optimal trade-off rate, k. Naomi should make this consistency check if she uses Figure 10.6.

Implicit in this bottom-up pairwise comparison process is the assumption that the choice of mix between two paired securities is not influenced by the proportions chosen in groupings (pairings) of other securities. A sufficient (but not necessary) condition to allow this is that covariances of securities in one grouping with respect to securities outside the grouping are all equal. This neutralizes the influence of varying mixes of securities in other parts of the portfolio. In relation to Figure 10.6 this amounts to the sufficient conditions

$$R_{78} = R_{13} = R_{14} = R_{23} = R_{24} \qquad [10.31]$$

$$R_{9\,10} = R_{15} = R_{16} = R_{25} = R_{26} = R_{35} = R_{36} = R_{45} = R_{46} \qquad [10.32]$$

In other words, there is nothing special about the correlation relationship between either of the UK common stocks (securities 1 and 2), and either of the US common stocks (securities 3 and 4). They share a common covariance as indicated by equation [10.31], with a composite security correlation coefficient R_{78} equal to associated base level R_{s1s2}. Further, there is nothing special about the correlation relationship between any of the common stocks 1 to 4 and the other two securities 5 and 6. They share a common covariance as indicated by equation [10.32]. This 'neutral covariance' assumption is not highly restrictive, and it can be relaxed. However, it does buy the convenience of being able to consider $S - 1$ pairwise conditional optimizations in diagrams of the form of Figure 10.7, rather than portfolio optimization via a quadratic programming algorithm. A special case worth noting is when the correlation coefficients R_{s1s2} are the same for all pairs of securities $s1$ and $s2$ within the complete set or a subset. In this case the choice of pairwise root structure is arbitrary – any choice will do. Any specific pairwise root structure like Figure 10.6 relaxes the rather strong assumption that all R_{s1s2} within the set or subset are the same, allowing differences in the R_{s1s2}. Choosing a specific pairwise structure is about choosing the differences in the R_{s1s2} which matter the most. The particular form of Figure 10.6 involves an R_{78} $(= R_{13} = R_{14} = R_{23} = R_{24})$ which need not be the same as $R_{9\ 10}$ $(= R_{15} = R_{16} = R_{25} = R_{35} = R_{36} = R_{45} = R_{46})$. This is a critical departure from an assumption of a common R_{s1s2} for the complete set but independent. Separate values for R_{12}, R_{34} and R_{56} are also implied. In a more general context, the pairwise structure of Figure 10.6 is not more restrictive than a structure which allows triplets or quadruplets or any other larger subset at any stage in the decision root. It is *less* restrictive. Any structure involving three or more roots merging at any given node can be re-expressed in a less restrictive pairwise form, or the separability simplifications of the three or more roots from a node used to work with a simplified pairwise root.

Sam's bottom-up composition process is actually a simple graphical form of dynamic programming (Bellman, 1957). However, the separability concept which Sam's process hinges on is more sophisticated, and less restrictive, than that normally used in dynamic programming. Separability as used in dynamic programming would require all $R_{s1s2} = 0$. For a discussion of the special features of a pairwise separability assumption as used here and its implications in other dynamic programming contexts, see Chapman (1974) or Chapman and Ward (1987).

An inferred V^2 modular decision analysis approach

Sam now suggested there was a variant of the neutral covariance modular decision analysis approach of the last section which Naomi should be aware of. It should not interest her directly in terms of her personal portfolio, but it might be of interest in the context of computer-based systems for some portfolio decision contexts, and it would help her to understand some further issues yet to be addressed. Sam suggested she consider it as if she was going to use a computer-based system for the simple $S = 6$ security context of the last section.

Sam asked Naomi to imagine that she had started as described on page 377 in terms of taking a view on the F_s values and recording these values, but that she did not bother with explicit V_s or R_{s1s2} estimation. Sam asked Naomi to imagine that she defined the decision root of Figure 10.6 on an intuitive basis, understanding the R_{s1s2} implications discussed in the last section, but not bothering to explicitly link the structure to R_{s1s2} values. Sam then asked Naomi to imagine that she uses a diagram like Figure 10.7 to define a linear locus of optional combinations of X_1 and X_2 to define E_7 for composite security 7 as in the last section, but without the V_7 scale or the Figure 10.2 cumulative probability distribution representations. That is, she explicitly considers how E_7 declines as she moves from $X_1 = 100$ to $X_1 = 90$, and so on, but she considers V_7 implicitly, without measuring V_1, V_2 or R_{12}. Sam then asked Naomi to imagine that she proceeds in this way to define composite securities $s = 8, \ldots, 11$, as in the last section, but with only implicit reference to V_s and R_{s1s2} throughout.

Sam then indicated that the $S - 1 = 5$ composite security definition decisions together with the six E_s estimates and a given X_{11} value for a dozen or so time periods would be enough information to use econometric methods and consumer behaviour theory to estimate V_{11}^2, provided V_{11}^2 was stable over time. Sam indicated that Naomi did not need to understand how this could be done in detail, but it was worth understanding how it could be done in outline. The basis of consumer behaviour theory is the notion of a utility (or preference) function which describes relative preferences (e.g. Green, 1970). In the present context, Naomi has a utility function of the form $U_{11}(X_1, \ldots, X_6)$ which measures relative preferences in terms of V_{11}^2. Consumer behaviour theory assumes these utility functions are well behaved, and they are maximized implicitly by consumers subject to a budget constraint. In the present context, the budget constraint is

$$E_1X_1 + E_2X_2 + E_3X_3 + E_4X_4 + E_5X_5 + E_6X_6 = E_{11}X_{11} \qquad [10.33]$$

Consumer behaviour theory assumes that the E_s (corresponding to commodity prices) change over time, and that the consumer (Naomi) changes the X_s in an optimal manner consistent with a stable utility function (V_{11}^2 function). This behaviour can be shown to correspond to the existence of a well-behaved set of demand functions of the form

$$X_1 = f_1(E_1, E_2, \ldots, E_6)$$
$$X_2 = f_2(E_1, E_2, \ldots, E_6)$$
$$\vdots \qquad \vdots$$
$$X_6 = f_6(E_1, E_2, \ldots, E_6)$$

The functional form of these demand equations f_1 to f_6 is linear if U_{11} is quadratic. Given a suitable data set, the system of demand equations can be fitted to the data set to estimate f_1 to f_6, which can be used to define U_{11}. A basic text on the economic theory is Katzner (1970). Byron (1970) deals with the separability implications. Brown and Deaton (1972) is a good review article of the field at that time. Any more up-to-date economics text and an econometric text like Kennedy (1998) will discuss implementation.

Neutral covariance is a special form of neutral want association, developed by Pearce (1964) to estimate such systems, and given a specific form to do this by Chapman (1975) which could be adapted for use here. The point of neutral want association is exploiting a special form of separability, defined in this case by Figure 10.6, to minimize the number of data points necessary for statistical estimation. It does this by allowing the use of partial demand functions which reflect the conditional optimization processes for each composite. For example, in relation to E_7, we have a partial demand equation of the form

$$X_1/X_2 = f_7(E_1, E_2) \qquad [10.34]$$

where

$$E_1X_1 + E_2X_2 = E_7X_7 \qquad [10.35]$$

with the function f_7 defined in terms of V_1, V_2 and R_{12}. For any size of S, $S - 1$ simple partial systems of this form can be used to estimate the complete system. At each stage in the partial demand equation estimation process, relatively few degrees of freedom are required and error terms reflect the separability structure, exploiting statistically (econometrically) the restricted form of U_{11} and the associated system of unconditional demand functions.

Sam finished this part of his presentation by making the point that a paper by Chapman and Ward (1992) concerned with computer-based security selection systems suggested using this implicit measurement of V_s and R_{s1s2} as a starting point. Sam was of the view this was not a good idea, because the dynamic aspects of V_s and R_{s1s2} which the forward factor tree addresses are of critical importance, and they make it important to be explicit about the V_s and R_{s1s2}. An explicit case against assuming stationarity of such functions is provided by Clarkson (1999). More generally, implicit values imply uncertainty which may be important. However, Sam thought Naomi should understand the potential for approaches which used utility theory as developed by economists in general as well as the neutral want form to model trader, manager or director behaviour, and use this to infer variance/covariance estimates or more general multiple-attribute evaluations. Some of her clients might be interested in using this line of development.

Investments with additional attributes

When Naomi makes choices between X_1 and X_2, the analysis of the last two subsections assumed only E_7 and V_7 were relevant. However, if Naomi is aware that security 1 is associated with an organization which has a particularly good record in relation to environmental issues, or socially aware employment policies, or supporting sports or charities of interest, Naomi might feel better investing in security 1 to an extent that makes her prepared to run a higher risk (for a higher expected return) than she would otherwise take. If Naomi is aware that security 2 is associated with an organization which has a particularly bad record in relation to similar issues, a similar feel-better effect might make her prepared to further increase X_1 and decrease X_2, running a still higher risk than she would otherwise take (for a higher return). Reversing the direction of these effects would lead to an optimum with a lower expected return (and a lower risk) than she would otherwise accept. The framework of Figure 10.7 makes it reasonably straightforward to consider relevant additional attributes like this explicitly, for each successive pair, without necessarily measuring any of them. That is, the explicit and implicit measurement approaches of the last two sections could be blended. Explicit consideration of additional attributes might be particularly relevant for security 5, the instant access account involving a useful liquidity characteristic which the other five securities of Figure 10.6 do not possess. This liquidity characteristic would become less important as X_5 was increased, resulting in a non-linear locus. Additional attributes might be still more relevant if Naomi's six investments, jointly with her partner, were:

- Investment 1: common stocks
- Investment 2: bonds
- Investment 3: paintings and etchings
- Investment 4: vintage cars
- Investment 5: a house in London
- Investment 6: a cottage in the country

and she and her partner had quite different views about the relative merits of the investments other than common stocks and bonds. For example, if Naomi is particularly keen on $s = 3$ and 5, while her partner has a stronger preference for $s = 4$ and 6, negotiating balanced trade-offs might be helped by the formal use of diagrams like Figure 10.7. This does not imply a need to measure the special attributes of owning paintings and etchings versus vintage cars. It simply implies it may be useful to determine an optimal combination consistent with the E versus V trade-off k for common stocks and bonds, and then address the extent to which movement from this position is desirable given these special attributes, in a manner consistent with a similar analysis for a house in London and a cottage in the country, and some related higher composite level decisions.

What is involved here in general is modular decision analysis making direct operational use for decision-taking purposes of neutral want association as a more general form of separability than neutral covariance. Neutral want association has been developed as a general framework for all consumer commodity choice decisions (Chapman, 1975), so this is a simple generalization. Its only significant impact is that the linearity of the locus in Figure 10.7 may be lost. In this form, or in the more specialized context of the last section, this approach provides a useful conceptual basis for the ratio-based rules of thumb many people use to manage investment portfolios. One example is a base case rule of thumb for a particular investor at a particular level of wealth like 'a 70:30 balance for common stocks and bonds' in normal market conditions (a rule that would have to alter with circumstances). Another example is a base case rule of thumb like 'a 60:30:10 balance for property, securities and "fun" investments', dependent on wealth and other factors. Depending on wealth, willingness to take risk, and a range of other factors, investors might use this kind of framework to assess and adjust suitable ratio-based rules of thumb.

In a corporate context, the focus of attention can be on understanding the role of E_s, V_s, and R_{s1s2} and the role of other investment attributes in the determination of rules of thumb of this kind used for real-time decisions (Chapman and Ward, 1992). Sam did not push this idea, but he finished this part of his presentation making sure Naomi was comfortable with the idea that the attributes or criteria of interest did not have to be restricted to E_s, V_s and R_{s1s2}. The utility theory which underlies a neutral want association structure is very general in the sense that any number of criteria may be involved, measured or unmeasured. It can be used to make decisions directly as in a Figure 10.7 context, or to capture revealed preferences via analysis of past decision choices using demand analysis models.

Sam indicated this was as far as he wanted to take the small, single-level portfolio special cases. In principle the concepts Sam had just introduced in the context of a small portfolio could be applied to larger and more complex portfolios managed in hierarchical structures.

Robustness Of Sam's System

With the previous ideas in mind, Sam wanted to finish his initial presentation to Naomi by suggesting how SINCOS might cope with further complexities of reality.

Coping with lack of Normality

The assumption that the B_s are Normally (Gaussian) distributed is very useful because it involves only two parameters, the mean and standard deviation (or variance). However, it should never be used without questioning the robustness of the assumption that the Normal distribution is appropriate. Markowitz (1959) pays considerable attention to the asymmetry of B_s distributions, in terms of different upside and downside semivariances. A downside semivariance interpretation of the V_s is possible, acknowledging a different upside semivariance for E_s estimation. However, lack of Normality is not just a question of different semivariances. The forward factor tree (Figure 10.5) approach to V_{df} estimation or V_{sf} estimation could give rise to up to nine modes (peaks) in the associated B_{df} probability distribution. More refined versions may reduce or eliminate this multimode effect. However, in general we are dealing with processes which can branch in two or more directions, rather than just a single-mode (one-peak) distribution. Clarkson (1999) reports, 'As expected, the frequency distribution of the 80 years of real annual returns for UK equities (with gross income reinvested) is distinctly bimodal with "fat tails". The shape of the distribution bears no resemblance whatsoever to the bell-shaped Normal distribution.'

Having made these points, Sam indicated that SINCOS does not require Normal distribution assumptions, and SINCOS could be used to test the appropriateness of such assumptions at any level in the analysis process. For example, observed E_s, A_s data couplets could be analysed using simple histogram frameworks, with computer software determining suitable class widths given the number of observations. Comparisons could be provided across $s = 1, \ldots, S_t$, to confirm that distribution shapes were similar (or not), risk efficiency being robust provided distribution asymmetries are similar. If distribution shapes are not similar, effective analysis becomes more complex unless other simplifying assumptions are made, but suitable alternative simplifications are feasible. For example, if the Figure 10.7 format is used in a modular decision analysis context, cumulative distribution comparisons in the form of Figure 10.2 can be made with any shape of distribution for the components and the resulting combinations, including dealing with components with opposite skews and other peculiarities which make a mean–variance approach quite unreliable. This could be viewed in terms of extending the consideration of E and V^2 to measures of skewness, and so on (higher moments), but a simpler view in operational terms is that E matters and the whole of the distribution defining E matters, so the whole cumulative curve needs to be considered.

The key point is that a pairwise separability structure assumption is not strongly restrictive, but it is restrictive. What it buys is an approach which exploits this restrictiveness to allow any number of attributes or criteria associated with a security to be considered in a systematic manner, including whole probability distributions. There is no need to be uncertain about the implications of a Normality assumption which clearly does not hold. Nor is there any need to be uncertain about the implications of the neutral want association assumption. Its implications can be examined in detail within any particular pairwise structure, and its alternatives, looking at any mix of measured and non-measured attributes or criteria.

Sam correctly presumed that Naomi did not want to consider these issues in depth. But he knew it was important to raise them, because it would be important to pursue them in the context of Naomi's clients. In general it is important to let people approach new ideas in a framework which is as familiar as possible, and to let them estimate uncertainty structures in the most convenient way. Most people in the finance field would see a mean–variance approach as familiar and convenient. However, SINCOS easily adapts to histogram-based approaches which are free of specific distribution assumptions. In general the authors favour approaches which are free of specific distribution assumptions, unless there are good grounds to believe such assumptions hold, and the convenience provided by the specific assumptions matters. In this case neither provision is met. By the time Naomi got to detailed discussions with potential clients, Sam knew she would want to be in position to drive home the seriously flawed nature of Normality assumptions and the strength of an approach which did not require these assumptions.

More complex securities, transaction costs and taxes

Common stocks purchased to hold without anticipated dividends are the simplest securities to deal with. They are central to the portfolio of most security-holding organizations viewed on a day-by-day portfolio management basis. However, a wide range of alternatives are usually important. Complications associated with dividends, transaction costs and taxes are inevitably very important. Dividend payments introduce minimal conceptual complications in terms of E_s estimation and A_s observation. However, arithmetically the complications are non-trivial, and effective management of complex tax structures can be very complicated.

Restricting the formal use of Markowitz models to retrospective analysis might seem a major handicap. However, Sam argued that direct prescriptive modelling of optimal portfolio trading is not feasible if tax considerations are addressed. The retrospective use of optimization models facilitates addressing these complexities. For example, it allows the overall tax liability position to unfold over the tax year, without early judgements about overall tax-effective behaviour disturbing individual decisions. SINCOS, or the systems it might lay alongside, could keep track of the changing tax position, to inform the relevant managers and directors of the emerging position. As part of the top-down strategy process at director level, appropriate guidance and instructions could be developed as the tax year progressed. The issues are important, but dealing with them is simplified by the framework of SINCOS, and SINCOS itself need not become more complicated. That is, managing the uncertainty associated with taxation, other transaction costs and dividend payments can be addressed alongside SINCOS, supported if appropriate by SINCOS, but there is no need to unduly complicate the basic role Sam's system plays.

Bonds, which may have coupon payments and may mature, raise similar issues. More complex securities, like futures, options and derivatives, can increase the scale of uncertainty and associated complexity in a more fundamental manner. In particular, the E_s, A_s couplets cannot be reduced to a V_s measure of risk because a situation approximating to Normality is not usually a tenable assumption. Because gearing is inherently involved, potential losses can exceed the assets managed.

Sam was candid about the need to involve specialist expertise to work out how his system would cope with these issues. However, he remained upbeat. They were an opportunity, not a problem, to be managed as such. In particular, the separability structure provided by a modular decision analysis approach meant choices between very complex derivative options and the like could be reduced to a tractable decision in a framework which makes very complex outcome distributions easy to deal with, whatever the shape or form of their probability distribution.

Alternative portfolio management hierarchy structures

Naomi could see that Sam's basic hierarchical system was clearly capable of extension or modification to fit with a variety of existing organizational arrangements. But, as Sam pointed out, adopting SINCOS could facilitate improvements to existing operational arrangements. This enhanced the value of SINCOS as a tool for managing and controlling organizational uncertainty.

Sam made the point that a major source of uncertainty (risk and opportunity) for most organizations is the way they manage devolution and autonomy with regard to decision taking, control and motivation. In the longer term this influenced an organization's ability to recruit, develop and retain suitable staff. Particularly for a security-trading organization, staff are an organization's really important investments, and the biggest source of real risk and opportunity. As Sam saw it, the rationale underlying his basic system highlighted the need to acknowledge and consider the relationship between the hierarchical arrangement of portfolio operations and the way the organization recruited, developed and retained staff. Reward structures and decision structures should be closely linked. This is because the uncertainty which underlies the risks and opportunities faced by the organization embraces ambiguity about who will be making investment decisions in the future and on what basis. How they are made today is important, but it is the tip of the iceberg. Sam's system encouraged the idea of defining a structure best suited to the operations of each organization from basic principles. The existing hierarchical structure for a client organization would be a starting point that may be sacred, but sacred or not, it could be worth review in relation to alternatives. For example, if there are three layers of managers, are they all necessary? Would it be better to use only two layers? This type of consideration may be heavily influenced by factors like ensuring career paths for high flyers at a junior manager level, managing the risk that the organization's best young managerial staff may leave before they have a chance to acquire the levels of remuneration and responsibility of senior positions.

Sam argued that whatever the organizational structure, it is important to assess the clarity of the job specification for the staff involved, appropriate staff development (including training), the extent to which the different aspects of each person's job involves common skills, and the extent to which the organization can avoid promoting people who are very good at one level into a higher level and a role for which they are ill-equipped. For example, if traders need very different skills to managers, and traders with a very high degree of these skills are rare, it may be sensible to ensure that very good traders are much better paid than most managers. Progression from trader to manager might be largely limited to people who are hired as manager material and given very restricted 'nursery trading portfolios' while they are learning that aspect of the business. Alternatively, the primary recruiting ground for both traders and managers might be support staff, and support staff recruitment and staff development might be specifically aimed at these two destinations as well as career support staff.

In terms of tailoring SINCOS and arriving at an appropriate hierarchical arrangement, the extent to which the different levels should exploit separability to operate autonomously is clearly a very important issue. If traders are establishing significant portfolio positions, senior management should want to know what these positions are and want to exercise responsible control, and they may want to direct significant changes in policy. Chapman and Ward (1992) provides a discussion with a focus on this issue. Quite extensive control can be exercised by higher levels in the form of top-down constraints on the allowable range for the loci like that illustrated in Figure 10.7. However, the opportunity provided by separability in investment decisions needs to be seized boldly and used effectively, not frittered away. In practice the sales of SINCOS would be critically dependent on the extent to which Naomi would be able to exploit the power of a generalized approach to separability.

The way forward

By now Naomi was convinced that Sam was on to something. However, the development of SINCOS into a saleable product would need careful management in relation to associated risks and opportunities for IBS. A particularly important issue would be the choice of business partners to help develop SINCOS.

Some of the biggest potential pay-offs to security holding and trading organizations might be related to organizational structure, payment, motivation, staff development and retention issues. It was clear to Naomi that IBS on its own could be too far out of its league to address all these issues in a credible manner for a major security holding and trading organization. At an early stage, uncertainty management for IBS with respect to the SINCOS product would have to address strategic partnerships or other approaches to putting together a credible team to deal with the issues SINCOS raised in a holistic manner. The big risk for IBS would be losing control to partners. Choosing a set of partners, structured so that none of them could run away with Sam's proposition, was a big issue. Those who sell uncertainty management systems, thought Naomi, need to practise what they preach in an equally effective manner.

Conclusion

Security market price uncertainty and associated risk are the traditional focus of portfolio analysis. This chapter outlines a powerful, practical approach to addressing them. However, it also goes a lot further. It should provide the reader with some understanding of the relevance of portfolio analysis to a wide range of application areas. Portfolios are ubiquitous. Portfolio analysis concepts are relevant whenever the combined effect of different sources of uncertainty is of interest and formal analysis may be useful. These concepts are also relevant as a conceptual basis for 'trained intuition' when formal analysis is not appropriate.

Risk efficiency

This chapter should help to consolidate the reader's understanding of the concept of risk efficiency, via its discussion in variance efficiency terms in Figure 10.1 and 10.3. Risk efficiency is at the core of uncertainty management. It was used extensively in earlier chapters, without the formal underpinning developed here. At the trader level of decision making, maximizing expected return should be the default solution unless the implied risk is too large to bear. Encouraging a bold and aggressive approach to taking risk is a key part of the rationale behind limiting direct consideration of diversification to the director and managing director level in Sam's basic system, the other part being the simplicity a focus on expected values allows. Putting it another way, the old adage 'don't put all your eggs in one basket' is a recommendation to diversify which has validity only if the separate baskets are not likely to be dropped at the same time. The traders all working for one manager in one market sector do not offer independent baskets, so it is better to forget about diversification to reduce risk at this level and go for expected return. This has direct analogies in terms of the suggested approach to aggressive risk taking in other chapters.

The role of separability

This chapter has also illustrated the role of separability in developing constructively simple analysis. It is particularly important in SINCOS and is what determines whether or not local optimization will collectively yield global optimization. In fact, separability is a core concept in any form of analysis. For example, the economic order quantity (EOQ) approach to inventory analysis in Chapter 2 assumes inventory sizing and management is separable from production planning and marketing. Just-in-time (JIT) approaches are founded on the premise that

destroying this separability is the best way forward. Nicola's real triumph was identifying a rationale for refining this separability without losing its benefits.

The idea of using a bottom-up form of analysis within a separability structure which allows conditional optimization to define composite investment decisions is conceptually important and a key aspect of managing uncertainty as ambiguity. Top-down allocations of organizational resources which are based on bottom-up composite proposals do not suffer from uncertainty about what the composites entail. However, if a bottom-up analysis has not been performed prior to top-down allocation, aggregate allocations have to be used. Such aggregates involve uncertainty to the extent that they fail to specify what lower-level decisions are involved. The problem is whether the top-down decomposition process involves a clear view of subsequent lower-level decomposition processes or not. For example, in the context of the allocation of funds to a portfolio of research and development activities, if the central decision maker allocates money to one area group with no controls on how the money is spent, a part of the risk is uncertainty about how that group will spend the money. Controls on each group's spending can be seen as part of the process of managing uncertainty. Another way to address the same question is to ask in advance how each group intends to spend its money before allocating it, basing allocations on this information, but with no immediate controls in mind, and then controlling in relation to the overall effectiveness of the group's planning and performance. A directly comparable approach to project management was considered in Chapter 6, and many other contexts involve similar issues.

Perhaps the most striking and important aspect of this chapter is the extent to which the analysis structure provided by separability also provides a vehicle for managing a wide range of uncertainties which go beyond the immediate focus. For example, security market price uncertainty is the immediate focus of the Markowitz model, but Sam's system addresses corporate structure, motivation and financial reward for staff, training, selection and retention of staff. From a trader's perspective, market uncertainty in his or her market sector is what portfolio analysis is about; from the managing directors' perspective, market risk is not an issue in a direct sense. Here are the key direct issues for the managing director:

• Organizational structure
• Reward structures with a view to motivation, attracting and keeping the right people, and losing the wrong people
• Reward structures with a view to making sure everyone is operating in the best interests of the organization
• Control procedures to ensure the impact of good performers is geared up and the impact of poor performers geared down
• Control processes to ensure any deviant behaviour is detected and stopped before it gets out of hand

These issues are comparatively simple in a security holding and trading organization with a separable hierarchy structure, but they are present in most other portfolio management contexts, and the issue of reward structures in relation to uncertainty management is a recurring theme in most other chapters of this book. In particular, the approach to rewarding traders is applicable more widely, and its principles are worth emphasizing. The basis of remuneration is the values of $(A_s - C)X_s$, directly realized gain less an average cost of capital, including return on a risk-free pseudo-security S_t. This embodies good luck specific to the trader and good luck general to the organization, both of which are filtered out to some extent via adjustments linked to V_t and A, in order to focus the trader's reward on good management and to compensate him or her for bad luck beyond their control. Similarly, the notion of linking the remuneration of managers and those above to those who work for them is applicable more widely, based on the same principle of distinguishing between good luck and good management, bad luck and bad management, what people are responsible for and what they are not responsible for.

Useful utility theory

Basic axiomatic and revealed preference forms of utility theory as used by economists in a wide range of contexts as well as the special-case neutral want association form used in this chapter can form the basis of useful approaches to security portfolio management. More important in the context of this book as a whole is the way they can underpin traditional MAVT approaches and more general multiple-attribute and multiple-criterion analysis, and both buyer (consumer) and supplier behaviour models. A holistic view of managing uncertainty can do without expected utility MAUT, but it should fully embrace more generally defined utility theory as used by economists. This chapter attempts to offer a glimpse of what is involved.

Embedding alternative scenarios

The F_i and F_{ij} factors open the door to embed scenario analysis, decision analysis, and risk identification approaches which are well developed in the project risk management literature (and the safety management literature). This link is important in terms of a holistic view of how all the concepts in this book can be reassembled in different ways depending on the context and starting position.

Another view of cube factors

The F_i and F_{ij} forward-looking factors illustrated in Figure 10.5 are a form of the cube factor (F^3) discussed in earlier chapters. In this case they relate to estimates based on a data set subjected to traditional statistical analysis. However, they address the difference between what the past data tells us about the future and a broader view of that future which we need to address, another perspective on known unknowns, unknown unknowns, and bias. All the suggestions about forward-looking factor analysis in this chapter could be applied to cube factors in other contexts.

A bold approach

The motto of the Chindits – the boldest measures are the safest – may seem inappropriate for an opening quote for a chapter on portfolio analysis. It may seem counter-intuitive. However, 'to boldly go' is the flavour of this chapter, and this book more generally. The Chindits were a very successful guerilla warfare force in Burma during World War II, highly international in composition. There is a monument in the park between MoD Main Building and the Thames in London which records their motto and notes, 'Chindits came from the armed forces of the UK, Burma, Hong Kong, India, Nepal, West Africa and the USA. They were supported by the RAF and the 1st Air Commando Group, 10th US Army Air Force. Victory was hastened by the Chindits exploits behind enemy lines. Four received the Victoria Cross.' Very difficult uncertainty management situations often require 'guerilla warfare', not traditional frontal attack, drawing forces (approaches) from a wide range of sources. The essence of uncertainty management is knowing which bold choices to make, given suitable diversification and hedging. Constructive simplicity is about being simple in bold terms, but not simplistic. Constructive complexity is about avoiding serious mistakes by addressing complexity that matters. Simplicity efficiency is about taking a bold approach to making constructive simplicity safe. The dynamic approach to risk efficiency outlined in Chapter 1 is a key component of these ideas. Perhaps better known than the motto of the Chindits is the motto of the SAS. 'Who dares wins' is similar in some respects, but it would not be appropriate as an opening quote for this chapter, and the difference is significant.

11 | Conrad's tale: Formulating strategy

Trying to get closer to what I don't know.
Eduardo Chillida

Introduction

This chapter is about looking at the big picture and assessing the way forward in broad terms. 'Formulating' strategy is used in the plain English sense 'setting forth systematically', rather than 'reducing to or expressing in a formula'. 'Strategy' is used in the sense of a complement to 'tactics', implying decision choices with long-term implications rather than decision choices with short-term implications. Some organizations distinguish 'short-term' and 'long-term' planning, but do not identify an intermediate 'medium term'. Effective uncertainty management usually involves distinguishing all three planning levels, each with different issues approached in different ways, using three separate forms of analysis. This chapter illustrates why.

In this three-level planning framework, separate treatment of planning levels does not imply independence between levels. There are clear downward dependencies: long-term decisions shape dependent medium-term decisions, which shape dependent short term decisions in obvious ways. There are also upward dependencies which are often overlooked, such as important implications for long-term strategy of short-term and medium-term decisions.

Strategy formulation also requires the integration of top-down and bottom-up strategy formulation processes in terms of management levels. That is, directors and senior managers and strategic planning departments have to shape strategy top-down, but effective strategy management also requires emergent strategy processes driven bottom-up. This chapter emphasizes the structure provided by an effective top-down approach, but recognizes the importance of integrating bottom-up approaches. Especially at a corporate strategy level, it is important to remember that ultimately everything is connected to everything else, and key connections are a major source of opportunities and threats. This makes keeping

strategy formulation simple and focused for everyone involved particularly difficult, but particularly rewarding. The notion of constructive simplicity in process
terms is a central concern for this chapter.

This chapter's tale involves a Canadian electric utility. In some respects its
strategy formulation problems are particularly difficult, which gives the tale useful
richness. In other respects its strategy formulation problems are particularly easy
to structure, which makes the tale effective. A particular interest in electric utilities is not necessary. The concepts developed in this chapter are of wider interest,
although how wide is an issue. Context is very important to strategic planning
processes.

Conrad's Situation

In the early 1990s Conrad was a consultant based in the UK. He was contracted to
advise Canelco, a Canadian electric utility owned by its provincial government, on
how best to embed the important issues associated with uncertainty management
into the corporate strategy formulation processes used by Canelco.

Conrad had the international reputation which led to his selection from a
worldwide market assessment of suitable consultants. However, he knew from the
outset that the director who had insisted on the study brief which he had to
address was not fully supported by Canelco's board. Three directors, Harry, Pat
and Dick, led by Harry, were openly hostile. This reflected an almost unanimous
senior management view that no significant changes in approach were needed,
and that Canelco managers understood the business better than anyone else, so
any changes should be their prerogative. Harry's responsibilities included oversight of the corporate strategic planning function. Pat's responsibilities included
oversight of all new plant projects. Dick's responsibilities included oversight of
day-to-day operations management and plant refurbishment projects. This trio
had oversight of three largely independent empires whose senior management
liked it that way and wanted to keep it that way. They saw no reason to change
what, in their view, they had done very successfully for decades. They were
incensed that anyone should even suggest that change might be necessary.

The Canelco director who initiated Conrad's study was Ivor. Ivor was 'the
board's catalyst for new thinking', as he described his role. Ivor had been recently
appointed on the insistence of Charles, the chairman of the board, to test the
status quo by challenging it where he thought there might be room for improvement. Ivor was 'the board's devil's advocate', as Charles put it. Ivor had yet to
prove he was not just 'a devil of a nuisance', as Harry referred to him in private
conversations with Dick, Pat and all their senior managers.

The hunch which motivated Ivor to pick on strategy formulation in relation to uncertainty management was the culture surrounding the managers reporting to Harry, Pat and Dick, as portrayed by a number of 'clues' Ivor had observed. Pat's managers seemed to favour big projects. Dick's managers liked big plants. Harry's managers seemed to favour big developments. They all liked detailed plans for many years ahead which assumed things would go as planned. When things didn't go as planned it was never anybody's fault within Canelco, and sometimes it wasn't clear who was responsible for sorting it out. Ivor was particularly concerned about several recent developments.

- Several small-output (low hydraulic pressure) hydroelectric plants owned by the utility for many years had been sold because they were 'unprofitable', but the new owners were making money with them.
- There was a proposal to build a major new hydro project and several new nuclear power stations, but the cases ignored long-term political and environmental concerns and uncertainties about full life-cycle costs which Ivor thought needed much more attention.
- There were political movements afoot to break up the effective monopoly currently enjoyed by Canelco, with similar pressure in other provinces and other countries. However, nothing had been done to even think about how to react to such a development, never mind attempting to build firewalls to contain it.

Ivor explained to Conrad that he had not indicated to anyone other than Charles what his hunch was based on. He saw no point in challenging 'the terrible trio', as he called them, on such issues directly. They were simply symptoms of an underlying culture and process problem which Ivor wanted to diagnose and cure. Ivor wanted Conrad to test Canelco's current processes and models for strategy formulation with respect to uncertainty management, and suggest enhancements or alternatives which would provide immediate improvements in corporate performance and help him to address the associated culture problems. Ivor wanted Conrad to proceed with as much tact as possible, but with clarity and frankness. Conrad would report to Ivor in the first instance, but subject to Ivor's approval, he would then report directly to the board.

Conrad began by talking to Harry, Pat, Dick and their staff, and reviewing a sizeable collection of documents they provided to illustrate the way they operated. He then prepared a presentation for the board to outline his preliminary findings and a recommended way forward. He tested his presentation for the board section by section on Ivor as it was developed. The following sections outline the form Conrad's presentation took when finally presented to the board, several months and a lot of lost weekends later, over a full day at a suitably isolated and comfortable location. What follows does not include the preliminaries or the comfort building or the explanations of issues discussed earlier in this book, just a distillation of the day's proceeding which concentrate on what the reader might find interesting, because it complements earlier insights or it builds on them to provide further new insights.

Planning Horizons

Conrad began his presentation by explaining that it would be useful to think in terms of three separate planning horizons which the utility had to address, which he would characterize as short term, medium term, and long term. Each of these planning horizons could be associated with a focus on different sorts of decisions, and some differences in appropriate forecasting paradigms.

The short term

Conrad indicated that by 'short-term planning horizon' he meant what Canelco's planning staff meant by a short-term planning horizon. Conrad indicated that like Canelco staff, he put an outer bound on the short term at about a year, but the exact boundary was flexible.

Short-term system planning for Canelco was concerned with issues requiring minute-by-minute or hour-by-hour decisions, such as which units to run, how much spinning reserve is appropriate to cope with unexpected surges in demand and outages, and so on. Demand for electric power is a key variable requiring short-term forecasting, but availability of plant is also important.

Models used for demand forecasting typically include: exponential smoothing (adaptive expectation) models which track a variable, predicting future values based on past observed values and their related forecasts; time series models, which identify systematic variations relating to trends and cycles; and regression (econometric) models, which use external or exogenous variables identifying causal relationships, like the effect on the demand for electric power of temperature, current level of economic activity, current price of electricity and substitute energy, and so on. All these approaches are well developed and established (Wood and Fildes, 1976).

The most effective short-term forecasting models are typically hybrid regression models incorporating all useful features of the above models. Effective use requires manual adjustments when factors not in the model are recognized, such as industrial action against major industrial consumers. Such models provide expected value point estimates and associated fit (forecasting) error probability distributions which can be used to define confidence bands. Such models are well understood relative to medium- and long-term models, and comparatively easy to use effectively. Canelco made effective use of state-of-the-art approaches to these models.

Models used for forecasting availability (reliability) of individual units are also well developed and established (Green and Bourne, 1972), and Canelco made effective use of state-of-the-art approaches.

The medium term

Conrad then indicated he believed it was important to decompose Canelco's 'long term', at the time everything beyond a year, into a 'medium term', bounding roughly 1 to 5 years, and a 'long term' defined as 5 years plus.

Medium-term system planning for any electric utility is concerned with issues requiring month-by-month or year-by-year decisions, such as which generation units to begin constructing, when to take on new non-utility generation or start a new conservation programme, which units to shut down for maintenance, which units to mothball, which units to retire, and so on. Demand for electric power is a key variable requiring medium-term forecasting. The issue in this context is peak demand within months or years, rather than hourly or daily demand. How long it will take to construct new plant is another key forecasting issue. Availability of existing plant in a time frame of months or years is also an issue.

As with short-term electricity demand forecasting, hybrid regression models incorporating smoothing effects, cycles, causal factors like temperature and economic variables tend to fit past data well, and are well understood (Wood and Fildes, 1976). Such models require reformulation for the peaks associated with different time period structures, and re-estimating, with significant changes in some of the individual variables involved. For example, average temperature may cease to be relevant, but population may become a useful explanatory variable. Such changes pose no significant difficulties. Given stable relationships and appropriate data, these top-down forecasting models work quite well. However, they cannot cope with significant new issues or structural changes, and they have limited value in the context of generating understanding for an uncertainty management process as distinct from a forecast.

A very important complement to these top-down forecasting models, widely used by Canelco and other electric utilities, are bottom-up or end-use models, which look at how much electricity refrigerators or air conditioning or other consumer and industrial uses involve, together with trends and cycles in associated use levels and efficiency levels. These bottom-up models provided significant insight into changes in the structure of the market and instruments available for 'active demand management' (encouraging consumers to use less electricity).

However, a significant difficulty posed by both top-down and bottom-up forecasting models is predicting the values of explanatory economic variables used to drive the forecasting process if the medium term is more than a few months. For example, the state of the economy and the prices of fuels are extremely difficult to predict five years out. This means that medium-term forecasts of demand for electricity need to reflect *in full* the substantial uncertainty associated with both the demand forecasting models and the exogenous variables that drive the models. If that uncertainty is understated or structurally biased, then planners can be expected to fail to identify the *full* range of options available in terms of responding to this uncertainty before and after implementation of a medium-term plan.

Uncertainty associated with medium-term forecasting of availability for existing plant was not addressed by Canelco, in the sense that losing the planned output of a major power station for a year or more was deemed a potential catastrophe with too low a probability for direct consideration via numerical modelling. However, judgemental processes were employed by senior managers to assess appropriate system reserve capacity to cope with this kind of event, or a major upsurge in demand. Part of Canelco's corporate culture was the notion 'we must keep the lights burning'. Conrad indicated that he believed meeting this objective was not an issue.

Uncertainty associated with forecasting the availability of new plant was a serious issue for Canelco, but it was not treated directly as such by Canelco, because it was masked by a conservative approach to availability of existing plant, and it was treated in terms of cost impacts.

The long term

Long-term system planning for any electric utility is concerned with issues such as what mix of hydro, nuclear and thermal units, by type, should be aimed for beyond the commitments associated with the medium-term planning horizon, and which of the specific proposed new generation units should be developed to the point where construction can begin. Demand for electric power remains a variable of interest, but the key issue now is full life-cycle cost per kilowatt-hour of electric power for different types of plant, together with associated threats and opportunities.

As with medium-term demand forecasting, hybrid regression models remain a useful basis for forecasting electric power demand. But this time predicting full life-cycle unit cost per kilowatt-hour for alternative sources of electric power is the central problem. For example, the state of the economy and the prices of fuels are even harder to predict 10 to 20 years out than 5 years out. And this time we also need to predict the capital cost of projects, including the effect of unplanned delays, changes in capital costs over time, decommissioning costs, and running cost changes, due to changes in load, technology and legislation, which can be even more difficult. Furthermore, we need to understand the relationships between these factors, some of these relationships being economic, some political and social. To attempt to deal with these complex relationships in a tractable manner, many organizations turn to scenario approaches for forecasting. Marsh (1991) provided a current synopsis of Shell International practice, Shell being an early pioneer of scenario approaches. They abandon the notion of point estimates with an associated error or confidence band. They focus instead on two or three scenarios which represent in a consistent way the credible extremes of the infinite number of possible futures.

Scenario approaches are a significant positive step. However, such approaches do not on their own resolve the difficulties facing electric utilities. Long-term forecasting needs to reflect the important correlations between drivers of the costs associated with different types of electric power generation in a manner scenario approaches fail to capture.

Conrad closed his discussion of the long-term system planning horizon by pointing out that it is particularly important to avoid allowing forecasting to be a passive process concerned with predicting a future which must be accepted, like it or not, what some call a 'predict and prepare' paradigm. Instead it was important to attempt the design of 'desirable futures' (Ackoff, 1974). Comprehensive uncertainty management processes can be used to attempt to achieve desirable futures, as well as to help avoid undesirable futures. Uncertainty was a problem, but it also reflects opportunities which must be seized to exercise control over Canelco's destiny, and this was the role of the board.

Conclusion

Conrad closed his introductory discussion of planning horizons as a whole by emphasizing Canelco's inability to forecast with any certainty beyond the very short term, and the quite profound difficulties associated with long-term forecasting of cost per kilowatt-hour for different sources of electric power. He noted that in addition to attempting to influence the shape of the future, the board had to shape Canelco's decision processes to deal with whatever the future brought in the long, medium and short term. This raised very difficult issues. He indicated he would now start to address these issues by turning his attention to long-term strategy formulation.

Long-Term Strategy Formulation

Conrad began by suggesting that long-term strategy formulation should start by asking the question, Where does Canelco want to be in about 20 years time, in terms of an appropriate mix of hydro and thermal units, by type? Canelco should be aiming for an agreed robust target mix of sources of electricity at a planning horizon of about 20 years, recognizing that in 5 years time the target will probably have moved. The issue was, In which direction should Canelco move knowing what they know now?

When Canelco had assessed where it planned to be in 20 years time, the result could be compared to, Where are we now? This would yield a prioritized list of projects which would fill the gap by closing those aspects of the gap of greatest concern. The retirement of plant reaching the end of its life cycle, or no longer economically feasible because of fuel and other operating costs, would be considered as part of this. Medium-term strategy formulation would then address what should be done over the next 5 years or so, given the priority list of new units emerging from the long-term strategy formulation process.

Each year both long- and medium-term strategy would have to be reviewed. Significant changes in long-term strategy might occur. However, medium-term strategy ought to be fairly stable. This ought to be an objective of long-term strategy formulation. For example, it was important not to delay new unit projects which were well advanced because demand had unexpectedly fallen. This was a none too subtle reference by Conrad to a recent nuclear power station project which had suffered massive cost increases largely attributable to such delays. Pat and Harry blamed changes in safety regulations during the pause in construction which could not have been anticipated (in their view), leading to a need to redesign the unit halfway through construction, with obvious serious knock-on implications. Ivor and Conrad saw the safety regulation changes as a development which should have been anticipated, and the resulting debacle as the result of a particularly glaring example of poor long/medium-term strategy formulation which would have to be remedied, worth mentioning now to remind all the other directors what they were addressing. Pat and Harry flushed when most of the other directors looked at them for a reaction, but they remained silent.

Keeping their attention to the long term for the moment, Conrad suggested there were a number of ingredients they needed before they could evaluate where they currently thought Canelco should be in 20 years time. These ingredients were a set of options, direct cost estimates for each option, and an understanding of the interdependencies between units. He would deal with these one at a time.

A set of options

Conrad indicated that a set of possible new units was an obvious place to start. The proposed new hydro station and the proposed two new nuclear power stations were obvious examples. Other examples included 'units' which provided equivalent power without construction cost investment by Canelco. He suggested two examples would be useful for illustrative purposes: conservation (e.g. encouraging lower demand via active demand management, via the sale of low-cost, low-energy consumption light bulbs), and non-utility generation (buying power from other power generators, including utilities in other provinces or in the US).

Conrad pointed out that they were under political pressure to consider both these options, whether they liked the idea or not, and he knew Harry had put a lot of effort into developing conservation and non-utility concepts to a viable stage.

Conrad indicated that in addition to the obvious fossil fuel alternatives, other renewable sources like wind power and solar power should be included, even if their inclusion was believed to be inappropriate at this stage. They needed to be able to explain why they were not going down these routes if that was the choice, and they needed to understand the exact nature of the gap between exclusion and inclusion in the portfolio of priority new units which would emerge.

Direct cost estimates for each option

Conrad indicated that options should be compared in terms of appropriate full life cycle cost on a 'levelized' cents per kilowatt hour (kWh) basis (annualized average cost as discussed in Chapter 8). Conrad suggested that levelized cost per kilowatt-hour could be defined to include the implications of uncertain political and social changes and indirect system costs. However, for the moment it would be useful to focus on actual direct costs, including fuel, other operating costs, and decommissioning costs.

One key aspect of these estimates was an unbiased view of the expected cost. A related concern was the potential for variability associated with this expected value. Pursuit of risk efficiency, the core concept in uncertainty management, required both.

Conrad suggested that expected values and their relationship with other measures of central tendency and an associated probability distribution are very important concepts to understand. To illustrate what was involved, and to provide a basis for numerical models used later, Conrad asked the board to assume their immediate concern was restricted to the provision of the last or marginal 6 gigawatts (GW) of nuclear power, all other aspects of a proposed plan being accepted for the moment. For illustrative convenience, he asked them to assume that this provision would involve two stations (each with multiple units) of 3 GW each, and the only alternative is an additional 3 GW of non-utility generation plus an additional 3 GW of conservation. Conrad suggested they assume specific sites were not being considered, and ignoring site specific issues itself introduces some uncertainty.

He then suggested they assume that the best estimate of the levelized cost of delivered power in 1992 Canadian cents per kilowatt-hour for a 3 GW nuclear station was indicated in Table 11.1. This tabular presentation could be associated

Table 11.1—Example cost distribution for a 3 GW nuclear power station: tabular form

1992 cents/kWh	Probability (density)	Product	Cumulative probability
4*	0.30	1.2	0.30
6	0.20	1.2	0.50
8	0.15	1.2	0.65
10	0.10	1.0	0.75
12	0.10	1.2	0.85
14	0.05	0.7	0.90
16	0.05	0.8	0.95
18	0.05	0.9	1.00
Expected cost (column sum)		8.2	

*Most likely cost 4 cents/kWh

with the rectangular histogram density form of Figure 11.1 and the cumulative probability curve of Figure 11.2. That is, the probability of 0.30 associated with 4 cents/kWh in Table 11.1 is associated with the range 3–5 cents/kWh for the density form of Figure 11.1, all values in this range being assumed to be equally likely. The trapezoidal cumulative form in Figure 11.2 follows directly from the rectangular histogram density form.

The most likely (modal) value, identified using Table 11.1 (or Figure 11.1) is the value with the highest probability, 4 (3–5) cents/kWh. The median value,

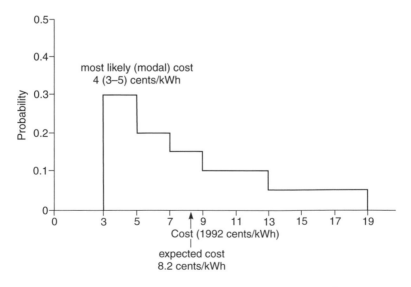

Figure 11.1—Example cost distribution for a 3 GW nuclear power station: rectangular histogram density form.

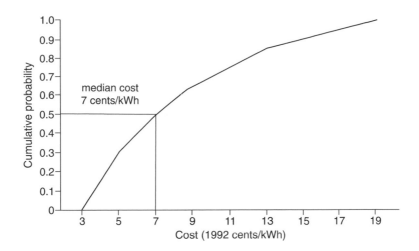

Figure 11.2—Example cost distribution for a 3 GW nuclear power station: cumulative form.

7 cents/kWh, identified using Figure 11.2, is the value with a 0.5 cumulative probability, a 50:50 chance of higher or lower values.

The expected value, 8.2 cents/kWh, was calculated as indicated in Table 11.1, weighting each possible value by its probability and summing these products. In formal terms this is the first moment about the origin of the density function of Figure 11.1, the point of balance if this distribution were to be cut out of a sheet of metal, a useful conceptual model. A fulcrum representing this point of balance is shown in Figure 11.1. Conrad indicated that probability values in Table 11.1 could have been estimated to the nearest 0.01 instead of the nearest 0.05, and more discrete values could be used to provide greater precision with associated smoother curves in the Figure 11.1 and Figure 11.2 formats. However, a limited level of precision makes the example easier to follow.

Conrad indicated that different probabilities could be argued for. The role of Table 11.1 and Figures 11.1 and 11.2 was simply illustrative. He did not wish to defend the values used. However, the 4 cents was consistent with Canelco's planning values and the shape and spread of the distribution illustrated was appropriate. The low most likely (modal) value, 4 (3–5) cents/kWh, a much higher median value, 7 cents/kWh, and a still higher expected value, 8.2 cents/kWh, are a consequence of the long right-hand tail in Figure 11.1. There is very limited scope for costs below the most likely, but there is considerable scope for higher costs, albeit with relatively low likelihood of such costs being realized. For example, a downturn in the demand for power from these last or marginal units, or loss of availability of power from these units, could occur for a wide range of reasons, and downturns in demand or losses in availability can generate substantial increases in the cost per kilowatt-hour.

Conrad then explained that if an estimation process is initiated on a deterministic (non-probabilistic) basis, people tend to produce an estimate fairly close to the most likely value, even if they incorporate contingency provisions of 20% or 30% or more, and there is no intention to produce an optimistically biased estimate. This is because each component tends to be identified in terms of a most likely value, and the sum of most likely values for all components will be a good deal less than the most likely overall value, as he would demonstrate shortly, unless all probability distributions are symmetric, which is hardly ever the case.

Conrad pointed out that the expected value is a best estimate of what should happen on average. Because of this and because of its additive properties, it should be the basis of estimation processes. Most likely values are of interest, especially because they tend to be the basis of deterministic estimation processes, but also because they sometimes approximate to reasonable targets (such as an initial 'no major problems' budget given to a project manager). Median values are of less interest. With skew to the right as indicated, median values always lie between most likely and expected values, since the probability of an outcome less than the expected value is always greater than 0.5, as illustrated in Figure 11.1

A key aspect of quantitative evaluation of uncertainty is the identification of an unbiased estimate of the expected value. If uncertainty is only partially considered, the spread of the probability distribution will be less, especially to the right in terms of Figure 11.1. As indicated by this numerical example, reasonably full consideration of uncertainty involving a significant skew leads to dramatic differences between most likely and expected values. Conrad knew this illustrated one reason why Pat's cost estimates for nuclear power were out by a factor of 2 or more. He also knew all the other board members would understand this message, but no one raised the issue at this stage.

Conrad then suggested that Table 11.2 and Figures 11.3 to 11.5 provide another example distribution, assumed to apply to an additional 3 GW of non-utility generation or conservation. Again a finer definition could be used, but the concern was simplicity to illustrate the issues. He reiterated that the numbers could be argued with, and he did not wish to defend them (this was an example only), but the shape and spread of the distribution illustrated in Table 11.2 and Figures 11.3

Table 11.2—Example cost distribution for 3 GW of conservation or non-utility power: tabular form

1992 cents/kWh	Probability (density)	Product	Cumulative probability
6	0.2	1.2	0.2
8*	0.5	4.0	0.7
10	0.3	3.0	1.0
Expected cost (column sum)		8.2	

*Most likely cost 8 cents/kWh

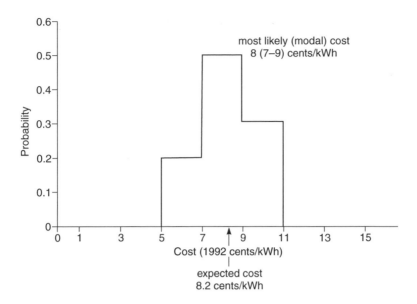

Figure 11.3—Example cost distribution for a 3 GW of conservation or non-utility power: rectangular histogram density.

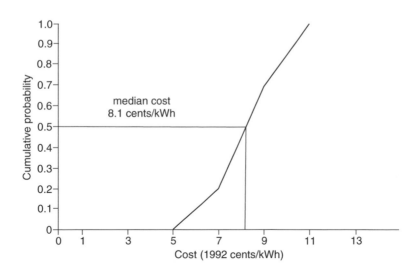

Figure 11.4—Example cost distribution for 3 GW of conservation or non-utility power: cumulative form.

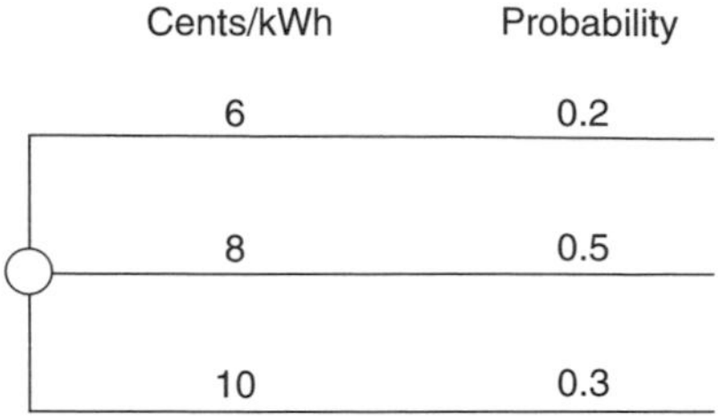

Cents/kWh	Probability
6	0.2
8	0.5
10	0.3

Figure 11.5—Example cost distribution for 3 GW of conservation or non-utility power: probability tree form.

to 11.5 was not unreasonable. There was scope for sizeable departures from the expected value in both directions, but much more symmetry than in the nuclear power case. As a result of this symmetry, most likely, median and expected values are very much closer, respectively 8, 8.1 and 8.2 cents/kWh. Even a substantial increase in uncertainty would not significantly affect the expected value, because of the near symmetry of the distribution. Figure 11.5 provided an alternative probability tree interpretation of the tabular information of Table 11.2, which explicitly treats the unit costs per kilowatt-hour of 6, 8 and 10 as discrete values. A similar reinterpretation of Table 11.1 was possible, these alternative interpretations being useful shortly.

The expected cost of 8.2 is the same as the expected cost for the nuclear power station example. In practice it might be higher or lower, but for illustrative purposes, nuclear, non-utility generation and conservation were all assumed to have the same expected cost, 8.2 cents/kWh.

Conrad then drove home an obvious point. The uplift from nuclear power's most likely cost of 4 cents/kWh to an expected cost of 8.2 cents/kWh is very large relative to the comparable 8 to 8.2 cents/kWh uplift for conservation and non-utility generation. This difference is generated by the long right-hand tail of Figure 11.1. The 'product' column of Table 11.1 shows the way extreme values influence expected values. For example, the 0.05 probability of 18 cents/kWh contributes almost a full 1 cent/kWh.

Conrad then emphasized that, in practice, estimation of distributions like those of Tables 11.1 and 11.2 would require considerable effort. The uncertainty involved should include a very wide range of technical and economic issues. It would be important to use a carefully structured approach to building up these distributions from component factors. It would also be important to use this process to develop an understanding of the relationships between different sources of uncertainty associated with the overall probability distribution for each potential type of electric power, or its equivalent in the case of conservation. As part of this process they needed to build up an understanding of the correlation between distributions for different types of electric power or its conservation equivalent. For example, the extent to which the unit costs of nuclear power and conservation may depart from current expectations in opposite directions would require careful study.

Conrad next indicated that the issue of correlation had to be addressed via a portfolio theory perspective. The basic idea encapsulated by portfolio models is 'don't put all your eggs in one basket'. In more formal terms, portfolio problems involve the allocation of money or some other resource to a set of possibilities when the uncertainty involved is significant and needs explicit attention. Particularly important is the relationship between allocations in terms of the patterns of positive or negative statistical dependence, or independence. Choosing the mix of sources of electric power by an electric utility was a classic portfolio problem. Many electric utilities recognize this explicitly and formally. For example, the UK CEGB (Central Electricity Generating Board) policy of building nuclear power stations based on several technologies has been explained as a deliberate attempt to spread the risk, to ensure that if significant nuclear power were required, at least one successful technology would be available. A diversification policy like this will increase expected cost. The concepts of risk efficiency and risk/expected cost balance apply here as elsewhere. In terms of a portfolio of sources of electric power, no utility can afford to go for the least expected cost solution in terms of a current view of cost per kilowatt-hour over the next 20 or 30 years. To do so would normally involve a single technology, which would almost inevitably prove a mistake. It is important to diversify. The trick is to diversify efficiently, with the least increase in expected cost for the greatest reduction in risk, and to stop this diversification process when risk has been reduced to an acceptable level.

Making portfolio models operational in any context is difficult, for a number of technical reasons. Even in the context of managing a portfolio of financial securities, the simplest classic portfolio problem, the task is very difficult. However, Conrad suggested Canelco could do so along the lines of some examples he would use to illustrate the nature of the issues which need to be addressed, and the implications if they were not addressed.

The key concept, developed first, is the role of dependence or lack thereof when combining uncertainty associated with two or more units of the same or different kinds. Statistical independence means that the outcome associated with one unit is not affected by or otherwise related to the outcome of another. It leads to a dramatic reduction in risk as more units are considered, because risks cancel out on average. Independence is the basis of spreading risk in insurance operations, for example. If one life insurance policyholder dies earlier than expected, it is equally likely that another will die later than expected, producing an acceptable average claims experience.

Positive dependence means that good (or bad) outcomes with one unit tend to occur at the same time as good (or bad) outcomes with another. Positive dependence means that the cancelling-out effect of independence is reduced or even lost altogether. If an insurance company specializes in earthquake risk in San Francisco, positive correlation puts them and their policyholders at risk, because the cancelling-out effects insurance companies have to achieve to be effective are lost.

Negative dependence means that good (or bad) outcomes with one unit tend to occur with bad (or good) outcomes for the other. Negative dependence means that the cancelling-out effect of independence is enhanced. Bookmakers attempt to ensure negative dependence on their portfolio of bets by changing the odds so that they get equal bets on either side of an outcome – a skilful bookmaker always keeps a balanced book.

Understanding how these concepts operate is not easy, but this understanding is central to understanding what is perhaps the most important uncertainty management issue in long-term strategy formulation.

Two nuclear power stations assuming independence

Table 11.3 illustrates a basic calculation of the probability distribution associated with the cost of power for two 3 GW nuclear power stations assuming independence, adding the distribution of Table 11.1 to itself and dividing by 2 to obtain an average cost. The 0.090 probability calculation component associated with 4 cents/kWh is the product of 0.30 × 0.30, the chance that both nuclear units will have a cost of 4 cents/kWh. The following first column 0.060 probability calculation component associated with 5 cents/kWh is the product of 0.30 × 0.20, the chance that one will have a cost of 4 cents/kWh, the other 6 cents/kWh, with a resulting average of 5 cents/kWh. In a similar manner, each column of probability

Table 11.3—Cost distribution for two 3 GW nuclear power stations assuming independence: basic calculation

1992 cents/kWh	Probability calculation components								Probability (density)	Cumulative probability
4	.090								0.0900	0.0900
5	.060	.06							0.1200	0.2100
6	.045	.04	.0450						0.1300	0.3408
7	.030	.03	.0300	.030					0.1200	0.4600
8	.030	.02	.0225	.020	.030				0.1225	0.5825
9	.015	.02	.0150	.015	.020	.0160			0.1000	0.6825
10	.015	.01	.0150	.010	.015	.0100	.0150		0.0850	0.8575
11	.015	.01	.0075	.010	.010	.0075	.0100	.0150	0.0850	0.8575
12		.01	.0075	.005	.010	.0050	.0075	.0100	0.0550	0.9125
13			.0075	.005	.005	.0050	.0050	.0075	0.0350	0.9475
14				.005	.005	.0025	.0050	.0050	0.0225	0.9700
15					.005	.0025	.0025	.0050	0.0150	0.9850
16						.0025	.0025	.0025	0.0075	0.9925
17							.0025	.0025	0.0050	0.9975
18								.0025	0.0025	1.0000

calculation components is associated with one cost value for the first unit, all possible values for the second unit, components in all columns being added across by row to yield the resulting probability density.

This calculation is precise and error free, using the standard calculus of probabilities, if the tabular representation of Table 11.1 is associated with a discrete probability tree as illustrated by Figure 11.5. It does involve a slight calculation error if it is recognized that the distributions are continuous as portrayed in Figure 11.1. Figures 11.6 and 11.7 illustrate why, and how corrections can be derived. Figure 11.6 indicates that integrating the uniform distribution associated with a cost of 4 (3–5) cents/kWh and a probability of 0.3 for the first unit with a similar distribution for the second results not in a probability of 0.09 being associated with a uniform distribution over the range 3.5 to 4.5, implicit in Table 11.3, but in a triangular distribution over the range 3.0 to 5.0. The rationale is comparable to the 'triangular' form of the discrete distribution associated with rolling two dice, each die having a uniform distribution. That is, for a single die the chance of 1, 2, 3, 4, 5 or 6 is 1/6, but for two dice the chance of rolling 2 is 1/36, the chance of rolling 3 is 2/36, and so on until the chance of 7, 7/36, the probabilities then declining in a symmetric manner. To correct this error, simple geometry shows we must allocate 1/8 of the 0.09 to the range 3.0 to 3.5, and a further 1/8 to the range 4.5 to 5.0, with similar corrections for all other probability calculation components in Table 11.3. Figure 11.7 indicates that some of these corrections cancel out, to leave a net correction equivalent to transferring 1/8 of the difference in adjacent probabilities from the higher class mark to the lower class mark. Table 11.4 implements this adjustment procedure. For example, the adjustment factor associated with 3 cents/kWh is 0.01125 (obtained by 0.0900/8), the adjustment

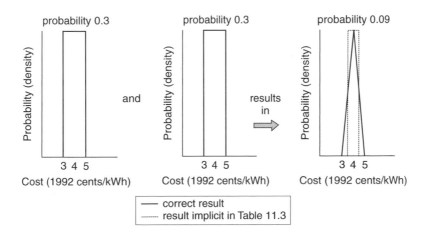

Figure 11.6—Calculation error associated with first probability calculation component of Table 11.3.

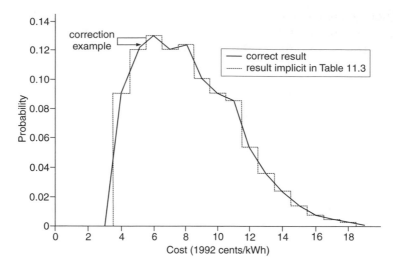

Figure 11.7—Net calculation error correction for Table 11.3.

factor associated with 4 cents/kWh is 0.00375 (obtained by (0.1200 − 0.0900)/8), and so on.

Conrad made the point that these adjustments are small, and understanding their basis was not necessary to understand what he was attempting to demonstrate. However, the corrections make some of what follows easier to understand,

Table 11.4—Cost distribution for two 3 GW nuclear power stations assuming independence with error correction

1992 cents/kWh	Density from Table 11.3	Adjustment factors		Adjusted density	Adjusted cumulative	Rounded cumulative	Rounded density
3		0.0112500		0.0112500	0.0112500	0.01	0.01
4	0.0900	0.0037500		0.0825000	0.0937500	0.09	0.08
5	0.1200	0.0012500		0.1175000	0.2112500	0.21	0.12
6*	0.1300			0.1275000	0.3387500	0.34	0.13
7	0.1200	0.0012500	0.003125	0.1215625	0.4603125	0.46	0.12
8	0.1225			0.1193750	0.5796875	0.58	0.12
9	0.1000	0.0028125		0.1015625	0.6812500	0.68	0.10
10	0.0900	0.0012500		0.0906250	0.7718750	0.77	0.09
11	0.0850	0.0006250		0.0818750	0.8537500	0.85	0.08
12	0.0550	0.0037500		0.0562500	0.9100000	0.91	0.06
13	0.0350	0.0025000		0.0359375	0.9459375	0.95	0.04
14	0.0225	0.0015625		0.0231250	0.9690625	0.97	0.02
15	0.0150	0.0009375		0.0150000	0.9840625	0.98	0.01
16	0.0075	0.0009375		0.0081250	0.9921875	0.99	0.01
17	0.0050	0.0002125		0.0050000	0.9971875	1.00	0.01
18	0.0025	0.0003125		0.0025000	0.9996875	1.00	0.00
19		0.0003125		0.0003125	1.0000000	1.00	0.00

*Most likely (modal) cost 6 cents/kWh, and expected cost 8.2 cent/kWh

and it was important to be confident that what a simple model indicates is sensible and robust. Those who are interested in the correction process at a technical level, and its implications for successive operations and computer software, should see Chapman and Cooper (1983a) or Cooper and Chapman (1987). Conventional Monte Carlo procedures provide a simple practical operational alternative to these discrete probability calculations. They involve sampling error rather than discrete approximation error, but it too can be controlled, by using large sample sizes, and Latin squares or hypercube approaches. To emphasize the need to avoid associating spurious accuracy with such distributions, and to simplify later discussion, rounded figures were provided in Table 11.4.

The result portrayed by Figure 11.7 is bimodal, with modal values of 6 and 8, the 6 being most likely. This is a consequence of the highly asymmetric modes of the Table 11.1 distribution. It is not of particular interest in terms of what this section is attempting to demonstrate, and it is lost in the format of the rounded Table 11.4 values, but Conrad was concerned to point out it was not an error – it is what should be expected if very skewed distributions are involved.

The expected cost of each of the nuclear power stations is 8.2 cents/kWh, and the expected cost indicated on Table 11.4 is also 8.2 cents/kWh. This illustrates a point made earlier, that expected values can be added to yield composite expected values if the distributions are independent, even if the distributions being added are not symmetric.

Conrad then noted that assuming independence results in a tighter distribution for the two power stations than that associated with a single station, and more symmetry, as illustrated in cumulative form by Figure 11.8. That is, the single-station curve suggests that the probability of a cost exceeding 15 cents/kWh is 0.10 (or a $1 - 0.10 = 0.90$ probability of staying below 15 cents/kWh), while the two-station curve suggests that the probability of a cost exceeding 15 cents/kWh is 0.025 (or a 0.975 probability of staying within 15 cents/kwh). This suggests a much tighter distribution for the two-station case.

Furthermore, the single-station curve has a median value of 7 cents/kWh as noted earlier, while the two-station case has a median of 7.8 cents/kWh, which is much closer to the expected cost of 8.2 cents/kWh. This suggests much more symmetry for the two-station case. A large number of successive additions assuming independence would lead to a continuing contraction of its spread (as measured by its variance, for example), as can be illustrated using simple mean–variance models.

The smooth cumulative probability curve associated with two stations in Figure 11.8 results from the shape of the corrected curve in Figure 11.7, using cumulative probability values provided by Table 11.4. All plotted points are shown to illustrate the minimal effect of this smoothing except in the range 3 to 4.5 cents/kWh. Had the correction procedure of Table 11.4 (Figure 11.7) not been used, the two curves of Figure 11.8 would not have met at 3 and 19 cents/kWh, which would have been confusing, both here and later.

Conrad noted that the most likely values for each of the nuclear power stations

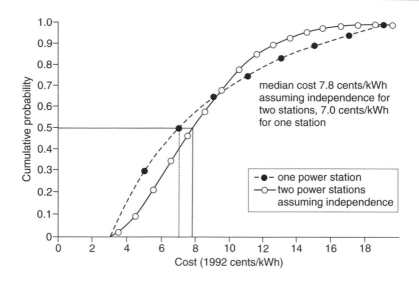

Figure 11.8—Comparison of cents/kWh cumulative probability distributions for one or two 3 GW nuclear power stations assuming independence.

is 4 cents/kWh, but the most likely value in Table 11.4 (Figure 11.7) is 6 cents/kWh, a 50% increase. This illustrates the point made earlier that most likely values are not additive. This effect is related to the loss of asymmetry as a result of addition assuming independence. Successive additions assuming independence will lead to expected, median and most likely values which coincide, as for the Normal distribution.

Two nuclear power stations assuming positive dependence

Statistical independence for the costs per kilowatt-hour of two nuclear power stations of the same kind is not a tenable assumption. Costs will be highly correlated in a positive manner. If one station costs more per kilowatt-hour (because construction costs are higher, decommissioning costs are higher, spent fuel disposal costs are higher, or lower levels of operation are achieved), the other is very likely to have a higher cost.

Perfect positive correlation (or 100% positive dependence) implies that the cumulative cost distribution for two units is exactly the same as the cumulative cost distribution for one unit. A comparison of the cost distributions assuming 100% positive dependence and assuming independence is illustrated by Figure 11.9, plotting the independence curve from Table 11.4, the 100% positive dependence curve from Figure 11.2, as for the cumulative curve of Figure 11.8.

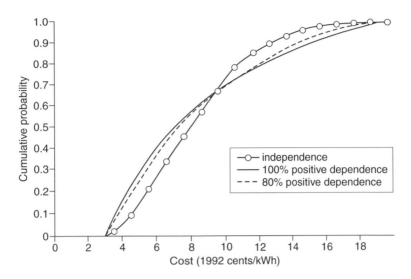

Figure 11.9—Comparison of cents/kWh cumulative probability distributions for two 3 GW nuclear power stations for different dependence levels.

While 100% positive dependence is closer to the truth than independence, 80% positive dependence might be a still more reasonable estimate. Figure 11.9 also shows a curve for 80% positive dependence, obtained by interpolating horizontally between the two solid curves. Figure 11.9 illustrates how positive dependence weakens the cancelling out of risk associated with independence when considering two or more units of a similar kind.

One unit of conservation and one unit of non-utility generation

Conrad then considered an alternative to two 3 GW nuclear units. He considered 3 GW of conservation and 3 GW of non-utility generation, using the distribution of Table 11.2. Table 11.5 illustrates the basic calculation associated with the cost of 6 GW from these two sources assuming independence, analogous to Table 11.3. Table 11.6 corrects the errors associated with this basic calculation, analogous to Table 11.4.

Positive statistical dependence for the costs of non-utility generation and conservation is unlikely. These costs should display significant negative correlation. If non-utility generation costs more, because fuel costs are higher for example, conservation will cost less, because higher electric power costs will make it easier to persuade customers to implement conservation.

Perfect negative correlation (or 100% negative dependence) means that any increase in one relative to the expected cost of 8.2 cents/kWh implies a counterbalancing decrease in the cost of the other, yielding a certain joint cost of 8.2 cents/kWh. A comparison of the cost distributions assuming 100% negative

Table 11.5—Cost distribution for 3 GW of conservation plus 3 GW of non-utility generation assuming independence: basic calculation

1992 cents/kWh	Probability calculation components			Probability (density)	Cumulative probability
6	0.04			0.04	0.04
7	0.10	0.10		0.20	0.24
8	0.06	0.25	0.06	0.37	0.61
9		0.15	0.15	0.30	0.91
10			0.09	0.09	1.00

Table 11.6—Cost distribution for 3 GW of conservation plus 3 GW of non-utility generation assuming independence with error correction

1992 cents/kWh	Density from Table 11.5	Adjustment factors	Adjusted density	Adjusted cumulative	Rounded cumulative	Rounded density
5		0.00500	0.00500	0.00500	0.01	0.01
6	0.04	0.02000	0.05500	0.06000	0.06	0.05
7	0.20	0.02125	0.20125	0.26125	0.26	0.20
8	0.37		0.34000	0.60125	0.60	0.34
9	0.30	0.00875	0.28250	0.88375	0.88	0.28
10	0.09	0.02625	0.10500	0.98875	0.99	0.11
11		0.01125	0.01125	1.00000	1.00	0.01

Expected cost 8.2 cents/kWh

dependence and assuming independence is illustrated by Figure 11.10, plotting a vertical line for the 100% negative dependence cumulative distribution at 8.2 cents/kWh, and the independence curve from Table 11.6.

The 100% negative dependence case might be much closer to the truth than independence, but there are reasons why a degree of independence needs to be considered. For example, the estimation processes for these two distributions will both be subject to errors, and these errors cannot be expected to display perfect negative correlation. Unlike the estimation errors associated with two similar nuclear power stations, very different issues are involved, and very different methodologies will be employed. In this case 80% negative dependence might seem a reasonable estimate, with an interpolated distribution shown in Figure 11.10 by the dotted curve.

Conditional specification: An alternative approach to dependence

The interpolation process used to obtain 80% positive and negative independence curves in Figures 11.9 and 11.10 can be a convenient way to capture dependence.

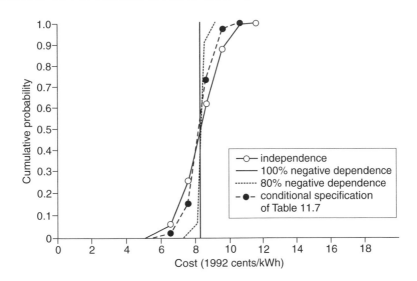

Figure 11.10—Comparison of cents/kWh cumulative probability distributions for 3 GW of conservation plus 3 GW of non-utility generation.

However, mental calibration of what percentage dependence means is necessary, and in some cases the percentage dependence concept which underlies inter- polation may not be appropriate. Similar arguments apply to the use of coefficient of correlation as an alternative to percentage dependence.

An alternative way to approach positive or negative dependence is illustrated by Figure 11.11. This provides an example of conditional specification of the cost of conservation given the cost of non-utility generation, presented in a probability tree format. In effect, the level of correlation is itself assigned a set of probabilities which can vary with the associated cost values. If non-utility generation costs 8 cents/kWh, the same probability distribution is assumed for conservation. But if non-utility generation costs only 6 cents/kWh, a relatively high probability of conservation costing 10 cents/kWh is assumed. And, if non-utility generation costs 10 cents/kWh, a relatively high probability of conservation costing 6 cents/kWh is assumed. For illustrative purposes, modest asymmetry of these conditional changes is assumed, but much greater asymmetry might be involved.

Table 11.7 computes the associated probability distribution. Correction pro- cedures are possible in this context, but they are more complex and they are not relevant to the present discussion. As with the other discrete probability models used to illustrate issues here, Monte Carlo sampling procedures can be used as an alternative computational tool in practice if this is more convenient.

Conrad noted that the expected cost is 8.12 cents/kWh, a decline relative to 8.2. Negative dependence in conditional form usually drags down the expected value, with positive dependence often having the opposite effect. More generally,

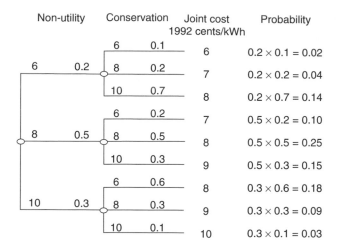

Figure 11.11—Example conditional specification of negative dependence between 3 GW of conservation and 3 GW of non-utility generation.

expected values need not be additive if dependence of this conditional kind is involved; see Cooper and Chapman (1987) for further examples.

Figure 11.10 portrays the result of Table 11.7 with a dashed curve. It corresponds to about 40% negative dependence, with important exceptions in the regions of 5 and 11 cents/kWh, when the conditional dependence curve converges to the independence case. The reason for this convergence is the possibility of 6 cents/kWh for both, and 10 cents/kWh for both, albeit with low probabilities. Conditional specification of dependence is the most general and flexible way to specify statistical dependence. The percentage dependence concept used earlier and other approaches to correlation involve assumptions which may not be appropriate in some circumstances.

Conrad then suggested that for their purposes it was appropriate to assume that the dashed curve on Figure 11.10 associated with Table 11.7 and the associated

Table 11.7—Cost distribution for 3 GW of conservation plus 3 GW of non-utility generation assuming conditional negative independence as in Figure 11.11

1992 cents/kWh	Probability calculation components			Probability (density)	Cumulative probability
6	0.02			0.02	0.02
7	0.04	0.10		0.14	0.16
8	0.14	0.25	0.18	0.57	0.73
9		0.15	0.09	0.24	0.97
10			0.03	0.03	1.00
Expected cost 8.12 cents/kWh					

specification of Figure 11.11 is more appropriate than the dotted 80% negative dependence curve of Figure 11.10. In particular, Conrad did not wish to overstate the case for negative dependence, because he wanted to show it was crucially important even in terms of the comparatively modest form illustrated by the dashed curve of Figure 11.10.

Comparing results involving positive and negative dependence

Conrad then moved on to a comparison between this result and the two nuclear power stations of Figure 11.9 assuming 80% positive dependence, illustrated by Figure 11.12. What this comparison clearly shows is a very much lower risk associated with the non-utility generation plus conservation approach. Figure 11.12 suggests that there is no chance of a cost greater than 11 cents/kWh for non-utility generation plus conservation, whereas there is a 0.23 chance this cost level will be exceeded for the two nuclear power stations (and a $1 - 0.23 = 0.77$ probability the cost will be less than 11).

What earlier discussion illustrates is that lower risk has two important components: a tighter distributions for each 3 GW unit, and negative dependence as opposed to positive dependence. In the case of these examples, the expected cost is approximately the same for the two nuclear power stations or the unit of conservation and the unit of non-utility generation, the latter being reduced slightly by the Figure 11.11 approach.

Risk efficiency and risk/expected cost balance

Conrad then explained that in practice, if the two nuclear units had a slightly higher expected cost than the conservation plus non-utility units, it would be very inefficient to choose them. If the conservation plus non-utility units had a slightly higher expected cost, choosing them would involve an efficient trade-off, trading a slightly higher expected cost for a significant reduction in risk. This suggests that any uncertainty about the probability distributions themselves implies Canelco ought to err on the side of conservation and non-utility generation. Canelco should only use an option like nuclear power, involving relatively high cost/kWh risk and correlation between station cost risks, if it has a very clear and unambiguous expected cost advantage. Furthermore, Canelco should increase the proportion of options which have relatively low cost/kWh risk and relatively less positive correlation between units well beyond the point where their expected cost is higher than that of higher-risk sources like nuclear, in order to obtain substantial reductions in risk for relatively low increases in expected cost. Canelco cannot afford to miss the opportunity to reduce risk to some extent. Finally, if

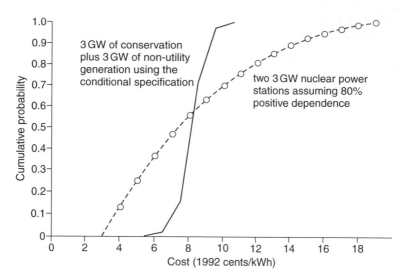

Figure 11.12—Comparison of cents/kWh cumulative probability distributions for two 3 GW nuclear power stations and 3 GW of conservation plus 3 GW of non-utility generation.

Canelco continues to reduce risk in this way, the expected cost of doing so will rise and the value of doing so will decrease, so Canelco must select a limiting point of balance. Those who are unwilling or unable to undertake any more than a minimum level of risk might wish to continue to reduce risk until it is very low, but this will involve a significant increase in expected cost. Electric utilities need not and should not take such an extreme position.

In terms of a classical graph (Figure 11.13) what ought to be done is first develop a portfolio of options on the risk-efficient boundary, and then move along the risk-efficient boundary until the preferred portfolio is reached. Conrad explained that Figure 11.13 is the basis for discussion of classical portfolio analysis (Markowitz, 1959). The feasible solution space represents all feasible combinations of sources of electric power, in terms of their expected cost, and their risk as measured by a surrogate variable like the variance of the associated probability distribution, a measure of spread. No matter how skilled the selection of a portfolio of sources of electric power, there is a lower limit to the expected cost for any given level of risk, and a lower limit to the risk for any given level of expected cost. Similarly, no matter how unskilled the selection of a portfolio of sources of electric power, there is an upper limit to the risk for any given level of expected cost. These limits define the boundaries of the feasible solution space, represented in Figure 11.13 as smooth (well behaved), although they need not be. The feasible solution space might have an irregular boundary and holes or voids in practice, and a set of discrete alternatives could lead to a solution space more appropriately viewed as a set of points or dots.

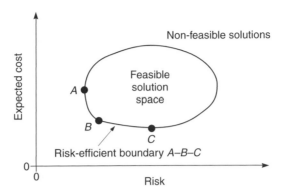

Figure 11.13—Classic portfolio analysis graph.

In Figure 11.13, point C represents a portfolio which involves minimizing expected cost. Point A represents a portfolio which involves minimizing risk. The risk efficient boundary between points A and C involves a trade-off between risk and expected cost. Whatever Canelco's view of risk, Canelco should select a solution on the risk-efficient boundary, as not to do so involves more risk for a given level of expected cost, or more expected cost for a given level of risk. Canelco should select the portfolio at point C on Figure 11.13 only if Canelco can afford to take the risk. This will involve a gamble on a single source of electric power, the sourse which *currently* has the lowest expected cost. No utility can afford such a gamble, so Canelco needs to move away from C towards B, stopping well short of A. Often the technology a utility is dealing with, or an appropriate view of economics or politics, implies a point such as B where the slope of the risk-efficiency boundary changes rapidly. In such cases a preferred solution at B is relatively uncontroversial. There is a considerable saving in risk for a minimal increase in expected cost by moving from C to B, but further reductions in risk are comparatively expensive.

Conrad emphasized that consideration of risk efficiency and the most appropriate risk/expected cost trade-off is central to all risk management. In the context of long-term planning for an electric utility, the issue is the mix of new sources to select, bearing in mind the risks inherent in existing sources as well as new sources. Thus far he had tried to explain this in terms of choices between new units at the margin.

Considering existing and proposed new units

Conrad then explained that this kind of analysis could and should be applied to the total portfolio of new power sources being considered and the total portfolio of existing sources which will still be operational at the planning horizon. The result would be a set of guidelines for the mix of electric power sources and equivalents (like conservation) at the planning horizon which provide risk efficiency at an appropriate level of risk. From this portfolio Canelco could derive a set of desirable additions to the current portfolio and a priority ordering of those additions. The modelling would not itself yield a prescriptive 'optimal' solution. It would provide the insight required to make a reasoned set of robust judgements.

If the 6 GW of nuclear power just considered were combined with the portfolio of all other existing and proposed new power units, a positive dependence level of less than 80% might be appropriate, but the high nuclear proportion in the portfolio of existing power units would require a high positive correlation. However, if the 6 GW of conservation plus non-utility generation just considered were combined with the portfolio of all existing and proposed new power units, a dependence level approaching zero might be appropriate, because non-utility power on its own would involve some positive correlation, but conservation on its own would involve negative correlation. That is, conservation plus non-utility involves less risk with respect to the 6 GW at the margin, but they also significantly reduce the risk associated with the total portfolio of power units, because, relative to the 6 GW of nuclear, they involve a significant degree of statistical independence with existing sources, allowing risks to cancel out. This illustrates the very strong impact on the risk associated with existing power sources arising from new sources of power with an important measure of independence because they are associated with different sources of risk.

Risk reduction: The importance of size and variety

While 3 GW is a practical size for a nuclear power station, conservation measures and non-utility generation are in practice going to involve much smaller units. This means 3 GW of conservation or 3 GW of non-utility generation will itself be a portfolio of components with its own dependence/independence characteristics. This will tend to reduce cost variability and centralize the expected value of the distribution illustrated in Table 11.2. More generally, lots of relatively small units with a variety of technologies means very much less exposure to risk than a limited number of units involving similar technology. Put the other way around, any new large units with a common technology will significantly increase the overall system risk relative to diversified smaller units, be they nuclear or hydro, for example.

Formal portfolio modelling with more than two possible allocations

Conrad explained that the formal modelling approach developed by Markowitz (1959) for any number of possible allocations (securities in a financial portfolio context, electricity generation units in the present context), uses quadratic programming (a form of mathematical programming) to consider all possible allocations simultaneously. Quadratic programming algorithms were developed to provide solutions to this model. Such models involve technical complications which his presentation did not need to address. However, the simple approach to considering a portfolio of two allocations he had used could be generalized to any number by building up a pairwise structure, and this is a practical proposition which could be developed within a framework developed in some detail in Chapter 10 and in Chapman and Ward (1992). This framework can be used to provide a basis for a more intuitive approach to portfolio risk management, which usually manifests itself in terms of constraints on the proportions of a portfolio that can be associated with any single allocation or set of allocations. For example, this framework could be used to assess regulatory or planning constraints of the form 'no more than x_1 percent of the supply capability of an electric utility should be of nuclear type 1, no more than x_2 percent of the supply capability of an electric utility should be of nuclear type 2, no more than x_3 percent of the supply capability of an electric utility should be of gas turbine type 1', and so on, for all possible sources of electric power. These constraints can reflect the board's intuitive view of the portfolio risks as well as external views. Considerable development of the framework described in Chapman and Ward (1992) would be required, but this development was a practical proposition. Moreover, even if such a framework was not made directly operational in formal terms, it could be used as a basis for understanding the nature and role of intuitively defined constraints on proportions of the x_i percentage form just suggested.

Decisions involving timing considerations

Conrad made the point that this portfolio modelling approach could, in principle, be extended to a multiperiod model which explicitly looked at the timing of all new plant decisions at the same time, in a manner comparable to Canelco's current linear programming models. He believed that in general these issues should be deferred to the medium term. However, any potential source of power at the horizon which involved important timing considerations should be treated as a set of options (perhaps mutually exclusive), which allowed consideration of key timing relationships. For example, there are important cost savings and associated simplifications in approvals processes if new thermal or nuclear power stations are on the sites of retired power stations. If an existing plant is due for retirement, replacing it on the planned retirement date might be the obvious choice, with related options involving early retirement, postponing retirement, or retirement followed by site preparation for a new plant.

Decisions involving option development

Conrad emphasized the need to see decisions about the development of options to the point where they could be rejected as unsuitable, put at the top of the queue for implementation, or simply put on the side for the moment, as part of the long-term strategic planning process. In terms of the project life cycle associated with development of an option, Conrad was arguing for early passes through the conception, design and planning stages (Chapman and Ward, 1997), all taking place within the strategic planning framework.

A focus on the portfolio problem

Conrad particularly emphasized the need to see the focus of the long-term planning process on 'the portfolio problem', in the sense of understanding the opportunities and threats associated with moving Canelco in different directions in terms of its major source of irreversible decisions, commitments to major power station construction. Minimizing the expected cost per kilowatt-hour of electricity at the planning horizon was the basic criterion which the portfolio modelling approach would address. But a core issue was diversification to reduce downside risk in a risk-efficient manner to the extent this was appropriate.

Deliverables from the long-term planning process

The deliverables provided by the long-term process could take the following form. Canelco's current views of the uncertainties associated with all possible sources of electric power over the next 20 years and beyond suggest an optimum portfolio of electric power sources (including existing and new sources) with the following targets and bounds:

Option number	Target proportion	Upper limit	Lower limit
1	X_{1t}	X_{1u}	X_{1l}
2	X_{2t}	X_{2u}	X_{2l}
etc.			

The target proportions reflect current best estimates of expected costs, risks associated with those expected costs which can be measured, and risks associated with those expected costs which are difficult or impossible to measure. Upper and lower limits on these targets reflect the imprecision of this planning process. Approvals would be sought to move towards the targets on a prioritized basis via the medium-term planning process on the understanding that changes in circumstances could lead to shifting the targets. However, a stable portfolio of projects under detailed development and implementation via the medium-term planning process is an important objective of this long term-process.

The upper limits for each of these power sources, together with a high load growth scenario and a pessimistic view of existing unit retirements, imply the following option capacities should be developed to the point where they are available for medium-term planning:

Option number	Capacity
1	Y_1
2	Y_2
etc.	

In effect, for each option category, the target total, less existing total, plus retirements, equals the shortfall that may in the future need to be added to get to the target result.

Medium-term planning processes can draw on these options, minimizing the expected life-cycle cost of added units within the guidelines provided by the target proportions and associated bounds. Part of this process will consider how far to develop options before decisions to begin construction. That is, the option development process begun in the long-term process will carry on in the medium-term process.

Conclusion

Conrad started to wind up his discussion of long-term strategy formulation by emphasizing he had used simple examples chosen for convenience, and analytical procedures which make the calculations transparent. In practice it would be sensible to use commercially available computer software which allows such calculations to be performed to whatever degree of precision is required to permit the comparison of all the alternatives of interest. It would be sensible to build up an understanding of the best mix of sources of power in a structured manner, and then further structure this understanding into guidelines for planning decisions, as just discussed. It would be important to address some significant complications in practice, such as a second nuclear power unit having a different cost distribution than the first because of economies of scale. Developing an operational set of models to deal effectively with these issues was a non-trivial task. The issues are not straightforward. However, it should be clear they are very important issues which cannot be overlooked without very great cost.

In practice it would also be important to develop at least two preferred portfolios of new electric power sources for the planning horizon, based on at least two (and preferably more) load growth scenarios to test the robustness of the process in terms of this key source of risk. It would be desirable to test other major impacts on the system as a whole in scenario terms, like a political decision to impose restrictions of one kind or another. That is, a portfolio analysis approach is essential to capture the risk management issues addressed here, but it does not replace the need for a more conventional scenario approach, which needs to underlie the portfolio analysis approach Conrad was proposing. And it does not replace the need for adjustments based on considerations which are not directly measurable.

In practice these target portfolios would play a role in defining a set of new power sources which should be developed to the stage where construction or implementation in some other sense can be initiated as part of the medium-term planning process, and the priority of each determined. Even quite major shifts in long-term system planning portfolios should not impact this set of readily implementable new sources and their priorities too much if the plans are reasonably robust. An important test of the validity of the process would be the stability of these developed options. Development costs of these options should not be incurred unless analysis indicates it is risk efficient to do so.

Medium-Term Strategy Formulation And Integration Upwards

Conrad began his treatment of the medium term by reminding everyone that long-term strategy formulation should provide a prioritized list of new plant requirements which reflected alternative load growth scenarios and other risks as well as anticipated plant retirements. Medium-term strategy formulation was about transforming this prioritized list into action plans which reflected commitments.

Action plans and action horizons

Associated with each commitment to action is an action plan and an action horizon. The action horizon is the time period requiring commitments to implement the action plan because of the need for lead times and the 'irreversible' or 'reversible at a cost' nature of associated decisions. Long lead time plant involves longer action horizons than short lead time plant. Conrad pointed out that the medium-term planning horizon would not be equated to an action horizon in this sense. For example, giving the go-ahead to a nuclear power station was now clearly recognized as a decision which ought to be seen as irreversible in the sense that it was not sensible to plan a slowdown, and a 9 or 10 year construction period was involved. However, a project involving building a gas turbine power plant with all permissions in place and the site prepared might be deferred for six months without comparable risks, and once the go-ahead was given, action horizons might be reasonably long for key components like the turbines and generators, but fairly short for the civil construction building materials, and virtually zero for the landscaping supplies.

This implied a need for an action plan which involved commitments appropriate to each part of the plan, embedded in a medium-term strategy which might cover a nominal medium-term planning horizon of 5 years or more. The utility needed to plan commitments as far ahead as necessary to optimize the action plan, recognizing that they could later alter aspects of the medium-term strategy if unfolding events suggested this was advisable. Indeed, they might have to alter action horizon plans, but this would be avoided to the extent that the costs warranted doing so. Detailed planning for implementation of an action plan was appropriate, but not for other parts of the medium-term strategy which did not involve commitments and might change.

It was in this context that Canelco had to address when to start the construction of new units, when to implement a new conservation programme, when to retire or mothball existing units, and so on. Canelco should select from options pre-selected and prioritized by the long-term system planning process. And given the importance of the action horizon distinction, options on the top of the list should be brought to a state such that they can be implemented as speedily as possible. This would be particularly important in the case of option components with very long lead times, as for nuclear power stations, when analysing linking the long and medium terms demonstrates it is risk efficient to do so.

Modelling load growth

What Conrad wanted to focus on next was how uncertainty modelling could help medium-term planning, and the nature of some of the issues involved. He indicated he would again use the basic probability tree arithmetic introduced earlier, dropping the correction process for simplicity.

The main message he wanted to get across, apart from the value of this kind of modelling, was that large units with long lead times involve a significant cost not normally attributed to them, which is associated with Canelco's inability to forecast precisely when their power will be needed. A set of small units with short lead times involves much less cost of this kind for the same total amount of power because the uncertainty associated with the gap between required power and provided power is very much less. In decision theory this cost is known as 'the value of information'. In the present context it is more appropriately termed 'the cost of uncertainty about demand', a cost which is a function of the size and lead time of the units being considered.

Figure 11.14 illustrates a probability tree of uncertain load growth (a variant of the semi-Markov processes used for analysis of pipe laying discussed in Chapter 4).

Figure 11.14 shows load growth in each of three 3 year periods in terms of probability tree branches associated with load growth of 0, 1 or 2 GW. It assumes some correlation over time: if load growth is zero in the first period, the chance that it will be zero in the second period is lower than it was in the first (0.2 rather than 0.3), and lower than it would be if first-period growth were 1 or 2 GW (0.3 or 0.4). This extends to third-period relationships in a similar manner.

Figure 11.14 reflects random shocks which may or may not be sustained over time, as Canelco should expect in practice. That is, over time there is some tendency to return to an underlying trend, although such returns may not occur. This is a form of what is sometimes called regression to the mean. The net effect over 9 years of the three levels of branches is computed by summing the growth over the branches. For example, zero growth in all three years yields zero growth over the 9 years. The probability of each outcome is the product of the associated branch probabilities. For example, the probability of zero growth over the 9 years is 0.006 (obtained by $0.3 \times 0.2 \times 0.1$).

This three-level tree can be collapsed to a single-level tree, shown in tabular form in Table 11.8, simply allocating each of the probabilities associated with an endpoint of the Figure 11.14 tree to its gigawatt value in the Table 11.8 'probability calculation components' column, and summing across rows. What is involved is repetitive addition of conditionally specified dependent probability distributions, a slight generalization of the treatment of adding conditionally dependent distributions in Table 11.7. The symmetry of the dependence pattern results in an expected growth in each time period of 1 GW, 3 GW over the 9 years, as indicated in Table 11.8.

Modelling the cost of uncertainty about demand

Conrad suggested the board assume that the 9 years coincides with the minimum construction period for a 3 GW nuclear power station, given design is complete and updated, permissions are in place, and so on. He suggested they assume that they wanted to model the implications of committing now to construction of this nuclear power station, with the tree of Figure 11.14 representing their current view of load growth over the next 9 years.

Conrad asked the board to further assume that contingency plans to cope with a departure from the expected load growth of 3 GW are reflected in the costs per kilowatt-hour associated with the possible load growth outcomes shown in

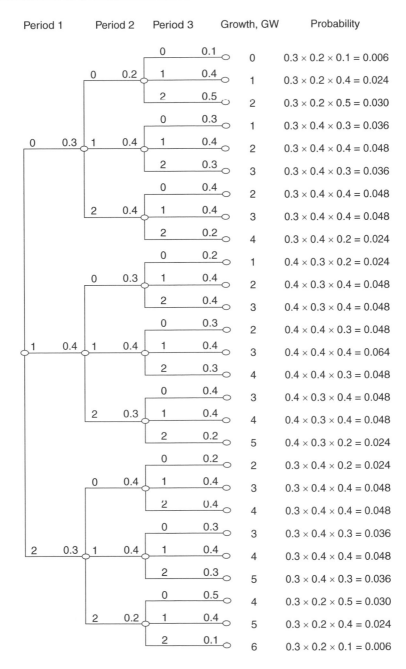

Figure 11.14—Example load growth probability tree for three 3 year periods.

Table 11.8—Load growth probability distributions for 9 years

Load growth (GW)	Probability calculation components									Probability (density)	Cumulative probability
0	.006									0.006	0.006
1	.024	.036		.024						0.084	0.090
2	.030	.048	.048	.048	.048		.024			0.246	0.336
3		.036	.048	.048	.064	.048	.048	.036		0.328	0.664
4		.024			.048	.048	.048	.048	.030	0.246	0.910
5						0.24		.036	.024	0.084	0.994
6									.006	0.006	1.000

Expected growth 3 GW, 1 GW every three years

Table 11.9. Suppose a load growth of 3 is associated with a cost per kilowatt-hour of 8, consistent with the 8.2 expected cost discussed earlier, and load growths of 2, 1 or 0 GW are associated with costs of 12, 15 and 20 cents/kWh, respectively. This reflects an assumption that if zero load growth occurs, the most effective contingency plans would involve using this nuclear power station, or existing base load plant, for shoulder periods, possibly shutting down lower merit order plant completely, or leaving some of the units incomplete, only recovering from this position some years later when existing plant retires if the zero growth continues, with less extreme variants on this theme if 1 or 2 GW growth occurs. It also reflects an assumption that the full cost is attributed to the nuclear power station in question. Similarly, suppose load growths of 4, 5 or 6 GW are associated with costs of 9, 10 and 10 cents/kWh respectively. This reflects an assumption that the utility would have to use a source like outdated peaking plant due to retire or new gas turbines to meet the unexpected load until the nuclear power station under consideration is on stream, the additional cost during this period being attributed to the nuclear power station cost per kilowatt-hour. It assumes that a second nuclear power station or some other base load equivalent would be initiated part way through the 9 year period if load growth looked as if it might exceed 3 GW, and the cost of being short of base load units or the equivalent after the nuclear power station in question comes on stream would be attributed to this second power source.

As with earlier examples, more precision could be used, different numbers could be argued for, and Conrad indicated he would not wish to defend the numbers used for illustrative purposes. But Table 11.9 reflects a realistic degree of asymmetry in the penalty costs associated with being early or late with a nuclear power station.

The more than 25% increase in expected cost per kilowatt-hour portrayed in Table 11.9, from 8 to 10.070, is clearly very important. This increase implies an expected cost per kilowatt-hour of 2.1 cents associated with imperfect knowledge

Table 11.9—Cost outcomes linked to load growth outcomes

Load growth (GW)	Cost (cents/kWh)	Probability (density) from Table 11.8	Product
0	20	0.006	0.120
1	15	0.084	1.260
2	12	0.246	2.952
3	8	0.328	2.624
4	9	0.246	2.214
5	10	0.084	0.840
6	10	0.006	0.060
Expected cost in cents/kWh (column total)			10.070

of demand growth in conjunction with a 9 year lead time for a nuclear power station, given a policy of building nuclear power stations in line with expected load growth. This increase suggests a policy for the medium-term planning process which involves never attempting to meet the whole of anticipated load growth with nuclear power stations, meeting such anticipated load growth at least in part with non-nuclear, and then bringing in nuclear stations to take over established base load. That is, deliberately lag the introduction of new nuclear plant. In simple terms, if being late is less expensive than being early, it pays to be late, although there are costs involved. The extent to which it pays to be late is a function of the relative penalties associated with being early or late. Further, if there is a way of meeting commitments which does not involve large units and lags, it will be worth paying a premium to use it.

Table 11.10 illustrates what the modelling of such a policy might imply, where 'notional' capacity growth from the end of year 9 is the planning base for starting construction. In the zero notional capacity growth case, zero load growth implies zero cost per kilowatt-hour. The gently rising costs if load growth is 1–3 GW more than planned capacity are consistent with Table 11.9. The expected value of 10.192 involves an increase in expected cost relative to the 10.070 of Table 11.9. Planning as if no growth will take place over 9 years is not an improvement on assuming a mean growth rate of 3 GW, as might be expected.

In the 1 and 2 GW notional capacity growth cases, appropriate numbers are drawn from the zero growth case and Table 11.9 to yield expected costs per kilowatt-hour of 9.688 and 9.384, respectively. These results suggest an optimal strategy that involves a capacity growth of less than 2 GW (say 1.75 GW) by the end of year 9. Given an expected increase in demand of 3 GW over 9 years, 1 GW every 3 years, this optimal strategy corresponds to a lag in capacity growth of about 4 years behind expected load growth. This lag would involve an expected cost saving per kilowatt-hour of about 7% relative to scheduling construction of 3 GW capacity to meet expected demand at the end of year 9. Even with this lag policy, the 9 year construction lead time involved, in conjunction with demand

Table 11.10—Cost outcomes linked to alternative amounts of notional capacity growth

Load growth (GW)	Probability (density) from Table 11.8	Cost (cents/kWh) given notional capacity growth at the end of the ninth year of			
		0 GW	1 GW	2 GW	3 GW
0	0.006	0	12	15	20
1	0.084	9	8	12	15
2	0.246	10	9	8	12
3	0.328	10	10	9	8
4	0.246	11	10	10	9
5	0.084	11	11	10	10
6	0.006	11	11	11	10
Expected cost (cents/kWh)		10.192	9.688	9.384	10.070

uncertainty, adds about 14% to the expected cost of 8.2 cents/kWh. If a short lead time option with an expected cost less than 114% of the cost of nuclear is available, it should be preferable.

The load growth distribution used for this example was assumed to be symmetric, to focus attention on the asymmetric penalty costs. If the load growth distribution were not symmetric, this would complicate the situation, but the same principles would apply. Conrad made the point that asymmetric functions, such as the one for cost illustrated here, are quite common, and some we can deal with effectively on an intuitive basis. For example, if someone purchases an advanced booking ticket (which does not allow changes) to make an important flight, say a close relative's wedding, being late for the flight may mean missing the wedding and losing the full cost of the ticket. In such a case it clearly makes sense to plan the journey to the airport to have an expected arrival time which is well before the flight departure. In general, an asymmetry of the penalty function means that it is sensible to set a target which is earlier or later depending upon the direction and degree of the asymmetry. In the ticket example, being late is very expensive. In the nuclear example, being early entails very high costs. However, it was not intuitively obvious that planning to bring nuclear power stations in later than needed was sensible. Indeed, it conflicted with the utility's traditional wish to bring them in early, 'to ensure the lights never went out'.

Integration upwards

Even the preferred option indicated by Table 11.10 involves a significant increase in the expected cost, and some increase in risk. Conrad suggested that an important issue is whether this expected cost and risk increase should be embedded in Table 11.1 and considered in the long-term planning process discussed earlier.

Normal practice would not involve attributing the additional costs associated with temporary use of gas-fired units to a nuclear station as assumed for Tables 11.9 and 11.10. Nor would normal practice attribute the full costs at the margin to the system of completing a nuclear power station prematurely as assumed for Tables 11.9 and 11.10. But if such costs must be borne by the system, and they stem from the particular nuclear power station decision, they need to be considered in the context of long-term planning if alternative sources do not involve such costs. Small hydro units or small gas-fired units, which could be constructed very quickly, do not involve such large additional costs and risk of this kind. In the latter case, relatively low capital cost and savings in fuel costs if the gas-fired units are not operated contribute to a reduction in penalty costs (over and above the shorter construction period). What this implied was the need for an 'integration upwards' process which adjusted the long-term strategy formulation process to reflect the impacts of medium-term strategy formulation.

Conrad suggested that the approach outlined earlier, based on Table 11.1, should be extended to consider these additional system costs and risks associated with new supply implementation lags. This might or might not involve embedding them directly in the cost per kilowatt-hour distributions of individual sources. The effect would have to be the same, however – a shift in the preferred mix away from sources with large capital costs and long lead times towards sources with low capital costs and short lead times.

In practice, models of this kind to assist an electric utility with medium-term system planning would have to examine reasonably complex decision rules associated with contingency responses, to develop appropriate rules and to provide a basis for the illustrative numbers of Tables 11.9 and 11.10.

Conrad finished his description of his proposed approach to the medium term by emphasizing the usefulness of explicit uncertainty modelling, the bias associated with omitted 'upward integration' adjustments, and the very different nature of the issues addressed and the models used relative to the long term. He made a particular point of emphasizing that the long-term planning process had to focus on portfolio issues in the sense of trade-offs between expected costs and risk exposure, while the medium term could focus on minimizing the expected cost of implementing the long-term strategy. This is analogous to an important distinction between the director and manager levels in the portfolio management process of Chapter 10. Only the top level needs to worry about expected value trade-offs with risk. Lower levels can focus on expected values.

Current practice compared to Conrad's proposed approach

Before leaving the medium term altogether, Conrad indicated this was an appropriate time to compare his proposed approach as outlined so far with current practice in Canelco and other utilities. Here are key points he developed in some detail for directors not fully aware of current Canelco practice.

Underestimation of variability in demand forecasts

Canelco had well-developed top-down and bottom-up demand forecasting models, as noted earlier. It used these models to make a 'joint medium-term and long-term demand forecast' in Conrad's terms, equating both to 'the long term' in current Canelco terminology. Canelco associated this demand forecast with a confidence band that was very narrow. It was misleadingly narrow because of the framing assumptions underlying the statistical models and presumptions about exogenous variables. In Conrad's view, this confidence band needed adjustment by at least 100%, probably 200% or more (an F^3 adjustment factor as discussed in Chapters 4 and 6).

Rejection of scenario approaches

Most other electric utilities had demand forecasting models which were comparable to but not as well developed as Canelco's. Most other utilities supplemented these models by scenario forecasting approaches (comparable to sizing plausible F^3 bands), an approach explicitly rejected by Canelco. The reason given by Canelco staff for rejecting scenario approaches was their lack of precision. One option was to believe staff and draw the conclusion that they were confusing precision and accuracy. Another option was to reject the staff explanation as a deliberate cover-up, and assume that what actually motivated Canelco staff rejection of scenario approaches was a misguided attempt to cling to a largely deterministic view of a very uncertain situation that they were not equipped to deal with. Canelco's whole approach was premised on the validity of narrow confidence bands for their demand forecast, and similarly narrow confidence bands for cost estimates and duration estimates. Conrad chose his language carefully, but made it crystal clear that Canelco staff demonstrated an unacceptably low level of competence in terms of managing uncertainty, unusual in the worldwide electric utility industry.

Cost estimation bias

Canelco assumed narrow error bands on demand forecasts over the medium and long term, cost per kilowatt-hour estimates for a preferred set of options, and on project durations. Given these narrow error bands, Canelco used elaborate linear programming models to minimize the expected cost of meeting demand over the medium term and the long term. These models simultaneously ordered the choices in Conrad's long-term planning sense, and timed their start of construction in Conrad's medium-term planning sense. They provided an optimal solution which involved massive new plant commitments, almost exclusively large nuclear power stations. However, the assumptions used involved a massive expected cost estimation bias in favour of nuclear, as Conrad's presentation had suggested. Simply looking at realistic probability distributions for direct costs as illustrated by Table 11.1 might uplift nuclear costs per kilowatt-hour by 100% or more. Other sources of bias considered, or about to be considered, might make an appropriate uplift of the expected cost of nuclear power 200% or more. Canelco's linear programming models would give an entirely different solution if expected cost estimate bias were corrected. Conrad believed nuclear power stations would play no part at all in such a revised solution.

Cost risk ignored

Bias associated with expected cost estimates was just a small part of the problems associated with Canelco's overall approach. Even if the biased expected costs issue was put on one side, and it was assumed that large nuclear power stations really did provide the lowest expected cost per kilowatt-hour over the long term as perceived now, to move Canelco to a predominantly nuclear portfolio of electric power sources was very risky. The conceptual basis provided by the linear programming framework ignores risk. Implicitly it assumes nuclear power will remain the lowest actual cost solution over the long term. There is no need to take such an extreme position. Most utilities also use linear programming models, but they use scenario analysis to test a range of demand and cost growth scenarios, and test proposed plans for robustness against the range of 'optimal' solutions which different assumptions produce. This can be a reasonably effective approach to managing risk. However, it does not address risk efficiently.

Conrad's approach

Conrad's approach would allow Canelco to identify a risk-efficient set of solutions for a range of demand growths and to assess in approximate terms a preferred mix of sources of power to aim for at the long-term horizon. It would also allow a coupled medium-term planning approach to minimizing the cost of meeting medium-term demand fluctuations while moving in the direction of the desired balance of sources at the long-term planning horizon. If Canelco adopted Conrad's approach, it could move from the bottom of the class to the top of the class in terms of industry standards in one step. What would flow from a full implementation of Conrad's approach was not just a different process for making decisions. Nor was it just a different solution. It was a different kind of process and a different kind of solution. Some of the differences should be self-evident already. Arguably the most profound differences had yet to be discussed.

Short-Term Strategy Formulation And Integration Upwards

Conrad began his treatment of the short term by reminding everyone that short-term strategy formulation was about 'keeping the lights on given the plant available'. This involved short-term demand and availability (reliability) issues.

Conrad indicated that Canelco's approach to demand forecasting for short-term planning purposes was 'at the top of the class' in terms of industry standards, and posed no concerns. Conrad then indicated that Canelco's approach to availability planning was good by industry standards so far as he was aware. Nevertheless, there was a serious problem which amplified concerns he had already identified. This problem affected short-term strategy formulation, but his immediate concern was its impact on medium-term and long-term planning, especially long-term planning. More specifically, it was necessary to revise how plant availability was assessed for a whole system, and to revise the attribution of reserve plant requirements and their costs.

Conrad indicated he would now illustrate how modelling could illuminate the nature of the issues involved and help to resolve them, using simple reliability/availability models and the discrete probability arithmetic introduced earlier without the correction process. Conrad suggested that one important message was that large units, and large numbers of units of a common type exposed to common mode failure, involve a greater need for system spare capacity than small units of different types. A related message is that this increase in system cost ought to be attributed to the large units (or large numbers of units of a common type) in terms of an increase in their expected life-cycle cost when choosing the desired mix of units. Another related message is that large units and large numbers of common units also increase the risk of major losses of availability. Unlike smaller capacity losses, it will not be economic to provide spare capacity for this eventuality. This risk ought to be reflected in the long-term portfolio modelling discussed earlier, because it is an important additional type of risk (although the customers rather than the utility bear the brunt of the cost, in the form of unreliable electricity service). For example, a constraint of the form 'no more than X_1 percentage of the supply capacity of the utility should be of nuclear power station type 1' might be appropriate, entirely driven by such risk considerations, with only the overall restriction of nuclear power as a whole being driven by the cost risk issues discussed earlier.

Modelling unplanned outage within one multi-unit nuclear power station

For illustrative purposes Conrad considered one of the 3 GW nuclear power stations used earlier, assuming it consisted of three units, all to the same specification. Conrad assumed the probability is 0.01 of a unit becoming unavailable in any month for unplanned reasons that are independent across units (such as damage caused by operator error restricted to a single unit). Conrad then assumed the probability is 0.005 of a unit becoming unavailable in any month for unplanned reasons that involve common-mode failures across units within the power station. If one unit is unavailable they all are, as would be the case if common systems failed. In practice both these probabilities would be functions of time since operation of the units began, so Conrad assumed for illustrative purposes that these probabilities are both averages over time. Intermediate levels of dependence might also require modelling in practice. Conrad acknowledged that both these probabilities might not be correct, but indicated that revisions would not alter the substance of what these numbers would illustrate.

Conrad indicated that Figure 11.15 shows a three-level probability tree associated with these assumptions, and Figure 11.16 shows the equivalent single-level collapsed tree. These trees and the associated rounded values indicate a high probability of no outage (0.965), a significant probability of one outage (0.030), and virtually no chance of two or more failures because of independent outage sources (0.0002965 + 0.0000010 rounded to 0.000). The probability of three failures due to common-mode failure of 0.005 is small, but large enough to be of serious concern given the consequences. In addition to the risk associated with losing all three units at the same time, Figure 11.16 shows that these common-mode failures contribute about a third of the expected number of outages in any month.

Conrad then assumed that any of these outages could be associated with the duration-of-outage probability tree associated with Table 11.11. The expected values from Figure 11.16 and Table 11.11 can be used to compute the expected unit months of outage per month of operation on start-up, 0.198 (obtained by 0.0449×4.4). This approximates the expected unit months of outage per month of operation once the system's operation has reached a steady state (which could be computed using a semi-Markov process). It is slightly higher than the result a steady-state calculation would provide, because when units are not available the probability of additional units becoming unavailable falls. Availability per unit using this result is 93.4% (obtained by $100 \times (3 - 0.198)/3$), about 95% if a steady-state calculation is used. This implies an increase in expected cost per kilowatt-hour of just over 5% to meet the expected level of outage. This increase is normally associated with the units in question through the standard treatment of availability.

The risk of losing large units requires a further increase in expected cost associated with additional reserve capacity provision to that required if smaller units were used, which is not normally associated with the units in question.

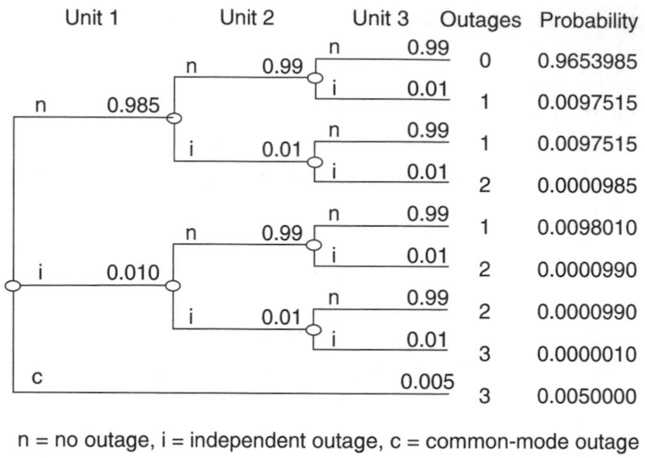

n = no outage, i = independent outage, c = common-mode outage

Figure 11.15—Example outage probability tree for a 3 GW nuclear power station with three 1 GW units: three-level probability tree.

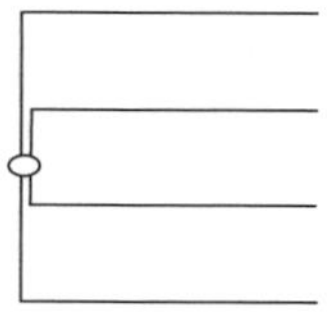

	Outages	Probability (density)	Cumulative probability	Rounded cumulative	Rounded probability
	0	0.9653985	0.9653985	0.965	0.965
	1	0.0293040	0.9947025	0.995	0.030
	2	0.0002965	0.9949990	0.995	0.000
	3	0.0050010	1.0000000	1.000	0.005

Expected number of outages   0.0449000   rounded to 0.045
Contribution of common mode   0.0150000   rounded to 0.015 (33%)

Figure 11.16—Collapsed single tree associated with Figure 11.15.

Table 11.11—Outage duration: example probability distribution

Outage duration (months)	Associated range	Probability	Product
0.5	0 to 1	0.4	0.2
2	1 to 3	0.3	0.6
6	3 to 12	0.2	1.2
24	12 or more	0.1	2.4
Expected value			4.4

Further, it requires another increase in cost, also not normally associated with the unit in question, associated with the risk of this increased reserve proving inadequate and requiring contingency demand management or other responses with significant costs borne by electricity consumers. The risk of being unable to meet demand is inevitably increased if larger units are used because reserve will not be scaled up in direct proportion – it would be uneconomic to do so.

Modelling unplanned outage for a set of nuclear power stations of a common type

Conrad then turned his attention to the situation if this 3 GW nuclear power station is one of four similar stations, each of three units, making a total of 12 units. He assumed that the same probabilities of independent and common-mode outage within a single station apply. He also assumed that 1 in 10 of the within-station common-mode outages involve a common-mode outage across stations. Such common-mode outages would include the discovery of design defects with safety implications requiring immediate shutdown of all stations, for example. One in ten is a monthly probability of only 0.0005, which is very low. However, the impact is substantial.

The implications of these across-station common-mode outages include a direct contribution to the expected cost of outages already costed in relation to station availability and normally included in the cost attributed to a nuclear power station, plus all the additional costs considered in the last section. They also include a very much larger system reserve to keep the consequences of such an outage acceptable, and the cost of this reserve is attributable to the use of a number of nuclear power stations of the same type, although it is not usually associated with them. More important is the large increase in expected cost associated with such common-mode failures that would be borne by customers; this cost should be considered when choosing the mix of sources of power, although this is not usually done. More important still, if the consequences of such a very large loss of availability are unacceptable for any reasonable increase in reserve capacity, from a regulator's perspective it may be critical to restrain a utility from undertaking any developments which imply any reasonable possibility of common-mode failure on this scale. That is, externally imposed constraints of the form 'no more than X_1 percentage of the available supply of a utility should be from nuclear power stations of type 1' may arise because of availability risk rather than the cost risk considered earlier. Such constraints might be imposed after a major incident, if the regulator is not aware of the possible implications in advance.

The additional reserve costs and the high costs of responses borne by consumers clearly need to be considered, and both the expected cost implications and the risk implications need to be considered and attributed to the nuclear power stations in the context of long-term system planning.

Modelling unplanned outage for small hydro units

Conrad then considered the situation if the 3 GW nuclear power station was replaced by 3 GW of small hydro, involving 300 relatively small units of similar sizes. He assumed the same probabilities of independent and common-mode outage apply, and the same outage duration distribution. In this case common-mode outage would include a drought affecting all 300 units, for example.

The impact of the large number of units in relation to independent sources of outage is a marked increase in the predictability of outage, apart from common-mode outage. Using the 95% availability figure, Conrad suggested they could expect about 15 of the 300 units out at any one time, with very little variation relative to the nuclear power station risk of having 0 or 1 of 3 units out at any one time for reasons not involving common mode outage. This means Canelco does not have to provide as much reserve for individual unit failures, with lower expected cost per kilowatt-hour implications, although Canelco would still have to worry about the risk of common-mode outage and its expected cost implications.

Conrad then considered the impact of the larger number of units in relation to the common-mode outages. For simplicity he assumed the same 0.005 probability of losing all 3 GW, with the risk that reserve capacity provision will prove inadequate, requiring contingency demand management responses with costs borne by electricity consumers. If Canelco reduced reserve provision because of the larger number of units and the more stable outage pattern, the cost implications of common-mode failure, in terms of costs borne by electricity customers, become even more serious than in the nuclear power station case. The costs associated with restoring hydropower are likely to be rather less than those associated with common-mode failures within a nuclear power station, but the short-term impact on the consumer is similar.

As with nuclear power stations, to some extent common-mode outages need to be considered in relation to all existing units, as well as all proposed new units. That is, a serious nuclear incident could lead to the recognition of design defects which result in all nuclear power stations being shut down, and a long-term drought might seriously affect most of an electric utility's hydro facilities. In practice the probability of common-mode outages on this scale, and on a smaller scale, may be very different for different sources of power. If, for example, nuclear power is very exposed to this kind of common-mode outage relative to hydro (or vice versa), then failing to address these issues biases the case for one option and against the other.

Modelling unplanned outage for a portfolio of electric power

Conrad next considered the situation if the four 3 GW nuclear power stations considered earlier are replaced by one 3 GW nuclear power station, the 3 GW of small hydro just discussed, 3 GW of gas-fired power, and 3 GW of conservation. What are the implications?

If the gas units are midway between the nuclear and small hydro units in terms of size, and the same probabilities apply, the situation with respect to the 3 GW of gas power will be intermediate in terms of the characteristics described earlier in relation to 3 GW of nuclear and 3 GW of small hydro. In this case, common-mode failure might involve loss of gas supply, for example. On the other hand, the 3 GW of conservation raises quite different issues. It might be argued that if conservation is unpredictable it should contribute to reserve requirements, but most demand management concerned with conservation is aimed at smoothing demand variations as well as reducing average consumption. This implies an expected cost reduction and a risk reduction in terms of the contribution of conservation to the portfolio considered by the long-term system planning process. Conservation contributes useful upside risk.

A key difference in the situation for the 12 GW as a whole is the absence of common-mode failures outside the nuclear, gas and hydro subsets. It is for this reason that regulators may wish to constrain the proportion of electricity produced from any single source which is subject to the possibility of common-mode failures. Again, this realization may follow a major outage.

Explicit risk sharing with customers

Conrad made the point that costs borne by customers should be considered by Canelco when determining strategy, but it might be appropriate to make it clear to customers that they bear the consequences because to do otherwise would involve increasing the cost per kilowatt-hour charge. That is, if customers wanted Canelco to in effect insure them against the consequences of major outages, Canelco would have to charge a premium that would involve expected costs plus administrative costs. Canelco might argue this would not be good value for customers.

Explicit costing of regulatory constraints

Conrad also made the point that costs associated with regulator/government constraints on the make-up of Canelco's portfolio imposed for reliability/

availability reasons would be passed on to the customers. Such costs could be identified, to test the appropriateness of the constraints, and to embed them in the long-term strategic planning process.

Conclusion

This kind of modelling of predominantly short-term availability issues is clearly a useful basis for considering short- and medium-term system planning issues. Of particular relevance here are the implications for long-term systems planning. The need for reserve capacity is a function of the size of the units involved, and the extent to which common-mode outage could occur. All reserve capacity costs should be attributed to types of unit, as should the risk of costs borne by electricity consumers as a consequence of involuntary demand management (or other responses), in terms of expected costs and risks. Risk may also require limits on the proportion of power provided by any single source in an overall system. These issues should be considered explicitly by Canelco within a long-term systems planning framework. Conrad's portfolio approach facilitates this.

Integrating Social, Environmental, Ethical and Political Issues

Conrad suggested the regulation issues which surfaced in the availability context of the last section were the tip of another important iceberg.

There was growing pressure on all electric utilities and their regulators to consider what economists call 'externalities' in relation to electric power generation, particularly those related to fossil fuel burning. Canelco staff had used carbon tax arguments to avoid consideration of fossil fuel plant, for example. If these issues are to be considered, they must be integrated with all the other considerations addressed by the long-term planning process, in a balanced manner. The framework of analysis must be capable of accommodating all such issues on a compatible basis. Conrad addressed how they could be considered within the framework for computing expected costs described in relation to Table 11.1 and the framework for dealing with associated risk described subsequently.

As an example, Conrad considered the social and environmental cost associated with nuclear power station incidents like Chernobyl, catastrophic releases of radioactivity, using probabilities and costs provided by the Goodman Group,

Boston, drawn from Pace (1990). He chose this example to expose a particular weakness in Canelco's current position.

Estimating expected costs and associated quantifiable risk

Estimates of deaths from Chernobyl, including on-site and latent cancers in the northern hemisphere, range from 28 000 to 140 000. Estimates of lingering illness range from 140 000 to 185 000. At $400 000 per illness and $4 000 000 per death, the total costs of the Chernobyl accident are estimated in the range of $400–580 billion. The probability of such an accident occurring based on US Nuclear Regulatory Commission estimates is 1/3333 per unit year. Multiplying this probability by this outcome and levelizing for average output of US reactors would add 2.0–3.1 cents/kWh (Pace, 1990). In expected cost terms, this might be interpreted as a cost of the order of 2.5 cents/kWh to be added to the costs considered in Table 11.1.

An East European incident, considered using US social costs and incident probabilities, is clearly a debatable basis for considering Canelco reactor incidents. The hybrid nature of this calculation adds uncertainty to the 2.0–3.1 cents/kWh provided by Pace (1990). Moreover, all the component figures are themselves subject to uncertainty, which is not reflected in the point estimates of the illness and death costs of any of the ranges. Probably a more meaningful estimate is a most likely (modal) value of the order of 2.5 cents with a 90% confidence range of the order of 1 to 10 cents. The implications of the greater scope for error on the high side demonstrated earlier in relation to expected values should be borne in mind: the implied expected cost might be in the range 3–4 cents/kWh. The risk implications of this very wide spread should also be borne in mind.

As pointed out by the Goodman Group, this social cost calculation is only a part of the full social cost and environmental cost associated with nuclear power. Other social costs which are amenable to economic evaluation like that just cited include cancers in nuclear power station workers caused by routine releases at most facilities (1.45 deaths per gigawatt-year), and incidents associated with radioactive waste storage, transport and disposal, decommissioning, and so on.

Non-quantifiable social and environmental costs

Many social costs of importance and many environmental issues are not amenable to economic evaluation. To help establish his Canadian credentials, Conrad supported the importance of this concern by quoting J. A. Cassilis (Ludvig von Miser, one of the pillars of the Austrian School of Economics):

> Economic calculation cannot comprehend things which are not sold and bought for money. What touches the human heart only, and does not induce other people to make sacrifices for its attainment, remains outside the pale of economic calculation. (Cassilis, 1991)

Conrad also quoted Cassilis himself:

> There is a danger in fixing the price of everything and knowing the value of nothing. (*ibid.*)

Conrad pointed out it should be clear that all the social and environmental cost issues which can be quantified in economic terms can be embedded in the nuclear power cost per kilowatt-hour distribution defined by Table 11.1. This should of course also be done for the equivalent of Table 11.2 and all other cost per kilowatt-hour distributions. He noted that this implies expected cost/risk trade-offs in social cost terms, which implies a need for external supervision of the long-term systems planning process by relevant regulators. The resulting mix of power sources can be interpreted as the preferred target portfolio in terms of all quantified issues. Bounds on the maximum proportion of power for any single source can be given a related rationale.

As part of the regulated review process associated with this long-term system planning exercise, verbal qualitative information about the implications of this mix can be considered, as part of the qualitative analysis process. Both qualitative issues and quantitative costs and benefits need to be considered, including complex issues which defy description in terms of simple cost per kilowatt-hour even if economic treatment is possible in part. For example, if there is too long a pause prior to building the next Canadian nuclear reactor, some people were quite properly concerned that the Canadian nuclear industry might deteriorate in a manner difficult to reverse. This has implications in terms of unemployment in the Canadian nuclear industry and the loss of an exporting industry, as well as implications for further electric power options for Canelco and other Canadian utilities. Adjustments to the mix can be identified in relation to the net effect of all the arguments. Such issues may have implications for prioritizing in the medium-term planning process and for operating constraints. Even if nuclear power has an unbiased cost per kilowatt-hour 3 or 4 times what has been assumed, maintaining a small stable nuclear position may be a very prudent investment for the long term.

Subsidies and taxes or constraints plus associated insurance

Most electric utilities do not and will not voluntarily include in their costs (as used for long-term planning or in associated medium- and short-term planning) the full social or environmental cost implications of their operations. One very sound reason for not doing so is that responsibility for a balanced approach from the perspective of all relevant parties to social and environmental costs is not part of their mandate. For example, in a private capacity all members of an electric utility's board might be of the view that taxes should be imposed on the burning of hydrocarbons, but the voluntary embedding of such costs in their corporate decision processes could be questioned, quite properly, by their electricity customers. This questioning could be particularly harsh if all other social and environmental costs were not considered in a balanced manner. This reason is quite sufficient. It can be argued that private or state-owned corporations which are 'responsible citizens' can justify to shareholders, regulators and governments the wisdom of such a stance.

If all electric utilities take this stance, it means that if the implications of environmental and social costs are to be considered in a short-, medium- and long-term planning context by electric utilities, there are two common ways of proceeding. One is to impose taxes such as a tax on carbon emissions. The other is to impose restrictions, like no more than X% of the total capacity may be coal-burning, no more than Y% of the total capacity may be nuclear, and so on. In both cases, the effect is to 'internalize' those external costs. A third approach involves recognizing the inherent value in electricity generation with fewer environmental and social costs, and providing subsidies, the flip side of a taxation-based approach. All three approaches could be used in combination.

The issue of subsidies and taxes or constraints can be addressed separately from the issue of a preferred mix of power sources. Taxes and subsidies can be given an interpretation which reflects government incentive priorities and revenue-raising priorities, full stop. Taxes on fuel for cars and other road vehicles raise all these issues. However, the expected cost of nuclear accidents raises another important set of issues involving implicit or explicit insurance. For example, if the expected cost of nuclear accidents is 2.5 cents/kWh, electricity customers do not pay Canelco this cost, and the government is implicitly providing full insurance in the insurer of last resort sense, then the government is subsidizing nuclear electric power at this level. If only partial insurance is provided by the government, all those at risk are subsidizing electricity to the extent of their risk exposure. If those at risk are the consumers of this electricity, they may see this position as appropriate risk sharing comparable to the extreme outage situation. However, this may not be the situation.

Conrad argued that Canelco and appropriate regulators and the government itself need to be clear about these issues, and they need to be explicit and honest about them. In his view it would be unethical to do otherwise. For example, if a government wishes to subsidize the cost of nuclear power, it might not tax nuclear power to meet the expected cost of disasters and other health problems. Instead, it might require utilities like Canelco to consider the expected cost in assessing the preferred mix, or constrain them to achieve similar results in terms of the proportion of nuclear, without insisting that the full expected cost be passed on to consumers. This is a clear subsidy if the electric utility would not or could not meet in full the consequences of a Chernobyl incident, and the costs would have to be borne by the government responsible. As compensations across national borders by national governments are likely to be involved in such incidents, and the costs involved are potentially so very large, prudent government policy on the part of all interested governments suggests international coordination, treating the financial transfers not as taxes, but as insurance premiums and claims.

Assuming the US Nuclear Regulatory Commission estimate of Chernobyl incidents of 1/3333 is of the correct order of magnitude, even 33 operating units implies such an incident every 100 years, while 333 units implies such an incident every 10 years, on average. Prudent insurance practice would not allow any individual, corporation or government to run a risk of large losses that the party responsible would not or could not meet. This is why most developed countries require third-party liability insurance of all automobile drivers by law, or provide back-up insurance through the licensing system. In the UK, driving a car without insurance involves heavy fines and can lead to a jail sentence. Operating a nuclear facility without insurance in place, implicitly if not explicitly, to meet all reasonable liability claims which may arise as a consequence of that operation involves directly analogous social and moral issues. Conrad emphasized this does not imply that all driving should be stopped, simply that those who benefit from the driving should pay, directly or indirectly, for insurance to compensate for any third parties who might be injured or killed or have their property damaged. Similarly, the points he had just made should not be taken to imply that all nuclear power stations should be closed, simply that those who benefit from the power should pay for any intentional and unintentional costs. The current difficulties associated with nuclear power stations in the former USSR could be attributed to a failure to take these issues on board at an international level.

Relative biases

Conrad explained that the 'externalities' example he used was nuclear power to counterbalance Canelco's current focus on 'externality' concerns about fossil fuel burning. Concerns about fossil fuel burning were receiving direct attention in many countries, including Canada, often without an equal concern for the environmental and social costs of other sources. All electric power sources should be considered in a balanced manner. In the context of his presentation it was not possible to assess whether the net effect of balanced consideration of both quantifiable and non-quantifiable issues would favour nuclear or fossil. However, it was very clear that not considering environmental and social costs in full involved a significant bias against cogeneration, hydro (particularly small hydro), other renewable sources, and conservation. Canelco had to address this bias. If Canelco did not do so, regulators would be under pressure to do so, and the result of leaving externalities to regulators might prove a very unhappy experience for Canelco.

Ethical issues as an opportunity

Conrad made the point that these social and environmental cost issues were very complex, and they were the source of major disputes and arguments, but they were not going to go away. Utilities like Canelco could see them as a threat to their agenda, and crisis manage them. However, he was of the view that Canelco's biggest threat was break-up and privatization, and its best defence against this was an exemplary ethical stance which separate privatized companies could not easily match.

The essence of his proposed approach was to invite all the relevant regulators to work with Canelco's strategic planners to assess full social and environmental expected costs and associated risk for all sources of electric power, use these results to determine the optimal mix of power sources to aim for and the pattern of their introduction, and formally negotiate an appropriate sharing of risk, taxes and subsidies. Constraints would probably not be necessary, but agreed constraints could be used as part of the agreed structure and processes.

A core part of the rationale was taking an ethical stance coupled to open processes to win the trust of regulators, consumers, and governments. Canelco could argue that a provincial-government-owned utility like Canelco could do this effectively, providing a solution which was risk efficient and balanced in terms of all the social and environmental issues. Canelco could argue that a market-driven alternative involving privatized separate players would be less efficient, less just, and less accountable. In effect, Canelco's biggest opportunity in the face of its most serious threat was the moral high ground. At present it was wasting this opportunity as well as ignoring the threat of privatization. And it was pursuing an unbalanced approach to environmental and social issues which could be its Achilles' heel in terms of the privatization/deregulation political processes.

A Crisis

When Conrad had finished his presentation and dealt with all the questions which followed, he was convinced that all members of the board could see the merit in what he was saying. However, Harry, Pat and Dick were clearly not going to admit it, and everyone bar Ivor was horrified by the extent to which Canelco's current stance was adrift from the strategy Conrad's proposed approach seemed to suggest. Discussion was defensive, and limited to points of clarification. The board agreed to discuss what to do about Conrad's report at a subsequent board meeting, after they had time to digest it. However, Conrad did not feel optimistic, and even Ivor was uncomfortable with the way the chairman, Charles, had reacted. It was clear that while Charles had expected Ivor to 'lift some rocks and expose some wildlife', he felt personally threatened by Conrad's presentation. Both Ivor and Conrad had a crisis on their hands. Prior to the next board meeting, two events precipitated a crisis for Canelco.

First, a further massive increase in the required budget provision for the nuclear power station mentioned earlier had to be sought. The press got hold of the story, and this made Charles and Pat particularly exposed. Second, Canelco had to revise its electricity demand forecast downwards, beyond its lower 'confidence bound', for the foreseeable future, because of a significant fall in actual demand, for reasons linked to demographic trend assumptions which were now clearly untenable. This was widely reported in the press, savaging Charles and Harry in particular.

Conrad's proposal was removed from the board's agenda, which now focused on crisis management. However, within the month, Charles was forced to resign. Ivor quickly found employment elsewhere. In the board shake-up which followed, Harry was sacked and Pat took early retirement.

The new board focused on dealing with the crisis, eventually with some success. However, none of the players wanted to generate the additional risks associated with significant change in corporate processes. The long-term plans changed to a massive extent, but the long-term planning process was not an immediate priority. The revisions to process that were made were in line with best practice in the electric utility industry, but they did not attempt to lead best practice. They were 'safe' in a risk-averse sense, but they did not seize the opportunities which Conrad had identified.

Conrad went on to pastures new and lost track of Canelco's progress. However, he remained convinced that the real crisis from a social and environmental perspective remained the lack of a conceptual framework for integrated joint management of the issues by those representing the interests of current consumers, other commercial interests, and the current and future societies bearing all the associated social and environmental costs. He was convinced that wholesale rejection of regulated government or private monopolies for the current breeds of deregulated utilities, railways and other similar organizations, in both North America and Europe, was not necessarily a step in the right direction. The ambiguities and uncertainties surrounding what constitute a best choice of structure and process, and how best to move towards a best choice of structure and process, seemed to him a challenge worth addressing. However, he was not clear about how to begin.

What was clear to Conrad was the need for structures and processes which allowed a balance to be struck between the various conflicting objectives and concerns. Even the regulators needed balanced control and motivation – who will regulate the regulators? For example, an exceptionally strong environmental regulator, concerned about greenhouse gasses, in concert with a strong allied green movement might restrict and unbalance the thermal portfolio and kill nuclear power, other interests might kill new hydro, and nobody might be motivated to make the necessary investment to make the resulting dependence on other renewable sources and 'conservation' effective. This might lead to very high electricity costs which induce energy-dependent industry to leave the province and start a spiral of decline in which virtually everyone in the province is a loser. At present nobody was managing such a risk, and nobody would until it was too late.

Conclusion

According to Irwin Stelzer's 'American Account' column in the *Sunday Times* (20 December 2001) the modernist Spanish sculptor Eduardo Chillida describes his art as 'trying to get closer to what I don't know'. Stelzer argues, 'Change don't to can't and you have the situation of those economists forced into the forecasting business.' For our purposes the original is better. Formulating strategy is not about trying to forecast particular futures and then prepare, it is about trying to get closer to the shape of possible futures and the nature of the best way to prepare for them and change them, to form and capture the most important opportunities as the primary concern, to neutralize or avoid any key threats as a secondary concern. Formulating strategy is much closer to sculpture and art than it is to forecasting and science. Good art needs passion, insight, imagination and technical skill. The material of this chapter is a contribution to the development of a generic process which is an effective add-in (not an add-on) to holistic strategic management in the way good risk management processes like the PRAM process discussed in Chapter 5 are an established add-in to holistic project management.

'Formulating strategy' was the term chosen for the title of this chapter to avoid a 'strategic planning' label for reasons set out by Mintzberg (1994) without claiming it dealt with strategic management as a whole. There is a vast literature on strategic management which this chapter has not touched on. Some of it, like Johnson and Scholes (1999) and Mintzberg, Ahlstrand and Lampel (1998), is centred on strategic management from a variety of perspectives which are weakly linked to the material of this chapter; some of it, like Dyson and O'Brien (1990), Friend and Hickling (1997) and Eden and Ackermann (1998), has stronger links because of some common process and modelling ideas; some of it, like Turner (1993), Partington (2000) and Murray-Webster and Thirty (2000), has stronger links because it is concerned about project-based management and the way programme management links project management and strategic management. The links to this wide literature offered in this chapter are focused on the way organizations can perceive and deal with uncertainty, demonstrating the way those whose focus is uncertainty in projects and programmes can interface with those who see strategic management from other perspectives. The links offered are incomplete in many respects. For example, the implementation aspects of strategic management is not addressed in terms of the concerns of the balanced scorecard literature, by Kaplan and Norton (1993b, 1996b) and Norreklit (2000) for example, although we hope it makes the need to do so clearer than earlier chapters which mentioned this literature. We also hope it makes the need to consider options outside the 'real options' framework clearer, in the medium- and long-term senses developed in this chapter, and in terms of their linkages.

This chapter is arguably the most important piece in the jigsaw puzzle of this book. It illustrates the importance of taking a corporate, holistic approach to uncertainty management which recognizes links between long-, medium- and short-term planning horizons, and related action horizons. While Conrad's consideration of Canelco's approach to strategy formulation reflects a specific context, most organizations share similar problems in terms of uncertainty about future costs, demand for their products, and appropriate choices for the product portfolio. Previous tales have been concerned with certain aspects of this uncertainty, but Conrad's tale addressed all these aspects and links between them.

To begin with, the tale illustrates the value of distinguishing between short-, medium- and longer-term planning horizons. Each horizon focuses attention on different kinds of decision, and warrants different forecasting paradigms. Typically, short-term planning is concerned with managing ongoing operations. Fluctuations in demand and availability of products, plant and materials are key considerations. Medium-term planning is concerned with the timing and introduction of new plant or products, when to retire old plant, maintenance programmes, and so on. Developing trends in demand, lead times for projects, availability of existing plant or products, and building competitive advantage are key considerations. Long-term planning is concerned with deciding where the company wants to be in terms of size and relative mix of investments in different products/markets, or modes of service delivery. Key considerations are survival, growth, demand for products, the whole-life cost of buildings and plant, developments in associated technology, and building a competitive advantage. Short-, medium- and long-term plans are clearly linked in a top-down fashion, with long-term plans influencing medium- and short-term plans. However, short- and medium-term planning issues may also have a bearing on long-term strategy.

In some respects, the structure of Canelco's activities is much simpler than most manufacturing firms. A single product is produced by a relatively small number of plants, whose variety is also limited. However, like any other company, Canelco has a need to forecast demand for its product, future costs, and its future operating environment. In Canelco, short-term demand forecasting was well developed. Medium-term forecasting needed greater use of regression models which relied more on tracking key exogenous variables than extrapolating from past observations. However, such medium-term forecasting needs to reflect *in full* the substantial uncertainty associated with forecasting models and the exogenous variables that drive the models. Long-term forecasting is particularly problematic for companies like Canelco because of the lengthy planning horizons involved. In these circumstances many companies use scenario approaches to explore credible extremes in the variety of possible futures. However, as Conrad's analysis shows, it is important to ensure these approaches recognize important correlations between key variables, such as production costs, and regulatory/political issues.

Arguably the persistent production of a narrow band of forecasts, whether for costs or demand, is symptomatic of a desire to reduce uncertainty so that appropriate strategies can be determined. This tends to result in a passive 'predict and prepare' approach to the future. Effective uncertainty management means confronting the extent of uncertainty head-on, and from a full appreciation of this, attempting to achieve desired futures as well as avoiding undesirable futures.

In addressing Canelco's approach to uncertainty management in strategy formulation, Conrad drew attention to three different considerations associated with the three planning horizons. In respect of long-term strategy, a key issue was recognizing and understanding the implications of correlation between the costs associated with operating multiple power units. This illustrates the use of portfolio analysis in a different context to the share dealing context described in Chapter 10. Conrad's analysis is perhaps easier to relate directly to the long-term management of a portfolio of business units, manufacturing plants or products. Canelco's choices in respect of power units again illustrates the importance of recognizing positive dependencies, and the substantial advantages of negative dependencies, between different activities.

In respect of the medium term, a key issue identified by Conrad was the costs associated with the inability to give precise forecasts of the demand for electricity (the product). In particular, the additional costs associated with demand being less than or greater than capacity provided were asymmetric – higher when capacity was greater than demand, and lower when capacity was less than demand. Accepting the asymmetry of these additional costs led to the insight that capacity should lag expected demand. A related insight was that it would be worth paying a premium for small-capacity units with short construction (lead) times. In this particular context, these insights warranted attention in the formulation of long-term strategy, illustrating an important bottom-up link between medium- and long-term planning.

Such considerations might well apply in other contexts, although the cost asymmetry might be reversed. For example, in many manufacturing businesses the cost of production exceeding demand might be less (not more) than the cost of production falling short of demand, particularly if no additional source of supply, perhaps via subcontracting, were available, or major competitors could take up the slack and capture customers. Similar considerations emerged in Chapter 9, where Tess's initial production capacity investment problem was just the starting point for development of long term-strategy.

In respect of the short term, demand forecasting in Canelco was not perceived by Conrad as a problem. Rather, the problem was the way availability of plant, and the need for reserve capacity, was assessed for the whole company. Conrad demonstrated that discrete probability arithmetic could be used to examine the probability of different numbers and durations of plant failures. This demonstrates that the need for reserve capacity increases as the size of units increases and their number decreases, and as the chance of common-mode failure increases.

An important point made by Conrad was that the cost of reserve capacity ought to be attributed to the plant (or activities) that causes it to be needed. Where reserve capacity is a significant element of costs, then this cost and related management options may need to be considered in the long-term planning process. Such conclusions are obviously generalizable to other contexts, although the consequences of plant (or product) failures may be less dramatic than for Canelco.

At all three levels of planning, Conrad used simple but plausible numerical examples and constructively simple analytical models which made calculations transparent. Although the models and the key issues were different at each level, the aim was the same – to clarify the implications of uncertainty for strategy formulation. The purpose of modelling as employed by Conrad was not to prescribe particular optimal strategies, but to provide insights which facilitate a reasoned set of robust judgements, and to highlight significant practical complications which need to be addressed. In particular, this includes consideration of non-quantifiable factors such as social and environmental costs. In Canelco's case this led Conrad to identify related ethical issues as a major opportunity for management, an opportunity which could address the significant threat of the privatization and break-up of Canelco itself. The unfortunate denouement of Conrad's work with Canelco illustrates how difficult it may be for organizations to accept advice which criticizes deeply entrenched shortcomings in uncertainty management. It also illustrates some of the likely consequences.

12   From concepts to culture

I would rather be an optimist proved wrong than a pessimist proved right.

Anon

Simplicity Efficiency

The more the authors explore the variety of approaches to uncertainty management and the complexity of the situations they address, the more the need to keep it simple in a constructive sense becomes obvious. The more time we spend running seminars for experienced managers who want to make direct use of what they learn immediately, the more it becomes obvious that we need to continually stress the need to add complexity only when it is effective and efficient to do so, and that what we are talking about is not rocket science, it is about systematic common sense. The emerging approach to constructive simplicity described in this book is concerned with achieving simplicity efficiency in respect of basic concepts and terminology, appropriate decision support processes, and embedded modelling approaches. The concept of simplicity efficiency, introduced in Chapter 1, is analogous to risk efficiency, another key concept employed throughout this book. Figure 12.1 is the simplicity efficiency equivalent of the Figure 10.3 depiction of risk efficiency.

Simplicity efficiency is about maximizing insight for any given level of complexity, and this applies to concepts, models and decision support processes. To achieve simplicity efficiency we need to employ concepts, models and processes which lie on the simplicity-efficient boundary rather than just any from the set of feasible alternatives. For example, in respect of concepts, 'risk' defined as 'probability times impact' is analogous to point *e* in a 'concept' interpretation of Figure 12.1. Risk defined as probability times impact is a feasible choice, but it excludes much more insightful (efficient and effective) perspectives. Risk defined as probability times impact is not a simplicity-efficient *concept*. This issue is central to Sarah's tale. As another example, probability impact matrices, as noted in Eddy's tale, are inefficient *models*, another choice like point *e* in Figure 12.1. *Processes* which are not designed to exploit a multiple-pass approach to modelling

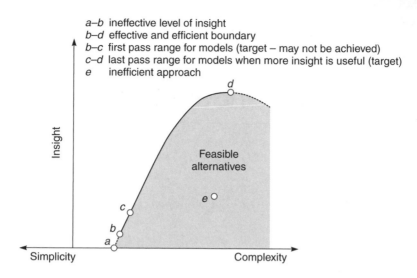

a–b ineffective level of insight
b–d effective and efficient boundary
b–c first pass range for models (target – may not be achieved)
c–d last pass range for models when more insight is useful (target)
e inefficient approach

Figure 12.1—Simplicity efficiency boundary.

uncertainty, as illustrated in a number of chapters, are further choices like point *e* in Figure 12.1.

In modelling terms simplicity-efficient choices involve being on the simplicity efficiency boundary *b–d* of Figure 12.1 for each modelling attempt. The simplicity-efficient range starts at point *b* because the range *a–b* is too simple to be effective. A first pass might start near the bottom as portrayed by the range *b–c* with subsequent passes moving up the range and a final pass coming close to *d* in the range *c–d* if constructive complexity proves worthwhile. Simplicity efficiency involves being bold about the high level of simplicity sought for models on a first pass, and being bold about the high level of insight sought for models on later passes if more insight is useful.

In process terms, simplicity-efficient choices involve being on the simplicity efficiency boundary *b–d* of Figure 12.1 for each process selection or development attempt. Some people may favour an initial process in the range *b–c*, with a view to working towards an ultimate process in the range *c–d*. However, there is a strong case for starting with a relatively sophisticated process (in the range *c–d*) to invest in insight about the nature of the issues being addressed, then moving towards a less insightful but simpler process once it is clear what the short cuts imply, a 'learn to walk before you try to run' strategy (Chapman and Ward, 1997). It is obvious we should not want to choose processes associated with points like *e* in Figure 12.1. However, it is less obvious where we should choose to be on the simplicity efficiency boundary. Simplicity efficiency in *model* terms involves progression from *b* to *c* to *d* on successive passes in a clearly defined way, but simplicity efficiency in *process* terms could involve proceeding either way, and simplicity efficiency in *concept* terms ought to go for something approaching *d* directly. There is no obvious argument for less insight than the maximum available given the foundation nature of concepts.

Basic Concepts

As noted in Chapter 1, a prerequisite for simplicity efficiency is a simple set of basic uncertainty concepts and associated terms which are common across different areas of application. In particular, we need to avoid terms and concepts which are restrictive, and which inhibit our approach because of framing assumptions. Table 12.1 summarizes the simple set of basic concepts and associated terms advocated in this book.

'Uncertainty', defined as 'lack of certainty', is an important starting point. Anything else is restrictive. Visualizing uncertainty in terms of 'variability' and 'ambiguity' is also important, with an ambiguous distinction between these two, and no prescriptive attempt to categorize ambiguity. Restrictive interpretations of uncertainty for management purposes, which argue that variability and ambiguity are inherently different and separable, and so require different treatment, are counterproductive. Tess's tale endeavours to clarify why directly, and all other tales do so indirectly.

The constructively simple approach to variability which this book advocates embraces part of the ambiguity associated with making decisions. If we do not understand why potential variability exists, because we have not yet thought it worthwhile identifying all the sources of variability and our potential responses to it, variability must embody ambiguity. The more we probe this variability with a view to understanding and managing it, the more we extract it from our working definition of variability and clarify it in terms of model structure. But model structure does not eliminate ambiguity. If constructive complexity is used effectively, it provides an effort-effective reduction in ambiguity, but a complete lack of ambiguity is not a feasible goal.

All the tales of this book should make it clear that ambiguity associated with working assumptions and framing assumptions is in general much more important than ambiguity associated with variability. We tend to ignore this kind of ambiguity because it is comparatively difficult. We are all guilty of concentrating on the issues which we know how to deal with, and like to deal with, ignoring those we do not know how to deal with, like Trevor in Chapter 3. Martha and Barney illustrate what can be done if we choose to model in terms of explicit working assumptions and structure in an area most marketing people deal with intuitively. Sarah and Eric illustrate what can be achieved in a safety context. Sam illustrates what might be achieved in a financial security portfolio management context.

Table 12.1—Basic uncertainty concepts and terminology

Concept	Definition
Uncertainty	Lack of certainty, involving variability and ambiguity
Variability	Uncertainty about the size of parameters which may result from lack of data, lack of detail, lack of definition, lack of experience, and so on, which may be quantified if this is useful
Ambiguity	The aspects of uncertainty not addressed in terms of variability
Cube factor (F^3)	The link between expected values defined in terms of variability and expected values considering known unknowns, unknown unknowns, and bias
Expected value	The best estimate of what should happen on average
Uncertainty management	Making decisions in the face of significant uncertainty
Risk	An implication of significant uncertainty, which may be upside (welcome) or downside (unwelcome)
Threat	A source of downside risk, with synonyms like 'hazard' or 'outage'
Opportunity	A source of upside risk
Risk efficiency	For any given decision the maximum level of expected performance in terms of all relevant criteria in an appropriately balance manner for a given level of risk, the risk level chosen reflecting a bold approach to risk associated with all relevant decisions over time
Simplicity efficiency	In respect of choices of concept, model or process, for a given level of complexity, the maximum level of insight in all relevant respects, the level of complexity chosen reflecting the pass involved (and its purpose) when models are involved
Constructive complexity	Additional complexity which is simplicity efficient

Key Modelling concepts

The basic guidelines for achieving simplicity efficiency in modelling are very simple: never use a complex model if a simpler one will do the job, and make sure the simplifying assumptions are the most appropriate simplifying assumptions. The operational requirements are not so simple, but they can be described to some extent in the following terms:

- Models should involve nested levels of complexity, a degree of modularity in terms of simplifying assumptions, so we can relax assumptions as necessary to increase complexity where it pays.
- Models in the set being used should not be mutually exclusive, incompatible or contradictory, requiring us to abandon what we have learned from the perspective of one model subset in order to move on to another.
- Model assumptions must not be opaque or hidden.
- Be clear about what working assumptions and framing assumptions are involved for all those parties involved in the decision process.
- Models should facilitate joint consideration of issues which are qualitatively modelled, quantitatively modelled, and external to the model.
- Models must not inhibit the consideration of any important issues.

In addition, the tales illustrate the value of three other features of constructively simple modelling: separability, portability and robustness.

Separability

Separability can be associated with basic concepts, as in the separability but lack of independence of opportunities and threats. However, separability is really defined and made operational as a modelling concept. It is a very powerful way of making things simpler without becoming simplistic. Tess's tale is the first to explore separability in relation to models directly. Sam and Conrad make extensive direct and explicit use of separability. However, separability was implicit in the approach to decomposing the probability of winning curves in Martha's tale, and separability is a useful framework for understanding correlation or other forms of variability dependence, a basic uncertainty modelling concern, as illustrated at a sophisticated level by Sam's tale, at a simple level by Martha's tale.

Portability

Portability is about how easy it is to transfer an approach from one context to another. In respect of modelling approaches, using Nicola's buffer model for inventories, or waiting time at an airport, or time between activities, is one illustration of what is involved. The use of simple discrete probability models throughout the tales is another. Models based on specific probability distributions or higher-moment representations of uncertainly can be useful, but if they are the conceptual basis or starting point for analysis, they can prove restrictive. In practice Monte Carlo simulation software is the most readily available and portable process for combining probability distributions (e.g. Grey, 1995).

Portability also has value beyond constructive simplicity. In terms of the toolbox of models needed to tackle all situations of interest, a high degree of portability means we do not need as many tools. We need a relatively small set of tools which are more flexible, more adaptable, more multi-purpose, the equivalent of Swiss army knives. And we can become more skilled in their use because there are fewer of them. Portable models (and processes) mean we can adapt our approach to each individual situation with greater ease, speed and confidence so that we can avoid serious errors of judgement. Everything we learn is more useful because it is more widely applicable. In the vernacular, our thinking is joined-up.

Robustness

Robustness concerns the nature of model assumptions. How critical are assumptions in relation to decision choices? Do particular assumptions matter or not? If they matter, it is important to understand in what way, and to what extent they matter. Nicola's tale is the most explicit exploration of this issue, but it also pervades other tales. The relationship between robustness and constructive simplicity may be too abstract to interest most readers, but in the authors' view it could prove useful territory to explore. In simple terms, constructive simplicity is an effective and efficient approach to achieving robustness.

Key Process Concepts

Constructive simplicity includes the idea of designed generic decision support processes for use with suitable adaptation to the circumstances, and guidance on that adaption. In our view, generic processes of this kind may be the real future for uncertainty management, in the sense that they are a promising route to mass use of the concepts discussed here. As consultants, Chapman and Ward have helped a number of organizations to solve specific uncertainty management problems (as in Nicola's tale), or to shape their specific uncertainty management analysis process (as in Martha's tale). However, it is widely available processes that are most likely to make constructive simplicity a common feature of uncertainty management in our view. In the context of project risk management, PRAM (Ian's tale) is a useful start, along with similar processes developed by the PMI (Project Management Institute, 2000), the Institute of Civil Engineers and the Faculty and Institute of Actuaries (Simon, 1998) and others. However, there are lots of other contexts which could use the same generic process concept, although the processes themselves might be very different. All chapters involve relevant ideas.

Well-developed generic but context-related processes like the PRAM process are probably best developed via synthesis from effective specific processes like the bidding process of Figure 3.12. This was the route to the PRAM process which was defined by a working party of 20 people representing leading-edge best practice in the UK (Simon, Hillson and Newland, 1997). It was based on the collective experience of this working party drawing on more specific project risk management processes. Some of these specific processes were developed by specific organizations for their own use in specific industries. Some were developed by specific consultants with broader applications in mind. But the process label 'generic' was explicitly used for the first time by the participants to emphasize the generality and portability being sought via the pooling of experience.

The focus phase

The focus phase is a key feature of the generic decision support process of Figure 1.1 and of specific-context generic processes like the PRAM process of Figure 5.1. The focus phase is about selecting a specific version of the generic best practice set to implement on a particular occasion. A key research question, explored to some extent in Chapman and Ward (1997) in relation to Figure 5.1, is What are the drivers which shape the optimal process choice? Example 'drivers' include: Where is the project in its project life cycle? How experienced is the organization in the use of project risk management? How much does the uncertainty matter? The most effective way to develop an understanding of these focus phase drivers seems to be generalization of the specific issues which shape effective approaches to individual cases. However, our current understanding of how to formalize the focus phase in an optimal manner is limited. We are talking craft, not science. The focus phase in Figure 1.1 is not usually identified as such in depictions of a general OR process. It is implicit. Each OR practitioner has their own view of it. At extremes some practitioners assume a traditional OR process starting position, informed by soft OR processes as appropriate, while others assume a specific soft OR process starting position, with traditional OR processes informing these process as appropriate (Chapman, 1992). The soft systems/soft OR community is now exploring 'multi-methodology' approaches which in effect use a focus phase to choose between and blend soft approaches to the starting position and subsequent quantitative modelling (Mingers and Gill, 1997), but a truly general focus phase for Figure 1.1 is going to be very elusive, and much more difficult to formalize than the focus phase for the PRAM process. However poorly defined is the nature of the focus phase, some key features of constructively simple processes are emerging, and Chapters 2 to 11 illustrate some of them. Many of them reflect constructively simple model characteristics.

Iterations

An iterative nature is one key feature of constructively simple decision support processes, with formal recognition of the need to seek different objectives on the first pass to those sought in later passes. The first pass is usually about sizing variability, to see if it might matter, and to reflect potential variability in an unbiased estimate of the expected outcome. If a very simple first-pass conservative estimate suggests expected values and variability do not matter, we should be able to ignore variability without further concern or further effort. If the first pass raises concerns, further passes are necessary. Designing the first and subsequent passes to reflect their purpose is part of the decision support process design, and part of the focus phase within a given process. One-shot standard decision support processes using standard models are hopelessly inefficient and ineffective.

From this perspective, making decisions involving uncertainty requires early framing and structuring choices couched in terms of modelling assumptions, to gain insight about objectives, priorities, and what is feasible. Strategic and tactical operational choices come later, in the light of understanding gained earlier in the decision support process. However, using a highly iterative process is essential because these two aspects are not really separable. Nicola's tale illustrates a basic form of this process. Tess's tale illustrates the importance of choosing an initial modelling framework which starts in the right place, avoiding blind alleys and problems defined to fit the tools available, rather than the other way around. A key feature of the way this perspective is developed here is the broad view of uncertainty. Variability is part of uncertainty, but a relatively trivial part for Nicola and Tess. Ambiguity about framing assumptions, structure, knowledge and data is much more important, and none of these considerations are really separable. The iterative nature of the process is the key to managing this lack of separability.

Separability

Separability linked to modelling separability is another key feature of constructively simple decision support processes. For example, separability has important implications with respect to different planning horizons, as explored in Sam's tale and Conrad's tale.

Portability

The portability of process ideas in terms of parts of processes or whole processes as well as model ideas and concepts is an important part of the constructive simplicity concept. For example, in Sarah's tale her ability to adapt project risk management process ideas to safety considerations contributed to the effectiveness and efficiency of both. Further, portions of specific or generic processes may be highly portable. For example, Eddy's tale describes a minimalist cost estimation process which can be embedded in the PRAM process and in other specific or generic processes concerned with marketing, safety or other quite different contexts, illustrated by the links between Chapters 3, 4 and 7.

Uncertainty Management Systems

Uncertainty management systems embrace standards, protocols, guidelines, procedures, decision-aiding software, database software, and embedded analytical processes. The embedded processes, and the models and concepts embedded in them, are the primary concern of this book.

However, to maximize their benefits, appropriate uncertainty management systems need to be built around constructively simple concept–process–model sets. Processes should be designed and then used to shape other aspects of management systems, in so far as this is feasible, not the other way round. System definition followed by development of concept–process–model sets involves a serious risk of inappropriate reverse dependencies. Established databases may shape the structure of thinking about uncertainty. Readily available software may shape the modelling of uncertainty. And standards which become set in stone may inhibit organizational learning to a terminal extent.

Those particularly interested in systems in their entirety may wish to extend constructive simplicity to embrace systems too, and consider constructively simple systems in the sense of Figure 12.1. This book does not attempt to do so. However, it may be useful to distinguish three kinds of systems: general modelling medium systems, specific modelling medium systems, and operating systems.

General modelling medium systems like @Risk, a risk modelling spreadsheet tool, are essential basic components of a sound systems environment. Grey (1995) provides advice on modelling using this kind of medium, and those involved in this kind of modelling need to use the range of advice appropriate to the general modelling mediums in use, like Grey. The generality and flexibility of these systems is important. An early move to more specialized and restrictive modelling systems to gain efficiency and ease of use can be a serious mistake.

Specific modelling medium systems like Sam's information and control system (Chapter 10) can provide serious competitive advantage. They are not essential basic components of operations unless competitors develop them first, in which case they can become vital. They are key potential threats when others have them and you do not. Modelling medium systems cover a wide range between simple spreadsheet environments and Sam's system, too wide to do them justice here. Operating systems should support the modelling medium systems without inhibiting their use more than necessary. Operating systems cover an even wider range, well beyond the scope of this book.

Sound modelling medium systems which are available and in common use, and which are effective and reasonably efficient, make a big difference to overall corporate performance. They may not need to be fine-tuned or optimized to a high degree. Effectiveness (doing the right things) is more important than efficiency (doing things right). But they need to do what matters tolerably well, with a tolerable level of effort. All organizations at the leading edge have sound modelling medium systems. It can be a serious handicap to have a modelling medium systems void, created for example by the lack of effective shared computer software which supports common processes with the flexibility to deal with the range of models needed.

Addressing Cultural Barriers To Uncertainty Management

Some important reasons for adopting constructively simple models and simplicity efficiency in associated decision support processes were discussed in Chapter 1. Hopefully all the tales have also demonstrated the potential benefits of constructive simplicity, as well as suggesting ways in which this can be achieved. However, the largest improvements in uncertainty management are likely to flow from the use of simplicity-efficient decision support processes, models and concepts because of their impact on an organization's uncertainty management culture. The term 'culture' is a convenient umbrella term which encompasses the implicit beliefs, values, convictions, and associated ways of doing things that are taken for granted and which pervade all organizations. Usually this culture is indirectly visible via physical manifestations such as routines, control systems, administrative structures, power structures, symbols, and company stories which make up what Johnson (1992) has termed the 'cultural web'.

In the authors' experience, some of the most significant barriers to effective uncertainty management are based on organizational culture. Sometimes these barriers are induced from outside the organization in the form of convictions, prejudices, biases, and routines of professional groups which can blinker thinking. The blinkers may arise from a wish to make decisions efficiently in a particular context according to recognized scientific or professional standards. But such blinkers may seriously limit our effectiveness. We may not even realize we are seeing the world from the back of a cave, with blinkered tunnel vision. Such professionally based convictions can strongly influence different groups within the same organization, making it very difficult to adopt holistic, enterprise-wide uncertainty management processes. However, most organizations also exhibit a number of more generic culture-based behaviours or 'conditions' inimical to effective uncertainty management. As an illustration, Table 12.2 lists a number of such culture-based conditions that we have observed in a variety of organizations. We do not suggest this list is complete, but it should be comprehensive enough to serve as a prompt for readers who want to develop a list for their own organization.

The conditions in Table 12.2 are grouped under four headings: dysfunctional behaviours, attitude to judgement, attitude to other parties, and organizational capability. Essentially these behaviours seem to evidence the difficulty management has in coping with complexity and uncertainty in decision making. Some of these conditions may seem mutually exclusive. For example, it might be assumed that an organization cannot simultaneously exhibit both po-faced pessimism and El Dorado optimism. In practice different parts of an organization can exhibit conflicting conditions like these two. However, half a dozen or so complementary cultural conditions seems to be the norm, in terms of a characterization of conditions significant enough to warrant attention and treatment.

Dysfunctional behaviours

The first group of conditions relate to general attitude to uncertainty and behaviours which might be thought to have some merit for individuals, but which give rise to significant disbenefits to the organization.

Po-faced pessimism

Po-faced pessimism, simplistic unmitigated pessimism, is normally limited to parts of organizations concerned with hazard or safety management. Even then it is usually an unfair cartoon characterization of those involved, by others who do not own the responsibility for explaining serious failures. However, a serious blame culture can encourage the development of po-faced pessimism across an organization. For example, it can result in bidding processes which are biased towards overpricing to avoid loss-making contracts, leading to bankruptcy via lack of work, as observed in Martha's tale. Constructively simple concepts, models and process should provide a simple cure in the context of each tale.

Table 12.2—Cultural conditions

Label	Description
Dysfunctional behaviours	
Po-faced pessimistic	Simplistic unmitigated pessimistic
El Dorado optimism	Simplistic unmitigated optimism
Muddled moderation	Simplistic unmitigated moderation
Conspiracy of optimism	Strong corporate pressures to avoid revealing bad news until you have to
Conspiracy of infallibility	Belief that crisis is unlikely and disaster is not possible
Naked emperor phenomenon	No one is prepared to acknowledge a high level of uncertainty which clearly exists
Management by misdirection	Constraint setting without appreciation of the consequences for other performance objectives
Attitude to judgement	
Irrational objectivity paradox	An obsession with objectivity when rationality should be seen as more important
Weak subjective skills	Undeveloped ability to make formal subjective judgements
Attitude to other parties	
Fair weather partnerships syndrome	Confidence in partnerships which are not designed to withstand major difficulties
Hands-off illusion	Belief that the transfer of uncertainty to other parties is generally effective and efficient
Hands-on illusion	Belief in retaining uncertainty which could be transferred to other parties effectively and efficiently
Organizational capability	
Disconnected left and right hands	The left hand doesn't know what the right hand is doing, in organizational terms
Complexity constipation	Permanent paralysis by analysis involving unconstructive complexity
Tunnel vision	Inability to see the big picture or the wood for the trees
Lack of focus	Inability to see the trees that matter in the wood
Wasted experience	The same mistakes made time after time
Propensity to panic	High levels of uncontrolled crisis and unhelpful fear
Self-healing deficiency	Lack of negative feedback loops to neutralize surprises
Self-harm syndrome	The presence of destructive internal pressures with positive feedback loops
Boredom	Lack of constructive tension, excitement and fun
Unenlightened intuition	Lack of intuitively applied expertise

El Dorado optimism

El Dorado optimism, simplistic unmitigated optimism, might seem to be a simple converse, and in some cases it may be. However, in a context like the Barings failure of the mid 1990s, it can be coupled to a lack of controls and inappropriate internal contracts, leading to and allowing a gambler's ruin form of escalating commitment, successively doubling up on bets. Sam's tale and Roger's tale illustrate relevant aspects of a constructively simple cure. The notion 'you might as well be hung for a sheep as a lamb' is not limited to the financial services sector. Many project managers and other managers take massive gambles against the odds because unless they 'luck in' they are going to be judged a failure anyway, due to a succession of earlier failures.

Muddled moderation

Muddled moderation, simplistic misguided moderation, is a common simplistic middle ground. Taking the right risks, avoiding the wrong risks, via a constructively simple approach, is the obvious cure here, applying the ideas of all ten tales. Distinguishing between 'unenlightened gambles' (beyond the gambler's ruin example) and 'enlightened gambles' (risk-efficient gambles) is the key issue here. These concepts have been discussed in a project management context (Chapman and Ward, 1997), but generalizing to other contexts has to address the lack of a well-defined generic process like the PRAM process in Figure 5.1 as a starting place, with the result that it may be necessary to start from Figure 1.1.

Conspiracy of optimism

A conspiracy of optimism, strong corporate pressures to avoid revealing bad news until you have to, is a more complex cultural condition. In many organizations this is associated with a can-do corporate culture, a Darwinian survival of the fittest struggle between projects, and a corporate culture which makes project team loyalty more important than loyalty to overall corporate goals. A range of other conditions may feed this, like a tendency to generate gambler's ruin situations. The difficult trick here is to preserve the positive aspect of a can-do spirit and a spirit of optimism while eliminating the downside effects. A concerted campaign to encourage risk-efficient choices is one way to start.

Conspiracy of infallibility

A conspiracy of infallibility is the belief that crisis is unlikely and disaster is not possible. It is particularly virulent and dangerous if naive uncertainty management approaches are introduced and applied without understanding the cube factor (F^3) concept introduced in Eddy's tale and developed or used in several other tales. It can fatally damage the credibility of formal uncertainty management processes, and set back organizations in a way which may prove terminal. A balance of self-confidence and humility is required, as well as enlightened intuition and a suitably large cube factor.

Naked emperor phenomenon

The naked emperor phenomenon describes situations where no one is prepared to acknowledge a high level of uncertainty which clearly exists. It is a label we apply to the all too common insistence of senior management on minimal uncertainty in estimates, tight ranges of the ±10% variety, and a culture which goes along with this mandate. The naked emperor phenomenon takes its name from the well-known fairy tale 'The Emperor's New Clothes'. The emperor's marvellous new clothes were a figment of his imagination, as pointed out by a child when the emperor appeared naked in public to show them off. A tight confidence bound, like ±10% on an early estimate of cost for a project worthy of uncertainty management, is as plausible as the emperor's new clothes.

The naked emperor phenomenon may be driven by a pathological dislike of uncertainty at the top. Most people dislike uncertainty. However, to flourish, this condition needs a yes-man culture, or an authoritarian culture which means people just don't comment on nonsense generated above. This can be an effective way to foster a corporate-wide conspiracy of optimism. In effect, the naked emperor phenomenon and a conspiracy of optimism are often different aspects of a shared underlying problem in organizations that suffer from them, and in such cases they need to be treated jointly. Internal contracts as devised by Roger may hold the key here. Culture change certainty needs to be managed from the top down as well as from the bottom up. This is a very common pair of conditions, usually found when simplistic risk management processes are employed, as illustrated by Ian's tale.

Sometimes a useful way to view the bottom line of uncertainty management is 'the effective management of expectations'. In a project uncertainty management context, expected values should move up *and down* as a project proceeds, within bounds that *consistently tighten* as time passes. If this does not happen, the uncertainty management process is failing. The focal point of the cure for the conspiracy of optimism is the minimalist estimation approach of Eddy's tale. However, equally important is the need to persuade the organization's senior management that preliminary estimates of project costs plus or minus a tight band like 10% are not feasible; +100% and −50% is more plausible. If excessively tight bands are mandated, the effect will be premeditated failure, if not in terms of cost then in terms of delivered performance or completion time.

Management by misdirection

A variant of the naked emperor phenomenon is management by misdirection; this involves setting constraints without appreciation of the consequences for other performance objectives. Uncertainly management at a corporate level has to pay attention to the time profile of performance. To the extent that any one measure such as cost is predefined (constrained), all associated uncertainty must be transformed into uncertainty and risk in terms of other aspects of performance. It is inevitable that attempts to constrain sets of performance measures (like cost and time) simultaneously result in additional uncertainty and risk for other performance aspects (like quality as defined by operating and maintenance costs, reliability, and non-monetary concerns like the satisfaction of employees, customers and others). A failure to understand the implications of constraints in term of transforming uncertainty and risk from one dimension into another is a common source of dysfunctional organizational behaviour. One way to address this problem is to use constructively simple decision support processes that recognize interdependencies between performance objectives and how different parties will be motivated to make trade-offs between different performance measures.

Attitudes to judgement

Irrational objectivity paradox

A very common condition, the irrational objectivity paradox is an obsession with objectivity when rationality should be seen as more important. This behaviour scorns the use of subjective estimates, particularly subjective probability estimates, as inherently unreliable and therefore of little value. This results in a preference for irrational 'objective' data which ignores uncertain (ambiguous) features of the real world context, rather than make use of rational subjective judgements which acknowledge these features. Eddy's tale introduced this problem as 'destructive objectivity', which operated as a barrier to more constructive, rational estimating that reflected beliefs about the decision context. The key to understanding how to deal with this condition is recognizing that making decisions is not science.

Most people with a physical science or engineering basic education see objectivity as an important virtue in any formal analysis. The need for reproducible results from physical science experiments if the science involved is good science, as inculcated in the first contact with physics at school, may be the early origins. A frequentist view of classical objective probabilities is based on the notion of sampling a finite number of times from a population which may be infinite to estimate a 'true' probability which in general is not knowable. However, the real world most of us live in most of the time is more akin to the worlds of Eddy or

Martha or Tess. Constructively simple probabilities as discussed in Eddy's tale are directly relevant to making decisions. Objective probabilities are not, although if available they may be used as a starting point, and their development may be appropriate if preliminary analysis suggests particular probabilities matter a great deal, and associated probability estimates need to be defensible. Formally modelling uncertainly about probabilities as well as outcomes in a multiple-pass approach is the key generalization. Successive estimation passes provide more insight by probing and refining the structure of the analysis as well as looking for more data if it is available, or the views of more people, if a structural decomposition lends itself to integrating the appropriate experience of different people. An infinite amount of time spent on an infinite number of passes involving an infinite number of people giving advice might lead to the perfect subjective probabilities, but this is an abstract special case of little direct practical interest.

Classical objective probabilities and classical Bayesian (objective or subjective) probabilities more generally may be useful in a constructively simple probability framework, but they should not be used without such a framework to make decisions. Mathematicians and statisticians may not warm to this idea, but practising engineers and applied economists should see its relevance immediately, as should anyone else who is concerned with practical uncertainty management. Constructively simple probability estimates are mathematically untidy, and lacking in mathematical elegance, from some perspectives. However, they are a simple, practical, systematic way to incorporate relevant judgements which can only be ignored if we are happy getting the right answer to the wrong problem. If practical right answers to the right problem are the concern, it is elegant as a simple way to link conditional probabilities to unconditional equivalents.

Weak subjective skills

Weak subjective skills, an undeveloped ability to make formal subjective judgements, often complements the irrational objectivity paradox. If people do not recognize the need to see formal judgements about probabilities and impacts as inherently subjective, they are not going to take steps to develop the skills needed to make effective subjective judgements. The minimalist approach of Eddy's tale addresses this need, perhaps to a sufficient degree if simple first- or second-pass approaches are all that is needed. But everyone involved in serious uncertainty management efforts needs a reasonably sophisticated understanding of the issues explored by books like *Judgement Under Uncertainty: Heuristics and Biases* (Kahneman, Slovic and Tversky, 1982). Deep uncertainty issues require deep skills development. Formal subjective judgement skills are an important part of the package.

Attitudes to other parties

A pervasive problem in all organizations is the agency problem involving uncertainty associated with selection of appropriate agents, moral hazard behaviour, and the extent of risk allocation. Much depends on the level of trust between parties, their motives, and the incentives operating.

Fair weather partnerships syndrome

The fair weather partnerships syndrome describes undue confidence in partnerships which are not designed to withstand major difficulties. It is a consequence of the current fashion for partnership approaches in the absence of enlightened intuition, and a lack of proven, effective frameworks for partnership management. Ian's tale and Roger's tale both address some of the issues, but they are not easy issues to deal with, and a lot of work needs to be done to understand them better. Roger's trigger contract and Ian's balanced incentive and risk sharing (BIARS) contract are a good starting point. Central aspects are the measurement of performance, and trade-offs between time, cost and performance. 'What doesn't get measured doesn't get managed' is a visible sign of failing fair weather partnerships when the going gets tough.

Hands-off illusion

The hands-off illusion, a belief that transfer of uncertainty to other parties is generally effective and efficient, is associated with an 'eyes-on hands-off' approach to contracting, often linked to the use of a single prime contractor who is supposed to take and manage all the risk. The most effective way to treat this condition involves starting from the perspective that such a contract is a special case of a partnership approach, and a generally ineffective special case. If a prime contractor is going to manage uncertainty on behalf of a client, the contractor needs a BIARS contract to motivate uncertainty management in the best interests of the client. Further, even a well-managed BIARS contract is likely to involve some surprises, which may benefit from hands-on client involvement, and could involve crises (serious surprises), even disasters (crises that are not contained), that definitely need hands-on client involvement. It is in the best interests of contractors as well as clients, more generally buyers and suppliers, to get this right.

Whether or not a partnership approach to contracting is applied, banishing the hands-off illusion is important. Appropriate unambiguous rules of engagement for intervention, and available resources to intervene effectively and efficiently, need to be addressed as part of any contract strategy. The hands-off illusion is dangerous because it is used to justify a lower than appropriate resourcing level for uncertainty management. Lower than appropriate levels of proactive prior management of uncertainty mean higher than appropriate levels of crisis management effort, and more potential for disasters. Lower than appropriate levels of resources for reactive management of uncertainty mean more crises become disasters. Higher opportunity costs overall are the result. It is not cost-effective to attempt to eliminate crises and disasters by prior planning, but it is important to reduce them to a cost-effective level. It is also important to be ready for the unexpected. Crisis and disaster will happen. If they don't, we are not trying hard enough.

Hands-on illusion

The hands-on illusion, a belief in retaining uncertainty which could be transferred to other parties effectively and efficiently, may be a relatively simple condition. It all depends on what is driving it. For example, if a large organization decides to self-insure accident damage to a vehicle fleet, it may be tempted to self-insure associated third-party liability. This could prove a public relations disaster if there occurs a high-profile accident involving a large damage claim that receives extensive media attention. Simple advice can avoid this kind of hands-on illusion. However, if a macho culture or a micromanagement obsession is driving a hands-on illusion, a cure may be very difficult indeed.

Organizational capability

This final group of conditions relates to general organizational capability in terms of the effectiveness of coordination and control systems, environmental scanning capability, and organizational learning. Simplicity efficiency in related decision support systems offers one way of alleviating these conditions.

Disconnected left and right hands

Disconnected left and right hands, where the left hand does not know what the right hand is doing, is a common organizational condition in a general sense, but it is also a direct implication of a failing uncertainty management process. An effective uncertainty management process is very much about everybody knowing what may happen as a result of bad luck or good luck involving any related activity or function. Martha's tale is directly concerned with this issue, but many others touch on it.

Complexity constipation

Complexity constipation, permanent paralysis by analysis involving destructive complexity, is in one sense another special case of unenlightened intuition. It deserves a special mention because 'keep it simple' is a mantra which needs routine repetition. Only add complexity when it serves a useful purpose is the corollary which needs to be kept in mind. Not being simplistic is the associated trap to avoid.

Tunnel vision

Tunnel vision, an inability to see the big picture or the wood for the trees, is another example of a common organizational condition in a general sense, but it is a direct implication of a failing uncertainty management process. Encouraging constructive insubordination, communicating upwards as well as downwards and across, is the cure within the framework provided by an effective uncertainty management process. But keeping it simple (not simplistic) is another essential part. Nicola's tale starts the demonstration of what is involved. Most of the other tales contribute, the most direct formal contribution coming from Conrad's tale.

Lack of focus

Lack of focus, an inability to see the trees that matter in the wood, can be viewed as a simple converse of tunnel vision. But it is common to find them together, characterized by refined solutions to the wrong problems, and detailed analysis of what people understand while the important issues are ignored because they seem too difficult. Curing this combination of lack of focus and tunnel vision is a central theme of constructive simplicity, in all of the tales.

Wasted experience

Wasted experience, where the same mistakes are made time after time, can be associated with a failure to develop the 'learning process' and 'learning organization' aspects of uncertainty management processes, as well as unenlightened intuition. Martha's tale and Sam's tale are particularly concerned with these issues, but so are Sarah's and several others.

Propensity to panic

Propensity to panic, evident by high levels of uncontrolled crises and unhelpful fear, is a sure sign of major uncertainty management process failure. Often this is driven top-down, by senior management making bad situations worse. In such situations there is no point doing anything until the ill-conceived pressure from the top is relieved. Propensity to panic can also be fuelled by unanticipated crises arising from a conspiracy of optimism or the naked emperor phenomenon and other conditions.

Self-healing deficiency

Self-healing deficiency, a lack of negative feedback loops to neutralize surprises, is directly concerned with recovery from damage inflicted by nasty surprises. As a simple example, if several key players in an organization suddenly leave, healthy organizations can move people up, sideways or down to fill the gap, but unhealthy organizations may be dependent on importing people who might induce positive feedback loops that make things worse. A sound uncertainty management process should recognize and addresses these issues.

Self-harm syndrome

Self-harm syndrome, the presence of destructive internal processes with positive feedback loops, is usually the consequence of perverse incentives, a failure of the psychological contracts and trust which glue an effective organization together. Uncertainty about the way people will behave can be seen as a central issue which has not been addressed. The outsourcing discussion in Roger's tale illustrates a simple version of this syndrome.

Boredom

Boredom, a lack of constructive tension, excitement and fun, can be attributed to uncertainty management process failure, and can be addressed by uncertainty management process design. Martha and Trevor, in their different but complementary ways, hint at what is involved here. As discussed in Roger's tale, appropriately designed internal incentive contracts can have effects beyond particular contracts in terms of providing a more pleasurable working environment which increases motivation and nurtures expertise.

Unenlightened intuition

Unenlightened intuition, a lack of intuitively applied expertise, can be associated with 'naive' levels of maturity in corporate uncertainty management as described by Hillson (1997). The implication is uncertainty management undertaken by 'amateurs' rather than 'professionals'. They may be gifted amateurs and enthusiastic amateurs, but they are not skilled professionals. This condition is a generalization of weak subjective skills. It needs to be treated via the implementation of appropriate processes and their evolution through Hillson's four stages until uncertainty management is natural, built into other processes. It also requires appropriate basic education, appropriate ongoing training, learning by doing with mentoring, an appropriate centre of excellence which can lead process development and the provision of internal consultancy as well as training, and a staff development and promotion approach which ensures expertise is managed creatively.

The skills required for a strong corporate capability in uncertainty management are similar to the skills required for a good internal operational research/ management science/information systems consultancy group. Some of the most successful groups of this kind are used as an elite training ground for future senior executive recruiting and development, as well as a core competitive weapon in their immediate role. The idea is to attract very bright younger staff as junior consultants, who will develop skills which remain very valuable when most of them move on to line management roles. Some will stay on in managing consultant roles, and some will become the custodians of processes, training and staff development. However, the spin-off of very effective line managers and future executives is a central feature. Leadership is a key issue for such groups. This is a classic potential problem which needs to be managed as an opportunity. Organizations which move everyone on to different jobs every two or three years have particular problems with this issue, although some have dealt with it very successfully by modifying their usual rules to some extent.

The aims of the tales

One aim of the ten tales is to demonstrate the potential organizational pay-off from a team made up of people like Nicola, Eddy, Martha, Ian and the others. Another aim is to illustrate the sophistication needed to use constructively simple approaches which provide constructive complexity when appropriate. The growth of MSc degrees in risk management (two at the University of Southampton School of Management, alongside three MSc degrees in operational research, management science, and information systems) demonstrates a growing awareness of the need to take uncertainty management seriously. However, the proportion of organizations at the leading edge is small, and lack of enlightened intuition is a common basic reason. Knowledge management might be seen as a more fashionable label for what is involved here. However, the authors prefer to view knowledge management as a product of enlightened intuition in conjunction with an effective concept–model–process–systems–culture set.

Culture Change Management

Culture change management can be seen as an important aspect of uncertainty management, or uncertainty management can be seen as can important aspect of culture change management. From either perspective, culture change management is important. Culture heavily influences the effectiveness and efficiency of uncertainty management.

One way to assess how well an organization manages uncertainty involves a 'concept to culture' framework. This framework was developed by Chapman as part of a recent review of project risk management practice within a client organization, using a rough approximation to a flexible 'grounded theory' approach (Strauss and Corbin, 1998). Structured interviews with senior managers designed to capture their views of organizational strengths and weakness, threats and opportunities, led to a set of six cultural conditions. These cultural conditions were then linked to current practice and to recommended alternatives in terms of a nested hierarchy of concepts, models, processes and systems. That is, the concerns at a cultural level were addressed as symptoms of issues at lower levels, with a hierarchy of issue linkages between culture, systems, processes, models and concepts. Recommendations for dealing with these issues addressed this hierarchical structure, together with associated strengths and opportunities which needed exploitation, as part of the process of taking the organization to the leading edge of project risk management best practice.

One way to initiate culture change is by creating a crisis. This notion is quite simple; to use a physical analogy, a crisis is an explosion which overcomes the inertia and friction that resist change. Once change starts, the momentum needs to be preserved, sustaining movement in the desired direction. One example of how this can be done involved an organization which suffered from the naked emperor phenomenon – no one was prepared to acknowledge a high level of uncertainty which clearly existed. A senior project manager was instrumental in the appointment of a consultant who had a robust reputation. The consultant prepared an analysis of the cost risk associated with the project manager's project. This project had to be proceeded with, for strategic reasons. The analysis demonstrated a cost variability risk the project manager would have to take that was several times what was normally allowed. The analysis also demonstrated that scope and other assumption conditions involved orders of magnitude more additional cost variability risk, which the directors would have to accept if they wanted the project to proceed.

The board could not accept the results, and the resulting crisis led to the consultant being sacked. But the board acknowledged that uncertainty was much more extensive than they had previously allowed, and agreed to set up an internal consultancy operation to assist project managers with risk management. This internal risk management function, in concert with project managers who understood the issues, gradually increased the extent to which cost variability and other associated risks were acknowledged, collectively and explicitly managing upwards the culture shift which they needed. Each step involved a new aspect of uncertainty measurement which could be defended one step at a time. For example, the implications of positive correlation between activity durations was established early on, with linked positive correlation of associated cost items. Then the implications of responses to earlier activity delays was established – reducing positive statistical dependence between duration estimates by throwing money at delays intensified the positive statistical dependence between costs. Subsequently a more comprehensive understanding of sources of uncertainty and additional cost variability associated with a flexible set of responses was introduced. The implications of scope definitions and other assumptions were left until last, finally reaching the position originally suggested by the consultant. A direct trip to the end goal was not feasible. A step-by-step journey initiated by the crisis eventually reached the original destination.

More generally, drivers which influence culture can be identified and used to change culture. A key driver is the nature of the contract used to interface between parties. These contracts may be psychological contracts, implicit understandings between people, or legal contracts between organizations. Different forms of contract require different uncertainty management systems to support associated uncertainty management. The uncertainty management systems used must be consistent with the contracts, and vice versa. The uncertainty management systems used are also direct drivers of the culture. If the systems facilitate the maintenance of a naked emperor phenomenon, it will persist. If the systems make such a phenomenon impossible, it will be eliminated. The standards, guidelines, protocols, procedures, decision-aiding software, database software and embedded processes are all part of the systems. But the processes, embedded models and concepts are the core.

Conclusion

Understanding and managing uncertainty is not a simple business. Simplistic perspectives put us in caves which seriously limit our view of outside and what is involved in decision making. To see the role of uncertainty in decision making from the hilltops in an unrestricted, mature, practical manner, we have to leave behind aspects of some conventional simplistic perspectives which inhibit a comprehensive general understanding. We have to weave together other aspects of conflicting or contradictory perspectives to form a unified perspective. This book is about one particular vision of what this involves. It is based on practical experience with real decisions, and the efforts to understand how best to make these decisions. Its central tenet is the notion of constructive simplicity. If constructive simplicity is the central theme of future developments in this area, and constructive complexity is the only kind of complexity introduced in practice, the authors are convinced we will be moving in the right direction. Where we will get to remains one of life's more interesting uncertainties. We hope you have enjoyed the ten tales about attempts to reach ten illustrative hilltops, and we hope they help you to climb your own particular choices of hilltop. We do not expect everyone to move in our chosen direction, but we hope this book will stimulate discussion among those who share some of our views, as well as helping those who simply wish to find their own way.

Bibliography

Abel, B. A. and Eberly, C. J. (1996) Optimal investment with costly reversibility. *Review of Economic Studies*, **63**, 581–93.

Abel, B. A., Dixit, K. A., Eberly, C. J. and Pindyck, S. R. (1996) Options, the value of capital, and investment. *Quarterly Journal of Economics*, **111**, 754–75.

Ackoff, R. L. (1974) *Redesigning the Future*, John Wiley & Sons, Chichester.

Ackoff, R. L. (1977) Optimization + objectivity = opt out. *European Journal of Operational Research*, **1**, 1–7.

Ackoff, R. L. (1979) Does the quality of life have to be quantified? *Journal of Operational Research*, **30**(1), 1–16.

Ackoff, R. L. (1986) *Management in Small Doses*, John Wiley & Sons, Chichester.

Ackoff, R. L. and Sasieni, M. W. (1968) *Fundamentals of Operations Research*, John Wiley & Sons, New York.

Arrow, K. J. (1961) Additive logarithmic demand functions and the Slutsky relations. *Review of Economic Studies*, **28**, 176–81.

Artto, K. A., Kahkonen, K. and Pitkanen, P. J. (2000) *Unknown Soldier Revisited: A Story of Risk Management*, Project Management Association Finland, Helsinki.

Atkinson, A. A., Waterhouse, J. H. and Wells, R. B. (1997) A stakeholder approach to strategic performance measurement. *Sloan Management Review*, Spring, pp. 25–37.

Baldwin, Y. C. (1982) Optimal sequential investment when capital is not readily reversible. *Journal of Finance*, **37**(3), 763–91.

Ballow, H. R. (1999) *Business Logistics Management*, 4th edn, Prentice Hall, Hemel Hempstead.

Barnes, N. M. L. (1988) Construction project management. *International Journal of Project Management*, **6**(2), 69–79.

Barwise, P., Marsh, P. R. and Wensley, R. (1989) Must finance and strategy clash? *Harvard Business Review*, **67**(5), 85–90.

Barzilai, J. (1997) Deriving weights from pairwise comparison matrices. *Journal of the Operational Research Society*, **48**, 1226–32.

Becker, H. S. (1983) Scenarios: a tool of growing importance to policy analysts in government and industry. *Technological Forecasting and Social Change*, **23**, 95–120.

Bellman, R. (1957) *Dynamic Programming*, Princeton University Press, Princeton NJ.

Belton, V. (1985) The use of a simple multiple-criteria model to assist in selection from a shortlist. *Journal of the Operational Research Society*, **36**(4), 265–74.

Belton, V. (1986) A comparison of the analytic hierarchy process and a simple multi-attribute value function. *European Journal of Operational Research*, **26**, 7–21.

Belton, V. (1990) Multiple criteria decision analysis – practically the only way to choose. In Hendry, L. C. and Eglese, R. W. (eds), *Operational Research Tutorial Papers*, Operational Research Society, Birmingham.

Belton, V. and Gear, T. (1982) On a shortcoming of Saaty's method of analytic hierarchies. *Omega, International Journal of Management Science*, **11**, 228–30.

Bernhard, R. H. (1984) Risk adjusted values, timing of uncertainty resolution, and the measurement of project worth. *Journal of Financial and Quantitative Analysis*, **19**(1), 83–99.

Bernstein, P. L. (1995) Awaiting the wildness. *Journal of Portfolio Management*, **21**, 1–2.

Bernstein, P. L. (1996) *Against the Gods: The Remarkable Story of Risk*, John Wiley & Sons, New York.

Black, F. and Scholes, M. (1973) The pricing of options and corporate liabilities. *Journal of Political Economy*, May–June, pp. 637–57.

Bontis, N., Dragonetti, N. C., Jacobsen, K. and Roos, G. (1999) The knowledge toolbox: a review of the tools available to measure and manage intangible resources. *European Management Journal*, **17**(4), 391–401.

Brans, J. P. and Vincke, P. (1985) A preference ranking method. *Management Science*, **31**, 647–56.

Brans, J. P., Vincke, P. and Mareschel, B. (1986) How to select and how to rank projects: the PROMETHEE method. *European Journal of Operational Research*, **24**, 228–38.

Brealey, A. R. and Myers, S. W. (1996) *Principles of Corporate Finance*, 5th edn, McGraw-Hill, Singapore.

Brewer, P. C., Chandra, G. and Hock, C. A. (1999) Economic value added (EVA): its uses and limitations. *SAM Advanced Management Journal*, **64**(2), 4–11.

Brown, A. and Deaton, A. (1972) Models of consumer behaviour. *Economic Journal*, **82**, 1145–1236.

Bunn, D. W. and Sato, A. A. (1993) Forecasting with scenarios. *European Journal of Operational Research*, **68**(3), 291–303.

Burke, C. (1992) Financial control of portfolio management decisions: discussant's comments. In Ezzamel, M. and Heathfield, D. (eds), *Perspectives on Financial Control: Essays in Memory of Kenneth Hilton*, Chapman & Hall, London.

Busby, J. S. and Pitts, C. G. C. (1997) Real options in practice: an exploratory survey of how finance officers deal with flexibility in capital appraisal. *Management Accounting Research*, **8**, 169–86.

Byron, R. P. (1970) A simple method for estimating demand systems under separability assumptions. *Review of Economic Studies*, **37**, 261–74.

Cassilis, J. A. (1991) Beyond the pale of economics: social responsibility, values and the environment. Paper for the Ottawa chapter of the IAEE, November 20.

Cather, H. (1997) Is the 'critical chain' the missing link? *Project Management Today*, Nov/Dec, pp. 22–25.

Chapman, C. B. (1974) Modular portfolio selection: an introduction. In Dickinson, J. P. (ed.), *Portfolio Analysis: Book of Readings*, Saxon House/Lexington Books, Farnborough.

Chapman, C. B. (1975) *Modular Demand Analysis: An Introduction in the Context of a Theoretical Basis for Consumer Demand Analysis*, Saxon House/Lexington Books, Farnborough.

Chapman, C. B. (1979) Large engineering project risk analysis. *IEEE Transactions on Engineering Management*, **26**, 78–86.

Chapman, C. B. (1984) Project risk management. In D. Lock (ed.), *Handbook of Project Management*, 2nd edn, Gower, Aldershot.

Chapman, C. B. (1988) Science, engineering and economics: OR at the interface. *Journal of the Operational Research Society*, **39**(1), 1–6.

Chapman, C. B. (1990) A risk engineering approach to project management. *International Journal of Project Management*, **8**(1), 5–16.

Chapman, C. B. (1992) My two cents worth on how OR should develop. *Journal of the Operational Research Society*, **43**(7), 647–64.

Chapman, C. B. (1997) Project risk analysis and management – PRAM the generic process. *International Journal of Project Management*, **15**(5), 273–81.

Chapman, C. B. (2000a) Two phase parametric discounting. In Turner, J. R. and Simister, S. J. (eds), *Handbook of Project Management*, 3rd edn, Gower, Aldershot.

Chapman, C. B. (2000b) Project risk management: the required changes to become project uncertainty management. In Slevin, D. P., Cleland, D. I. and Pinto, J. K. (eds), *Proceedings of the Project Management Institute Research Conference*, Paris, pp. 241–45, PMI, Newtown Square PA.

Chapman, C. B. and Cooper, D. F. (1983a) Risk engineering: basic controlled interval and memory models. *Journal of the Operational Research Society*, **34**(1), 51–60.

Chapman, C. B. and Cooper, D. F. (1983b) Parametric discounting. *Omega, International Journal of Management Science*, **11**(3), 303–10.

Chapman, C. B. and Cooper, D. F. (1985) A programmed equity redemption approach to the finance of public projects. *Managerial and Decision Economics*, **6**(2), 112–18.

Chapman, C. B. and Howden, M. (1997) Two phase parametric and probabilistic NPV calculations, with possible deferral of disposal of UK Nuclear Waste as an example. *Omega, International Journal of Management Science*, **25**(6), 707–14.

Chapman, C. B. and Ward, S. C. (1987) Modular decision analysis – a production scheduling illustration. *Journal of the Operational Research Society*, **38**(9), 803–14.

Chapman, C. B. and Ward, S. C. (1988) Developing competitive bids: a framework for information processing. *Journal of the Operational Research Society*, **39**(2), 123–34.

Chapman, C. B. and Ward, S. C. (1992) Financial control of portfolio management decisions. In Ezzamel, M. and Heathfield, D. (eds), *Perspectives on Financial Control: Essays in Memory of Kenneth Hilton*, Chapman & Hall, London.

Chapman, C. B. and Ward, S. C. (1996) Valuing the flexibility of alternative sources of power generation. *Energy Policy*, **24**(2), 129–36.

Chapman, C. B. and Ward, S. C. (1997) *Project Risk Management: Processes, Techniques and Insights*, John Wiley & Sons, Chichester.

Chapman, C. B. and Ward, S. C. (2000) Estimation and evaluation of uncertainty: a minimalist first pass approach. *International Journal of Project Management*, **18**(6), 369–83.

Chapman, C. B., Cooper, D. F. and Cammaert, A. B. (1984) Model and situation specific OR methods: risk engineering reliability analysis of an LNG facility. *Journal of the Operational Research Society*, **35**(1), 27–35.

Chapman, C. B., Cooper, D. F. and Page, M. J. (1987) *Management for Engineers*, John Wiley & Sons, Chichester.

Chapman, C. B., Ward, S. C. and Bennell, J. A. (2000) Incorporating uncertainty in competitive bidding. *International Journal of Project Management*, **18**(5), 337–47.

Chapman, C. B., Ward, S. C. and Curtis, B. (1989) Risk theory for contracting. In Uff, J. and Capper, P. (eds), *Construction Contract Policy: Improved Procedures and Practice*, Centre of Construction Law and Management, King's College, London.

Chapman, C. B., Ward, S. C. and Curtis, B. (1991) On the allocation of risk in construction projects. *International Journal of Project Management*, **9**(3), 140–47.

Chapman, C. B., Ward, S. C. and Hawkins, C. (1984) Pricing models: a case study in practical OR. *Journal of the Operational Research Society*, **35**(7), 597–603.

Chapman, C. B., Ward, S. C. and Klein, J. H. (1991) Theoretical versus applied models: the newsboy problem. *Omega, International Journal of Management Science*, **19**(14), 197–206.

Chapman, C. B., Ward, S. C., Cooper, D. F. and Page, M. J. (1984) Credit policy and inventory control. *Journal of the Operational Research Society*, **8**(12), 1055–65.

Chapman, C. B., Cooper, D. F., Debelius, C. A. and Pecora, A. G. (1985) Problem-solving methodology design on the run. *Journal of the Operational Research Society*, **36**(9), 769–78.

Checkland, P. (1981) *Systems Thinking, Systems Practice*, John Wiley & Sons, Chichester.

Checkland, P. B. and Scholes, J. (1990) *Soft Systems Methodology in Action*, John Wiley & Sons, Chichester.

Chelst, K. and Bodily, S. E. (2000) Structured risk management: filling a gap in decision analysis education. *Journal of the Operational Research Society*, **51**, 1420–32.

Christopher, M. (1998) *Logistics and Supply Chain Management: Strategies for Reducing Cost and Improving Service*, 2nd edn, Financial Times Management, London.

Clark, P. and Chapman, C. B. (1987) The development of computer software for risk analysis: a decision support system development case study. *European Journal of Operational Research*, **29**(3), 252–61.

Clarkson, R. (1999) The long-term case for UK equities. *The Actuary*, December, pp. 16–17.

Claxton, G. (1997) *Hare Brain, Tortoise Mind: Why Intelligence Increases When You Think Less*. Fourth Estate, London.

Cohen, R. and Durnford, F. (1986) Forecasting for inventory control: an example of when 'simple means better'. *Interfaces*, **16**(6), 95–99.

Cook, S. and Slack, N. (1991) *Making Management Decisions*, 2nd edn, Prentice Hall, Hemel Hempstead.

Cook, S. D. N. and Brown, J. S. (1999) Bridging epistemologies: the generative dance between organisational knowledge and organisational knowing. *Organisation Science*, **10**(4), 381–400.

Cooper, D. F. and Chapman, C. B. (1987) *Risk Analysis for Large Projects*, John Wiley & Sons, Chichester.

Copeland, E. and Keenan, T. (1998a) How much is flexibility worth? *McKinsey Quarterly*, **2**, 39–49.

Copeland, E. and Keenan, T. (1998b) Making real options real. *McKinsey Quarterly*, **3**, 128–41.

Cross, R. and Baird, L. (2000) Technology is not enough: improving performance by building organisational memory. *Sloan Management Review*, **41**(3), 69–78.

Curtis, B., Ward, S. C. and Chapman, C. B. (1991) *Roles, Responsibilities and Risks in Management Contracting*. Special Publication 81, Construction Industry Research and Information Association (CIRIA), London.

Daellenbach, H. G. and George, J. A. (1978) *Introduction to Operations Research Techniques*, Allyn and Bacon, Boston.

Diffenbach, J. (1982) Influence diagrams for complex strategic issues. *Strategic Management Journal*, **3**, 133–46.

Dixit, A. K. and Pindyck, R. S. (1994) *Investment Under Uncertainty*, Princeton University Press, Princeton NJ.

Dixit, A. K. and Pindyck, R. S. (1995) The real options approach to capital investment. *Harvard Business Review*, May/June, pp. 105–15.

DoE (1994) *Review of Radioactive Waste Management Policy Preliminary Conclusions: A Consultative Document*, Radioactive Substances Division, Department of the Environment.

Dorfman, R., Samuelson, P. A. and Solow, R. M. (1958) *Linear Programming and Economic Analysis*, McGraw-Hill, New York.

Dowie, J. (1999) Against risk. *Risk Decision and Policy*, **4**(1), 57–73.

Dyer, J. S. (1990) Remarks on the analytic hierarchy process. *Management Science*, **36**, 249–58.

Dyer, J. S. and Sarin, R. (1981) Relative risk aversion. *Management Science*, **28**, 875–86.

Dyson, R. G. and O'Brien, F. A. (1990) *Strategic Development: Methods and Models*, John Wiley & Sons, Chichester.

Eden, C. (1988) Cognitive mapping: a review. *European Journal of Operational Research*, **36**, 1–13.

Eden, C. (1994) Cognitive mapping and problem structuring for system dynamics model building. *System Dynamics Review*, **10**, 257–76.

Eden, C. and Ackermann, F. (1998) *Making Strategy: The Journey of Strategic Management*, Sage, London.

Eilon, S. (1979) Mathematical modelling for management. In *Aspects of Management*, 2nd edn, Pergamon, Oxford.

Einhorn, H. J. and Hogarth, R. M. (1981) Behavioral decision theory: processes of judgment and choice. *Annual Review of Psychology*, **32**, 53–88.

Elrod, R. and Moss, S. E. (1994) Adversarial decision making: benefits or losses. *Omega, International Journal of Management Science*, **22**(3), 283–89.

Elton, J. and Roe, J. (1998) Bringing discipline to project management. *Harvard Business Review*, March/April, pp. 153–59.

Fishburn, P. (1970) *Utility Theory for Decision Making*, John Wiley & Sons, New York.

Fishburn, P. (1988) *Nonlinear Preference and Utility Theory*, Johns Hopkins University Press, Baltimore MD.

French, S. (1988) *Decision Theory: An Introduction to the Mathematics of Rationality*, Ellis Horwood, Chichester.

French, S. (1991) Recent mathematical developments in decision analysis. *IMA Journal of Mathematics Applied in Business and Industry*, **3**, 1–12.

Friedman, L. (1956) A competitive bidding strategy. *Operations Research*, **4**, 104–12.

Friend, J. K. and Hickling, A. (1997) *Planning Under Pressure: The Strategic Choice Approach*, 2nd edn, Butterworth-Heinemann, Oxford.

Frigo, L. and Krumwiede, R. (2000) The balanced scorecard, a winning performance measurement system. *Strategic Finance*, January, pp. 50–54.

Fripp, J. (1985) How effective are models? *Omega, International Journal of Management Science*, **13**(1), 19–28.

Frisch, D. and Clemen, R. T. (1994) Beyond expected utility: rethinking behavioural decision research. *Psychological Bulletin*, **116**, 46–54.

Garud, R., Kumaraswamy, A. and Nayyar, P. (1998) Real options or fool's gold? Perspective makes the difference. *Academy of Management Review*, **23**, 212–14.

Godfrey, P. C. and Hill, C. W. L. (1995) The problem of unobservables in strategic management research. *Strategic Management Journal*, **7**(16), 519–33.

Godfrey, P. S. (1996) *Control of Risk: A Guide to the Systematic Management of Risk from Construction*, Construction Industry Research and Information Association (CIRIA), London.

Goldratt, E. M. (1997) *Critical Chain*, North River Press, Great Barrington MA.

Goldratt, E. M. and Cox, S. (1992) *The Goal*, 2nd edn, North River Press, Great Barrington MA.

Goodwin, P. and Wright, G. (1998) *Decision Analysis for Management Judgement*, 2nd edn, John Wiley & Sons, Chichester.

Gorman, W. M. (1959) Separable utility and aggregation. *Econometrica*, **27**, 469–81.

Gorman, W. M. (1963) Additive logarithmic preferences: a further note. *Review of Economic Studies*, **30**, 56–62.

Gorman, W. M. (1968) The structure of utility functions. *Review of Economic Studies*, **35**, 367–90.

Gorman, W. M. (1968) Conditions for additive separability. *Econometrica*, **36**, 605–9.

Graham, J. D. (2001) Decision-analytic refinement of the precautionary principle. *Journal of Risk Research*, **4**(2), 127–42.

Green, A. E. and Bourne, A. J. (1972) *Reliability Technology*, Wiley-Interscience, New York.

Green, H. A. J. (1964) *Aggregation in Economic Analysis: An Introductory Survey*, Princeton University Press, Princeton NJ.

Green, H. A. J. (1970) *Consumer Theory*, Penguin, London.

Green, S. D. (2001) Towards an integrated script for risk and value management. *Project Management*, **7**(1), 52–58.

Grey, S. (1995) *Practical Risk Assessment for Project Management*, John Wiley & Sons, Chichester.

Hadley, G. (1964) *Nonlinear and Dynamic Programming*, Addison-Wesley, Reading MA.

Hammond, J. S., Keeney, R. L. and Raiffa, H. (1998) The hidden traps in decision making. *Harvard Business Review*, Sept/Oct, pp. 47–58.

Hartman, F. T. (2000) *Don't Park Your Brain Outside – A Practical Guide to Adding Shareholder Value With SMART Management*, Project Management Institute, Newton Square PA.

Harwood, I. A. (2002) Developing scenarios for post merger and acquisition integration: a grounded theory of 'risk bartering'. PhD thesis, School of Management, University of Southampton.

Hawkins, C. J. and Pearce, D. W. (1971) *Capital Investment Appraisal*, Macmillan, London.

Henig, M. I. and Buchanan, J. T. (1996) Solving MCDM problems: process concepts. *Journal of Multi-Criteria Decision Analysis*, **5**, 3–21.

Hershey, J. C., Kunreuther, H. L. and Schoemaker, P. J. H. (1988) Sources of bias in assessment procedures for utility functions. In Bell, D. E., Raiffa, H. and Tversky, A. (eds), *Decision Making: Descriptive, Normative and Prescriptive Interactions*, Cambridge University Press, Cambridge.

Hertz, D. B. (1964) Risk analysis in capital investment. *Harvard Business Review*, **42**(1), 95–106.

Hertz, D. B. and Thomas, H. (1983) *Risk Analysis and Its Applications*, John Wiley & Sons, New York.

Hillier, F. S. (1963) The derivation of probabilistic information for the evaluation of risky investments. *Management Science*, April, pp. 443–51.

Hillson, D. A. (1997) Toward a risk maturity model. *International Journal of Project and Business Risk Management*, **1**(1), 35–45.

HMSO (1991) *Economic Appraisal in Central Government: A Technical Guide for Government Departments*, HMSO, London, ISBN 0115600345.

Hodder, E. and Triantis, J. A. (1990) Valuing flexibility as a complex option. *Journal of Finance*, **45**(2), 549–66.

Hood, C. and Jones, D. K. C. (1996) *Accident and Design: Contemporary Debates in Risk Management*, UCL Press, London.

Horowitz, I. (1970) *Decision Making and the Theory of the Firm*, Holt, Rinehart and Winston, New York.

Houthakkar, H. S. (1960) Additive preferences. *Econometrica*, **29**, 244–57.

Institute of Chartered Accountants in England and Wales (1999) *No Surprises: A Case for Better Risk Reporting*, ICAEW, London.

Johnson, G. (1992) Managing strategic change: strategy, culture and action. *Long Range Planning*, **25**(1), 28–36.

Johnson, G. and Scholes, K. (1999) *Exploring Corporate Strategy*, 5th edn, Prentice Hall, Hemel Hempstead.

Joy, O. M. and Bradley, J. O. (1973) A note on sensitivity analysis of rates of return. *Journal of Finance*, **28**, 1255–61.

Kahn, H. and Wiener, A. J. (1967) *The Year 2000: A Framework for Speculation on the Next Thirty-Three Years*, Macmillan, New York.

Kahn, R. N. (1995) Fixed-income risk modelling in the 1990s. *Journal of Portfolio Management*, **22**, 94–101.

Kahkonen, K. and Artto, K. A. (1997) *Managing Risks in Projects*, Spon, London.

Kahneman, D. and Lovallo, D. (1993) Timid choices and bold forecasts: a cognitive perspective on risk taking. *Management Science*, **39**(1), 17–31.

Kahneman, D. and Tversky, A. (1979) Prospect theory: an analysis of decision under risk. *Econometrica*, **47**, 263–91.

Kahneman, D., Slovic, P. and Tversky, A. (1982) *Judgement under Uncertainty: Heuristics and Biases*, Cambridge Press, Cambridge MA.

Kaplan, R. S. and Atkinson, A. (1998) *Advanced Management Accounting*, 3rd edn, Prentice Hall, Englewood Cliffs NJ.

Kaplan, R. S. and Norton, D. P. (1992) The balanced scorecard – measures that drive performance. *Harvard Business Review*, Jan/Feb, pp. 71–79.

Kaplan, R. S. and Norton, D. P. (1993a) Putting the balanced scorecard to work. *Harvard Business Review*, Sept/Oct, pp. 134–47.

Kaplan, R. S. and Norton, D. P. (1993b) Using the balanced scorecard as a strategic management system. *Harvard Business Review*, Sept/Oct, pp. 75–85.

Kaplan, R. S. and Norton, D. P. (1996a), *The Balanced Scorecard: Translating Strategy into Action*, Harvard Business School Press, Boston MA.

Kaplan, R. S. and Norton, D. P. (1996b) Linking the balanced scorecard to strategy. *California Management Review*, **39**(1), 71–79.

Kaplan, S. (1997) The words of risk analysis. *Risk Analysis*, **17**, 407–17.

Katzner, D. W. (1970) *Static Demand Theory*, Macmillan, London.

Keasey, K., Hudson, R. and Littler, K. (1998) *The Intelligent Guide to Stock Market Investments*, John Wiley & Sons, Chichester.

Keefer, D. L. and Bodily, S. E. (1983) Three point approximations for continuous random variables. *Management Science*, **29**(5), 595–609.

Keeney, R. L. (1981) Analysis of preference dependencies among objectives. *Operational Research*, **29**, 11105–20.

Keeney, R. L. (1982) Decision analysis: an overview. *Operations Research*, **30**, 803–38.

Keeney, R. L. and Raiffa, H. (1976) *Decisions with Multiple Objectives*, John Wiley & Sons, New York.

Keeney, R. L. and von Winterfeldt, D. (2001) Appreciating the precautionary principle – a decision analysis perspective. *Journal of Risk Research*, **4**(2), 191–202.

Kennedy, P. (1998) *A Guide to Econometrics,* 4th edn, MIT Press, Cambridge MA.

Kester, W. C. (1984) Today's options for tomorrow's growth. *Harvard Business Review*, March/April, pp. 153–60.

Khan, A. M. and Shih, C. T. (1988) Judgmental decision models as alternatives to optimisation: the case of spousal selection. *Journal of the Operational Research Society*, **35**, 453–57.

Kheifet, L. I., Hester G. L. and Banerjee G. L. (2001) The precautionary principle and EMF: implementation and evaluation. *Journal of Risk Research*, **4**(2), 113–26.

King, M. and Mercer, A. (1985) Problems in determining bidding strategies. *Journal of the Operational Research Society*, **36**, 915–23.

King, M. and Mercer, A. (1991) Distributions in competitive bidding. *Journal of the Operational Research Society*, **42**(2), 151.

Knight, F. (1921) *Risk, Uncertainty and Profit*, Houghton Mifflin, Boston.

Kogut, B. and Kulatilaka, N. (1994) Options thinking and platform investments: investing in opportunity. *California Management Review*, **36**, Winter, pp. 52–70.

Kotler, P. (1984) *Marketing Management,* fifth edition, Prentice Hall, Hemel Hempstead.

Kuhn, T. (1962) *The Structure of Scientific Revolution*, University of Chicago Press, Chicago IL.

Kulatilaka, N. and Marcus, A. J. (1992) Project valuation under uncertainty: when does DCF fail? *Journal of Applied Corporate Finance*, **5**(3), 92–100.

Kulatilaka, N. and Perotti, E. C. (1998) Strategic growth options. *Management Science*, **4**(5), 1021–31.

Leslie, K. J. and Michaels, M. P. (1997) The real power of real options. *McKinsey Quarterly*, No. 3, pp. 4–23.

Levy, D. (1994) Chaos theory and strategy: theory, application, and managerial implications. *Strategic Management Journal*, **15**, 167–78.

Lilien, G. L. and Kotler, P. (1983) *Marketing Decision Making*, Harper and Row, New York.

Little, J. D. C. (1970) Models and managers: the concept of a decision calculus. *Management Sciences*, **16**(8), B466–85.

Lohmann, J. R. and Baksh, S. N. (1993) The IRR and payback period and their relative performance in common capital budgeting decision procedures for dealing with risk. *Engineering Economist*, **39**(1), 17–48.

Lootsma, F. A. (1990) The French and the American school in multi-criteria decision analysis. *Operational Research*, **24**, 263–85.

Lootsma, F. A. (1993) Scale sensitivity in the multiplicative AHP and SMART. *Journal of Multi-Criteria Decision Analysis*, **2**, 87–110.

MacKay, D. B., Bowen, W. M. and Zinnes, J. L. (1996) A Thurstonian view of the analytic hierarchy process. *European Journal of Operational Research*, **89**, 427–44.

MacNulty, A. A. R. (1977) Scenario development for corporate planning. *Futures*, **9**(2), 128–38.

March, J. G. and Shapiro, Z. (1987) Managerial perspectives on risk and risk taking. *Management Science*, **33**(11), 1404–18.

Mareschal, B. and Brans, J. P. (1988) Geometrical representation for MDCA (GAIA). *European Journal of Operational Research*, **34**, 69–77.

Markowitz, H. (1959) *Portfolio Selection: Efficient Diversification of Investments*, John Wiley & Sons, New York.

Marsh, B. (1991) Coping with uncertainty: rational investment. Paper presented at 'Chaos, Forecasting and Risk Assessment', Joint Strategic and Operational Research Society Conference, London, February.

McGrath, R. G. (1997) A real options logic for initiating technology positioning investments. *Academy of Management Review*, **22**(4), 974–96.

McGrath, R. G. (1998) Only fools rush in? Using real options reasoning to inform the theory of technology strategy: response to Garud, Kumaraswamy and Nayyar. *Academy of Management Review*, **23**, 214–17.

McGrath, R. G. (1999) Falling forward: real options reasoning and entrepreneurial failure. *Academy of Management Review*, **24**(1), 13–30.

Miles, L. D. (1961) *Techniques of Value Analysis and Engineering*, McGraw-Hill, New York.

Miller, G. A. (1956) The magical number seven plus or minus two: some limits on our capacity for processing information. *Psychological Review*, **63**, 81–97.

Miller, R. and Lessard, D. R. (2000) *The Strategic Management of Large Engineering Projects: Shaping Institutions, Risk and Governance*, MIT Press, Cambridge MA.

Mingers, J. and Gill, A. (1997) *Methodology: The Theory and Practice of Combining Management Science Methodologies*, John Wiley & Sons, Chichester.

Mintzberg, H. (1994) *The Rise and Fall of Strategic Planning*, Prentice Hall, New York.

Mintzberg, H., Ahlstrand, B. and Lampel, J. (1998) *Strategy Safari*, Prentice Hall, Hemel Hempstead.

Moder, J. J. and Philips, C. R. (1970) *Project Management with CPM and PERT*, Van Nostrand, New York.

Modigliani, F. and Miller, M. H. (1958) The cost of capital, corporate finance and the theory of investment. *American Economic Review*, **48**, 261–97.

Mooraj, A., Oyon, D. and Hostettler, D. (1999) The balanced scorecard: a necessary good or an unnecessary evil? *European Management Journal*, **17**(5), 481–91.

Moore, P. G. and Thomas, H. (1973) The rev counter decision. *Operational Research Quarterly*, **24**, 337–51.

Moore, P. G. and Thomas, H. (1976) *Anatomy of Decisions*, Penguin, London.

Morris, P. W. G. and Hough, G. H. (1987) *The Anatomy of Major Projects*, John Wiley & Sons, Chichester.

Murray-Webster, R. and Thirty, M. (2000) Managing programmes of projects. In Turner, J. R. and Simister, S. J. (eds), *Gower Handbook of Project Management*, 3rd edn, Gower, Aldershot.

Myers, S. C. (1976) Using simulation for risk analysis. In Myers, S. C. (ed.) *Modern Developments in Financial Management*, Dryden Press, Hinsdale IL.

Myers, S. C. (1984) Finance theory and financial strategy. *Interfaces*, **14**(1) Jan/Feb, 126–37.

Nau, F. and Smith, E. (1995) Valuing risky projects: option pricing theory and decision analysis. *Management Science*, **41**(5), 795–816.

Norreklit, H. (2000) The balance on the balanced scorecard – a critical analysis of the sum of its assumptions. *Management Accounting Research*, **11**(1), 65–88.

Olve, N., Roy J. and Wetter, M. (1999) *Performance Drivers: A Practical Guide to Using the Balanced Scorecard*, John Wiley & Sons, Chichester.

Pace (1990) *Environmental Costs of Electricity*, Pace University Center for Environmental Legal Studies, Oceana Publications, New York.

Partington, D. (2000) Implementing strategy through programmes of projects. In Turner, J. R. and Simister, S. J. (Eds) *Gower Handbook of Project Management*, 3rd edn, Gower, Aldershot.

Pearce, I. F. (1964) *A Contribution to Demand Analysis*, Oxford University Press, Oxford.

Pettigrew, A. M. and Whipp, R. (1991) *Managing Change for Competitive Success*, Basil Blackwell, Oxford.

Phillips, L. D. (1982) Requisite decision modelling: a case study. *Journal of the Operational Research Society*, **33**, 303–11.

Phillips, L. D. (1989) Decision analysis in the 1990s. In Shahani, A. and Stainton, R. (eds), *Tutorial Papers in Operational Research*, Operational Research Society, Birmingham.

Pidd, M. (1996) *Tools for Thinking: Modelling in Management Science*, John Wiley & Sons, Chichester.

Pidd, M. (2001) The futures of OR. *Journal of the Operational Research Society*, **52**(11), 1181–90.

Pindyck, S. R. (1988) Irreversible investment, capacity choice, and the value of the firm. *American Economic Review*, **78**, 969–85.

Project Management Institute (2000) *A Guide to the Project Management Body of Knowledge*, 2000 edition, Project Management Institute, Newtown Square PA.

Raiffa, H. (1968) *Decision Analysis: Introductory Lectures on Choices Under Uncertainty*, Addison-Wesley, Reading MA

Railtrack Safety and Standards Directorate (1999) *Railway Safety Case Version 22*, Volume 2, *Supporting Information*, Railtrack Safety and Standards Directorate, London.

Railtrack Safety and Standards Directorate (2000) *Railway Group Year End Safety Performance Report*, Railtrack Safety and Standards Directorate, London.

Rand, G. K. (2000) Critical chain: the theory of constraints applied to project management. *International Journal of Project Management*, **18**(3), 173–78.

Reinhardt, U. E. (1973) Break-even analysis for Lockheed's TriStar: an application of financial theory. *Journal of Finance*, **28**, 821–38.

Rivett, P. (1994) *The Craft of Decision Modelling*, John Wiley & Sons, Chichester.

Roberts, E. B. (1977) Strategies for effective implementation of complex corporate models. *Interfaces*, **8**(8), 26–33.

Roberts, J. (2000) From know-how to show-how? Questioning the role of information and communication technologies in knowledge transfer. *Technology Analysis and Strategic Management*, **12**(4), 429–43.

Robichek, A. A. and Van Horne, J. C. (1967) Abandonment value and capital budgeting. *Journal of Finance*, **22**, 577–89.

Rosenbloom, E. S. (1996) A probabilistic interpretation of the final rankings in AHP. *European Journal of Operational Research*, **96**, 371–78.

Rosenhead, J. R. (1989) *Rational Analysis for a Problematic World*, John Wiley & Sons, Chichester.

Ruthkopf, M. H. (1983) *Auctions, Bidding and Contracting: Uses and Theory*, New York University Press, New York.

Saaty, T. L. (1977) A scaling method for priorities in hierarchical structures. *Journal of Mathematical Psychology*, **15**, 234–81.

Saaty, T. L. (1980) *The Analytic Hierarchy Process*, McGraw-Hill, New York.

Saaty, T. L. (1990a) An exposition of the AHP in reply to the paper: remarks on the analytic hierarchy process. *Management Science*, **36**, 259–68.

Saaty, T. L. (1990b) How to make a decision: the analytic hierarchy process. *European Journal of Operational Research*, **48**, 9–26.

Saaty, T. L. (1994) Highlights and critical points in the theory and application of the analytical hierarchy process. *European Journal of Operational Research*, **74**, 426–47.

Saaty, T. L. (1997) A scaling method for priorities in hierarchical structure. *Journal of Mathematical Psychology*, **15**, 234–81.

Saaty, T. L. and Kearns, K. P. (1985) *Analytical Planning: The Organization of Systems*, Pergamon, Oxford.

Saaty, T. L. and Vargas, L. G. (1987) Uncertainty and rank order in the analytic hierarchy process. *European Journal of Operational Research*, **32**, 107–17.

Saavides, S. (1994) Risk analysis in investment appraisal. *Project Appraisal*, **9**(1), 3–18.

Sadin, P. (1999) Dimensions of the precautionary principle. *Human and Ecological Risk Assessment*, **5**, 889–907.

Sasieni, M. W., Yaspan, A. and Friedman, L. (1959) *Operations Research: Methods and Problems*, John Wiley & Sons, New York.

Schoemaker, P. J. H. (1992) How to link strategic vision to core capabilities. *Sloan Management Review*, **34**(1), 67–72.

Schoemaker, P. J. H. (1995) Scenario planning: a tool for strategic thinking. *Sloan Management Review*, **36**(2), 25–40.

Schoner, B. and Wedley, W. C. (1989) Ambiguous criteria weights in AHP: consequences and solutions. *Decision Science*, **20**, 462–75.

Schwarz, M. (1999) *The evolution of strategic ideas: the interplay between the evolution of strategic ideas and corporate culture*. PhD thesis, School of Management, University of Southampton.

Sharpe, W. F. (1964) Capital asset prices: a theory of market equilibrium under conditions of risk. *Journal of Finance*, September, pp. 425–42.

Shoham, A. (1998) Export performance: a conceptualization and empirical assessment. *Journal of International Marketing*, **6**(3), 59–81.

Shoham, A. (1999) Bounded rationality, planning standardization of international strategy, and export performance: a structural model examination. *Journal of International Marketing*, **7**(2), 24–50.

Simon, H. A. (1979) Rational decision-making in business organisations. *American Economic Review*, **69**, 493–513.

Simon, O. (1998) *RAMP Risk Analysis and Management for Projects*, Institution of Civil Engineers and the Faculty and Institute of Actuaries, Thomas Telford, London.

Simon, P., Hillson, D. and Newland, K. (1997) *PRAM Project Risk Analysis and Management Guide*, Association for Project Management, Norwich.

Simpson, L. (1996) Do decision makers know what they prefer? MAVT and ELECTRE II. *Journal of the Operational Research Society*, **47**, 919–29.

Slack, N., Chambers, S. and Johnston, R. (2001) *Operations Management*, 3rd edn, Prentice Hall, London.

Slater, S. F., Reddy, V. K., and Zwirlein, T. J. (1998) Evaluating strategic investments: implementing discounted cash flow analysis with option analysis. *Industrial Marketing Management*, **27**(5), 447–58.

Slevin, D. P., Cleland, D. I. and Pinto, J. K. (2000) *Project Management Research at the Turn of the Millennium.* Proceedings of the Project Management Institute Research Conference, Paris, PMI, Newton Square PA.

Smith, H. T. J. and Ankum, L. A. (1993) A real options and game-theoretic approach to corporate investment strategy under competition. *Financial Management*, **22**(3), 241–50.

Smith, J. E. and Nau, R. F. (1995) Valuing risky projects: option pricing theory and decision analysis. *Management Science*, **41**(5), 795–816.

Smith, J. Q. (1988) *Decision Analysis – a Bayesian Approach*, Chapman & Hall, London.

Starbuck, W. H. and Milliken F. J. (1988) Challenger: fine tuning the odds until something breaks. *Journal of Management Studies,* **25**(4), 319–40.

Staw, M. B. (1981) The escalation of commitment to a course of action. *Academy of Management Review*, **6**(4) 577–87.

Stewart, T. J. (1981) A descriptive approach to multiple criteria decision-making. *Journal of the Operational Research Society*, **32**, 45–53.

Stewart, T. J. (1992) A critical survey on the status of multiple criteria decision making theory and practice. *Omega, International Journal of Management Science*, **20**, 569–86.

Stewart, T. J. (1995) Simplified approaches for multiple criteria decision making under uncertainty. *Journal of Multi-Criteria Decision Analysis*, **4**, 246–58.

Stewart, T. J. (1996) Robustness of additive value function methods in MCDM. *Journal of Multi-Criteria Decision Analysis*, **5**, 301–9.

Steyn, H. (2001) An investigation into the fundamentals of critical chain project scheduling. *International Journal of Project Management*, **19**(6), 363–70.

Strauss, A. and Corbin, J. (1998) *Basics of Qualitative Research: Techniques and Procedures for Developing Grounded Theory*, 2nd edn, Sage, Newbury Park CA

Strotz, R. H. (1957) The empirical implication of the utility tree. *Econometrica*, **25**, 269–80.

Taha, H. A. (1971) *Operations Research: An Introduction*, Macmillan, New York.

Target, D. (1996) *Analytical Decision Making*, Pitman, London.

Tocher, K. D. (1977) Planning systems. *Philosophical Transactions of the Royal Society of London*, **A287**, 425–41.

Toft, B. and Renolds, S. (1997) *Learning from Disaster: A Management Approach*, Perpetuity Press, Leicester.

Trigeorgis, L. (1993) Real options and interactions with financial flexibility, *Financial Management*, **22**(3), 202–24.

Trigeorgis, L. (1997) *Real options: Managerial Flexibility and Strategy in Resource Allocation*, MIT Press, Cambridge MA.

Turner, B. A. and Pidgeon, N. F. (1997) *Man Made Disaster*, Butterworth-Heinnmann, Oxford.

Turner, J. R. (1993) *The Handbook of Project-based Management*, McGraw-Hill, London.

Tweedley, N. (1995) *Wining the Bid – A Manager's Guide to Competitive Bidding*, Financial Times Pitman, London.

United Nations (1992) Declaration on Environment and Development LFNCED document A/CONF. 151/5 Rev. 1, 13 June, United Nations Conference on Environment and Development, Rio de Janeiro. Reprinted in *International Legal*, **31**, 874–79.

US Nuclear Regulatory Commission Reactor Safety Study (1975) An assessment of accident risk in US commercial nuclear power plants, WASH-1400, NUREG-75/014.

Van Horne, J. C. (1971) A note on biases in capital budgeting introduced by inflation. *Journal of Financial and Quantitative Analysis*, **6**, 653–58.

Van Huylenbroeck, G. (1995) The conflict analysis method: bridging the gap between ELECTRE, PROMETHEE and ORESTE. *European Journal of Operational Research*, **82**, 490–502.

Vanston, J. H. Jr., Fisbie, W. P., Lopreato, S. C. and Poston D. L. Jr (1977) Alternate scenario planning, *Technological Forecasting and Social Change*, **10**, 159–80.

Vargas, L. G. (1990) An overview of the analytic hierarchy process and its applications. *European Journal of Operational Research*, **48**, 2–8.

Von Winterfeldt, D. and Edwards, W. (1986) *Decision Analysis and Behavioural Research*, Cambridge University Press, Cambridge.

Wallingford, B. A. (1967) A survey and comparison of portfolio selection problems. *Journal of Financial and Quantitative Analysis*, **2**, 85–106.

Ward, K. and Grundy, T. (1996) The strategic management of corporate value. *European Management Journal*, **14**(3), 321–30.

Ward, S. C. (1989) Arguments for constructively simple models. *Journal of the Operational Research Society*, **40**(2), 141–53.

Ward, S. C. (1999) Assessing and managing important risks. *International Journal of Project Management*, **17**, 331–36.

Ward, S. C. and Chapman, C. B. (1988) Developing competitive bids: a framework for information processing. *Journal of the Operational Research Society*, **39**(2), 123–34.

Ward, S. C. and Chapman, C. B. (1991) Extending the use of risk analysis in project management. *International Journal of Project Management*, **9**(2), 117–23.

Ward, S. C. and Chapman, C. B. (1994a) The efficient allocation of risk in contracts. *Omega, International Journal of Management Science*, **22**(6), 537–52.

Ward, S. C. and Chapman, C. B. (1994b) A risk management perspective on the project life cycle. *International Journal of Project Management*, **13**(3), 145–50.

Ward, S. C. and Chapman, C. B. (1995) Evaluating fixed price incentive contracts. *Omega, International Journal of Management Science*, **23**(1), 49–62.

Ward, S. C. and Chapman, C. B. (2002) Transforming project risk management into project uncertainty management. *International Journal of Project Management*, **21**(2), forthcoming.

Ward, S. C., Chapman, C. B. and Curtis, B. (1991) On the allocation of risk in construction projects. *International Journal of Project Management*, **9**(3) 140–47.

Ward, S. C., Chapman, C. B. and Klein, J. H. (1991) Theoretical versus applied models: the newsboy problem. *Omega, International Journal of Management Science*, **19**(4), 197–206.

Ward, S. C., Curtis, B. and Chapman, C. B. (1991a) Objectives and performance in construction projects. *Construction Management and Economics*, **9**, 343–53.

Ward, S. C., Curtis, B. and Chapman, C. B. (1991b) The advantages of management contracting – a critical analysis. *Journal of Construction Engineering and Management*, **117**(2), 195–211.

Ward, S. C., Klein, J. H., Avison, D., Powell, P. and Keen, J. (1997) Flexibility and the management of uncertainty. *International Journal of Project and Business Risk Management*, **1**(2), 131–45.

Waters, C. D. J. (1991) *An Introduction to Operations Management*, Addison-Wesley, Reading MA.

Weiss, H. H. (1987) An accuracy range system of uncertain appraisal. *Engineering Economist*, **32**(3), 197–216.

Williams, T. M. (1997) *Managing and Modelling Complex Projects*, Kluwer, London.

Wood, D. and Fildes, R. (1976) *Forecasting for Business: Methods and Applications*, Longman, New York.

Wright, G. (1984) *Behavioral Decision Theory*. Penguin, Harmondsworth.

Wynn, H. (1999) RSS99 debates 'risk'. *Royal Statistical Society News*, **27**(2), 1–2.

Yahya, S. and Kingsman, B. (1999) Vendor rating for an entrepreneur development programme: a case study using the analytic hierarchy process method. *Journal of the Operational Research Society*, **50**(9) 916–30.

Zahedi, F. (1986) The analytic hierarchy process – a survey of the method and its applications. *Interfaces*, **16**, 96–108.

Index